ACCA

UDY TEXT

DIPLOMA IN INTERNATIONAL FINANCIAL REPORTING

BPP Learning Media is the **sole ACCA Platinum Approved Learning Partner – content** for the Diploma in International Financial Reporting. **In this 2010 study text:**

- We **include** the revised IASs and IFRSs
- We **discuss** the **best strategies** for studying for your exams
- We **highlight** the **most important elements** in the syllabus and the **key skills** you will need
- We **signpost** how each chapter links to the syllabus and the study guide
- We **provide** lots of **exam focus points** demonstrating what the examiner will want you to do
- We **emphasise key points** in regular **fast forward summaries**
- We **test your knowledge** of what you've studied in **quick quizzes**
- We **examine your understanding** in our **exam question bank**
- We **reference all the important topics** in our **full index**

FOR EXAMS IN 2011

BPP LEARNING MEDIA

Seventh edition November 2010

ISBN 9780 7517 8323 0
(Previous edition 9780 7517 6694 3)
e-ISBN 9780 7517 8830 3

British Library Cataloguing-in-Publication Data
A catalogue record for this book
is available from the British Library

Published by

BPP Learning Media Ltd
BPP House, Aldine Place
London W12 8AA

www.bpp.com/learningmedia

Printed in the United Kingdom

Your learning materials, published by BPP Learning Media Ltd, are printed on paper sourced from sustainable, managed forests.

We are grateful to the Association of Chartered Certified Accountants for permission to reproduce past examination questions. The suggested solutions in the exam answer bank have been prepared by BPP Learning Media Ltd, unless where otherwise stated.

Contents

A note about copyright

Dear Customer

What does the little © mean and why does it matter?

Your market-leading BPP books and course materials do not write and update themselves. People write them: on their own behalf or as employees of an organisation that invests in this activity. Copyright law protects their livelihoods. It does so by creating rights over the use of the content.

Breach of copyright is a form of theft – as well being a criminal offence in some jurisdictions, it is potentially a serious breach of professional ethics.

With current technology, things might seem a bit hazy but, basically, without the express permission of BPP Learning Media:

- Photocopying our materials is a breach of copyright
- Scanning, ripcasting or conversion of our digital materials into different file formats, uploading them to facebook or emailing them to your friends is a breach of copyright

You can, of course, sell your books, in the form in which you have bought them – once you have finished with them. (Is this fair to your fellow students? We update for a reason.)

And what about outside the UK? BPP Learning Media strives to make our materials available at prices students can afford by local printing arrangements, pricing policies and partnerships which are clearly listed on our website. A tiny minority ignore this and indulge in criminal activity by illegally photocopying our material or supporting organisations that do. If they act illegally and unethically in one area, can you really trust them?

Learning to Learn Accountancy

BPP's ground-breaking **Learning to Learn Accountancy** book is designed to be used both at the outset of your ACCA studies and throughout the process of learning accountancy. It challenges you to consider how you study and gives you helpful hints about how to approach the various types of paper which you will encounter. It can help you **focus your studies on the subject and exam**, enabling you to **acquire knowledge, practise and revise efficiently and effectively**.

How the BPP ACCA-approved Study Text can help you pass

BPP Learning Media – the sole Platinum Approved Learning Partner - content

As ACCA's **sole Platinum Approved Learning Partner – content**, BPP Learning Media gives you the **unique opportunity** to use **examiner-reviewed** study materials for the 2011 exams. By incorporating the examiner's comments and suggestions regarding the depth and breadth of syllabus coverage, the BPP Learning Media Study Text provides excellent, **ACCA-approved** support for your studies.

Tackling studying

Studying can be a daunting prospect, particularly when you have lots of other commitments. The **different features** of the text, the **purposes** of which are explained fully on the **Chapter features** page, will help you whilst studying and improve your chances of **exam success**.

Developing exam awareness

Our Texts are completely **focused** on helping you pass your exam.

Our advice on **Studying for the Diploma in International Financial Reporting (DipIFR)** outlines the **content** of the paper, the **necessary skills** the examiner expects you to demonstrate and any **brought forward knowledge** you are expected to have.

Exam focus points are included within the chapters to highlight when and how specific topics were examined, or how they might be examined in the future.

Using the Syllabus and Study Guide

You can find the syllabus, Study Guide and other useful resources for DipIFR on the ACCA web site:

www.accaglobal.com/members/qualifications/dipifr/

The Study Text covers **all aspects** of the syllabus to ensure you are as fully prepared for the exam as possible.

Testing what you can do

Testing yourself helps you develop the skills you need to pass the exam and also confirms that you can recall what you have learnt.

We include **Questions** – lots of them - both within chapters and in the **Exam Question Bank**, as well as **Quick Quizzes** at the end of each chapter to test your knowledge of the chapter content.

Chapter features

Each chapter contains a number of helpful features to guide you through each topic.

Topic list

Topic list	Syllabus reference

Tells you what you will be studying in this chapter and the relevant section numbers, together the ACCA syllabus references.

Introduction – Puts the chapter content in the context of the syllabus as a whole.

Study Guide – Links the chapter content with ACCA guidance.

Exam Guide – Highlights how examinable the chapter content is likely to be and the ways in which it could be examined.

Knowledge brought forward from earlier studies – What you are assumed to know from previous studies/exams.

FAST FORWARD – Summarises the content of main chapter headings, allowing you to preview and review each section easily.

Examples – Demonstrate how to apply key knowledge and techniques.

Key terms – Definitions of important concepts that can often earn you easy marks in exams.

Exam focus points – Tell you when and how specific topics were examined, or how they may be examined in the future.

Question – Give you essential practice of techniques covered in the chapter.

Chapter Roundup – A full list of the Fast Forwards included in the chapter, providing an easy source of review.

Quick Quiz – A quick test of your knowledge of the main topics in the chapter.

Exam Question Bank – Found at the back of the Study Text with more comprehensive chapter questions. Cross referenced for easy navigation.

Studying for the Diploma in International Financial Reporting

Aim

To develop knowledge, understanding and application of International Financial Reporting Standards and the concepts and principles which underpin them.

Objectives

On completion of the Diploma candidates should be able to:

- Understand and explain the structure of the international professional and conceptual framework of accounting
- Apply relevant financial reporting standards to key elements of financial reports
- Identify and apply disclosure requirements for companies relating to the presentation of financial reports and notes
- Prepare financial statements of single entities and account for their key elements complying with specified International Financial Reporting Standards and other related pronouncements
- Prepare group financial statements (excluding statements of cash flows for groups) including subsidiaries, associates and joint ventures

Position of the course within the overall portfolio of ACCA's qualification framework

Dip IFR builds on the technical and/or practical knowledge acquired from recognised country specific accountancy qualifications or relevant work experience. The course introduces the candidate to the wider international framework of accounting and the system of standard setting.

This conversion course concentrates on the application of conceptual and technical financial accounting knowledge that candidates have already obtained to the specific requirements of financial reporting under international professional regulation and standards.

Dip IFR also provides essential international financial reporting knowledge and principles that will prepare candidates for the increasingly global market place and keep them abreast of international developments and how they might apply to the companies and businesses.

The prerequisite knowledge for Dip IFR can come from:

- A relevant degree plus two years' work experience
- Three years' work experience
- ACCA affiliate status
- ACCA Certificate in International Financial Reporting plus two years' work experience

Approach to examining the syllabus

The format of the examination is different from exams in 2011 onwards. The examination is a three hour paper in two sections. The questions within the examination are all compulsory thereby ensuring that a candidate is examined on all the main syllabus areas within any one examination session. The examination will comprise the following:

The first question will be one compulsory 40 mark question covering group accounting and individual company adjustments

The following three questions will be 20 mark questions covering a variety of accounting standards.

An individual question may often involve elements that relate to different areas of the syllabus. For example a question on the preparation of financial statements for public issue could include elements relating to several accounting standards. In scenario questions candidates may be expected to comment on management's chosen accounting treatment and determine a more appropriate one, based on circumstances described in the question.

Some International Financial Reporting Standards are very detailed and complex. In the Dip IFR exam candidates need to be aware of the principles and key elements of these Standards. Candidates will also be expected to have an appreciation of the background and need for international accounting financial reporting and issues related to harmonisation of accounting in a global context.

The overall passmark for the Diploma in International Financial Reporting is 50%.

	Number of marks
One compulsory question	40
Choice of 3 from 4 questions	60
	100

Additional information

Candidates need to be aware that the cut off date for the new examinable regulations to be examined is 30 September of the preceding year. This means that new regulations issued up to 30 September 2010 (for example) are examinable in all exams sat in 2011, but regulations issued after 30 September 2010 will only be examined in 2012.

A pilot paper demonstrating the effects of the 2010 syllabus changes is currently available on the ACCA website here:

http://www.accaglobal.com/members/qualifications/dipifr/assessment/past_papers

Syllabus and Study Guide

1 **International sources of authority**

(a) The structure of the International Accounting Standards Board (IASB)
(b) The standard setting process
(c) The role of the International Financial Reporting Interpretations Committee
(d) Progress towards international harmonisation
(e) The accounting framework
(f) The first time adoption of International Financial Reporting Standards

2 **Elements of financial statements**

(a) Property, plant and equipment
(b) Intangible assets
(c) Goodwill
(d) Current assets including inventories
(e) Construction contracts
(f) Liabilities
(g) Financial instruments
(h) Provisions and contingencies
(i) Employment and post-employment benefits
(j) Current and deferred tax
(k) Biological assets and agricultural produce
(l) Share-based payment
(m) Exploration and evaluation expenditures

3 **Presentation and additional disclosures**

(a) Events after the reporting date
(b) Earnings per share
(c) Related party disclosures
(d) Interim financial reporting
(e) Effects of changes in foreign exchange rates
(f) Operating segments

4 **Preparation of external financial reports for combined entities and joint ventures**

(a) Definitions of subsidiaries, investments in associates and joint ventures
(b) Preparation of consolidated statements of financial position, statements of comprehensive income and statements of changes in equity
(c) Equity accounting
(d) Proportionate consolidation and joint ventures

Excluded topics

The following topics are specifically excluded from the syllabus.

- Partnership and branch financial statements
- Complex group structures including sub-subsidiaries or mixed groups and foreign subsidiaries
- Piece-meal acquisitions, disposal of subsidiaries and group reconstructions
- Financial statements of banks and similar financial institutions
- Statements of cash flows

- Schemes of reorganisation/reconstruction
- Company/share valuation
- Accounting for insurance entities
- International financial reporting exposure drafts and discussion drafts
- The international public sector perspective
- Multi-employer benefit schemes
- Share-based payment transactions with cash alternatives

Key areas of the syllabus

The key topic areas are as follows.

- International sources of authority
- Elements of financial statements
- Presentation of accounts and additional disclosures
- Preparation of external reports for combined entities and joint ventures

Relevant topics

The ACCA recommends the following material.

- International Accounting Standards Board. **International Financial Reporting Standards** IASB Publications (2010)
- Ernst and Young International GAAP 2010

Wider reading

Wider reading is absolutely essential, especially regular study of relevant articles from ACCA's *Student Accountant*. Of particular relevance are articles written by the Dip IFR examiner, Paul Robins. These are available on the ACCA website in the Dip IFR section:

www.accaglobal.com/members/qualifications/dipifr/assessment/technical_articles/

Examinable Documents

International Accounting Financial Reporting Standards		Chapter reference
Framework	Framework for the Preparation and Presentation of Financial Statements	2
IAS 1 (revised)	Presentation of financial statements	15
IAS 2 (revised)	Inventories	7
IAS 7 (revised)	Statements of cash flows	19
IAS 8 (revised)	Accounting policies, changes in accounting estimates and errors	16
IAS 10 (revised)	Events after the reporting period	16
IAS 11 (revised)	Construction contracts	7
IAS 12 (revised)	Income taxes	11
IAS 16 (revised)	Property, plant and equipment	4
IAS 17 (revised)	Leases	5
IAS 18 (revised)	Revenue	3
IAS 19	Employee benefits	9
IAS 20	Accounting for government grants and disclosure of government assistance	4
IAS 21 (revised)	The effects of changes in foreign exchange rates	12
IAS 23 (revised)	Borrowing costs	4
IAS 24 (revised)	Related party disclosures	18
IAS 27 (revised)	Consolidated and separate financial statements	20
IAS 28 (revised)	Investment in associates	23
IAS 31 (revised)	Interests in joint ventures	24
IAS 32 (revised)	Financial instruments: Presentation	10
IAS 33	Earnings per share	17
IAS 34	Interim financial reporting	15
IAS 36	Impairment of assets	4
IAS 37	Provisions, contingent liabilities and contingent assets	8
IAS 38	Intangible assets	6
IAS 39 (revised)	Financial instruments: recognition and measurement	10
IAS 40	Investment property	4
IAS 41	Agriculture	13
IFRS 1	First time adoption of International Financial Reporting Standards	1
IFRS 2	Share-based payment	14
IFRS 3 (revised)	Business combinations	21
IFRS 5	Non-current assets held for sale and discontinued operations	16

International Accounting Financial Reporting Standards		Chapter reference
IFRS 6	Exploration for and evaluation of mineral resources	13
IFRS 7	Financial instruments: disclosures	10
IFRS 8	Operating segments	18

Diploma in International Financial Reporting
Study Guide

INTERNATIONAL SOURCES OF AUTHORITY

1 The International accounting standards board and the regulatory framework

- Discuss the need for international financial reporting standards and possible barriers to this process
- Explain the structure and constitution of the IASB and the standard setting process
- Identify the purpose and functions of the IFRS Interpretations Committee
- Understand and interpret the Financial Reporting Framework
- Account for the first-time adoption of International Financial Reporting Standards

ELEMENTS OF FINANCIAL STATEMENTS

2 REVENUE RECOGNITION

- Outline the principles of the timing of revenue recognition
- Explain the concept of substance over form in relation to recognising sales revenue
- Discuss the various points in the production and sales cycle where it may, depending on circumstances, be appropriate to recognise gains and losses – give examples of this
- Describe the IASB's approach to revenue recognition

3 NON-CURRENT ASSETS – TANGIBLE

- Define the initial cost of a non-current asset (including a self-constructed asset) and apply this to various examples of expenditure, distinguishing between capital and revenue items
- Identify pre-conditions for the capitalisation of borrowing costs
- Describe, and be able to identify, subsequent expenditures that may be capitalised
- State and appraise the effects of the IASB's rules for the revaluation of property, plant and equipment (IAS 16)
- Account for gains and losses on the disposal of revalued assets
- Calculate depreciation on:
  - revalued assets, and
  - assets that have two or more major items or significant parts
- Apply the provisions of accounting standards relating to government grants and government assistance
- Describe the criteria that need to be present before non-current assets are classified as held for sale, either individually or in a disposal group (IFRS 5)
- Account for non-current assets and disposal groups that are held for sale
- Discuss the way in which the treatment of investment properties differs from other properties
- Apply the requirements of international accounting standards to investment property.

4 IMPAIRMENT OF ASSETS

- Define the recoverable amount of an asset; define impairment losses
- Give examples of, and be able to identify, circumstances that may indicate that an impairment of an asset has occurred
- Describe what is meant by a cash-generating unit
- State the basis on which impairment losses should be allocated, and allocate a given impairment loss to the assets of a cash-generating unit (IAS 36)

5 LEASES

- Define the essential characteristics of a lease
- Describe and apply the method of determining a lease type (ie an operating or finance lease)
- Explain the effect on the financial statements of a finance lease being incorrectly treated as an operating lease
- Account for operating leases in the financial statements of the lessor and the lessee
- Account for finance leases in the financial statements of the lessor and lessee
- Outline the principles of accounting standards for leases and the main disclosure requirements
  Note: the net cash investment method will not be examined

6 INTANGIBLE ASSETS AND GOODWILL

- Discuss the nature and possible accounting treatments of both internally generated and purchased goodwill
- Distinguish between goodwill and other intangible assets
- Define the criteria for the initial recognition and measurement of intangible assets
- Explain the subsequent accounting treatment, including the principle of impairment tests in relation to purchased goodwill
- Identify the circumstances in which negative goodwill arises, and its subsequent accounting treatment
- Describe and apply the requirements of international accounting standards to internally generated assets other than goodwill (eg research and development)
- Describe the method of accounting specified by the IASB for the exploration for and evaluation of mineral resources

7 INVENTORIES AND CONSTRUCTION CONTRACTS

- Measure and value inventories (IAS 2)
- Define a construction contract and describe why recognising profit before completion is generally considered to be desirable; discuss if this may be profit smoothing (IAS 11)
- Describe the ways in which contract revenue and contract cost may be recognised
- Calculate and disclose the amounts to be shown in the financial statements for construction contracts

8 FINANCIAL INSTRUMENTS

- Account for debt instruments, equity instruments and the allocation of finance costs
- Account for fixed interest rate and convertible bonds
- Discuss the definition and classification of a financial instrument
- Discuss the measurement issues relating to financial instruments (IAS 39)
- Explain the current measurement proposals for financial instruments including the use of current values, hedging and the treatment of gains and losses
- Describe the nature of the presentation and disclosure requirements relating to financial instruments (IAS 32 and IFRS 7)
- Discuss the key areas where consensus is required on the accounting treatment of financial instruments

9 LIABILITIES – PROVISIONS, CONTINGENT ASSETS AND LIABILITIES

- Explain why an accounting standard on provisions is necessary – give examples of previous abuses in this area
- Define provisions, legal and constructive obligations, past events and the transfer of economic benefits
- State when provision may and may not be made, and how they should be accounted for
- Explain how provisions should be measured (IAS 37)
- Define contingent assets and liabilities – give examples and describe their accounting treatment
- Identify and account for
  - Onerous contracts
  - Environmental and similar provisions
- Discuss the validity of making provisions for future repairs or renewals

10 ACCOUNTING FOR EMPLOYMENT AND POST-EMPLOYMENT BENEFIT COSTS

- Describe the nature of defined contribution, multi-employers and defined benefits schemes
- Explain the recognition and measurement of defined benefit schemes under current proposals
- Account for defined benefit schemes including the amounts shown in the financial statements (and notes to the accounts)

11 TAXATION IN FINANCIAL STATEMENTS

- Account for current tax liabilities and assets in accordance with international accounting standards
- Describe the general principles of government sales taxes (eg VAT or GST)
- Explain the effect of taxable temporary differences on accounting and taxable profits
- Outline the principles of accounting for deferred tax
- Identify and account for the IASB requirements relating to deferred tax assets and liabilities
- Calculate and record deferred tax amounts in the financial statements.

12 THE EFFECTS OF CHANGES IN FOREIGN CURRENCY EXCHANGE RATES

- Discuss the recording of transactions and translation of monetary/non-monetary items at the reporting date for individual entities in accordance with relevant accounting standards
- Distinguish between reporting and functional currencies

- Determine an entity's functional currency

13 AGRICULTURE

- Recognise the scope of international accounting standards for agriculture
- Discuss the recognition and measurement criteria including the treatment of gains and losses, and the inability to measure fair value reliably
- Identify and explain the treatment of government grants, and the presentation and disclosure of information relating to agriculture
- Report on the transformation of biological assets and agricultural produce at the point of harvest and account for agriculture related government grants

14 SHARE-BASED PAYMENT

- Understand the term 'share-based payment' (IFRS 2)
- Discuss the key issue that measurement of the transaction should be based on fair value
- Explain the difference between cash-settled share-based payment transactions and equity-settled share-based payment transactions
- Identify the principles applied to measuring both cash and equity settled share-based payment transactions
- Compute the amounts that need to be recorded in the financial statements when an entity carries out a transaction where the payment is share-based

15 EXPLORATION AND EVALUATION EXPENDITURES

- Outline the need for an accounting standard in this area and clarify its scope
- Give examples of elements of cost that might be included in the initial measurement of exploration and evaluation assets
- Describe how exploration and evaluation assets should be classified and reclassified
- Explain when and how exploration and evaluation assets should be tested for impairment

PRESENTATION OF ACCOUNTS AND ADDITIONAL DISCLOSURES

16 PRESENTATION OF THE INCOME STATEMENT AND STATEMENT OF COMPREHENSIVE INCOME

- State the objectives of international accounting standards governing presentation of financial statements
- Describe the structure and content of income statements and statements of comprehensive income, including continuing operations
- Discuss 'fair presentation' and the accounting concepts/principles
- Recognise the content and format of interim financial statements (IAS 34)

17 EARNINGS PER SHARE

- Recognise the importance of comparability in relation to the calculation of earnings per share (EPS) and its importance as a stock market indicator
- Explain why the trend of EPS may be a more accurate indicator of performance than a company's profit trend
- Define earnings
- Calculate the EPS in the following circumstances:
  - basic EPS
  - where there has been a bonus issue of shares/stock split during the year, and
  - where there has been a rights issues of shares during the year
- Explain the relevance to existing shareholders of the diluted EPS, and describe the circumstances that will give rise to a future dilution of the EPS
- Compute the diluted EPS in the following circumstances:
  - where convertible debt or preference shares are in issue
  - where share options and warrants exist
- Identify anti-dilutive circumstances

18 ACCOUNTING POLICIES, CHANGES IN ACCOUNTING ESTIMATES AND ERRORS

- Distinguish between and account for adjusting and non-adjusting events after the reporting period (IAS 10)
- Identify items requiring separate disclosure, including their accounting treatment and required disclosures
- Recognise the circumstances where a change in accounting policy is justified
- Define prior period adjustments and 'errors' and account for the correction of errors and changes in accounting policies (IAS 8)

19 RELATED PARTY DISCLOSURES

- Define and apply the definition of related parties in accordance with international accounting standards
- Describe the potential to mislead users when related party transactions are accounted for
- Explain the disclosure requirements for related party transactions

20 OPERATING SEGMENTS

- Discuss the usefulness and problems associated with the provision of segment information
- Define an operating segment

- Identify reportable segments (including applying the aggregation criteria and quantitative thresholds)

PREPARATION OF EXTERNAL REPORTS FOR COMBINED ENTITIES AND JOINT VENTURES

21 PREPARATION OF GROUP CONSOLIDATED EXTERNAL REPORTS

- Explain the concept of a group and the purpose of preparing consolidated financial statements
- Explain and apply the definition of subsidiary companies (IAS 27)
- Identify the circumstances and reasoning when subsidiaries should be excluded from consolidated financial statements
- Prepare a consolidated statement of financial position for a simple group dealing with pre and post acquisition profits, non-controlling interests and goodwill.
- Explain the need for using coterminous year-ends and uniform accounting polices when preparing consolidated financial statements and describe how it is achieved in practice
- Prepare a consolidated income statement, statement of comprehensive income and statement of changes in equity for a simple group, including an example where an acquisition occurs during the year where there is a non-controlling interest

22 BUSINESS COMBINATIONS – INTRA-GROUP ADJUSTMENTS

- Explain why intra-group transactions should be eliminated on consolidation
- Report the effects of intra-group trading and other transactions including:
  - unrealised profits in inventory and non-current assets
  - intra-group loans and interest and other intra-group charges, and
  - intra-group dividends

23 BUSINESS COMBINATIONS – FAIR VALUE ADJUSTMENTS

- Explain why it is necessary for both the consideration paid for a subsidiary and the subsidiary's identifiable assets and liabilities to be accounted for at their fair values when preparing consolidated financial statements (IFRS 3)
- Prepare consolidated financial statements dealing with fair value adjustments (including their effect on consolidated goodwill) in respect of:
  - Depreciating and non-depreciating non-current assets
  - Inventory
  - Monetary liabilities
  - Assets and liabilities (including contingencies), not included in the subsidiary's own statement of financial position

24 BUSINESS COMBINATIONS – ASSOCIATES AND JOINT VENTURES (IAS 28 AND 31)

- Define associates and joint ventures (ie jointly controlled operations, assets and entities)
- Distinguish between equity accounting and proportional consolidation
- Describe and prepare accounts under the two formats of proportional consolidation
- Prepare consolidated financial statements to include a single subsidiary and an associated company or a joint venture (both allowed methods).

Analysis of past papers

The analysis below shows the elements of the syllabus which have been examined so far under the current paper including the pilot paper. Further details can be found in the exam focus points in the relevant chapters.

Covered in Text chapter		Pilot Paper 2010	June 2010	Dec 2009	June 2009	Dec 2008	June 2008	Dec 2007	June 2007	Dec 2006	June 2006	Dec 2005	June 2005	Dec 2004	June 2004
	International sources of authority														
1	The IASB and the regulatory framework														
2	Conceptual framework for financial reporting														✓
	Elements of financial statements														
3	Revenue recognition		✓✓	✓	✓	✓	✓	✓	✓			✓			✓
4	Accounting for tangible non-current assets	✓	✓✓ ✓	✓✓✓	✓✓	✓	✓	✓✓	✓	✓					
5	Accounting for leases	✓✓	✓	✓✓	✓✓	✓	✓	✓	✓		✓	✓			
6	Intangible non-current assets and goodwill	✓	✓			✓	✓✓	✓✓	✓	✓	✓	✓			
7	Inventories and construction contracts		✓	✓	✓✓	✓		✓		✓	✓	✓			✓
8	Provisions and contingencies	✓✓		✓✓	✓✓	✓✓	✓✓	✓	✓	✓		✓		✓	
9	Employee benefits				✓					✓			✓		
10	Financial instruments	✓✓ ✓	✓	✓	✓	✓	✓	✓		✓	✓✓✓	✓	✓✓		✓
11	Accounting for taxation		✓✓	✓✓✓	✓			✓✓		✓✓					✓
12	Foreign currency translation	✓	✓				✓						✓		
13	Accounting for agriculture and mineral resources						✓							✓	
14	Share-based payment	✓		✓				✓	✓		✓				
	Presentation of accounts and additional disclosures														
15	Presentation of published financial statements			✓	✓	✓	✓	✓	✓	✓	✓	✓	✓	✓	✓
16	Reporting financial performance	✓		✓✓	✓	✓	✓				✓		✓	✓	
17	Earnings per share													✓	
18	Miscellaneous standards: related party disclosures and segment reporting				✓									✓	
19	Statement of cash flows					✓							✓		
	Financial reports for combined entities and joint ventures														
20	Constitution of a group	✓	✓	✓	✓	✓	✓	✓	✓	✓	✓	✓	✓	✓	✓
21	The consolidated statement of financial position		✓			✓		✓	✓				✓	✓	
22	The consolidated statement of comprehensive income	✓		✓	✓		✓			✓	✓	✓	✓		✓
23	Accounting for associates		✓		✓		✓							✓	✓
24	Accounting for joint ventures														

P A R T

A

International sources of authority

1

The IASB and the regulatory framework

Topic list	Syllabus reference
1 Impact of globalisation	1(d)
2 Steps to harmonisation	1(d)
3 International Accounting Standards Board (IASB)	1(a), (b), (c)
4 Generally Accepted Accounting Principles (GAAP)	1(a)
5 Other international influences	1(a), (b)
6 Scope and application of IASs/IFRSs	1(a), (b)
7 Progress towards global harmonisation	1(d)
8 Benefits of and barriers to global harmonisation	1(d)
9 Feedback on the IASB	1(a)
10 IFRS 1: First-time adoption of International Financial Reporting Standards	1(f)

Introduction

In this chapter we are concerned with the IASB's relationship with other bodies, with the way it operates and how IFRSs are produced.

Later in this text we look at some of the theory behind what appears in the accounts. The most important document in this area is the IASB's *Framework for the preparation and presentation of financial statements*. Since it was published, all IFRSs have been based on the principles it contains.

Study Guide

Section 1 – The International accounting standards board and the regulatory framework

- Discuss the need for international financial reporting standards and possible barriers to this process
- Explain the structure and constitution of the IASB and the standard setting process
- Account for the first-time adoption of International Financial Reporting Statements

1 Impact of globalisation

FAST FORWARD

The need for harmonised financial reporting standards arises as a result of the globalisation of business activities and operations. Harmonised financial reporting standards are intended to provide:

- A platform for wider investment choice
- A more efficient capital market
- Lower cost of capital
- Enhanced business development

The current reality is that the world's **capital markets operate** more and more freely **across borders**. The impacts of rapid globalisation are epitomised by the words of Paul Volker, Chairman of the IFRS Foundation Trustees in November 2002, in a speech to the World Congress of Accountants.

> 'Developments over the past year and more have strongly reinforced the logic of achieving and implementing high-quality international accounting standards. In an age when capital flows freely across borders, it simply makes sense to account for economic transactions, whether they occur in the Americas, Asia, or Europe, in the same manner. Providing improved transparency and comparability will certainly help ensure that capital is allocated efficiently. Not so incidentally, generally accepted international standards will reduce the cost of compliance with multiple national standards.'

As the modern business imperative moves towards the globalisation of operations and activities, there is an underlying commercial logic that also requires a **truly global capital market.** Harmonised financial reporting standards are intended to provide:

- A platform for wider investment choice
- A more efficient capital market
- Lower cost of capital
- Enhanced business development

Globally, users of financial statements need **transparent** and **comparative information** to help them **make economic decisions**.

Since 2005 EU listed companies have been required to use IFRSs to prepare their consolidated financial statements. This is an important step towards eventual harmonisation.

Exam focus point

The June 2004 paper required candidates to discuss lack of commonality between IFRSs and the requirements of securities exchanges in USA and Japan.

2 Steps to harmonisation

FAST FORWARD

Harmonisation remains a long and on-going process and you should be aware of the background surrounding this.

The following timeline briefly summarises the development of the international accounting standards setting structure and the issue of international financial reporting standards.

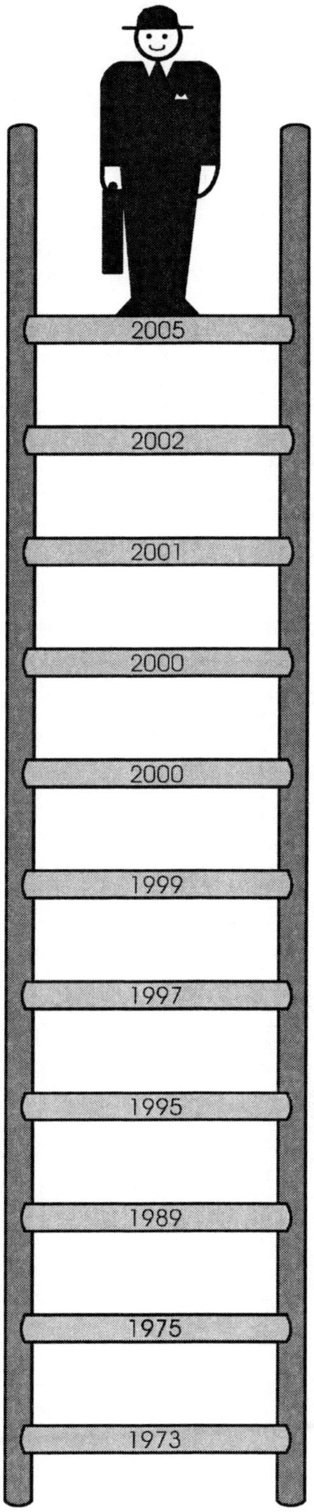

2005	EU listed companies must use IAS/IFRS in respect of their consolidated financial statements for accounting periods beginning on or after 1 January 2005.
2002	SIC renamed International Financial Reporting Interpretations Committee (IFRIC). Europe requires implementation of IFRS for listed companies starting 2005.
2001	Workload of IASC grows and leads to restructuring. In April 2001, new IASB assumes standards setting responsibilities. Existing IASs and SICs adopted by IASB.
2000	IOSCO recommends that its members allow incoming multi-national issuers to use IASC core standards to prepare their financial standards for cross-border offerings and listings.
2000	US Securities and Exchange Commission recommends that IASs should now be accepted for use in cross-border listings, without reconciliation to results under US GAAP.
1999	Standards Interpretations Committee (SIC) set up to tackle difficulties in agreeing how IASs should be used in practice.
1997	The International Monetary Fund (IMF) and the G7 Finance Ministers encourage support for IAS to "strengthen the international financial architecture".
1995	Agreement between International Organisation of Securities Commission (IOSCO) and IASC to develop a set of core standards.
1989	European Accounting Federation supports international harmonisation and greater involvement in IASC.
1975	First International Accounting Standard published.
1973	IASC formed to develop International Accounting Standards.

3 International Accounting Standards Board (IASB)

FAST FORWARD

You should be able to describe the **organisations of the IASB** and its relationship with intergovernmental bodies, professional accounting bodies, national standard settings bodies and IOSCO.

The International Accounting Standards Board is an independent, privately-funded accounting standard setter based in London. Contributors include major accounting firms, private financial institutions, industrial companies throughout the world, central and development banks, and other international and professional organisations.

In March 2001 the IASC Foundation was formed as a not-for-profit corporation incorporated in the USA. In 2010 it changed its name to IFRS Foundation. The IFRS Foundation is the parent entity of the IASB.

From April 2001 the IASB assumed accounting standard setting responsibilities from its predecessor body, the International Accounting Standards Committee (IASC). This restructuring was based upon the recommendations made in the *Recommendations on Shaping IASC for the Future.* In essence, the restructuring was driven by the need to increase the level of resourcing owing to an increasing workload.

3.1 How the IASB is made up

The 15 members of the IASB come from nine countries and have a variety of backgrounds with a mix of auditors, preparers of financial statements, users of financial statements and an academic.

3.2 Objectives of the IASB

The formal objectives of the IASB are to:

(a) **Develop**, in the public interest, a **single set** of high quality, understandable and **enforceable global accounting standards** that require high quality, transparent and comparable information in financial statements and other financial reporting to help participants in the various **capital markets** of the world and other users of the **information** to make **economic decisions**

(b) **Promote** the use and **rigorous application** of those standards

(c) Work actively with national standard-setters to bring about **convergence** of national accounting standards and IFRSs to **high quality solutions**

Exam focus point

Knowledge of the objectives of the IASB are important so as to provide you with the background to IFRS.

3.3 Structure of the IASB

The structure of the IASB can be illustrated by the following diagram:

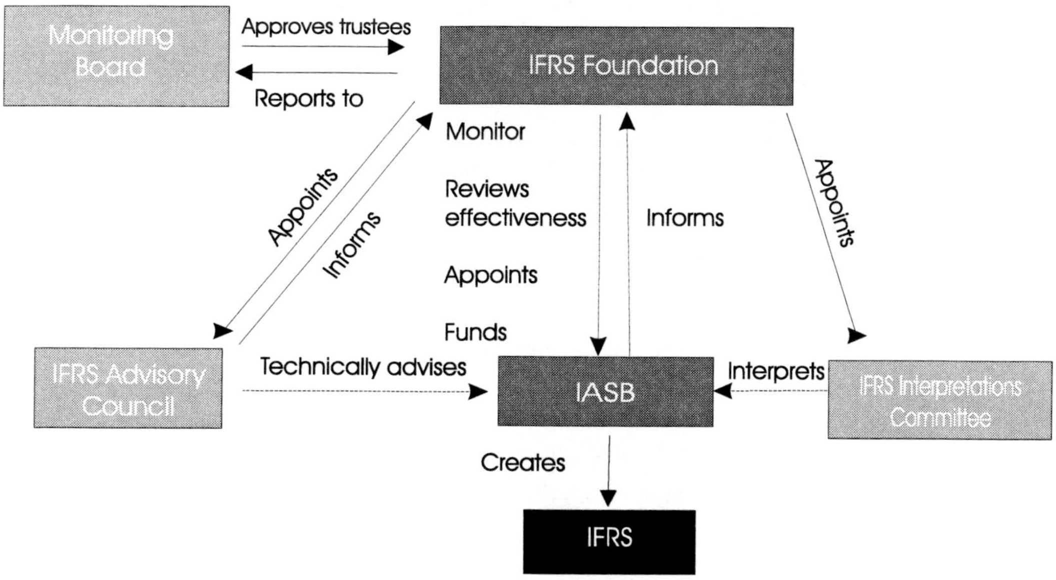

3.3.1 IFRS Foundation

The IFRS Foundation is made up of twenty-two Trustees, who essentially monitor and fund the IASB, the IFRS Advisory Council and the IFRS Interpretations Committee. The Trustees are appointed from a variety of geographic and functional backgrounds according to the following procedure:

(a) The International Federation of Accountants (IFAC) suggested candidates to fill five of the twenty-two Trustee seats and international organisations of preparers, users and academics each suggested one candidate.

(b) The remaining fourteen Trustees are 'at-large' in that they were not selected through the constituency nomination process.

3.3.2 IFRS Advisory Council

The IFRS Advisory Council (formerly the Standards Advisory Council, or SAC) is essentially a forum used by the IASB to consult with the outside world. It consults with national standard setters, academics, user groups and a host of other interested parties to advise the IASB on a range of issues, from the IASB's work programme for developing new IFRSs, to giving practical advice on the implementation of particular standards.

3.3.3 IFRS Interpretations Committee

The IFRS Interpretations Committee (formerly IFRIC) provides guidance on specific practical issues in the interpretation of IFRSs. The IFRS Interpretations Committee is discussed in more detail in sections 3.6 – 3.7 below.

3.4 Scope and authority of IFRSs

The IASB achieves its objectives primarily by developing and publishing IFRSs and promoting the use of those standards in general purpose financial statements and other financial reporting.

IFRSs set out **recognition, measurement, presentation and disclosure requirements** dealing with transactions and events that are important in general purpose financial statements. IFRSs are based on the IASB *Framework,* which:

- Addresses the **concepts** underlying the information presented in general purpose financial statements
- Facilitates the **consistent** and logical formulation of IFRSs
- Provides a basis for the use of **judgement** in resolving accounting issues.

IFRSs are designed to apply to the general purpose financial statements and other financial reporting of all profit-oriented entities.

General purpose financial statements are directed towards the common information needs of a **wide range of users**, for example, shareholders, suppliers, employees and the public at large. The objective of financial statements is to provide information about the financial position, performance and cash flows of an entity that is useful to those users in making **economic decisions**.

A complete set of financial statements includes:

- A statement of financial position
- A statement of comprehensive income
- A statement of all changes in equity, showing only owner changes in equity (Non-owner changes are in the statement of comprehensive income)
- A statement of cash flows
- Accounting policies and explanatory notes

The term 'financial statements' includes a complete set of financial statements prepared for an interim or annual period, and condensed financial statements for an interim period. In the interest of timeliness and cost, and to avoid repeating information previously reported, an entity may provide less information in its interim financial statements than in its annual financial statements. IAS 34 *Interim financial reporting* prescribes the minimum content of complete or condensed financial statements for an interim period.

Many of the IASs produced by the old IASC allowed entities to make a choice between 'benchmark treatments' and 'allowed alternatives'. By contrast, the IASB has shifted the emphasis away from allowing entities a choice between accounting treatments, and is reconsidering all those IASs where choices are permitted. Its objective is either to reduce the number of options available to choose from, or to eliminate the element of choice altogether. This is in line with the IASB's emphasis on reporting like transactions and events in a like way, and reporting different transactions and events differently.

Any limitation of scope of an IFRS will be made clear in the standard.

3.5 IFRS due process

FAST FORWARD

You must understand the **due process** involved in producing international standards, their scope and application and moved by the IASB to interpret them. You should keep an eye on the work of the IASB in the accountancy press and Internet, so you are completely up to date.

IFRSs are developed through an international due process that involves accountants, financial analysts and other users of financial statements, the business community, stock exchanges, regulatory and legal authorities, academics and other interested individuals and organisations from around the world. The IASB consults the IFRS Advisory Council in public meetings on major projects, agenda decisions and work priorities, and discusses technical matters in meetings that are open to public observation.

The overall agenda of the IASB will initially be set by discussion with the IFRS Advisory Council. The process for developing an individual standard would involve the following steps.

Step 1 During the early stages of a project, IASB may establish an **Advisory Committee** to give advice on issues arising in the project. Consultation with the Advisory Committee and the Standards Advisory Council occurs throughout the project.

Step 2 IASB may develop and publish **Discussion Papers** for public comment.

Step 3 Following the receipt and review of comments, IASB would develop and publish an **Exposure Draft** for public comment.

Step 4 Following the receipt and review of comments, the IASB would issue a final **International Financial Reporting Standard**.

The period of exposure for public comment is normally 90 days. However, in exceptional circumstances, proposals may be issued with a comment period of 60 days.

Exam focus point

The above seems to lend itself to a small question.

3.6 Interpretation of IASs/IFRSs

The IFRS Interpretations Committee assists the IASB by improving existing Standards. It was established in July 2010, and replaced the IFRIC (International Financial Reporting Interpretations Committee), which had itself replaced the Standing Interpretations Committee (SIC) in 2002.

The IFRS Interpretations Committee has two main responsibilities:

- Review, on a timely basis, newly identified financial reporting issues not specifically addressed in IFRSs
- Clarify issues where unsatisfactory or conflicting interpretations have developed, or seem likely to develop in the absence of authoritative guidance, with a view to reaching a consensus on the appropriate treatment.

The IFRS Interpretations Committee also helps the IASB move towards international harmonisation by working with its equivalent national-level bodies (such as the UITF in the UK).

The IFRS Interpretations Committee, like the IASB itself, adopts a **principle-based approach**. Its intention is to provide guidance that is in line with the rest of the IFRSs. It therefore bases itself, like each of the individual Standards, first and foremost on the IASB *Framework*. It will then look at any relevant IASs for principles applying the *Framework* to that particular area. It is absolutely essential to the work of the IFRS Interpretations Committee that its interpretations are in line with IASB *Framework* principles, rather than any other accounting principles.

The IFRS Interpretations Committee then in turn informs the IASB of any inadequacies that it finds in the *Framework* or in existing IFRSs. If it believes that they should be modified or that a new Standard should be developed, the IFRS Interpretations Committee informs the IASB so that it can consider whether or not to do so. This helps to ensure that the *Framework* and existing IFRSs are kept up to date for the actual financial reporting issues that the IFRS Interpretations Committee has found with them.

The IFRS Interpretations Committee develops its interpretations through a due process of consultation and debate which includes making Draft Interpretations available for public comment. The IFRS Interpretations Committee's Interpretations that it makes publically available are the consensus views that it has reached as a result of this process.

Exam focus point

The role of the IFRS Interpretations Committee is another area which could form the basis of a small question.

3.6.1 Authority and application of IFRS Interpretations Committee Interpretations

IFRS Interpretations Committee Interpretations carry the same authority as IFRSs, in the sense that they set out consensus views that entities must adhere to if they describe their financial statements as being prepared in accordance with IFRS.

IFRS Interpretations Committee Interpretations are applicable from the date of issue or if they specify one, from their effective date. Some Interpretations may contain 'transitional provisions' that apply to their first application.

An Interpretation then ceases to apply when it is overridden by a new IFRS (or other authoritative IASB document). When this happens, this would be mentioned in the Exposure Draft of the new, overriding IFRS (or other document). The IASB would then inform the IFRS Interpretations Committee when this happens.

3.7 IFRS Interpretations Committee due process

Interpretations of IFRS are developed through an international due process that involves accountants, financial analysts and other users of financial statements, the business community, stock exchanges, regulatory and legal authorities, the business community, stock exchanges, regulatory and legal authorities, academics and other interested individuals and organisations from around the world. The **IFRS Interpretations Committee discusses technical matters in meetings that are open to public observation**. The due process for each project normally, but not necessarily, involves the following steps (the steps that are required under the terms of the Constitution are indicated by an asterisk*):

(a) Staff work to identify and review all the issues associated with the topic and to consider the application of the IASB's *Framework* to the issues

(b) Study of national accounting requirements and practice and an exchange of views about the issues with national standard setters, including national committees that have responsibility for interpretations of national standards

(c) Publication of a draft Interpretation for public comment if no more than three of the IFRS Interpretations Committee's members have voted against the proposal *

(d) Consideration of all comments received on a draft Interpretation within a reasonable period of time *

(e) Approval by the IFRS Interpretations Committee of an Interpretation if no more than three of the IFRS Interpretations Committee's members have voted against the Interpretation after considering public comments on the draft Interpretation *

(f) Approval of the Interpretation by at least eight votes of the Board *

3.8 Comment periods

The IASB issues each Exposure Draft of a Standard and discussion documents for public comment, with a normal comment period of 120 days. In certain circumstances, the Board may expose proposals for a much shorter period. However, such limited periods would be used only in extreme circumstances. Draft IFRS Interpretations Committee Interpretations are exposed for a 60-day comment period.

3.9 Co-ordination with national standard setters

Close co-ordination between IASB due process and due process of national standard setters is important to the success of the IASB's mandate.

The IASB is exploring ways in which to integrate its due process more closely with national due process. Such integration may grow as the relationship between IASB and national standard setters evolves. In particular, the IASB is exploring the following procedure for projects that have international implications.

(a) IASB and national standard setters would co-ordinate their work plans so that when the IASB starts a project, national standard setters would also add it to their own work plans so that they can play a full part in developing international consensus. Similarly, where national standard setters start projects, the IASB would consider whether it needs to develop a new Standard or review its existing Standards. Over a reasonable period, the IASB and national standard setters should aim to review all standards where significant differences currently exist, giving priority to the areas where the differences are greatest.

(b) National standards setters would not be required to vote for IASB's preferred solution in their national standards, since each country remains free to adopt IASB standards with amendments or to adopt other standards. However, the existence of an international consensus is clearly one factor that members of national standard setters would consider when they decide how to vote on national standards.

(c) The IASB would continue to publish its own Exposure Drafts and other documents for public comment.

(d) National standard setters would publish their own exposure document at approximately the same time as IASB Exposure Drafts and would seek specific comments on any significant divergences between the two exposure documents. In some instances, national standard setters may include in their exposure documents specific comments on issues of particular relevance to their country or include more detailed guidance than is included in the corresponding IASB document.

(e) National standard setters would follow their own full due process, which they would ideally choose to integrate with the IASB's due process. This integration would avoid unnecessary delays in completing standards and would also minimise the likelihood of unnecessary differences between the standards that result.

3.9.1 IASB liaison members

Seven of the full-time members of the IASB have formal liaison responsibilities with national standard setters in order to promote the convergence of national accounting standards and International Accounting Standards. The IASB envisages a partnership between the IASB and these national standard setters as they work together to achieve convergence of accounting standards world-wide.

The countries with these liaison members are Australia and New Zealand, Canada, France, Germany, Japan, UK and USA.

In addition all IASB members have contact responsibility with national standards setters not having liaison members and many countries are also represented on the Standards Advisory Council.

Exam focus point

It is wise to bear in mind any points relating to harmonisation and what is happening to achieve it.

3.10 Opportunities for input

The development of an IAS involves an open, public process of debating technical issues and evaluating input sought through several mechanisms. Opportunities for interested parties to participate in the development of IASs would include, depending on the nature of the project:

(a) Participation in the development of views as a member of the IFRS Advisory Council
(b) Participation in advisory groups
(c) Submission of a comment letter in response to a discussion document
(d) Submission of a comment letter in response to an Exposure Draft
(e) Participation in public hearings
(f) Participation in field visits and field tests

The IASB publishes an **annual report** on its activities during the past year and priorities for next year. This report provides a basis and opportunity for comment by interested parties.

IASB reports on its technical projects in its quarterly newsletter, *IASB Insight* and on its Website. IASB publishes a report on IASB decisions immediately after each IASB meeting in its newsletter *IASB Update.* Do visit the IASB website on a regular basis.

4 Generally Accepted Accounting Principles (GAAP)

FAST FORWARD

GAAP, as a term, prevalent in recent years signifies **all the rules, from whatever source, which govern accounting**.

We also need to consider some important terms which you will meet in your financial accounting studies.

- Local (national) company legislation
- National and international accounting standards
- Statutory requirements in other countries (particularly the US)
- Stock exchange requirements

The expression GAAP may or may not have statutory or legal authority or definition, depending on the country involved, eg it does not have statutory authority in the UK, but does so in the USA.

GAAP is in fact a **dynamic concept** and changes constantly as circumstances alter through new legislation, standards and practice.

The problem of what is 'generally accepted' is not easy to settle, because new practices will obviously not be generally adopted yet. The criteria for a practice being 'generally accepted' will depend on factors such as whether the practice is addressed by financial reporting standards or legislation, and whether other companies have adopted the practice. Most importantly perhaps, the question should be whether the practice is consistent with the needs of the users and the objective of financial reporting and whether it is consistent with the 'true and fair' concept.

4.1 True and fair view (or presented fairly)

It is a requirement of both national legislation (in some countries) and International Standards on Auditing that the financial statements should give a true and fair view of (or 'present fairly, in all material respects') the financial position of the enterprise as at the end of the financial year.

4.1.1 True and fair 'override'

The terms 'true and fair view' and 'present fairly, in all material aspects' are not defined in accounting or auditing standards. Despite this, a company's managers may depart from any of the provisions of accounting standards if these are inconsistent with the requirement to give a true and fair view. This is commonly referred to as the **'true and fair override'**. It has been treated as an important **loophole** in the law in different countries and has been the cause of much argument and dissatisfaction within the accounting profession.

5 Other international influences

FAST FORWARD

The EC, the UN, the IFAC, the OECD and the FASB all influence the harmonisation process.

Exam focus point

This section is very much background. There may be one or two points you may be able to use in a question on a topic for example, such as, harmonisation.

The role of the EC and IOSCO is also useful background knowledge.

5.1 European Commission (EC)

The EC regulations form one part of a broader programme for the harmonisation of company law in member states. The commission is uniquely the only organisation to produce international standards of accounting practice which are legally enforceable, in the form of directives which must be included in the national legislation of member states.

However, the EC has also acknowledged the role of the IASB in harmonising world-wide accounting rules.

In June 2000, the EC announced a proposal to **require** all listed companies in member states to **use** IASs for their consolidated financial statements by 2005.

To this end the IASB undertook an improvements project, dealing with revisions to IAS, for example in the area of materiality, presentation, leases, related parties and earnings per share. This has been matched in, for example, the UK, by a convergence project, bringing UK GAAP into line with IFRSs where these are better.

5.2 United Nations (UN)

The UN has a Commission and Centre on Transnational Reporting Corporations through which it gathers information concerning the activities and reporting of multinational companies. The UN processes are highly **political** and probably reflect the **attitudes of the governments** of developing countries to multinationals.

5.3 International Federation of Accountants (IFAC)

The IFAC is a **private sector body** established in 1977 and which now consists of over 100 professional accounting bodies from around 80 different countries. The IFAC's main objective is to **co-ordinate** the **accounting profession** on a **global scale** by issuing and establishing international standards on auditing, management accounting, ethics, education and training.

5.4 Organisation for Economic Co-operation and Development (OECD)

The OECD supports the work of the IASB but also undertakes its **own research** into accounting standards via *ad hoc* working groups. For example, in 1976 the OECD issued guidelines for multinational companies on financial reporting and non-financial disclosures. The OECD appears to work on behalf of **developed countries** to protect them from the extreme proposals of the UN. The OECD has also entered the debate on corporate governance.

5.5 International Organisation of Securities Commissions (IOSCO)

IOSCO is the representative of the world's securities markets regulators. **High quality information** is vital for the operation of an **efficient capital market**, and differences in the quality of the accounting policies and their enforcement between countries leads to inefficiencies between markets. IOSCO has been active in encouraging and promoting the improvement and quality of IASs over the last ten years. Most recently, this commitment was evidenced by the agreement between IFRS and IOSCO to work on a programme of 'core standards' which could be used by publicly listed entities when offering securities in foreign jurisdictions.

The '**core standards' project** resulted in fifteen new or revised IASs and was **completed** in **1999** with the issue of IAS 39 *Financial instruments: recognition and measurement.* IOSCO spent a year reviewing the results of the project and released a report in May 2000 which recommended to all its members that they allow multinational issuers to use IASs, as supplemented by reconciliation, disclosure and interpretation where necessary to address outstanding substantive issues at a national or regional level.

IASB staff and IOSCO continue to work together to resolve outstanding issues and to identify areas where new IASB standards are needed.

5.6 Financial Accounting Standards Board (FASB)

The US standard setter, the FASB and the IASB have been undertaking a project of harmonisation between US GAAP and IFRS.

In September 2002, both parties acknowledged their commitment to the process of developing accounting standards that can be used for domestic and international purposes. Both the FASB and the IASB have worked together to make amendments to current accounting standards in the short term, and to work together on a long term basis to ensure new standards issued are compatible.

The FASB is a important influence on the current and future work of the ISAB.

6 Scope and application of IASs/IFRSs

6.1 Scope

Any limitation of the applicability of a specific IAS/IFRS is made clear within that standard. IASs/IFRSs are **not intended to be applied to immaterial items, nor are they retrospective**. Each individual IAS/IFRS lays out its scope at the beginning of the standard.

6.2 Application

Within each individual country **local regulations** govern, to a greater or lesser degree, the issue of financial statements. These local regulations include accounting standards issued by the national regulatory bodies and/or professional accountancy bodies in the country concerned.

The IASs/IFRSs **concentrate on essentials** and are designed not to be too complex, otherwise they would be impossible to apply on a worldwide basis.

IASs/IFRSs do not override local regulations on financial statements. Members of the IASB should simply disclose the fact where IASs/IFRSs are complied with in all material respects. Members of the IASB in individual counties will attempt to persuade local authorities, where current regulations deviate from IASs/IFRSs, that the benefits of harmonisation make local change worthwhile.

In relation to the above Exam focus point, the following is our **brief summary** of the main points included in ACCA's suggested solution

- It is difficult if not impossible to comply with both local regulations /statutes as well as IAS/IFRS.
- In the past the regulatory bodies have either amended their standards and/or lobbied for changes in the regulations/statutes.
- Financial statements do not comply with the requirements of IAS, as per IAS 1, unless all IASs are complied with
- It is not appropriate to try to rectify non-compliance by resorting to disclosure or explanatory material.
- A pragmatic and practical response may be to prepare two sets of financial statements
  - Set 1 For local filing purposes and complying with local regulations
  - Set 2 For international publication purposes and complying with IASs/IFRSs.

Note. The company might also resort to the true and fair override as per Paragraph 4.1.1 above.

7 Progress towards global harmonisation

FAST FORWARD

You need to be aware of all the issues surrounding harmonisation.

Exam focus point

Harmonisation is always a hot topic and hence could come up in your exam as a small discursive question.

You should try to keep up to date by reading publications such as the Financial Times, the Economist and articles posted on the ACCA website.

Close co-ordination between IASB due process and due process of national standard setters is important to the success of the IASB's mandate.

The IASB is exploring ways of further integrating its due process with that of national standard setters. This integration may grow as the relationship between IASB and national standard setters evolves. In particular, the IASB is exploring the following procedure for projects that have international implications.

(a) IASB and national standard setters would co-ordinate their work plans so that when the IASB starts a project, national standard setters would also add it to their own work plans so that they can play a full part in developing international consensus. Similarly, where national standard setters start projects, the IASB would consider whether it needs to develop a new Standard or review its existing Standards. Over a reasonable period, the IASB and national standard setters should aim to review all standards where significant differences currently exist, giving priority to the areas where the differences are greatest.

(b) National standards setters would not be required to vote for IASB's preferred solution in their national standards, since each country remains free to adopt IASB standards with amendments or to adopt other standards. However, the existence of an international consensus is clearly one factor that members of national standard setters would consider when they decide how to vote on national standards.

(c) The IASB would continue to publish its own Exposure Drafts and other documents for public comment.

(d) National standard setters would publish their own exposure document at approximately the same time as IASB Exposure Drafts and would seek specific comments on any significant divergences between the two exposure documents. In some instances, national standard setters may include in their exposure documents specific comments on issues of particular relevance to their country or include more detailed guidance than is included in the corresponding IASB document.

(e) National standard setters would follow their own full due process, which they would ideally choose to integrate with the IASB's due process. This integration would avoid unnecessary delays in completing standards and would also minimise the likelihood of unnecessary differences between the standards that result.

7.1 IASB liaison members

Seven of the full-time members of the IASB have formal liaison responsibilities with national standard setters in order to promote the convergence of national accounting standards and International Accounting Standards. The IASB envisages a partnership between the IASB and these national standard setters as they work together to achieve convergence of accounting standards worldwide.

The countries with these liaison members are Australia and New Zealand, Canada, France, Germany, Japan, UK and USA.

In addition all IASB members have contact responsibility with national standards setters not having liaison members and many countries are also represented on the Standards Advisory Council.

7.2 World-wide effect of IASs and the IASB

The IASB, and before it the IASC, has now been in existence for around 25 years, and it is worth looking at the effect it has had in that time.

As far as Europe is concerned, the consolidated financial statements of many of Europe's top multinationals are already prepared in conformity with national requirements, EC directives and IASs. These developments have been given added impetus by the internationalisation of capital markets. As discussed, IASs/IFRSs have been implemented in EU since 2005.

In Japan, the influence of the IASB had, until recently, been negligible. This was mainly because of links in Japan between tax rules and financial reporting. The Japanese Ministry of Finance set up a working committee to consider whether to bring national requirements into line with IASs/IFRSs. The Tokyo Stock Exchange has announced that it will accept financial statements from foreign issuers that conform with home country standards, which would include IFRS.

The Japanese standpoint was widely seen as an attempt to attract foreign issuers, in particular companies from Hong Kong and Singapore. As these countries base their accounting on international standards, this action is therefore implicit acknowledgement by the Japanese Ministry of Finance of IAS/IFRS requirements.

In **America**, the Securities and Exchange Commission (SEC) agreed in 1993 to allow foreign issuers (of shares, etc) to follow IAS/IFRS treatments on certain issues, including cash flow statements under IAS 7. The overall effect is that, where an IAS/IFRS treatment differs from US GAAP, these treatments will now be acceptable. The SEC is now supporting the IASB because it wants to attract foreign listings.

In certain countries, the application of IASs/IFRs is **mandatory** for all domestic listed companies. The following provides an example of some of the countries, but the schedule is not exhaustive: Barbados, Cyprus, Georgia, Jamaica, Jordan, Kenya, Kuwait, Malawi, Mauritius, Nepal, Peru, Serbia and Trinidad and Tobago.

Countries that implemented IFRS for the 2005 European ruling in respect of the consolidated financial statements of public listed companies include Austria, Belgium, Czech Republic, Denmark, Estonia, Finland, France, Germany, Greece, Hungary, Iceland, Ireland, Italy, Liechtenstein, Lithuania, Luxembourg,

Netherlands, Norway, Poland, Portugal, Slovenia, Slovak Republic, Spain, Sweden and the United Kingdom.

Many non-European counties also require their listed companies to adopt IFRS. These include Australia, Bahamas, Bahrain, Chile, Costa Rica, Egypt, Hong Kong, Kenya, Kuwait, Mauritius, New Zealand, and South Africa; the list is not exhaustive.

There are some countries where the implementation of IASs/IFRSs is **not mandatory but discretionary**. These include Aruba, Bermuda, Bolivia, Botswana, Cayman Islands, Dominica, El Salvador, Gibraltar, Laos, Lesotho, Swaziland, Switzerland, Turkey, Uganda, Zambia and Zimbabwe.

In December 2009, the Japanese FSA announced that Japanese listed companies would be allowed to use IFRSs from 31 March 2010.

However, there are several countries where the **use of IASs/IFRSs are not permitted**. The following are some of the countries, but the list is not exhaustive: Argentina, Bangladesh, Canada, India, Indonesia, Iran, Japan, South Korea, Malaysia, Pakistan, Saudi Arabia, Senegal, Taiwan, Thailand, Tunisia and Vietnam.

7.3 Harmonisation in Europe

The objective of the European Commission (EC) is to build a fully integrated, globally competitive market. A key element of this is the harmonisation of company law across the member states. In line with this the **EC aims to establish a level playing field for financial reporting**, supported by an effective enforcement regime. The commission is uniquely the only organisation whose accounting standards are legally enforceable, in the form of directives which must be included in the national legislation of member states. However, the directives have been criticised as they might become constraints on the application of world-wide standards, and might bring accounting standardisation and harmonisation into the political arena.

The EC adopted a regulation stating that from 2005 consolidated accounts of listed companies have been required to comply with IFRSs. The implications of this measure are far reaching. However, member states currently have the discretion to extend the implementation of IAS/IFRS to include non-listed companies. In the UK, for example, small companies report under UK GAAP, with many taking advantage of the reduced disclosure requirements of the FRSSE (Financial Reporting Standard for Smaller Entities). The IASB has recently issued the IFRS for SMEs (Small and Medium-sized Entities), which is an important step toward the introduction of IFRS for all companies.

Many commentators believe that in the light of the EC's commitment to IFRS it is only a matter of time before national standard setting bodies like the UK's ASB are, in effect, replaced by the IASB, with national standards falling into disuse. However, the IASB will continue to need input and expertise from valued national standard setters like the ASB.

7.4 IFRS in the USA

Convergence between IFRS and US GAAP is **one of the bigger issues** in the global implementation of IFRS. At present, all US entities must file accounts prepared under US GAAP. However, in 2002 the IASB and its US equivalent, the FASB (Financial Accounting Standards Board) did agree to harmonise their work plans, and to work towards reducing the differences between IFRS and US GAAP.

In **2008 the Securities and Exchange Commission (SEC) issued a 'roadmap'** for the use of IFRS, proposing the eventual mandatory use of IFRS for all US public companies by 2014. At present, only *overseas* issuers of securities are allowed to file accounts under IFRS (without having to provide a reconciliation to US GAAP).

The SEC's 'roadmap' would allow some companies the option of using IFRS from 2010. It envisages phasing in IFRS by requiring companies to file accounts under both IFRS and US GAAP for the two years 2012-2014, after which accounts would be prepared under IFRS alone. The SEC has said that it will make its final decision on timings in 2011.

7.5 Rules-based versus principles-based financial reporting standards

Exam focus point

The expressions 'rules-based' and 'principles-based' may be used in a question. Ensure you understand what they mean.

US GAAP is an example of a rules-based approach. It consists of a large number of specific accounting standards, and each standard contains a large number of rules (as well as exceptions to the rules), attempting to prescribe treatments for every possible situation that might arise. However, in 2002 the incoming chairman of the **FASB** signalled his support for a **shift to a principles-based approach**:

> 'I understand the US environment where there has been such a proliferation of rules. I like the principles-based approach but some people have exaggerated the differences. You are always going to have rules but the question is: 'Where do I start?' You can never have a rule for everything and at that point you have to go back to principles.'
>
> Bob Hertz, FASB Chairman (*Financial Times*, 27 May 2002)

The US has accordingly begun to develop a principles-based approach, which coincides with its move toward adoption of IFRS, which are themselves principles-based.

A principles-based approach then, is one where the individual standards can be clearly seen to be applications of the approach to accounting adopted by the standards as a whole. Thus each individual IAS/IFRS applies the IASB *Framework*, and each standard is an individual reflection of the whole. Specificity at the level of detail is sacrificed for clarity in terms of the overall approach.

Accountants working under **IFRS** are required, then, to use **more professional judgement** than under a rules-based approach. There may not be a specific rule that applies to the event that they need to report, so they need to use judgement in applying the principles contained in the relevant IFRS. It is the view of the IASB that this will result in better quality financial reporting. Accounts will have to be **true to the overall principles of IFRS**, rather than to an individual rule that may not be appropriate for the event being reported, and which may therefore end up with an accounting treatment that is not true to the intentions of IFRS as a whole.

7.6 Brief comparison of IFRS v UK GAAP v US GAAP

To provide you with some practical perspective, here is a **very brief comparison** between IAS, UK GAAP and US GAAP requirements regarding three financial reporting areas.

Subject	UK GAAP	US GAAP	IFRS
Inventory valuation	The **LIFO** method is **not** permitted under UK GAAP, so the stock must be valued using a method such as FIFO (first in first out).	In the USA stock may be valued using the **LIFO** (last in first out) method. Under this method, assuming prices are rising, closing stock has a lower value than using FIFO.	IAS 2 (revised) requires use of FIFO or average methods for ordinarily interchangeable items.
Development expenditure	Development expenditure should be written off in year of expenditure, except in certain circumstances where it may be deferred.	Development expenditure must be recognised in profit and loss under all circumstances.	Under IAS 38 (revised) development costs are capitalised if certain criteria are met.

7.7 UK Accounting Standards Board Convergence Approach

In the UK a detailed comparison has been carried out between international and UK accounting standards which has been documented in what is called *The Convergence Handbook.*

The following statement is taken from *The Convergence Handbook.*

> 'The ASB is working with the IASB and other national standard setters in order to seek improvements in IFRS and convergence of national and international standards. The ASB is one of several national standard setters that have a formal liaison relationship with the IASB. This relationship involves regular meetings and other consultations as well as several joint standard setting projects, including the ASB's joint project with the IASB on reporting financial performance.
>
> The ASB intends to align UK accounting standards with IFRS whenever practicable. It proposes to do this, in the main, by a phased replacement of existing UK standards with new UK standards based on the equivalent IFRS.'

We quote again from Sir David Tweedie's previously-mentioned article.

> 'The UK is part of an increasingly global economy, and its prosperity depends upon inward and outward capital flows to facilitate investment and promote economic growth. Adopting international standards will remove a hurdle in the way of developments that offer the prospects of benefits for the UK investor and for UK business as a whole.'

8 Benefits of and barriers to global harmonisation

FAST FORWARD

There are **benefits** to international harmonisation but also **barriers** to its achievement.

Exam focus point

Given the nature of the Dip IFR syllabus and its objectives, it is worthwhile being adequately prepared to handle a question in this area.

We have now comprehensively covered the international regulatory framework and the role of the IASB, and shall now look at the benefits of harmonisation and the problems to achieving this.

Question — Harmonisation

In terms of financial reporting standards, what do you think are:

(a) The benefits of international harmonisation?
(b) The barriers to international harmonisation?

Answer

(a) Benefits of global harmonisation

The benefits of harmonisation will be based on the benefits to users and preparers of accounts, as follows.

(i) Investors, both individual and corporate, would like to be able to compare the financial results of different companies internationally as well as nationally in making investment decisions.

(ii) Multinational companies would benefit from harmonisation for many reasons including the following.

(1) Better access would be gained to foreign investor funds.
(2) Management control would be improved, because harmonisation would aid internal communication of financial information.

(3) Appraisal of foreign enterprises for take-overs and mergers would be more straightforward.

(4) It would be easier to comply with the reporting requirements of overseas stock exchanges.

(5) Preparation of group accounts would be easier.

(6) A reduction in audit costs might be achieved.

(7) Transfer of accounting staff across national borders would be easier.

(iii) Governments of developing countries would save time and money if they could adopt international standards and, if these were used internally, governments of developing countries could attempt to control the activities of foreign multinational companies in their own country. These companies could not 'hide' behind foreign accounting practices which are difficult to understand.

(iv) Tax authorities. It will be easier to calculate the tax liability of investors, including multinationals who receive income from overseas sources.

(v) Regional economic groups usually promote trade within a specific geographical region. This would be aided by common accounting practices within the region.

(vi) Large international accounting firms would benefit as accounting and auditing would be much easier if similar accounting practices existed throughout the world.

(b) Barriers to harmonisation

(i) Different purposes of financial reporting. In some countries the purpose is solely for tax assessment, while in others it is for investor decision-making.

(ii) Different legal systems. These prevent the development of certain accounting practices and restrict the options available.

(iii) Different user groups. Countries have different ideas about who the relevant user groups are and their respective importance. In the USA investor and creditor groups are given prominence, while in Europe employees enjoy a higher profile.

(iv) Needs of developing countries. Developing countries are obviously behind in the standard setting process and they need to develop the basic standards and principles already in place in most developed countries.

(v) Nationalism is demonstrated in an unwillingness to accept another country's standard.

(vi) Cultural differences result in objectives for accounting systems differing from country to country.

(vii) Unique circumstances. Some countries may be experiencing unusual circumstances which affect all aspects of everyday life and impinge on the ability of companies to produce proper reports, for example hyperinflation, civil war, currency restriction and so on.

(viii) The lack of strong accountancy bodies. Many countries do not have strong independent accountancy or business bodies which would press for better standards and greater harmonisation.

9 Feedback on the IASB

We will begin by looking at some of the feedback and issues relating to IFRSs, particularly where they offer a choice of treatment.

9.1 Financial reporting standards and choice

In favour of accounting standards (both national and international), the following points can be made.

- They reduce or eliminate confusing variations in the methods used to prepare accounts.
- They provide a focal point for debate and discussions about accounting practice.

- They oblige companies to disclose the accounting policies used in the preparation of accounts.
- They are a less rigid alternative to enforcing conformity by means of legislation.
- They have obliged companies to disclose more accounting information than they would otherwise have done if accounting standards did not exist, for example IAS 33 *Earnings per share.* Many companies are reluctant to disclose information which is not required by national legislation.

However, the following arguments may be put forward against standardisation and in favour of choice.

- Standards may be subject to lobbying or government pressure (in the case of national standards). For example, in the USA, the accounting standard FAS 19 on the accounts of oil and gas companies led to a powerful lobby of oil companies, which persuaded the SEC (Securities and Exchange Commission) to step in. FAS 19 was then suspended.
- Many national standards are not based on a conceptual framework of accounting, although IASs are.
- There may a trend towards rigidity, and away from flexibility in applying the rules.

9.2 Political problems

Exam focus point

Again, this area may provide useful material in addressing a question on harmonisation.

Any international body, whatever its purpose or activity, faces enormous political difficulties in attempting to gain international consensus and the IASB is no exception to this. How can the IASB reconcile the financial reporting situation between economies as diverse as third-world developing countries and sophisticated first-world industrial powers?

Developing countries are suspicious of the IASB, believing it to be dominated by the USA. They are being catered for to some extent by the development of a standard on agriculture, which is generally of much more relevance to such countries.

There are also tensions between the UK/US model of financial reporting and the European model. The UK/US model is based around investor reporting, whereas the European model is mainly concerned with tax rules, so shareholder reporting has a much lower priority.

As discussed earlier, there are also tensions between US GAAP which is rules-based and IAS/IFRS which are principles-based.

The break-up of the former USSR and the move in many Eastern European countries to free-market economies has also created difficulties. It is likely that these countries will have to 'catch up' to international standards as their economies stabilise, although it is obvious good progress is being made.

You must keep up to date with the IASB's progress and the problems it encounters in the financial press, as well as on the IASB website.

10 IFRS 1: First-time adoption of International Financial Reporting Standards

FAST FORWARD

You need to be aware of the technical requirements and practical managerial issues of implementing IFRS for the first time.

Exam focus point

Your examiner has stated that you are unlikely to be examined on the *detail* of IFRS 1. However, it is still an examinable document for Dip IFR, so you should read and work through this section so that you are ready for anything the examiner might ask you on it.

IFRS 1 sets out the precise way in which companies should implement a change from local accounting standards (their previous GAAP) to IASs and IFRSs. One of the main reasons for issuing a new standard was that listed companies in the EU were required to prepare their consolidated financial statements in accordance with IFRSs from 2005 onwards.

The standard is intended to ensure that an entity's first IFRS financial statements contain high quality information that: is transparent for users and comparable over all periods presented; provides a suitable starting point for accounting under IFRSs; and can be generated at a cost that does not exceed the benefits to users.

Key terms

Date of transition to IFRSs. The beginning of the earliest period for which an entity presents full comparative information under IFRSs in its first IFRS financial statements.

Deemed cost An amount used as a surrogate for cost or depreciated cost at a given date.

Fair value The amount for which an asset could be exchanged, or a liability settled, between knowledgeable, willing parties in an arm's length transaction.

First IFRS financial statements The first annual financial statements in which an entity adopts International Financial Reporting Standards (IFRSs), by an explicit and unreserved statement of compliance with IFRSs.

Opening IFRS statement of financial position An entity's statement of financial position (published or unpublished) at the date of transition to IFRSs.

Previous GAAP The basis of accounting that a first time adopter used immediately before adopting IFRSs.

Reporting period The latest period covered by financial statements or by an interim financial report. *(IFRS 1)*

IFRS 1 **only applies** where an entity prepares IFRS financial statements **for the first time**. Changes in accounting policies made by an entity that already applies IFRSs should be dealt with by applying either IAS 8 or specific transitional requirements in other standards.

10.1 Making the transition to IFRS

An entity should:

(a) Select accounting policies that comply with IFRSs at the end of the reporting period for the entity's first IFRS financial statements.

(b) Prepare an opening IFRS statement of financial position at the date of transition to IFRSs. This is the starting point for subsequent accounting under IFRSs. The date of transition to IFRSs is the beginning of the earliest comparative period presented in an entity's first IFRS financial statements.

(c) Disclose the effect of the change in the financial statements.

10.2 Example: reporting period and opening IFRS statement of financial position

A listed company has a 31 December year-end and will be required to comply with IFRSs from 1 January 2009.

Required

What is the date of transition to IFRSs?

10.3 Solution

The company's first IFRS financial statements will be for the year ended 31 December 2009.

IFRS 1 requires that at least one year's comparative figures are presented in the first IFRS financial statements. The comparative figures will be for the year ended 31 December 2008.

Therefore the date of transition to IFRSs is 1 January 2008 and the company prepares an opening IFRS statement of financial position at this date.

10.4 Preparing the opening IFRS statement of financial position

IFRS 1 states that in its opening IFRS statement of financial position an entity shall:

(a) Recognise all assets and liabilities whose recognition is required by IFRSs

(b) Not recognise items as assets or liabilities if IFRSs do not permit such recognition

(c) Reclassify items that it recognised under previous GAAP as one type of asset, liability or component of equity, but are a different type of asset liability or component of equity under IFRSs

(d) Apply IFRS in measuring all recognised assets and liabilities

This involves restating the statement of financial position prepared at the same date under the entity's previous GAAP so that it complies with IASs and IFRSs in force at the end of the reporting period. In our example above, the company prepares its opening IFRS statement of financial position 1 January 2008, following accounting policies that comply with IFRSs in force at 31 December 2009.

The accounting policies that an entity uses in its opening IFRS statement of financial position may differ from those it used for the same date using its previous GAAP. The resulting adjustments are recognised directly in retained earnings (in equity) at the date of transition. (This is because the adjustments arise from events and transactions before the date of transition to IFRS.)

10.5 Exemptions from other IFRSs

A business may elect to use any or all of a range of exemptions. These enable an entity not to apply certain requirements of specific accounting standards retrospectively in drawing up its opening IFRS statement of financial position. Their purpose is to ensure that the cost of producing IFRS financial statements does not exceed the benefits to users.

10.5.1 Business combinations

IFRS 3 need not be applied retrospectively to business combinations that occurred before the date of the opening IFRS statement of financial position. This has the following consequences.

(a) Combinations keep the same classification (eg acquisition, uniting of interests) as in the previous GAAP financial statements.

(b) All acquired assets and liabilities are recognised other than:

  (i) Some financial assets and financial liabilities derecognised under the previous GAAP (derivatives and special purpose entities must be recognised);

  (ii) Assets (including goodwill) and liabilities that were not recognised under previous GAAP and would not qualify for recognition under IFRSs.

  Any resulting change is recognised by adjusting retained earnings (ie equity) unless the change results from the recognition of an intangible asset that was previously subsumed within goodwill.

(c) Items which do not qualify for recognition as an asset or liability under IFRSs must be excluded from the opening IFRS statement of financial position. For example, intangible assets that do not qualify for separate recognition under IAS 38 must be reclassified as part of goodwill.

(d) The carrying amount of goodwill in the opening IFRS statement of financial position is the same as its carrying amount under previous GAAP. However, goodwill must be tested for impairment at the transition date.

10.5.2 Property, plant and equipment

An entity may measure an item of property, plant and equipment at its fair value at the transition date and then use the fair value as its deemed cost at that date.

An entity may use a previous GAAP revaluation (or a valuation for the purpose of a privatisation or initial public offering) as the deemed cost at the transition date, so long as the revaluation was broadly comparable to fair value or depreciated replacement cost at the date of the valuation.

These exemptions are also available for:

(a) Investment properties measured under the cost model in IAS 40 *Investment property*

(b) Intangible assets that meet the recognition criteria and the criteria for revaluation in IAS 38 *Intangible assets*

10.5.3 Employee benefits

Under IAS 19 an entity may elect to use a 'corridor' approach that leaves some actuarial gains and losses unrecognised. A first time adopter may elect to recognise all cumulative actuarial gains and losses at the date of transition to IFRSs, even if it uses the corridor approach for later actuarial gains and losses. If this election is used it must apply to all plans.

10.5.4 Cumulative translation differences

IAS 21 requires some exchange differences to be classified as a separate component of equity, for example differences arising when the financial statements of a foreign operation are translated. The cumulative translation differences must be included in the gain or loss on disposal of the foreign operation. Under the exemption, the cumulative translation differences for all foreign operations are deemed to be zero at the transition date. The gain or loss on a subsequent disposal of a foreign operation will exclude translation differences that arose before the transition date. Later translation differences will be included.

10.5.5 Compound financial instruments

IAS 32 requires compound financial instruments to be split at inception into separate liability and equity components. If the liability component is no longer outstanding at the date of the translation to IFRSs, the split is not required.

10.5.6 Designation of previously recognised financial instruments

When financial instruments are first recognised, they may be designated as financial assets or financial liabilities 'at fair value through profit or loss' or as 'available for sale' under IAS 39. An entity may make such a designation at the date of transition to IFRSs.

10.5.7 Share-based payment transactions

An entity is encouraged, but not required to apply IFRS 2 to:

(a) Equity instruments that were granted and vested before the date of transition to IFRSs or 1 January 2005 (whichever is the later)

(b) Liabilities arising from share-based payment transactions that were settled before the date of transition to IFRSs

10.5.8 Financial instruments disclosures

In January 2010 IFRS 1 was amended to provide limited exemption from comparative IFRS 7 disclosures, so that first-time adopters of IFRSs have the same exemptions as existing IFRS preparers.

10.6 Exceptions to retrospective application of other IFRSs

IFRS 1 prohibits retrospective application of some other aspects of IFRSs.

(a) Derecognition of financial assets and financial liabilities: the requirements in IAS 39 are applied prospectively from 1 January 2001 (the effective date of IAS 39). This means that financial assets and liabilities derecognised under previous GAAP before this date are not recognised.

(b) Hedge accounting: the conditions to qualify for hedge accounting apply prospectively from the date of transition to IFRSs.

(c) Estimates: Estimates under IFRSs at the date of transition must be consistent with those made at the same date under previous GAAP, (after adjustments to reflect any difference in accounting policies), unless there is objective evidence that those estimates were in error.

Question

Russell Co will adopt International Financial Reporting Standards (IFRSs) for the first time in its financial statements for the year ended 31 December 20X9.

In its previous financial statements for 31 December 20X7 and 20X8, which were prepared under local GAAP, the company made a number of routine accounting estimates, including accrued expenses. It also recognised a general provision for liabilities, calculated at a fixed percentage of its retained earnings for the year. This is required under its local GAAP.

Subsequently, some of the accruals were found to be overestimates and some were found to be underestimates.

Required

Discuss how the matters above should be dealt with in the IFRS financial statements of Russell Co for the year ended 31 December 20X9.

Answer

Provided that the routine accounting estimates have been made in a manner consistent with IFRSs no adjustments are made in the first IFRS financial statements. The only exception to this is if the company has subsequently discovered that these estimates were in error. Although there were some overestimates and some underestimates, this is probably not the case here.

The general provision is a different matter. This provision would definitely not have met the criteria for recognition under IAS 37 and therefore it will not be recognised in the opening IFRS statement of financial position (1 January 20X8) or at subsequent year-ends.

10.7 Presentation and disclosure

An entity's first IFRS financial statements must include at least one year of comparative information.

Comparative information need not comply with IAS 32 and IAS 39; instead the entity may apply its previous GAAP and disclose this fact together with the nature of the main adjustments that would make the information comply with IAS 32 and IAS 39.

An entity must also explain the effect of the transition from previous GAAP to IFRSs on its financial position, financial performance and cash flows by providing reconciliations:

(a) Of equity reported under previous GAAP to equity under IFRSs at the date of transition and at the reporting date

(b) Of the profit or loss reported under previous GAAP to profit or loss reported under IFRSs for the period

The reconciliations must give sufficient detail to enable users to understand the material adjustments to the statement of financial position and the statement of comprehensive income.

If an entity presented a statement of cash flows under its previous GAAP, it should also explain the material adjustments to the statement of cash flows.

If an entity recognised or reversed any impairment losses for the first time in preparing its opening IFRS statement of financial position, it must provide the disclosures that IAS 36 *Impairment of assets* would have required if the entity had recognised those impairment losses or reversals in the period beginning with the date of transition to IFRSs.

If an entity corrects errors made under previous GAAP, the reconciliations must distinguish the correction of errors from changes in accounting policies.

Where fair value has been used as deemed cost for a non-current asset in the opening IFRS statement of financial position as deemed cost for a non-current asset, the financial statements must disclose the aggregate of fair values and the aggregate adjustments to the carrying amounts reported under previous GAAP for each line in the opening IFRS statement of financial position.

10.8 Interim financial reports

IFRS 1 applies to any interim financial report that an entity presents under IAS 34 *Interim financial reporting* for part of the period covered by the first IFRS financial statements.

Where interim financial reports are presented, an entity should provide the same reconciliations required for full financial statements and described in 10.4 above. Material adjustments to the statement of cash flows, if any, should also be disclosed.

10.9 Managing the change to International Standards

The implementation of the technical changes above is likely to entail careful management in most companies. Here are some of the change management considerations that should be addressed.

(a) **Accurate assessment of the task involved**. Underestimation or wishful thinking may hamper the effectiveness of the conversion and may ultimately prove inefficient.

(b) **Proper planning**. This should take place at the overall project level, but a detailed task analysis could be drawn up to control work performed.

(c) **Human resource management**. The project must be properly structured and staffed.

(d) **Training**. Where there are skills gaps, remedial training should be provided.

(e) **Monitoring and accountability**. A relaxed 'it will be alright on the night' attitude could spell danger. Implementation progress should be monitored and regular meetings set up so that participants can personally account for what they are doing as well as flag up any problems as early as possible. Project drift should be avoided.

(f) **Achieving milestones**. Successful completion of key steps and tasks should be appropriately acknowledged, ie what managers call 'celebrating success', so as to sustain motivation and performance.

(g) **Physical resourcing**. The need for IT equipment and office space should be properly assessed.

(h) **Process review**. Care should be taken not to perceive the change as a one-off quick fix. Any charge in future systems and processes should be assessed and properly implemented.

(i) **Follow-up procedures**. As with general good management practice, the follow up procedures should be planned in to make sure that the changes stick and that any further changes are identified and addressed.

10.10 Section summary

You need to be able to advise an entity making the change from previous GAAP to IFRSs on:

- The general rules (including the date of the opening IFRS statement of financial position)
- The exemptions available
- How to deal with estimates in previous financial statements
- Explaining the effects of the change on the financial statements (preparing reconciliations)
- The practical aspects of managing the change

Chapter Roundup

- The need for harmonised financial reporting standards arises as a result of the globalisation of business activities and operations. Harmonised financial reporting standards are intended to provide:
  - A platform for wider investment choice
  - A more efficient capital market
  - Lower cost of capital
  - Enhanced business development
- Harmonisation remains a long and on-going process and you should be aware of the background surrounding this.
- It is sometimes argued that companies should be given a choice in matters of financial reporting on the grounds that accounting standards are detrimental to the quality of such reporting. There are arguments on both sides.
- You should be able to describe the **organisation of the IASB** and its relationships with intergovernmental bodies, professional accountancy bodies, national standard setting bodies and IOSCO.
- You must understand the **due process** involved in producing international standards, their scope and application and moves by the IASB to interpret them. You should keep an eye on the work of the IASB in the accountancy press and Internet, so you are completely up to date.
- GAAP, as a term, prevalent in recent years signifies **all the rules, from whatever source, which govern accounting**.
- The EC, the UN, the IFAC, the OECD and the FASB all influence the harmonisation process.
- You need to be aware of all the issues surrounding harmonisation.
- There are **benefits** to international harmonisation but also **barriers** to its achievement
- You need to be aware of the technical requirements and practical managerial issues of implementing IFRS for the first time.

Quick Quiz

1 What recent decisions will have a beneficial effect on global harmonisation?

2 One objective of the IASB is to promote the preparation of financial statements using the euro.

True ☐ False ☐

3 What development at the IASB aids users' interpretation of IFRSs?

4 Which of the following arguments is not in favour of accounting standards, but is in favour of accounting choice?

A They reduce variations in methods used to produce accounts
B They oblige companies to disclose their accounting policies
C They are a less rigid alternative to legislation
D They may tend towards rigidity in applying the rules

Answers to Quick Quiz

1 The IOSCO endorsement, and the EC proposal that listed companies should use IAS by 2005.

2 False

3 The formation of an IFRS Interpretations Committee.

4 D The other arguments are all in favour of accounting standards.

Now try the questions below from the Exam Question Bank

Number	Level	Marks	Time
Q1	Introductory	n/a	n/a
Q2	Introductory	n/a	n/a
Q3	Introductory	n/a	n/a

Conceptual framework for financial reporting

2

Topic list	Syllabus reference
1 The need for a conceptual framework	1(e)
2 The IASB's *Framework*	1(e)
3 The objective of financial statements	1(e)
4 Underlying assumptions	1(e)
5 Qualitative characteristics of financial statements	1(e)
6 The elements of financial statements	1(e)
7 Recognition of the elements of financial statements	1(e)
8 Measurement of the elements of financial statements	1(e)

Introduction

The need for a **formal conceptual framework** is driven by the desire to ensure that **accounting standards** are **not produced** in a haphazard and **fire-fighting manner**.

The IASB Framework envisages its role in being used for **standard setting purposes**, **interpretation** and **application** of standards and dealing with **issues** are not covered in standards.

Study Guide

Section 1 – The international accounting standards board and the regulatory framework

- Understand and interpret the IASB *Framework for the Preparation and Presentation of Financial Statements*

Exam Guide

The contents of this chapter provide the essential building blocks of the International Financial Reporting Standards. Careful study of this material will be very helpful to later work as you proceed through this textbook.

1 The need for a conceptual framework

FAST FORWARD

The financial reporting process is concerned with providing information that is **useful** in the business and economic **decision-making process**. Therefore a conceptual framework will form the **theoretical basis** for determining which events should be accounted for, how they should be measured and how they should be communicated to the user.

Key term

A **conceptual framework**, in the field we are concerned with, is a statement of generally accepted theoretical principles which form the frame of reference for financial reporting. These theoretical principles provide the basis for the development of new accounting standards and the evaluation of those already in existence.

Although it is theoretical in nature, a conceptual framework for financial reporting has highly practical final aims.

The **danger of not having a conceptual framework** is demonstrated in the way some countries' standards have developed over recent years; standards tend to be produced in a **haphazard and fire-fighting way**. Where an agreed framework exists, the standard-setting body act as an architect or designer, rather than a fire-fighter, building accounting rules on the foundation of sound, agreed basic principles.

The lack of a conceptual framework also means that fundamental principles are tackled more than once in different standards, thereby producing **contradictions** and **inconsistencies** in basic concepts, such as those of prudence and matching. This leads to ambiguity and it affects the true and fair concept of financial reporting.

Another problem with the lack of a conceptual framework has become apparent in the USA. The large number of highly detailed standards produced by the Financial Accounting Standards Board (FASB) has created a financial reporting environment governed by **specific rules rather than general principles**. This would be avoided if a cohesive set of principles were in place.

A conceptual framework can also bolster standard setters **against political pressure** from various 'lobby groups' and interested parties. Such pressure would only prevail if it was acceptable under the conceptual framework.

1.1 Advantages and disadvantages of a conceptual framework

Advantages

(a) The situation is **avoided** whereby standards are being developed on a **patchwork** basis, where a particular accounting problem is recognised as having emerged, and resources were then channelled into standardising accounting practice in that area, without regard to whether that particular issue was necessarily the most important issue remaining at that time without standardisation.

(b) As stated above, the development of certain standards (particularly national standards) have been subject to considerable political interference from interested parties. Where there is a conflict of interest between user groups on which policies to choose, policies deriving from a conceptual framework will be **less open** to criticism that the standard-setter buckled to **external pressure**.

(c) Some standards may concentrate on the **income statement** whereas some may concentrate on the **valuation of net assets** (statement of financial position).

Disadvantages

(a) Financial statements are intended for a **variety of users**, and it is not certain that a single conceptual framework can be devised which will suit all users.

(b) Given the **diversity of user requirements**, there may be a need for a variety of accounting standards, each produced for a **different purpose** (and with different concepts as a basis).

(c) It is not clear that a conceptual framework makes the task of preparing and then implementing standards any easier than without a framework.

2 The IASB'S *Framework*

FAST FORWARD

The IASB's *Framework* provides a **conceptual framework** for all IASs/IFRSs.

In July 1989 the IASB (then IASC) produced a document, *Framework for the preparation and presentation of financial statements* (*'Framework'*). The *Framework* is, in effect, the **conceptual** framework upon which all IASs are based and hence which determines how financial statements are prepared and the information they contain.

The *Framework* consists of several sections or chapters, following on after a preface and introduction. These chapters are as follows.

- The objective of financial statements.
- Underlying assumptions
- Qualitative characteristics of financial statements
- The elements of financial statements
- Recognition of the elements of financial statements
- Measurement of the elements of financial statements
- Concepts of capital and capital maintenance

We will look briefly at the preface and introduction to the *Framework* as these will place the document in context with the rest of what you have studied for this paper and in particular the context of the *Framework* in the IASB's approach to developing IASs.

2.1 Preface

The preface to the *Framework* points out the **fundamental reason** why financial statements are **produced worldwide**, ie to **satisfy the requirements of external users**, but that practice varies due to the individual pressures in each country. These pressures may be social, political, economic or legal, but they result in variations in practice from country to country, including the form of statements, the definition of their component parts (assets, liabilities etc), the criteria for recognition of items and both the scope and disclosure of financial statements.

It is these differences which the IASB wishes to narrow by **harmonising** all aspects of financial statements, including the regulations governing their accounting standards and their preparation and presentation.

The preface emphasises the way **financial statements are used to make economic decisions** and thus financial statements should be prepared to this end. The types of economic decisions for which financial statements are likely to be used include the following.

- Decisions to buy, hold or sell equity investments
- Assessment of management stewardship and accountability

- Assessment of the enterprise's ability to pay employees
- Assessment of the security of amounts lent to the enterprise
- Determination of taxation policies
- Determination of distributable profits and dividends
- Inclusion in national income statistics
- Regulations of the activities of enterprises

Any additional requirements imposed by national governments for their own purposes should not affect financial statements produced for the benefit of other users.

The *Framework* recognises that financial statements can be prepared using a **variety of models**. Although the most common is based on historical cost and a nominal unit of currency (ie pound sterling, US dollar etc), the *Framework* can be applied to financial statements prepared under a range of models.

The introduction to the *Framework* lays out the purpose, status and scope of the document. It then looks at different users of financial statements and their information needs.

2.1.1 Purpose and status

The introduction gives a list of the purposes of the *Framework*.

(a) Assist the Board of the IASB in the **development of future IASs** and in its review of existing IASs.

(b) Assist the Board of the IASB in **promoting harmonisation** of regulations, accounting standards and procedures relating to the presentation of financial statements by providing a basis for reducing the number of alternative accounting treatments permitted by IASs.

(c) Assist **national standard-setting bodies** in developing national standards.

(d) Assist **preparers of financial statements** in applying IASs and in dealing with topics that have yet to form the subject of an IAS.

(e) Assist **auditors** in forming an opinion as to whether financial statements conform with IASs.

(f) Assist **users of financial statements** in interpreting the information contained in financial statements prepared in conformity with IASs.

(g) Provide those who are interested in the work of IASB with **information** about its approach to the formulation of IASs (now IFRSs).

The *Framework* is not an IAS and so does not overrule any individual IAS. In the (rare) cases of conflict between an IAS and the *Framework*, the **IAS will prevail**. These cases will diminish over time as the *Framework* will be used as a guide in the production of future IASs. The *Framework* itself will be revised occasionally depending on the experience of the IASB in using it.

2.1.2 Scope

The *Framework* deals with:

(a) The **objective** of financial statements

(b) The **qualitative characteristics** that determine the usefulness of information in financial statements

(c) The **definition, recognition and measurement** of the elements from which financial statements are constructed

(d) Concepts of **capital and capital maintenance**

The *Framework* is concerned with **'general purpose' financial statements** (ie a normal set of annual statements), but it can be applied to other types of accounts. A complete set of financial statements includes:

(a) A statement of financial position
(b) A statement of comprehensive income
(c) A statement of changes in financial position (eg a statement of cash flows)
(d) Notes, other statements and explanatory material

Supplementary information may be included, but some items are not included, namely commentaries and reports by the directors, the chairman, management etc.

All types of financial reporting entities are included (commercial, industrial, business; public or private sector).

Key term

> A **reporting entity** is an entity for which there are users who rely on the financial statements as their major source of financial information about the enterprise. *(Framework)*

2.1.3 Users and their information needs

Users of accounting information consist of investors, employees, lenders, suppliers and other trade creditors, customers, government and their agencies and the public. Their needs are as follows.

(a) **Investors** are the providers of risk capital

- (i) Information is required to help make a decision about buying or selling shares, taking up a rights issue and voting.
- (ii) Investors must have information about the level of dividend, past, present and future and any changes in share price.
- (iii) Investors will also need to know whether the management has been running the company efficiently.
- (iv) As well as the position indicated by the statements and earnings per share (EPS), investors will want to know about the liquidity of comprehensive income, statement of financial position of the company, the company's future prospects, and how the company's shares compare with those of its competitors.

(b) **Employees** need information about the security of employment and future prospects for jobs in the company, and to help with collective pay bargaining.

(c) **Lenders** need information to help them decide whether to lend to a company. They will also need to check that the value of any security remains adequate, that the interest repayments are secure, that the cash is available for redemption at the appropriate time and that any financial restrictions (such as maximum debt/equity ratios) have not been breached.

(d) **Suppliers** need to know whether the company will be a good customer and pay its debts.

(e) **Customers** need to know whether the company will be able to continue producing and supplying goods.

(f) **Government's** interest in a company may be one of creditor or customer, as well as being specifically concerned with compliance with tax and company law, ability to pay tax and the general contribution of the company to the economy.

(g) The **public** at large would wish to have information for all the reasons mentioned above, but it could be suggested that it would be impossible to provide general purpose accounting information which was specifically designed for the needs of the public.

Financial statements cannot meet all these users' needs, but financial statements which meet the **needs of investors** (providers of risk capital) will meet most of the needs of other users.

The *Framework* emphasises that the preparation and presentation of financial statements is primarily the **responsibility of an enterprise's management**. Management also has an interest in the information appearing in financial statements.

2.1.4 IAS 1 Presentation of financial statements

Much of what IAS 1 states in relation to accounting policies and the formats of financial statements repeats the contents of the *Framework* document. IAS 1 is considered in detail in Chapter 15. Please note that IAS 1 was revised in September 2007. The new requirements in terms of format and terminology are explained in more detail in Chapter 15. Broadly, the changes mean that the balance sheet will be referred to as the 'statement of financial position', and the income statement as the 'statement of comprehensive income'.

3 The objective of financial statements

FAST FORWARD

The **objective of financial statements** is to meet the needs of users.

The *Framework* states that:

> 'The objective of financial statements is to provide information about the financial position performance and changes in financial position of an enterprise that is useful to a wide range of users in making economic decisions.'

Such financial statements will meet the needs of most users. The information is, however, **restricted**.

(a) It is based on **past events** not expected future events.
(b) It does not necessarily contain **non-financial information**.

The statements also show the results of **management's stewardship**.

3.1 Financial position, performance and changes in financial position

It is important for users to assess the **ability of an enterprise to produce cash and cash equivalents** to pay employees, lenders etc.

Financial position information is affected by the following and information about each one can aid the user.

(a) **Economic resources controlled**: to predict the ability to generate cash
(b) **Financial structure**: to predict borrowing needs, the distribution of future profits/cash and likely success in raising new finance
(c) **Liquidity and solvency**: to predict whether financial commitments will be met as they fall due (liquidity relates to short-term commitments, solvency is longer-term)

Key terms

Liquidity. The availability of sufficient funds to meet deposit withdrawals and other financial commitments as they fall due.

Solvency. The availability of cash over the longer term to meet financial commitments as they fall due. *(Framework)*

In all these areas, the capacity to adapt to changes in the environment in which the enterprise operates is very important.

Financial performance (statement of comprehensive income) information, particularly profitability, is used to assess potential changes in the economic resources the enterprise is likely to control in future. Information about performance variability is therefore important.

Changes in financial position (statement of cash flows) information is used to assess the enterprise's investing, financing and operating activities. They show the enterprise's ability to produce cash and the needs which utilise those cash flows.

All parts of the financial statements are **interrelated**, reflecting different aspects of the same transactions or events. Each statement provides different information; none can provide all the information required by users.

Exam focus point

Many of the terms such as accruals, going concern, prudence etc may appear familiar based on your previous studies and professional work. However, you must take on board the fact that the IASB definitions, though similar, may contain subtle but important differences.

Study the key terms in this chapter carefully and understand precisely what they mean and also what they do not mean.

4 Underlying assumptions

FAST FORWARD

Accruals and **going concern** are the two underlying assumptions in preparing financial statements.

We have already met the two assumptions discussed here.

4.1 Accruals basis

Key term

Accruals basis. The effects of transactions and other events are recognised when they occur (and not as cash or its equivalent is received or paid) and they are recorded in the accounting records and reported in the financial statements of the periods to which they relate. *(Framework)*

Financial statements prepared under the accruals basis show users past transactions involving cash and also obligations to pay cash in the future and resources which represent cash to be received in the future.

4.2 Going concern

Key term

Going concern. The enterprise is normally viewed as a going concern, that is, as continuing in operation for the foreseeable future. It is assumed that the enterprise has neither the intention nor the necessity of liquidation or of curtailing materially the scale of its operations. *(Framework)*

It is assumed that the enterprise has no intention to liquidate or curtail major operations. If it did, then the financial statements would be prepared on a **different (disclosed) basis.**

5 Qualitative characteristics of financial statements

FAST FORWARD

The important **qualitative characteristics** of the financial statements are:

- Understandability
- Relevance
- Reliability
- Comparability

The *Framework* states that qualitative characteristics are the attributes that make the information provided in financial statements useful to users. The four principal qualitative characteristics are **understandability, relevance, reliability and comparability**.

5.1 Understandability

Users must be able to understand financial statements. They are assumed to have some business, economic and accounting knowledge and to be able to apply themselves to study the information properly. **Complex matters should not be left out** of financial statements simply due to its difficulty if it is relevant information.

5.2 Relevance

The **predictive and confirmatory roles** of information are interrelated.

Key term

Relevance. Information has the quality of relevance when it influences the economic decisions of users by helping them evaluate past, present or future events or confirming, or correcting, their past evaluations. *(Framework)*

Information on financial position and performance is often used to predict future position and performance and other things of interest to the user, eg likely dividend, wage rises. The **manner of showing information** will enhance the ability to make predictions, eg by highlighting unusual items.

5.3 Materiality

The relevance of information is affected by its **nature and materiality**.

Key term

Materiality. Information is material if its omission or misstatement could influence the economic decisions of users taken on the basis of the financial statements. *(Framework)*

Information may be judged relevant simply because of its nature (eg remuneration of management). In other cases, both the nature and materiality of the information are important. Materiality is not a primary qualitative characteristic itself (like reliability or relevance), because it is merely a threshold or cut-off point.

Exam focus point

Qualitative characteristics of financial statements could be examined as a discursive part of a question.

5.4 Reliability

Information must also be reliable to be useful. The user must be able to depend on it being a **faithful representation**.

Key term

Reliability. Information has the quality of reliability when it is free from material error and bias and can be depended upon by users to represent faithfully that which it either purports to represent or could reasonably be expected to represent. *(Framework)*

Even if information is relevant, if it is very unreliable it may be **misleading to recognise it**, eg a disputed claim for damages in a legal action.

5.4.1 Faithful representation

Information must represent faithfully the transactions it purports to represent in order to be reliable. There is a risk that this may not be the case, not due to bias, but due to **inherent difficulties in identifying the transactions** or finding an **appropriate method of measurement or presentation**. Where measurement of the financial effects of an item is so uncertain, enterprises should not recognise such an item, eg internally generated goodwill.

5.4.2 Substance over form

Exam focus point

The requirements of the IASB Framework in terms of recording the substance of transactions is frequently examined as part of a longer question.

Faithful representation of a transaction is only possible if it is accounted for according to its **substance and economic reality**, not with its legal form.

Key term

Substance over form. The principle that transactions and other events are accounted for and presented in accordance with their substance and economic reality and not merely their legal form. *(Framework)*

5.4.3 Neutrality

Information must be **free from bias** to be reliable. Neutrality is lost if the financial statements are prepared so as to influence the user to make a judgement or decision in order to achieve a predetermined outcome.

5.4.4 Prudence

Uncertainties exist in the preparation of financial information, eg the collectability of doubtful receivables. These uncertainties are recognised through disclosure and through the application of prudence. Prudence does not, however, allow the creation of hidden reserves or excessive provisions, understatement of assets or income or overstatement of liabilities or expenses.

5.4.5 Completeness

Financial information must be complete, within the **restrictions of materiality and cost**, to be reliable. Omission may cause information to be misleading.

5.5 Comparability

Users must be able to compare an enterprise's financial statements:

(a) **Through time** to identify trends

(b) **With other enterprise's statements**, to evaluate their relative financial position, performance and changes in financial position

The consistency of treatment is therefore important across like items over time, within the enterprise and across all enterprises.

The **disclosure of accounting policies** is particularly important here. Users must be able to distinguish between different accounting policies in order to be able to make a valid comparison of similar items in the accounts of different entities.

Comparability is **not the same as uniformity**. Enterprises should change accounting policies if they become inappropriate.

Corresponding information for **preceding periods** should be shown to enable comparison over time.

5.6 Constraints on relevant and reliable information

5.6.1 Timeliness

Information may become irrelevant if there is a delay in reporting it. There is a **balance between timeliness and the provision of reliable information**. Information may be reported on a timely basis when not all aspects of the transaction are known, thus compromising reliability.

If every detail of a transaction is known, it may be too late to publish the information because it has become irrelevant. The overriding consideration is how best to satisfy the economic decision-making needs of the users.

5.6.2 Balance between benefits and cost

This is a pervasive constraint, not a qualitative characteristic. When information is provided, its benefits must exceed the costs of obtaining and presenting it. This is a **subjective area** and there are other difficulties: others than the intended users may gain a benefit; also the cost may be paid by someone other than the users. It is therefore difficult to apply a cost-benefit analysis, but preparers and users should be aware of the constraint.

5.6.3 Balance between qualitative characteristics

A **trade off between qualitative characteristics** of often necessary, the aim being to achieve an appropriate balance to meet the objective of financial statements. It is a matter for professional judgement as to the relative importance of these characteristics in each case.

5.7 True and fair view/fair presentation

The *Framework* does not attempt to define these concepts directly. It does state, however, that the application of the **principal 'qualitative' characteristics** and of **appropriate accounting standards** will usually result in financial statements which show a true and fair view, or present fairly.

6 The elements of financial statements

FAST FORWARD

The elements of financial statements can be broken down into:

- **Financial position** (statement of financial position): assets, liabilities, equity
- **Financial performance** (statement of comprehensive income): income, expenses

Transactions and other events are grouped together in broad **classes** and in this way their financial effects are shown in the financial statements. These broad classes are the elements of financial statements. The *Framework* lays out these elements as follows.

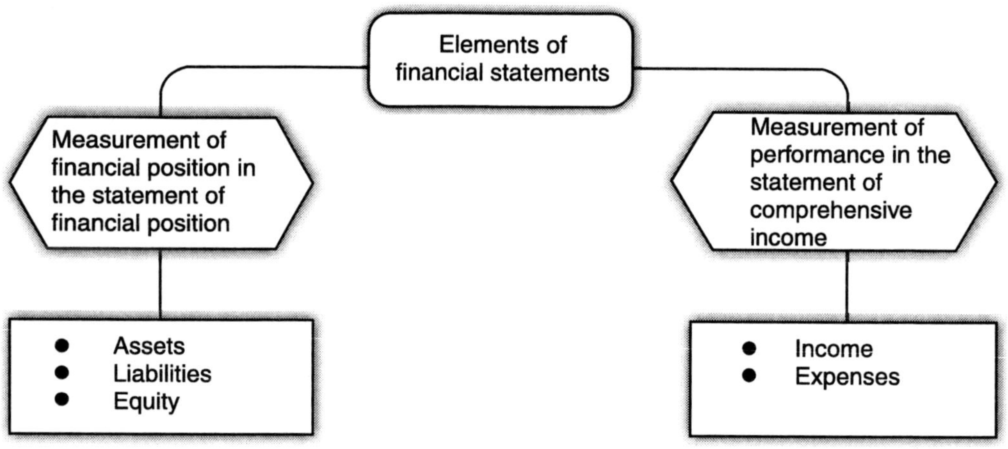

A process of **sub-classification** then takes place for presentation in the financial statements, eg assets are classified by their nature or function in the business to show information in the best way for users to take economic decisions.

Exam focus point

The pilot paper included a question requiring explanation of why the elements of assets and liabilities are of particular importance within the context of the IASB Framework. Candidates were also required to critically discuss their definitions giving examples of where current accepted practice may be at odds with these definitions.

The IASB definitions of asset, liability, provision, future economic benefit and obligation are important and must be thoroughly understood.

6.1 Financial position

We need to define the three terms listed under this heading above.

Key terms

- **Asset**. A resource controlled by an enterprise as a result of past events and from which future economic benefits are expected to flow to the enterprise.
- **Liability**. A present obligation of the enterprise arising from past events, the settlement of which is expected to result in an outflow from the enterprise of resources embodying economic benefits.
- **Equity.** The residual interest in the assets of the enterprise after deducting all its liabilities.

(Framework)

These definitions are important, but they do not cover the **criteria for recognition** of any of these items, which are discussed in the next section of this chapter. This means that the definitions may include items which would not actually be recognised in the statement of financial position because they fail to satisfy recognition criteria particularly, as we will see below, the **probable flow of any economic benefit** to or from the business.

Whether an item satisfies any of the definitions above will depend on the **substance and economic reality** of the transaction, not merely its legal form. Consider finance leases, for instance.

6.2 Assets

We can look in more detail at the components of the definitions given above.

Key term

> **Future economic benefit.** The potential to contribute, directly or indirectly, to the flow of cash and cash equivalents to the enterprise. The potential may be a productive one that is part of the operating activities of the enterprise. It may also take the form of convertibility into cash or cash equivalents or a capability to reduce cash outflows, such as when an alternative manufacturing process lowers the cost of production. *(Framework)*

Assets are usually employed to produce goods or services for customers; customers will then pay for these. **Cash itself** renders a service to the enterprise due to its command over other resources.

The existence of an asset, particularly in terms of **control**, is not reliant on:

(a) **Physical form** (hence patents and copyrights); *nor*
(b) **Legal rights** (hence leases).

Transactions or events **in the past** give rise to assets; those expected to occur in the future do not in themselves give rise to assets. For example, an intention to purchase a non-current asset does not, in itself, meet the definition of an asset.

6.3 Liabilities

Again we can look more closely at some aspects of the definition. An essential characteristic of a liability is that the enterprise has a **present obligation**.

Key term

> **Obligation.** A duty or responsibility to act or perform in a certain way. Obligations may be legally enforceable as a consequence of a binding contract or statutory requirement. Obligations also arise, however, from normal business practice, custom and a desire to maintain good business relations or act in an equitable manner. *(Framework)*

It is important to distinguish between a present obligation and a **future commitment**. A management decision to purchase assets in the future does not, in itself, give rise to a present obligation.

Settlement of a present obligation will involve the enterprise giving up resources embodying economic benefits in order to satisfy the claim of the other party. This may be done in various ways, not just by payment of cash.

Liabilities must arise from **past transactions or events**. In the case of, say, recognition of future rebates to customers based on annual purchases, the sale of goods in the past is the transaction that gives rise to the liability.

6.3.1 Provisions

Is a provision a liability?

Key term

> **Provision.** A present obligation which satisfies the rest of the definition of a liability, even if the amount of the obligation has to be estimated. *(Framework)*

Question — **Framework**

Consider the following situations. In each case, do we have an asset or liability within the definitions given by the *Framework?* Give reasons for your answer.

(a) Hugo Co has purchased a patent for $20,000. The patent gives the company sole use of a particular manufacturing process which will save $3,000 a year for the next five years.

(b) Lantos Co paid Zophia $10,000 to set up a car repair shop, on condition that priority treatment is given to cars from the company's fleet.

(c) Deals on Wheels Co provides a warranty with every car sold.

Answer

(a) This is an asset, albeit an intangible one. There is a past event, control and future economic benefit (through cost savings).

(b) This cannot be classified as an asset. Lantos Co has no control over the car repair shop and it is difficult to argue that there are 'future economic benefits'.

(c) This is a liability; the business has taken on an obligation. It would be recognised when the warranty is issued rather than when a claim is made.

6.4 Equity

Equity is defined above as a **residual**, but it may be sub-classified in the statement of financial position. This will indicate legal or other restrictions on the ability of the enterprise to distribute or otherwise apply its equity. Some reserves are required by statute or other law, eg for the future protection of creditors. The amount shown for equity depends on the **measurement of assets and liabilities.** It has nothing to do with the market value of the enterprise's shares.

6.5 Performance

Profit is used as a **measure of performance**, or as a basis for other measures (eg EPS). It depends directly on the measurement of income and expenses, which in turn depend (in part) on the concepts of capital and capital maintenance adopted.

The elements of income and expense are therefore defined.

Key terms

- **Income**. Increases in economic benefits during the accounting period in the form of inflows or enhancements of assets or decreases of liabilities that result in increases in equity, other than those relating to contributions from equity participants.
- **Expenses**. Decreases in economic benefits during the accounting period in the form of outflows or depletions of assets or incurrences of liabilities that result in decreases in equity, other than those relating to distributions to equity participants.

(Framework)

Income and expenses can be **presented in different ways** in the income statement, to provide information relevant for economic decision-making. For example, distinguish between income and expenses which arise in the ordinary course of operations and those which do not.

Items of income and expense can be **distinguished** from each other or **combined** with each other.

Both **revenue** and **gains** are included in the definition of income. **Revenue** arises in the course of ordinary activities of an enterprise.

Key term

Gains. Increases in economic benefits. As such they are no different in nature from revenue. *(Framework)*

Gains include those arising on the disposal of non-current assets. The definition of income also includes **unrealised gains**, eg on revaluation of marketable securities.

6.6 Expenses

As with income, the definition of expenses includes losses as well as those expenses that arise in the course of ordinary activities of an enterprise.

Key term

> **Losses**. Decreases in economic benefits. As such they are no different in nature from other expenses. *(Framework)*

Losses will include those arising on the disposal of non-current assets. The definition of expenses will also include **unrealised losses**, eg exchange rate effects on borrowings.

6.7 Capital maintenance adjustments

A **revaluation** gives rise to an increase or decrease in equity.

Key term

> **Revaluation.** Restatement of assets and liabilities. *(Framework)*

These increases and decreases meet the definitions of income and expenses. They are **not included** in the income statement under certain concepts of capital maintenance, however, but rather in equity.

6.8 Section summary

Make sure you learn the important definitions.

- Financial position:
  - Assets
  - Liabilities
  - Equity
- Financial performance:
  - Income
  - Expenses

7 Recognition of the elements of financial statements

FAST FORWARD

> Items which meet the definition of assets or liabilities may still not be recognised in financial statements because they must also meet certain **recognition criteria**.

As noted above, items which meet the definition of assets or liabilities may still not be recognised in financial statements because they must also meet certain **recognition criteria**.

Key term

> **Recognition.** The process of incorporating an item into the statement of financial position or statement of comprehensive income that meets the definition of an element and satisfies the following for recognition:
>
> (a) it is probable that any future economic benefit associated with the item will flow to or from the enterprise; and
>
> (b) the item has a cost or value that can be measured with reliability. *(Framework)*

Regard must be given to **materiality** (see paragraph 5.3).

7.1 Probability of future economic benefits

Probability here means the **degree of uncertainty** that the future economic benefits associated with an item will flow to or from the enterprise. This must be judged on the basis of the **characteristics of the entity's environment** and the **evidence available** when the financial statements are prepared.

7.2 Reliability of measurement

The cost or value of an item, in many cases, **must be estimated**. The *Framework* states, however, that the use of reasonable estimates is an essential part of the preparation of financial statements and does not undermine their reliability. Where no reasonable estimate can be made, the item should not be recognised, although its existence should be disclosed in the notes, or other explanatory material.

Items may still qualify for recognition **at a later date** due to changes in circumstances or subsequent events.

7.3 Recognition of items

We can summarise the recognition criteria for assets, liabilities, income and expenses, based on the definition of recognition given above.

Item	Recognised in	When
Asset	The statement of financial position	It is probable that the future economic benefits will flow to the enterprise and the asset has a cost or value that can be measured reliably.
Liability	The statement of financial position	It is probable that an outflow of resources embodying economic benefits will result from the settlement of a present obligation and the amount at which the settlement will take place can be measured reliably.
Income	The statement of comprehensive income	An increase in future economic benefits related to an increase in an asset or a decrease of a liability has arisen that can be measured reliably.
Expenses	The statement of comprehensive income	A decrease in future economic benefits related to a decrease in an asset or an increase of a liability has arisen that can be measured reliably.

8 Measurement of the elements of financial statements

FAST FORWARD

Measurement of elements in financial statements involves selection of one/more of:

- Historical cost
- Current cost
- Realisable (settlement) value
- Present value

Measurement is defined as follows.

Key term

Measurement. The process of determining the monetary amounts at which the elements of the financial statements are to be recognised and carried in the statement of financial position and statement of comprehensive income. *(Framework)*

This involves the selection of a particular **basis of measurement**. A number of these are used to different degrees and in varying combinations in financial statements. They include the following.

Key terms

- **Historical cost.** Assets are recorded at the amount of cash or cash equivalents paid or the fair value of the consideration given to acquire them at the time of their acquisition. Liabilities are recorded at the amount of proceeds received in exchange for the obligation, or in some circumstances (for example, income taxes), at the amounts of cash or cash equivalents expected to be paid to satisfy the liability in the normal course of business.
- **Current cost.** The amount of cash or cash equivalents that would have to be paid if the same or an equivalent asset was acquired currently.

  The undisclosed amount of cash or cash equivalents that would be required to settle an obligation currently.

Key terms (cont'd)

- **Realisable (settlement) value.**
  - **Realisable value**. The amount of cash or cash equivalents that could currently be obtained by selling an asset in an orderly disposal.
  - **Settlement value**. The undiscounted amounts of cash or cash equivalents expected to be paid to satisfy the liabilities in the normal course of business.
- **Present value**. A current estimate of the present discounted value of the future net cash flows in the normal course of business. *(Framework)*

Historical cost is the most commonly adopted measurement basis, but this is usually combined with other bases, eg inventory is carried at the lower of cost and net realisable value.

Chapter Roundup

- The financial reporting process is concerned with providing information that is **useful** in the business and economic **decision-making process.** Therefore a conceptual framework will form the **theoretical basis** for determining which events should be accounted for, how they should be measured and how they should be communicated to the user.
- The IASB's *Framework* provides a **conceptual framework** for all IASs/IFRSs.
- The **objective of financial statements** is to meet the needs of users.
- **Accruals** and **going concern** are the two underlying assumptions in preparing financial statements.
- The important **qualitative characteristics** of financial statements are:
  - Understandability
  - Relevance
  - Reliability
  - Comparability
- The elements of financial statements can be broken down into:
  - **Financial position** (statement of financial position): assets, liabilities, equity
  - **Financial performance** (statement of comprehensive income): income, expenses
- Items which meet the definition of assets or liabilities may still not be recognised in financial statements because they must also meet certain **recognition criteria**.
- **Measurement** of elements in financial statements involves selection of one/more of:
  - Historical cost
  - Current cost
  - Realisable (settlement) value
  - Present value

Quick Quiz

1 Define a 'conceptual framework'.
2 What are the advantages and disadvantages of a conceptual framework?
3 The needs of which category of user are paramount when preparing financial statements?
4 Define 'relevance'.
5 In which two ways should users be able to compare an enterprise's financial statements?
6 A provision can be a liability. True or false?
7 Define 'recognition'.
8 The cost or value of items in the financial statements is never estimated. True or false?
9 What is the most common basis of measurement used in financial statements?
10 What are the main criticisms of the IASB's approach to a conceptual framework (rather than the document itself)?

Answers to Quick Quiz

1 This is a statement of generally accepted theoretical principles, which form the frame of reference for financial reporting.

2 *Advantages*

- Standardised accounting practice
- Less open to criticism
- Concentrate on statement of comprehensive income or statement of financial position, as appropriate

Disadvantages

- Variety of users, so not all with be satisfied
- Variety of standards for different purposes
- Preparing and implementing standards not necessarily any easier

3 Needs of investors

4 Information has relevance when it influences the economic decisions of users by helping them evaluate past, present or future events or confirming (or correcting) their past evaluations.

5
- Through time to identify trends
- With other enterprise's statements

6 It satisfies the rest of the definition of a liability but the amount may need to be estimated.

7 See Key Term Para 7.

8 False. Monetary values are often estimated.

9 Historical cost.

10
- Overall approach
- Definitions of assets and liabilities

Now try the questions below from the Exam Question Bank

Number	Level	Marks	Time
Q4	Introductory	n/a	n/a
Q5	Introductory	n/a	n/a

PART B

Elements of financial statements

√Revenue recognition

3

Topic list	Syllabus reference
1 Revenue recognition (IAS 18)	2

Introduction

Revenue is the **gross inflow** of **economic benefits** during the period arising in the course of the ordinary activities of an enterprise when those inflows result in increases in equity, other than increases relating to contributions from equity participants.

Study Guide

Section 2 – Revenue recognition

- Outline the principles of the timing of revenue recognition
- Explain the concept of substance over form in relation to recognising sales revenue
- Discuss the various points in the production and sales cycle where it may, depending on circumstances be appropriate to recognise gains and losses – give examples of this
- Describe the IASB's approach to revenue recognition within its *Framework* and compare this to the requirements of IAS 18 *Revenue*

1 Revenue recognition

FAST FORWARD

Revenue recognition is straightforward in most business transactions, but some situations are more complicated. It is necessary to determine the **substance of each transaction, rather than the legal form**.

Exam focus point

The principles of IAS 18 *Revenue* are frequently examined, with questions in December 2005, June 2007, December 2007, June 2008 and June 2010. The June 2010 exam included an entire question on IAS 18. About a third of the marks were for explaining the principles of the Standard, with the rest of the marks being for applying IAS 18 to specific scenarios.

1.1 Introduction

Accruals accounting is based on the **matching of costs with the revenue they generate**. It is crucially important under this convention that we can establish the point at which revenue may be recognised so that the correct treatment can be applied to the related costs. For example, the costs of producing an item of finished goods should be carried as an asset in the statement of financial position until such time as it is sold; they should then be written off as a charge to the trading account. Which of these two treatments should be applied cannot be decided until it is clear at what moment the sale of the item takes place.

The decision has a **direct impact on profit** since under the **prudence concept** it would be unacceptable to recognise the profit on sale until a sale had taken place in accordance with the **criteria of revenue recognition**.

Revenue is of course open to manipulation. The latest scandal is at Satyam Computer Services in India where the Chairman recently admitted that profits were massively inflated for years and that in the quarter to 30 September 2008 revenue was overstated by 78%. How this got past the auditors has yet to be explained, but it does illustrate why rules on revenue recognition are needed.

1.2 Point of sale

BASIC REQUIREMENT

Revenue is generally recognised as **earned at the point of sale**, because at that point four criteria will generally have been met.

- The product or service has been **provided to the buyer**.
- The buyer has **recognised his liability** to pay for the goods or services provided. The converse of this is that the seller has recognised that ownership of goods has passed from himself to the buyer.
- The buyer has indicated his **willingness to hand over cash** or other assets in settlement of his liability.
- The **monetary value** of the goods or services has been established.

At earlier points in the business cycle there will not generally be firm evidence that the above criteria will be met. Until work on a product is complete, there is a risk that some flaw in the manufacturing process will necessitate its writing off; even when the product is complete there is no guarantee that it will find a buyer. There is **uncertainty** whether the inventory will yield **future economic benefit**, and the inventory may need to be written off from the statement of financial position.

At later points in the **business cycle**, for example when cash is received for the sale, the recognition of revenue may occur in a period later than that in which the related costs were charged. Revenue recognition would then depend on fortuitous circumstances, such as the cash flow of a company's receivables, and might fluctuate misleadingly from one period to another. Again, if collection of payments from any receivable is uncertain, an allowance or provision may need to be set up.

The above may be depicted by the following diagram.

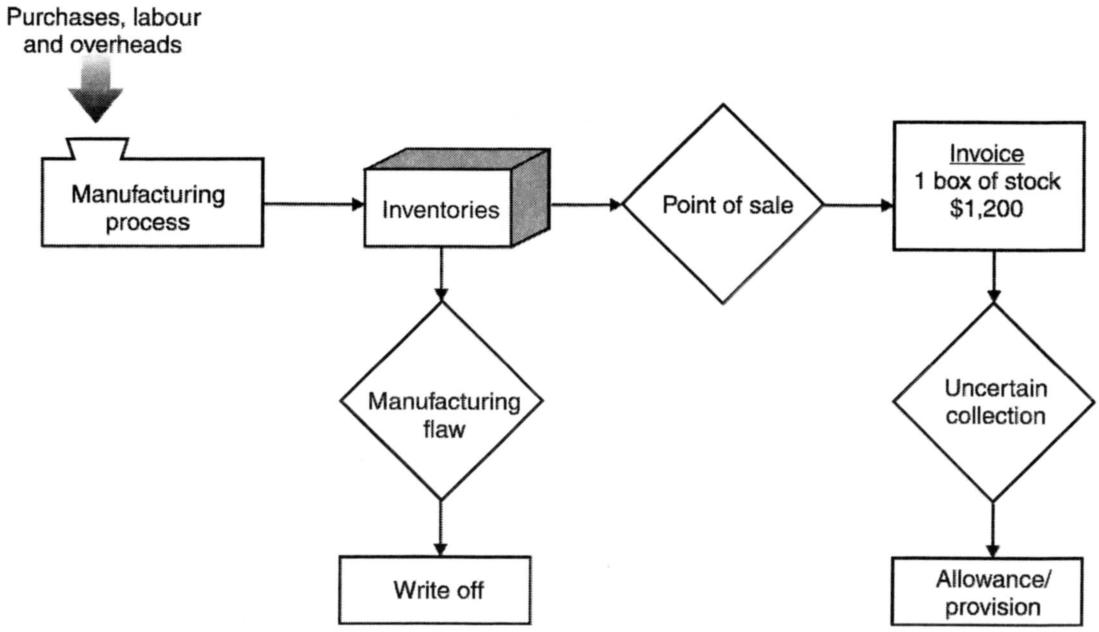

There are however, times when revenue is **recognised at other times than at the completion of a sale**. For example, in the recognition of profit on long-term construction contracts. Under IAS 11 *Construction contracts* contract revenue and contract costs associated with the construction contract should be recognised as revenue and expenses respectively by reference to the **stage of completion** of the **contract activity** at the reporting date.

(a) Owing to the length of time taken to complete such contracts, to defer taking profit into account until completion may result in the income statement reflecting, not so much a fair view of the activity of the company during the year, but rather the results relating to contracts which have been completed by the year end.

(b) Revenue in this case is recognised when production on, say, a section of the total contract is complete, even though no sale can be made until the whole is complete.

1.3 IAS 18 *Revenue*

IAS 18 governs the recognition of revenue in specific (common) types of transaction. Generally, recognition should be when it is probable that **future economic benefits** will flow to the entity and when these benefits can be **measured reliably**.

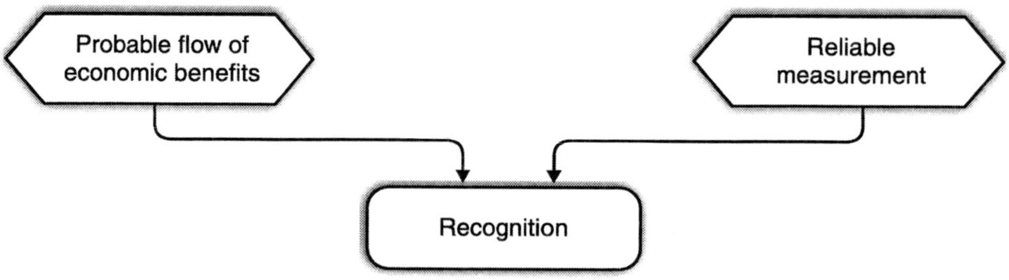

Income, as defined by the IASB's *Framework* document, includes both revenues and gains. Revenue is income arising in the ordinary course of an entity's activities and it may be called different names, such as sales, fees, interest, dividends or royalties.

1.4 Scope

FAST FORWARD

IAS 18 *Revenue* is concerned with the **recognition of revenues** arising from fairly common transactions or events.

- The sale of goods
- The rendering of services
- The use by others of enterprise assets yielding interest, royalties and dividends

Interest, royalties and dividends are included as income because they arise from the use of an enterprise's assets by other parties.

Key terms

Interest is the charge for the use of cash or cash equivalents or amounts due to the enterprise.

Royalties are charges for the use of non-current assets of the enterprise, eg patents, computer software and trademarks.

Dividends are distributions of profit to holders of equity investments, in proportion with their holdings, of each relevant class of capital. *(IAS 18)*

The standard specifically **excludes** various types of revenue arising from leases, insurance contracts, changes in value of financial instruments or other current assets natural increases in agricultural assets and mineral ore extraction.

1.5 Definitions

The following definitions are given in the standard.

Key terms

Revenue is the gross inflow of economic benefits during the period arising in the course of the ordinary activities of an enterprise when those inflows result in increases in equity, other than increases relating to contributions from equity participants.

Fair value is the amount for which an asset could be exchanged, or a liability settled, between knowledgeable, willing parties in an arm's length transaction. *(IAS 18)*

Revenue **does not include** sales taxes, value added taxes or goods and service taxes which are only collected for third parties, because these do not represent an economic benefit flowing to the entity. The same is true for revenues collected by an agent on behalf of a principal. Revenue for the agent is only the commission received for acting as agent.

1.6 Measurement of revenue

FAST FORWARD

Generally revenue is recognised when the entity has transferred to the buyer the **significant risks and rewards of ownership** and when the revenue can be **measured reliably**.

When a transaction takes place, the amount of revenue is usually decided by the **agreement of the buyer and seller**. The revenue is actually measured, however, as the **fair value of the consideration received**, which will take account of any trade discounts and volume rebates.

ARMS LENGTH TRANSACTION

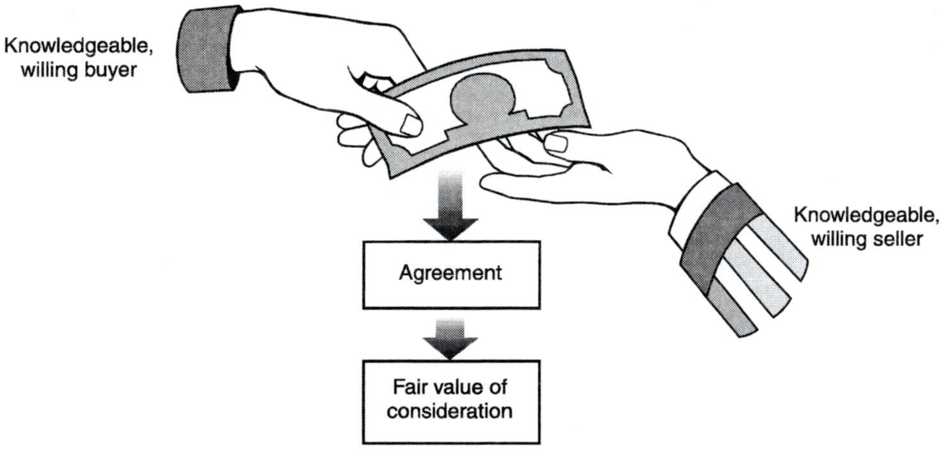

1.7 Identification of the transaction

Normally, each transaction can be looked at **as a whole**. Sometimes, however, transactions are more complicated, and it is necessary to break a transaction down into its **component parts**. For example, a sale may include the transfer of goods and the provision of future servicing, the revenue for which should be deferred over the period the service is performed.

At the other end of the scale, **seemingly separate transactions must be considered together** if apart they lose their commercial meaning. An example would be to sell an asset with an agreement to buy it back at a later date. The second transaction cancels the first and so both must be considered together.

Exam focus point

The June 2010 paper included a whole question on the requirements of IAS 18, just as the December 2005 paper had done. The candidate had to outline the requirements of the standard, compare definition of revenue with that in *Framework* and apply IAS 18 to the specific transactions. Revenue recognition was also examined in June 2007, December 2007 and June 2008.

1.8 Sale of goods

Revenue from the sale of goods should only be recognised when *all* these conditions are satisfied.

(a) The entity has transferred the **significant risks and rewards** of ownership of the goods to the buyer

(b) The entity has **no continuing managerial involvement** to the degree usually associated with ownership, and no longer has effective control over the goods sold

(c) The amount of revenue can be **measured reliably**

(d) It is probable that the **economic benefits** associated with the transaction will flow to the entity

(e) The **costs incurred** in respect of the transaction can be measured reliably

The transfer of risks and rewards can only be decided by examining each transaction. Mainly, the transfer occurs at the same time as either the **transfer of legal title**, or the **passing of possession** to the buyer – this is what happens when you buy something in a shop.

If **significant risks and rewards remain with the seller**, then the transaction is *not* a sale and revenue cannot be recognised, for example if the receipt of the revenue from a particular sale depends on the buyer receiving revenue from his own sale of the goods.

It is possible for the seller to retain only an **'insignificant' risk of ownership** and for the sale and revenue to be recognised. The main example here is where the seller retains title only to ensure collection of what is owed on the goods. This is a common commercial situation, and when it arises the revenue should be recognised on the date of sale.

The probability of the entity receiving the revenue arising from a transaction must be assessed. It may only become probable that the economic benefits will be received when an uncertainty is removed, for example government permission for funds to be received from another country. Only when the uncertainty is removed should the revenue be recognised. This is in contrast with the situation where revenue has already been recognised but where the **collectability of the cash** is brought into doubt. Where recovery has ceased to be probable, the amount should be recognised as an expense, *not* an adjustment of the revenue previously recognised. These points also refer to services and interest, royalties and dividends below.

Matching should take place, ie the **revenue** and **expenses** relating to the **same transaction** should be **recognised** at the **same time**. It is usually easy to estimate expenses at the date of sale (eg warranty costs, shipment costs, etc). Where they cannot be estimated reliably, then revenue cannot be recognised; any consideration which has already been received is treated as a liability. Remember the definition of an asset and that revenue is recognised only when it is probably that the economic benefit associated with the transaction will flow to the enterprise.

Exam focus point

> The June 2006 paper included as part of a question, a sale and repurchase transaction, requiring the student to identify and explain why this did not constitute a sale under IAS 18. The December 2008 paper tested students on the matching of revenue to warranty costs.

1.9 Rendering of services

When the outcome of a transaction involving the rendering of services can be estimated reliably, the associated revenue should be recognised by reference to the **stage of completion of the transaction** at the reporting date. The outcome of a transaction can be estimated reliably when *all* these conditions are satisfied.

(a) The amount of revenue can be **measured reliably**

(b) It is probable that the **economic benefits** associated with the transaction will flow to the entity

(c) The **stage of completion** of the transaction at the end of the reporting period can be measured reliably

(d) The **costs incurred** for the transaction and the costs to complete the transaction can be measured reliably

The parties to the transaction will normally have to agree the following before an entity can make reliable estimates.

(a) Each party's **enforceable rights** regarding the service to be provided and received by the parties

(b) The **consideration** to be exchanged

(c) The **manner and terms of settlement**

There are various methods of determining the **stage of completion** of a transaction, but for practical purposes, when services are performed by an indeterminate number of acts over a period of time, revenue should be recognised on a **straight line basis** over the period, unless there is evidence for the use of a more appropriate method. If one act is of more significance than the others, then the significant act should be carried out *before* revenue is recognised.

In uncertain situations, when the outcome of the transaction involving the rendering of services cannot be estimated reliably, the standard recommends a **no loss/no gain approach**. Revenue is recognised only to the extent of the expenses recognised that are recoverable.

This is particularly likely during the **early stages of a transaction**, but it is still probable that the entity will recover the costs incurred. So the revenue recognised in such a period will be equal to the expenses incurred, with no profit.

Obviously, if the **costs** are **not likely** to **be reimbursed**, then they must be recognised as an **expense immediately**. When the uncertainties cease to exist, revenue should be recognised as laid out in Section 1.6 above.

1.10 Reporting the substance of the transaction

In some cases, what initially appears to be a sale transaction may turn out to be something different and a sale should not be recognised. It is important that the substance of the transaction is reported and not just its legal form. In other words, you need to understand exactly what is happening with a single transaction or series of transactions.

For example, MacDougal Drinks sold 100 barrels of Brew No 1 to the Scots Bank, on 30 June 2009 for $100 per barrel. When Brew No 1 is mature in two years time it will be worth $500 per barrel. MacDougal retains custody of the barrels. The sale contract contains a clause requiring MacDougal to repurchase the barrels on 30 June 2011 for $150 per barrel.

How should this transaction be recognised?

Solution

Often, the substance of a transaction can only be determined by looking at all transactions relating to an item as a whole.

In this case, MacDougal sells his barrels to the Scots Bank which would appear to be a standard transaction. However, on maturity of the barrels, he repurchases them from the bank. It is important to note that he does not physically give the barrels to the bank, they are still kept at his premises.

Normally once an item is sold, the goods are transferred and the seller transfers the risks and rewards of ownership to the purchaser. This does not happen in this case. MacDougal still retains physical ownership and with the option of buying the barrels back at below their market price, retains the rewards of ownership.

In substance, this transactions is not a sale. Rather, it is a loan from Scots Bank to MacDougal, secured on the inventory.

The accounting for this transaction is to continue to recognise the barrels as inventory and record the cash received from the bank as the proceeds of a loan. The difference between the $100 'sales' price and the $150 repurchase price should be accounted for as loan interest over the two year period of the loan. No sale has taken place.

1.11 Realised profit

The realisation concept states that revenue and profits should not be anticipated, but should be recognised by inclusion in the income statement only when **realised** in the form either of **cash**, or of other assets the ultimate cash realisation of which can be assessed with reasonable certainty.

Unfortunately there is no standard definition of realised profits. It could be said that they are such profits or losses of a company as fall to be treated as realised in accordance with principles generally accepted at the time when the accounts are prepared.

The language of accounting has recently moved away from the concept of realisation to focus instead on whether the **conditions** have been **met** for an **item** to be **recognised** in the financial statements. In this regard we have progressed from an income statement approach to a **statement of financial position-driven approach** as fostered by the **IASB**. We review this in the section below.

This IASB approach acknowledges the concept of matching, but views **recognition** in terms of including items in the financial statements in the periods to which they **relate** rather than the period of payment or receipt.

IAS 1 specifically notes that the application of the matching concept does not allow the **recognition** of items in the statement of financial position which do not meet the **definition of assets and liabilities.**

Key terms

- **Asset**. A resource controlled by an enterprise as a result of past events and from which future economic benefits are expected to flow to the enterprise.
- **Liability.** A present obligation of the enterprise arising from past events, the settlement of which is expected to result in an outflow from the enterprise of resources embodying economic benefits.

Exam focus point

> The definitions of assets and liabilities (examined in detail in the previous chapter) are at the very heart of financial reporting and you must learn it properly.
>
> The IASB's approach to revenue recognition is fundamental to your examinations.

1.12 Interest, royalties and dividends

When others use the enterprise's assets yielding interest, royalties and dividends, the revenue should be recognised on the bases set out below when:

(a) it is probable that the **economic benefits** associated with the transaction will flow to the enterprise; and

(b) the amount of the revenue can be **measured reliably**.

The revenue is recognised on the following bases.

(a) **Interest** is recognised on a **time proportion** basis that takes into account the **effective yield** on the asset

(b) **Royalties** are recognised on an **accruals** basis in accordance with the **substance** of the **relevant agreement**

(c) **Dividends** are recognised when the **shareholder's right to receive payment** is established

It is unlikely that you would be asked about anything as complex as this in the exam, but you should be aware of the basic requirements of the standard. The **effective yield** on an asset mentioned above is the rate of interest required to discount the stream of future cash receipts expected over the life of the asset to equate to the initial carrying amount of the asset.

Royalties are usually recognised on the same basis that they accrue **under the relevant agreement.** Sometimes the true substance of the agreement may require some other systematic and rational method of recognition.

Once again, the points made above about **probability and collectability** on sale of goods also apply here.

1.13 IFRS improvements

Improvements in 2009 included an addition to IAS 18 giving guidance on the Issue of when an entity is acting as a principal. An entity is acting as a principal when:

(a) the entity has primary responsibility for providing goods or services to the customer
(b) the entity has inventory risk before or after the customer order, during shipping or on return
(c) the entity has latitude in establishing prices, either directly or indirectly
(d) the entity bears the customers credit risk for the amount receivable from the customer

1.14 Disclosure

The following items should be disclosed.

(a) The **accounting policies** adopted for the recognition of revenue, including the methods used to determine the stage of completion of transactions involving the rendering of services

(b) The amount of each **significant category of revenue** recognised during the period including revenue arising from:

  (i) The sale of goods
  (ii) The rendering of services
  (iii) Interest
  (iv) Royalties
  (v) Dividends

(c) The amount of revenue arising from **exchanges of goods or services** included in each significant category of revenue

Any **contingent gains or losses**, such as those relating to warranty costs, claims or penalties should be treated according to IAS 10 *Events after the reporting period* (covered in Chapter 15).

Question

Recognition

Given that prudence is the main consideration, discuss under what circumstances, if any, revenue might be recognised at the following stages of a sale.

(a) Goods are acquired by the business which it confidently expects to resell very quickly.
(b) A customer places a firm order for goods.
(c) Goods are delivered to the customer.
(d) The customer is invoiced for goods.
(e) The customer pays for the goods.
(f) The customer's cheque in payment for the goods has been cleared by the bank.

Answer

(a) A sale must never be recognised before the goods have even been ordered by a customer. There is no certainty about the value of the sale, nor when it will take place, even if it is virtually certain that goods will be sold.

(b) A sale must never be recognised when the customer places an order. Even though the order will be for a specific quantity of goods at a specific price, it is not yet certain that the sale transaction will go through. The customer may cancel the order, the supplier might be unable to deliver the goods as ordered or it may be decided that the customer is not a good credit risk.

(c) A sale will be recognised when delivery of the goods is made only when:

(i) the sale is for cash, and so the cash is received at the same time; or
(ii) the sale is on credit and the customer accepts delivery (eg by signing a delivery note).

(d) The critical event for a credit sale is usually the despatch of an invoice to the customer. There is then a legally enforceable debt, payable on specified terms, for a completed sale transaction.

(e) The critical event for a cash sale is when delivery takes place and when cash is received; both take place at the same time.

It would be too cautious or 'prudent' to await cash payment for a credit sale transaction before recognising the sale, unless the customer is a high credit risk and there is a serious doubt about his ability or intention to pay.

(f) It would again be over-cautious to wait for clearance of the customer's cheques before recognising sales revenue. Such a precaution would only be justified in cases where there is a very high risk of the bank refusing to honour the cheque.

Chapter Roundup

- **Revenue recognition** is straightforward in most business transactions, but some situations are more complicated. It is necessary to determine the **substance of each transaction, rather than the legal form**.
- IAS 18 *Revenue* is concerned with the **recognition of revenues** arising from fairly common transactions or events.
  - The sale of goods
  - The rendering of services
  - The use by others of enterprise assets yielding interest, royalties and dividends
- Generally revenue is recognised when the enterprise has transferred to the buyer the **significant risks and rewards of ownership** and when the revenue can be **measured reliably**.

Quick Quiz

1 Revenue recognition is governed by IAS?

2 Revenue should be measured at the .... value of the .... received or receivable.

3 Explain in no more than 40 words, when revenue from sale of goods should be recognised.

Answers to Quick Quiz

1 IAS 18

2 Fair, consideration

3 Revenue from the **sale of goods** should be recognised when the **significant risks** and **rewards** of ownership have been **transferred** to the buyer, the seller has lost effective control and the amount of revenue can be measured reliably.

Now try the questions below from the Exam Question Bank

Number	Level	Marks	Time
Q6	Examination	25	45 mins

p.482

Accounting for tangible non-current assets

4

Topic list	Syllabus reference
1 IAS 16 Property, plant and equipment	2(a)
2 IAS 20 Government grants	2(a)
3 IAS 40 Investment property	2(a)
4 IAS 36 Impairment of assets	2(a)-(e)
5 IAS 23 Borrowing costs	2(a), (e), (f)

Introduction

IAS 16 should be familiar to you from your earlier studies, as should the mechanics of accounting for depreciation, revaluations of long-term (non-current) assets and disposals of non-current assets. Some questions are given here for revision purposes.

IAS 20 on government grants is a straightforward standard and you should have few problems with it.

IAS 40 deals with investment properties, which can be treated differently from other property under IAS 16.

IAS 36 on impairment is a topical standard.

IAS 16, 36 and **40** have recently been revised.

Study Guide

Section 3 – Non-current assets – tangible

- Define the initial cost of a non-current asset (including a self-constructed asset) and apply this to various examples of expenditures distinguishing between capital and revenue items
- Identify pre-conditions for capitalisation of borrowing costs
- Describe and be able to identify subsequent expenditures that may be capitalised
- State and appraise the effects of the IASB's rules for the revaluation of property, plant and equipment
- Account for gains and losses on the disposal of revalued assets
- Calculate depreciation on:
  - revalued assets, and
  - assets that have two or more major items or significant parts
- Describe the criteria that need to be present before non-current assets are classified as held for sale, either individually or in a disposal group
- Account for non-current assets and disposal groups that are held for sale
- Apply the provisions of accounting standards relating to government grants and government assistance
- Discuss the ways in which the treatment of investment properties differs from other properties
- Apply the requirements of international accounting standards to investment properties

Section 4 – Impairment of assets

- Define the recoverable amount of an asset; define impairment losses
- Give examples of, and be able to identify, circumstances that may indicate than an impairment of an asset has occurred
- Describe what is meant by a cash-generating unit
- State the basis on which impairment losses should be allocated, and allocate a given impairment loss to the asset of a cash-generating unit

1 IAS 16 Property, plant and equipment

FAST FORWARD

IAS 16 *Property, plant and equipment* covers all aspects of accounting for property, plant and equipment. This represents the bulk of items which are **'tangible' non-current assets**.

Exam focus point

Revaluation as part of financial statement preparation was tested in December 2004, June 2005, December 2006 and December 2007.

The treatment and accounting for property, plant and equipment was examined in June 2004. In June 2007, one question examined self constructed assets and disposal of assets.

1.1 Scope

IAS 16 should be followed when accounting for property, plant and equipment *unless* another international accounting standard requires a **different treatment**.

IAS 16 **does not apply** to the following.

(a) Biological assets related to agricultural activity
(b) Mineral rights and mineral reserves, such as oil, gas and other non-regenerative resources

However, it does apply to property, plant and equipment used to develop these assets.

1.2 Definitions

The standard gives a large number of definitions.

Key terms

- **Property, plant and equipment** are tangible assets that:
  - are held for use in the production or supply of goods or services, for rental to others, or for administrative purposes; and
  - are expected to be used during more than one period.
- **Cost** is the amount of cash or cash equivalents paid or the fair value of the other consideration given to acquire an asset at the time of its acquisition or construction.
- **Residual value** is the net amount which the entity expects to obtain for an asset at the end of its useful life after deducting the expected costs of disposal.
- **Entity specific value** is the present value of the cash flows an entity expects to arise from the continuing use of an asset and from its disposal at the end of its useful life, or expects to incur when settling a liability.
- **Fair value** is the amount for which an asset could be exchanged between knowledgeable, willing parties in an arm's length transaction.
- **Carrying amount** is the amount at which an asset is recognised in the statement of financial position after deducting any accumulated depreciation and accumulated impairment losses.
- An **impairment loss** is the amount by which the carrying amount of an asset exceeds its recoverable amount.
- **Depreciation** is the result of systematic allocation of the depreciable amount of an asset over its estimated useful life. Depreciation for the accounting period is charged to net profit or loss for the period either directly or indirectly.
- **Useful life** is one of two things.
  - The period over which a depreciable asset is expected to be used by the entity, or
  - The number of production or similar units expected to be obtained from the asset by the entity. *(IAS 16)*

1.3 Recognition

In this context, recognition simply means incorporation of the item in the business's accounts, in this case as a non-current asset. The recognition of property, plant and equipment depends on two criteria.

(a) It is probable that **future economic benefits** associated with the asset will flow to the entity
(b) The cost of the asset to the entity can be **measured reliably**

These recognition criteria apply to **subsequent expenditure** as well as costs incurred initially. There are no longer any separate criteria for recognising subsequent expenditure.

Property, plant and equipment can amount to **substantial amounts** in financial statements, affecting the presentation of the company's financial position (in the statement of financial position) and the profitability of the entity, through depreciation and also if an asset is wrongly classified as an expense and taken to the statement of comprehensive income.

1.3.1 First criterion: future economic benefits

The **degree of certainty** attached to the flow of future economic benefits must be assessed. This should be based on the evidence available at the date of initial recognition (usually the date of purchase). The entity should thus be assured that it will receive the rewards attached to the asset and it will incur the associated risks, which will only generally be the case when the rewards and risks have actually passed to the entity. Until then, the asset should not be recognised.

1.3.2 Second criterion: cost measured reliably

It is generally easy to measure the cost of an asset as the **transfer amount on purchase**, ie what was paid for it. **Self-constructed assets** can also be measured easily by adding together the purchase price of all the constituent parts (labour, material etc) paid to external parties.

1.4 Separate items

Most of the time assets will be identified individually, but this will not be the case for **smaller items**, such as tools, dies and moulds, which are sometimes classified as inventory and written off as an expense.

Major components or spare parts, should also be recognised as property, plant and equipment.

For very **large and specialised items**, an apparently single asset should be broken down into its composite parts. This occurs where the different parts have different useful lives and different depreciation rates are applied to each part, eg an aircraft, where the body and engines are separated as they have different useful lives.

1.5 Safety and environmental equipment

When such assets as these are acquired they will qualify for recognition where they enable the entity to **obtain future economic benefits** from related assets in excess of those it would obtain otherwise. The recognition will only be to the extent that the carrying amount of the asset and related assets does not exceed the total recoverable amount of these assets.

1.6 Initial measurement

Once an item of property, plant and equipment qualifies for recognition as an asset, it will initially be **measured at cost**.

1.6.1 Components of cost

The standard lists the components of the cost of an item of property, plant and equipment.

- **Purchase price**, less any trade discount or rebate
- **Import duties** and non-refundable purchase taxes
- **Directly attributable costs** of bringing the asset to working condition for its intended use, eg:
  - The cost of site preparation
  - Initial delivery and handling costs
  - Installation costs
  - Testing
  - Professional fees (architects, engineers)
- Initial estimate of the unavoidable cost of dismantling and removing the asset and restoring the site on which it is located

The revised IAS 16 provides **additional guidance on directly attributable** costs included in the cost of an item of property, plant and equipment.

(a) These costs bring the asset to the location and working conditions necessary for it to be capable of operating in the manner intended by management, including those costs to test whether the asset is functioning properly.

(b) They are determined after deducting the net proceeds from selling any items produced when bringing the asset to its location and condition.

The revised standard also states that income and related expenses of operations that are **incidental** to the construction or development of an item of property, plant and equipment should be **recognised** in the income statement.

The following costs **will not be part of the cost** of property, plant or equipment unless they can be attributed directly to the asset's acquisition, or bringing it into its working condition.

- Administration and other general overhead costs
- Start-up and similar pre-production costs
- Initial operating losses before the asset reaches planned performance

All of these will be recognised as an **expense** rather than an asset.

In the case of **self-constructed assets**, the same principles are applied as for acquired assets. If the entity makes similar assets during the normal course of business for sale externally, then the cost of the asset will be the cost of its production under IAS 2 *Inventories*. This also means that abnormal costs (wasted material, labour or other resources) are excluded from the cost of the asset. An example of a self-constructed asset is when a building company builds its own head office.

1.6.2 Exchanges of assets

The revised IAS 16 specifies that exchange of items of property, plant and equipment, regardless of whether the assets are similar, are measured at **fair value**, **unless the exchange transaction lacks commercial substance** or the fair value of neither of the assets exchanged can be **measured reliably**. If the acquired item is not measured at fair value, its cost is measured at the carrying amount of the asset given up.

Expenditure incurred in replacing or renewing a component of an item of property, plant and equipment must be **recognised in the carrying amount of the item**. The carrying amount of the replaced or renewed component must be derecognised. A similar approach is also applied when a separate component of an item of property, plant and equipment is identified in respect of a major inspection to enable the continued use of the item.

1.7 Measurement subsequent to initial recognition

The standard offers two possible treatments here, essentially a choice between keeping an asset recorded at **cost** or revaluing it to **fair value**.

Cost model

Carry the asset at its cost less any accumulated depreciation and any accumulated impairment loss.

Revaluation model

- Carry the asset at a revalued amount, being its fair value at the date of the revaluation less any subsequent accumulated depreciation and subsequent accumulated impairment losses.
- Revaluations shall be made regularly enough so that the carrying amount approximates to fair value at the reporting date.

The revised IAS 16 specifies that the revaluation model is available only if the fair value of the asset can be measured reliably.

1.7.1 Revaluation model

The **market value** of land and buildings usually represents fair value, assuming existing use and line of business. Such valuations are usually carried out by professionally qualified valuers.

In the case of **plant and equipment**, fair value can also be taken as **market value**. Where a market value is not available, however, depreciated replacement cost should be used. There may be no market value where types of plant and equipment are sold only rarely or because of their specialised nature (ie they would normally only be sold as part of an ongoing business).

The frequency of valuation depends on the **volatility of the fair values** of individual items of property, plant and equipment. The more volatile the fair value, the more frequently revaluations should be carried out. Where the current fair value is very different from the carrying value then a revaluation should be carried out.

Most importantly, when an item of property, plant and equipment is revalued, **the whole class of assets to which it belongs should be revalued.**

All the items within a class should be **revalued at the same time**, to prevent selective revaluation of certain assets and to avoid disclosing a mixture of costs and values from different dates in the financial statements. A rolling basis of revaluation is allowed if the revaluations are kept up to date and the revaluation of the whole class is completed in a short period of time.

How should any **increase in value** be treated when a revaluation takes place? The debit will be the increase in value in the statement of financial position, but what about the credit? IAS 16 requires the increase to be credited to a **revaluation surplus** (ie part of owners' equity), *unless* the increase is reversing a previous decrease which was recognised as an expense. To the extent that this offset is made, the increase is recognised as income; any excess is then taken to the revaluation reserve.

1.8 Example: revaluation reserve

Binkie Co has an item of land carried in its books at $13,000. Two years ago a slump in land values led the company to reduce the carrying value from $15,000. This was taken as an expense in profit or loss. There has been a surge in land prices in the current year, however, and the land is now worth $20,000.

Account for the revaluation in the current year.

Solution

The double entry is:

DEBIT	Asset value (statement of financial position)	$7,000	
CREDIT	Profit or loss		$2,000
	Revaluation surplus		$5,000

The case is similar for a **decrease in value** on revaluation. Any decrease should be recognised as an expense, except where it offsets a previous increase taken as a revaluation surplus in owners' equity. Any decrease greater than the previous upwards increase in value must be taken as an expense in profit or loss.

1.9 Example: revaluation decrease

Let us simply swap round the example given above. The original cost was $15,000, revalued upwards to $20,000 two years ago. The value has now fallen to $13,000.

Account for the decrease in value.

Solution

The double entry is:

DEBIT	Revaluation surplus	$5,000	
DEBIT	Profit or loss	$2,000	
CREDIT	Asset value (statement of financial position)		$7,000

There is a further complication when a **revalued asset is being depreciated**. As we have seen, an upward revaluation means that the depreciation charge will increase. Normally, a revaluation surplus is only realised when the asset is sold, but when it is being depreciated, part of that surplus is being realised as the asset is used. The amount of the surplus realised is the difference between depreciation charged on the revalued amount and the (lower) depreciation which would have been charged on the asset's original cost. **The entity can then choose to transfer this amount to retained (ie realised) earnings but *not* through the income statement.**

1.10 Example: revaluation and depreciation

Crinckle Co bought an asset for $10,000 at the beginning of 20X6. It had a useful life of five years. On 1 January 20X8 the asset was revalued to $12,000. The expected useful life has remained unchanged (ie three years remain).

Account for the revaluation and state the treatment for depreciation from 20X8 onwards.

Solution

On 1 January 20X8 the carrying value of the asset is $10,000 – (2 × $10,000 ÷ 5) = $6,000. For the revaluation:

DEBIT	Asset value	$6,000	
CREDIT	Revaluation surplus		$6,000

The depreciation for the next three years will be $12,000 ÷ 3 = $4,000, compared to depreciation on cost of $10,000 ÷ 5 = $2,000. So each year, the extra $2,000 can be treated as part of the surplus which has become realised:

DEBIT	Revaluation surplus	$2,000	
CREDIT	Retained earnings		$2,000

This is a movement on owners' equity only, not an item in the income statement.

1.11 Cost model: Depreciation

FAST FORWARD

The **cost of a non-current asset**, less its estimated residual value, is allocated fairly between accounting periods by means of depreciation. The provision for depreciation is both:

- Charged against profit
- Deducted from the value of the non-current asset in the statement of financial position

The need to depreciate non-current assets arises from the **accruals assumption**. If money is expended in purchasing an asset then the amount expended must at some time be charged against profits. If the asset is one which contributes to an entity's revenue over a number of accounting periods it would be inappropriate to charge any single period (eg the period in which the asset was acquired) with the whole of the expenditure. Instead, some method must be found of spreading the cost of the asset over its useful economic life.

This view of depreciation as a process of allocation of the cost of an asset over several accounting periods is the view adopted by IAS 16. It is worth mentioning here two **common misconceptions** about the purpose and effects of depreciation.

(a) It is sometimes thought that the net book value (NBV) of an asset is equal to its net realisable value and that the object of charging depreciation is to **reflect the fall in value of an asset over its life**.

This misconception is the basis of a common, but incorrect, argument which says that freehold properties (say) need not be depreciated in times when property values are rising. It is true that historical cost statements of financial position often give a misleading impression when a property's NBV is much below its market value, but in such a case it is open to a business to incorporate a revaluation into its books, or even to prepare its accounts based on current costs. This is a separate problem from that of allocating the property's cost over successive accounting periods.

(b) Another misconception is that depreciation is provided **so that an asset can be replaced at the end of its useful life**. This is not the case.

  (i) If there is no intention of replacing the asset, it could then be argued that there is no need to provide for any depreciation at all.

  (ii) If prices are rising, the replacement cost of the asset will exceed the amount of depreciation provided.

The standard states that:

- The **depreciable amount** of an item of property, plant and equipment should be allocated on a systematic basis over its useful life.
- The **depreciation method** used should reflect the pattern in which the asset's economic benefits are consumed by the entity.
- The **depreciation charge** for each period should be recognised as an expense unless it is included in the carrying amount of another asset.

Land and buildings are dealt with separately even when they are acquired together because land normally has an unlimited life and is therefore not depreciated. In contrast buildings do have a limited life and must be depreciated. Any increase in the value of land on which a building is standing will have no impact on the determination of the building's useful life.

Depreciation is usually treated as an **expense**, but not where it is absorbed by the entity in the process of producing other assets. For example, depreciation of plant and machinery can be incurred in the production of goods for sale (inventory items). In such circumstances, the depreciation is included in the cost of the new assets produced.

1.11.1 Review of useful life

The following factors should be considered when **estimating the useful life** of a depreciable asset.

- Expected physical **wear and tear**
- **Obsolescence**
- Legal or other **limits on the use** of the assets

Once decided, the useful life should be **reviewed at least every financial year** end and depreciation rates adjusted for the current and future periods if expectations vary significantly from the original estimates. The effect of the change should be disclosed in the accounting period in which the change takes place.

The assessment of useful life requires **judgement** based on previous experience with similar assets or classes of asset. When a completely new type of asset is acquired (ie through technological advancement or through use in producing a brand new product or service) it is still necessary to estimate useful life, even though the exercise will be much more difficult.

The standard also points out that the physical life of the asset might be longer than its useful life to the entity in question. One of the main factors to be taken into consideration is the **physical wear and tear** the asset is likely to endure. This will depend on various circumstances, including the number of shifts for which the asset will be used, the entity's repair and maintenance programme and so on. Other factors to be considered include obsolescence (due to technological advances in production or due to a reduction in demand for the product the asset produces) and legal restrictions, eg length of a related lease.

1.11.2 Review of depreciation method

FAST FORWARD

IAS 16 *Property, plant and equipment* provides the basic rules on **depreciation**, including important definitions of depreciation, depreciable assets, useful life and depreciable amount, all of which you should learn. You should be familiar with methods of depreciation from your earlier studies.

The **depreciation method** should also be reviewed **at least at each financial year end** and, if there has been a significant change in the expected pattern of economic benefits from those assets, the method should be changed to suit this changed pattern. When such a change in depreciation method takes place the change should be accounted for as a **change in accounting estimate** and the depreciation charge for the current and future periods should be adjusted.

1.11.3 Impairment of asset values

An **impairment loss** should be treated in the same way as a **revaluation decrease** ie the decrease should be **recognised as an expense**. However, a revaluation decrease (or impairment loss) should be charged directly against any related revaluation surplus to the extent that the decrease does not exceed the amount held in the revaluation surplus in respect of that same asset.

A **reversal of an impairment** loss should be treated in the same way as a **revaluation increase**, ie a revaluation increase should be recognised as income to the extent that it reverses a revaluation decrease or an impairment loss of the same asset previously recognised as an expense.

1.11.4 Disclosure

An accounting policy note should disclose the **valuation bases** used for determining the amounts at which depreciable assets are stated, along with the other accounting policies (see IAS 1).

IAS 16 also requires the following to be disclosed for each major class of depreciable asset:

- Depreciation methods used
- Useful lives or the depreciation rates used
- Total depreciation allocated for the period
- Gross amount of depreciable assets and the related accumulated depreciation

1.12 Retirements and disposals

FAST FORWARD

When a non-current asset is **sold**, there is likely to be a profit or loss on disposal. This is the difference between the net sale price of the asset and its net book value at the time of disposal.

When an asset is permanently **withdrawn from use, or sold or scrapped**, and no future economic benefits are expected from its disposal, it should be withdrawn from the statement of financial position.

Gains or losses are the difference between the estimated net disposal proceeds and the carrying amount of the asset. They should be recognised as income or expense in the profit or loss.

1.13 Derecognition

An entity is required to **derecognise the carrying amount** of an item of property, plant or equipment that it disposes of on the date the **criteria for the sale of goods** in IAS 18 *Revenue* would be met. This also applies to parts of an asset.

An entity cannot classify as revenue (ie in the top line of the income statement) a gain it realises on the disposal of an item of property, plant and equipment.

1.14 Disclosure

The standard has a long list of disclosure requirements, for each class of property, plant and equipment.

(a) **Measurement bases** for determining the gross carrying amount (if more than one, the gross carrying amount for that basis in each category)

(b) **Depreciation methods** used

(c) **Useful lives** or depreciation rates used

(d) **Gross carrying amount** and accumulated depreciation (aggregated with accumulated impairment losses) at the beginning and end of the period

(e) **Reconciliation** of the carrying amount at the beginning and end of the period showing:

(i) Additions
(ii) Disposals
(iii) Acquisitions through business combinations (see Chapter 21)
(iv) Increases/decreases during the period from revaluations and from impairment losses
(v) Impairment losses recognised in profit or loss
(vi) Impairment losses reversed in profit or loss
(vii) Depreciation
(viii) Net exchange differences (from translation of statements of foreign entity)
(ix) Any other movements.

The financial statements should also disclose the following.

(a) Any recoverable amounts of property, plant and equipment
(b) Existence and amounts of **restrictions on title**, and items pledged as security for liabilities
(c) Accounting policy for **the estimated costs of restoring the site**
(d) Amount of expenditures on account of **items in the course of construction**
(e) Amount of commitments to **acquisitions**

Revalued assets require further disclosures.

(a) Basis used to revalue the assets
(b) Effective date of the revaluation
(c) Whether an independent valuer was involved
(d) Nature of any indices used to determine replacement cost
(e) Carrying amount of each class of property, plant and equipment that would have been included in the financial statements had the assets been carried at cost less accumulated depreciation and accumulated impairment losses.
(f) Revaluation surplus, indicating the movement for the period and any restrictions on the distribution of the balance to shareholders.

The standard also **encourages disclosure** of additional information, which the users of financial statements may find useful.

(a) The carrying amount of temporarily idle property, plant and equipment
(b) The gross carrying amount of any fully depreciated property, plant and equipment that is still in use
(c) The carrying amount of property, plant and equipment retired from active use and held for disposal
(d) The fair value of property, plant and equipment when this is materially different from the carrying amount

The following format (with notional figures) is commonly used to disclose non-current assets movements.

	Total	*Land and buildings*	*Plant and equipment*
	$	$	$
Cost or valuation			
At 1 January 20X4	50,000	40,000	10,000
Revaluation surplus	12,000	12,000	–
Additions in year	4,000	–	4,000
Disposals in year	(1,000)	–	(1,000)
At 31 December 20X4	65,000	52,000	13,000
Depreciation			
At 1 January 20X4	16,000	10,000	6,000
Charge for year	4,000	1,000	3,000
Eliminated on disposals	(500)	–	(500)
At 31 December 20X4	19,500	11,000	8,500
Net book value			
At 31 December 20X4	45,500	41,000	4,500
At 1 January 20X4	34,000	30,000	4,000

Question

Non-current assets

(a) In a statement of financial position prepared in accordance with IAS 16, what does the net book value (carrying value) represent?

(b) In a set of financial statements prepared in accordance with IAS 16, is it correct to say that the net book value (carrying value) figure in a statement of financial position cannot be greater than the market (net realisable) value of the partially used asset as at the end of the reporting period? Explain your reasons for your answer.

Answer

(a) In simple terms the net book value of an asset is the cost of an asset less the 'accumulated depreciation', that is all depreciation charged so far. It should be emphasised that the main purpose of charging depreciation is to ensure that profits are fairly reported. Thus depreciation is concerned with the statement of comprehensive income rather than the statement of financial position. In consequence the net book value figure in the statement of financial position can be quite arbitrary. In particular, it does not necessarily bear any relation to the market value of an asset and is of little use for planning and decision making.

An obvious example of the disparity between net book value and market value is found in the case of buildings, which may be worth more than ten times as much as their net book value.

(b) Net book value can in some circumstances be higher than market value (net realisable value). IAS 16 *Property, plant and equipment* states that the value of an asset cannot be greater than its 'recoverable amount'. However 'recoverable amount' as defined in IAS 16 is the amount recoverable from further use. This may be higher than the market value.

This makes sense if you think of a specialised machine which could not fetch much on the secondhand market but which will produce goods which can be sold at a profit for many years.

Exam focus point

Tangible non-current assets have been tested in December 2008, June 2008, December 2007 & June 2007, and in the groups question in December 2006. It would be advisable to make sure that you know this area well.

2 IAS 20 Government grants

FAST FORWARD

It is common for entities to receive government grants for various purposes (grants may be called subsidies, premiums, etc). They may also receive other types of assistance which may be in many forms. The treatment of government grants is covered by IAS 20 *Accounting for government grants and disclosure of government assistance.*

Key term

Government grants have been examined recently in the December 2008 and December 2007 papers.

2.1 Scope

IAS 20 does ***not*** cover the following situations.

- Accounting for government grants in financial statements reflecting the effects of **changing prices**
- Government assistance given in the form of **'tax breaks'**
- Government acting as **part-owner** of the entity

2.2 Definitions

These definitions are given by the standard.

Key terms

- **Government.** Government, government agencies and similar bodies whether local, national or international.
- **Government assistance.** Action by government designed to provide an economic benefit specific to an entity or range of entities qualifying under certain criteria.
- **Government grants.** Assistance by government in the form of transfers of resources to an entity in return for past or future compliance with certain conditions relating to the operating activities of the entity. They exclude those forms of government assistance which cannot reasonably have a value placed upon them and transactions with government which cannot be distinguished from the normal trading transactions of the entity.
- **Grants related to assets**. Government grants whose primary condition is that an entity qualifying for them should purchase, construct or otherwise acquire non-current assets. Subsidiary conditions may also be attached restricting the type or location of the assets or the periods during which they are to be acquired or held.
- **Grants related to income**. Government grants other than those related to assets.
- **Forgivable loans.** Loans which the lender undertakes to waive repayment of under certain prescribed conditions.
- **Fair value**. The amount for which an asset could be exchanged, or a liability settled, between knowledgeable, willing parties in an arm's length transaction. *(IAS 20)*

You can see that there are many **different forms** of government assistance: both the type of assistance and the conditions attached to it will vary. Government assistance may have encouraged an entity to undertake something it would not otherwise have done.

How will the receipt of government assistance affect the financial statements?

(a) An appropriate method must be found to account for any **resources transferred**.

(b) The extent to which an entity has **benefited** from such assistance during the reporting period should be shown.

2.3 Government grants

An entity should not recognise government grants (including non-monetary grants at fair value) until it has **reasonable assurance** that:

- The entity will comply with any **conditions** attached to the grant
- The entity will **actually receive** the grant

Even if the grant has been received, this does not prove that the conditions attached to it have been or will be fulfilled.

It makes no difference in the treatment of the grant whether it is received in cash or given as a reduction in a liability to government, ie the **manner of receipt is irrelevant**.

Any related **contingency** should be recognised under IAS 37 *Provisions, contingent liabilities and contingent assets*, once the grant has been recognised.

In the case of a **forgivable loan** (as defined in the key terms above) from government, it should be treated in the same way as a government grant when it is reasonably assured that the entity will meet the relevant terms for forgiveness.

2.3.1 Accounting treatment of government grants

There are two methods which could be used to account for government grants, and the arguments for each are given in IAS 20.

Capital approach	Income approach
Credit the grant directly to shareholders' interests	The grant is credited to the income statement over one or more periods.

Question — Capital approach or income approach

Can you think of the different arguments used in support of each method?

Answer

The standard gives the following arguments in support of each method.

Capital approach

(a) The grants are a **financing device**, so should go through the statement of financial position. In the income statement they would simply offset the expenses which they are financing. No repayment is expected by the Government, so the grants should be credited directly to shareholders' interests.

(b) Grants are **not earned**, they are incentives without related costs, so it would be wrong to take them to the income statement.

Income approach

(a) The grants are **not received from shareholders** so should not be credited directly to shareholders' interests.

(b) Grants are **not given or received for nothing**. They are earned by compliance with conditions and by meeting obligations. There are therefore associated costs with which the grant can be matched in the income statement as these costs are being compensated by the grant.

(c) Grants are an extension of **fiscal policies** and so as income taxes and other taxes are charged against income, so grants should be credited to income.

IAS 20 requires grants to be recognised under the income approach, ie grants are recognised as income over the relevant periods to match them with related costs which they have been received to compensate. This should be done on a systematic basis. **Grants should not, therefore, be credited directly to shareholders' interests.**

It would be against the accruals assumption to credit grants to income on a receipts basis, so a **systematic basis of matching** must be used. A receipts basis would only be acceptable if no other basis was available.

It will usually be easy to identify the **costs related to a government grant**, and thereby the period(s) in which the grant should be recognised as income, ie when the costs are incurred. Where grants are received in relation to a depreciating asset, the grant will be recognised over the periods in which the asset is depreciated *and* in the same proportions.

Question

Recognition

Arturo Co receives a government grant representing 50% of the cost of a depreciating asset which costs $40,000. How will the grant be recognised if Arturo Co depreciates the asset:

(a) over four years straight line; or
(b) at 40% reducing balance?

The residual value is nil. The useful life is four years.

Answer

The grant should be recognised in the same proportion as the depreciation.

(a) *Straight line*

		Depreciation	*Grant income*
		$	$
Year	1	10,000	5,000
	2	10,000	5,000
	3	10,000	5,000
	4	10,000	5,000

(b) *Reducing balance*

		Depreciation	*Grant income*
		$	$
Year	1	16,000	8,000
	2	9,600	4,800
	3	5,760	2,880
	4 (remainder)	8,640	4,320

In the case of **grants for non-depreciable assets**, certain obligations may need to be fulfilled, in which case the grant should be recognised as income over the periods in which the cost of meeting the obligation is incurred. For example, if a piece of land is granted on condition that a building is erected on it, then the grant should be recognised as income over the building's life.

There may be a **series of conditions** attached to a grant, in the nature of a package of financial aid. An entity must take care to identify precisely those conditions which give rise to costs which in turn determine the periods over which the grant will be earned. When appropriate, the grant may be split and the parts allocated on different bases.

An entity may receive a grant as compensation for expenses or losses which it has **already incurred**. Alternatively, a grant may be given to an entity simply to provide immediate financial support where no future related costs are expected. In cases such as these, the grant received should be recognised as income of the period in which it becomes receivable.

2.3.2 Non-monetary government grants

A non-monetary asset may be transferred by government to an entity as a grant, for example a piece of land, or other resources. The **fair value** of such an asset is usually assessed and this is used to account for both the asset and the grant. Alternatively, both may be valued at a nominal amount.

2.3.3 Presentation of grants related to assets

There are two choices here for how government grants related to assets (including non-monetary grants at fair value) should be shown in the statement of financial position.

(a) Set up the grant as **deferred income.**

(b) **Deduct the grant** in arriving at the **carrying amount** of the asset.

These are considered to be acceptable alternatives and we can look at an example showing both.

Example: accounting for grants related to assets

A company receives a 20% grant towards the cost of a new item of machinery, which cost $100,000. The machinery has an expected life of four years and a nil residual value. The expected profits of the company, before accounting for depreciation on the new machine or the grant, amount to $50,000 per annum in each year of the machinery's life.

Solution

The results of the company for the four years of the machine's life would be as follows.

(a) *Reducing the cost of the asset*

	Year 1	*Year 2*	*Year 3*	*Year 4*	*Total*
	$	$	$	$	$
Profits					
Profit before depreciation	50,000	50,000	50,000	50,000	200,000
Depreciation*	20,000	20,000	20,000	20,000	80,000
Profit	30,000	30,000	30,000	30,000	120,000

*The depreciation charge on a straight line basis, for each year, is ¼ of $(100,000 – 20,000) = $20,000.

Statement of financial position at reporting date (extract)

	$	$	$	$
Non-current asset at cost	80,000	80,000	80,000	80,000
Depreciation	20,000	40,000	60,000	80,000
Net book value	60,000	40,000	20,000	–

(b) *Treating the grant as deferred income*

	Year 1	*Year 2*	*Year 3*	*Year 4*	*Total*
	$	$	$	$	$
Profits					
Profit before grant & dep'n	50,000	50,000	50,000	50,000	200,000
Depreciation	(25,000)	(25,000)	(25,000)	(25,000)	(100,000)
Grant	5,000	5,000	5,000	5,000	20,000
Profit	30,000	30,000	30,000	30,000	120,000

Statement of financial position at reporting date (extract)

	Year 1	*Year 2*	*Year 3*	*Year 4*
	$	$	$	$
Non-current asset at cost	100,000	100,000	100,000	100,000
Depreciation	(25,000)	(50,000)	(75,000)	(100,000)
Net book value	75,000	50,000	25,000	–
Deferred income				
Government grant deferred income	15,000	10,000	5,000	–

Whichever of these methods is used, the **cash flows** in relation to the purchase of the asset and the receipt of the grant are often disclosed separately because of the significance of the movements in cash flow.

2.3.4 Presentation of grants related to income

FAST FORWARD

You should understand the arguments supporting the **income approach and the capital approach** to the treatment of government grants. You should be able to show both methods of dealing with **grants related to assets.**

These grants are a credit to profit or loss, but there is a choice in the method of disclosure.

Method (a)	Method (b) Income approach
Present as a separate credit or under a general heading, eg 'other income'	Deduct from the related expense

Some would argue that offsetting income and expenses in the in profit or loss for the year is not good practice. Others would say that the expenses would not have been incurred had the grant not been available, so offsetting the two is acceptable. Although both methods are acceptable, disclosure of the grant may be necessary for a **proper understanding** of the financial statements, particularly the effect on any item of income or expense which is required to be separately disclosed.

2.3.5 Repayment of government grants

If a grant must be repaid it should be accounted for as a **revision of an accounting estimate** (see IAS 8).

Repayment of a grant related to income

- Apply first against any unamortised deferred income set up in respect of the grant.
- Any excess should be recognised immediately as an expense.

Repayment of a grant related to an asset

- Increase the carrying amount of the asset or reduce the deferred income balance by the amount repayable.
- The cumulative additional depreciation that would have been recognised to date in the absence of the grant should be immediately recognised as an expense.

It is possible that the circumstances surrounding repayment may require a review of the **asset value** and an impairment of the new carrying amount of the asset.

2.4 Government assistance

Some forms of government assistance are excluded from the definition of government grants.

(a) Some forms of government assistance **cannot reasonably have a value placed on them**, eg free technical or marketing advice, provision of guarantees.

(b) There are transactions with government which **cannot be distinguished from the entity's normal trading transactions**, eg government procurement policy resulting in a portion of the entity's sales. Any segregation would be arbitrary.

Disclosure of such assistance may be necessary because of its significance; its nature, extent and duration should be disclosed. Loans at low or zero interest rates are a form of government assistance, but the imputation of interest does not fully quantify the benefit received.

2.5 Disclosure

Disclosure is required of the following.

- **Accounting policy** adopted, including method of presentation
- **Nature and extent** of government grants recognised and other forms of assistance received
- **Unfulfilled conditions and other contingencies** attached to recognised government assistance

3 IAS 40 Investment property

FAST FORWARD

An entity may own land or a building **as an investment** rather than for use in the business. It may therefore generate cash flows largely independently of other assets which the entity holds.

Exam focus point

The December 2003 paper tested the application of IAS 40 within a group accounting scenario. IAS 40 was also tested in December 2006, but has not been tested since then.

3.1 Definitions

Consider the following definitions.

Key terms

Investment property is property (land or a building – or part of a building – or both) held (by the owner or by the lessee under a finance lease) to earn rentals or for capital appreciation or both, rather than for:

(a) Use in the production or supply of goods or services or for administrative purposes, or
(b) Sale in the ordinary course of business

Owner-occupied property is property held by the owner (or by the lessee under a finance lease) for use in the production or supply of goods or services or for administrative purposes.

Fair value is the amount for which an asset could be exchanged between knowledgeable, willing parties in an arm's length transaction.

Cost is the amount of cash or cash equivalents paid or the fair value of other consideration given to acquire an asset at the time of its acquisition or construction.

Carrying amount is the amount at which an asset is recognised in the statement of financial position.

A property interest that is held by a lessee under an **operating lease** may be classified and accounted for as an **investment property**, if and only if the property would otherwise meet the definition of an investment property and the lessee uses the IAS 40 **fair value model**. This classification is available on a property-by-property basis.

Examples of investment property include:

(a) **Land held for long-term capital appreciation** rather than for short-term sale in the ordinary course of business

(b) A **building** owned by the reporting entity (or held by the entity under a finance lease) and **leased out under an operating lease**

Question — Investment

Rich Co owns a piece of land. The directors have not yet decided whether to build a factory on it for use in its business or to keep it and sell it when its value has risen.

Would this be classified as an investment property under IAS 40?

Answer

Yes. If an entity has not determined that it will use the land either as an owner-occupied property or for short-term sale in the ordinary course of business, the land is considered as being held for capital appreciation.

3.2 IAS 40

FAST FORWARD

IAS 40 *Investment property* defines investment property as property **held to earn rentals or for capital appreciation** or both, rather than for:

- Use in production or supply of goods or services
- Sale in the ordinary course of business

Entities can choose between:

- A **fair value model**, with changes in fair value being measured
- A **cost model** – usual treatment under IAS 16

IAS 40 was published in March 2000 and has recently been revised. Its objective is to prescribe the accounting treatment for investment property and related disclosure requirements.

You now know what an investment property is under IAS 40. Below are examples of things that are **not investment property** under IAS 40.

Type of non-investment property	Applicable IAS
Property intended for sale in the ordinary course of business	IAS 2 *Inventories*
Property being constructed or developed on behalf of third parties	IAS 11 *Construction contracts*
Owner-occupied property	IAS 16 *Property, plant and equipment*
Property leased to another entity under a finance lease	IAS 11 *Leases*

3.3 Recognition

Investment property should be recognised as an asset when **two conditions** are met.

(a) It is **probable** that the **future economic benefits** that are associated with the investment property will **flow to the entity**.

(b) The **cost** of the investment property can be **measured reliably**.

3.4 Initial measurement

An investment property should be measured initially at its **cost,** including transaction costs.

A property interest held under a lease and classified as an investment property shall be accounted for **as if it were a finance lease**. The asset is recognised at the lower of the fair value of the property and the present value of the minimum lease payments. An equivalent amount is recognised as a liability.

3.5 Measurement subsequent to initial recognition

IAS 40 requires an entity to **choose between two models.**

- **The fair value model**
- **The cost model**

Whatever policy it chooses should be applied to **all of its investment property**.

Where an entity chooses to classify a property held under an **operating lease** as an investment property, there is **no choice**. The **fair value model must be used** for **all the entity's investment property**, regardless of whether it is owned or leased.

3.5.1 Fair value model

(a) After initial recognition, an entity that chooses the **fair value model** should measure all of its investment property at fair value, except in the extremely rare cases where this cannot be measured reliably. In such cases it should apply the IAS 16 cost model.

(b) A gain or loss arising from a change in the fair value of an investment property should be recognised in net profit or loss for the period in which it arises.

(c) The fair value of investment property should reflect market conditions at the reporting date.

This was the first time that the IASB has allowed a fair value model for non-financial assets. This is not the same as a revaluation, where increases in carrying amount above a cost-based measure are recognised as revaluation surplus. Under the fair-value model **all** changes in fair value are recognised in the income statement.

The standard elaborates on **issues relating to fair value.**

(a) Fair value assumes that an arm's length transaction has taken place between '**knowledgeable, willing parties'**, ie both buyer and seller are reasonably informed about the nature and characteristics of the investment property.

(b) A willing buyer is **motivated but not compelled** to buy. A willing seller is neither an over-eager nor a forced seller, nor one prepared to sell at any price or to hold out for a price not considered reasonable in the current market.

(c) **Fair value is not the same as 'value in use'** as defined in IAS 36 *Impairment of assets*. Value in use reflects factors and knowledge specific to the entity, while fair value reflects factors and knowledge relevant to the market.

(d) In determining fair value an entity **should not double count assets**. For example, elevators or air conditioning are often an integral part of a building and should be included in the investment property, rather than recognised separately.

(e) In those rare cases where the **entity cannot determine the fair value of an investment property reliably**, the cost model in **IAS 16** must be applied until the investment property is disposed of. The **residual value must be assumed to be zero**.

3.5.2 Cost model

The cost model is the **cost model in IAS 16.** Investment property should be measured at **depreciated cost, less any accumulated impairment losses.** An entity that chooses the cost model should **disclose the fair value of its investment property.**

3.5.3 Changing models

Once the entity has chosen the fair value or cost model, it should apply it to all of its investment property. It **should not change from one model to the other unless the change will result in a more appropriate presentation**. IAS 40 states that it is highly unlikely that a change from the fair value model to the cost model will result in a more appropriate presentation.

Exam focus point

Revaluation of investment properties and the fair value model is a popular topic and may be examined as part of a longer question.

3.6 Transfers

Transfers to or from investment property should **only** be made **when there is a change in use**. For example, owner occupation commences so the investment property will be treated under IAS 16 as an owner-occupied property.

When there is a transfer from investment property carried at fair value to owner-occupied property or inventories, the property's cost for subsequent accounting under IAS 16 or IAS 2 should be its fair value at the date of change of use.

Conversely, an owner-occupied property may become an investment property and need to be carried at fair value. An entity should apply IAS 16 up to the date of change of use. It should treat any difference at that date between the carrying amount of the property under IAS 16 and its fair value as a revaluation under IAS 16.

3.7 Disposals

An investment property should be derecognised on disposal or when it is permanently withdrawn from use and no future economic benefits are expected from its disposal.

Any **gain or loss** on disposal is the difference between the net disposal proceeds and the carrying amount of the asset. It should generally be **recognised as income or expense in the profit or loss**.

Compensation from third parties for investment property that was impaired, lost or given up shall be recognised in profit or loss when the compensation becomes receivable.

3.8 Disclosure requirements

These relate to:

- Choice of fair value model or cost model
- Whether property interests held as operating leases are included in investment property
- Criteria for classification as investment property
- Assumptions in determining fair value
- Use of independent professional valuer (encouraged but not required)
- Rental income and expenses
- Any restrictions or obligations

3.8.1 Fair value model – additional disclosures

An entity that adopts this must also disclose a **reconciliation** of the carrying amount of the investment property at the beginning and end of the period.

3.8.2 Cost model – additional disclosures

These relate mainly to the depreciation method. In addition, an entity which adopts the cost model **must disclose the fair value** of the investment property.

3.9 Decision tree

The decision tree below summarises which IASs apply to various kinds of property.

Exam focus point

Consider learning this decision tree – it will help you tackle most of the problems you are likely to meet in the exam!

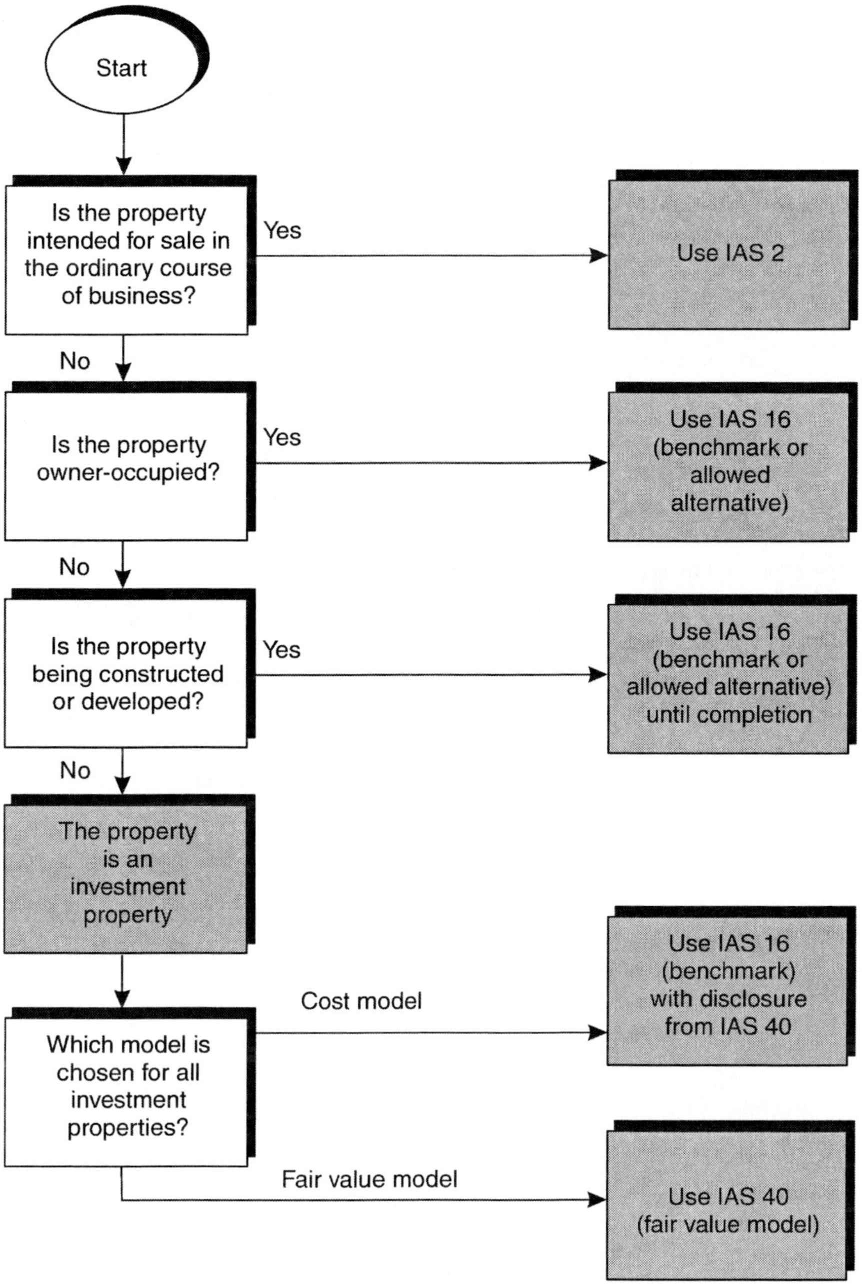

4 IAS 36 Impairment of assets

FAST FORWARD

Impairment is determined by comparing the carrying amount of the asset with its recoverable value.

There is an established principle that assets should not be carried at more than their recoverable amount. An entity should write down the carrying value of an asset to its recoverable amount if the carrying value of an asset is not recoverable in full. IAS 36 puts in place a detailed methodology for carrying out impairment reviews and related accounting treatments and disclosures.

Exam focus point

The December 2003 paper required candidates to:

- Describe the circumstances where an impairment loss is deemed to have occurred and explain why an impairment review should be undertaken
- Discuss the matters to be considered in assessing whether an asset may be impaired.

IAS 36 was also examined in December 2006, and 2007 and December 2007.

4.1 Scope

IAS 36 applies to all tangible, intangible and financial assets **except** inventories, assets arising from construction contracts, deferred tax assets, assets arising under IAS 19 *Employee benefits* and financial assets within the scope of IAS 32 *Financial instruments: Presentation*. This is because those IASs already have rules for recognising and measuring impairment. Note also that IAS 36 does not apply to non-current assets held for sale, which are dealt with under IFRS 5 *Non-current assets held for sale and discontinued operations*.

Key terms

- **Impairment:** a fall in the value of an asset, so that its 'recoverable amount' is now less than its carrying amount in the statement of financial position.
- **Carrying amount**: is the net value at which the asset is included in the statement of financial position (ie after deducting accumulated depreciation and any impairment losses). *(IAS 36)*

The basic principle underlying IAS 36 is relatively straightforward. If an asset's value in the accounts is higher than its realistic value, measured as its 'recoverable amount', the asset is judged to have suffered an impairment loss. It should therefore be reduced in value, by the amount of the **impairment loss**. The amount of the impairment loss should be **written off against profit** immediately.

The main accounting issues to consider are therefore as follows.

(a) How is it possible to **identify when** an impairment loss may have occurred?
(b) How should the **recoverable amount** of the asset be measured?
(c) How should an 'impairment loss' be **reported in the accounts**?

4.2 Identifying a potentially impaired asset

An entity should assess at the end of each reporting period whether there are any indications of impairment to any assets. The concept of **materiality** applies, and only material impairment needs to be identified.

If there are indications of possible impairment, the entity is required to make a formal estimate of the **recoverable amount** of the assets concerned.

IAS 36 suggests how **indications of a possible impairment** of assets might be recognised. The suggestions are based largely on common sense.

(a) **External sources of information**

   (i) A fall in the asset's market value that is more significant than would normally be expected from passage of time over normal use.
   (ii) A significant change in the technological, market, legal or economic environment of the business in which the assets are employed.
   (iii) An increase in market interest rates or market rates of return on investments likely to affect the discount rate used in calculating value in use.
   (iv) The carrying amount of the entity's net assets being more than its market capitalisation.

(b) **Internal sources of information**: evidence of obsolescence or physical damage, adverse changes in the use to which the asset is put, or the asset's economic performance

Even if there are no indications of impairment, the following assets must **always** be tested for impairment annually.

(a) An intangible asset with an **indefinite useful life**
(b) **Goodwill** acquired in a business combination

4.3 Measuring the recoverable amount of the asset

FAST FORWARD

The recoverable amount of an asset is the higher of the asset's **fair value less costs to sell** and **its value in use**. When is it not possible to calculate the recoverable amount of a single asset, then that of its **cash generating unit** should be measured instead.

What is an asset's recoverable amount?

Key term

The **recoverable amount of an asset** should be measured as the *higher value* of:

(a) The asset's fair value less costs to sell; and
(b) Its value in use. *(IAS 36)*

An asset's fair value less costs to sell is the amount net of selling costs that could be obtained from the sale of the asset. Selling costs include sales transaction costs, such as legal expenses.

(a) If there is **an active market** in the asset, the net selling price should be based on the **market value**, or on the price of recent transactions in similar assets.
(b) If there is **no active market** in the assets it might be possible to **estimate** a net selling price using best estimates of what 'knowledgeable, willing parties' might pay in an arm's length transaction.

Net selling price **cannot** be reduced, however, by including within selling costs any **restructuring or reorganisation expenses**, or any costs that have already been recognised in the accounts as liabilities.

The concept of 'value in use' is very important.

Key term

The **value in use** of an asset is measured as the present value of estimated future cash flows (inflows minus outflows) generated by the asset, including its estimated net disposal value (if any) at the end of its expected useful life.

The cash flows used in the calculation should be **pre-tax cash flows** and a **pre-tax discount rate** should be applied to calculate the present value.

The calculation of **value in use** must reflect the following.

(a) An estimate of the **future cash flows** the entity expects to derive from the asset
(b) Expectations about **possible variations** in the amount and timing of future cash flows
(c) The **time value of money**
(d) The price for bearing the **uncertainty** inherent in the asset, and
(e) **Other factors** that would be reflected in pricing future cash flows from the asset

Calculating a value in use therefore calls for estimates of future cash flows, and the possibility exists that an entity might come up with **over-optimistic estimates** of cash flows. The IAS therefore states the following.

(a) Cash flow projections should be based on **'reasonable and supportable' assumptions**.
(b) Projections of cash flows, normally up to a maximum period of five years, should be based on the most **recent budgets or financial forecasts**.
(c) Cash flow projections beyond this period should be obtained by extrapolating short-term projections, using either a **steady or declining growth rate** for each subsequent year (unless a rising growth rate can be justified). The long term growth rate applied should not exceed the average long term growth rate for the product, market, industry or country, unless a higher growth rate can be justified.

4.4 Composition of estimates of future cash flows

These should include the following.

(a) Projections of **cash inflows** from **continuing use** of the asset

(b) Projections of **cash outflows** necessarily incurred to **generate the cash inflows** from continuing use of the asset

(c) **Net cash flows** received/paid on **disposal** of the asset at the end of its useful life

There is an underlying principle that future cash flows should be estimated for the asset in its current condition. Future cash flows relating to restructurings to which the entity is not yet committed, or to future costs to add to, replace part of, or service the asset are excluded.

Estimates of future cash flows should **exclude** the following.

(a) Cash inflows/outflows from financing activities
(b) Income tax receipts/payments

The amount of net cash inflow/outflow on **disposal** of an asset should assume an arm's length transaction.

Foreign currency future cash flows should be forecast in the currency in which they will arise and will be discounted using a rate appropriate for that currency. The resulting figure should then be translated into the reporting currency at the spot rate at the end of each reporting period.

The **discount rate** should be a current pre-tax rate (or rates) that reflects the current assessment of the time value of money and the risks specific to the asset. The discount rate should not include a risk weighting if the underlying cash flows have already been adjusted for risk.

4.5 Recognition and measurement of an impairment loss

The rule for assets at historical cost is:

Rule to learn

If the recoverable amount of an asset is lower than the carrying amount, the carrying amount should be reduced by the difference (ie the impairment loss) which should be charged as an expense in the income statement.

The rule for assets held at a revalued amount (such as property revalued under IAS 16) is:

Rule to learn

The impairment loss is to be treated as a revaluation decrease under the relevant IAS.

In practice this means:

- To the extent that there is a revaluation surplus held in respect of the asset, the impairment loss should be charged to revaluation surplus.
- Any excess should be charged to the income statement.

The IAS goes into quite a large amount of detail about the important concept of cash generating units. As a basic rule, the recoverable amount of an asset should be calculated for the **asset individually**. However, there will be occasions when it is not possible to estimate such a value for an individual asset, particularly in the calculation of value in use. This is because cash inflows and outflows cannot be attributed to the individual asset.

If it is not possible to calculate the recoverable amount for an individual asset, the recoverable amount of the asset's cash generating unit should be measured instead.

Key term

A cash generating unit is the smallest identifiable group of assets for which independent cash flows can be identified and measured.

Question — Cash generating unit I

Can you think of some examples of how a cash generating unit would be identified?

Answer

Here are two possibilities.

(a) A mining company owns a private railway that it uses to transport output from one of its mines. The railway now has no market value other than as scrap, and it is impossible to identify any separate cash inflows with the use of the railway itself. Consequently, if the mining company suspects an impairment in the value of the railway, it should treat the mine as a whole as a cash generating unit, and measure the recoverable amount of the mine as a whole.

(b) A bus company has an arrangement with a town's authorities to run a bus service on four routes in the town. Separately identifiable assets are allocated to each of the bus routes, and cash inflows and outflows can be attributed to each individual route. Three routes are running at a profit and one is running at a loss. The bus company suspects that there is an impairment of assets on the loss-making route. However, the company will be unable to close the loss-making route, because it is under an obligation to operate all four routes, as part of its contract with the local authority. Consequently, the company should treat all four bus routes together as a cash generating unit, and calculate the recoverable amount for the unit as a whole.

Question — Cash generating unit II

Minimart belongs to a retail store chain Maximart. Minimart makes all its retail purchases through Maximart's purchasing centre. Pricing, marketing, advertising and human resources policies (except for hiring Minimart's cashiers and salesmen) are decided by Maximart. Maximart also owns 5 other stores in the same city as Minimart (although in different neighbourhoods) and 20 other stores in other cities. All stores are managed in the same way as Minimart. Minimart and 4 other stores were purchased 5 years ago and goodwill was recognised.

What is the cash-generating unit for Minimart?

Answer

In identifying Minimart's cash-generating unit, an entity considers whether, for example:

(a) Internal management reporting is organised to measure performance on a store-by-store basis.
(b) The business is run on a store-by-store profit basis or on a region/city basis.

All Maximart's stores are in different neighbourhoods and probably have different customer bases. So, although Minimart is managed at a corporate level, Minimart generates cash inflows that are largely independent from those of Maximart's other stores. Therefore, it is likely that Minimart is a cash-generating unit.

Question — Cash generating unit III

Mighty Mag Publishing Co owns 150 magazine titles of which 70 were purchased and 80 were self-created. The price paid for a purchased magazine title is recognised as an intangible asset. The costs of creating magazine titles and maintaining the existing titles are recognised as an expense when incurred. Cash inflows from direct sales and advertising are identifiable for each magazine title. Titles are managed by customer segments. The level of advertising income for a magazine title depends on the range of titles in the customer segment to which the magazine title relates. Management has a policy to abandon old titles before the end of their economic lives and replace them immediately with new titles for the same customer segment.

What is the cash-generating unit for an individual magazine title?

Answer

It is likely that the recoverable amount of an individual magazine title can be assessed. Even though the level of advertising income for a title is influenced, to a certain extent, by the other titles in the customer segment, cash inflows from direct sales and advertising are identifiable for each title. In addition, although titles are managed by customer segments, decisions to abandon titles are made on an individual title basis.

Therefore, it is likely that individual magazine titles generate cash inflows that are largely independent one from another and that each magazine title is a separate cash-generating unit.

If an active market exists for the output produced by the asset or a group of assets, this asset or group should be identified as a cash generating unit, even if some or all of the output is used internally.

Cash generating units should be identified consistently from period to period for the same type of asset unless a change is justified.

The group of net assets less liabilities that are considered for impairment should be the same as those considered in the calculation of the recoverable amount. (For the treatment of goodwill and corporate assets see below.)

4.6 Example: Recoverable amount and carrying amount

Fourways Co is made up of four cash generating units. All four units are being tested for impairment.

(a) Property, plant and equipment and separate intangibles would be allocated to be cash generating units as far as possible.

(b) Current assets such as inventories, receivables and prepayments would be allocated to the relevant cash generating units.

(c) Liabilities (eg payables) would be deducted from the net assets of the relevant cash generating units.

(d) The net figure for each cash generating unit resulting from this exercise would be compared to the relevant recoverable amount, computed on the same basis.

4.7 Goodwill and the impairment of assets

4.7.1 Allocating goodwill to cash-generating units

Goodwill acquired in a business combination does not generate cash flows independently of other assets. It must be **allocated** to each of the acquirer's **cash-generating units** (or groups of cash-generating units) that are expected to benefit from the synergies of the combination. Each unit to which the goodwill is so allocated should:

(a) Represent the **lowest level** within the entity at which the goodwill is monitored for internal management purposes

(b) Not be **larger than a reporting segment** determined in accordance with IAS 14 *Segment reporting*

It may be impractical to complete the allocation of goodwill before the first reporting date after a business combination, particularly if the acquirer is accounting for the combination for the first time using provisional values (see Chapter 6). The initial allocation of goodwill must be completed before the end of the first reporting period after the acquisition date.

4.7.2 Testing cash-generating units with goodwill for impairment

There are two situations to consider.

(a) Where goodwill has been allocated to a cash-generating unit

(b) Where it has not been possible to allocate goodwill to a specific cash-generating unit, but only to a group of units

A cash-generating unit to which goodwill has been allocated is tested for impairment annually. The **carrying amount** of the unit, including goodwill, is **compared with the recoverable amount**. If the carrying amount of the unit exceeds the recoverable amount, the entity must recognise an impairment loss.

Where goodwill relates to a cash-generating unit but has not been allocated to that unit, the unit is tested for impairment by **comparing its carrying amount** (excluding goodwill) **with its recoverable amount**. The entity must recognise an impairment loss if the carrying amount exceeds the recoverable amount.

The annual impairment test may be performed at any time during an accounting period, but must be performed at the **same time every year**.

4.8 Corporate assets

Corporate assets are group or divisional assets such as a head office building, computer equipment or a research centre. Essentially, corporate assets are assets that do not generate cash inflows independently from other assets, hence their carrying amount cannot be fully attributed to a cash-generating unit under review.

In testing a cash generating unit for impairment, an entity should identify all the corporate assets that relate to the cash-generating unit.

(a) If a portion of the carrying amount of a corporate asset **can be allocated** to the unit on a reasonable and consistent basis, the entity compares the carrying amount of the unit (including the portion of the asset) with its recoverable amount.

(b) If a portion of the carrying amount of a corporate asset **cannot be allocated** to the unit on a reasonable and consistent basis, the entity:

  (i) Compares the carrying amount of the unit (excluding the asset) with its recoverable amount and recognises any impairment loss

  (ii) Identifies the smallest group of cash-generating units that includes the cash-generating unit to which the asset belongs and to which a portion of the carrying amount of the asset can be allocated on a reasonable and consistent basis

  (iii) Compares the carrying amount of that group of cash-generating units (including the portion of the asset allocated to the group of units) with the recoverable amount of the group of units and recognises any impairment loss

4.9 Accounting treatment of an impairment loss

If, and only if, the recoverable amount of an asset is less than its carrying amount in the statement of financial position, an impairment loss has occurred. This loss should be **recognised immediately**.

(a) The asset's **carrying amount** should be reduced to its recoverable amount in the statement of financial position.

(b) The **impairment loss** should be recognised immediately in the income statement (unless the asset has been revalued in which case the loss is treated as a revaluation decrease).

After reducing an asset to its recoverable amount, the **depreciation charge** on the asset should then be based on its new carrying amount, its estimated residual value (if any) and its estimated remaining useful life.

An impairment loss should be recognised for a **cash generating unit** if (and only if) the recoverable amount for the cash generating unit is less than the carrying amount in the statement of financial position for all the assets in the unit. When an impairment loss is recognised for a cash generating unit, the loss should be allocated between the assets in the unit in the following order.

(a) First, to any assets that are obviously damaged or destroyed
(b) Next, to the **goodwill** allocated to the cash generating unit
(c) Then to all other assets in the cash-generating unit, on a **pro rata basis**

In allocating an impairment loss, the carrying amount of an asset should not be reduced below the highest of:

(a) Its fair value less costs to sell
(b) Its value in use (if determinable)
(c) Zero

Any remaining amount of an impairment loss should be recognised as a liability if required by other IASs.

4.10 Example 1: impairment loss

A company that extracts natural gas and oil has a drilling platform in the Caspian Sea. It is required by legislation of the country concerned to remove and dismantle the platform at the end of its useful life. Accordingly, the company has included an amount in its accounts for removal and dismantling costs, and is depreciating this amount over the platform's expected life.

The company is carrying out an exercise to establish whether there has been an impairment of the platform.

(a) Its carrying amount in the statement of financial position is $3m.
(b) The company has received an offer of $2.8m for the platform from another oil company. The bidder would take over the responsibility (and costs) for dismantling and removing the platform at the end of its life.
(c) The present value of the estimated cash flows from the platform's continued use is $3.3m.
(d) The carrying amount in the statement of financial position for the provision for dismantling and removal is currently $0.6m.

What should be the value of the drilling platform in the statement of financial position, and what, if anything, is the impairment loss?

Solution

Fair value less costs to sell	=	$2.8m
Value in use	=	PV of cash flows from use less the carrying amount of the provision/liability = $3.3m – $0.6m = $2.7m
Recoverable amount	=	Higher of these two amounts, ie $2.8m
Carrying value	=	$3m
Impairment loss	=	$0.2m

The carrying value should be reduced to $2.8m

4.11 Example 2: impairment loss

A company has acquired another business for $4.5m: tangible assets are valued at $4.0m and goodwill at $0.5m.

An asset with a carrying value of $1m is destroyed in a terrorist attack. The asset was not insured. The loss of the asset, without insurance, has prompted the company to assess whether there has been an impairment of assets in the acquired business and what the amount of any such loss is.

The recoverable amount of the business (a single cash generating unit) is measured as $3.1m.

Solution

There has been an impairment loss of $1.4m ($4.5m – $3.1m).

The impairment loss will be recognised in profit or loss. The loss will be allocated between the assets in the cash generating unit as follows.

(a) A loss of $1m can be attributed directly to the uninsured asset that has been destroyed.
(b) The remaining loss of $0.4m should be allocated to goodwill.

The carrying value of the assets will now be $3m for tangible assets and $0.1m for goodwill.

4.12 Reversal of an impairment loss

The annual assessment to determine whether there may have been some impairment should be **applied to all assets**, including assets that have already been impaired in the past.

In some cases, the recoverable amount of an asset that has previously been impaired might turn out to be **higher** than the asset's current carrying value. In other words, there might have been a reversal of some of the previous impairment loss.

(a) The reversal of the impairment loss should be **recognised immediately** as income in the profit or loss.

(b) The carrying amount of the asset should be increased to its **new recoverable amount**.

Rule to learn

An impairment loss recognised for an asset in prior years should be reversed if, and only if, there has been a change in the estimates used to determine the asset's recoverable amount since the last impairment loss was recognised.

The asset cannot be revalued to a carrying amount that is higher than its value would have been if the asset had not been impaired originally, ie its **depreciated carrying value** had the impairment not taken place. Depreciation of the asset should now be based on its new revalued amount, its estimated residual value (if any) and its estimated remaining useful life.

An exception to this rule is for **goodwill**. An impairment loss for goodwill should not be reversed in a subsequent period.

Question

Reversal of impairment loss

A cash generating unit comprising a factory, plant and equipment etc and associated purchased goodwill becomes impaired because the product it makes is overtaken by a technologically more advanced model produced by a competitor. The recoverable amount of the cash generating unit falls to $60m, resulting in an impairment loss of $80m, allocated as follows.

	Carrying amounts before impairment	*Carrying amounts after impairment*
	$m	$m
Goodwill	40	
Patent (with no market value)	20	
Tangible non-current assets (market value $60m)	80	60
Total	140	60

After three years, the entity makes a technological breakthrough of its own, and the recoverable amount of the cash generating unit increases to $90m. The carrying amount of the tangible non-current assets had the impairment not occurred would have been $70m.

Required

Calculate the reversal of the impairment loss.

Answer

The reversal of the impairment loss is recognised to the extent that it increases the carrying amount of the tangible non-current assets to what it would have been had the impairment not taken place, ie a reversal of the impairment loss of $10m is recognised and the tangible non-current assets written back to $70m. Reversal of the impairment is not recognised in relation to the goodwill and patent because the effect of the external event that caused the original impairment has not reversed – the original product is still overtaken by a more advanced model.

4.13 Disclosure

IAS 36 calls for substantial disclosure about impairment of assets. The information to be disclosed includes the following.

(a) For each class of assets, the amount of **impairment losses recognised** and the amount of any **impairment losses recovered** (ie reversals of impairment losses)

(b) For each individual asset or cash generating unit that has suffered a **significant impairment loss**, details of the nature of the asset, the amount of the loss, the events that led to recognition of the loss, whether the recoverable amount is fair value less costs to sell or value in use, and if the recoverable amount is value in use, the basis on which this value was estimated (eg the discount rate applied)

4.13.1 Compensation for the impairment or loss of items

An entity may receive monetary or non-monetary compensation from third parties for the impairment or loss of items of property, plant and equipment. The compensation may be used to restore the asset. Examples include:

- Reimbursement by insurance companies after an impairment of items of plant and equipment
- Physical replacement of an impaired or lost asset

The accounting treatment is as follows.

(a) Impairments of items of property, plant and equipment should be recognised under IAS 36, disposals should be recognised under IAS 16.

(b) Monetary or non-monetary compensation from third parties for items of property etc that were impaired, lost or given up, should be included in the profit or loss.

(c) The cost of assets restored, purchased, constructed as a replacement or received as compensation should be determined and presented under IAS 16.

4.14 Section summary

The main aspects of IAS 36 to consider are:

- **Indications** of impairment of assets
- **Measuring recoverable amount**, as net selling price or value in use
- **Measuring value in use**
- **Cash generating units**
- **Accounting treatment** of an impairment loss, for individual assets and cash generating units
- **Reversal** of an impairment loss

5 IAS 23 Borrowing costs

FAST FORWARD

IAS 23 *Borrowing costs* looks at the treatment of borrowing costs, particularly where the related borrowings are applied to the **construction of certain assets**. These are what are usually called 'self-constructed assets', where an enterprise builds its own inventory of non-current assets over a substantial period of time. IAS 23 requires eligible borrowing costs to be capitalised into the cost of the asset.

Exam focus point

The examiner will expect you to be able to actually calculate finance costs to be capitalised. This has been tested in the past.

5.1 Definitions

IAS 23 *Borrowing costs* was revised in March 2007. Previously it gave a choice of methods in dealing with borrowing costs: capitalisation or expense. The revised standard requires capitalisation.

Only two definitions are given by the standard.

Key terms

- **Borrowing costs**. Interest and other costs incurred by an entity in connection with the borrowing of funds.
- **Qualifying asset**. An asset that necessarily takes a substantial period of time to get ready for its intended use or sale. *(IAS 23)*

The standard lists what may be **included in borrowing costs**.

- Interest on bank overdrafts and short-term and long-term borrowings
- Amortisation of discounts or premiums relating to borrowings
- Amortisation of ancillary costs incurred in connection with the arrangement of borrowings
- Finance charges in respect of finance leases recognised in accordance with IAS 17
- Exchange differences arising from foreign currency borrowings to the extent that they are regarded as an adjustment to interest costs

Depending on the circumstances, any of the following may be qualifying assets.

- Inventories
- Manufacturing plants
- Power generation facilities
- Intangible assets
- Investment properties

Financial assets and inventories that are manufactured, or otherwise produced over a short period of time are **not qualifying assets**. Assets that are ready for their intended use or sale when purchased are not qualifying assets.

5.2 Recognition

Borrowing costs should be capitalised if they are directly attributable to the acquisition, construction or production of a qualifying asset as part of its cost. Other borrowing costs are expensed as incurred.

Those borrowing costs directly attributable to the acquisition, construction or production of a qualifying asset are costs that **would have been avoided** had the expenditure on the qualifying asset not been made. This is obviously straightforward where funds have been borrowed for the financing of one particular asset.

Difficulties arise, however, where the enterprise uses a **range of debt instruments** to finance a wide range of assets, so that there is no direct relationship between particular borrowings and a specific asset. For example, all borrowings may be made centrally and then lent to different parts of the group or enterprise. Judgement is therefore required, particularly where further complications can arise (eg foreign currency loans).

Once the relevant borrowings are identified, which relate to a specific asset, then the **amount of borrowing costs eligible for capitalisation** will be the actual borrowing costs incurred on those borrowings during the period, *less* any investment income on the temporary investment of those borrowings. It would not be unusual for some or all of the funds to be invested before they are actually used on the qualifying asset.

Question — Borrowing costs

On 1 January 20X9 Stremans Co borrowed $1.5m to finance the production of two assets, both of which were expected to take a year to build. Production started during 20X9. The loan facility was drawn down on 1 January 20X9, and was utilised as follows, with the remaining funds invested temporarily.

	Asset A	*Asset B*

	$'000	$'000
1 January 20X9	250	500
1 July 20X9	250	500

The loan rate was 9% and Stremans Co can invest surplus funds at 7%.

Required

Ignoring compound interest, calculate the borrowing costs which may be capitalised for each of the assets and consequently the cost of each asset as at 31 December 20X9.

Answer

		Asset A	*Asset B*
		$	$
Borrowing costs			
To 30 June 20X9	$250,000/$500,000 × 9% × 6/12	11,250	22,500
To 31 December 20X9	$500,000/$1,000,000 × 9% × 6/12	22,500	45,000
		33,750	67,500
Less investment income			
To 30 June 20X9	$250,000/$500,000 × 7% × 6/12	(8,750)	(17,500)
		25,000	50,000
Cost of assets			
Expenditure incurred		500,000	1,000,000
Borrowing costs		25,000	50,000
		525,000	1,050,000

In a situation where **borrowings are obtained generally**, but are applied in part to obtaining a qualifying asset, then the amount of borrowing costs eligible for capitalisation is found by applying the 'capitalisation rate' to the expenditure on the asset.

The **capitalisation rate** is the weighted average of the borrowing costs applicable to the enterprise's borrowings that are outstanding during the period, *excluding* borrowings made specifically to obtain a qualifying asset. However, there is a cap on the amount of borrowing costs calculated in this way: it must not exceed actual borrowing costs incurred.

Sometimes one overall weighted average can be calculated for a group or enterprise, but in some situations it may be more appropriate to use a weighted average for borrowing costs for **individual parts of the group or enterprise**.

Question

Capitalisation

Acruni Co had the following loans in place at the beginning and end of 20X6.

	1 January 20X6	*31 December 20X6*
	$m	$m
10% Bank loan repayable 20X8	120	120
9.5% Bank loan repayable 20X9	80	80
8.9% debenture repayable 20X7	–	150

The 8.9% debenture was issued to fund the construction of a qualifying asset (a piece of mining equipment), construction of which began on 1 July 20X6.

On 1 January 20X6, Acruni Co began construction of a qualifying asset, a piece of machinery for a hydro-electric plant, using existing borrowings. Expenditure drawn down for the construction was: $30m on 1 January 20X6, $20m on 1 October 20X6.

Required

Calculate the borrowing costs to be capitalised for the hydro-electric plant machine.

Answer

Capitalisation rate = weighted average rate = $(10\% \times \frac{120}{120+80}) + (9.5\% \times \frac{80}{120+80}) = 9.8\%$

Borrowing costs $= (\$30m \times 9.8\%) + (\$20m \times 9.8\% \times 3/12)$
$= \$3.43m$

5.2.1 Carrying amount exceeds recoverable amount

A situation may arise whereby the carrying amount (or expected ultimate cost) of the qualifying asset exceeds its recoverable amount or net realisable value. In these cases, the carrying amount must be **written down or written off**, as required by other IASs. In certain circumstances (again as allowed by other IASs), these amounts may be written back in future periods.

5.2.2 Commencement of capitalisation

An entity can start to capitalise borrowing costs on the **commencement date**. This is the date when the following conditions are met:

(a) Expenditure on the asset is being incurred
(b) Borrowing costs are being incurred
(c) Activities are undertaken that are necessary to prepare the asset for its intended use or sale

Expenditure must result in the payment of cash, transfer of other assets or assumption of interest-bearing liabilities. **Deductions from expenditure** will be made for any progress payments or grants received in connection with the asset. IAS 23 allows the **average carrying amount** of the asset during a period (including borrowing costs previously capitalised) to be used as a reasonable approximation of the expenditure to which the capitalisation rate is applied in the period. Presumably more exact calculations can be used.

Activities necessary to prepare the asset for its intended sale or use extend further than physical construction work. They encompass technical and administrative work prior to construction, eg obtaining permits. They do *not* include holding an asset when no production or development that changes the asset's condition is taking place, eg where land is held without any associated development activity.

5.2.3 Suspension of capitalisation

If active development is **interrupted for any extended periods**, capitalisation of borrowing costs should be suspended for those periods.

Suspension of capitalisation of borrowing costs is not necessary for **temporary delays** or for periods when substantial technical or administrative work is taking place.

5.2.4 Cessation of capitalisation

Once substantially all the activities necessary to prepare the qualifying asset for its intended use or sale are complete, then capitalisation of borrowing costs should cease. This will normally be when **physical construction of the asset is completed**, although minor modifications may still be outstanding.

The asset may be completed in **parts or stages**, where each part can be used while construction is still taking place on the other parts. Capitalisation of borrowing costs should cease for each part as it is completed. The example given by the standard is a business park consisting of several buildings.

5.2.5 Disclosure

The following should be disclosed in the financial statements in relation to borrowing costs.

(a) Amount of borrowing costs **capitalised during the period**

(b) **Capitalisation rate** used to determine the amount of borrowing costs eligible for capitalisation

5.3 Section summary

- IAS 23 was amended in March 2007 and requires borrowing costs on qualifying assets to be capitalised.
- Borrowing costs can be capitalised when an entity
  - Incurs expenditure for an asset
  - Incurs borrowing costs
  - Undertakes activities that are necessary to prepare the asset for its intended use or sale.

Chapter Roundup

- IAS 16 *Property, plant and equipment* covers all aspects of accounting for property, plant and equipment. This represents the bulk of items which are **'tangible' non-current assets**.
- The **cost of a non-current asset**, less its estimated residual value, is allocated fairly between accounting periods by means of depreciation. The provision for depreciation is both:
  - Charged against profit
  - Deducted from the value of the non-current asset in the statement of financial position
- IAS 16 *Property, plant and equipment* provides the basic rules on **depreciation**, including important definitions of depreciation, depreciable assets, useful life and depreciable amount, all of which you should learn. You should be familiar with methods of depreciation from your earlier studies.
- When a non-current asset is **sold**, there is likely to be a profit or loss on disposal. This is the difference between the net sale price of the asset and its net book value at the time of disposal.
- It is common for entities to receive government grants for various purposes (grants may be called subsidies, premiums, etc). They may also receive other types of assistance which may be in many forms. The treatment of government grants is covered by IAS 20 *Accounting for government grants and disclosure of government assistance.*
- You should understand the arguments supporting the **income approach and the capital approach** to the treatment of government grants. You should be able to show both methods of dealing with **grants related to assets**.
- An entity may own land or a building *as an investment* rather than for use in the business. It may therefore generate cash flows largely independently of other assets which the entity holds.
- IAS 40 *Investment property* defines investment property as property **held to earn rentals or for capital appreciation** or both, rather than for:
  - Use in production or supply of goods or services
  - Sale in the ordinary course of business
- Entities can choose between:
  - A **fair value model**, with changes in fair value being measured
  - A **cost model** – usual treatment under IAS 16
- Impairment is determined by comparing the carrying amount of the asset with its recoverable value.
- The recoverable amount of an asset is the higher of the asset's **fair value less costs to sell** and **its value in use**. When it is not possible to calculate the recoverable amount of a single asset, then that of its **cash generating unit** should be measured instead.
- IAS 23 *Borrowing costs* at the treatment of borrowing costs, particularly where the related borrowings are applied to the **construction of certain assets**. These are what are usually called 'self-constructed assets', where an enterprise builds its own inventory or non-current assets over a substantial period of time. IAS 23 required eligible borrowing costs to be capitalised into the cost of the asset.

Quick Quiz

1 Define depreciation.

2 Which of the following elements can be included in the production cost of a non-current asset?

(a) Purchase price of raw materials
(b) Architect's fees
(c) Import duties
(d) Installation costs

3 Market value can usually be taken as fair value.

True ☐ False ☐

4 Define impairment.

5 Investment properties must always be shown at fair value.

True ☐ False ☐

6 What is the correct treatment for property being constructed for future use as investment property?

Answers to Quick Quiz

1 See Para 1.2

2 All of them.

3 True

4 See Para 5.1

5 False. The cost model may be used, provided it is used consistently.

6 Use IAS 16 until construction is complete, then IAS 40.

Now try the question below from the Exam Question Bank

Number	Level	Marks	Time
Q7	Examination	25	45 mins

5

Accounting for leases

Topic list	Syllabus reference
1 Types of lease	2(a)
2 Lessees	2(a)
3 Lessors	2(a)

Introduction

Leasing transactions are extremely common so this is an important practical subject. **Lease accounting is regulated by IAS 17**, which was introduced because of abuses in the use of lease accounting by companies.

These companies effectively 'owned' an asset and 'owed' a debt for its purchase, but showed neither the asset nor the liability on the statement of financial accounts because they were not required to do so. This is called **'off balance sheet finance'**, a term which you will meet again later in this Text.

Study Guide

Section 5 – Leases

- Define the essential characteristics of a lease
- Describe and apply the method of determining a lease type (ie an operating or finance lease)
- Explain the effect on the financial statements of a finance lease being incorrectly treated as an operating lease
- Account for operating leases in financial statements of the lessor and lessee
- Account for finance leases in the financial statements of the lessor and lessee
- Outline the principles of IAS 17 and its main disclosure requirements. *Note*. The net cash investment method will not be examined

Exam Guide

You are likely to be asked about the detailed accounting treatment. as well as for critical comment and discussion. Issues of substance over form are a key area for this exam.

1 Types of lease

FAST FORWARD

A finance lease is a means of acquiring the long-term use of an asset, whereas an operating lease is a short-term rental agreement. However, substance over form is important in distinguishing between them.

Exam focus point

Lease accounting is examined frequently and has been tested as part of a longer question in almost every examination, including the recent pilot paper for exams in 2011.

1.1 What is a lease?

Where goods are acquired other than on immediate cash terms, arrangements have to be made in respect of the future payments on those goods. In the simplest case of **credit sales**, the purchaser is allowed a period of time (say one month) to settle the outstanding amount and the normal accounting procedure in respect of receivables/payables will be adopted. However, in recent years there has been considerable growth in leasing agreements (some types of lease are called **hire purchase agreements** in some countries).

IAS 17 *Leases* standardises the accounting treatment and disclosure of assets held under lease.

In a leasing transaction there is a **contract** between the lessor and the lessee for the hire of an asset. The lessor retains legal ownership but conveys to the lessee the right to use the asset for an agreed period of time in return for specified rentals. IAS 17 defines a lease and recognises two types.

Key terms

- **Lease.** An agreement whereby the lessor conveys to the lessee in return for rent the right to use an asset for an agreed period of time.
- **Finance lease.** A lease that transfers substantially all the risks and rewards incident to ownership of an asset. Title may or may not eventually be transferred.
- **Operating lease.** A lease other than a finance lease. *(IAS 17)*

A **finance lease** may be a **hire purchase agreement**. (The difference is that under a hire purchase agreement the customer eventually, after paying an agreed number of instalments, becomes entitled to exercise an option to purchase the asset. Under other leasing agreements, ownership remains forever with the lessor.)

In this chapter the **user** of an asset will often be referred to simply as the **lessee**, and the **supplier** as the **lessor**. You should bear in mind that identical requirements apply in the case of hirers and vendors respectively under hire purchase agreements.

To expand on the definition above, a finance lease should be presumed if at the inception of a lease the **present value of the minimum lease payments** is approximately equal to the **fair value of the leased asset**.

The present value should be calculated by using the **interest rate implicit in the lease.**

Key terms

- **Minimum lease payments.** The payments over the lease term that the lessee is or can be required to make, excluding contingent rent, costs for services and taxes to be paid by and be reimbursed to the lessor, together with:

  (a) For a lessee, any amounts guaranteed by the lessee or by a party related to the lessee

  (b) For a lessor, any residual value guaranteed to the lessor by one of the following.

    (i) The lessee
    (ii) A party related to the lessee
    (iii) An independent third party financially capable of meeting this guarantee

  However, if the lessee has the option to purchase the asset at a price which is expected to be sufficiently lower than fair value at the date the option becomes exercisable for it to be reasonably certain, at the inception of the lease, that the option will be exercised, the minimum lease payments comprise the minimum payments payable over the lease term to the expected date of exercise of this purchase option and the payment required to exercise it.

- **Interest rate implicit in the lease.**

  The discount rate that, at the inception of the lease, causes the aggregate present value of

  (a) The minimum lease payments, and
  (b) The unguaranteed residual value

  to be equal to the sum of

  (a) The fair value of the leased asset, and
  (b) Any initial direct costs.

- **Initial direct costs** are **incremental costs** that are directly attributable to **negotiating** and **arranging** a lease, except for such costs incurred by manufacturer or dealer lessors. Examples of initial direct costs include amounts such as **commissions, legal fees** and relevant internal costs.

- **Lease term.** The non-cancellable period for which the lessee has contracted to lease the asset together with any further terms for which the lessee has the option to continue to lease the asset, with or without further payment, when at the inception of the lease it is reasonably certain that the lessee will exercise the option.

- A **non-cancellable lease** is a lease that is cancellable only in one of the following situations.

  (a) Upon the occurrence of some remote contingency
  (b) With the permission of the lessor
  (c) If the lessee enters into a new lease for the same or an equivalent asset with the same lessor
  (d) Upon payment by the lessee of an additional amount such that, at inception, continuation of the lease is reasonably certain

- The **inception of the lease** is the earlier of the date of the lease agreement and the date of commitment by the parties to the principal provisions of the lease. As at this date:

  (a) A lease is classified as either an operating lease or a finance lease; and

  (b) In the case of a finance lease, the amounts to be recognised at the start of lease term are determined.

Key terms (cont'd)

- **Economic life** is either:

  (a) The period over which an asset is expected to be economically usable by one or more users, or

  (b) The number of production or similar units expected to be obtained from the asset by one or more users.

- **Useful life** is the estimated remaining period, from the beginning of the lease term, without limitation by the lease term, over which the economic benefits embodied in the asset are expected to be consumed by the entity.

- **Guaranteed residual value** is:

  (a) For a lessee, that part of the residual value which is guaranteed by the lessee or by a party related to the lessee (the amount of the guarantee being the maximum amount that could, in any event, become payable).

  (b) For a lessor, that part of the residual value which is guaranteed by the lessee or by a third party unrelated to the lessor who is financially capable of discharging the obligations under the guarantee.

- **Unguaranteed residual value** is that portion of the residual value of the leased asset, the realisation of which by the lessor is not assured or is guaranteed solely by a party related to the lessor.

- **Gross investment in the lease** is the aggregate of:

  (a) The minimum lease payments receivable by the lessor under a finance lease, and
  (b) Any unguaranteed residual value accruing to the lessor.

- **Net investment in the lease** is the gross investment in the lease discounted at the interest rate implicit in the lease.

- **Unearned finance income** is the difference between:

  (a) The gross investment in the lease, and
  (b) The net investment in the lease.

- The **lessee's incremental borrowing rate of interest** is the rate of interest the lessee would have to pay on a similar lease or, if that is not determinable, the rate that, at the inception of the lease, the lessee would incur to borrow over a similar term, and with a similar security, the funds necessary to purchase the asset.

- **Contingent rent** is that portion of the lease payments that is not fixed in amount but is based on a factor other than just the passage of time (eg percentage of sales, amount of usage, price indices, market rates of interest). *(IAS 17)*

There are further definitions in IAS 17, but (fortunately!) these go beyond the scope of your syllabus.

1.2 Accounting for operating leases

FAST FORWARD

Operating lease are **rental agreements** and all instalments are charged against profit.

Operating leases do not really pose an accounting problem. The lessee pays amounts periodically to the lessor and these are **charged to the income statement**. The lessor treats the leased asset as a non-current asset and depreciates it in the normal way. Rentals received from the lessee are credited to the income statement in the lessor's books.

1.3 Accounting for finance leases

FAST FORWARD

Under **finance leases**:

- Assets acquired should be capitalised
- Interest element of instalments should be charged against profit.

Where the lessee is offered an incentive such as a **rent-free period** or **cashback incentive**, this is effectively a **discount**, which will be spread over the period of the operating lease in accordance with the accruals principle. For instance, if a company entered into a 4-year operating lease but was not required to make any payments until year 2, the total payments to be made over years 2-4 should be charged evenly over years 1-4.

Where a cashback incentive is received, the total amount payable over the lease term, less the cashback, should be charged evenly over the term of the lease. This can be done by crediting the cashback received to deferred income and releasing it to profit or loss over the lease term.

For assets held under **finance leases** (including hire purchase) this accounting treatment would not disclose the reality of the situation. If a **lessor** leases out an asset on a finance lease, the asset will probably never be seen on his premises or used in his business again. It would be inappropriate for a lessor to record such an asset as a non-current asset. In reality, what he owns is a **stream of cash flows receivable** from the lessee. **The asset is an amount receivable rather than a non-current asset.**

Similarly, a **lessee** may use a finance lease to fund the 'acquisition' of a major asset which he will then use in his business perhaps for many years. **The substance of the transaction is that he has acquired a non-current asset**, and this is reflected in the accounting treatment prescribed by IAS 17, even though in law the lessee may never become the owner of the asset.

The following summary diagram should help you when deciding whether a lease is an operating lease or a finance lease.

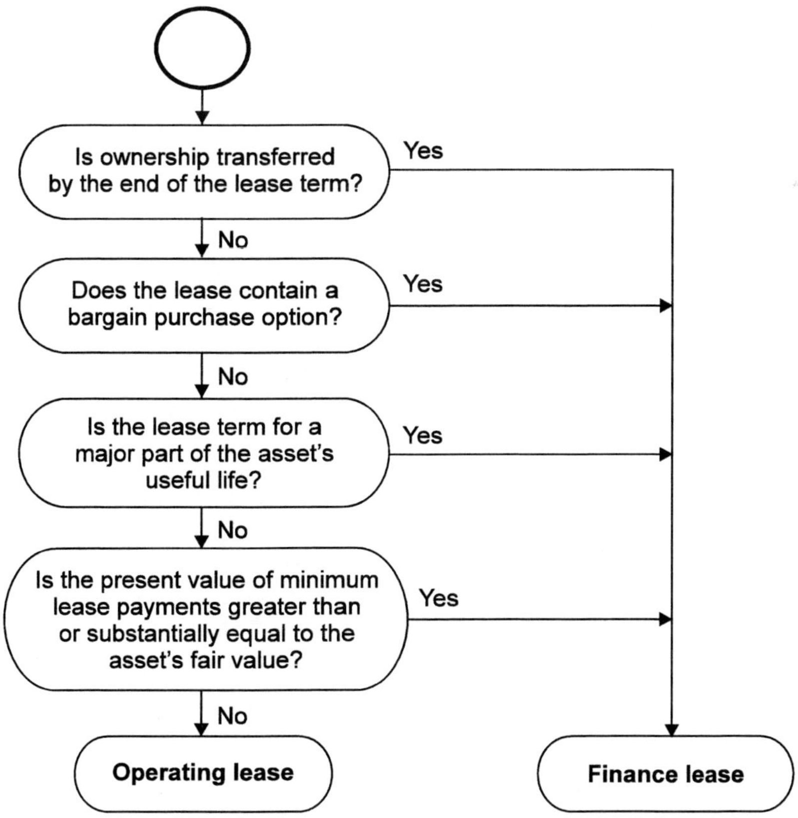

The revised IAS 17 stated that when classifying a lease of **land and buildings** the **land** element is normally classified as an **operating lease unless title passes to the lessee** at the end of the contract. This was amended (effective from January 2010) to give entities the **option** to treat a long lease of land as a **finance lease**.

Exam focus point

Questions on leasing could involve a discussion of the reasons for the different accounting treatments of operating and finance leases, from the perspectives of both the lessor and the lessee. Practical questions could involve preparation of the relevant ledger accounts and/or extracts from the financial statements.

2 Lessees

FAST FORWARD

You must be aware of the disclosure requirements for lessees under finance leases and operating leases.

2.1 Accounting treatment for finance leases

IAS 17 requires that, when an asset changes hands under a **finance lease**, **lessor and lessee should account for the transaction as though it were a credit sale.** In the lessee's books therefore the lease asset is capitalised:

DEBIT Asset account
CREDIT Lessor (liability) account

The amount to be recorded in this way is the **lower of** the **fair value** and the **present value** of the **minimum lease payments**.

A variant approach which produces the same net result is to debit the asset account with the fair value, and to debit an **interest suspense account** with the total amount of interest or finance charges payable under the agreement and to credit a lessor account with the total amount (capital and interest) payable under the agreement. We will see below how this affects the year end accounting entries.

IAS 17 states that it is not appropriate to show liabilities for leased assets as deductions from the leased assets. A distinction should be made between **current and non-current** lease liabilities, if the entity makes this distinction for other liabilities.

The asset should be **depreciated** (on the bases set out in IASs 16 and 38) over the shorter of:

- The lease term
- The asset's useful life

If there is reasonable certainty of eventual ownership of the asset, then it should be depreciated over its useful life.

2.2 Apportionment of rental payments

When the lessee makes a rental payment it will comprise two elements.

(a) An **interest charge** on the finance provided by the lessor. This proportion of each payment is interest payable and interest receivable in the income statements of the lessee and lessor respectively.

(b) A repayment of part of the **capital cost** of the asset. In the lessee's books this proportion of each rental payment must be debited to the lessor's account to reduce the outstanding liability. In the lessor's books, it must be credited to the lessee's account to reduce the amount owing (the debit of course is to cash).

The accounting problem is to decide what proportion of each instalment paid by the lessee represents interest, and what proportion represents a repayment of the capital advanced by the lessor. There are two apportionment methods you may encounter:

- The actuarial method
- The sum-of-the-digits method

Exam focus point

An examination question would always make it clear which method should be used. In theory, the aim is that the income statement finance charge should reduce over the lease term in line with the outstanding liability.

Your examiner has stated that the sum-of-the-digits method is less likely to be examined than the actuarial method.

The **actuarial method** is the best and most scientific method. It derives from the common-sense assumption that the interest charged by a lessor company will equal the rate of return desired by the company, multiplied by the amount of capital it has invested. The required rate of return is described as the **effective interest rate.**

(a) At the beginning of the lease the capital invested is equal to the fair value of the asset (less any initial deposit paid by the lessee).

(b) This amount reduces as each instalment is paid. It follows that the interest accruing is greatest in the early part of the lease term, and gradually reduces as capital is repaid. In this section, we will look at a simple example of the actuarial method.

The **sum-of-the-digits** method approximates to the actuarial method, splitting the total interest (without reference to a rate of interest) in such a way that the greater proportion falls in the earlier years. The procedure is as follows.

(a) Assign a digit to each instalment. The digit 1 should be assigned to the final instalment, 2 to the penultimate instalment and so on.

(b) Add the digits. A quick method of adding the digits is to use the formula $\frac{n(n+1)}{2}$ where n is the number of instalments. If there are twelve instalments, then the sum of the digits will be 78. For this reason, the sum of the digits method is sometimes called the **rule of 78**.

(c) Calculate the interest charge included in each instalment. Do this by multiplying the total interest accruing over the lease term by the fraction:

$$\frac{\text{Digit applicable to the instalment}}{\text{Sum of the digits}}$$

2.3 Example: apportionment methods

On 1 January 20X0 Bacchus Co, wine merchants, buys a small bottling and labelling machine from Silenus Co under a finance lease. The cash price of the machine was $7,710 while the amount to be paid was $10,000. The agreement required the immediate payment of a $2,000 deposit with the balance being settled in four equal annual instalments commencing on 31 December 20X0. The charge of $2,290 represents interest of 15% per annum, calculated on the remaining balance of the liability during each accounting period. Depreciation on the plant is to be provided for at the rate of 20% per annum on a straight line basis assuming a residual value of nil.

You are required to show the breakdown of each instalment between interest and capital, using in turn each of the apportionment methods described above.

Solution

In this example, enough detail is given to use any of the apportionment methods. In an examination question, you would normally be directed to use one method specifically.

(a) **Sum-of-the-digits method**

Each instalment is allocated a digit as follows.

Instalment	*Digit*
1st (20X0)	4
2nd (20X1)	3
3rd (20X2)	2
4th (20X3)	1
	10

Or using the formula, $\frac{4 \times 5}{2}$ = 10.

The $2,290 interest charges can then be apportioned.

		$
1st instalment	$2,290 × 4/10	916
2nd instalment	$2,290 × 3/10	687
3rd instalment	$2,290 × 2/10	458
4th instalment	$2,290 × 1/10	229
		2,290

The breakdown is then as follows.

	1st instalment	*2nd instalment*	*3rd instalment*	*4th instalment*
	$	$	$	$
Interest	916	687	458	229
Capital repayment (balance)	1,084	1,313	1,542	1,771
	2,000	2,000	2,000	2,000

(b) **Actuarial method**

Interest is calculated as 15% of the outstanding *capital* balance at the beginning of each year. The outstanding capital balance reduces each year by the capital element comprised in each instalment. The outstanding capital balance at 1 January 20X0 is $5,710 ($7,710 fair value less $2,000 deposit).

	Total	*Capital*	*Interest*
	$	$	$
Capital balance at 1 Jan 20X0		5,710	
1st instalment (interest = $5,710 × 15%)	2,000	1,144	856
Capital balance at 1 Jan 20X1		4,566	
2nd instalment (interest = $4,566 × 15%)	2,000	1,315	685
Capital balance at 1 Jan 20X2		3,251	
3rd instalment (interest = $3,251 × 15%)	2,000	1,512	488
Capital balance at 1 Jan 20X3		1,739	
4th instalment (interest = $1,739 × 15%)	2,000	1,739	261
	8,000		2,290
Capital balance at 1 Jan 20X4		–	

2.4 Interest suspense account

Where an interest suspense account is used (see Paragraph 2.1), the double entry for finance lease instalments is as follows (assuming that the actuarial method is used in the example above).

(a)	DEBIT	Asset account	$7,710	
		Interest suspense	$2,290	
	CREDIT	Lessor payable: Silenus		$10,000

Being entries required to record acquisition of asset under finance lease

(b)	DEBIT	Lessor payable: Silenus	$2,000	
	CREDIT	Bank		$2,000

Being instalment payment recorded in full

(c)	DEBIT	Interest payable/finance charges (profit or loss)	$856	
	CREDIT	Interest suspense account		$856

Being year end adjustment to ensure that the year's interest/finance charges are charged to the income statement

The equivalent entries where a suspense account is not used might be as follows.

(a)	DEBIT	Asset account	$7,710	
	CREDIT	Lessor payable: Silenus		$7,710
(b)	DEBIT	Lessor payable: Silenus	$2,000	
	CREDIT	Bank		$2,000
(c)	DEBIT	Interest payable/finance charges (profit or loss)	$856	
	CREDIT	Lessor payable: Silenus		$856

Entry (c) ensures that the interest element is recorded and is an annual adjustment. It is, of course, possible to make the full correct entry as each instalment is paid:

DEBIT	Interest payable/finance charges (profit or loss)	$856	
	Lessor payable: Silenus	$1,144	
CREDIT	Bank		$2,000

However, in practice in many companies the interest/finance charge calculation is only made annually when preparing published accounts.

Thus, at the year end, whatever system is used during the year, the balance on the lessor payable (where appropriate, less the balance on the interest suspense account) will represent the outstanding capital liability. Future interest/finance charges are not a true liability as the capital could be paid off at any time, thus avoiding these charges.

Question — Accounting entries

Dundas Co purchased a machine under a finance lease on 1 January 20X6. The agreement provided for an immediate payment of $2,000, following by five equal instalments of $3,056, each instalment to be paid on 30 June and 31 December respectively. The cash price of the machine was $10,000. Dundas estimated that it would have a useful economic life of five years, and its residual value would then be $1,000. At the end of the lease, ownership will pass to Dundas Co.

In apportioning interest to respective accounting periods, the company uses the 'sum of digits' method.

Required

(a) Write up the following ledger accounts for each of the three years to 31 December 20X6, 20X7 and 20X8 respectively.

- (i) Machine lease payable account
- (ii) Machine lease interest account

(b) Show the following extracts from the statement of financial position relating to the machine as at 31 December 20X6, 20X7 and 20X8 respectively.

- (i) Non-current term assets: machine at net book value
- (ii) Current payables: obligation under finance lease
- (iii) Non-current payables: obligation under finance lease

Answer

(a) (i) MACHINE LEASE PAYABLE ACCOUNT

		$			$
20X6			*20X6*		
1.1	Bank	2,000	1.1	Machine	10,000
30.6	Bank	3,056	1.1	Machine interest	7,280

31.12	Bank	3,056			
31.12	Balance c/d	9,168			
		17,280			17,280
20X7			*20X7*		
30.6	Bank	3,056	1.1	Balance b/d	9,168
31.12	Bank	3,056			
31.12	Balance c/d	3,056			
		9,168			9,168
20X8			*20X8*		
30.6	Bank	3,056	1.1	Balance b/d	3,056

(ii) MACHINE LEASE INTEREST ACCOUNT

		$			$
20X6			*20X6*		
1.1	Machine HP Loan a/c	7,280	31.12	Profit or loss	4,368
			31.12	Balance c/d	2,912
		7,280			7,280
20X7			*20X7*		
1.1	Balance b/d	2,912	31.12	Profit or loss	2,427
			31.12	Balance c/d	485
		2,912			2,912
20X8			*20X8*		
1.1	Balance b/d	485	31.12	Profit or loss	485

Working

		$
Sum of the digits = 5 + 4 + 3 + 2 + 1 = 15 (5 half year periods)		
Interest charge 20X6	$= \$7{,}280 \times \frac{5+4}{15}$	4,368
Interest charge 20X7	$= \$7{,}280 \times \frac{3+2}{15}$	2,427
Interest charge 20X8	$= \$\$7{,}280 \times \frac{1}{15}$	485
		7,280

(b) (i) *Non-current assets: machines at net book value*

		$
At 31.12.X6	Machines at cost	10,000
	Accumulated depreciation	1,800
	Net book value	8,200
At 31.12.X7	Machines at cost	10,000
	Accumulated depreciation	3,600
	Net book value	6,400
At 31.12.X8	Machines at cost	10,000
	Accumulated depreciation	5,400
	Residual value	4,600

Working

Depreciation: cost	10,000
residual value	1,000
	9,000
Economic life*	5 years

Annual depreciation charge on a straight-line basis $= \frac{\$9{,}000}{5}$

$= \$1{,}800$ per year

* *Note.* Eventual ownership is certain – see para 2.1.

(ii) *Current payables: obligation under finance lease*

			$
	At 31.12.X6		3,685
	At 31.12.X7		2,571
	At 31.12.X8		–
	Workings		
			$
	31.12.X6	Balance per loan account	9,168
		Less due in 20X8	(3,056)
		Less interest element	(2,427)
			3,685
	31.12.X7	Balance per loan account	3,056
		Less interest element	(485)
			2,571
(iii)	*Non-current payables: obligation under finance lease*		
			$
	At 31.12.X6		2,571
	At 31.12.X7		–
	At 31.12.X8		–

For working see (b)(ii) above.

2.5 Disclosure requirements for lessees

IAS 17 (revised) requires the following disclosures by lessees in respect of finance leases:

- The **net carrying amount** at the reporting date for each class of asset
- A **reconciliation** between the total of minimum lease payments at the reporting date, and their present value. In addition, an entity should disclose the total of minimum lease payments at the reporting date, and their present value, for each of the following periods:
  - Not later than one year
  - Later than one year and not later than five years
  - Later than five years
- **Contingent rents** recognised as income in the period
- Total of **future minimum sublease payments** expected to be received under non-cancellable subleases at the reporting date
- A **general description** of the lessee's material leasing arrangements
- The accumulated allowance for uncollectible minimum lease payments receivable

IAS 17 encourages (but does not require) further disclosures, as appropriate.

2.6 Example: lessee disclosures

These disclosure requirements will be illustrated for Bacchus Co (above example). We will assume that Bacchus Co makes up its accounts to 31 December and uses the actuarial method to apportion finance charges.

Solution

The company's accounts for the first year of the lease, the year ended 31 December 20X0, would include the information given below.

STATEMENT OF FINANCIAL POSITION AS AT 31 DECEMBER 20X0 (EXTRACTS)

	$	$

Non-current assets		
Assets held under finance leases		
Plant and machinery at cost	7,710	
Less accumulated depreciation (20% × $7,710)	(1,542)	
		6,168
Non-current liabilities		
Obligations under finance leases		
$(1,512 + 1,739)		3,251
Current liabilities		
Obligations under finance leases		1,315

(Notice that only the outstanding **capital** element is disclosed under liabilities, ie the total of the minimum lease payments with future finance charges separately deducted.)

INCOME STATEMENT/STATEMENT OF COMPREHENSIVE INCOME
FOR THE YEAR ENDED 31 DECEMBER 20X0 (EXTRACT)

	$
Interest payable and similar charges	
Interest on finance leases	856

2.7 Example: 6-monthly payments

Now let us see what would change if Bacchus was not required to pay a deposit but had to pay $1,250 every 6 months for 4 years. We will use the same interest rate and calculate the amounts for the first year's financial statements.

	$
Balance 1 January 20X0	7,710
Interest to 30 June 20X0 (7,710 × 15% × 6/12)	478
Instalment paid 30 June 20X0	(1,250)
Balance 30 June 20X0	7,038
Interest to 31 December 20X0 (7,038 × 15% × 6/12)	528
Instalment paid 31 December 20X0	(1,250)
Balance 31 December 20X0	6,316
Interest to 30 June 20X1 (6,316 × 15% × 6/12)	478
Instalment paid 30 June 20X1	(1,250)
Balance 30 June 20X1	5,544
Interest to 31 December 20X0 (5,544 × 15% × 6/12)	416
Instalment paid 31 December 20X1	(1,250)
Balance 31 December 20X1	4,710

Financial statement extracts at 31 December 20X0:

	$
Non-current assets (as above)	6,168
Non-current liabilities	
Obligations under finance leases	4,710
Current liabilities	
Obligations under finance leases (6,316 – 4,710)	1,606
Income statement: interest payable (578 + 528)	1,106

2.8 Operating leases: disclosure requirements for lessees

For **operating leases** the disclosures are as follows.

(a) The total of future minimum lease payments under non-cancellable operating leases for each of the following periods:

   (i) Not later than one year
   (ii) Later than one year and not later than five years
   (iii) Later than five years

(b) Total contingent rents recognised as income in the period.

(c) A general description of the lessor's leasing arrangements.

The following diagram gives a useful summary of the **accounting treatment for a finance lease by a lessee.**

2.9 Accounting for a finance lease by a lessee

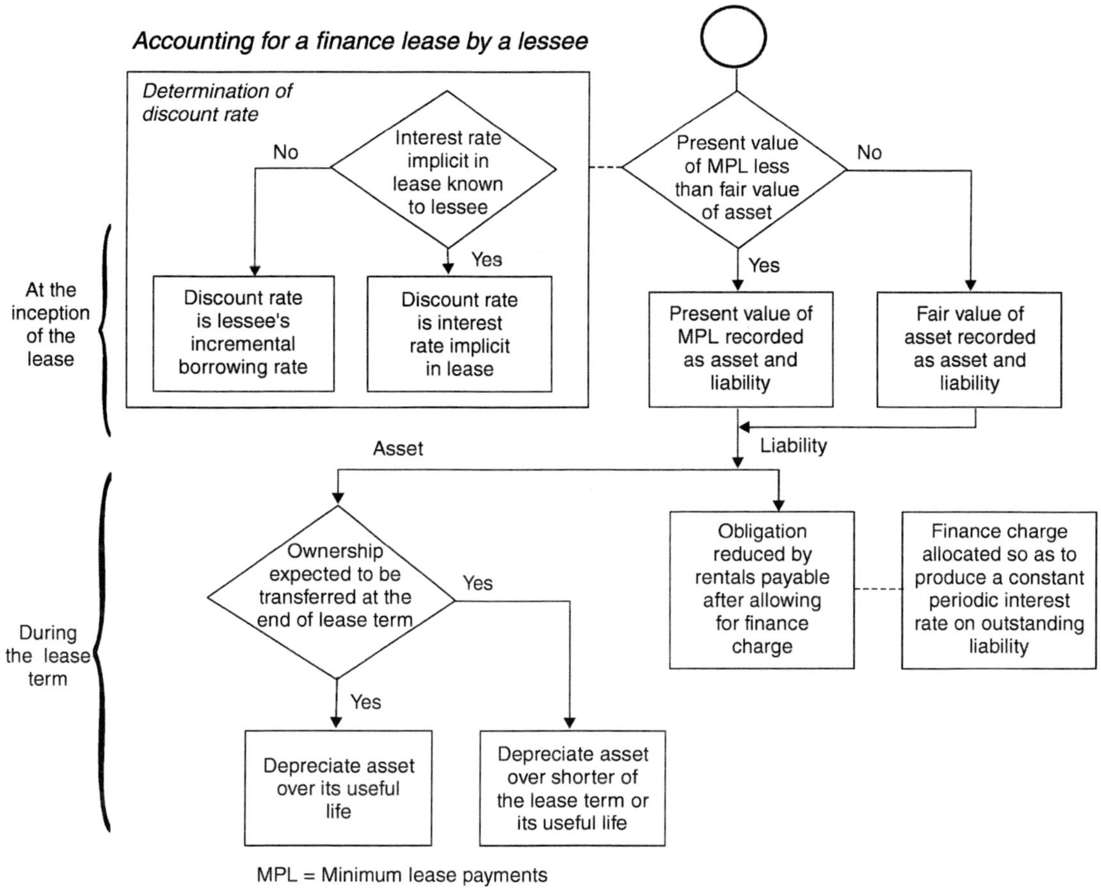

3 Lessors

FAST FORWARD

Lessor accounting:

- Finance leases: record the amount due from the lessor in the statement of financial position at the net investment in the lease, recognise finance income to give a constant periodic rate of return.
- Operating leases: record as long-term asset and depreciate over useful life, record income on a straight-line basis over the lease term, unless another systematic basis is more representative of the pattern of the use benefit in relation to the item leased

To a certain extent at least, the accounting treatment of leases adopted by lessors will be a **mirror image** of that used by lessees.

3.1 Finance leases

Several of the **definitions** given in Section 1 of this chapter are relevant to lessor accounting in particular and you should go back and look at them.

- Unguaranteed residual value
- Gross investment in the lease
- Unearned finance income
- Net investment in the lease

3.2 Accounting treatment

IAS 17 requires the **amount due from the lessee** under a finance lease to be recorded in the statement of financial position of a lessor as a receivable at the amount of the **net investment in the lease**.

The **recognition of finance income** under a finance lease should normally be based on a pattern to give a **constant periodic rate of return** on the lessor's net investment outstanding in respect of the finance lease in each period. In arriving at the constant periodic rate of return, a reasonable approximation may be made.

The lease payments (excluding costs for services) relating to the accounting period should be applied against the gross investment in the lease, so as to **reduce both the principal and the unearned finance income**.

The **estimated unguaranteed residual values** used to calculate the lessor's gross investment in a lease should be reviewed regularly. If there has been a reduction in the value, then the income allocation over the lease term must be revised. Any reduction in respect of amounts already accrued should be recognised immediately.

Initial direct costs incurred by lessors (eg commissions, legal fees and other costs that are directly attributable to negotiating and arranging a lease) are included in the initial measurement of the finance lease receivable.

3.3 Manufacturer/dealer lessors

IAS 17 (revised) looks at the situation where manufacturers or dealers offer customers the choice of either buying or leasing an asset. There will be two types of income under such a lease.

(a) Profit/loss equal to that from an **outright sale** (normal selling price less any discount)
(b) **Finance income** over the lease term

IAS 17 requires the following treatment.

(a) Recognise the **selling profit/loss** in income for the period as if it was an outright sale.
(b) If **interest rates are artificially low**, restrict the selling profit to that which would apply had a commercial rate been applied.
(c) Recognise **costs** incurred in connection with negotiating and arranging a lease as an **expense** when the **selling profit** is recognised (at the start of the lease term).

3.4 Lessors' disclosures for finance leases

The following should be disclosed.

- A **reconciliation** between the total gross investment in the lease at the year end, and the present value of minimum lease payments receivable at the year end. In addition, an entity should disclose the total gross investment in the lease and the present value of minimum lease payments receivable at the year end, for each of the following periods:
  - Not later than one year
  - Later than one year and not later than five years
  - Later than five years
- Unearned finance income
- The unguaranteed residual values accruing to the benefit of the lessor
- The accumulated allowance for uncollectible minimum lease payments receivable
- Contingent rents recognised in income
- A general description of the lessor's material leasing arrangements

3.5 Operating leases

3.5.1 Accounting treatment

An **asset** held for use in operating leases by a lessor should be recorded as a long-term asset and depreciated over its useful life. The basis for depreciation should be consistent with the lessor's policy on similar non-lease assets and follow the guidance in IAS 16.

Income from an operating lease, excluding charges for services such as insurance and maintenance, should be recognised on **a straight-line basis** over the period of the lease (even if the receipts are not on such a basis), unless another systematic and rational basis is more representative of the time pattern in which the benefit from the leased asset is receivable.

Initial direct costs incurred by lessors in negotiating and arranging an operating lease should be **added to the carrying amount** of the leased asset and recognised as an expense over the lease term on the same basis as lease income, ie capitalised and amortised over the lease term.

Lessors should refer to IAS 36 in order to determine whether a leased asset has become impaired.

A lessor who is a **manufacturer or dealer** should not recognise any selling profit on entering into an operating lease because it is not the equivalent of a sale.

3.5.2 Lessors' disclosures for operating leases

The following should be disclosed.

- For each class of asset, the **gross carrying amount**, the accumulated depreciation and accumulated impairment losses at the year end:
  - Depreciation recognised in income for the period
  - Impairment losses recognised in income for the period
  - Impairment losses reversed in income for the period
- The **future minimum lease** payments under non-cancellable operating leases in the aggregate and for each of the following periods:
  - Not later than one year
  - Later than one year and not later than five years
  - Later than five years
- Total **contingent rents** recognised in income
- A **general description** of the lessor's leasing arrangements

3.6 Sale and leaseback transactions

In a sale and leaseback transaction, an asset is sold by a vendor and then the same asset is **leased back** to the same vendor. The lease payment and sale price are normally interdependent because they are negotiated as part of the same package. The accounting treatment for the lessee or seller should be as follows, depending on the type of lease involved.

(a) In a sale and leaseback transaction which results in a **finance lease**, any apparent profit or loss (that is, the difference between the sale price and the previous carrying value) should be deferred and amortised in the financial statements of the seller/lessee over the lease term. It should not be recognised as income immediately.

(b) If the leaseback is an **operating lease**:

  (i) Any profit or loss should be recognised immediately, provided it is clear that the transaction is established at a **fair value.**

  (ii) Where the **sale price is below fair value**, any profit or loss should be recognised immediately except that if the apparent loss is compensated by future lease payments at below market price it should to that extent be deferred and amortised over the period for which the asset is expected to be used.

(iii) If the **sale price is above fair value**, the excess over fair value should be deferred and amortised over the period over which the asset is expected to be used.

In addition, for an operating lease where the fair value of the asset at the time of the sale is less than the **carrying amount**, the loss (carrying value less fair value) should be recognised immediately.

The buyer or lessor should account for a sale and leaseback in the **same way as other leases**.

The **disclosure requirements** for both lessees and lessors should force disclosure of sale and leaseback transactions. IAS 1 should be considered.

Chapter Roundup

- A finance lease is a means of acquiring the long-term use of an asset, whereas an operating lease is a short-term rental agreement. However, substance over form is important in distinguishing between them.
- **Operating leases** are **rental agreements** and all instalments are charged against profit.
- Under **finance leases**:
  - Assets acquired should be capitalised
  - Interest element of instalments should be charged against profit.
- You must be aware of the disclosure requirements for lessees under finance leases and operating leases.
- Lessor accounting:
  - Finance leases: record the amount due from the lessor in the statement of financial position at the net investment in the lease, recognise finance income to give a constant periodic rate of return.
  - Operating leases: record as long-term asset and depreciate over useful life, record income on a straight-line basis over the lease term, unless another systematic basis is more representative of the pattern of the use benefit in relation to the item leased.

Quick Quiz

1 (a) ....leases transfer substantially all the risks and rewards of ownership.

(b) ....leases are usually short-term rental agreements with the lessor being responsible for the repairs and maintenance of the asset.

2 A business acquires an asset under a finance lease. What is the double entry?

3 What is the formula to calculate each period's interest using the sum of digits?

4 List the disclosures required under IAS 17 for lessees.

5 A lorry has an expected useful life of six years. It is acquired under a four year finance lease. Over which period should it be depreciated?

6 A company leases a photocopier under an operating lease which expires in June 20X2. Its office is leased under an operating lease due to expire in January 20X3. How should past and future operating leases be disclosed in its 31 December 20X1 accounts?

Answers to Quick Quiz

1 (a) Finance leases
(b) Operating leases

2 DEBIT Asset account
CREDIT Lessor account

3 $$\frac{\text{Digit applicable to the instalment}}{\text{Sum of the digits}} \times \text{Total finance charge}$$

4 See Para 2.5.

5 The four year term, unless eventual ownership of the lorry is reasonably certain, in which case it should be depreciated over its useful life of six years.

6 The total operating lease rentals charged though profit or loss should be disclosed. The payments committed to should be disclosed analysing them between those falling due in the next year and the second to fifth years.

Now try the question below from the Exam Question Bank

Number	Level	Marks	Time
Q8	Examination	25	45 mins
Q9	Examination	25	45 mins

Intangible non-current assets and goodwill

6

Topic list	Syllabus reference
1 IAS 38 Intangible assets	2(b)
2 Goodwill (IFRS 3)	2(c)

Introduction

We begin our examination of intangible non-current assets with a discussion of a recently revised IAS on the subject (**IAS 38**).

Goodwill and its treatment is a controversial area, as is the accounting for items similar to goodwill, such as brands. Goodwill is very important in **group accounts** and we will look at it again in Part D.

Study Guide

Section 6 – Intangible assets and goodwill

- Discuss the nature and possible accounting treatments of both internally generated and purchased goodwill
- Distinguish between goodwill and other intangible assets
- Define the criteria for the initial recognition and measurement of intangible assets
- Explain the subsequent accounting treatment, including the principle of impairment tests in relation to purchased goodwill
- Identify the circumstances in which negative goodwill arises, and its subsequent accounting treatment
- Describe and apply the requirements of international accounting standards to internally generated assets other than goodwill (eg research and development)

Exam Guide

IAS 38 *Intangible assets* is a very examinable area, and is likely to come up in some form or other in every exam.

1 IAS 38 Intangible assets

FAST FORWARD

Intangible assets are defined by IAS 38 as non-monetary assets without physical substance. They must be:

– **Identifiable**
– **Controlled** as a result of a past event
– Able to provide **future economic benefits**

IAS 38 *Intangible assets* was originally published in September 1998. It was revised in 2008 to reflect changes introduced by the revision of IFRS 3 *Business combinations*.

There are three broad kinds of intangible asset dealt with in this chapter of your Study Text: purchased intangibles, internally generated intangibles (such as development costs), and intangibles acquired in a business combination (dealt with by IFRS 3).

1.1 The objectives of the standard

(a) To establish the criteria for when an intangible asset may or should be **recognised**
(b) To specify how intangible assets should be **measured**
(c) To specify the **disclosure requirements** for intangible assets

1.2 Scope

IAS 38 applies to all intangible assets with certain **exceptions**: deferred tax assets (IAS 12), leases that fall within the scope of IAS 17, financial assets, insurance contracts, assets arising from employee benefits (IAS 19), non-current assets held for sale, and mineral rights and exploration and extraction costs for minerals (although *some* of this material *is* covered by IAS 38). It does *not* apply to goodwill acquired in a business combination, which is dealt with under IFRS 3 *Business combinations*.

1.3 Definition of an intangible asset

The definition of an intangible asset is a key aspect of the standard, because the rules for deciding whether or not an intangible asset may be **recognised** in the accounts of an entity are based on the definition of what an intangible asset is.

Key term

> An **intangible asset** is an identifiable non-monetary asset without physical substance The asset must be:
>
> (a) controlled by the entity as a result of events in the past, and
> (b) something from which the entity expects future economic benefits to flow. *(IAS 38)*

Examples of items that might be considered as intangible assets include computer software, patents, copyrights, motion picture films, customer lists, franchises and fishing rights. An item should not be recognised as an intangible asset, however, unless it **fully meets the definition** in the standard. The guidelines go into great detail on this matter.

1.4 Intangible asset: must be identifiable

An intangible asset must be identifiable in order to distinguish it from goodwill. With non-physical items, there may be a problem with **'identifiability'**.

(a) If an intangible asset is **acquired separately through purchase**, there may be a transfer of a legal right that would help to make an asset identifiable.

(b) An intangible asset may be identifiable if it is **separable**, ie if it could be rented or sold separately. However, 'separability' is not an essential feature of an intangible asset.

1.5 Intangible asset: control by the entity

Another element of the definition of an intangible asset is that it must be under the control of the entity as a result of a past event. The entity must therefore be able to enjoy the future economic benefits from the asset, and prevent the access of others to those benefits. A **legally enforceable right** is evidence of such control, but is not always a *necessary* condition.

(a) Control over **technical knowledge or know-how** only exists if it is protected by a **legal right**.

(b) The skill of employees, arising out of the benefits of **training costs**, are most unlikely to be recognisable as an intangible asset, because an entity does not control the future actions of its staff.

(c) Similarly, **market share and customer loyalty** cannot normally be intangible assets, since an entity cannot control the actions of its customers.

1.6 Intangible asset: expected future economic benefits

An item can only be recognised as an intangible asset if economic benefits are expected to flow in the future from ownership of the asset. Economic benefits may come from the **sale** of products or services, or from a **reduction in expenditures** (cost savings).

An intangible asset, when recognised initially, must be measured at **cost**. It should be recognised if, and only if **both** the following occur.

(a) It is probable that the **future economic benefits** that are attributable to the asset will **flow to the entity.**

(b) The **cost can be measured reliably**.

Management has to exercise its judgement in assessing the degree of certainty attached to the flow of economic benefits to the entity. External evidence is best.

(a) If an intangible asset is **acquired separately**, its cost can usually be measured reliably as its purchase price (including incidental costs of purchase such as legal fees, and any costs incurred in getting the asset ready for use).

(b) When an intangible asset is acquired as **part of a business combination** (ie an acquisition or takeover), the cost of the intangible asset is its fair value at the date of the acquisition.

IFRS 3 explains that the fair value of intangible assets acquired in business combinations can normally be measured with sufficient reliability to be **recognised separately** from goodwill.

Quoted market prices in an active market provide the most reliable estimate of the fair value of an intangible asset. If no active market exists for an intangible asset, its fair value is the amount that the entity would have paid for the asset, at the acquisition date, in an arm's length transaction between knowledgeable and willing parties, on the basis of the best information available. In determining this amount, an entity should consider the outcome of recent transactions for similar assets. There are techniques for estimating the fair values of unique intangible assets (such as brand names) and these may be used to measure an intangible asset acquired in a business combination.

In accordance with IAS 20, intangible assets acquired by way of government grant and the grant itself may be recorded initially either at cost (which may be zero) or fair value.

1.7 Exchanges of assets

If one intangible asset is exchanged for another, the cost of the intangible asset is measured at fair value unless:

(a) The exchange transaction lacks commercial substance, or
(b) The fair value of neither the asset received nor the asset given up can be measured reliably.

Otherwise, its cost is measured at the carrying amount of the asset given up.

1.8 Internally generated goodwill

Rule to learn

Internally generated goodwill may **not** be recognised as an **asset**.

The standard deliberately precludes recognition of internally generated goodwill because it requires that, for initial recognition, the cost of the asset rather than its fair value should be capable of being measured reliably and that it should be identifiable and controlled. Thus you do not recognise an asset which is subjective and cannot be measured reliably.

1.9 Research and development costs

FAST FORWARD

Development costs must be recognised as an asset if they meet certain criteria.

1.9.1 Research

Research activities by definition do not meet the criteria for recognition under IAS 38. This is because, at the research stage of a project, it cannot be certain that future economic benefits will probably flow to the entity from the project. There is too much uncertainty about the likely success or otherwise of the project. **Research costs should therefore be written off as an expense as they are incurred**.

Examples of research costs

(a) Activities aimed at obtaining new knowledge
(b) The search for, evaluation and final selection of, applications of research findings or other knowledge
(c) The search for alternatives for materials, devices, products, processes, systems or services
(d) The formulation, design evaluation and final selection of possible alternatives for new or improved materials, devices, products, systems or services

1.9.2 Development

Development costs **may qualify** for recognition as intangible assets provided that the following **strict criteria** can be demonstrated.

(a) The technical feasibility of completing the intangible asset so that it will be available for use or sale.

(b) Its intention to complete the intangible asset and use or sell it.
(c) Its ability to use or sell the intangible asset.
(d) How the intangible asset will generate probable future economic benefits. Among other things, the entity should demonstrate the existence of a market for the output of the intangible asset or the intangible asset itself or, if it is to be used internally, the usefulness of the intangible asset.
(e) Its ability to measure the expenditure attributable to the intangible asset during its development reliably.

In contrast with research costs development costs are incurred at a later stage in a project, and the probability of success should be more apparent. Examples of development costs include the following.

(a) The design, construction and testing of pre-production or pre-use prototypes and models
(b) The design of tools, jigs, moulds and dies involving new technology
(c) The design, construction and operation of a pilot plant that is not of a scale economically feasible for commercial production
(d) The design, construction and testing of a chosen alternative for new or improved materials, devices, products, processes, systems or services

1.9.3 Other internally generated intangible assets

The standard **prohibits** the recognition of **internally generated brands**, **mastheads**, **publishing titles and customer lists** and similar items as intangible assets. These all fail to meet one or more (in some cases all) the definition and recognition criteria and in some cases are probably indistinguishable from internally generated goodwill.

1.9.4 Cost of an internally generated intangible asset

FAST FORWARD

Intangible assets should be initially measured at cost, but subsequently they can be carried out at cost of at a revalued amount.

The costs allocated to an internally generated intangible asset should be only costs that can be **directly attributed** or allocated on a reasonable and consistent basis to creating, producing or preparing the asset for its intended use. The principles underlying the costs which may or may not be included are similar to those for other non-current assets and inventory.

The cost of an internally generated intangible asset is the sum of the **expenditure incurred from the date when** the intangible asset first **meets the recognition criteria**. If, as often happens, considerable costs have already been recognised as expenses before management could demonstrate that the criteria have been met, this earlier expenditure should not be retrospectively recognised at a later date as part of the cost of an intangible asset.

Exam focus point

The treatment of development costs was examined in December 2003, June 2010 and the Pilot Paper for exams in 2011. Internally developed brands and other intangibles were examined in December 2005 and June 2006. As part of another June 2006 question candidates were required to explain why certain intangibles not recognised at entity level are recognised in the consolidated financial statements.

The capitalisation of intangibles was also tested in December 2007 and June 2008 as small parts of a longer question.

Question

Treatment

Doug Co is developing a new production process. During 20X9, expenditure incurred was $100,000, of which $90,000 was incurred before 1 December 20X9 and $10,000 between 1 December 20X9 and 31 December 20X9. Doug Co can demonstrate that, at 1 December 20X9, the production process met the criteria for recognition as an intangible asset. The recoverable amount of the know-how embodied in the process is estimated to be $50,000.

How should the expenditure be treated?

Answer

At the end of 20X9, the production process is recognised as an intangible asset at a cost of $10,000. This is the expenditure incurred since the date when the recognition criteria were met, that is 1 December 20X9. The $90,000 expenditure incurred before 1 December 20X9 is expensed, because the recognition criteria were not met. It will never form part of the cost of the production process recognised in the statement of financial position.

1.10 Recognition of an expense

All expenditure related to an intangible which does not meet the criteria for recognition either as an identifiable intangible asset or as goodwill arising on an acquisition should be **expensed as incurred**. The IAS gives examples of such expenditure.

- Start up costs
- Training costs
- Advertising costs
- Business relocation costs

Prepaid costs for services, for example advertising or marketing costs for campaigns that have been prepared but not launched, can still be recognised as a **prepayment**.

1.11 Measurement of intangible assets subsequent to initial recognition

The standard allows two methods of valuation for intangible assets after they have been first recognised.

Applying the **cost model**, an intangible asset should be **carried at its cost**, less any accumulated amortisation and less any accumulated impairment losses.

The **revaluation model** allows an intangible asset to be carried at a revalued amount, which is its **fair value** at the date of revaluation, less any subsequent accumulated amortisation and any subsequent accumulated impairment losses.

(a) The fair value must be able to be measured reliably with reference to an **active market** in that type of asset.

(b) The **entire class** of intangible assets of that type must be revalued at the same time (to prevent selective revaluations).

(c) If an intangible asset in a class of revalued intangible assets cannot be revalued because there is **no active market** for this asset, the asset should be carried at its **cost less any accumulated amortisation and impairment losses**.

(d) Revaluations should be made with such **regularity** that the carrying amount does not differ from that which would be determined using fair value at the reporting date.

Point to note

> This treatment is **not** available for the **initial recognition** of intangible assets. This is because the cost of the asset must be reliably measured.

The guidelines state that there **will not usually be an active market** in an intangible asset; therefore the revaluation model will usually not be available. For example, although copyrights, publishing rights and film rights can be sold, each has a unique sale value. In such cases, revaluation to fair value would be inappropriate. A fair value might be obtainable however for assets such as fishing rights or quotas or taxi cab licences.

Where an intangible asset is revalued upwards to a fair value, the amount of the revaluation should be credited directly to equity under the heading of a **revaluation surplus**.

However, if a revaluation surplus is a **reversal of a revaluation decrease** that was previously charged against income, the increase can be recognised as income.

Where the carrying amount of an intangible asset is revalued downwards, the amount of the **downward revaluation** should be charged as an expense against income, unless the asset has previously been revalued upwards. A revaluation decrease should be first charged against any previous revaluation surplus in respect of that asset.

Question

Downward revaluation

An intangible asset is measured by a company at fair value. The asset was revalued by $400 in 20X8, and there is a revaluation surplus of $400 in the statement of financial position. At the end of 20X9, the asset is valued again, and a downward valuation of $500 is required.

Required

State the accounting treatment for the downward revaluation.

Answer

In this example, the downward valuation of $500 can first be set against the revaluation surplus of $400. The revaluation surplus will be reduced to 0 and a charge of $100 made as an expense in 20X9.

When the revaluation model is used, and an intangible asset is revalued upwards, the cumulative revaluation **surplus may be transferred to retained earnings** when the surplus is eventually realised. The surplus would be realised when the asset is disposed of. However, the surplus may also be realised over time as the **asset is used** by the entity. The amount of the surplus realised each year is the difference between the amortisation charge for the asset based on the revalued amount of the asset, and the amortisation that would be charged on the basis of the asset's historical cost. The realised surplus in such case should be transferred from revaluation surplus directly to retained earnings, and should not be taken through the income statement.

1.12 Useful life

An entity should **assess** the useful life of an intangible asset, which may be **finite or indefinite**. An intangible asset has an indefinite useful life when there is **no foreseeable limit** to the period over which the asset is expected to generate net cash inflows for the entity.

Many factors are considered in determining the useful life of an intangible asset, including: expected usage; typical product life cycles; technical, technological, commercial or other types of obsolescence; the stability of the industry; expected actions by competitors; the level of maintenance expenditure required; and legal or similar limits on the use of the asset, such as the expiry dates of related leases. Computer software and many other intangible assets normally have short lives because they are susceptible to technological obsolescence. However, uncertainty does not justify choosing a life that is unrealistically short.

The useful life of an intangible asset that arises from **contractual or other legal rights** should not exceed the period of the rights, but may be shorter depending on the period over which the entity expects to use the asset.

1.13 Amortisation period and amortisation method

An intangible asset with a finite useful life should be amortised over its **expected useful life.**

(a) Amortisation should start when the asset is **available for use**.

(b) Amortisation should cease at the earlier of the date that the asset is classified **as held for sale** in accordance with IFRS 5 *Non-current assets held for sale and discontinued operations* and the date that the asset is **derecognised**.

(c) The amortisation method used should reflect the **pattern in which the asset's future economic benefits are consumed**. If such a pattern cannot be predicted reliably, the straight-line method should be used.

(d) The amortisation charge for each period should normally be recognised **in profit or loss**.

The **residual value** of an intangible asset with a finite useful life is **assumed to be zero** unless a third party is committed to buying the intangible asset at the end of its useful life or unless there is an active market for that type of asset (so that its expected residual value can be measured) and it is probable that there will be a market for the asset at the end of its useful life.

The amortisation period and the amortisation method used for an intangible asset with a finite useful life should be **reviewed at each financial year-end**.

1.14 Intangible assets with indefinite useful lives

An intangible asset with an indefinite useful life **should not be amortised**. (IAS 36 requires that such an asset is tested for impairment at least annually.)

The useful life of an intangible asset that is not being amortised should be **reviewed each year** to determine whether it is still appropriate to assess its useful life as indefinite. Reassessing the useful life of an intangible asset as finite rather than indefinite is an indicator that the asset may be impaired and therefore it should be tested for impairment.

Question — Intangible asset

It may be difficult to establish the useful life of an intangible asset, and judgement will be needed. Consider how to determine the useful life of a *purchased* brand name.

Answer

Factors to consider would include the following.

(a) Legal protection of the brand name and the control of the entity over the (illegal) use by others of the brand name (ie control over pirating)

(b) Age of the brand name

(c) Status or position of the brand in its particular market

(d) Ability of the management of the entity to manage the brand name and to measure activities that support the brand name (eg advertising and PR activities)

(e) Stability and geographical spread of the market in which the branded products are sold

(f) Pattern of benefits that the brand name is expected to generate over time

(g) Intention of the entity to use and promote the brand name over time (as evidenced perhaps by a business plan in which there will be substantial expenditure to promote the brand name)

1.15 Disposals/retirements of intangible assets

An intangible asset should be eliminated from the statement of financial position when it is disposed of or when there is no further expected economic benefit from its future use. On disposal the gain or loss arising from the **difference between the net disposal proceeds and the carrying amount** of the asset should be taken to profit or loss as a gain or loss on disposal (ie treated as income or expense).

1.16 Disclosure requirements

The standard has fairly extensive disclosure requirements for intangible assets. The financial statements should disclose the **accounting policies** for intangible assets that have been adopted.

For **each class of intangible assets**, disclosure is required of the following.

- The **method of amortisation** used
- The **useful life** of the assets or the amortisation rate used
- The **gross carrying amount**, the **accumulated amortisation** and the **accumulated impairment losses** as at the beginning and the end of the period
- The line in the statement of comprehensive income in which any amortisation of intangible assets is included
- A **reconciliation of the carrying amount** as at the beginning and at the end of the period (additions, retirements/disposals, revaluations, impairment losses, impairment losses reversed, amortisation charge for the period, net exchange differences, other movements)
- The carrying amount of **internally-generated intangible assets**

The financial statements should also disclose the following.

- In the case of intangible assets that are assessed as having an indefinite useful life, the carrying amounts and the reasons supporting that assessment
- For intangible assets acquired by way of a **government grant** and initially recognised at fair value, the **fair value initially recognised**, the **carrying amount**, and whether they are carried under the **cost model** or the **revaluation model** for subsequent remeasurements
- The carrying amount, nature and remaining amortisation period of any intangible asset that is **material to the financial statements of the entity as a whole**
- The existence (if any) and amounts of intangible assets whose **title is restricted** and of intangible assets that have been **pledged as security** for liabilities
- The amount of any **commitments for the future acquisition of intangible assets**

Where intangible assets are accounted for at revalued amounts, disclosure is required of the following.

- The **effective date of the revaluation** (by class of intangible assets)
- The **carrying amount** of revalued intangible assets
- The carrying amount that would have been shown (by class of assets) **if the cost model had been used**, and the amount of amortisation that would have been charged
- The amount of any **revaluation surplus** on intangible assets, as at the beginning and end of the period, and movements in the surplus during the year (and any restrictions on the distribution of the balance to shareholders)
- The methods and significant assumptions applied in estimating assets' fair values

The financial statements should also disclose the amount of research and development expenditure that have been charged as expenses of the period.

1.17 Section summary

- An intangible asset should be recognised if, and only if, it is probable that future economic benefits will flow to the entity and the cost of the asset can be measured reliably.
- An asset is initially recognised at cost and subsequently carried either at cost or revalued amount.
- Costs that do not meet the recognition criteria should be expensed as incurred.
- An intangible asset with a finite useful life should be amortised over its useful life. An intangible asset with an indefinite useful life should not be amortised.

Question — R&D

As an aid to your revision, list the examples given in IAS 38 of activities that might be included in either research or development.

Answer

IAS 38 gives these examples.

Research

- Activities aimed at obtaining new knowledge
- The search for applications of research findings or other knowledge
- The search for product or process alternatives
- The formulation and design of possible new or improved product or process alternatives

Development

- The evaluation of product or process alternatives
- The design, construction and testing of pre-production prototypes and models
- The design of tools, jigs, moulds and dies involving new technology
- The design, construction and operation of a pilot plant that is not of a scale economically feasible for commercial production

2 Goodwill (IFRS 3)

FAST FORWARD

Purchased goodwill arising on consolidation is retained in the statement of financial position as an intangible asset under IFRS 3. It must then be reviewed annually for impairment.

2.1 What is goodwill?

Goodwill is **created by good relationships** between a business and its customers.

(a) By building up a **reputation** (by word of mouth perhaps) for high quality products or high standards of service

(b) By **responding promptly and helpfully** to queries and complaints from customers

(c) Through the **personality of the staff** and their attitudes to customers

The value of goodwill to a business might be **extremely significant**. However, goodwill is not usually valued in the accounts of a business at all, and we should not normally expect to find an amount for goodwill in its statement of financial position. For example, the welcoming smile of the bar staff may contribute more to a bar's profits than the fact that a new electronic cash register has recently been acquired. Even so, whereas the cash register will be recorded in the accounts as a non-current asset, the value of staff would be ignored for accounting purposes.

On reflection, we might agree with this omission of goodwill from the accounts of a business.

(a) The goodwill is **inherent** in the business but it has not been paid for, and it does not have an 'objective' value. We can guess at what such goodwill is worth, but such guesswork would be a matter of individual opinion, and not based on hard facts.

(b) Goodwill **changes** from day to day. One act of bad customer relations might damage goodwill and one act of good relations might improve it. Staff with a favourable personality might retire or leave to find another job, to be replaced by staff who need time to find their feet in the job, etc. Since goodwill is continually changing in value, it cannot realistically be recorded in the accounts of the business.

2.2 Purchased goodwill

FAST FORWARD

Purchased goodwill is shown in the statement of financial position because it has been paid for. It has no tangible substance, and so it is an intangible non-current asset. **Internally-generated goodwill** cannot be recognised as an asset but other internally-generated assets may be, eg R & D.

There is one exception to the general rule that goodwill has no objective valuation. This is **when a business is sold**. People wishing to set up in business have a choice of how to do it – they can either buy their own long-term assets and inventory and set up their business from scratch, or they can buy up an existing business from a proprietor willing to sell it. When a buyer purchases an existing business, he will have to purchase not only its long-term assets and inventory (and perhaps take over its accounts payable and receivable too) but also the goodwill of the business.

2.3 How is the value of purchased goodwill decided?

FAST FORWARD

If a business has **goodwill**, it means that the value of the business as a going concern is greater than value of its separate tangible assets. The valuation of goodwill is extremely subjective and fluctuates constantly. For this reason, non-purchased goodwill is **not** shown as an asset in the statement of financial position.

When a business is sold, there is likely to be some purchased goodwill in the selling price. But **how is the amount of this purchased goodwill decided**?

This is not really a problem for accountants, who must simply record the goodwill in the accounts of the new business. The value of the goodwill is a **matter for the purchaser and seller to agree upon in fixing the purchase/sale price**. However, two methods of valuation are worth mentioning here.

(a) The seller and buyer agree on a price for the business **without specifically quantifying the goodwill.** The purchased goodwill will then be the difference between the price agreed and the value of the tangible net assets in the books of the new business.

(b) However, the calculation of goodwill often precedes the fixing of the purchase price and becomes a **central element of negotiation**. There are many ways of arriving at a value for goodwill and most of them are related to the profit record of the business in question.

No matter how goodwill is calculated within the total agreed purchase price, the goodwill shown by the purchaser in his accounts will be **the difference between the purchase consideration and his own valuation of the tangible net assets acquired**. If A values his tangible net assets at $40,000, goodwill is agreed at $21,000 and B agrees to pay $61,000 for the business but values the tangible net assets at only $38,000, then the goodwill in B's books will be $61,000 – $38,000 = $23,000.

2.4 IFRS 3 Business combinations

IFRS 3 covers the accounting treatment of goodwill acquired in a business combination.

Key term

Goodwill. Future economic benefits arising from assets that are not capable of being individually identified and separately recognised. *(IFRS 3)*

Goodwill acquired in a business combination is **recognised as an asset** and is initially measured at **cost**. Cost of goodwill is the excess of the cost of the combination over the acquirer's interest in the net fair value of the acquiree's identifiable assets, liabilities and contingent liabilities.

After initial recognition goodwill acquired in a business combination is measured **at cost less any accumulated impairment losses**. It is **not amortised**. Instead it is tested for impairment at least annually, in accordance with IAS 36 *Impairment of assets.*

Negative goodwill arises when the acquirer's interest in the net fair value of the acquiree's identifiable assets, liabilities and contingent liabilities exceeds the cost of the business combination. IFRS 3 refers to negative goodwill as the 'excess of acquirer's interest in the net fair value of acquiree's identifiable assets, liabilities and contingent liabilities over cost'.

Negative goodwill can arise as the result of **errors** in measuring the fair value of either the cost of the combination or the acquiree's identifiable net assets. It can also arise as the result of a **bargain purchase**.

Where there is negative goodwill, an entity should first **reassess** the amounts at which it has measured both the cost of the combination and the acquiree's identifiable net assets. This exercise should identify any errors.

Any negative goodwill remaining should be **recognised immediately in profit or loss** (that is, in the income statement).

IFRS 3 requires extensive **disclosures**. These include a **reconciliation** of the carrying amount of goodwill at the beginning and end of the period, showing separately:

(a) The gross amount and accumulated impairment losses at the beginning of the period
(b) Additional goodwill recognised during the period
(c) Impairment losses recognised during the period
(d) Net exchange differences arising during the period, and
(e) The gross amount and accumulated impairment losses at the end of the period

Exam focus point

Goodwill recognition and impairment is a key aspect of group accounts preparation. You should expect it to be examined very frequently.

Question

Characteristics of goodwill

What are the main characteristics of goodwill which distinguish it from other intangible non-current assets? To what extent do you consider that these characteristics should affect the accounting treatment of goodwill? State your reasons.

Answer

Goodwill may be distinguished from other intangible non-current assets by reference to the following characteristics.

(a) It is incapable of realisation separately from the business as a whole.
(b) Its value has no reliable or predictable relationship to any costs which may have been incurred.
(c) Its value arises from various intangible factors such as skilled employees, effective advertising or a strategic location. These indirect factors cannot be valued.
(d) The value of goodwill may fluctuate widely according to internal and external circumstances over relatively short periods of time.
(e) The assessment of the value of goodwill is highly subjective.

It could be argued that, because goodwill is so different from other intangible non-current assets it does not make sense to account for it in the same way. Thus the capitalisation and amortisation treatment would not be acceptable. Furthermore, because goodwill is so difficult to value, any valuation may be misleading, and it is best eliminated from the statement of financial position altogether. However, there are strong arguments for treating it like any other intangible non-current asset. This issue remains controversial.

Chapter Roundup

- **Intangible assets** are defined by **IAS 38** as non-monetary assets without physical substance. They must be:
  - **Identifiable**
  - **Controlled** as a result of a past event
  - Able to provide **future economic benefits**
- Development costs must be recognised as an asset if they meet certain criteria.
- Intangible assets should initially be measured at cost, but subsequently they can be carried at **cost or at a revalued amount**.
- Purchased goodwill arising on consolidation is retained in the statement of financial position as an intangible asset under IFRS 3. It must then be reviewed annually for impairment.
- Purchased goodwill is shown in the statement of financial position because it has been paid for. It has no tangible substance, and so it is an intangible non-current asset. **Internally-generated goodwill** cannot be recognised as an asset but other internally-generated assets may be, eg R & D.
- If a business has **goodwill**, it means that the value of the business as a going concern is greater than the value of its separate tangible assets. The valuation of goodwill is extremely subjective and fluctuates constantly. For this reason, non-purchased goodwill is **not** shown as an asset in the statement of financial position.

Quick Quiz

1 Intangible assets can only be recognised in a company's accounts if:
   - It is probable that .... will flow to the entity
   - The cost can be ....
2 What are the criteria which must be met before development expenditure can be deferred?
3 Start up costs must be expensed.

   True ☐ False ☐
4 Peggy buys Phil's business for $30,000. The business assets are a bar valued at $20,000, inventories at $3,000 and receivables of $3,000. How much is goodwill valued at?
5 What method of accounting for goodwill arising on consolidation is required by IFRS 3?
6 How should negative goodwill be accounted for under IFRS 3?

Answers to Quick Quiz

1 Future economic benefits. Measured reliably.

2 See Para 1.9.2

3 True

4 $30,000 – $20,000 – $3,000 – $3,000 = $4,000

5 Cost less impairment losses

6 Recognised in profit or loss immediately

Now try the question below from the Exam Question Bank

Number	Level	Marks	Time
Q10	Examination	25	45 mins

7

Inventories and construction contracts

Topic list	Syllabus reference
1 Inventories and short-term WIP (IAS 2)	2(d)
2 IAS 11 Construction contracts	2(e)

Introduction

Inventory and short-term work-in-progress valuation has a direct impact on a company's gross profit and it is usually a material item in any company's accounts. This is therefore an important subject area. If you have any doubts about accounting for inventories and methods of inventory valuation you would be advised to go back to your earlier study material and revise this topic.

Section 1 of this chapter goes over some of this ground again, concentrating on the effect of IAS 2. Section 2 goes on to discuss a new area, construction contracts, which are effectively long-term work in progress. You should find this topic fairly logical as long as you work through the examples and question carefully.

Study Guide

Section 7 – Inventories and construction contracts

- Measure and value inventories
- Define a construction contract and describe why recognising profit before completion is generally considered to be desirable; discuss if this may be profit smoothing (IAS 11)
- Describe the ways in which contract revenue and contract cost may be recognised
- Calculate and disclose the amounts to be shown in the financial statements for construction contracts

Exam Guide

Construction contracts are a good test of double entry and are likely to be tested as part of a longer question.

1 Inventories and short-term WIP (IAS 2)

FAST FORWARD

IAS 2 *Inventories* requires that the statement of financial position should show **inventories** classified in a manner appropriate to the entity. Common **classifications** are:

– Merchandise
– Product supplies
– Materials
– Work in progress
– Finished goods

1.1 Introduction

In most businesses the value put on inventory is an important factor in the determination of profit. Inventory valuation is, however, a highly subjective exercise and consequently there is a wide variety of different methods used in practice.

1.2 IAS 2 (revised) Inventories

IAS 2 was revised in December 2003. It lays out the required accounting treatment for inventories (sometimes called stocks) under the historical cost system. The major area of contention is the cost **value of inventory** to be recorded. This is recognised as an asset of the entity until the related revenues are recognised (ie the item is sold) at which point the inventory is recognised as an expense (ie cost of sales). Part or all of the cost of inventories may also be expensed if a write-down to **net realisable value** is necessary. The revised IAS also provides guidance on the cost formulas that are used to assign costs to inventories.

In other words, the fundamental accounting assumption of **accruals** requires costs to be matched with associated revenues. In order to achieve this, costs incurred for goods which remain unsold at the year end must be carried forward in the statement of financial position and matched against future revenues.

1.3 Scope

The following items are **excluded** from the scope of the standard.

- Work in progress under **construction contracts** (covered by IAS 11 *Construction contracts,* see Section 2)
- **Financial instruments** (ie shares, bonds)
- **Biological assets**

Certain inventories are exempt from the standard's **measurement rules**, ie those held by:

- Producers of **agricultural and forest products**
- **Commodity-broker traders**

1.4 Definitions

The standard gives the following important definitions.

Key terms

- **Inventories** are assets:
  - held for sale in the ordinary course of business;
  - in the process of production for such sale; or
  - in the form of materials or supplies to be consumed in the production process or in the rendering of services.
- **Net realisable value** is the estimated selling price in the ordinary course of business less the estimated costs of completion and the estimated costs necessary to make the sale.
- **Fair value** is the amount for which an asset could be exchanged or a liability settled between knowledgeable, willing parties in an arm's length transaction. (*IAS 2*)

Inventories can **include** any of the following.

- **Goods purchased and held for resale**, eg goods held for sale by a retailer, or land and buildings held for resale
- **Finished goods** produced
- **Work in progress** being produced
- Materials and supplies awaiting use in the production process (**raw materials**)

1.5 Measurement of inventories

The standard states that '**Inventories should be measured at the lower of cost and net realisable value**.'

Exam focus point

This is a very important rule and you will be expected to apply it in the exam.

1.6 Cost of inventories

The cost of inventories will consist of all costs of:

- **Purchase**
- **Costs of conversion**
- **Other costs** incurred in bringing the inventories to their **present location and condition**

1.6.1 Costs of purchase

The standard lists the following as comprising the costs of purchase of inventories:

- **Purchase price** *plus*
- **Import duties** and other taxes *plus*
- Transport, handling and any other cost **directly attributable** to the acquisition of finished goods, services and materials *less*
- **Trade discounts**, rebates and other similar amounts

1.6.2 Costs of conversion

Costs of conversion of inventories consist of two main parts.

(a) Costs **directly related** to the units of production, eg direct materials, direct labour

(b) Fixed and variable **production overheads** that are incurred in converting materials into finished goods, allocated on a systematic basis.

You may have come across the terms 'fixed production overheads' or 'variable production overheads' elsewhere in your studies. The standard defines them as follows.

Key terms

- **Fixed production overheads** are those indirect costs of production that remain relatively constant regardless of the volume of production, eg the cost of factory management and administration.
- **Variable production overheads** are those indirect costs of production that vary directly, or nearly directly, with the volume of production, eg indirect materials and labour. *(IAS 2)*

The standard emphasises that fixed production overheads must be allocated to items of inventory on the basis of the **normal capacity of the production facilities**. This is an important point.

(a) **Normal capacity** is the expected achievable production based on the average over several periods/seasons, under normal circumstances.

(b) The above figure should take account of the capacity lost through **planned maintenance**.

(c) If it approximates to the normal level of activity then the **actual level of production** can be used.

(d) **Low production** or **idle plant** will *not* result in a higher fixed overhead allocation to each unit.

(e) **Unallocated overheads** must be recognised as an expense in the period in which they were incurred.

(f) When production is **abnormally high**, the fixed production overhead allocated to each unit will be reduced, so avoiding inventories being stated at more than cost.

(g) The allocation of variable production overheads to each unit is based on the **actual use** of production facilities.

1.6.3 Other costs

Any other costs should only be recognised if they are incurred in bringing the inventories to their **present location and condition**.

The standard lists types of cost which **would not be included** in cost of inventories. Instead, they should be recognised as an **expense** in the period they are incurred.

(a) **Abnormal amounts** of wasted materials, labour or other production costs

(b) **Storage costs** (except costs which are necessary in the production process before a further production stage)

(c) **Administrative overheads** not incurred to bring inventories to their present location and conditions

(d) **Selling costs**

1.6.4 Techniques for the measurement of cost

Two techniques are mentioned by the standard, both of which produce results which **approximate to cost**, and so both of which may be used for convenience.

(a) **Standard costs** are set up to take account of normal production values: amount of raw materials used, labour time etc. They are reviewed and revised on a regular basis.

(b) **Retail method**: this is often used in the retail industry where there is a large turnover of inventory items, which nevertheless have similar profit margins. The only practical method of inventory valuation may be to take the total selling price of inventories and deduct an overall average profit margin, thus reducing the value to an approximation of cost. The percentage will take account of reduced price lines. Sometimes different percentages are applied on a department basis.

1.7 Cost formulae

Cost of inventories should be assigned by **specific identification** of their individual costs for:

(a) Items that are **not ordinarily interchangeable**

(b) Goods or services produced and segregated for **specific projects**

Specific costs should be attributed to individual items of inventory when they are segregated for a specific project, but not where inventories consist of a large number of interchangeable (ie identical or very similar) items. In the latter case the rule is as specified below.

1.7.1 Interchangeable items

Rule to learn

The cost of inventories should be assigned by using the **first-in, first-out (FIFO)** or **weighted average** cost formulas. The LIFO formula (last in, first out) is **not permitted** by IAS 2.

You should be familiar with these methods from your previous studies. Under the weighted average cost method, a recalculation can be made after each purchase, **or alternatively only at the period end**.

1.8 Net realisable value (NRV)

FAST FORWARD

Full details are required of inventory carried at **NRV** as well as the reversal of any previous write down.

As a general rule assets should not be carried at amounts greater than those expected to be realised from their sale or use. In the case of inventories this amount could fall below cost when items are **damaged or become obsolete**, or where the **costs to completion have increased** in order to make the sale.

In fact we can identify the principal situations in which **NRV is likely to be less than cost**, ie where there has been:

(a) An **increase in costs** or a **fall in selling price**
(b) A **physical deterioration** in the condition of inventory
(c) **Obsolescence** of products
(d) A decision as part of the company's marketing strategy to manufacture and sell products at a **loss**
(e) **Errors in production or purchasing**

A write down of inventories would normally take place on an item by item basis, but similar or related items may be **grouped together**. This grouping together is acceptable for, say, items in the same product line, but it is not acceptable to write down inventories based on a whole classification (eg finished goods) or a whole business.

The assessment of NRV should take place **at the same time** as estimates are made of selling price, using the most reliable information available. Fluctuations of price or cost should be taken into account if they relate directly to **events after the reporting period,** which confirm conditions existing at the end of the period.

The reasons why inventory is held must also be taken into account. Some inventory, for example, may be held to satisfy a firm contract and its NRV will therefore be the **contract price**. Any additional inventory of the same type held at the period end will, in contrast, be assessed according to general sales prices when NRV is estimated.

Net realisable value must be reassessed at the end of each period and compared again with cost. If the NRV has risen for inventories held over the end of more than one period, then the previous write down must be **reversed** to the extent that the inventory is then valued at the lower of cost and the new NRV. This may be possible when selling prices have fallen in the past and then risen again.

On occasion a write down to NRV may be of such size, incidence or nature that it must be **disclosed separately**.

You are the accountant at Water Pumps Co, and you have been asked to calculate the valuation of the company's inventory at cost at its year end of 30 April 20X9.

Water Pumps manufactures a range of pumps. The pumps are assembled from components bought by Water Pumps (the company does not manufacture any parts).

The company does not use a standard costing system, and work in progress and finished goods are valued as follows.

(a) Material costs are determined from the product specification, which lists the components required to make a pump.

(b) The company produces a range of pumps. Employees record the hours spent on assembling each type of pump, this information is input into the payroll system which prints the total hours spent each week assembling each type of pump. All employees assembling pumps are paid at the same rate and there is no overtime.

(c) Overheads are added to the inventory value in accordance with IAS 2 *Inventories*. The financial accounting records are used to determine the overhead cost, and this is applied as a percentage based on the direct labour cost.

For direct labour costs, you have agreed that the labour expended for a unit in work in progress is half that of a completed unit.

The draft accounts show the following materials and direct labour costs in inventory.

	Raw materials	*Work in progress*	*Finished goods*
Materials ($)	74,786	85,692	152,693
Direct labour ($)		13,072	46,584

The costs incurred in April, as recorded in the financial accounting records, were as follows.

	$
Direct labour	61,320
Selling costs	43,550
Depreciation and finance costs of production machines	4,490
Distribution costs	6,570
Factory manager's wage	2,560
Other production overheads	24,820
Purchasing and accounting costs relating to production	5,450
Other accounting costs	7,130
Other administration overheads	24,770

For your calculations assume that all work in progress and finished goods were produced in April 20X5 and that the company was operating at a normal level of activity.

Required

Calculate the value of overheads which should be added to work in progress and finished goods in accordance with IAS 2 *Inventories*.

Note. You should include details and a description of your workings and all figures should be calculated to the nearest $.

Answer

Calculation of overheads for inventories

Production overheads are as follows.

	$
Depreciation/finance costs	4,490
Factory manager's wage	2,560
Other production overheads	24,820
Accounting/purchasing costs	5,450
	37,320

Direct labour = $61,320

$\therefore$ Production overhead rate = $\frac{37,320}{61,320}$ = 60.86%

Inventory valuation

	Raw materials	*WIP*	*Finished goods*	*Total*
	$	$	$	$
Materials	74,786	85,692	152,693	313,171
Direct labour	–	13,072	46,584	59,656
Production overhead (at 60.86% of labour)	–	7,956	28,351	36,307
	74,786	106,720	227,628	409,134

1.9 Consistency – different cost formulae for inventories

FAST FORWARD

The use of **LIFO** is **prohibited** under the revised IAS 2.

IAS 2 allows two cost formulae (FIFO or weighted average cost) for inventories that are ordinarily interchangeable or are not produced and segregated for specific projects. The issue is whether an entity may use different cost formulae for different types of inventories.

IAS 2 provides that an entity should use **the same cost formula for all inventories having similar nature and use to the entity.** For inventories with different nature or use (for example, certain commodities used in one business segment and the same type of commodities used in another business segment), different cost formulas may be justified. A difference in geographical location of inventories (and in the respective tax rules), by itself, is not sufficient to justify the use of different cost formulas.

2 IAS 11 Construction contracts

FAST FORWARD

The rules of calculating accounting entries on **construction contracts** can be summarised as follows.

- Sales revenue is based upon the stage of completion.
- Calculate profit to date and cost of sales is a balancing figure
- Foreseeable losses are recognised immediately.
- The finanancial position (amounts due from/(to) customers) is calculated as:

Costs to date	X
Profit (losses) to date	X
Progress billings	(X)
	X

2.1 Introduction

Imagine that you are the accountant at a construction company. Your company is building a large tower block that will house offices, under a contract with an investment company. It will take three years to build the block and over that time you will obviously have to pay for building materials, wages of workers on the building, architects' fees and so on. You will receive periodic payments from the investment company at various predetermined stages of the construction. How do you decide, in each of the three years, **what to include as income and expenditure** for the contract in the statement of comprehensive income?

This is the problem tackled by IAS 11 *Construction contracts*.

2.2 Example: construction contract

A numerical example might help to illustrate the problem. Suppose that a contract is started on 1 January 20X5, with an estimated completion date of 31 December 20X6. The final contract price is $1,500,000. In the first year, to 31 December 20X5:

(a) Costs incurred amounted to $600,000.

(b) Half the work on the contract was completed.

(c) Certificates of work completed have been issued, to the value of $750,000. (*Note.* It is usual, in a construction contract, for a qualified person such as an architect or engineer to inspect the work completed, and if it is satisfactory, to issue certificates. This will then be the notification to the customer that progress payments are now due to the contractor. Progress payments are commonly the amount of valuation on the work certificates issued, minus a precautionary retention of 10%).

(d) It is estimated with reasonable certainty that further costs to completion in 20X6 will be $600,000.

What is the contract profit in 20X5, and what entries would be made for the contract at 31 December 20X5 if:

(a) Profits are deferred until the completion of the contract?

(b) A proportion of the estimated revenue and profit is credited to profit or loss in 20X5?

Solution

(a) If profits were deferred until the completion of the contract in 20X6, the revenue and profit recognised on the contract in 20X5 would be nil, and the value of work in progress on 31 December 20X5 would be $600,000. IAS 11 takes the view that this policy is unreasonable, because in 20X6, the total profit of $300,000 would be recorded. Since the contract revenues are earned throughout 20X5 and 20X6, a profit of nil in 20X5 and $300,000 in 20X6 would be contrary to the accruals concept of accounting.

(b) **It is fairer to recognise revenue and profit throughout the duration of the contract.**

As at 31 December 20X5 revenue of $750,000 should be matched with cost of sales of $600,000 in the statement of comprehensive income, leaving an attributable profit for 20X5 of $150,000.

The only entry in the statement of financial position as at 31 December 20X5 is a receivable of $750,000 recognising that the company is owed this amount for work done to date. No balance remains for work in progress, the whole $600,000 having been recognised in cost of sales.

2.3 What is a construction contract?

A contract which needs IAS 11 treatment does not have to last for a period of more than one year. The main point is that the contract activity **starts in one financial period and ends in another**, thus creating the problem: to which of two or more periods should contract income and costs be allocated? In fact the definition given in the IAS of a construction contract is very straightforward.

Key term

> **Construction contract.** A contract specifically negotiated for the construction of an asset or a combination of assets that are closely interrelated or interdependent in terms of their design, technology and function or their ultimate purpose or use. *(IAS 11)*

The standard differentiates between fixed price contracts and cost plus contracts.

Key terms

> - **Fixed price contract.** A contract in which the contractor agrees to a fixed contract price, or a fixed rate per unit of output, which in some cases is subject to cost escalation clauses.
> - **Cost plus contract.** A construction contract in which the contractor is reimbursed for allowable or otherwise defined costs, plus a percentage of these costs or a fixed fee.

Construction contracts may involve the building of one asset, eg a bridge, or a series of interrelated assets eg an oil refinery. They may also include **rendering of services** (eg architects) or restoring or demolishing an asset.

2.4 Combining and segmenting construction contracts

The standard lays out the factors which determine whether the construction of a **series of assets** under one contract should be treated as several contracts.

- **Separate proposals** are submitted for each asset
- **Separate negotiations** are undertaken for each asset; the customer can accept/reject each individually
- **Identifiable costs and revenues** can be separated for each asset

There are also circumstances where a **group of contracts** should be treated as **one single construction contract**.

- The group of contracts are negotiated as a **single package**
- Contracts are **closely interrelated**, with an overall profit margin
- The contracts are performed **concurrently** or **in a single sequence**

2.5 Contract revenue

Contract revenue will be the **amount specified in the contract**, subject to variations in the contract work, incentive payments and claims *if* these will probably give rise to revenue and *if* they can be reliably measured. The result is that contract revenue is measured at the **fair value** of received or receivable revenue.

The standard elaborates on the types of uncertainty, which depend on the outcome of future events, that affect the **measurement of contract revenue**.

- An **agreed variation** (increase/decrease)
- **Cost escalation clauses** in a fixed price contract (increase)
- **Penalties** imposed due to delays by the contractor (decrease)
- **Number of units** varies in a contract for fixed prices per unit (increase/decrease)

In the case of any variation, claim or incentive payment, two factors should be assessed to determine whether contract revenue should be recognised.

- Whether it is **probable** that the customer will accept the variation/claim, or that the contract is sufficiently advanced that the performance criteria will be met
- Whether the amount of the revenue can be **measured reliably**

2.6 Contract costs

Contract costs consist of:

- Costs relating **directly** to the contract

- Costs attributable to general contract activity which can be **allocated** to the contract, such as insurance, cost of design and technical assistance not directly related to a specific contract and construction overheads
- Any other costs which can be **charged to the customer** under the contract, which may include general administration costs and development costs

Costs that **relate directly** to a specific contract include the following.

- **Site labour costs**, including site supervision
- Costs of **materials** used in construction
- **Depreciation** of plant and equipment used on the contract
- Costs of **moving** plant, equipment and materials to and from the contract site
- Costs of **hiring** plant and equipment
- Costs of **design and technical assistance** that are directly related to the contract
- Estimated costs of **rectification and guarantee work**, including expected warranty costs
- **Claims from third parties**

General contract activity costs should be **allocated systematically and rationally**, and all costs with similar characteristics should be treated **consistently**. The allocation should be based on the **normal level** of construction activity. Borrowing costs may be attributed in this way (see IAS 23: Chapter 10).

Some costs **cannot be attributed** to contract activity and so the following should be **excluded** from construction contract costs.

- **General administration costs** (unless reimbursement is specified in the contract)
- **Selling costs**
- **R&D** (unless reimbursement is specified in the contract)
- **Depreciation** of idle plant and equipment not used on any particular contract

2.7 Recognition of contract revenue and expenses

Revenue and costs associated with a contract should be recognised according to the stage of completion of the contract at the end of the reporting period, but *only when* the **outcome of the activity can be estimated reliably**. If a loss is predicted on a contract, then it should be recognised immediately. This is often known as the **percentage of completion method**.

A reliable estimate of the outcome of a construction contract can only be made when **certain conditions** have been met, and these conditions will be different for fixed price and cost plus contracts.

- **Fixed price contracts**
  - Probable that economic benefits of the contract will flow to the entity
  - Total contract revenue can be reliably measured
  - Stage of completion at the period end and costs to complete the contract can be reliably measured
  - Costs attributable to the contract can be identified clearly and be reliably measured (actual costs can be compared to previous estimates)
- **Cost plus contracts**
  - Probable that economic benefits of the contract will flow to the entity
  - Costs attributable to the contract (whether or not reimbursable) can be identified clearly and be reliably measured

The **percentage of completion method** is an application of the accruals assumption. Contract revenue is matched to the contract costs incurred in reaching the stage of completion, so revenue, costs and profit are attributed to the proportion of work completed.

We can **summarise** the treatment as follows.

- Recognise **contract revenue** as revenue in the accounting periods in which the work is performed

- Recognise **contract costs** as an expense in the accounting period in which the work to which they relate is performed
- Any **expected excess** of total contract costs over total contract revenue should be recognised as an expense immediately
- Any costs incurred which relate to **future activity** should be recognised as an asset if it is probable that they will be recovered (often called contract work in progress, ie amounts due from the customer)
- Where amounts have been recognised as contract revenue, but their **collectability** from the customer becomes doubtful, such amounts should be recognised as an expense, not a deduction from revenue

2.8 When can reliable estimates be made?

IAS 11 only allows contract revenue and costs to be recognised when the outcome of the contract can be predicted, ie when it is probable that the economic benefits attached to the contract will flow to the entity. IAS 11 states that this can only be when a contract has been agreed which establishes the following.

- The **enforceable rights** of each party in respect of the asset to be constructed
- The **consideration** that is to be exchanged
- **Terms and manner of settlement**

In addition, the entity should have an **effective internal financial budgeting and reporting system**, in order to review and revise the estimates of contract revenue and costs as the contract progresses.

2.9 Determining the stage of completion

How should you decide on the stage of completion of any contract? The standard lists several methods.

- **Proportion of contract costs incurred** for work carried out to date
- **Surveys** of work carried out
- **Physical proportion** of the contract work completed

2.10 Example: stage of completion

Centrepoint Co have a fixed price contract to build a tower block. The initial amount of revenue agreed is $220m. At the beginning of the contract on 1 January 20X6 our initial estimate of the contract costs is $200m. At the end of 20X6 our estimate of the total costs has risen to $202m.

During 20X7 the customer agrees to a variation which increases expected revenue from the contract by $5m and causes additional costs of $3m. At the end of 20X7 there are materials stored on site for use during the following period which cost $2.5m.

We have decided to determine the stage of completion of the contract by calculating the proportion that contract costs incurred for work to date bear to the latest estimated total contract costs. The contract costs incurred at the end of each year were 20X6: $52.52m, 20X7: $154.2m (including materials in store), 20X8 $205m.

Required

Calculate the stage of completion for each year of the contract and show how revenues, costs and profits will be recognised in each year.

Solution

We can summarise the financial data for each year end during the construction period as follows.

	20X6	*20X7*	*20X8*
	$'000	$'000	$'000
Initial amount of revenue agreed in the contract	220,000	220,000	220,000
Variation	–	5,000	5,000
Total contract revenue	220,000	225,000	225,000

	20X6	*20X7*	*20X8*
	$'000	$'000	$'000
Contract costs incurred to date	52,520	154,200	205,000
Contract costs to complete	149,480	50,800	–
Total estimated contract costs	202,000	205,000	205,000
Estimated profit	18,000	20,000	20,000
Stage of completion	26.0%	74.0%	100.0%

The stage of completion has been calculated using the formula:

$$\frac{\text{Contract costs incurred to date}}{\text{Total estimated contract costs}}$$

The stage of completion in 20X7 is calculated by deducting the $2.5m of materials held for the following period from the costs incurred up to that year end, ie $154.2m – $2.5m = $151.7m. $151.7m/$205m = 74%.

Revenue, expenses and profit will be recognised in profit or loss as follows.

		To date	*Recognised in prior years*	*Recognised in current year*
		$'000	$'000	$'000
20X6	Revenue ($220m × 26%)	57,200		
	Costs ($202m × 26%)	52,520		
		4,680		
20X7	Revenue ($225m × 74%)	166,500	57,200	109,300
	Costs ($205m × 74%)	151,700	52,520	99,180
		14,800	4,680	10,120
20X8	Revenue ($225m × 100%)	225,000	166,500	58,500
	Costs ($205m × 100%)	205,000	151,700	53,300
		20,000	14,800	5,200

You can see from the above example that, when the stage of completion is determined using the contract costs incurred to date, only contract costs reflecting the work to date should be included in costs incurred to date.

- Exclude costs relating to **future activity**, eg cost of materials delivered but not yet used
- Exclude payments made to subcontractors **in advance** of work performed

2.11 Outcome of the contract cannot be reliably estimated

When the contract's outcome cannot be reliably estimated the following treatment should be followed.

- Only recognise revenue to the extent of contract costs incurred which are expected to be **recoverable**
- Recognise contract costs as an **expense** in the period they are incurred

This **no profit/no loss approach** reflects the situation near the beginning of a contract, ie the outcome cannot be reliably estimated, but it is likely that costs will be recovered.

Contract costs which **cannot be recovered** should be recognised as an expense straight away. IAS 11 lists the following situations where this might occur.

- The contract is **not fully enforceable**, ie its validity is seriously questioned
- The completion of the contract is subject to the outcome of **pending litigation or legislation**
- The contract relates to properties which will probably be **expropriated or condemned**
- The customer is **unable to meet its obligations** under the contract
- The contractor **cannot complete** the contract or in any other way meet its obligations under the contract

Where these **uncertainties cease to exist,** contract revenue and costs should be recognised as normal, ie by reference to the stage of completion.

2.12 Recognition of expected losses

Any loss on a contract should be **recognised as soon as it is foreseen**. The loss will be the amount by which total expected contract revenue is exceeded by total expected contract costs. The loss amount is not affected by whether work has started on the contract, the stage of completion of the work or profits on other contracts (unless they are related contracts treated as a single contract).

2.13 Changes in estimates

The effect of any change in the estimate of contract revenue or costs or the outcome of a contract should be accounted for as a **change in accounting estimate** under IAS 8 *Accounting policies, changes in accounting estimates and errors.*

2.14 Example: changes in estimates

The example below shows the effect of a change in estimate of costs on the figures that appear in the statement of comprehensive income and statement of financial position.

Battersby Co enters into a three-year contract.

Estimated revenue = \$20,000
Estimated total cost = \$16,000.

However, during Year 2, management revises its estimate of total costs incurred and thus the outcome of the contract. As a result, during Year 2, a loss is recognised on the contract for the year, even though the contract will still be profitable overall.

	Year 1	*Year 2*	*Year 3*
	\$	\$	\$
Estimated revenue	20,000	20,000	20,000
Estimated total cost	16,000	18,000	18,000
Estimated total profit	4,000	2,000	2,000
Cost incurred to date	\$8,000	\$13,500	\$18,000
Percentage of completion	50%	75%	100%
Recognised profit/(loss) for year	\$2,000	(\$500)	\$500
Cumulative recognised profit	\$2,000	\$1,500	\$2,000

Progress billings of \$8,000, \$8,000 and \$4,000 are made on the last day of each year and are received in the first month of the following year. The asset at the end of each year is:

	Year 1	*Year 2*	*Year 3*
	\$	\$	\$
Costs incurred	8,000	13,500	18,000
Recognised profits	2,000	2,000	2,500
(Recognised losses)		(500)	(500)
(Progress billings)	(8,000)	(16,000)	(20,000)
Amount recognised as an asset/(liability)	2,000	(1,000)	0

In addition, at each year end, the entity recognises a trade receivable for the amount outstanding at the end of the year of \$8,000, \$8,000 and \$4,000.

2.15 Section summary

In valuing long-term contracts and the other disclosures required under IAS 11, an organised approach is essential. The following suggested method breaks the process down into five logical steps.

Step 1 **Compare the contract value** and the **total costs** expected to be incurred on the contract. If a loss is foreseen (that is, if the costs to date plus estimated costs to completion exceed the contract value) then it must be charged against profits. If a loss has already been charged in previous years, then only the difference between the loss as previously and currently estimated need be charged.

Step 2 Using the percentage completed to date (or other formula given in the question), calculate sales revenue **attributable** to the contract for the period (for example percentage complete × total contract value, less of course, revenue taken in previous periods).

Step 3 **Calculate the cost of sales** on the contract for the period.

	$
Total contract costs × percentage complete (or follow instructions in question)	X
Less any costs charged in previous periods	(X)
	X
Add foreseeable losses in full (not previously charged)	X
Cost of sales on contract for the period	X

Step 4 **Deduct the cost of sales** for the period as calculated above (including any foreseeable loss) from the sales revenue calculated at step 2 to give profit (loss) recognised for the period.

Step 5 **Calculate amounts due to/from** customers as per the working on the previous page.

	$
Contract costs incurred to date	X
Recognised profits/(losses) to date	X
	X
Progress billings to date	(X)
Amounts due from/(to) customers	X

Note: This represents unbilled revenue. Unpaid billed revenue will be shown under trade receivables.

2.16 Summary of accounting treatment

The following summarises the accounting treatment for long-term contracts – **make sure that you understand it.**

2.16.1 Statement of comprehensive income (income statement)

(a) **Revenue and costs**

(i) Sales revenue and associated costs should be recorded in the income statement section as the contract activity progresses.

(ii) Include an appropriate proportion of total contract value as sales revenue in the income statement.

(iii) The costs incurred in reaching that stage of completion are matched with this sales revenue, resulting in the reporting of results which can be attributed to the proportion of work completed.

(iv) Sales revenue is the value of work carried out to date.

(b) **Profit recognised in the contract**

(i) It must reflect the proportion of work carried out.

(ii) It should take into account any known inequalities in profitability in the various stages of a contract.

2.16.2 Statement of financial position

(a) **Inventories**

	$
Costs to date	X
Plus recognised profits	(X)
	X
Less recognised losses	(X)
	X
Less progress billings	(X)
Amount due from customers	X

(b) **Receivables**

	$
Unpaid progress billings	X

(c) **Payables**. Where (a) gives a net 'amount due to customers' this amount should be included in payables under 'payments on account'.

Question — Construction contract

The main business of Santolina Co is construction contracts. At the end of September 20X9 there is an uncompleted contract on the books, details of which are as follows.

CONTRACT B	
Date commenced	1.4.X7
Expected completion date	23.12.X9
	$
Final contract price	290,000
Costs to 30.9.X9	210,450
Value of work certified to 30.9.X9	230,000
Progress billings to 30.9.X9	210,000
Cash received to 30.9.X9	194,000
Estimated costs to completion at 30.9.X9	20,600

Required

Prepare calculations showing the amount to be included in the statement of financial position at 30 September 20X9 in respect of the above contract.

Answer

Contract B is a construction contract and will be included in the statement of financial position at cost plus attributable profit less progress billings.

The estimated final profit is:

	$
Final contract price	290,000
Less: costs to date	(210,450)
estimated future costs	(20,600)
Estimated final profit	58,950

The attributable profit is found as follows.

$$\text{Estimated final profit} \times \frac{\text{Work certified}}{\text{Total contract price}}$$

$$\$58{,}950 \times \frac{230{,}000}{290{,}000}$$

Attributable profit = $46,753

Long-term contract work in progress

CONTRACT B

	$
Costs to date	210,450
Attributable profit	46,753
	257,203
Progress billings	(210,000)
Amount due from customers	47,203
Trade receivables	16,000

Exam focus point

A question is more likely to be set on construction contracts than on inventory, simply because they are a higher-level topic. Construction contracts lend themselves to computational questions, and have been examined in recent years as part of a financial statements preparation question (question 1), although they could also be examined with a discussion requirement.

Question

IAS 11 calculations

Haggrun Co has two contracts in progress, the details of which are as follows.

	Happy (profitable)	*Grumpy (loss-making)*
	$'000	$'000
Total contract price	300	300
Costs incurred to date	90	150
Estimated costs to completion	135	225
Progress payments invoiced and received	116	116

Required

Show extracts from the statement of comprehensive income and the statement of financial position for each contract, assuming they are both:

(a) 40% complete; and
(b) 36% complete.

Answer

Happy contract

(a) *40% complete*

	$'000
Statement of comprehensive income (Extract)	
Revenue (300 × 40%)	120
Cost of sales ((90+ 135) × 40%)	(90)
Profit to date (W)	30

Working

Profit to date

	$'000
Total contract price	300
Costs to date	(90)
Cost to completion	(135)
Total expected profit	75
Profit to date (75 × 40%)	30

Statement of financial position (Extract)

	$'000
Costs to date	90
Profit recognised to date	30
Progress billings	(116)
Amount due from customers	4

(b) *36% complete*

	$'000
Statement of comprehensive income (Extract)	
Revenue (300 × 36%)	108
Cost of sales (((90 + 135) × 36%))	(81)
Profit to date (75 × 36%)	27
Statement of financial position	
Costs to date	90
Profit recognised to date	27
Progress billings	(116)
Amount due from customers	1

Grumpy contract

(a) *40% complete*

	$'000
Statement of comprehensive income (Extract)	
Revenue (300 × 40%)	120
Cost of sales*	(195)
Foreseeable loss (W)	(75)

Working

	$'000
Total contract revenue	300
Costs to date	(150)
Costs to complete	(225)
Foreseeable loss	(75)
Statement of financial position (Extract)	
Costs to date	150
Foreseeable loss	(75)
Progress billings	(116)
Amounts due to customers	(41)

	$'000
* Costs to date (150 + 225) × 40%	150
Forseeable loss (75) × 60%**	45
	195

** The other 40% is taken into account in costs to date. We make this adjustment to bring in the **whole** of the foreseeable loss.

(b) *36% complete*

	$'000
Statement of comprehensive income (Extract)	
Revenue (300 × 36%)	108
Cost of sales*	(183)
Foreseeable loss	(75)
Statement of financial position (Extract)	
Costs to date	150
Foreseeable loss	(75)
Progress billings	(116)
Amount due to customers	(41)

	$'000
* Costs to date (150 + 225) × 36%	135
Forseeable loss (75) × 64%**	48
	183

Chapter roundup

- IAS 2 *Inventories* requires that the statement of financial position should show **inventories** classified in a manner appropriate to the entity. Common **classifications** are:
  - Merchandise
  - Production supplies
  - Materials
  - Work in progress
  - Finished goods
- Full details are required of inventory carried at **NRV** as well as the reversal of any previous write down.
- The use of **LIFO** is **prohibited** under the revised IAS 2.
- The rules for calculating accounting entries on **construction contracts** can be summarised as follows.
  - Sales revenue is based upon the stage of completion.
  - Calculate profit to date and cost of sales is a balancing figure.
  - Foreseeable losses are recognised immediately.
  - The financial position amount (amounts due from/(to) customers) is calculated as:

Costs to date	X
Profits (losses) to date	X
Progress billings	(X)
	X

Quick quiz

1 Net realisable value = Selling price **less** .... **less** ....

2 Which inventory costing method is allowed under IAS 2?
   (a) FIFO
   (b) LIFO

3 Any expected loss on a construction contract must be recognised, in full, in the year it was identified.

   True ☐

   False ☐

4 List the five steps to be taken when valuing construction contracts.

5 Which items in the statement of comprehensive income and statement of financial position are potentially affected by construction contracts?

Answers to quick quiz

1 Net realisable value = selling price costs to completion less costs necessary to make the sale.

2 (a) FIFO. LIFO is not allowed.

3 True

4 See paragraph 2.15

5 Statement of comprehensive income: revenue and cost of sales.
   Statement of financial position: inventories, receivables, payables.

Now try the question below from the Exam Question Bank

Number	Level	Marks	Time
11	Introductory	n/a	n/a

Provisions and contingencies

8

Topic list	Syllabus reference
1 Provisions	2(h)
2 Provisions for restructuring	2(h)
3 Contingent liabilities and contingent assets	2(h)

Introduction

You will have come across provisions and contingencies in your earlier studies or professional work. However, you may be asked in more detail about IAS 37 for this paper, given that the relevant Study Guide section is fairly detailed.

Study Guide

Section 9 – Liabilities

- Explain why an accounting standard on provisions is necessary – give examples of previous abuses in this area
- Define provisions, legal and constructive obligations, past events and the transfer of economic benefits
- State when provisions may and may not be made, and how they should be accounted for
- Explain how provisions should be measured
- Define contingent assets and liabilities – give examples and describe their accounting treatment
- Identify and account for:
  - onerous contracts
  - environmental and similar provisions
- Discuss the validity of making provisions for future repairs or renewals

Exam Guide

This is a very important area and has been always been popular with Dip IFR examiners. IAS 37 came up in June 2007, December 2007, June 2008, December 2008, December 2009 and the Pilot Paper for exams in 2011. It can be examined either as part of a calculation question, or as part of a discussion question.

1 Provisions

FAST FORWARD

Under **IAS 37** a **provision** should be recognised when:

- An entity has a **present obligation**, legal or constructive
- It is probable that a **transfer of resources embodying economic benefits** will be required to settle it
- A **reliable estimate** can be made of its amount.

Financial statements must include **all the information necessary for an understanding of the company's financial position**. Provisions, contingent liabilities and contingent assets are 'uncertainties' that must be accounted for consistently if we are to achieve this understanding.

1.1 Objective

IAS 37 *Provisions, contingent liabilities and contingent assets* aims to ensure that appropriate **recognition criteria** and **measurement bases** are applied to provisions, contingent liabilities and contingent assets and that **sufficient information** is disclosed in the **notes** to the financial statements to enable users to understand their nature, timing and amount.

1.2 Provisions

You will be familiar with provisions for depreciation and doubtful debts from your earlier studies. The sorts of provisions addressed by IAS 37 are, however, rather different.

Before IAS 37, there was no accounting standard dealing with provisions. Companies wanting to show their results in the most favourable light used to make large 'one off' provisions in years where a high level of underlying profits was generated. These provisions, often known as 'big bath' provisions, were then available to shield expenditure in future years when perhaps the underlying profits were not as good. In other words, provisions were used for profit smoothing. Profit smoothing is misleading.

Important

> The key aim of IAS 37 is to ensure that **provisions are made only** where there are valid grounds for them.

IAS 37 views a provision as a liability.

Key terms

> A **provision** is a **liability** of uncertain timing or amount.
>
> A **liability** is an obligation of an entity to transfer economic benefits as a result of past transactions or events. *(IAS 37)*

The IAS distinguishes provisions from other liabilities such as trade payables and accruals. This is on the basis that for a provision there is **uncertainty** about the timing or amount of the future expenditure. Whilst uncertainty is clearly present in the case of certain accruals the uncertainty is generally much less than for provisions.

1.3 Recognition

IAS 37 states that a provision should be **recognised** as a liability in the financial statements when:

- An entity has a **present obligation** (legal or constructive) as a result of a past event
- It is probable that a **transfer of economic benefits** will be required to settle the obligation
- A **reliable estimate** can be made of the obligation

1.4 Meaning of obligation

It is fairly clear what a legal obligation is. However, you may not know what a **constructive obligation** is.

Key term

> IAS 37 defines a **constructive obligation** as
>
> 'An obligation that derives from an entity's actions where:
>
> - by an established pattern of past practice, published policies or a sufficiently specific current statement the entity has indicated to other parties that it will accept certain responsibilities; and
> - as a result, the entity has created a valid expectation on the part of those other parties that it will discharge those responsibilities.' *(IAS 37)*

Question — Provision

In which of the following circumstances might a provision be recognised?

(a) On 13 December 20X9 the board of an entity decided to close down a division. The accounting date of the company is 31 December. Before 31 December 20X9 the decision was not communicated to any of those affected and no other steps were taken to implement the decision.

(b) The board agreed a detailed closure plan on 20 December 20X9 and details were given to customers and employees.

(c) A company is obliged to incur clean up costs for environmental damage (that has already been caused).

(d) A company intends to carry out future expenditure to operate in a particular way in the future.

Answer

(a) No provision would be recognised as the decision has not been communicated and could still be avoided.

(b) A provision would be made in the 20X9 financial statements.

(c) A provision for such costs is appropriate because the obligation arises from a past event.

(d) No present obligation exists and under IAS 37 no provision would be appropriate. This is because the entity could avoid the future expenditure by its future actions, maybe by changing its method of operation.

1.4.1 Probable transfer of economic benefits

For the purpose of the IAS, a transfer of resources embodying economic benefits is regarded as **'probable'** if the event is **more likely than not** to occur. This appears to indicate a probability of more than 50%. However, the standard makes it clear that where there is a number of similar obligations the probability should be based on considering the population as a whole, rather than one single item.

1.4.2 Example: transfer of economic benefits

If a company has entered into a warranty obligation then the probability of transfer of resources embodying economic benefits may well be extremely small in respect of one specific item. However, when considering the population as a whole the probability of some transfer of resources is quite likely to be much higher. If there is a **greater than 50% probability** of some transfer of economic benefits then a **provision** should be made for the **expected amount**.

1.4.3 Measurement of provisions

Important

> The amount recognised as a provision should be the best estimate of the expenditure required to settle the present obligation at the end of the reporting period.

The estimates will be determined by the **judgement** of the entity's management supplemented by the experience of similar transactions.

Allowance is made for **uncertainty**. Where the provision being measured involves a large population of items, the obligation is estimated by weighting all possible outcomes by their associated probabilities, ie **expected value**.

Question

Warranty

Parker Co sells goods with a warranty under which customers are covered for the cost of repairs of any manufacturing defect that becomes apparent within the first six months of purchase. The company's past experience and future expectations indicate the following pattern of likely repairs.

% of goods sold	*Defects*	*Cost of repairs if all items suffered from these defects* $m
75	None	–
20	Minor	1.0
5	Major	4.0

What is the provision required?

Answer

The cost is found using 'expected values' (75% × $nil) + (20% × $1.0m) + (5% × $4.0m) = $400,000.

Where the effect of the **time value of money** is material, the amount of a provision should be the **present value** of the expenditure required to settle the obligation. An appropriate **discount** rate should be used.

The discount rate should be a pre-tax rate that reflects current market assessments of the time value of money. The discount rate(s) should not reflect risks for which future cash flow estimates have been adjusted.

Example

A company knows that when it ceases a certain operation in 5 years time it will have to pay environmental cleanup costs of $5m.

The provision to be made now will be the present value of $5m in 5 years time.

The relevant discount rate in this case is 10%.

Therefore a provision will be made for:

	$
$5m × 0.62092*	3,104,600

* The discount rate for 5 yeas at 10%.

The following year the provision will be:

$5m × 0.68301	3,415,050
	310,450

The increase in the second year of $310,450 will be charged to profit or loss. It is referred to as the **unwinding** of the discount. This is accounted for as a finance cost.

1.4.4 Future events

Future events which are reasonably expected to occur (eg new legislation, changes in technology) may affect the amount required to settle the entity's obligation and should be taken into account.

1.4.5 Expected disposal of assets

Gains from the expected disposal of assets should not be taken into account in measuring a provision.

1.4.6 Reimbursements

Some or all of the expenditure needed to settle a provision may be expected to be recovered from a third party. If so, the **reimbursement should be recognised only when it is virtually certain that reimbursement will be received if the entity settles the obligation**.

- The reimbursement should be treated as a separate asset, and the amount recognised should not be greater than the provision itself.
- The provision and the amount recognised for reimbursement may be netted off in profit or loss.

1.4.7 Changes in provisions

Provisions should be **reviewed at the end of each reporting period** and adjusted to reflect the current best estimate. If it is no longer probable that a transfer of resources will be required to settle the obligation, the provision should be reversed.

1.4.8 Use of provisions

A provision should be used only for expenditures for which the provision was originally recognised. Setting expenditures against a provision that was originally recognised for another purpose would conceal the impact of two different events.

1.4.9 Future operating losses

Provisions should not be recognised for future operating losses. They do not meet the definition of a liability and the general recognition criteria set out in the standard.

1.4.10 Onerous contracts

If an entity has a contract that is onerous, the present obligation under the contract **should be recognised and measured** as a provision. An example might be vacant leasehold property. The entity is under an obligation to maintain the property but is receiving no income from it.

Key term

An **onerous contract** is a contract entered into with another party under which the unavoidable costs of fulfilling the terms of the contract exceed any revenues expected to be received from the goods or services supplied or purchased directly or indirectly under the contract and where the entity would have to compensate the other party if it did not fulfil the terms of the contract. *(IAS 37)*

1.5 Examples of possible provisions

It is easier to see what IAS 37 is driving at if you look at examples of those items which are possible provisions under this standard. Some of these we have already touched on.

(a) **Warranties**. These are argued to be genuine provisions as on past experience it is probable, ie more likely than not, that some claims will emerge. The provision must be estimated, however, on the basis of the class as a whole and not on individual claims. There is a clear legal obligation in this case.

(b) **Major repairs**. In the past it has been quite popular for companies to provide for expenditure on a major overhaul to be accrued gradually over the intervening years between overhauls. Under IAS 37 this is no longer possible as IAS 37 would argue that this is a mere intention to carry out repairs, not an obligation. The entity can always sell the asset in the meantime. The only solution is to treat major assets such as aircraft, ships, furnaces etc as a series of smaller assets where each part is depreciated over shorter lives. Thus any major overhaul may be argued to be replacement and therefore capital rather than revenue expenditure.

(c) **Self insurance**. A number of companies have created a provision for self insurance based on the expected cost of making good fire damage etc instead of paying premiums to an insurance company. Under IAS 37 this provision is no longer justifiable as the entity has no obligation until a fire or accident occurs. No obligation exists until that time.

(d) **Environmental contamination**. If the company has an environmental policy such that other parties would expect the company to clean up any contamination or if the company has broken current environmental legislation then a provision for environmental damage must be made.

(e) **Decommissioning or abandonment costs**. When an oil company initially purchases an oilfield it is put under a legal obligation to decommission the site at the end of its life. Prior to IAS 37 most oil companies set up the provision gradually over the life of the field so that no one year would be unduly burdened with the cost.

IAS 37, however, insists that a legal obligation exists on the initial expenditure on the field and therefore a liability exists immediately. This would appear to result in a large charge to profit and loss in the first year of operation of the field. However, the IAS takes the view that the cost of purchasing the field in the first place is not only the cost of the field itself but also the costs of putting it right again. Thus all the costs of decommissioning may be capitalised.

(f) **Restructuring**. This is considered in detail below.

Exam focus point

The examples given above are the sort of situation you may get in the exam.

2 Provisions for restructuring

FAST FORWARD

One of the main purposes of IAS 37 was to target abuses of provisions for restructuring. Accordingly, IAS 37 lays down **strict criteria** to determine when such a provision can be made.

Key term

IAS 37 defines a **restructuring** as:

A programme that is planned and is controlled by management and materially changes one of two things.

- The scope of a business undertaken by an entity
- The manner in which that business is conducted *(IAS 37)*

The IAS gives the following **examples** of events that may fall under the definition of restructuring.

- The **sale or termination** of a line of business
- The **closure of business locations** in a country or region or the **relocation** of business activities from one country region to another
- **Changes in management structure**, for example, the elimination of a layer of management
- **Fundamental reorganisations** that have a material effect on the **nature and focus** of the entity's operations

The question is whether or not an entity has an obligation – legal or constructive – at the end of the reporting period. For this to be the case:

- An entity must have a **detailed formal plan** for the restructuring
- It must have **raised a valid expectation** in those affected that it will carry out the restructuring by starting to implement that plan or announcing its main features to those affected by it

Important

A mere management decision is not normally sufficient. Management decisions may sometimes trigger off recognition, but only if earlier events such as negotiations with employee representatives and other interested parties have been concluded subject only to management approval.

Where the restructuring involves the **sale of an operation** then IAS 37 states that no obligation arises until the entity has entered into a **binding sale agreement**. This is because until this has occurred the entity will be able to change its mind and withdraw from the sale even if its intentions have been announced publicly.

2.1 Costs to be included within a restructuring provision

The IAS states that a restructuring provision should include only the **direct expenditures** arising from the restructuring, which are those that are both:

- **Necessarily entailed** by the restructuring; and
- Not associated with the **ongoing activities** of the entity.

The following costs should specifically **not** be included within a restructuring provision.

- **Retraining** or relocating continuing staff
- **Marketing**
- **Investment in new systems** and distribution networks

2.2 Disclosure

Disclosures for provisions fall into two parts.

- Disclosure of details of the **change in carrying value** of a provision from the beginning to the end of the year
- Disclosure of the **background** to the making of the provision and the uncertainties affecting its outcome

Question — Provision

In which of the following circumstances might a provision be recognised?

(a) On 13 December 20X9 the board of an entity decided to close down a division. The accounting date of the company is 31 December. Before 31 December 20X9 the decision was not communicated to any of those affected and no other steps were taken to implement the decision.

(b) The board agreed a detailed closure plan on 20 December 20X9 and details were given to customers and employees.

(c) A company is obliged to incur clean up costs for environmental damage (that has already been caused).

(d) A company intends to carry out future expenditure to operate in a particular way in the future.

Answer

(a) No provision would be recognised as the decision has not been communicated.

(b) A provision would be made in the 20X9 financial statements.

(c) A provision for such costs is appropriate.

(d) No present obligation exists and under IAS 37 no provision would be appropriate. This is because the entity could avoid the future expenditure by its future actions, maybe by changing its method of operation.

3 Contingent liabilities and contingent assets

FAST FORWARD

An entity **should not recognise** a **contingent asset or liability**, but they **should be disclosed**.

Now you understand provisions it will be easier to understand contingent assets and liabilities.

Key term

IAS 37 defines a **contingent liability** as:

- A possible obligation that arises from past events and whose existence will be confirmed only by the occurrence or non-occurrence of one or more uncertain future events not wholly within the control of the entity; or
- A present obligation that arises from past events but is not recognised because:
  - It is not probable that an outflow of resources embodying economic benefits will be required to settle the obligation; or
  - The amount of the obligation cannot be measured with sufficient reliability. *(IAS 37)*

As a rule of thumb, probable means more than 50% likely. If an obligation is probable, it is not a contingent liability – instead, a provision is needed.

3.1 Treatment of contingent liabilities

Contingent liabilities **should not be recognised in financial statements** but they **should be disclosed**. The required disclosures are:

- A brief description of the nature of the contingent liability
- An estimate of its financial effect
- An indication of the uncertainties that exist
- The possibility of any reimbursement

3.2 Contingent assets

Key term

IAS 37 defines a **contingent asset** as:

A possible asset that arises from past events and whose existence will be confirmed by the occurrence or non-occurrence of one or more uncertain future events not wholly within control of the entity. *(IAS 37)*

A contingent asset must not be recognised. Only when the realisation of the related economic benefits is **virtually certain** should recognition take place. At that point, **the asset is no longer a contingent asset!**

3.3 Disclosure

3.3.1 Disclosure: contingent liabilities

A **brief description** must be provided of all material contingent liabilities unless they are likely to be remote. In addition, provide

- An estimate of their **financial effect**
- Details of **any uncertainties**
- The possibility of any reimbursement

3.3.2 Disclosure: contingent assets

Contingent assets must only be disclosed in the notes if they are **probable**. In that case a brief description of the contingent asset should be provided along with an estimate of its likely financial effect.

3.4 'Let out'

IAS 37 permits reporting entities to avoid disclosure requirements relating to provisions, contingent liabilities and contingent assets if they would be expected to **seriously prejudice** the position of the entity in dispute with other parties. However, this should only be employed in **extremely rare** cases. Details of the general nature of the provision/contingencies must still be provided, together with an explanation of why it has not been disclosed.

3.5 Flow chart

You must practise the questions below to get the hang of IAS 37. But first, study the flow chart, taken from IAS 37, which is a good summary of its requirements concerning provisions and contingent liabilities.

Exam focus point

If you know this flow chart then you should be able to deal with most questions you are likely to meet in an exam.

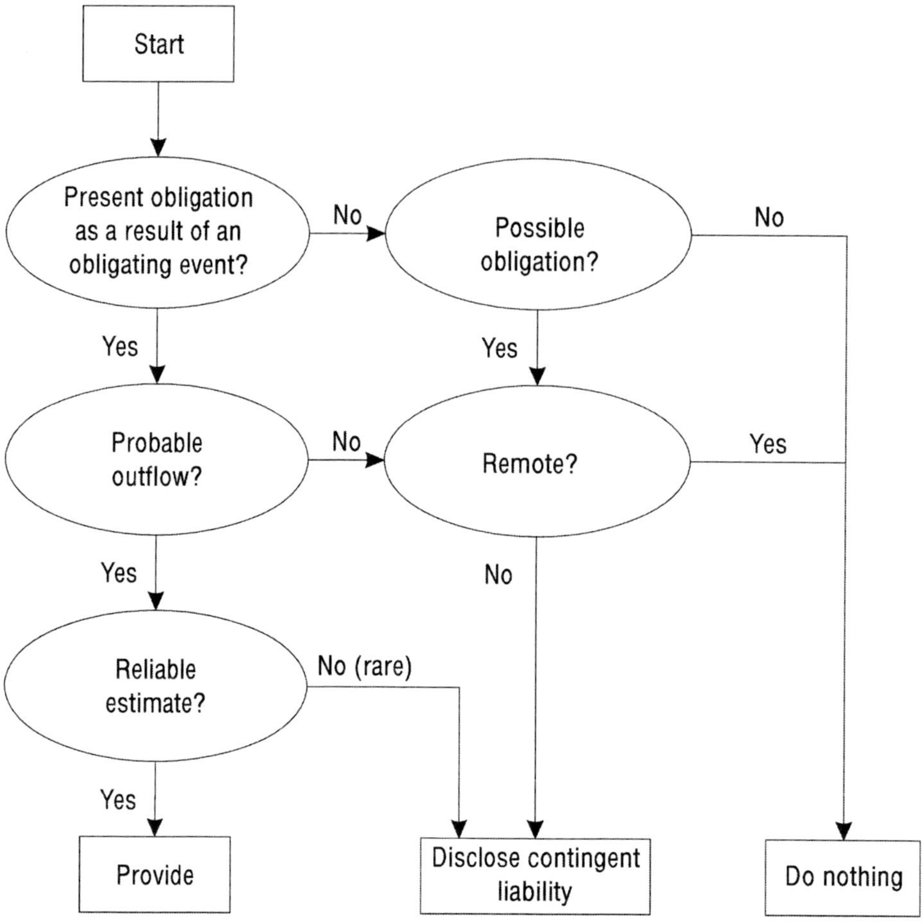

Question

Accounting treatment

During 20X0 Smack Co gives a guarantee of certain borrowings of Pony Co, whose financial condition at that time is sound. During 20X1, the financial condition of Pony Co deteriorates and at 30 June 20X1 Pony Co files for protection from its creditors.

What accounting treatment is required:

(a) At 31 December 20X0?
(b) At 31 December 20X1?

Answer

(a) *At 31 December 20X0*

There is a present obligation as a result of a past obligating event. The obligating event is the giving of the guarantee, which gives rise to a legal obligation. However, at 31 December 20X0 no transfer of resources is probable in settlement of the obligation.

No provision is recognised. The guarantee is disclosed as a contingent liability unless the probability of any transfer is regarded as remote.

(b) *At 31 December 20X1*

As above, there is a present obligation as a result of a past obligating event, namely the giving of the guarantee.

At 31 December 20X1 it is probable that a transfer of resources will be required to settle the obligation. A provision is therefore recognised for the best estimate of the obligation.

Question — Recognition of provision

Warren Co gives warranties at the time of sale to purchasers of its products. Under the terms of the warranty the manufacturer undertakes to make good, by repair or replacement, manufacturing defects that become apparent within a period of three years from the date of the sale. Should a provision be recognised?

Answer

Warren Co **cannot avoid** the cost of repairing or replacing all items of product that manifest manufacturing defects in respect of which warranties are given before the end of the reporting period, and a provision for the cost of this should therefore be made.

Warren Co is obliged to repair or replace items that fail within the entire warranty period. Therefore, in respect of **this year's sales**, the obligation provided for at the end of the reporting period should be the cost of making good items for which defects have been notified but not yet processed, **plus** an estimate of costs in respect of the other items sold for which there is sufficient evidence that manufacturing defects **will** manifest themselves during their remaining periods of warranty cover.

Question — Accounting treatment

After a wedding in 20X0 ten people died, possibly as a result of food poisoning from products sold by Callow Co. Legal proceedings are started seeking damages from Callow but it disputes liability. Up to the date of approval of the financial statements for the year to 31 December 20X0, Callow's lawyers advise that it is probable that it will not be found liable. However, when Callow prepares the financial statements for the year to 31 December 20X1 its lawyers advise that, owing to developments in the case, it is probable that it will be found liable.

What is the required accounting treatment:

(a) At 31 December 20X0?
(b) At 31 December 20X1?

Answer

(a) *At 31 December 20X0*

On the basis of the evidence available when the financial statements were approved, there is no obligation as a result of past events. No provision is recognised. The matter is disclosed as a contingent liability unless the probability of any transfer is regarded as remote.

(b) *At 31 December 20X1*

On the basis of the evidence available, there is a present obligation. A transfer of resources in settlement is probable.

A provision is recognised for the best estimate of the amount needed to settle the present obligation.

3.6 Section summary

- The objective of IAS 37 is to ensure that **appropriate recognition criteria and measurement** bases are **applied to provisions and contingencies** and that sufficient information is **disclosed**.

- The IAS seeks to ensure that provisions are **only recognised** when a **measurable obligation** exists. It includes detailed rules that can be used to ascertain when an obligation exists and how to measure the obligation.
- The standard attempts to **eliminate** the **'profit smoothing'** which has gone on before it was issued.

Chapter Roundup

- Under **IAS 37**, a **provision** should be recognised
  - When an entity has a **present obligation**, legal or constructive
  - It is probable that a **transfer of resources embodying economic benefits** will be required to settle it
  - A **reliable estimate** can be made of its amount
- One the main purposes of IAS 37 was to target abuses of provisions for restructuring. Accordingly, IAS 37 lays down **strict criteria** to determine when such a provision can be made.
- An entity **should not recognise a contingent asset or liability**, but they **should be disclosed.**

Quick Quiz

1 A provision is a .... of .... timing or amount.

2 A programme is undertaken by management which converts the previously wholly owned chain of restaurants they ran into franchises. Is this restructuring?

3 Define contingent asset and contingent liability.

4 How should decommissioning costs on an oilfield be accounted for under IAS 37?

5 'Provisions for major overhauls should be accrued for over the period between overhauls'. Is this correct?

Answers to Quick Quiz

1 Liability of uncertain timing or amount

2 Yes. The manner in which the business is conducted has changed

3 Refer to paragraphs 3.1 and 3.2

4 They should be capitalised as part of the initial expenditure on the oilfield.

5 No. It is not correct. See paragraph 1.5.

Now try the questions below from the Exam Question Bank

Number	Level	Marks	Time
12	Examination	25	45 mins

9

Employee benefits

Topic list	Syllabus reference
1 IAS 19 Employee benefits	2(i)
2 Short-term employee benefits	2(i)
3 Post-employment benefits	2(i)
4 Defined contribution plans	2(i)
5 Defined benefit plans: recognition and measurement	2(i)
6 Defined benefit plans: other matters	2(i)
7 Special cases	2(i)
8 Other issues and recent developments	2(i)

Introduction

An increasing number of companies and other entities now provide a **pension and other employee benefits** as part of their employees' remuneration package. In view of this trend, it is important that there is standard best practice for the way in which employee benefit costs are **recognised, measured, presented and disclosed** in the sponsoring entities' accounts.

Study Guide

Section 10 – Accounting for employment and post-employment benefit costs

- Describe the nature of defined contribution, multi-employers and defined benefits schemes
- Explain the recognition and measurement of defined benefit schemes under current proposals
- Account for defined benefit schemes including the amounts shown in the financial statements,(and notes to the accounts)

Exam Guide

This part of the syllabus refers specifically to retirement benefit costs. The Standard, IAS 19, covers more than just retirement benefits. As the syllabus does not exclude the further details of IAS 19, the full standard is covered in this chapter.

1 IAS 19 Employee benefits

FAST FORWARD

IAS 19 *Employee benefits* is a long and complex standard covering both short-term and long-term (post employment) benefits. The complications arise when dealing with **post-employment benefits.**

Exam focus point

This is a very difficult topic. Employee benefit costs are inherently complex and their accounting is both **problematic and controversial**. A section B question wholly on IAS 19 was included in the June 2009 and June 2005 papers.

IAS 19 (revised) *Employee benefits* has replaced the previous IAS 19 *Retirement benefit costs*. Note the increased scope of the new standard, which covers **all employee benefit costs**, except share-based payment, not only retirement benefit (pension) costs. Before we look at IAS 19, we should consider the nature of employee benefit costs and why there is an accounting problem which must be addressed by a standard.

1.1 The conceptual nature of employee benefit costs

When a company or other entity employs a new worker, that worker will be offered a **package of pay and benefits.** Some of these will be short-term and the employee will receive the benefit at about the same time as he or she earns it, for example basic pay, overtime etc. Other employee benefits are **deferred**, however, the main example being retirement benefits (ie a pension).

The cost of these deferred employee benefits to the employer can be viewed in various ways. They could be described as **deferred salary** to the employee. Alternatively, they are a **deduction** from the employee's true gross salary, used as a tax-efficient means of saving. In some countries, tax efficiency arises on retirement benefit contributions because they are not taxed on the employee, but they are allowed as a deduction from taxable profits of the employer.

1.2 Accounting for employee benefit costs

Accounting for **short-term employee benefit costs** tends to be quite straightforward, because they are simply recognised as an expense in the employer's financial statements of the current period.

Accounting for the cost of **deferred employee benefits** is much more difficult. This is because of the large amounts involved, as well as the long time scale, complicated estimates and uncertainties. In the past, entities accounted for these benefits simply by charging the income statements of the employing entity on the basis of actual payments made. This led to substantial variations in reported profits of these entities and disclosure of information on these costs was usually sparse.

1.3 IAS 19 Employee benefits

IAS 19 is intended to prescribe the following.

(a) **When** the cost of employee benefits should be **recognised as a liability or an expense**
(b) The **amount** of the liability or expense that should be recognised

As a basic rule, the standard states the following.

(a) A **liability** should be recognised when an employee has provided a service in exchange for benefits to be received by the employee at some time in the future.

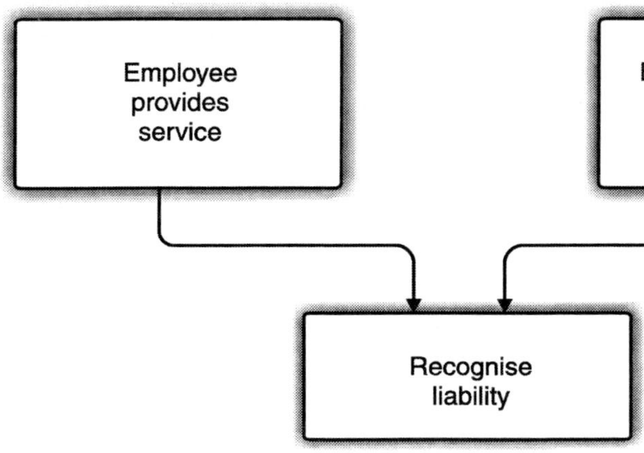

(b) An **expense** should be recognised when the entity enjoys the economic benefits from a service provided by an employee regardless of when the employee received or will receive the benefits from providing the service.

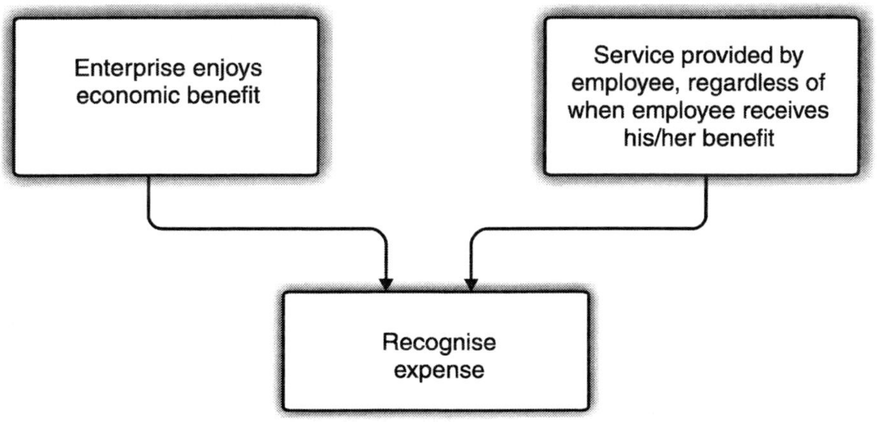

The basic problem is therefore fairly straightforward. An entity will often enjoy the **economic benefits** from the services provided by its employees in advance of the employees receiving all the employment benefits from the work they have done, for example they will not receive pension benefits until after they retire.

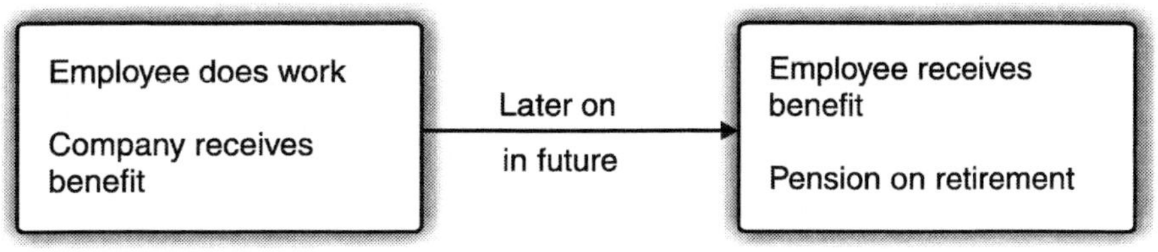

1.4 Categories of employee benefits

The standard recognises four categories of employee benefits, and proposes a different accounting treatment for each. These four categories are as follows.

1 **Short-term benefits** including:

- Wages and salaries
- Social security contributions
- Paid annual leave
- Paid sick leave
- Paid maternity/paternity leave
- Profit shares and bonuses paid within 12 months of the year end
- Paid jury service
- Paid military service
- Non-monetary benefits, eg medical care, cars, free goods

2 **Post-employment benefits**, eg pensions and post-employment medical care

3 **Other long-term benefits**, eg profit shares, bonuses or deferred compensation payable later than 12 months after the year end, sabbatical leave, long-service benefits

4 **Termination benefits**, eg early retirement payments and redundancy payments

Benefits may be paid to the employees themselves, to their dependants (spouses, children, etc) or to third parties.

1.5 Definitions

IAS 19 uses a great many important definitions. They are grouped together here, but you should refer back to them as necessary as you work through the rest of this chapter.

Key terms

Employee benefits are all forms of consideration given by an entity in exchange for service rendered by employees.

Short-term employee benefits are employee benefits (other than termination benefits) which fall due wholly within twelve months after the end of the period in which the employees render the related service.

Post-employment benefits are employee benefits (other than termination benefits) which are payable after the completion of employment.

Post-employment benefit plans are formal or informal arrangements under which an entity provides post-employment benefits for one or more employees.

Defined contribution plans are post-employment benefit plans under which an entity pays fixed contributions into a separate entity (a fund) and will have no legal or constructive obligation to pay further contributions if the fund does not hold sufficient assets to pay all employee benefits relating to employee service in the current and prior periods.

Defined benefit plans are post-employment benefit plans other than defined contribution plans.

Multi-employer plans are defined contribution plans (other than state plans) or defined benefit plans (other than state plans) that:

(a) pool the assets contributed by various entities that are not under common control, and

(b) use those assets to provide benefits to employees of more than one entity, on the basis that contribution and benefit levels are determined without regard to the identity of the entity that employs the employees concerned.

Other long-term employee benefits are employee benefits (other than post-employment benefits and termination benefits) which do not fall due wholly within twelve months after the end of the period in which the employees render the related service.

Termination benefits are employee benefits payable as a result of either:

(a) an entity's decision to terminate an employee's employment before the normal retirement date, or
(b) an employee's decision to accept voluntary redundancy in exchange for those benefits.

Vested employee benefits are employee benefits that are not conditional on future employment.

Key terms (cont)

The **present value of a defined benefit** obligation is the present value, without deducting any plan assets, of expected future payments required to settle the obligation resulting from employee service in the current and prior periods.

Current service cost is the increase in the present value of the defined benefit obligation resulting from employee service in the current period.

Interest cost is the increase during a period in the present value of a defined benefit obligation which arises because the benefits are one period closer to settlement.

Plan assets comprise:

(a) Assets held by a long-term employee benefit fund; and
(b) Qualifying insurance policies

The **return on plan assets** is interest, dividends and other revenue derived from the plan assets, together with realised and unrealised gains or losses on the plan assets, less any cost of administering the plan and loess any tax payable by the plan itself.

Actuarial gains and losses comprise:

(a) Experience adjustments (the effects of differences between the previous actuarial assumptions and what has actually occurred), and
(b) The effects of changes in actuarial assumptions.

Past service cost is the increase in the present value of the defined benefit obligation for employee service in prior periods, resulting in the current period from the introduction of, or changes to, post-employment benefits or other long-term employee benefits. Past service cost may be either positive (where benefits are introduced or changed so that the present value of the defined benefit obligation increases) or negative (where existing benefits are changed so that the present value of the defined benefit obligation decreases).

(IAS 19)

1.6 Asset ceiling test

The revisions to IAS 19 in May 2002 seek to prevent what the IASB regards as a 'counter-intuitive' result produced by the interaction of two aspects of the existing IAS 19.

(a) Permission to defer recognition of actuarial gains and losses.
(b) Imposition of an upper limit on the amount that can be recognised as an asset (the asset ceiling).

The issue affects only those entities that have, at the beginning or end of the accounting period, a surplus in a defined benefit plan that, based on the current terms of the plan, the entity cannot fully recover through refunds or reductions in future contributions.

The issue is the impact of the wording of the asset ceiling.

(a) Sometimes a gain is recognised when a pension plan is in surplus only because of the deferring and amortising of an actuarial loss or added past service cost in the current period.
(b) Conversely, a loss may be recognised because of a deferral of actuarial gains.

The revisions to IAS 19 introduced a limited amendment that would prevent gains (losses) from being recognised solely as a result of past service cost or actuarial losses (gains) arising in the period. No change is currently proposed to the general approach of allowing deferral of actuarial gains and losses. During its deliberations on the amendments to IAS 19, the IASB concluded that there were further conceptual and practical problems with these provisions. The IASB intends to conduct a comprehensive review of these aspects of IAS 19 as part of its work on convergence of accounting standards across the world.

IAS 19 states that pension plan assets (surpluses) are measured at the **lower** of:

- The net asset or liability as calculated

AND

- The total of
  - Any cumulative unrecognised actuarial losses and past service costs
  - The present value or any economic benefits available in the form of refunds from the plan or reductions in future contributions to the plan

1.7 Example: asset ceiling test

Celia, a limited liability company, has a defined benefit plan. The following information is available as at 31 December 20X8

	$m
Fair value of plan assets	380
Present value of pension liability	320
Present value of future refunds and reductions in future contributions	28
Unrecognised actuarial losses	32
Unrecognised past service costs	20

Required

Calculate the amount of the asset that is to be recognised in the financial statements as at 31 December 20X8.

Solution

The amount that can be recognised is the lower of:

	$m
Present value of pension liability	320
Fair value of plan assets	(380)
	(60)
Unrecognised actuarial losses	(32)
Unrecognised past service costs	(20)
Surplus (pension plan asset)	(112)

	$m
Unrecognised actuarial losses	32
Unrecognised past service costs	20
Present value of future refunds and reductions in future contributions	28
	80

Therefore the amount of the asset recognised is restricted to $80m.

1.8 Section summary

There are **two key issues** or problems to consider.

- It may be necessary to rely on **actuarial assumptions** about what the future amount of benefits payable will be.
- If benefits are payable later than 12 months after the end of the accounting period, the future benefits payable should be **discounted** to a present value.

2 Short-term employee benefits

FAST FORWARD

Accounting for short-term employee benefits is fairly straightforward, because there are **no actuarial assumptions** to be made, and there is **no requirement to discount** future benefits (because they are all, by definition, payable no later than 12 months after the end of the accounting period).

2.1 Recognition and measurement

The rules for short-term benefits are essentially an application of **basic accounting principles and practice**.

(a) **Unpaid short-term employee benefits** as at the end of an accounting period should be recognised as an accrued expense. Any short-term benefits **paid in advance** should be recognised as a prepayment (to the extent that it will lead to, eg a reduction in future payments or a cash refund).

(b) The **cost of short-term employee benefits** should be recognised as an **expense** in the period when the economic benefit is given, as employment costs (except insofar as employment costs may be included within the cost of an asset, eg property, plant and equipment).

2.2 Short-term absences

There may be **short-term accumulating compensated absences**. These are absences for which an employee is paid, and if the employee's entitlement has not been used up at the end of the period, they are carried forward to the next period. An example is paid holiday leave, where any unused holidays in one year are carried forward to the next year. The cost of the benefits of such absences should be **charged as an expense** as the employees render service that increases their entitlement to future compensated absences.

There may be **short-term non-accumulating compensated absences**. These are absences for which an employee is paid when they occur, but an **entitlement to the absences does not accumulate**. The employee can be absent, and be paid, but only if and when the circumstances arise. Examples are maternity/paternity pay, (in most cases) sick pay, and paid absence for jury service.

2.3 Example: Unused holiday leave

A company gives its employees an annual entitlement to paid holiday leave. If there is any unused leave at the end of the year, employees are entitled to carry forward the unused leave for up to 12 months. At the end of 20X9, the company's employees carried forward in total 50 days of unused holiday leave. Employees are paid $100 per day.

Required

State the required accounting for the unused holiday carried forward.

Solution

The short-term accumulating compensated absences should be recognised as a cost in the year when the entitlement arises, ie in 20X9.

Question — Sick leave

Plyman Co has 100 employees. Each is entitled to five working days of paid sick leave for each year, and unused sick leave can be carried forward for one year. Sick leave is taken on a LIFO basis (ie firstly out of the current year's entitlement and then out of any balance brought forward).

As at 31 December 20X8, the average unused entitlement is two days per employee. Plyman Co expects (based on past experience which is expected to continue) that 92 employees will take five days or less sick leave in 20X9, the remaining eight employees will take an average of 6½ days each.

Required

State the required accounting for sick leave.

Answer

Plyman Co expects to pay an additional 12 days of sick pay as a result of the unused entitlement that has accumulated at 31 December 20X8, ie 1½ days × 8 employees. Plyman Co should recognise a liability equal to 12 days of sick pay.

2.4 Profit sharing or bonus plans

Profit shares or bonuses payable within 12 months after the end of the accounting period should be recognised as an expected cost when the entity has a **present obligation to pay it**, ie when the employer has no real option but to pay it. This will usually be when the employer recognises the profit or other performance achievement to which the profit share or bonus relates.

2.5 Example: Profit sharing plan

Mooro Co runs a profit sharing plan under which it pays 3% of its net profit for the year to its employees if none have left during the year. Mooro Co estimates that this will be reduced by staff turnover to 2.5% in 20X9.

Required

Which costs should be recognised by Mooro Co for the profit share?

Solution

Mooro Co should recognise a liability and an expense of 2.5% of net profit.

2.6 Disclosure

There are **no specific disclosure requirements for short-term employee benefits** in the proposed standard.

3 Post-employment benefits

FAST FORWARD

There are two **types of post-employment benefit** plan:

- Defined contribution plans
- Defined benefit plans

Defined contribution plans are simple to account for as the benefits are defined by the contributions made.

Defined benefit plans are much more difficult to deal with as the benefits are promised, they define the contributions to be made.

Many employers provide post-employment benefits for their employees after they have stopped working. **Pension schemes** are the most obvious example, but an employer might provide post-employment death benefits to the dependants of former employees, or post-employment medical care.

Post-employment benefit schemes are often referred to as '**plans**'. The 'plan' receives regular contributions from the employer (and sometimes from current employees as well) and the money is invested in assets, such as stocks and shares and other investments. The post-employment benefits are paid out of the income from the plan assets (dividends, interest) or from money from the sale of some plan assets.

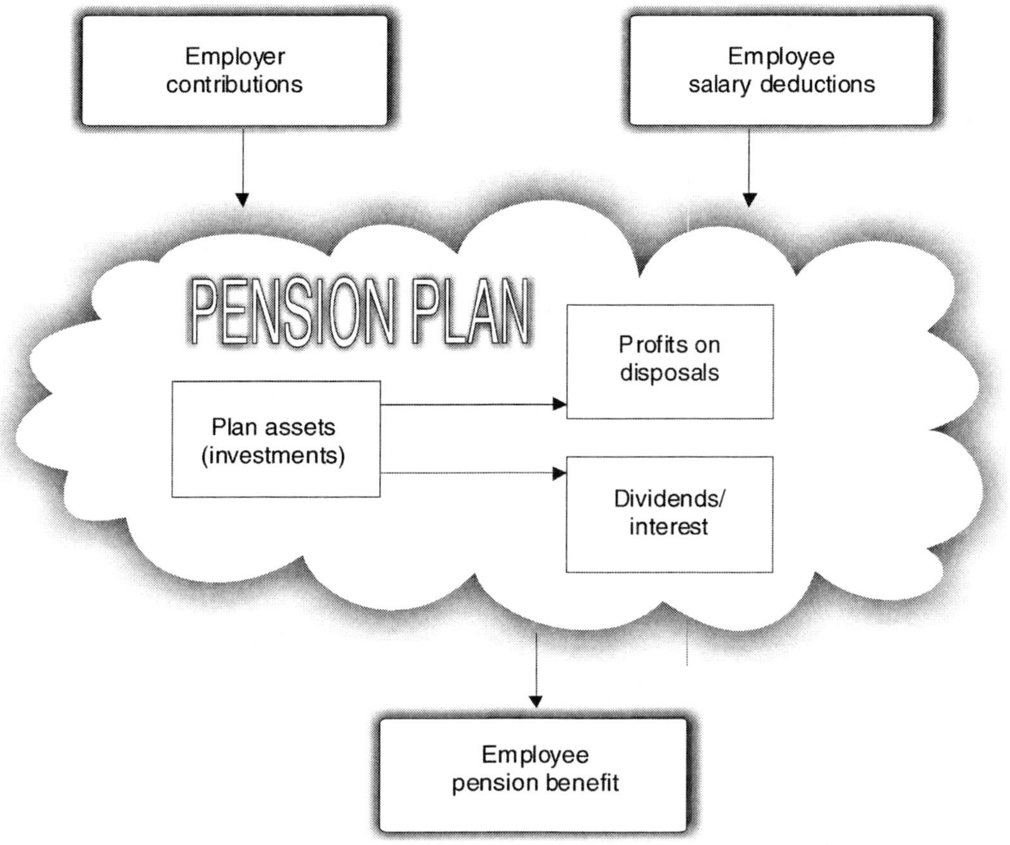

There are two types or categories of post-employment benefit plan, as given in the definitions in Section 1 above.

(a) **Defined contribution plans**. With such plans, the employer (and possibly current employees too) pay regular contributions into the plan of a given or 'defined' amount each year. The contributions are invested, and the size of the post-employment benefits paid to former employees depends on how well or how badly the plan's investments perform. If the investments perform well, the plan will be able to afford higher benefits than if the investments performed less well.

(b) **Defined benefit plans**. With these plans, the size of the post-employment benefits is determined in advance, ie the benefits are 'defined'. The employer (and possibly current employees too) pay contributions into the plan, and the contributions are invested. The size of the contributions is set at an amount that is expected to earn enough investment returns to meet the obligation to pay the post-employment benefits. If, however, it becomes apparent that the assets in the fund are insufficient, the employer will be required to make additional contributions into the plan to make up the expected shortfall. On the other hand, if the fund's assets appear to be larger than they need to be, and in excess of what is required to pay the post-employment benefits, the employer may be allowed to take a 'contribution holiday' (ie stop paying in contributions for a while).

It is important to make a clear distinction between the following.

(a) **Funding** a defined benefit plan, ie paying contributions into the plan
(b) **Accounting for** the cost of funding a defined benefit plan

Before we examine accounting for both these types of scheme, we need to mention a couple of other issues addressed by the standard.

3.1 Multi-employer plans

These were defined above. IAS 19 requires an entity to **classify** such a plan as a defined contribution plan or a defined benefit plan, depending on its terms (including any constructive obligation beyond those terms).

For a multi-employer plan that is a **defined benefit plan**, the entity should account for its proportionate share of the defined benefit obligation, plan assets and cost associated with the plan in the same way as for any other defined benefit plan and make full disclosure.

When there is **insufficient information** to use defined benefit accounting, then the multi-employer plan should be accounted for as a defined contribution plan and additional disclosures made (that the plan is in fact a defined benefit plan and information about any known surplus or deficit).

3.2 State plans

These plans are **established by legislation** to cover some or all entities and are operated by government or its agent. These plans cannot be controlled or influenced by the entity. State plans should be treated in the same way as multi-employer plans by the entity.

3.3 Insurance benefits

Insurance premiums paid by an employer to fund an employee post-employment benefit plan should be accounted for as **defined contributions** to the plan, *unless* the employer, has a legal or constructive obligation to pay the employee benefits directly when they fall due, *or* to make further payments in the event that the insurance company does not pay all the post-employment benefits (relating to service given in prior years and the current period) for which insurance has been paid.

3.4 Examples: Insurance benefits

For example, Employer A pays insurance premiums to fund post-employment medical care for former employees. It has no obligation beyond paying the annual insurance premiums. The premium paid each year should be accounted for as a defined contribution.

Employer B similarly pays insurance premiums for the same purpose, but retains the liability to pay for the medical benefits itself. In the case of Employer B, the rights under the insurance policy should be recognised as an asset, and it should account for the obligation to employees as a liability as if there were no insurance policy.

3.5 Section summary

- There are two categories of **post-retirement benefits**:
  - Defined contribution schemes
  - Defined benefit schemes
- **Defined contribution schemes** provide benefits commensurate with the fund available to produce them.
- **Defined benefit schemes** provide promised benefits and so contributions are based on estimates of how the fund will perform.
- **Defined contribution scheme costs** are easy to account for and this is covered in the next section.

4 Defined contribution plans

Accounting for payments into defined contribution plans is straightforward.

(a) The **obligation** is determined by the amount paid into the plan in each period.

(b) There are no actuarial assumptions to make.

(c) If the obligation is settled in the current period (or at least no later than 12 months after the end of the current period) there is **no requirement for discounting**.

IAS 19 requires the following:

(a) **Contributions** to a defined contribution plan should be recognised as an **expense** in the period they are payable (except to the extent that labour costs may be included within the cost of assets).

(b) Any liability for **unpaid contributions** that are due as at the end of the period should be recognised as a **liability** (accrued expense).

(c) Any **excess contributions** paid should be recognised as an asset (prepaid expense), but only to the extent that the prepayment will lead to, eg a reduction in future payments or a cash refund.

In the (unusual) situation where contributions to a defined contribution plan do not fall due entirely within 12 months after the end of the period in which the employees performed the related service, then these should be **discounted**. The discount rate to be used is discussed below in Section 5.9.

Disclosure requirements

(a) A **description** of the plan
(b) The amount recognised as an **expense** in the period

5 Defined benefit plans: recognition and measurement

Accounting for defined benefit plans is much more complex. The complexity of accounting for defined benefit plans stems largely from the following factors.

(a) The future benefits (arising from employee service in the current or prior years) **cannot be estimated exactly**, but whatever they are, the employer will have to pay them, and the liability should therefore be recognised now. To estimate these future obligations, it is necessary to use **actuarial assumptions**.

(b) The obligations payable in future years should be valued, by discounting, on a **present value** basis. This is because the obligations may be settled in many years' time.

(c) If actuarial assumptions change, the amount of required contributions to the fund will change, and there may be **actuarial gains or losses**. A contribution into a fund in any period is not necessarily the total for that period, due to actuarial gains or losses.

Most of the definitions given in the standard (shown in Section 1) are to do with defined benefit plans.

5.1 Outline of the method

FAST FORWARD

There is a **six-step method** for accounting for the expenses and liability of a defined benefit pension plan.

An outline of the method used for an employer to account for the expenses and obligation of a defined benefit plan is given below. The stages will be explained in more detail later.

Step 1 **Actuarial assumptions** should be used to make a reliable estimate of the amount of future benefits employees have earned from service in relation to the current and prior years. Assumptions include, for example, assumptions about employee turnover, mortality rates, future increases in salaries (if these will affect the eventual size of future benefits such as pension payments).

Step 2 These **future benefits** should be attributed to service performed by employees in the current period, and in prior periods, using the **Projected Unit Credit Method**. This gives a total present value of future benefit obligations arising from past and current periods of service.

Step 3 The **fair value** of any plan assets should be established.

Step 4 The size of any **actuarial gains or losses** should be determined, and the amount of these that will be recognised.

Step 5 If the benefits payable under the plan have been improved, the **extra cost arising from past service** should be determined.

Step 6 If the **benefits payable** under the plan have been reduced or cancelled, the resulting gain should be determined.

5.2 Constructive obligation

IAS 19 makes it very clear that it is not only its legal obligation under the formal terms of a defined benefit plan that an entity must account for, but also for any **constructive obligation** that it may have. A constructive obligation, which will arise from the entity's informal practices, exist when the entity has no realistic alternative but to pay employee benefits, for example if any change in the informal practices would cause unacceptable damage to employee relationships.

We will look at all the steps in Section 5.1, but we will begin by covering the mathematics involved in the Projected Unit Credit Method.

5.3 The Projected Unit Credit Method

FAST FORWARD

Future benefits are attributed to services performed by employees using the **Projected Unit Credit Method**.

With this method, it is assumed that each period of service by an employee gives rise to an **additional unit of future benefits**. The present value of that unit of future benefits can be calculated, and attributed to the period in which the service is given. The units, each measured separately, build up to the overall obligation. The accumulated present value of (discounted) future benefits will incur interest over time, and an interest expense should be recognised.

In practice, the mathematics will be complex. Here is a simplified example, using figures rounded to whole numbers.

5.4 Example: Projected unit credit method

An employer pays a lump sum to employees when they retire. The lump sum is equal to 1% of their salary in the final year of service, for every year of service they have given.

(a) An employee is expected to work for 5 years (actuarial assumption)
(b) His salary is expected to rise by 8% pa (actuarial assumption)
(c) His salary in 20X1 is $10,000
(d) The discount rate applied is 10% pa

Required

Calculate the amounts chargeable to each of years 20X1 to 20X5 and the closing obligation each year, assuming no change in actuarial assumptions.

Solution

Since his salary in 20X1 is $10,000, his salary in 20X5 is expected to be $13,605. His lump sum entitlement is therefore expected to be $136 for each year's service, ie $680 in total.

Using the Projected Unit Credit Method, and assuming that the actuarial assumptions do not change over any of 20X1 to 20X5, and that the employees do leave at the end of 20X5, the calculations are as follows.

Future benefit attributable to:	*20X1*	*20X2*	*20X3*	*20X4*	*20X5*
	$	$	$	$	$
Prior years	0	136	272	408	544
Current year					
(1% of final salary)	136	136	136	136	136
Prior and current years total	136	272	408	544	680

The future benefit builds up to $680 over the five years, at the end of which the employee is expected to leave and the benefit is payable.

These figures, however, are not discounted. The benefit attributable to the current year should be discounted, in this example at 10%, from the end of 20X5.

	20X1	*20X2*	*20X3*	*20X4*	*20X5*
	$	$	$	$	$
Opening obligation (note 1)	–	93	204	336	494
Interest (note 2)	–	9	20	34	50*
Current service cost (note 3)	93	102	112	124	136
Closing obligation (note 4)	93	204	336	494	680

* There is a rounding error of $1 in the calculations. To make the total add up to $680, the interest of $49.4 has therefore been rounded up to $50 in compensation.

Notes

1 The opening obligation is the closing obligation of the previous period, brought forward.

2 Interest is charged on this opening obligation to the current year.

3 The current service cost is the future obligation attributed to the current period (in this example $136 in each year).

4 The closing obligation is the total of the opening obligation brought forward, the interest charge on that amount and the current year service cost.

5 The calculations in the example above assume that actuarial forecasts are exactly correct. If these were to prove incorrect (which is likely in practice), there could be an adjustment to make, resulting in an actuarial gain or an actuarial loss.

5.5 Interest cost

The interest cost in the income statement is the **present value of the defined benefit obligation** as at the start of the year **multiplied by the discount rate**.

Note that the interest charge is *not* the opening statement of financial position liability multiplied by the discount rate, because the liability is stated after deducting the market value of the plan assets and after making certain other adjustments, for example for actuarial gains or losses. Interest is the **obligation** multiplied by the discount rate.

5.6 The statement of financial position

In the statement of financial position, the amount recognised as a **defined benefit liability** (which may be a negative amount, ie an asset) should be the total of the following.

(a) The **present value of the defined obligation** at the reporting date, **plus**

(b) Any **actuarial gains** or minus any **actuarial losses** that have not yet been recognised, **minus**

(c) Any **past service cost** not yet recognised (if any), **minus**

(d) The **fair value of the assets of the plan** as at the reporting date (if there are any) out of which the future obligations to current and past employees will be directly settled

If this total is a **negative amount**, there is a statement of financial position asset and this should be shown in the statement of financial position as the **lower** of (a) and (b) below.

(a) The figure as calculated above

(b) The total of the present values of:

(i) Any unrecognised actuarial losses and past service costs
(ii) Any refunds expected from the plan
(iii) Any reductions in future contributions to the plan because of the surplus

The determination of a discount rate is covered below.

5.7 The statement of comprehensive income

The **expense** that should be recognised in the income statement for post-employment benefits in a defined benefit plan is the total of the following.

(a) The **current service cost**
(b) **Interest**
(c) The **expected return on any plan assets**
(d) The actuarial gains or losses, to the extent that they are recognised
(e) **Past service cost** to the extent that it is recognised
(f) The effect of any **curtailments** or **settlements**

5.8 Attributing benefit to periods of service

Consider a situation where a defined benefit plan provides for annual pensions for former employees on retirement. The size of the pension is 2.5% of the employee's salary in his/her final year, for each full year of service. The pension is payable from the age of 65.

The post-employment benefit for each employee is an annual pension of 2.5% of his/her final year's salary for every full year of service. This annual payment obligation should first be converted to a present 'lump sum' value *as at the retirement date*, using actuarial assumptions. Having established an obligation as at the expected retirement date, the **current service cost** is calculated as the present value of that obligation, ie the present value of monthly pension payments of 2.5% of final salary, multiplied by the number of years of service up to the reporting date.

For example, if an employee is expected to earn $10,000 in his final year of employment, and is expected to live for 15 years after retirement, the benefit payable for each year of employment would be calculated as the discounted value, as at retirement date, of $250 per annum for 15 years. This should then be converted to a present value (as at the reporting date) to determine the current service cost for the year for that employee.

Probabilities should be taken into consideration in the calculations. Suppose that a benefit of $1,000 for every year of service is payable to employees when they retire at the age of 60, provided that they remain with the employer until they retire (ie that they don't leave to work for someone else). Suppose also that an employee joins the firm at the age of 40, with 20 years to work to retirement.

The benefit attributable to each year of service is $1,000 **multiplied by the probability** that the employee will remain with the employer until he/she is 60. Since the benefit is payable at retirement as a lump sum, it should be discounted to a present value as at the reporting date to determine the current service cost for a given year. The obligation should be calculated as the present value of $40,000 (40 years × $1,000) **multiplied by the same probability**.

No added obligations arise **after all significant post-employment benefits have vested**; in other words, no extra post-benefit obligations arise after an employee has already done everything necessary to qualify in full for the post-employment benefit. Suppose for example that employees have an entitlement to a lump sum payment on retirement of $2,000 for every year they have worked, up to a maximum of 10 years, ie a maximum lump sum payment of $20,000. The benefit vests after 10 years.

In accounting for this **lump sum benefit on retirement**, a benefit of $2,000 should be attributed to each of the first ten years of an employee's service. The current service cost in each of the ten years should be the present value of $2,000. If an employee has 25 years to go to retirement from the time he/she joins the firm, there should be a service cost in each of the first ten years, and none in the 15 years thereafter (other than the interest cost on the obligation).

Question — Service periods

Under Hibbo Co's plan, all employees are paid a lump sum retirement benefit of $100,000. They must be still employed aged 55 after 20 years' service, *or* still employed at the age of 65, no matter what their length of service.

Required

State how this benefit should be attributed to service periods.

Answer

This answer is in three parts.

(a) In the case of those employees joining before age 35, service first leads to benefits under this plan at the age of 35, because an employee could leave at the age of 30 and return at the age of 33, with no effect on the amount/timing of benefits. In addition, service beyond age 55 will lead to no further benefits. Therefore, for these employees Hibbo Co should allocate $100,000 ÷ 20 = $5,000 to each year between the ages of 35 and 55.

(b) In the case of employees joining between the ages of 35 and 45, service beyond 20 years will lead to no further benefit. For these employees, Hibbo Co should allocate $100,000 ÷ 20 = $5,000 to each of the first 20 years.

(c) Employees joining at 55 exactly will receive no further benefit past 65, so Hibbo Co should allocate $100,000 ÷ 10 = $10,000 to each of the first 10 years.

The current service cost and the present value of the obligation for all employees reflect the probability that the employee may not complete the necessary period of service.

5.9 Actuarial assumptions

FAST FORWARD

Actuarial assumptions made should be unbiased and based on market expectations.

Discount rates used should be determined by reference to market yields on high-quality fixed-rate corporate bonds.

Actuarial assumptions are needed **to estimate the size of the future (post-employment) benefits** that will be payable under a defined benefits scheme. The main categories of actuarial assumptions are as follows.

Demographic assumptions	Financial assumptions
• Mortality rates before and after retirement	• Discount rates to apply
• Rate of employee turnover	• Expected return on plan assets
• Early retirement	• Future salary levels (allowing for seniority and promotion as well as inflation)
• Claim rates under medical plans for former employees	• Future rate of increase in medical costs (not just inflationary cost rises, but also cost rises specific to medical treatments and to medical treatments required given the expectations of longer average life expectancy)

The standard requires actuarial assumptions to be neither too cautious nor too imprudent: they should be **'unbiased'**. They should also be based on **'market expectations'** at the reporting date, over the period during which the obligations will be settled.

The **discount rate** adopted should be determined by reference to **market yields** (at the reporting date) on high quality fixed-rate corporate bonds. In the absence of a 'deep' market in such bonds, the yields on comparable government bonds should be used as reference instead. The maturity of the corporate bonds that are used to determine a discount rate should have a term to maturity that is consistent with the expected maturity of the post-employment benefit obligations, although a single weighted average discount rate is sufficient.

The guidelines comment that there may be some difficulty in obtaining a **reliable yield for long-term maturities**, say 30 or 40 years from now. This should not, however, be a significant problem: the present value of obligations payable in many years time will be relatively small and unlikely to be a significant proportion of the total defined benefit obligation. The total obligation is therefore unlikely to be sensitive to errors in the assumption about the discount rate for long-term maturities (beyond the maturities of long-term corporate or government bonds).

5.10 Actuarial gains or losses

FAST FORWARD

Actuarial gains and losses arise for several reasons, but IAS 19 requires only a portion to be recognised, to avoid volatility in the accounts.

Actuarial gains or losses arise because of the following.

- **Actual events** (eg employee turnover, salary increases) differ from the actuarial assumptions that were made to estimate the defined benefit obligations.
- **Actuarial assumptions are revised** (eg a different discount rate is used, or a different assumption is made about future employee turnover, salary rises, mortality rates, and so on)
- **Actual returns on plan assets** differ from expected returns

Since actuarial assumptions are rarely going to be exact, some actuarial gains or losses are inevitable. The proposed standard suggests that, given the inevitability of actuarial gains or losses, they **should not be recognised unless they appear 'significant'**. They are not sufficient to warrant recognition if they fall within a tolerable range or 'corridor'.

The standard requires the following.

(a) An entity should, as a **general rule**, recognise actuarial gains and losses as an item of income or expense (profit or loss), and as part of the deferred benefit liability (statement of financial position).

(b) However, only a portion of such actuarial gains or losses (as calculated above) should be recognised if the **net cumulative actuarial gains/losses exceed** the *greater* of:

    (i) 10% of the present value of the opening defined benefit obligation (ie before deducting plan assets), and

    (ii) 10% of the fair value of the opening plan assets.

A separate calculation should be made for each defined benefit plan: two or more plans should not be aggregated.

The excess calculated under Paragraph 5.10(b) should be **divided by the expected average remaining working lives of participating employees** to give the portion of actuarial gains and losses to be recognised.

However, IAS 19 allows any systematic method to be adopted if it results in **faster recognition** of actuarial gains and losses. The same basis must be applied to both gains and losses and applied consistently between periods.

5.10.1 Immediate recognition – amendment to IAS 19

In December 2004, the IASB issued an amendment to IAS 19. This allows an entity to **recognise actuarial gains and losses immediately** in the period in which it arises, outside profit and loss. These gains and losses need to be presented in the **statement of comprehensive income** as 'other comprehensive income'. If the entity adopts this approach, it must do so:

- For all of its defined benefits plans
- For all of its actuarial gains and losses

This makes IAS 19 more convergent with the UK standard, FRS 17.

In addition, the amendment requires **improved disclosures**, including many also required by FRS 17, and slightly eases the methods whereby the amounts recognised in the consolidated financial statements have to be allocated to individual group companies for the purposes of their own reporting under IFRSs.

5.11 Past service cost

A past service cost arises when an entity either introduces a defined benefits plan or **improves the benefits payable** under an existing plan. As a result, the entity has taken on additional obligations that it has not hitherto provided for. For example, an employer might decide to introduce a medical benefits scheme for former employees. This will create a new defined benefit obligation, that has not yet been provided for. How should this obligation be accounted for?

A past service cost may be in respect of either **current employees or past employees**. IAS 19 has introduced a different accounting treatment for past service costs, according to whether they relate to **current employees or past employees**.

Past employees

The **past service cost** should be **recognised** as **part** of the **defined benefit liability** in the balance sheet.

For the income statement, the past service cost should be **amortised** on a **straight line basis** over the **average period** until the **benefits become vested.**

Current employees

If the change affects them, the past service cost should be recognised in full immediately the plan is introduced or improved (ie because they are immediately 'vested'), as part of the defined benefit liability and as an expense (in full) to the financial period.

Question — Past service costs

Watkins Co operates a pension plan that provides a pension of 2% of final salary for every year of service and the benefits become vested after five years' service. On 1 January 20X6 Watkins Co improved the pension to 2.5% of final salary for every year of service starting from 1 January 20X2.

At the date of improvement, the present value of the additional benefits for service from 1 January 20X2 to 1 January 20X6 is as follows.

	$m
Employees with more than 5 years' service at 1/1/X6	300
Employees with less than 5 years' service at 1/1/X6 (average period until vesting = 3 years	240
	540

Required

State the correct accounting treatment for past service costs.

Answer

Watkins Co should recognise $300m immediately, because these benefits are already vested. $240m should be recognised on a straight-line basis over three years from 1 January 20X6.

5.12 Plan assets

The contributions into a plan by the employer (and employees) are invested, and the plan builds up assets in the form of stocks and shares, etc. The **fair value of these plan assets** are deducted from the defined benefits obligation, in calculating the liability in the statement of financial position. This makes sense, because the employer is not liable to the defined benefits scheme to the extent that the assets of the fund are sufficient to meet those obligations.

The standard includes the following specific requirements.

(a) The fair value of the plan assets should be **net of any transaction costs** that would be incurred in selling them.

(b) The plan assets should **exclude any contributions due** from the employer but not yet paid.

5.13 Return on plan assets

FAST FORWARD

The difference between the **expected return and actual return on plan assets** must be calculated.

It is also necessary to recognise the distinction between:

(a) The **expected return** on the plan assets, which is an actuarial assumption, and
(b) The **actual return** made by the plan assets in a financial period.

The **expected return** on the plan assets is a component element in the income statement, not the actual returns. The **difference between the expected return and the actual return** may also be included in the income statement, but within the actuarial gains or losses. This difference will only be reported if the actuarial gains or losses are outside the 10% corridor for these gains or losses, otherwise they will not be included in the expense item because they are not regarded as significant.

5.14 Example: plan assets

At 1 January 20X2 the fair value of the assets of a defined benefit plan was valued at $1m. Net cumulative actuarial gains and losses were $76,000.

On 31 December 20X2, the plan received contributions from the employer of $490,000 and paid out benefits of $190,000.

After these transactions, the fair value of the plan's assets at 31 December 20X2 were $1.5m. The present value of the defined benefit obligation was $1,479,200 and actuarial losses on the obligation for 20X2 were $6,000.

The expected return on the plan assets (net of investment transaction costs) is 8% per annum.

The reporting entity made the following estimates at 1 January 20X2, based on market prices at that date.

	%
Dividend/interest income (after tax payable by fund)	9.25
Realised and unrealised gains (after tax) on plan assets	2.00
Administration costs	(1.00)
	10.25

Required

Calculate the expected and actual return on plan assets, calculate any actuarial gain or loss and state the required accounting.

Solution

The expected and actual return for 20X2 are as follows.

	$
Return on $1m held for 12 months at 10.25%	102,500
Return on $(490,000 – 190,000) = $300,000	
for 6 months at 5% (ie 10.25% annually compounded every 6 months)	15,000
Expected return on plan assets	117,500

	$
Fair value of plan assets at 31/12/X2	1,500,000
Less fair value of plan assets at 1/1/X2	1,000,000
Less contributions received	(490,000)
Add benefits paid	190,000
Actual return on plan assets	200,000

Actuarial gain = $(200,000 – 117,500) = $82,500.

∴ Cumulative net unrecognised actuarial gains = $(76,000 + 82,500 – 6,000) = $152,500.

The limits of the corridor are set at the *greater* of:

(a) 10% × $1,500,000 = $150,000, and
(b) 10% × $1,479,200 = $147,920.

In 20X3 the entity should recognise an actuarial gain of $(152,500 – 150,000) = $2,500, divided by the expected average remaining working life of the relevant employees.

For 20X3, the expected return on plan assets will be based on market expectations at 1/1/X3 for returns over the entire life of the obligation.

The following accounting treatment is required.

Statement of comprehensive income

In the **statement of comprehensive income**, an expected return on fund assets of $117,500 will be recognised, together with an actuarial gain of $2,500 divided by the expected average remaining useful life of the employees.

Statement of financial position

In the **statement of financial position**, the defined benefit liability will adjust the defined benefit obligation as at 31 December 20X2. The unrecognised actuarial gain (ie the gain within the 10% corridor) should be added, and the market value of the plan assets as at that date should be subtracted.

5.15 Section summary

The recognition and measurement of defined benefit plan costs are complex issues.

- Learn the **outline method** of accounting (see Paragraph 5.3)
- Learn the calculations for the **Projected Unit Credit Method**
- Learn the recognition method for the:
  - Statement of financial position (SOFP)
  - Statement of comprehensive income (SOCI)

6 Defined benefit plans: other matters

FAST FORWARD

You should know how to deal with **curtailments** and **settlements.**

This section looks at the presentation and disclosure of defined benefit plans, but we begin here by looking at the special circumstances of curtailment and settlements.

6.1 Curtailments and settlements

A **curtailment** occurs when an entity cuts back on the benefits available under a defined benefit scheme, so that there is either a significant reduction in the number of employees eligible for the post-employment benefits (eg because a large number of staff have been made redundant due to a plant closure), or there is a reduction in the post-employment benefits that will be given for the future service of current employees.

A **settlement** occurs either when an employer pays off its post-employment benefit obligations in exchange for making a lump sum payment, or when an employer reduces the size of post-employment benefits payable in the future in respect of **past service**.

A curtailment and settlement might **happen together**, for example when an employer brings a defined benefit plan to an end by settling the obligation with a one-off lump sum payment and then scrapping the plan.

Gains or losses arising from the curtailment or settlement of a defined benefit plan should be **recognised in full in the financial year that they occur**. These gains or losses will comprise the following.

- Any **change in the present value of the future obligations** of the entity as a result of the curtailment or settlement
- Any **change in the fair value of the plan assets** as a consequence of the curtailment or settlement
- Any related **actuarial gains/losses** and **past service cost** that had not previously been recognised

An entity should **remeasure the obligation** (and the related plan assets, if any) using current actuarial assumptions, before determining the effect of a curtailment or settlement.

Question

Discontinued

Hewsan Co discontinues a business segment. Employees of the discontinued segment will earn no further benefits (ie this is a curtailment without a settlement). Using current actuarial assumptions (including current market interest rates and other current market prices) immediately before the curtailment, the Hewsan Co had a defined benefit obligation with a net present value of \$500,000, plan assets with a fair value of \$410,000 and net cumulative unrecognised actuarial gains of \$25,000. The entity had first adopted IAS 19 (revised) one year earlier. This increased the net liability by \$50,000, which the entity chose to recognise over five years (this is permitted under the transitional provisions). The curtailment reduces the net present value of the obligation by \$50,000 to \$450,000.

Required

Show the required treatment for the curtailment.

Answer

Of the previously unrecognised actuarial gains and transitional amounts, 10% (\$50,000/\$500,000) relates to the part of the obligation that was eliminated through the curtailment. Therefore, the effect of the curtailment is as follows.

	Before curtailment	*Curtailment gain*	*After curtailment*
	\$'000	\$'000	\$'000
Net present value of obligation	500.0	(50.0)	450.0
Fair value of plan assets	(410.0)	–	(410.0)
	90.0	(50.0)	40.0
Unrecognised actuarial gains	25.0	(2.5)	22.5
Unrecognised transitional amount (\$50,000 × 4/5)	(40.0)	4.0	(36.0)
Net liability recognised in statement of financial position	75.0	(48.5)	26.5

6.2 Suggested approach and questions

The suggested approach to defined benefit schemes is to deal with the change in the obligation and asset in the following order, building up the disclosure notes:

SOCI: Statement of comprehensive income
SOFP: Statement of financial position

Step	Item	Recognition
1	**Record opening figures:** • Asset • Obligation • Any unrecognised gains and losses	
2	**Interest cost** • Based on discount rate and PV obligation at start of period. • Should also reflect any changes in obligation during period.	DEBIT *Interest cost (SOCI) (x% × b/d obligation)* CREDIT *PV defined benefit obligation (SOFP)*
3	**Expected return on plan assets** • Based on long-term expectations as advised by actuary and asset value at start of period. • Technically, the expected return is also time apportioned on contributions less benefits paid in the period.	DEBIT *Plan assets (SOFP)* CREDIT *Exp'd return on plan assets (SOCI) (y% × b/d assets)*
4	**Current service cost** • Increase in the present value of the obligation resulting from employee service in the current period.	DEBIT *Current service cost (SOCI)* CREDIT *PV defined benefit obligation (SOFP)*
5	**Contributions** • As advised by actuary.	DEBIT *Plan assets (SOFP)* CREDIT *Company cash*
6	**Benefits** • Actual pension payments made.	DEBIT *PV defined benefit obligation (SOFP)* CREDIT *Plan assets (SOFP)*
7	**Past service cost** • Increase in PV obligation as a result of introduction or improvement of benefits. • Past service cost is *vested* when any minimum employment period has been completed.	**Vested benefits:** DEBIT *Past service cost (SOCI)* CREDIT *PV defined benefit obligation (SOFP)* **Non-vested benefits:** DEBIT *Unrecognised past service cost (SOFP)* CREDIT *PV defined benefit obligation (SOFP)* The unrecognised past service cost is amortised through profit or loss straight line over the average period until the minimum employment period is completed.
8	**Actuarial gains and losses** • Arising from annual valuations of obligation and asset. • On obligation, differences between actuarial assumptions and actual experience during the period, or changes in actuarial assumptions. • On assets, differences between expected and actual return.	(a) *(only if using corridor approach):* recognise unrecognised gains/losses b/d outside 10% corridor in profit or loss over average remaining working lives of employees. (b) Calculate carried down actuarial gains/losses from statement of financial position workings. Recognise in: – Unrecognised gains/losses, *or* – Profit or loss directly, *or* – Retained earnings directly according to accounting policy.
9	**Disclose in accordance with the standard**	See comprehensive question.

Question

During the year ended 30 November 20X3, the directors of Pole decided to form a defined benefit pension scheme for the employees of the company and contributed cash of $160 million to it. The following details relate to the scheme at 30 November 20X3:

	$m
Present value of obligation	208
Fair value of plan assets	200
Current service cost	176
Interest cost – scheme liabilities	32
Expected return on pension scheme assets	16

The only entry in the financial statements made to date is in respect of the cash contribution which has been included in trade receivables. The directors have been uncertain as to how to deal with the above pension scheme in the consolidated financial statements because of the significance of the potential increase in the charge to profit or loss (in the income statements) relating to the pension scheme. They wish to recognise any actuarial gain immediately.

Required

Show how the defined benefit pension scheme should be dealt with in the financial statements for the year ended 30 November 20X3.

Answer

The defined benefit pension scheme is treated in accordance with IAS 19 *Employee benefits.*

The pension scheme has a deficit of liabilities over assets:

	$m
Fair value of plan assets	200
Less: present value of obligation	(208)
	(8)

The deficit is reported as a liability in the statement of financial position.

The statement of comprehensive income for the year includes:

	$m
Current service cost	176
Interest cost	32
Expected return on plan assets	(16)
	192

The company proposes to recognise the $24,000,000 actuarial gain, although under IAS 19 it is not required to do so. IAS 19 requires actuarial gains and losses at the end of the previous accounting period to be recognised using the '10% corridor approach'. Alternatively, they may be recognised more quickly, or immediately. There were no actuarial gains or losses at the start of the current period.

However, recognising the gain provides useful information to users of the financial statements, given that the pension scheme is new and results in a significant additional charge to profit or loss. Under IAS 19 an actuarial gain cannot be recognised in profit or loss, but must be taken to equity (reserves). The statement of changes in equity for the year includes:

	$m
Actuarial gain on defined benefit pension scheme assets	24

Adjustment to the financial statements:

DEBIT	Retained earnings	$168 million
CREDIT	Receivables	$160 million
CREDIT	Defined benefit pension scheme liability	$8 million

Working

	$m
Scheme assets:	
Contributions paid	160
Expected return on plan assets	16
Actuarial gain (balancing figure)	24
Fair value of plan assets	200
Scheme liabilities:	
Current service cost	176
Interest cost	32
Present value of obligation	208
Net pension liability	8

Exam focus point

It would be useful for you to do one last question on accounting for post employment defined benefit schemes. Questions on these are likely in the exam.

Question

Comprehensive

For the sake of simplicity and clarity, all transactions are assumed to occur at the year end.

The following data applies to the post employment defined benefit compensation scheme of an entity.

Expected return on plan assets: 12% (each year)
Discount rate: 10% (each year)
Present value of obligation at start of 20X2: $1m
Market value of plan assets at start of 20X2: $1m

The following figures are relevant.

	20X2	*20X3*	*20X4*
	$'000	$'000	$'000
Current service cost	140	150	150
Benefits paid out	120	140	150
Contributions paid by entity	110	120	120
Present value of obligation at year end	1,200	1,600	1,700
Market value of plan assets at year end	1,250	1,450	1,610

Required

Show how the reporting entity should account for this defined benefit plan in each of years 20X2, 20X3 and 20X4. Actuarial gains and losses outside the 10% corridor are to be recognised in full in profit or loss for the year.

Answer

The actuarial gain or loss is established as a balancing figure in the calculations, as follows.

Present value of obligation

	20X2	*20X3*	*20X4*
	$'000	$'000	$'000
PV of obligation at start of year	1,000	1,200	1,600
Interest cost (10%)	100	120	160
Current service cost	140	150	150
Benefits paid	(120)	(140)	(150)
Actuarial (gain)/loss on obligation: balancing figure	80	270	(60)
PV of obligation at end of year	1,200	1,600	1,700

Market value of plan assets

	20X2	*20X3*	*20X4*
	$'000	$'000	$'000
Market value of plan assets at start of year	1,000	1,250	1,450
Expected return on plan assets (12%)	120	150	174
Contributions	110	120	120
Benefits paid	(120)	(140)	(150)
Actuarial gain/(loss) on plan assets: balancing figure	140	70	16
Market value of plan assets at year end	1,250	1,450	1,610

10% corridor

The next step is to determine whether the actuarial gains or losses exceed the tolerance limit of the 10% corridor. The 10% limit is 10% of the higher amount of the PV of the opening obligation (before deducting the plan assets) and the opening plan assets.

	20X2	*20X3*	*20X4*
	$'000	$'000	$'000
Limit of corridor	100	125	160
Unrecognised actuarial gains/(losses)	–	60	(140)
Actuarial gain/(loss) for year: obligation	(80)	(270)	60
Actuarial gain/(loss) for year: plan assets	140	70	16
Sub-total	60	(140)	(64)
Actuarial gain/(loss) realised	–	–	–
Unrecognised actuarial gains/(losses)	60	(140)	(64)

The actuarial loss recognised in 20X2 is nil. This is because the figure for the cumulative unrecognised actuarial gains/losses at the start of 20X2 is nil. This is less than the corridor limit of $100,000.

Similarly, the actuarial loss recognised in 20X3 is nil. This is because the figure for cumulative unrecognised actuarial gains brought forward at the **beginning** of the year of $60,000 is less than the corridor limit of $125,000.

In the statement of financial position, the liability that is recognised is calculated as follows.

	20X2	*20X3*	*20X4*
	$'000	$'000	$'000
Present value of obligation	1,200	1,600	1,700
Market value of plan assets	1,250	1,450	1,610
	(50)	150	90
Unrecognised actuarial gains/(losses)	60	(140)	(64)
Liability/(asset) in statement of financial position	10	10	26

The statement of comprehensive income will recognise the following.

	20X2	*20X3*	*20X4*
	$'000	$'000	$'000
Current service cost	140	150	150
Interest cost	100	120	160
Expected return on plan assets	(120)	(150)	(174)
Net actuarial (gain)/loss recognised in the year			
Expense recognised in profit or loss	120	120	136

7 Special cases

We have now covered the major parts of IAS 19 (revised), but the standard goes on to discuss certain other matters which we will cover briefly here. The transitional arrangements are quite important due to the **long-term effect** of post-retirement benefits and we will look at these at the end of the section.

7.1 Other long-term employment benefits

There may be other long-term employment benefits, in addition to post-employment benefits. These include **bonuses** and **profit shares** payable 12 months or more after the reporting date, and **long-term sabbatical leave**.

The standard requires these benefits to be accounted for **in the same way as post-employment defined benefits**, but with two major differences.

(a) **Actuarial gains or losses** should be recognised in full immediately in the financial year they become apparent, and there should be no 10% corridor.

(b) All **past service cost** for current as well as past employees should be recognised as an expense in full immediately.

There are no specific disclosure requirements with respect to these benefits.

7.2 Termination benefits

Termination benefits are benefits to employees arising as a consequence of **termination of their employment**. An example is the payment of a lump sum to an employee who volunteers for early retirement.

The standard recommends that these costs should be recognised in full as a liability and an expense in the financial period when the entity recognises a **demonstrable obligation** to pay those benefits at some time in the future. Evidence of a demonstrable obligation would be a formal plan (eg a plan for voluntary redundancy) drawn up and communicated to the people affected.

If the termination is to take place over 12 months after the reporting date, the termination benefits should be **discounted**. The discount rate should be found as detailed elsewhere in the standard.

Where an offer is made to encourage **voluntary redundancy**, the calculation should be based on the number of employees expected to accept.

8 Other issues and recent developments

8.1 Problems with IAS 19

Accounting for employee benefits, particularly retirement benefits, has been seen as **problematic** in the following respects:

(a) **Income statement (statement of comprehensive income) treatment.** It has been argued that the complexity of the presentation makes the treatment hard to understand and the splitting up of the various components is arbitrary.

(b) **Fair value and volatility.** The fair value of plan assets may be volatile, and values in the statement of financial position may fluctuate. However, not all those fluctuations are recognised in the statement of financial position.

(c) **Fair value and economic reality.** Fair value, normally market value, is used to value plan assets. This may not reflect economic reality, because fair values fluctuate in the short term, while pension scheme assets and liabilities are held for the long term. It could be argued that plan assets should be valued on an actuarial basis instead.

(d) **Problems in determining the discount rate used in measuring the defined benefit obligation.** Guidance is contradictory.

FAST FORWARD

An **ED** contains proposals on termination benefits, and a recent **Discussion Paper** proposes improvements to accounting for employee benefits.

An Exposure Draft issued in June 2005 proposed amendments to IAS 19.

Key term

Termination benefits are defined as employee benefits provided in connection with the termination of an employee's employment. 'Involuntary' termination benefits arise from an entity's decision to terminate an employee's employment, whereas 'voluntary' termination benefits arise from an employee's decision to accept voluntary termination.

8.2 ED proposals

(a) Termination benefits are to be defined as employee benefits provided **in connection with the termination of an employee's employment**.

(b) Termination benefits may be **either 'involuntary'** (provided as a result of an entity's decision to terminate an employee's employment) **or 'voluntary'** (offered for a short period of time in exchange for an employee's decision to accept voluntary termination).

(c) Benefits offered to encourage employees to leave service early are voluntary termination benefits **only if they are offered for a short period.**

(d) **A liability and expense** for **voluntary** termination benefits should be **recognised** when the **employee accepts the entity's offer** to those termination benefits.

(e) A liability and expense **for involuntary termination benefits**, except where provided in exchange for the employees' future services, should be **recognised when the entity has a plan of termination that it has communicated to the employees** and the plan meets the criteria specified in the Standard.

(f) **Involuntary termination benefits** are provided in exchange for employees' future services if they:

   (i) Are **incremental** to what the employees would otherwise be entitled to receive (ie benefits are not provided in accordance with the terms of an ongoing benefit plan)

   (ii) Do not **vest** until the employment is **terminated**

   (iii) Are provided to employees who will be **retained beyond the minimum retention period**. The minimum retention period will normally be the period of notice an entity is required to provide employees in advance of terminating their employment

(g) Where **involuntary** termination benefits are provided in exchange for employees' future service the termination benefits are **recognised as a liability and expense over the period of future service**.

(h) Where termination benefits are provided as an **enhancement** of retirement benefits the liability and expense recognised initially includes **only the value of the additional benefits** that arise from the provision of the termination benefits.

8.3 Discussion Paper

In March 2008, the IASB issued a Discussion Paper *Preliminary Views on Amendments to IAS 19 Employee Benefits.* The purpose of the Discussion Paper is to improve accounting in the short-term for employee benefits in the light of criticisms of the current IAS 19 by users and preparers of financial statements, including the US SEC and the EU's European Financial Reporting Advisory Group (that approves IFRS for use in the EU). In the long term, the IASB intends to produce a common IASB-FASB standard, but recognises that this will take many years to complete.

8.3.1 Scope

Because the Paper is a short-term measure, its **scope is limited to** the following areas.

(a) Deferred recognition of some gains and losses arising from defined benefit plans

(b) Presentation of changes in value of the defined benefit obligation and assets

(c) Accounting for benefits that are based on contributions and a promised return
(d) Accounting for benefit promises with a 'higher of' option.

However, the IASB recognises that the scope **could be expanded** to include items such as:

(a) **Recognition of the obligation based on the 'benefit' formula.** This current approach means that unvested benefits are recognised as a liability which is inconsistent with other IFRSs.
(b) **Measurement of the obligation.** The 'projected unit credit method' (as defined before) is used which is based on expected benefits (including salary increases). Alternative approaches include accumulated benefit, projected benefit, fair value and settlement value.
(c) **Presenting of a net defined benefit obligation.** Defined benefit plan assets and liabilities are currently presented net on the grounds that the fund is not controlled (which would require consolidation of the fund).
(d) **Multi-employer plans.** Current accounting is normally for the entity's proportionate share of the obligation, plan assets and costs as for a single-employer plan, but an exemption is currently provided where sufficient information is not available, and defined contribution accounting can be used instead. Should the exemption be removed?

8.3.2 Preliminary discussions

(a) **Deferred recognition**

- (i) This (ie the corridor method) is to be eliminated. Actuarial gains and losses to be recognised in the period incurred.
- (ii) The actual return on assets would not be divided into expected return and actuarial gain/loss.
- (iii) Past service costs would be recognised in the period of plan amendment.

(b) **Presentation of changes in value of the defined benefit obligation and assets**

Possible options are as follows:

- (i) Show all in profit or loss in the period incurred
- (ii) Include all costs of service in profit or loss, all other changes in other comprehensive income
- (iii) Re-measurements arising from changes in financial assumptions (that is, changes in the discount rate for liabilities and changes in plan assets) in other comprehensive income, all other changes in profit or loss.

(c) **Benefits based on contributions plus a promised return on assets**

- (i) Arguably these are not faithfully represented under current approach
- (ii) It is proposed to measure the liability for contribution-based promises at fair value (as a separate category; as consideration of the projected unit credit method approach to measuring the defined benefit liability itself deferred to a later date)
- (iii) Changes are to be disaggregated into a service cost and other value changes (but both recognised in profit or loss).

(d) **Benefit promises with a 'higher of' option**

- (i) These occur where a plan member will receive the higher of a defined benefit pension or contributions plus a promised return on assets.
- (ii) In substance there is an embedded option/guarantee.
- (iii) The liability may be underestimated under the current IAS 19 approach.
- (iv) It is proposed to separate out the 'higher of' option and separately measure it at fair value assuming the terms of the benefit promise do not change (with all changes in the option value recognised in profit or loss).

8.3.3 ASB and discount rate

Some of the above issues have been considered in a January 2008 Discussion Paper from the UK Accounting Standards Board in the context of FRS 17 *Retirement benefits*.

Curently the techniques used to quantify pension liabilities rely on a number of assumptions, including the return that is expected to be made on assets in the time before the benefit will be paid. The paper notes that this is not appropriate because it does not reflect the present economic burden of the liability. The proposal in the Discussion Paper is that the liability should be **quantified** for financial reporting purposes **at an assessment of the cost of settling the benefit**, which will typically **reflect all future cash flows**. Information about the riskiness of the liability would be conveyed by disclosure rather than by adjusting the liability. According **the cash flows should be discounted at the risk-free rate**.

8.4 Exposure Draft: Defined benefit plans

In April 2010, the IASB published for public comment an exposure draft (ED) of proposed amendments to IAS 19 *Employee Benefits*. The proposals would amend the accounting for defined benefit plans through which some employers provide **long-term employee benefits**, such as pensions and post-employment medical care.

In defined benefit plans, employers bear the risk of increases in costs and of possible poor investment performance.

The ED proposes improvements to the recognition, presentation, and disclosure of defined benefit plans. The ED does not address measurement of defined benefit plans or the accounting for contribution-based benefit promises.

8.4.1 Elimination of 'corridor' and other methods of recognition

All estimated changes in the cost of providing defined benefits and all changes in the value of plan assets would be **recognised immediately.** Methods which defer some of these gains and losses, including the corridor method, would no longer be allowed.

8.4.2 New presentation approach

A new approach to presentation is proposed. This would distinguish between the different types of gains and losses arising from defined benefit plans.

Recognise in profit or loss	Recognise in other comprehensive income
• Current service cost • Past service costs • Finance cost (ie net interest on the net defined benefit liability) – as part of finance costs in profit or loss	Re-measurements, that is: • Actuarial gains and losses on the obligation • Actual return on plan assets (excluding application of interest to asset included in net defined benefit obligation) • Any effect of the asset ceiling test

8.4.3 Improved disclosures

The exposure draft proposes improved disclosures, focused on specified objectives, including disclosures about:

(a) The characteristics of an entity's defined benefit plans and the amounts in the financial statements resulting from those plans.

(b) Risk arising from defined benefit plans, including sensitivity analyses of changes in demographic risk.

(c) Participation in multi-employer plans.

The proposal to require immediate recognition of actuarial gains and losses would mean that the proposed standard would not require disclosures about deferred recognition of those items.

Chapter Roundup

- IAS 19 *Employee benefits* is a long and complex standard covering both short-term and long-term (post employment) benefits. The complications arise when dealing with **post-employment benefits**.
- Accounting for short-term employee benefits is fairly straightforward, because there are **no actuarial assumptions** to be made, and there is **no requirement to discount** future benefits (because they are all, by definition, payable no later than 12 months after the end of the accounting period)
- There are **two types of post-employment benefit plan**:
  - Defined contribution plans
  - Defined benefit plans
- **Defined contribution plans** are simple to account for as the benefits are defined by the contributions made.
- **Defined benefit plans** are much more difficult to deal with as the benefits are promised, they define the contributions to be made.
- There is a **six-step method** for accounting for the expenses and liability of a defined benefit pension plan.
- Future benefits are attributed to services performed by employees using the **Projected Unit Credit Method**.
- **Actuarial assumptions** made should be unbiased and based on market expectations.
- **Discount rates** used should be determined by reference to market yields on high-quality fixed-rate corporate bonds.
- **Actuarial gains and losses** arise for several reasons, but IAS 19 requires only a portion to be recognised, to avoid volatility in the accounts.
- The difference between the **expected return and actual return on plan assets** must be calculated.
- You should know how to deal with **curtailments** and **settlements**.
- An **ED** contains proposals on termination benefits, and a recent **Discussion Paper** proposes improvements to accounting for employee benefits.

Quick Quiz

1. What are the five categories of employee benefits given by IAS 19?
2. What is the difference between defined contribution and defined benefit plans?
3. What is a 'constructive obligation' compared to a legal obligation?
4. How should a defined benefit expense be recognised in the income statement?
5. What causes actuarial gains or losses?
6. How should termination benefits be recognised?

   A Provided for as part of the costs of employment when incurred
   B Part of a special provision for future liabilities
   C Recognised in full as a liability and expense when a future obligation is recognised
   D Amortised over the period of employment

7. How should equity compensation benefits be treated?

Answers to Quick Quiz

1
- Short-term
- Post-employment
- Other long-term
- Termination
- Equity compensation

2 See Section 3

3 A constructive obligation exists when the entity has no realistic alternative than to pay employee benefits.

4 Current service cost + interest + expected return + recognised actuarial gains/losses + past service cost + curtailments or settlements.

5 See Section 5.10

6 C Recognised in full as a liability and an expense in the accounting period when the entity recognises a demonstrable obligation to pay the benefits in the future.

7 Amount held at the beginning and end of the period, and amounts issued to the scheme, or employees, during the period.

Now try the questions below from the Exam Question Bank

Number	Level	Marks	Time
Q13	Introductory	n/a	n/a

Financial instruments

10

Topic list	Syllabus reference
1 Financial instruments	2(g)
2 Presentation of financial instruments	2(g)
3 Recognition of financial instruments	2(g)
4 Measurement of financial instruments	2(g)
5 Hedge accounting	2(g)
6 Reducing complexity	2(g)
7 Amended reclassification rules	2(g)
8 IFRS 9 and other current issues	2(g)
9 Disclosure of financial instruments	2(g)

Introduction

Financial instruments sounds like a daunting subject, and indeed this is a complex and controversial area. The numbers involved in financial instruments are often huge, but don't let this put you off. In this chapter we aim to simplify the topic as much as possible and to focus on the important issues.

IFRS 9, the most recent standard on financial instruments is a work in progress and only replaces with certain parts of IAS 39. In addition, it is not yet in force. Accordingly, it is dealt with as a current issue, and in terms of contrasts with IAS 39.

Study Guide

Section 8 – Financial Instruments

- Account for debt instruments, equity instruments and the allocation of finance costs
- Account for fixed interest rate and convertible bonds
- Discuss the definition and classification of a financial instrument
- Discuss the measurement issues relating to financial instruments
- Explain the current measurement proposals for financial instruments including the use of current values, hedging and the treatment of gains and losses
- Describe the nature of the disclosures requirements relating to financial instruments
- Discuss the key areas where consensus is required on the accounting treatment of financial instruments

Exam Guide

This topic is highly controversial and therefore likely to be examined. It can be examined in any part of the exam; the groups question would lend itself to a focus on calculations, while the remaining questions lend themselves to a more discursive requirement.

Exam focus point

Although the complexity of this topic makes it a highly likely subject for an exam question, there are limits as to how complicated and detailed a question the examiner can set. You should therefore concentrate on the essential points. Financial instruments have mainly been examined as part of a larger question. Candidates have been asked to explain the specific financial reporting implications of particular financial instruments.

The December 2007 paper included a whole question with discursive and numerical parts on IAS 32 and IAS 39. The June 2008 paper tested convertible bonds as part of a longer question, and in December 2008 a longer question tested hedge accounting rules in respect of a derivative. The Pilot Paper for exams in 2011 examined financial instruments in more than one place.

1 Financial instruments

FAST FORWARD

Financial instruments can be very complex, particularly **derivative instruments**, although **primary instruments** are more straightforward.

1.1 Background

If you read the financial press you will probably be aware of **rapid international expansion** in the use of financial instruments. These vary from straightforward, traditional instruments, eg bonds, through to various forms of so-called 'derivative instruments'.

We can perhaps summarise the reasons why a project on the accounting for financial instruments was considered necessary as follows.

(a) The **significant growth of financial instruments** over recent years has outstripped the development of guidance for their accounting.

(b) The topic is of **international concern**, other national standard-setters are involved as well as the IASB.

(c) There have been recent **high-profile disasters** involving derivatives (eg Barings) which, while not caused by accounting failures, have raised questions about accounting and disclosure practices.

There are four Standards on financial instruments:

(a) IAS 32 *Financial instruments: Presentation*, which deals with:

  (i) The classification of financial instruments between liabilities and equity
  (ii) Presentation of certain compound instruments

(b) IFRS 7 *Financial instruments: Disclosures*, which revised, simplified and incorporated disclosure requirements previously in IAS 32.

(c) IAS 39 *Financial instruments: Recognition and measurement*, which deals with:
   (i) Recognition and derecognition
   (ii) The measurement of financial instruments
   (iii) Hedge accounting

(d) IFRS 9 *Financial Instruments*, issued in November 2009, replaced certain parts of IAS 39, in particular with respect to the classification of financial assets. This standard is a work in progress and in due course will be developed further to fully replace IAS 39.

1.2 Definitions

The most important definitions are common to all four Standards.

FAST FORWARD

The important definitions to understand are:

- **Financial asset**
- **Financial liability**
- **Equity instrument**

Key terms

Financial instrument. Any contract that gives rise to both a financial asset of one entity and a financial liability or equity instrument of another entity.

Financial asset. Any asset that is:

(a) Cash
(b) An equity instrument of another entity
(c) A contractual right to receive cash or another financial asset from another entity; or to exchange financial instruments with another entity under conditions that are potentially favourable to the entity, or
(d) A contract that will or may be settled in the entity's own equity instruments and is:
   (i) A non-derivative for which the entity is or may be obliged to receive a variable number of the entity's own equity instruments; or
   (ii) A derivative that will or may be settled other than by the exchange of a fixed amount of cash or another financial asset for a fixed number of the entity's own equity instruments.

Financial liability. Any liability that is:

(a) A contractual obligation:
   (i) To deliver cash or another financial asset to another entity, or
   (ii) To exchange financial instruments with another entity under conditions that are potentially unfavourable; or
(b) A contract that will or may be settled in the entity's own equity instruments and is:
   (i) A non-derivative for which the entity is or may be obliged to deliver a variable number of the entity's own equity instruments; or
   (ii) a derivative that will or may be settled other than by the exchange of a fixed amount of cash or another financial asset for a fixed number of the entity's own equity instruments.

Equity instrument. Any contract that evidences a residual interest in the assets of an entity after deducting all of its liabilities.

Fair value is the amount for which an asset could be exchanged, or a liability settled, between knowledgeable, willing parties in an arm's length transaction

Key terms (cont'd)

> **Derivative.** A financial instrument or other contract with all three of the following characteristics:
>
> (a) Its value changes in response to the change in a specified interest rate, financial instrument price, commodity price, foreign exchange rate, index of prices or rates, credit rating or credit index, or other variable (sometimes called the 'underlying')
>
> (b) It requires no initial net investment or an initial net investment that is smaller than would be required for other types of contracts that would be expected to have a similar response to changes in market factors; and
>
> (c) It is settled at a future date. *(IAS 32 and IAS 39)*

Exam focus point

> These definitions are very important – particularly the first three – so understand them.

We should clarify some points arising from these definitions. Firstly, one or two terms above should be themselves defined.

(a) A '**contract**' need not be in writing, but it must comprise an agreement that has 'clear economic consequences' and which the parties to it cannot avoid, usually because the agreement is enforceable in law.

(b) An '**entity**' here could be an individual, partnership, incorporated body or government agency.

The definitions of **financial assets and financial liabilities** may seem rather circular, referring as they do to the terms financial asset and financial instrument. The point is that there may be a chain of contractual rights and obligations, but it will lead ultimately to the receipt or payment of cash *or* the acquisition or issue of an equity instrument.

Examples of **financial assets** include:

(a) Trade receivables
(b) Options
(c) Shares (when used as an investment).

Examples of **financial liabilities** include:

(a) Trade payables
(b) Debenture loans payable
(c) Redeemable preference (non-equity) shares
(d) Forward contracts standing at a loss.

As we have already noted, financial instruments include both of the following.

(a) **Primary instruments**: eg receivables, payables and equity securities

(b) **Derivative instruments**: eg financial options, futures and forwards, interest rate swaps and currency swaps, **whether recognised or unrecognised**

IAS 32 makes it clear that the following items are *not* financial instruments.

- **Physical assets**, eg inventories, property, plant and equipment, leased assets and intangible assets (patents, trademarks etc)
- **Prepaid expenses**, deferred revenue and most warranty obligations
- Liabilities or assets that are **not contractual** in nature
- Contractual rights/obligations that **do not involve transfer of a financial asset**, eg commodity futures contracts, operating leases

Question — Why not?

Can you give the reasons why the first two items listed above do not qualify as financial instruments?

Answer

Refer to the definitions of financial assets and liabilities given above.

(a) **Physical assets**: control of these creates an opportunity to generate an inflow of cash or other assets, but it does not give rise to a present right to receive cash or other financial assets.

(b) **Prepaid expenses, etc**: the future economic benefit is the receipt of goods/services rather than the right to receive cash or other financial assets.

(c) **Deferred revenue, warranty obligations**: the probable outflow of economic benefits is the delivery of goods/services rather than cash or another financial asset.

Contingent rights and obligations meet the definition of financial assets and financial liabilities respectively, even though many do not qualify for recognition in financial statements. This is because the contractual rights or obligations exist because of a past transaction or event (eg assumption of a guarantee).

1.3 Derivatives

A **derivative** is a financial instrument that **derives** its value from the price or rate of an underlying item. Common **examples** of derivatives include:

(a) **Forward contracts**: agreements to buy or sell an asset at a fixed price at a fixed future date

(b) **Futures contracts**: similar to forward contracts except that contracts are standardised and traded on an exchange

(c) **Options**: rights (but not obligations) for the option holder to exercise at a pre-determined price; the option writer loses out if the option is exercised

(d) **Swaps**: agreements to swap one set of cash flows for another (normally interest rate or currency swaps)

The nature of derivatives often gives rise to **particular problems**. The **value** of a derivative (and the amount at which it is eventually settled) depends on **movements** in an underlying item (such as an exchange rate). This means that settlement of a derivative can lead to a very different result from the one originally envisaged. A company which has derivatives is exposed to **uncertainty and risk** (potential for gain or loss) and this can have a very material effect on its financial performance, financial position and cash flows.

Yet because a derivative contract normally has **little or no initial cost**, under traditional accounting it **may not be recognised** in the financial statements at all. Alternatively it may be recognised at an amount which bears no relation to its current value. This is clearly **misleading** and leaves users of the financial statements unaware of the **level of risk** that the company faces. IASs 32 and 39 were developed in order to correct this situation.

1.4 Section summary

- Four accounting standards are relevant:
  - **IAS 32**: *Financial instruments: Presentation*
  - **IFRS 7**: *Financial instruments: Disclosures*
  - **IAS 39**: *Financial instruments: Recognition and measurement*
  - **IFRS 9**: *Financial instruments* (a 'work in progress')
- The definitions of **financial asset, financial liability** and **equity instrument** are fundamental to the standards.
- Financial instruments include:
  - **Primary** instruments
  - **Derivative** instruments

2 Presentation of financial instruments

2.1 Objective

The objective of IAS 32 is:

'to enhance financial statement users' understanding of the significance of on-balance sheet and off-balance sheet financial instruments to an entity's financial position, performance and cash flows.'

2.2 Scope

IAS 32 should be applied in the presentation of **all types of financial instruments**, whether recognised or unrecognised.

Certain items are **excluded**.

- Interests in subsidiaries (IAS 27: Chapter 20)
- Interests in associates (IAS 28: Chapter 23)
- Interests in joint ventures (IAS 31: Chapter 24)
- Pensions and other post-retirement benefits (IAS 19: Chapter 9)
- Insurance contracts
- Contracts for contingent consideration in a business combination
- Contracts that require a payment based on climatic, geological or other physical variables
- Financial instruments, contracts and obligations under share-based payment transactions (IFRS 2: Chapter 14)

2.3 Liabilities and equity

FAST FORWARD

Financial instruments must be classified as **liabilities** or **equity** according to their **substance.**

The critical feature of a financial liability is the **contractual obligation to deliver cash** or another financial asset.

The main thrust of IAS 32 here is that financial instruments should be presented according to their **substance**, **not merely their legal form**. In particular, entities which issue financial instruments should classify them (or their component parts) as **either financial liabilities, or equity**.

The classification of a financial instrument as a liability or as equity depends on the following.

- The substance of the contractual arrangement on initial recognition
- The definitions of a financial liability and an equity instrument

How should a **financial liability be distinguished from an equity instrument**? The critical feature of a **liability** is an **obligation** to transfer economic benefit. Therefore a financial instrument is a financial liability if there is a **contractual obligation** on the issuer either to deliver cash or another financial asset to the holder or to exchange another financial instrument with the holder under potentially unfavourable conditions to the issuer.

The financial liability exists **regardless of the way in which the contractual obligation will be settled**. The issuer's ability to satisfy an obligation may be restricted, eg by lack of access to foreign currency, but this is irrelevant as it does not remove the issuer's obligation or the holder's right under the instrument.

Where the above critical feature is *not* met, then the financial instrument is an **equity instrument**. IAS 32 explains that although the holder of an equity instrument may be entitled to a *pro rata* share of any distributions out of equity, the issuer does *not* have a contractual obligation to make such a distribution.

Although substance and legal form are often **consistent with each other**, this is not always the case. In particular, a financial instrument may have the legal form of equity, but in substance it is in fact a liability. Other instruments may combine features of both equity instruments and financial liabilities.

For example, many entities issue **preferred shares** which must be **redeemed** by the issuer for a fixed (or determinable) amount at a fixed (or determinable) future date. Alternatively, the holder may have the right to require the issuer to redeem the shares at or after a certain date for a fixed amount. In such cases, the issuer has an **obligation**. Therefore the instrument is a **financial liability** and should be classified as such.

The classification of the financial instrument is made when it is **first recognised** and this classification will continue until the financial instrument is removed from the entity's statement of financial position.

2.4 Contingent settlement provisions

An entity may issue a financial instrument where the way in which it is settled depends on:

(a) The occurrence or non-occurrence of uncertain future events, or
(b) The outcome of uncertain circumstances,

that are beyond the control of both the holder and the issuer of the instrument. For example, an entity might have to deliver cash instead of issuing equity shares. In this situation it is not immediately clear whether the entity has an equity instrument or a financial liability.

Such financial instruments should be classified as **financial liabilities** unless the possibility of settlement is remote.

2.5 Settlement options

When a derivative financial instrument gives one party a **choice** over how it is settled (eg, the issuer can choose whether to settle in cash or by issuing shares) the instrument is a **financial asset** or a **financial liability** unless **all the alternative choices** would result in it being an equity instrument.

2.6 Compound financial instruments

FAST FORWARD

Compound instruments are split into **equity** and **liability** components and presented accordingly in the statement of financial position.

Some financial instruments contain both a liability and an equity element. In such cases, IAS 32 requires the component parts of the instrument to be **classified separately**, according to the substance of the contractual arrangement and the definitions of a financial liability and an equity instrument.

One of the most common types of compound instrument is **convertible debt**. This creates a primary financial liability of the issuer and grants an option to the holder of the instrument to convert it into an equity instrument (usually ordinary shares) of the issuer. This is the economic equivalent of the issue of conventional debt plus a warrant to acquire shares in the future.

Although in theory there are several possible ways of calculating the split, the following method is recommended by IAS32:

(a) Calculate the value for the liability component.
(b) Deduct this from the instrument as a whole to leave a residual value for the equity component.

The reasoning behind this approach is that an entity's equity is its residual interest in its assets amount after deducting all its liabilities.

The **sum of the carrying amounts** assigned to liability and equity will always be equal to the carrying amount that would be ascribed to the instrument **as a whole**.

2.7 Example: valuation of compound instruments

Rathbone Co issues 2,000 convertible bonds at the start of 20X2. The bonds have a three year term, and are issued at par with a face value of $1,000 per bond, giving total proceeds of $2,000,000. Interest is payable annually in arrears at a nominal annual interest rate of 6%. Each bond is convertible at any time up to maturity into 250 common shares.

When the bonds are issued, the prevailing market interest rate for similar debt without conversion options is 9%. At the issue date, the market price of one common share is $3. The dividends expected over the three year term of the bonds amount to 14c per share at the end of each year. The risk-free annual interest rate for a three year term is 5%.

Required

What is the value of the equity component in the bond?

Solution

The liability component is valued first, and the difference between the proceeds of the bond issue and the fair value of the liability is assigned to the equity component. The present value of the liability component is calculated using a discount rate of 9%, the market interest rate for similar bonds having no conversion rights, as shown.

	$
Present value of the principal: $2,000,000 payable at the end of three years ($2m × 0.772)*	1,544,000
Present value of the interest: $120,000 payable annually in arrears for three years ($120,000 × 2.531)*	303,725
Total liability component	1,847,720
Equity component (balancing figure)	152,280
Proceeds of the bond issue	2,000,000

* These figures can be obtained from discount and annuity tables (0.772 = DF 3 years @ 9%; 2.531 = AF 3 years @ 9%).

The split between the liability and equity components remains the same throughout the term of the instrument, even if there are changes in the **likelihood of the option being exercised.** This is because it is not always possible to predict how a holder will behave. The issuer continues to have an obligation to make future payments until conversion, maturity of the instrument or some other relevant transaction takes place.

2.8 Treasury shares

If an entity **reacquires its own equity instruments**, those instruments ('treasury shares') shall be **deducted from equity**. No gain or loss shall be recognised in profit or loss on the purchase, sale, issue or cancellation of an entity's own equity instruments. Consideration paid or received shall be recognised directly in equity.

2.9 Interest, dividends, losses and gains

As well as looking at statement of financial position presentation, IAS 32 considers how financial instruments affect the profit or loss (and movements in equity). The treatment varies according to whether interest, dividends, losses or gains relate to a financial liability or an equity instrument.

(a) Interest, dividends, losses and gains relating to a financial instrument (or component part) classified as a **financial liability** should be recognised as **income or expense** in profit or loss.

(b) Distributions to holders of a financial instrument classified as an **equity instrument** should be **debited directly to equity** by the issuer.

(c) **Transaction costs** of an equity transaction shall be accounted for as a **deduction from equity** (unless they are directly attributable to the acquisition of a business, in which case they are accounted for under IFRS 3).

You should look at the requirements of IAS 1 *Presentation of financial statements* for further details of disclosure, and IAS 12 *Income taxes* for disclosure of tax effects.

2.10 Offsetting a financial asset and a financial liability

A financial asset and financial liability should **only** be **offset**, with the net amount reported in the statement of financial position, when an entity:

(a) Has a legally enforceable right of set off, *and*

(b) Intends to settle on a net basis, or to realise the asset and settle the liability simultaneously, ie at the same moment.

This will reflect the expected **future cash flows** of the entity in these specific circumstances. In all other cases, financial assets and financial liabilities are presented separately.

2.11 Amendment to IAS 32: Puttable financial instruments and obligations arising on liquidation

This amendment was issued in February 2008. The changes deal with puttable financial instruments and the effect obligations that arise on liquidation have on determining whether an instrument is debt or equity.

IAS 32 requires that if the holder of a financial instrument can require the issuer to redeem it for cash it should be classified as a liability. Some ordinary shares and partnership interests allow the holder to 'put' the instrument (that is to require the issuer to redeem it in cash). Such shares might more usually be considered as equity, but application of IAS 32 results in their being classified as liabilities.

The amendment would requires entities to classify such instruments as equity, so long as they meet certain conditions. The amendment further requires that instruments imposing an obligation on an entity to deliver to another party a pro rata share of the net assets only on liquidation should be classified as equity.

2.12 Section summary

- Financial instruments issued to raise capital must be classified as **liabilities** or **equity**
- The **substance** of the financial instrument is more important than its **legal form**
- The **critical feature of a financial liability** is the contractual obligation to deliver cash or another financial instrument
- **Compound instruments** are split into equity and liability parts and presented accordingly
- **Interest, dividends, losses and gains** are treated according to whether they relate to an equity instrument or a financial liability

3 Recognition of financial instruments

FAST FORWARD

IAS 39 *Financial instruments: recognition and measurement* is a controversial standard.

The IAS states that **all financial assets and liabilities** should be **recognised in the statement of financial position, including derivatives.**

The recognition of financial assets is being amended by IFRS 9 *Financial Instruments.* IFRS 9 is a work in progress. It is dealt with in a separate section towards the end of this chapter.

IAS 39 *Financial instruments: Recognition and measurement* establishes principles for recognising and measuring financial assets and financial liabilities.

Exam focus point

The examiner has stated that in the exam you can answer in accordance with IFRS 9 or IAS 39, although examiner's answers will be prepared on the basis of IFRS 9. **If you are applying IAS 39**, you should **state in your answer that you are doing so**.

3.1 Scope

IAS 39 applies to **all entities** and to **all types of financial instruments except** those specifically excluded, as listed below.

(a) Investments in **subsidiaries, associates, and joint ventures** that are accounted for under IASs 27, 28 and 31

(b) **Leases** covered in IAS 17

(c) **Employee benefit plans** covered in IAS 19

(d) **Insurance contracts**

(e) Equity instruments **issued by the entity** eg ordinary shares issued, or options and warrants

(f) **Financial guarantee** contracts

(g) **Contracts for contingent consideration** in a business combination, covered in IFRS 3

(h) Contracts requiring payment based on climatic, geological or other **physical variables**

(i) **Loan commitments** that cannot be settled net in cash or another financial instrument

(j) Financial instruments, contracts and obligations under **share based payment transactions,** covered in IFRS 2

Note also that financial assets will be dealt with under IFRS 9 when this comes into force.

3.2 Initial recognition

Financial instruments should be recognised in the statement of financial position when the entity becomes a party to the **contractual provisions of the instrument**.

Point to note

An important consequence of this is that all derivatives should be in the statement of financial position.

Notice that this is **different** from the recognition criteria in the *Framework* and in most other standards. Items are normally recognised when there is a probable inflow or outflow of resources and the item has a cost or value that can be measured reliably.

3.3 Example: initial recognition

An entity has entered into two separate contracts.

(a) A firm commitment (an order) to buy a specific quantity of iron.

(b) A forward contract to buy a specific quantity of iron at a specified price on a specified date, provided delivery of the iron is not taken.

Contract (a) is a **normal trading contract**. The entity does not recognise a liability for the iron until the goods have actually been delivered. (Note that this contract is not a financial instrument because it involves a physical asset, rather than a financial asset.)

Contract (b) is a **financial instrument**. Under IAS 39, the entity recognises a financial liability (an obligation to deliver cash) on the **commitment date**, rather than waiting for the closing date on which the exchange takes place.

Note that planned future transactions, no matter how likely, are not assets and liabilities of an entity – the entity has not yet become a party to the contract.

3.4 Derecognition

Derecognition is the removal of a previously recognised financial instrument from an entity's statement of financial position.

An entity should derecognise a **financial asset** when:

(a) The **contractual rights** to the cash flows from the financial asset **expire**, or

(b) The entity **transfers substantially all the risks and rewards of ownership** of the financial asset to another party.

Question

Can you think of an example of a situation in which:

(a) An entity has transferred substantially all the risks and rewards of ownership?
(b) An entity has retained substantially all the risks and rewards of ownership?

Answer

IAS 39 and IFRS 9 include the following examples:

(a) (i) An unconditional sale of a financial asset
(ii) A sale of a financial asset together with an option to repurchase the financial asset at its fair value at the time of repurchase

(b) (i) A sale and repurchase transaction where the repurchase price is a fixed price or the sale price plus a lender's return
(ii) A sale of a financial asset together with a total return swap that transfers the market risk exposure back to the entity

Exam focus point

The principle here is that of **substance over form**.

An entity should derecognise a **financial liability** when it is **extinguished** – ie, when the obligation specified in the contract is discharged or cancelled or expires.

It is possible for only **part** of a financial asset or liability to be derecognised. This is allowed if the part comprises:

(a) only specifically identified cash flows; or
(b) only a fully proportionate (pro rata) share of the total cash flows.

For example, if an entity holds a bond it has the right to two separate sets of cash inflows: those relating to the principal and those relating to the interest. It could sell the right to receive the interest to another party while retaining the right to receive the principal.

On derecognition, the amount to be included in net profit or loss for the period is calculated as follows:

Formula to learn

	$	$
Carrying amount of asset/liability (or the portion of asset/liability) transferred		X
Less: Proceeds received/paid	X	
Any cumulative gain or loss reported in equity	X	
		(X)
Difference to net profit/loss		X

Where only part of a financial asset is derecognised, the carrying amount of the asset should be allocated between the part retained and the part transferred based on their relative fair values on the date of transfer. A gain or loss should be recognised based on the proceeds for the portion transferred.

3.5 Section summary

- **All financial assets** and **liabilities** should be **recognised in the statement of financial position**, including derivatives.
- Financial assets should be derecognised when the **rights to the cash flows** from the asset **expire** or where **substantially all the risks and rewards of ownership are transferred** to another party.
- Financial liabilities should be derecognised when they are **extinguished**.

4 Measurement of financial instruments

Exam focus point

> The ACCA examiner has indicated that questions on financial assets will be set with IFRS 9 in mind (see Section 9), but answers in terms of IAS 39 will be acceptable. IAS 39 still applies to liabilities. As stated before, if you base your answers on IAS 39, you must state that you are doing so.

FAST FORWARD

> **Financial assets** should **initially** be measured at **cost = fair value.**
>
> Subsequently they should be re-measured to fair value except for
>
> (a) Loans and receivables not held for trading
> (b) Other **held-to-maturity investments**
> (c) **Financial assets** whose value **cannot be reliably measured**

Note. These categories will be simplified when IFRS 9 (see Section 9) comes into force

4.1 Initial measurement

Financial instruments are initially measured at the **fair value** of the consideration given or received (ie, **cost) plus** (in most cases) **transaction costs** that are **directly attributable** to the acquisition or issue of the financial instrument.

The **exception** to this rule is where a financial instrument is designated as **at fair value through profit or loss** (this term is explained below). In this case, **transaction costs** are **not** added to fair value at initial recognition.

The fair value of the consideration is normally the transaction price or market prices. If market prices are not reliable, the fair value may be **estimated** using a valuation technique (for example, by discounting cash flows).

4.2 Subsequent measurement

Subsequent measurement of financial assets is dealt with in Section 9 on IFRS 9, but the IAS 39 rules are included for completeness, in an Appendix at the end of this Text.

A term you will meet in connection with both financial assets and liabilities, and in both IFRS 9 and IAS 39 is **amortised cost.** Under IFRS 9, financial assets are measured either at amortised cost, using the **effective interest method**, or at fair value.

Key terms

> **A financial asset or liability at fair value through profit or loss** meets either of the following conditions:
>
> (a) It is classified as held for trading. A financial instrument is classified as held for trading if it is:
> (i) Acquired or incurred principally for the purpose of selling or repurchasing it in the near term
> (ii) Part of a portfolio of identified financial instruments that are managed together and for which there is evidence of a recent actual pattern of short-term profit-taking, or
> (iii) A derivative (unless it is a designated and effective hedging instrument).
>
> (b) Upon initial recognition it is designated by the entity as at fair value through profit or loss. An entity may only use this designation in severely restricted circumstances:
> (i) It **eliminates** or significantly **reduces** a measurement or recognition **inconsistency** (mismatch) that would otherwise arise.
> (ii) A **group of** financial assets/liabilities is managed and its performance is evaluated **on a fair value basis.**
>
> **Held-to-maturity investments** are non-derivative financial assets with fixed or determinable payments and fixed maturity that an entity has the positive intent and ability to hold to maturity other than:

Key terms (cont'd)

(a) Those that the entity upon initial recognition designates as at fair value through profit or loss
(b) Those that the entity designates as available for sale
(c) Those that meet the definition of loans and receivables

Loans and receivables are non-derivative financial assets with fixed or determinable payments that are not quoted in an active market, other than:

(a) Those that the entity intends to sell immediately or in the near term, which should be classified as held for trading and those that the entity upon initial recognition designates as at fair value through profit or loss
(b) Those that the entity upon initial recognition designates as available-for-sale, or
(c) Those for which the holder may not recover substantially all of the initial investment, other than because of credit deterioration, which shall be classified as available for sale

An interest acquired in a pool of assets that are not loans or receivables (for example, an interest in a mutual fund or a similar fund) is not a loan or a receivable.

Available-for-sale financial assets are those financial assets that are not:

(a) Loans and receivables originated by the entity,
(b) Held-to-maturity investments, or
(c) Financial assets at fair value through profit or loss. *(IAS 39)*

After initial recognition, all financial assets should be **remeasured to fair value**, without any deduction for transaction costs that may be incurred on sale or other disposal, except for:

(a) Loans and receivables
(b) Held to maturity investments
(c) Investments in equity instruments that do not have a quoted market price in an active market and whose fair value cannot be reliably measured and derivatives that are linked to and must be settled by delivery of such unquoted equity instruments

Loans and receivables and **held to maturity investments** should be measured at **amortised cost** using the **effective interest method**.

Key terms

Amortised cost of a financial asset or financial liability is the amount at which the financial asset or liability is measured at initial recognition minus principal repayments, plus or minus the cumulative amortisation of any difference between that initial amount and the maturity amount, and minus any write-down (directly or through the use of an allowance account) for impairment or uncollectability.

The **effective interest method** is a method of calculating the amortised cost of a financial instrument and of allocating the interest income or interest expense over the relevant period.

The **effective interest rate** is the rate that exactly discounts estimated future cash payments or receipts through the expected life of the financial instrument to the net carrying amount of the financial asset or liability. (*IAS 39*)

4.3 Example: Amortised cost

On 1 January 20X1 Abacus Co purchases a debt instrument for its fair value of $1,000. The debt instrument is due to mature on 31 December 20X5. The instrument has a principal amount of $1,250 and the instrument carries fixed interest at 4.72% that is paid annually. (The effective interest rate is 10%.)

How should Abacus Co account for the debt instrument over its five year term?

Solution

Abacus Co will receive interest of \$59 (1,250 × 4.72%) each year and \$1,250 when the instrument matures.

Abacus must allocate the discount of \$250 and the interest receivable over the five year term at a constant rate on the carrying amount of the debt. To do this, it must apply the effective interest rate of 10%.

The following table shows the allocation over the years:

Year	*Amortised cost at beginning of year*	*Profit or loss: Interest income for year (@10%)*	*Interest received during year (cash inflow)*	*Amortised cost at end of year*
	\$	\$	\$	\$
20X1	1,000	100	(59)	1,041
20X2	1,041	104	(59)	1,086
20X3	1,086	109	(59)	1,136
20X4	1,136	113	(59)	1,190
20X5	1,190	119	(1,250+59)	–

Each year the carrying amount of the financial asset is increased by the interest income for the year and reduced by the interest actually received during the year.

Investments whose **fair value cannot be reliably measured** should be measured at **cost**.

4.4 Classification

There is a certain amount of flexibility in that **any** financial instrument can be designated as fair value through profit or loss. However, this is a **once and for all choice** and has to be made on initial recognition. Once a financial instrument has been classified in this way it **cannot be reclassified**, even if it would otherwise be possible to measure it at cost or amortised cost.

In contrast, it is quite difficult for an entity **not** to remeasure financial instruments to fair value.

Exam focus point

Notice that derivatives **must** be remeasured to fair value. This is because it would be misleading to measure them at cost.

For a financial instrument to be held to maturity it must meet several extremely narrow criteria. The entity must have a **positive intent** and a **demonstrated ability** to hold the investment to maturity. These conditions are not met if:

(a) The entity intends to hold the financial asset for an undefined period

(b) The entity stands ready to sell the financial asset in response to changes in interest rates or risks, liquidity needs and similar factors (unless these situations could not possibly have been reasonably anticipated)

(c) The issuer has the right to settle the financial asset at an amount significantly below its amortised cost (because this right will almost certainly be exercised)

(d) It does not have the financial resources available to continue to finance the investment until maturity

(e) It is subject to an existing legal or other constraint that could frustrate its intention to hold the financial asset to maturity

In addition, an **equity** instrument is **unlikely** to meet the criteria for classification as held to maturity.

There is a **penalty** for selling or reclassifying a 'held-to-maturity' investment other than in certain very tightly defined circumstances. If this has occurred during the **current** financial year or during the **two preceding** financial years **no** financial asset can be classified as held-to-maturity.

If an entity can no longer hold an investment to maturity, it is no longer appropriate to use amortised cost and the asset must be re-measured to fair value. **All** remaining held-to-maturity investments must also be re-measured to fair value and classified as available-for-sale (see above).

4.5 Subsequent measurement of financial liabilities

After initial recognition, all financial liabilities should be measured at **amortised cost**, with the exception of financial liabilities at fair value through profit or loss (including most derivatives). These should be measured at **fair value**, but where the fair value **is not capable of reliable measurement**, they should be measured at **cost**.

Question — Measurement

Galaxy Co issues a bond for $503,778 on 1 January 20X2. No interest is payable on the bond, but it will be held to maturity and redeemed on 31 December 20X4 for $600,000. The bond has **not** been designated as at fair value through profit or loss.

Required:

Calculate the charge to profit or loss of Galaxy Co for the year ended 31 December 20X2 and the balance outstanding at 31 December 20X2.

Answer

The bond is a 'deep discount' bond and is a financial liability of Galaxy Co. It is measured at amortised cost. Although there is no interest as such, the difference between the initial cost of the bond and the price at which it will be redeemed is a finance cost. This must be allocated over the term of the bond at a constant rate on the carrying amount.

To calculate amortised cost we need to calculate the effective interest rate of the bond:

$$\frac{600{,}000}{503{,}778} = 1.191 \text{ over three years}$$

To calculate an annual rate, we take the cube root, $(1.191)^{1/3} = 1.06$, so the annual interest rate is 6%.

The charge to the income statement is $30,226 (503,778 × 6%)

The balance outstanding at 31 December 20X2 is $534,004 (503,778 + 30,226)

4.6 Gains and losses

Instruments at **fair value through profit or loss**: gains and losses are recognised **in profit or loss**.

Available for sale financial assets: gains and losses are recognised **directly in equity** through the statement of changes in equity. When the asset is derecognised the cumulative gain or loss previously recognised in equity should be recognised in profit and loss.

Financial instruments carried at **amortised cost**: gains and losses are recognised **in profit and loss** as a result of the amortisation process and when the asset is derecognised.

Financial assets and financial liabilities that are **hedged items**: special rules apply (discussed later in this chapter).

Question — Finance cost 1

On 1 January 20X3 Deferred issued $600,000 loan notes. Issue costs were $200. The loan notes do not carry interest, but are redeemable at a premium of $152,389 on 31 December 20X4. The effective finance cost of the debentures is 12%.

What is the finance cost in respect of the loan notes for the year ended 31 December 20X4?

A $72,000
B $76,194
C $80,613
D $80,640

Answer

C The premium on redemption of the preferred shares represents a finance cost. The effective rate of interest must be applied so that the debt is measured at amortised cost (IAS 39).

At the time of issue, the loan notes are recognised at their net proceeds of $599,800 (600,000 – 200).

The finance cost for the year ended 31 December 20X4 is calculated as follows:

	B/f	*Interest @ 12%*	*C/f*
	$	$	$
20X3	599,800	71,976	671,776
20X4	671,776	80,613	752,389

Question

Finance cost 2

On 1 January 20X5, an entity issued a debt instrument with a coupon rate of 3.5% at a par value of $6,000,000. The directly attributable costs of issue were $120,000. The debt instrument s repayable on 31 December 2011 at a premium of $1,100,000.

What is the total amount of the finance cost associated with the debt instrument?

A $1,470,000
B $1,590,000
C $2,570,000
D $2,690,000

Answer

D

	$
Issue costs	120,000
Interest $6,000,000 × 3.5% × 7	1,470,000
Premium on redemption	1,100,000
Total finance cost	2,690,000

Question

Classification

During the financial year ended 28 February 20X5, MN issued the two financial instruments described below. For *each* of the instruments, identify whether it should be classified as debt or equity, **explaining in not more than 40 words each** the reason for your choice. In each case you should refer to the relevant International Accounting Standard or International Financial Reporting Standard.

(i) Redeemable preferred shares with a coupon rate 8%. The shares are redeemable on 28 February 20X9 at premium of 10%

(ii) A grant of share options to senior executives. The options may be exercised from 28 February 20X8.

Answer

(i) **Debt.** The preference shares require regular distributions to the holders but more importantly have the debt characteristic of being redeemable. Therefore according to IAS 32 *Financial instruments: Presentation* they must be classified as debt.

(ii) **Equity.** According to IFRS 2 *Share based payment* the grant of share options must be recorded as equity in the statement of financial position. It is an alternative method of payment to cash for the provision of the services of the directors.

Question — Hybrid financial instrument

On 1 January 20X1, EFG issued 10,000 5% convertible bonds at their par value of $50 each. The bonds will be redeemed on 1 January 20X6. Each bond is convertible at the option of the holder at any time during the five year period. Interest on the bond will be paid annually in arrears.

The prevailing market interest rate for similar debt without conversion options at the date of issue was 6%.

At what value should the equity element of the hybrid financial instrument be recognised in the financial statements of EFG at the date of issue?

Answer

Top tip The method to use here is to find the present value of the principal value of the bond, $500,000 (10,000 × $50) and the interest payments of $25,000 annually (5% × $500,000) at the market rate for non-convertible bonds of 6%, using the discount factor tables. The difference between this total and the principal amount of $500,000 is the equity element.

	$
Present value of principal $500,000 × 0.747	373,500
Present value of interest $25,000 × 4.212	105,300
Liability value	478,800
Principal amount	500,000
Equity element	21,200

Question — Subsequent measurement

After initial recognition, all financial liabilities should be measured at amortised cost.

True ☐ False ☐

Answer

False. Some may be measured at fair value if certain criteria are net.

Question — Types of investment

Ellesmere Co entered into the following transactions during the year ended 31 December 20X3:

(1) Entered into a speculative interest rate option costing $10,000 on 1 January 20X3 to borrow $6,000,000 from AB Bank commencing 31 March 20X5 for 6 months at 4%. The value of the option at 31 December 20X3 was $15,250.

(2) Purchased 6% debentures in FG Co on 1 January 20X3 (their issue date) for $150,000 as an investment. Ellesmere Co intends to hold the debentures until their redemption at a premium in 5 year's time. The effective rate of interest of the bond is 8.0%.

(3) Purchased 50,000 shares in ST Co on 1 July 20X3 for $3.50 each as an investment. The share price on 31 December 20X3 was $3.75.

Required

Show the accounting treatment and relevant extracts from the financial statements for the year ended 31 December 20X3. Ellesmere Co only designates financial assets as at fair value through profit or loss where this is unavoidable.

Answer

STATEMENT OF FINANCIAL POSITION (EXTRACTS)

	$
Financial assets:	
Interest rate option (W1)	15,250
6% debentures in FG Co (W2)	153,000
Shares in EG Co (W3)	187,500

STATEMENT OF COMPREHENSIVE INCOME (EXTRACTS)

	$
Finance income:	
Gain on interest rate option (W1)	5,250
Effective interest on 6% debentures (W2)	12,000

Workings

1 *Interest rate option*

This is a derivative and so it must be treated as at fair value through profit or loss.

Initial measurement (at cost):

DEBIT	Financial asset	$10,000	
CREDIT	Cash		$10,000

At 31.12.20X3 (re-measured to fair value)

DEBIT	Financial asset ($15,250 – $10,000)	$5,250	
CREDIT	Profit or loss		$5,250

2 *Debentures*

On the basis of the information provided, this can be treated as a held-to-maturity investment.

Initial measurement (at cost):

DEBIT	Financial asset	$150,000	
CREDIT	Cash		$150,000

At 31.12.20X3 (amortised cost):

DEBIT	Financial asset (150,000 × 8%)	$12,000	
CREDIT	Finance income		$12,000
DEBIT	Cash (150,000 × 6%)	$9,000	
CREDIT	Financial asset		$9,000

Amortised cost at 31.12.20X3:

(150,000 + 12,000 – 9,000) = $153,000

3 *Shares*

These are treated as an available for sale financial asset (shares cannot normally be held to maturity and they are clearly not loans or receivables).

Initial measurement (at cost):

DEBIT	Financial asset (50,000 × $3.50)	$175,000	
CREDIT	Cash		$175,000

At 31.12.20X3 (re-measured to fair value)

DEBIT	Financial asset ((50,000 × $3.75) – $175,000))	$12,500	
CREDIT	Equity		$12,500

4.7 Impairment and uncollectability of financial assets

Note. Impairment is still governed by IAS 39.

At each year end, an entity should assess whether there is any objective evidence that a financial asset or group of assets is impaired.

Question — **Impairment**

Give examples of indications that a financial asset or group of assets may be impaired.

Answer

IAS 39 lists the following:

(a) Significant financial difficulty of the issuer

(b) A breach of contract, such as a default in interest or principal payments

(c) The lender granting a concession to the borrower that the lender would not otherwise consider, for reasons relating to the borrower's financial difficulty

(d) It becomes probable that the borrower will enter bankruptcy

(e) The disappearance of an active market for that financial asset because of financial difficulties

Where there is objective evidence of impairment, the entity should **determine the amount** of any impairment loss.

4.7.1 Financial assets carried at amortised cost

The impairment loss is the **difference** between the asset's **carrying amount** and its **recoverable amount**. The asset's recoverable amount is the present value of estimated future cash flows, discounted at the financial instrument's **original** effective interest rate.

The amount of the loss should be **recognised in profit or loss.**

If the impairment loss decreases at a later date (and the decrease relates to an event occurring **after** the impairment was recognised) the reversal is recognised in profit or loss. The carrying amount of the asset must not exceed the original amortised cost.

4.7.2 Financial assets carried at cost

Unquoted equity instruments are carried at cost if their fair value cannot be reliably measured. The impairment loss is the difference between the asset's **carrying amount** and the **present value of estimated future cash flows**, discounted at the current market rate of return for a similar financial instrument. Such impairment losses cannot be reversed.

4.7.3 Investments in equity instruments (IEI)

Investments in equity instruments are carried at fair value and gains and losses are recognised directly in equity. Any impairment loss on investments in equity instruments should be **removed from equity** and **recognised in net profit or loss for the period** even though the financial asset has not been derecognised.

The impairment loss is the difference between its **acquisition cost** (net of any principal repayment and amortisation) and **current fair value** (for equity instruments) or recoverable amount (for debt instruments), less any impairment loss on that asset previously recognised in profit or loss.

Impairment losses relating to equity instruments cannot be reversed. Impairment losses relating to debt instruments may be reversed if, in a later period, the fair value of the instrument increases and the increase can be objectively related to an event occurring after the loss was recognised.

4.8 Example: Impairment

Broadfield Co purchased 5% debentures in X Co on 1 January 20X3 (their issue date) for $100,000. The term of the debentures was 5 years and the maturity value is $130,525. The effective rate of interest on the debentures is 10% and the company has classified them as a held-to-maturity financial asset.

At the end of 20X4 X Co went into liquidation. All interest had been paid until that date. On 31 December 20X4 the liquidator of X Co announced that no further interest would be paid and only 80% of the maturity value would be repaid, on the original repayment date.

The market interest rate on similar bonds is 8% on that date.

Required

(a) What value should the debentures have been stated at just before the impairment became apparent?

(b) At what value should the debentures be stated at 31 December 20X4, after the impairment?

(c) How will the impairment be reported in the financial statements for the year ended 31 December 20X4?

Solution

(a) The debentures are classified as a held-to-maturity financial asset and so they would have been stated at amortised cost:

	$
Initial cost	100,000
Interest at 10%	10,000
Cash at 5%	(5,000)
At 31 December 20X3	105,000
Interest at 10%	10,500
Cash at 5%	(5,000)
At 31 December 20X4	110,500

(b) After the impairment, the debentures are stated at their recoverable amount (using the **original** effective interest rate of 10%):

80% × $130,525 × 0.751 = $78,419

(c) The impairment of $32,081 ($110,500 – $78,419) should be recorded:

DEBIT Statement of comprehensive income	$32,081	
CREDIT Financial asset		$32,081

4.9 Section summary

- On initial recognition, financial instruments are measured at **cost**.
- Subsequent measurement depends on how a financial asset is **classified**.
- Financial assets at **fair value through profit or loss** are measured at **fair value**; gains and losses are recognised in **profit or loss**.
- **Available for sale** assets are measured at **fair value**; gains and losses are taken to **equity**.
- **Loans and receivables** and **held to maturity** investments are measured at **amortised cost**; gains and losses are recognised in **profit or loss**.
- Financial **liabilities** are normally measured at **amortised cost**, unless they have been classified as at fair value through profit or loss.

5 Hedge accounting

FAST FORWARD

Hedge accounting is allowed in certain strictly defined circumstances.

5.1 Introduction

IAS 39 **requires hedge accounting** where there is a **designated hedging relationship** between a hedging instrument and a hedged item. It is **prohibited otherwise**.

Key terms

Hedging, for accounting purposes, means designating one or more hedging instruments so that their change in fair value is an offset, in whole or in part, to the change in fair value or cash flows of a hedged item.

A **hedged item** is an asset, liability, firm commitment, or forecasted future transaction that:

(a) exposes the entity to risk of changes in fair value or changes in future cash flows, and that
(b) is designated as being hedged.

A **hedging instrument** is a designated derivative or (in limited circumstances) another financial asset or liability whose fair value or cash flows are expected to offset changes in the fair value or cash flows of a designated hedged item. (A non-derivative financial asset or liability may be designated as a hedging instrument for hedge accounting purposes only if it hedges the risk of changes in foreign currency exchange rates.)

Hedge effectiveness is the degree to which changes in the fair value or cash flows of the hedged item attributable to a hedged risk are offset by changes in the fair value or cash flows of the hedging instrument. (*IAS 39*)

In simple terms, entities hedge to reduce their exposure to risk and uncertainty, such as changes in prices, interest rates or foreign exchange rates. Hedge accounting recognises hedging relationships by allowing (for example) losses on a hedged item to be offset against gains on a hedging instrument.

Generally only assets, liabilities etc that involve external parties can be designated as hedged items. The foreign currency risk of an intragroup monetary item (eg payable/receivable between two subsidiaries) may qualify as a hedged item in the group financial statements if it results in an exposure to foreign exchange rate gains or losses that are not fully eliminated on consolidation. This can happen (per IAS 21) when the transaction is between entities with different functional currencies.

In addition the foreign currency risk of a highly probable group transaction may qualify as a hedged item if it is in a currency other than the functional currency of the entity and the foreign currency risk will affect profit or loss.

5.2 Example: Hedging

A company owns inventories of 20,000 gallons of oil which cost $400,000 on 1 December 20X3.

In order to hedge the fluctuation in the market value of the oil the company signs a futures contract to deliver 20,000 gallons of oil on 31 March 20X4 at the futures price of $22 per gallon.

The market price of oil on 31 December 20X3 is $23 per gallon and the futures price for delivery on 31 March 20X4 is $24 per gallon.

Required

Explain the impact of the transactions on the financial statements of the company:

(a) Without hedge accounting
(b) With hedge accounting.

Solution

The futures contract was intended to protect the company from a fall in oil prices (which would have reduced the profit when the oil was eventually sold). However, oil prices have actually risen, so that the company has made a loss on the contract.

Without hedge accounting:

The futures contract is a derivative and therefore must be remeasured to fair value under IAS 39. The loss on the futures contract is recognised in profit or loss:

DEBIT	Profit or loss (20,000 × 24 – 22)	$40,000	
CREDIT	Financial liability		$40,000

With hedge accounting:

The loss on the futures contract is recognised in the profit or loss as before.

The inventories are revalued to fair value:

	$
Fair value at 31 December 20X4 (20,000 × 23)	460,000
Cost	(400,000)
Gain	60,000

The gain is also recognised in profit or loss:

DEBIT	Inventory	$60,000	
CREDIT	Profit or loss		$60,000

The net effect on the profit or loss is a gain of $20,000 compared with a loss of $40,000 without hedging.

The **standard** identifies three types of **hedging relationship**.

Key terms

Fair value hedge: a hedge of the exposure to changes in the fair value of a recognised asset or liability, or an identified portion of such an asset or liability, that is attributable to a particular risk and could affect profit or loss.

Cash flow hedge: a hedge of the exposure to variability in cash flows that

(a) Is attributable to a particular risk associated with a recognised asset or liability (such as all or some future interest payments on variable rate debt) or a highly probable forecast transaction (such as an anticipated purchase or sale), and that

(b) Could affect profit or loss.

Hedge of a net investment in a foreign operation: IAS 21 defines a net investment in a foreign operation as the amount of the reporting entity's interest in the net assets of that operation. (*IAS 39*)

The hedge in the example above is a **fair value hedge** (it hedges exposure to changes in the fair value of a recognised asset: the oil).

5.3 Conditions for hedge accounting

Before a hedging relationship qualifies for hedge accounting, **all** of the following **conditions** must be met.

(a) The hedging relationship must be **designated at its inception as a hedge** based on the entity's risk management objective and strategy. There must be formal documentation (including identification of the hedged item, the hedging instrument, the nature of the risk that is to be hedged and how the entity will assess the hedging instrument's effectiveness in offsetting the exposure to changes in the hedged item's fair value or cash flows attributable to the hedged risk).

(b) The hedge is expected to be **highly effective** in achieving offsetting changes in fair value or cash flows attributable to the hedged risk. (Note: the hedge need not necessarily be *fully* effective. A highly effective hedge is one that is 80% – 125% effective.)

(c) For **cash flow hedges**, a **forecast transaction** that is the subject of the hedge must be **highly probable** and must present an exposure to variations in cash flows that could ultimately affect profit or loss.

(d) The effectiveness of the hedge can be **measured reliably**.

(e) The hedge is **assessed** on an ongoing basis (annually) and has been **effective during the reporting period**.

5.4 Accounting treatment

5.4.1 Fair value hedges

The **gain or loss** resulting from **re-measuring** the hedging instrument at fair value is **recognised in profit or loss**.

The gain or loss on the hedged item attributable to the **hedged risk** should **adjust the carrying amount** of the hedged item and be **recognised in profit or loss**.

5.4.2 Cash flow hedges

The portion of the gain or loss on the hedging instrument that is determined to be an **effective** hedge shall be **recognised directly in equity** through the statement of changes in equity.

The **ineffective portion** of the gain or loss on the hedging instrument should be **recognised in profit or loss**.

When a hedging transaction results in the recognition of an asset or liability, changes in the value of the hedging instrument recognised in equity either:

(a) Are adjusted against the carrying value of the asset or liability, or

(b) Affect the profit or loss at the same time as the hedged item (for example, through depreciation or sale).

5.5 Example: Cash flow hedge

Bets Co signs a contract on 1 November 20X1 to purchase an asset on 1 November 20X2 for €60,000,000. Bets reports in US$ and hedges this transaction by entering into a forward contract to buy €60,000,000 on 1 November 20X2 at US$1: €1.5.

Spot and forward exchange rates at the following dates are:

	Spot	*Forward (for delivery on 1.11.X2)*
1.11.X1	US$1: €1.45	US$1: €1.5
31.12.X1	US$1: €1.20	US$1: €1.24
1.11.X2	US$1: €1.0	US$1: €1.0 (actual)

Required

Show the double entries relating to these transactions at 1 November 20X1, 31 December 20X1 and 1 November 20X2.

Solution

Entries at 1 November 20X1

The value of the forward contract at inception is zero so no entries recorded (other than any transaction costs), but risk disclosures will be made.

The contractual commitment to buy the asset would be disclosed if material (IAS 16).

Entries at 31 December 20X1

Gain on forward contract:

	$
Value of contract at 31.12.X1 (€60,000,000/1.24)	48,387,097
Value of contract at 1.11.X1 (€60,000,000/1.5)	40,000,000
Gain on contract	8,387,097

Compare to movement in value of asset (unrecognised):

Increase in $ cost of asset

(€60,000,000/1.20 – €60,000,000/1.45)	$8,620,690

As this is higher, the hedge is deemed fully effective at this point:

DEBIT Financial asset (Forward a/c)	$8,387,097	
CREDIT Equity		$8,387,097

Entries at 1 November 20X2

Additional gain on forward contract

	$
Value of contract at 1.11.X2 (€60,000,000/1.0)	60,000,000
Value of contract at 31.12.X1 (€60,000,000/1.24)	48,387,097
Gain on contract	11,612,903

Compare to movement in value of asset (unrecognised):

Increase in $ cost of asset

(€60,000,000/1.0 – €60,000,000/1.2)	$10,000,000

Therefore, the hedge is not fully effective during this period, but is still highly effective (and hence hedge accounting can be used):

$10,000,000/ $11,612,903 = 86% which is within the 80% – 125% bandings.

DEBIT Financial asset (Forward a/c)	$11,612,903	
CREDIT Equity		$10,000,000
CREDIT Profit or loss		$1,612,903

Purchase of asset at market price

DEBIT Asset (€60,000,000/1.0)	$60,000,000	
CREDIT Cash		$60,000,000

Settlement of forward contract

DEBIT Cash	$20,000,000	
CREDIT Financial asset (Forward a/c)		$20,000,000

Realisation of gain on hedging instrument

The cumulative gain of $18,387,097 recognised in equity:

- Is transferred to profit or loss as the asset is used, ie over the asset's useful life; or
- Adjusts the initial cost of the asset (reducing future depreciation).

5.6 Section summary

- **Hedge accounting** means designating one or more instruments so that their change in fair value is **offset** by the change in fair value or cash flows of another item.
- **Hedge accounting** is permitted in certain circumstances, provided the hedging relationship is **clearly defined**, **measurable** and actually **effective**.

- There are three types of hedge: **fair value** hedge; **cash flow** hedge; hedge of a **net investment in a foreign operation.**
- The accounting treatment of a hedge **depends on its type**.

6 Reducing complexity

FAST FORWARD

Many users and preparers of accounts have found financial instruments to be **complex.** The IASB has issued a Discussion Paper, which aims at reducing complexity.

6.1 Background

You may have found this chapter difficult. Question practice will help. It may be of some comfort to know that students are not alone in finding **financial instruments complex.** Preparers of financial statements, their users and auditors, have all found this to be the case.

In March 2008, the IASB issued a Discussion Paper *Reducing complexity in reporting financial instruments.* The Discussion Paper is also being considered for comment by the US Financial Accounting Standards Board (FASB). In fact this is a joint project between the IASB and FASB.

6.2 Objective

The objective of the joint project is to **develop less complex and principle-based standards** on accounting for financial instruments. The Discussion Paper aims to gather information in order to assist with this project.

6.3 Summary

The Discussion Paper covers the following matters.

(a) The main **causes of complexity** in financial instrument accounting: multiple measurement methods

(b) **A long-term solution** for reducing complexity and improving financial instrument accounting: measure all financial instruments at **fair value**

(c) Three possible approaches for the medium term:

 (i) Amending the current measurement requirements
 (ii) Replacing the existing measurement requirements
 (iii) Simplifying hedge accounting requirements

The determination of fair value and the classification of financial instruments as debt or equity are not discussed, as these matters are dealt with in separate projects.

6.4 Reasons for complexity in accounting for financial instruments

As the Discussion Paper acknowledges, the main reason for complexity in accounting for financial instruments is the **many different ways in which they can be measured**. A table lists twenty-four! The measurement method depends on:

(a) The applicable financial reporting standard
(b) The categorisation of the financial instrument under IAS 39 *Financial instruments: Recognition and measurement*
(c) Whether hedge accounting has been applied

6.5 Long-term solution: fair value

The Discussion Paper maintains the view that **fair value is the only measure that is appropriate for all types of financial instruments**, and that a full fair value model would be much simpler to apply than the current mixed model. A single measurement method would, it is argued:

(a) Significantly reduce complexity
(b) Make reported information easier to understand
(c) Improve the comparability of reported information between entities and between periods

6.5.1 IAS 39 requirements no longer needed

Fair value measurement for all financial instruments would mean that the following **requirements of IAS 39 could be dispensed with:**

(a) **Classification** of financial instruments into:

    (i) Fair value through profit or loss
    (ii) Available for sale
    (iii) Held-to-maturity
    (iv) Loans and receivables

(b) **Accounting for transfers** between the above categories

(c) Identification and quantification of **impairments**

6.5.2 Unresolved problems

The Discussion Paper acknowledges that a single measurement method would not resolve all of the current problems and notes that it would not be possible to achieve the long-term solution of measuring all financial instruments at fair value until the following issues have been resolved:

(a) **Presentation.** How should the effects of changes in fair values be presented in earnings?
(b) **Disclosure**. What information about financial instruments should be disclosed?
(c) **Measurement**. What is the definition of fair value and how should it be measured?
(d) **Scope.** What is the appropriate definition of a financial instrument and which financial instruments, if any, should be outside the scope of a standard?

6.6 Intermediate approaches

The long-term solution of measuring all financial instruments at **fair value** must be **postponed until certain other projects have been completed**. Accordingly, an intermediate solution must be found. The Discussion Paper proposes three intermediate approaches.

6.6.1 Amending the current measurement requirements

It is proposed to reduce the number of categories of financial instruments (see 7.5.1 above) and/or to simplify or eliminate some of the current requirements or restrictions.

6.6.2 Replacing the existing measurement requirements

This approach would involve replacing the existing measurement requirements with a fair value measurement principle, which would make fair value through profit or loss the default category. An exemption would be available, whereby some financial instruments could be measured at amortised cost. (This approach follows that proposed in the IASB Exposure Draft of an *IFRS for Small and medium-sized entities.)*

6.6.3 Simplifying hedge accounting requirements

The hedge accounting requirements would be simplified in one of the following ways.

(a) One or more of the existing hedge accounting models would be eliminated or replaced (eg with a less complex fair value hedging model).

(b) The current hedge accounting models would be maintained and simplified (eg by changing the requirements for assessing effectiveness, hedging of portions and partial term hedges.

6.6.4 Benefits of intermediate approach

(a) Reduced complexity
(b) Greater relevance in information provided to users
(c) Consistency with the long-term solution of measuring all financial instruments at fair value
(d) Benefits outweighing costs

6.7 Section summary

- Financial instruments are found to be complex, mainly because there are so many different measurement methods.
- The IASB has addressed this in a Discussion Paper.
- In the long term all financial instruments will be measured at fair value.
- Solutions are proposed for the medium term.

7 Amended reclassification rules

FAST FORWARD

Changes to IAS 39 introduced in October 2008 permit entities to **reclassify non-derivative financial assets out of the 'fair value through profit or loss' and 'available-for-sale' categories** in limited circumstances. Additional disclosures are required.

In October 2008, the IASB published amendments to IAS 39 *Financial instruments: recognition and measurement* and IFRS 7 *Financial instruments: disclosures.* The IASB had come under pressure, to bring the reclassification of financial assets into line with US GAAP, thus creating a 'level playing field'. The amendments were effective from 1 July 2008.

7.1 Scope

The amendment only applies to reclassification of some non-derivative financial assets recognised in accordance with IAS 39. Reclassification is not permitted for financial liabilities, derivatives and financial assets that are designated as at fair value through profit or loss (FVTPL) on initial recognition under the 'fair value option'.

The amendments therefore **only permit reclassification of debt and equity financial assets** subject to meeting specified criteria. They **do not permit reclassification into FVTPL**.

7.2 Criteria for reclassification out of fair value through profit or loss and available for sale

The criteria vary depending on whether the asset would have met the definition of 'loans and receivables' if it had not been classified as FVTPL or available for sale (AFS) on initial recognition.

(a) If the debt instrument would have met the definition of loans and receivables, had it not been required to be classified as held for trading at initial recognition, it may be classified out of FVTPL **provided the entity has the intention and ability to hold the asset for the foreseeable future or until maturity**.

(b) If a debt instrument was classified as AFS, but would have met the definition of loans and receivables if it had not been designated as AFS, it may be reclassified to the loans and receivables category **provided the entity has the intention and ability to hold the financial asset for the foreseeable future or until maturity**.

(c) Other debt instruments or any equity instruments may be reclassified from FVTPL to AFS or, in the case of debt instruments only from FVTPL to held to maturity (HTM) **if the financial assets are no longer held for selling in the short term**. Such cases will be rare.

7.3 Measurement at the reclassification date

Reclassified assets must be measured at the **fair value of the financial asset at the date of reclassification**.

(a) Previously recognised gains and losses cannot be reversed.

(b) The fair value at the date of reclassification becomes the new cost, or amortised cost of the financial asset.

7.4 Measurement after the reclassification date

After the reclassification date, **the normal IAS 39 requirements apply**. For example, in the case of financial assets measured at amortised cost, a **new effective interest rate** will be determined. If a fixed rate debt is reclassified as loans and receivables and held to maturity, this effective interest rate will be used as the discount rate for future impairment calculations.

For assets reclassified out of AFS, amounts previously recognised in other comprehensive income must be reclassified to profit or loss.

7.4.1 Exception

Reclassified debt instruments are treated differently. If, after the instrument has been reclassified, an entity increases its estimate of recoverability of future cash flows, the carrying amount is not adjusted upwards (in accordance with existing IAS 39 rules). Instead, a **new effective interest rate must be applied from that date** on. This enables the increase in recoverability of cash flows to be recognised over the expected life of the financial asset.

7.5 Disclosures

Disclosures, covered by IFRS 7, are not important for your Dip IFR studies. You should be aware that IFRS 7 has been amended to require additional disclosures for reclassifications that fall within the scope of the above amendments. They relate to the amounts reclassified in and out of each category, the fair values of reclassified assets, fair value gains or losses recognised in the period of reclassification and any new effective interest rate.

8 IFRS 9 and other current issues

FAST FORWARD

IFRS 9 *Financial Instruments* was issued in November 2009, and **replaced** and **simplified** certain parts of **IAS 39**, particularly with respect to the classification of financial assets. This standard is a work in progress and will be developed further in due course to fully replace IAS 39.

8.1 Background

It has been the IASB's intention to replace IAS 39 with a principle-based standard for some time, due to criticism of the complexity of IAS 39, which is difficult to understand, apply and interpret. The ED follows a Discussion Paper in March 2008 (*Reducing Complexity in Reporting Financial Instruments*).

The replacement of IAS 39 has become more urgent after the financial crisis. The IASB and US FASB set up a Financial Crisis Advisory Group (FCAG) to advise on how improvements in financial reporting could help enhance investor confidence in financial markets.

As a result the project to replace IAS 39 has been divided into 3 phases:

Phase 1: *Classification and Measurement.* IFRS 9 was issued in November 2009, but only applies to assets, not liabilities.

Phase 2: *Impairment Methodology.* An Exposure Draft *Financial Instruments: Amortised Cost and Impairment* was issued in November 2009 (see below).

Phase 3: *Hedging.* An Exposure Draft is pending.

The standard has been criticised, notably by the European Union, who warned that the new rules could lead to greater volatility in accounts, undermining broader financial stability, and postponed its EU adoption.

8.2 Definitions and scope

The scope of IFRS 9 is the same as that of IAS 39, and the IFRS 9 definitions relating to financial assets are the same as those in IAS 39.

8.3 Recognition of financial assets

On **recognition**, IFRS 9 requires that financial assets are classified as measured at either:

- **Amortised cost**, or
- **Fair value**

This classification is made on the basis of both:

(a) The **entity's business model** for managing the financial assets, and
(b) The **contractual cash flow** characteristics of the financial asset.

A financial asset is classified as measured at amortised cost where:

(a) The objective of the business model within which the asset is held is to hold assets in order to collect contractual cash flows and

(b) The contractual terms of the financial asset give rise on specified dates to cash flows that are solely payments of principal and interest on the principal outstanding.

An application of these rules means that **equity investments may not be classified as measured at amortised cost** and must be measured at fair value. This is because contractual cash flows on specified dates are not a characteristic of equity instruments. In addition, all derivatives are measured at fair value.

A **debt instrument** may be classified as measured at either amortised cost or fair value **depending on whether it meets the criteria above**. Even where the criteria are met at initial recognition, a debt instrument may be classified as measured at fair value through profit or loss if doing so eliminates or significantly reduces a measurement or recognition inconsistency (sometimes referred to as an 'accounting mismatch') that would otherwise arise from measuring assets or liabilities or recognizing the gains and losses on them on different bases.

8.3.1 Business model test in more detail

IFRS 9 introduces a business model test that requires an entity to assess whether its **business objective for a debt instrument is to collect the contractual cash flows of the instrument as opposed to realising its fair value change from sale prior to its contractual maturity**. Note the following key points:

(a) The assessment of a 'business model' is not made at an individual financial instrument level.

(b) The assessment is based on how key management personnel actually manage the business, rather than management's intentions for specific financial assets.

(c) An entity may have more than one business model for managing its financial assets and the classification need not be determined at the reporting entity level. For example, it may have one portfolio of investments that it manages with the objective of collecting contractual cash flows and another portfolio of investments held with the objective of trading to realise changes in fair value. It would be appropriate for entities like these to carry out the assessment for classification purposes at portfolio level, rather than at entity level.

(d) Although the objective of an entity's business model may be to hold financial assets in order to collect contractual cash flows, the entity need not hold all of those assets until maturity. Thus an entity's business model can be to hold financial assets to collect contractual cash flows even when sales of financial assets occur.

8.3.2 Business model test: examples

The following examples, from the Application Guidance to IFRS 9, are of situations where the objective of an entity's business model may be to hold financial assets to collect the contractual cash flows.

Example 1

An entity holds investments to collect their contractual cash flows but would sell an investment in particular circumstances, perhaps to fund capital expenditure, or because the credit rating of the instrument falls below that required by the entity's investment policy.

Analysis

Although an entity may consider, among other information, the financial assets' fair values from a liquidity perspective (ie the cash amount that would be realised if the entity needs to sell assets), the entity's objective is to hold the financial assets and collect the contractual cash flows. Some sales would not contradict that objective. If sales became frequent, the entity might be required to reconsider whether the sales were consistent with an objective of collecting contractual cash flows.

Example 2

An entity has a business model with the objective of originating loans to customers and subsequently to sell those loans to a securitisation vehicle. The securitisation vehicle issues instruments to investors.

The originating entity controls the securitisation vehicle and thus consolidates it. The securitisation vehicle collects the contractual cash flows from the loans and passes them on to its investors in the vehicle.

It is assumed for the purposes of this example that the loans continue to be recognised in the consolidated statement of financial position because they are not derecognised by the securitisation vehicle.

Analysis

The consolidated group originated the loans with the objective of holding them to collect the contractual cash flows.

However, the originating entity has an objective of realising cash flows on the loan portfolio by selling the loans to the securitisation vehicle, so for the purposes of its separate financial statements it would not be considered to be managing this portfolio in order to collect the contractual cash flows.

Example 3

An entity's business model is to purchase portfolios of financial assets, such as loans. Those portfolios may or may not include financial assets with incurred credit losses. If payment on the loans is not made on a timely basis, the entity attempts to extract the contractual cash flows through various means – for example, by contacting the debtor through mail, telephone, etc.

In some cases, the entity enters into interest rate swaps to change the interest rate on particular financial assets in a portfolio from a floating interest rate to a fixed interest rate.

Analysis

The objective of the entity's business model is to hold the financial assets and collect the contractual cash flows. The entity does not purchase the portfolio to make a profit by selling them.

The same analysis would apply even if the entity does not expect to receive all of the contractual cash flows (eg some of the financial assets have incurred credit losses).

Moreover, the fact that the entity has entered into derivatives to modify the cash flows of the portfolio does not in itself change the entity's business model. If the portfolio is not managed on a fair value basis, the objective of the business model could be to hold the assets to collect the contractual cash flows.

8.3.3 Contractual cash flow test in more detail

The requirement in IFRS 9 to assess the contractual cash flow characteristics of a financial asset is based on the concept that **only instruments with contractual cash flows of principal and interest on principal (may qualify for amortised cost measurement.** By interest, IFRS 9 means consideration for the time value of money and the credit risk associated with the principal outstanding during a particular period of time.

Question — **Contractual cash flows**

Would an investment in a convertible loan qualify to be measured at amortised cost under IFRS 9?

Answer

No because of the inclusion of the conversion option which is not deemed to represent payments of principal and interest

Measurement at amortised cost is permitted when the cash flows on a loan are entirely fixed (eg a fixed interest rate loan or zero coupon bond), or where interest is floating (eg a GBP loan where interest is contractually linked to GBP LIBOR), or combination of fixed and floating (eg where interest is LIBOR plus a fixed spread).

8.3.4 Examples of instruments that pass the contractual cash flows test

The following instruments satisfy the IFRS 9 criteria

(a) A variable rate instrument with a stated maturity date that permits the borrower to choose to pay three- month LIBOR for a three-month term or one-month LIBOR for a one-month term

(b) A fixed term variable market interest rate bond where the variable interest rate is capped

(c) A fixed term bond where the payments of principal and interest are linked to an unleveraged inflation index of the currency in which the instrument is issued

8.3.5 Examples of instruments that do not pass the contractual cash flows test

The following instruments do not satisfy the IFRS 9 criteria

(a) A bond that is convertible into equity instruments of the issuer

(b) A loan that pays an inverse floating interest rate (eg 8% minus LIBOR)

Note that the IFRS 9 requirement to classify financial assets on recognition as one of two types is **a significant simplification** of the previous IAS 39 rules. These required financial assets to be classified as one of four types, being:

- At fair value through profit or loss
- Held to maturity
- Available for sale, and
- Loans and receivables

8.4 Re-classification of financial assets

Although on initial recognition financial instruments must be classified in accordance with the requirements of IFRS 9, in some cases they may be subsequently reclassified. IFRS 9 requires that **when an entity changes its business model for managing financial assets, it should reclassify all affected financial assets.** This reclassification applies only to debt instruments, as equity instruments must be classified as measured at fair value.

The application guidance to IFRS 9 includes examples of circumstances when a reclassification is required or is not permitted.

8.4.1 Examples: Reclassification permitted

Reclassification is permitted in the following circumstances, because a **change in the business model** has taken place:

(a) An entity has a portfolio of commercial loans that it holds to sell in the short term. The entity acquires a company that manages commercial loans and has a business model that holds the loans in order to collect the contractual cash flows. The portfolio of commercial loans is no longer for sale, and the portfolio is now managed together with the acquired commercial loans and all are held to collect the contractual cash flows.

(b) A financial services firm decides to shut down its retail mortgage business. That business no longer accepts new business and the financial services firm is actively marketing its mortgage loan portfolio for sale.

8.4.2 Examples: Reclassification not permitted

Reclassification is **not permitted** in the following circumstances, because a **change in the business model has not taken place.**

(a) A change in intention related to particular financial assets (even in circumstances of significant changes in market conditions)

(b) A temporary disappearance of a particular market for financial assets

(c) A transfer of financial assets between parts of the entity with different business models.

8.5 Initial measurement

IFRS 9 requires that financial assets are initially measured at the **fair value of consideration given.** In the case of financial assets classified as measured at amortised cost, transaction costs directly attributable to the acquisition of the financial asset increase this amount.

8.6 Subsequent measurement

Financial assets are subsequently measured at :

- **Fair value** with changes in value normally recognised in profit or loss, or
- **Amortised cost** with interest recognised in profit or loss

8.6.1 Financial assets measured at fair value

Where a financial asset is classified as measured at fair value, fair value is established at each period end by reference to either the market price, where the instrument is quoted, or valuation techniques otherwise. IFRS 9 also states that in some cases, cost may be the best estimate of fair value.

Any changes in fair value are normally recognised in profit or loss. There is an **exception** to this rule where the financial asset is an investment in an **equity instrument not held for trading**. In this case the entity can make an irrevocable election to recognise changes in the fair value in **other comprehensive income.**

8.7 Example: Asset measurement

On 8 February 20X8 Orange Co acquires an investment in the shares of Lemon Co with the intention of holding it in the long term. The investment cost $850.000. At Orange Co's year end of 31 March 20X8, the market price of the investment is $900,000. How is the asset initially and subsequently measured?

Orange Co has elected to recognise changes in the fair value of the equity investment in other comprehensive income.

Solution

- The asset is initially recognised at the fair value of the consideration, being $850,000
- At the period end it is remeasured to $900,000
- This results in the recognition of $50,000 in other comprehensive income

8.8 Financial assets measured at amortised cost

IFRS 9 does not define amortised cost, but it refers to the definition of this and other relevant terms in IAS 39.

Comparison table

The following table shows the extent to which IFRS 9 simplifies the IAS 39 definitions.

Old IAS 39 Category	Measured at	Gains and losses
Financial asset at fair value through profit or loss	Fair value	Profit or loss
Available for sale financial asset	Fair value	Other comprehensive income
Financial asset held to maturity	Amortised cost	Profit or loss
Loans and receivables	Amortised cost	Profit or loss

8.9 Embedded derivatives

Where the host contract is a financial asset within the scope of the standard, the classification and **measurement rules of the standard are applied to the entire hybrid contract**.

This is a simplification of the IAS 39 rules, which required that an embedded derivative be **separated from its host contract** and accounted for as a derivative under certain conditions.

8.10 Exposure Draft: Amortised cost and impairment

This exposure draft, published in November 2009 is Phase 2 of the revision of IAS 39, IFRS 9 on assets being Phase 1 and hedging being Phase 3.

8.10.1 Why change?

Both IFRS and US GAAP currently use **an 'incurred loss' model** for the impairment of financial assets. This model assumes that all loans will be repaid until evidence to the contrary, that is until the occurrence of an event that triggers an impairment indicator. Only at this point is the impaired loan written down to a lower value. The global financial crisis has led to criticism of this approach for many reasons, including that it leads to an overstatement of interest revenue in the periods prior to the occurrence of a loss event, and produces deficient information.

8.10.2 Amortised cost

The ED set out principles to calculate amortised cost including:

(a) Defining the objective of amortised cost measurement for both financial assets and financial liabilities

(b) Explaining the measurement principles in determining amortised cost

(c) Articulating more clearly the application of these principles to variable rate instruments

Specifically:

(a) The ED states that the objective of amortised cost is 'to provide information about the effective return on a financial asset or financial liability by allocating interest revenue or interest expense over the expected life of the financial instrument'

(b) It contains more guidance on amortised cost of a variable instrument (ie it is the constant spread of a variable rate financial instrument that amortised cost applies to).

8.10.3 Impairment

Under the proposals, the 'incurred loss' model would be replaced with an approach **whereby expected losses are recognised throughout the life of the loan** (or other financial asset measured at amortised cost), and not just after a loss event has been identified. This is known as an expected cash flow (ECF) approach. Note the following:

(a) The ECF approach uses forward-looking cash flows that incorporate expected future credit losses throughout the term of a financial asset (eg a loan). In contrast to the existing incurred loss approach, the ECF approach would not require identification of impairment indicators or triggering events and would result in earlier recognition of credit losses.

(b) The effective interest rate will include an initial estimate of any expected credit losses. Credit losses will be held in a separate allowance account. Losses due to changes in cash flow estimates disclosed as a separate line item. If the item is considered uncollectable, write-offs will be made directly to the financial asset account.

8.10.4 Example: Expected losses

The following example is taken from the notes to a meeting of a joint IASB-FASB committee in March 2009.

An entity has a portfolio of 1,000 identical loans for $2,500 made on 1 January 20X1. Each loan has a contractual interest rate of 16 percent and requires interest payments of $400 on each December 31 for 9 years, followed by a payment of $2,900 on December 31 of the tenth year. The loans cannot be pre-paid. There are no transaction costs, fees, or origination costs. As a result, the effective interest rate as defined in IAS 39 is the same as the contractual rate.

Management estimates that no loans will default in 20X1 or 20X2. Beginning in 20X3, loans will default at an annual rate of about 9 percent. If that expectation is correct, then the rate of return from the portfolio will be approximately 9.07 percent.

There are several ways that an expected loss approach might be implemented. For purposes of this paper we have made two assumptions to fully integrate the approach into the loan accounting. First, the amount reported as interest income should continue to represent the contractual amount from outstanding loans. Second, the objective of the expected loss computation is to report the 9.07 percent expected return described earlier. With those assumptions, the expected loss approach is consistent with the underlying principles of loan accounting in IAS 39, except that it includes expected future credit losses.

Assuming again that losses occur as expected, selected amounts in the entity's financial statements would be:

Expected Loss Model

	Loans, net of allowance	*Interest income*	*Loan loss expense (incurred)*	*Expected loss adjustment*	*Interest less loan loss*	*Return, net of loan loss*
31/12/X1	2,326,689	400,000	0	173,311	226,689	9.07%
31/12/X2	2,137,662	400,000	0	189,027	210,973	9.07%
31/12/X3	1,967,496	364,000	225,000	-54,834	193,834	9.07%
31/12/X4	1,814,300	331,600	202,500	-49,304	178,404	9.07%
31/12/X6	1,676,812	302,000	185,000	-47,512	164,512	9.07%

31/12/X7	1,553,658	275,200	167,500	-44,346	152,046	9.07%
31/12/X8	1,443,737	250,800	152,500	-42,579	140,879	9.07%
31/12/X9	1,346,248	228,400	140,000	-42,511	130,911	9.07%
31/12/Y0	1,260,320	208,000	127,500	-41,572	122,072	9.07%
31/12/Y1	0	189,600	115,000	-39,680	114,280	9.07%

Alternative presentation

Below is an alternative presentation for the first two years to show how the figures are calculated:

	$
1.1.20X1 Loans	2,500,000
Interest 20X1 (16%) (using the full effective and contractual rate)	400,000
31.12.20X1 Interest received	(400,000)
Loss adjustment (400,000 – 226,689*)	(173,311)
31.12.20X1 c/f	2,326,689

* Interest calculated using the "loss adjusted rate of 9.06756% on the carrying value (9.06756% × 2,500,000)

	$
1.1.20X2 b/f	2,326,689
Interest 20X2 (16%) (using the full effective and contractual rate**)	400,000
31.12.20X2 Interest received	(400,000)
Loss adjustment (400,000 – 210,973***)	(189,027)
31.12.20X2 c/f	2,137,662

** Loss adjustment is actually credited to an allowance account, so offset against the loan asset on the statement of financial position. The interest continues to be calculated on the loan balance of $2,500,000.

*** The loss adjusted interest is calculated on the balance brought forward net of the allowance.

Then when losses start to be incurred in the third year:

	$
1.1.20X3 b/f	2,137,662
Loans in default written off ($2,500,000 × 9%)	(225,000)
Interest 20X3 (16%) (using the full effective and contractual rate****)	364,000
31.12.20X3 Interest received	(364,000)
Loss adjustment (364,000 – 193,834***** – 225,000******)	54,834
31.12.20X3 c/f	1,967,496

**** The contract/effective interest is now applied only to the remaining loans $2,275,000 ($2,500,000 –$225,000)

***** The loss adjusted interest is calculated as (9.06756% ×2,137,662)

******The loans written off will be debited to the loss allowance account

8.10.5 Disclosures

The ED would require **extensive disclosures provide investors with an understanding of the loss estimates** that an entity judges necessary and to enable users to evaluate the financial effect of interest revenue and expense, and the quality of financial assets including credit risk. These include:

(a) Mandatory use of an **allowance account** to account for credit losses

(b) **Detail about estimates** and changes in estimates; reconciliation of changes in an entity's non-performing assets, that is financial assets more than ninety days overdue or considered uncollectible.

(c) Information about the **origination and maturity** of financial assets

(d) The results of **'stress testing'**, if this is performed for internal risk management. (Stress testing is where management look at how robust a particular financial instrument is in certain extreme cases.)

The following disclosures must be made on the face of the statement of comprehensive income:

Gross interest revenue (effective interest method before initial credit losses)	X
Reduction due to allocation of initial expected credit losses	(X)
Net (must be shown)	X
Gains/(losses) due to changes in estimates	X/(X)
Interest expense	(X)

8.10.6 Possible consequences

The proposals represent a **significant change from current practice.** The IASB acknowledges that their application would probably result in significant systems and operational challenges such as developing reliable estimates of cash flows over the expected lives of financial assets. Accordingly, the IASB proposes that the IFRS resulting from ED will not become mandatory until about three years after it is issued.

9 Disclosure of financial instruments

FAST FORWARD

IFRS 7 specifies the **disclosures** required for financial instruments. The standard requires qualitative and quantitative disclosures about exposure to risks arising from financial instruments and specifies minimum disclosures about credit risk, liquidity risk and market risk.

Exam focus point

Skim through for background only – disclosures are unlikely to be tested in detail.

The IASB maintains that users of financial instruments need information about an entity's exposures to risks and how those risks are managed, as this information can **influence a user's assessment of the financial position and financial performance of an entity** or of the amount, timing and uncertainty of its **future cash flows.**

There have been new techniques and approaches to measuring risk management, which highlighted the need for guidance.

Accordingly, IFRS 7 *Financial instruments: Disclosures* was issued in August 2005. The standard revises, enhances and replaces the disclosures in IAS 30 and IAS 32. The presentation aspects of IAS 32 are retained, and IAS 32 has been renamed *Financial instruments: Presentation.*

9.1 General requirements

The extent of disclosure required depends on the extent of the entity's use of financial instruments and of its exposure to risk. It **adds to the requirements previously in IAS 32** by requiring:

- Enhanced statement of financial position and statement of comprehensive income disclosures
- Disclosures about an allowance account when one is used to reduce the carrying amount of impaired financial instruments.

The standard requires **qualitative and quantitative disclosures about exposure to risks** arising from financial instruments, and specifies minimum disclosures about **credit risk**, **liquidity risk** and **market risk**.

9.2 Objective

The objective of the IFRS is to require entities to provide disclosures in their financial statements that enable users to evaluate:

(a) The significance of financial instruments for the entity's financial position and performance

(b) The nature and extent of risks arising from financial instruments to which the entity is exposed during the period and at the reporting date, and how the entity manages those risks.

The principles in IFRS 7 complement the principles for recognising, measuring and presenting financial assets and financial liabilities in IAS 32 *Financial instruments: Presentation* and IAS 39 *Financial instruments: Recognition and Measurement*.

9.3 Classes of financial instruments and levels of disclosure

The entity must group financial instruments into classes **appropriate to the nature of the information disclosed**. An entity must decide in the light of its circumstances how much detail it provides. Sufficient information must be provided to permit reconciliation to the line items presented in the statement of financial position.

9.3.1 Statement of financial position

The following must be disclosed.

(a) **Carrying amount** of financial assets and liabilities by IAS 39 category

(b) **Reason for any reclassification** between fair value and amortised cost (and vice versa)

(c) **Details** of the assets and exposure to risk where the entity has made a **transfer** such that part or all of the financial assets do not qualify for derecognition.

(d) The **carrying amount** of financial assets the entity has **pledged as collateral** for liabilities or contingent liabilities and the associated terms and conditions.

(e) When financial assets are impaired by credit losses and the entity records the impairment in a separate account (eg an **allowance account** used to record individual impairments or a similar account used to record a collective impairment of assets) rather than directly reducing the carrying amount of the asset, it must disclose a **reconciliation** of changes in that account during the period for each class of financial assets.

(f) The **existence of multiple embedded derivatives**, where compound instruments contain these.

(g) Defaults and breaches.

9.3.2 Statement of comprehensive income

The entity must disclose the following **items of income, expense, gains or losses**, either on the face of the financial statements or in the notes.

(a) Net gains/losses by IAS 39 category (broken down as appropriate: eg interest, fair value changes, dividend income)

(b) Interest income/expense

(c) Impairments losses by class of financial asset

9.3.3 Other disclosures

Entities must disclose in the summary of **significant accounting policies** the measurement basis used in preparing the financial statements and the other accounting policies that are relevant to an understanding of the financial statements.

Disclosures must be made relating to **hedge accounting**, as follows:

(a) Description of hedge

(b) Description of financial instruments designated as **hedging instruments** and their fair value at the reporting date

(c) The **nature of the risks** being hedged

(d) For **cash flow hedges**, periods **when the cash flows will occur** and when will affect profit or loss

(e) For fair value hedges, gains or losses on the hedging instrument and the hedged item

(f) The **ineffectiveness recognised in profit or loss** arising from cash flow hedges and net investments in foreign operations

Disclosures must be made relating to **fair value**:

(a) **By class** in a way that allows comparison to statement of financial position value in the statement of financial position. (Financial assets and liabilities may only be offset to the extent that their carrying amounts are offset in the statement of financial position.)

(b) The **methods and assumptions** used, for example by reference to an active market, and any change in these assumptions. If the market for a financial instrument is not active, a valuation technique, as per IAS 39, must be used. There could be a difference between the fair value at initial recognition and the amount that would be determined using the valuation technique. The accounting policy for recognising that difference in profit or loss, the aggregate difference yet to be recognised in profit or loss at the beginning and end of the period and a reconciliation of the changes in the balance of this difference, should be disclosed, as in the following example.

9.3.4 Example: Fair value disclosures

Background

On 1 January 20X1 an entity purchases for $15 million financial assets that are not traded in an active market. The entity has only one class of such financial assets.

The transaction price of $15 million is the fair value at initial recognition.

After initial recognition, the entity will apply a valuation technique to establish the financial assets fair value. This valuation technique includes variables other than data from observable markets.

At initial recognition, the same valuation technique would have resulted in an amount of $14 million, which differs from fair value by $1 million.

The entity has existing differences of $5 million at 1 January 20X1.

Application of requirements

The entity's 20X2 disclosure would include the following:

Accounting policies

The entity uses the following valuation technique to determine the fair value of financial instruments that are not traded in an active market: [description of technique, not included in this example]. Differences may arise between the fair value at initial recognition (which, in accordance with IAS 39, is generally the transaction price) and the amount determined at initial recognition using the valuation technique. Any such differences are [description of the entity's accounting policy].

In the notes to the financial statements

As discussed in note X, the entity uses [name of valuation technique] to measure the fair value of the following financial instruments that are not traded in an active market. However, in accordance with IAS 39, the fair value of an instrument at inception is generally the transaction price. If the transaction price differs from the amount determined at inception using the valuation technique, that difference is [description of the entity's accounting policy]. The differences yet to be recognised in profit or loss are as follows:

	31 Dec 20X2	*31 Dec 20X1*
	$m	$m
Balance at beginning of year	5.3	5.0
New transactions		1.0
Amounts recognised in profit or loss during the year	(0.7)	(0.8)
Other increases		0.2
Other decreases	(0.1)	(0.1)
Balance at end of year	4.5	5.3

Disclosures of fair value are **not required** if carrying value is a reasonable approximation to fair value, or if fair value cannot be measured reliably.

9.4 Nature and extent of risks arising from financial instruments

In undertaking transactions in financial instruments, an entity may assume or transfer to another party one or more of **different types of financial risk** as defined below. The disclosures required by the standard show the extent to which an entity is exposed to these different types of risk, relating to both recognised and unrecognised financial instruments.

Credit risk	The risk that one party to a financial instrument will cause a financial loss for the other party by failing to discharge an obligation.
Currency risk	The risk that the fair value or future cash flows of a financial instrument will fluctuate because of changes in foreign exchange rates.
Interest rate risk	The risk that the fair value or future cash flows of a financial instrument will fluctuate because of changes in market interest rates.
Liquidity risk	The risk that an entity will encounter difficulty in meeting obligations associated with financial liabilities.
Loans payable	Loans payable are financial liabilities, other than short-term trade payables on normal credit terms.
Market risk	The risk that the fair value or future cash flows of a financial instrument will fluctuate because of changes in market prices. Market risk comprises three types of risk: currency risk, interest rate risk and other price risk.
Other price risk	The risk that the fair value or future cash flows of a financial instrument will fluctuate because of changes in market prices (other than those arising from interest rate risk or currency risk), whether those changes are caused by factors specific to the individual financial instrument or its issuer, or factors affecting all similar financial instruments traded in the market.
Past due	A financial asset is past due when a counterparty has failed to make a payment when contractually due.

9.4.1 Qualitative disclosures

For each type of risk arising from financial instruments, an entity must disclose:

(a) The **exposures to risk** and how they arise

(b) Its objectives, policies and processes for managing the risk and the methods used to measure the risk

(c) Any **changes** in (a) or (b) from the previous period

9.4.2 Quantitative disclosures

For each financial instrument risk, **summary quantitative data** about risk exposure must be disclosed. This should be based on the information provided internally to key management personnel. More information should be provided if this is unrepresentative.
Information about **credit risk** must be disclosed by class of financial instrument:

(a) Maximum exposure at the year end

(b) Any collateral pledged as security

(c) In respect of the amount disclosed in (b), a description of collateral held as security and other credit enhancements

(d) Information about the credit quality of financial assets that are neither **past due** nor impaired

(e) Financial assets that are past due or impaired, giving an age analysis and a description of collateral held by the entity as security.

(f) Collateral and other credit enhancements obtained, including the nature and carrying amount of the assets and policy for disposing of assets not readily convertible into cash

For **liquidity risk** entities must disclose:

(a) A maturity analysis of financial liabilities
(b) A description of the way risk is managed

Disclosures required in connection with **market risk** are:

(a) Sensitivity analysis, showing the effects on profit or loss of changes in each market risk
(b) If the sensitivity analysis reflects interdependencies between risk variables, such as interest rates and exchange rates the method, **assumptions and limitations** must be disclosed

9.5 Capital disclosures

Certain disclosures about **capital** are required. An entity's capital does not relate solely to financial instruments, but has more general relevance. Accordingly, those disclosures are included in IAS 1, rather than in IFRS 7.

Chapter Roundup

- Financial instruments can be very complex, particularly **derivative instruments**, although **primary instruments** are more straightforward.
- The important definitions to understand are:
  - **Financial asset**
  - **Financial liability**
  - **Equity instrument**
- Financial instruments must be classified as **liabilities** or **equity** according to their **substance**
- The critical feature of a financial liability is the **contractual obligation to deliver cash** or another financial asset.
- **Compound instruments** are split into **equity** and **liability** components and presented accordingly in the statement of financial position.
- **IAS 39** *Financial instruments: recognition and measurement* is a controversial standard.
- The IAS states that **all financial assets and liabilities** should be **recognised in the statement of financial position, including derivatives.**
- Financial assets are now also accounted for under IFRS 9. The recognition of financial assets is being amended by IFRS 9 *Financial Instruments.* IFRS 9 is a work in progress.
- **Financial assets** should **initially** be measured at **cost = fair value**.
- Subsequently they should be **re-measured to fair value** except for

  (a) Loans and receivables not held for trading
  (b) Other **held-to-maturity investments**
  (c) **Financial assets** whose value **cannot be reliably measured**

- **Hedge accounting** is allowed in certain strictly defined circumstances.
- Many users and preparers of accounts have found financial instruments to be **complex.** The IASB has recently issued a Discussion Paper, which aims at reducing complexity.
- Changes to IAS 39 introduced in October 2008 permit entities to **reclassify non-derivative financial assets out of the 'fair value through profit or loss' and 'available-for-sale' categories** in limited circumstances. Additional disclosures are required.
- **IFRS 9** ***Financial Instruments*** was issued in November 2009, and **replaced** and **simplified** certain parts of **IAS 39**, particularly with respect to the classification of financial assets. This standard is a work in progress and will be developed further in due course to fully replace IAS 39.
- **IFRS 7** specifies the **disclosures** required for financial instruments. The standard requires quantitative and qualitative disclosures about exposure to risks arising from financial instruments and specifies minimum disclosures about credit risk, liquidity risk and market risk.

Quick Quiz

1 Which four issues are dealt with by IAS 32?

2 What items are *not* financial instruments according to IAS 32?

3 What is the critical feature used to identify a financial liability?

4 How should compound instruments be presented in the statement of financial position?

5 Define interest rate risk and credit risk.

6 When should a financial asset be de-recognised?

7 How are financial instruments initially measured?

8 What is hedging?

9 Name the three types of hedging relationship identified by IAS 39.

10 How are financial assets measured under IFRS 9, subsequent to initial recognition?

11 How are embedded derivatives treated under IFRS 9?

Answers to Quick Quiz

1 Classification; presentation; offsetting and disclosure

2 Physical assets; prepaid expenses; non-contractual assets or liabilities; contractual rights not involving transfer of assets

3 The contractual obligation to deliver cash or another financial asset to the holder

4 By calculating the present value of the liability component and then deducting this from the instrument as a whole to leave a residual value for the equity component

5 See Key Terms, Section 3.4

6 Financial assets should be derecognised when the rights to the cash flows from the asset expire or where substantially all the risks and rewards of ownership are transferred to another party.

7 At cost

8 See Key Terms, Section 6.1

9 Fair value hedge; cash flow hedge; hedge of a net investment in a foreign operation

10 At amortised cost or fair value.

11 Where the host contract is a financial asset within the scope of the standard, the , the classification and measurement rules of the standard are applied to the entire hybrid contract.

Now try the questions below from the Exam Question Bank

Number	Level	Marks	Time
Q14	Introductory	n/a	n/a
Q15	Examination	25	45 mins

Accounting for taxation

Topic list	Syllabus reference
1 Current tax	2(j)
2 Deferred tax	2(j)
3 Taxable temporary differences	2(j)
4 Deductible temporary differences	2(j)
5 Measurement and recognition of deferred tax	2(j)
6 Taxation in company accounts	2(j)
7 Deferred taxation and business combinations	2(j)

Introduction

In almost all countries entities are taxed on the basis of their trading income. In some countries this may be called corporation or corporate tax, but we will follow the terminology of IAS 12 *Income taxes* and call it **income tax**.

There are two main systems for taxing corporate income: the **classical system** and the **imputation system**: go back to your earlier study material if necessary. For this chapter we will assume a classical system. Of course, each country will be different in its tax legislation and its method of accounting for taxation may reflect this.

There are two aspects of income tax which must be accounted for: **current tax** and **deferred tax**. Current tax is revised briefly in Section 1. The rest of this chapter is concerned with deferred tax, which students invariably find difficult.

Section 6 introduces a new aspect of deferred tax, relating to **business combinations**. This represents one of the most complex areas of deferred tax.

Note. Throughout this chapter we will assume a current corporate income tax rate of 30% and a current personal income tax rate of 20%, unless otherwise stated.

Study guide

Section 11 – Taxation in financial statements

- Account for current tax liabilities and assets in accordance with international accounting standards
- Describe the general principles of government sales taxes (eg VAT or GST)
- Explain the effect of taxable temporary differences on accounting and taxable profits
- Outline the principles of accounting for deferred tax
- Identify and account for the IASB requirements relating to deferred tax assets and liabilities
- Calculate and record deferred tax amounts in the financial statements
- *Note.* Throughout this chapter we will assume a current corporate income tax rate of 30% and a current personal income tax rate of 20%.

Exam guide

Be prepared for a whole question on deferred tax, as happened on the Pilot Paper, when you were asked to discuss the conceptual basis for its accounting treatment and to calculate the deferred tax provision after making adjustments. The December 2009 paper notably contained a 12-mark requirement focusing on deferred tax.

1 Current tax

Taxation in company accounts consists broadly of indirect government sales taxes (eg VAT or GST), and direct taxes on company income. Sales tax is relatively straightforward to account for. Revenue and expenses are stated net of sales tax, with the result that sales tax does not generally affect the income statement. The statement of financial position will generally include a payable representing the current liability for sales tax.

The rest of this chapter will deal with the effect on the financial statements of direct taxes on company income.

1.1 Current tax in the financial statements

FAST FORWARD

Taxation consists of **two components.**

- Current tax
- Deferred tax

Current tax is ordinarily straightforward. Complexities arise, however, when we consider the future tax consequences of what is going on in the accounts now. This is an aspect of tax called deferred tax, which we will look at in the next section. IAS 12 *Income taxes* covers both current and deferred tax. The parts relating to current tax are fairly brief, because this is the simple and uncontroversial area of tax.

1.2 Definitions

These are some of the definitions given in IAS 12. We will look at the rest later.

Key terms

Accounting profit. Net profit or loss for a period before deducting tax expense.

Taxable profit (tax loss). The profit (loss) for a period, determined in accordance with the rules established by the taxation authorities, upon which income taxes are payable (recoverable).

Tax expense (tax income). The aggregate amount included in the determination of net profit or loss for the period in respect of current tax and deferred tax.

> **Current tax**. The amount of income taxes payable (recoverable) in respect of the taxable profit (tax loss) for a period. *(IAS 12)*

Remember the difference between current and deferred tax.

(a) **Current tax** is the amount *actually payable* to the tax authorities in relation to the trading activities of the entity during the period.

(b) **Deferred tax** is an *accounting measure*, used to match the tax effects of transactions with their accounting impact and thereby produce less distorted results.

1.3 Recognition of current tax liabilities and assets

FAST FORWARD

> **Current tax** is the amount payable to the tax authorities in relation to the trading activities during the period. It is generally straightforward.

IAS 12 requires any **unpaid tax** in respect of the current or prior periods to be recognised as a **liability**.

Conversely, any **excess tax** paid in respect of current or prior periods over what is due should be recognised as an asset.

Question — Current tax

In 20X8 Darton Co had taxable profits of $120,000. In the previous year (20X7) income tax on 20X7 profits had been estimated as $30,000.

Required

Calculate tax payable and the charge for 20X8 if the tax due on 20X7 profits was subsequently agreed with the tax authorities as:

(a) $35,000
(b) $25,000

Any under or over payments are not settled until the following year's tax payment is due.

Answer

(a)

	$
Tax due on 20X8 profits ($120,000 × 30%)	40,000
Underpayment for 20X7	5,000
Tax charge and liability	45,000

(b)

	$
Tax due on 20X8 profits (as above)	40,000
Overpayment for 20X7	(5,000)
Tax charge and liability	35,000

Alternatively, the rebate due could be shown separately as income in the statement of comprehensive income and as an asset in the statement of financial position. An offset approach like this is, however, most likely.

Taking this a stage further, IAS 12 also requires recognition as an asset of the benefit relating to any tax loss that can be **carried back** to recover current tax of a previous period. This is acceptable because it is probable that the benefit will flow to the entity *and* it can be reliably measured.

1.4 Example: Tax losses carried back

In 20X7 Eramu Co paid $50,000 in tax on its profits. In 20X8 the company made tax losses of $24,000. The local tax authority rules allow losses to be carried back to offset against current tax of prior years.

Required

Show the tax charge and tax liability for 20X8.

Solution

Tax repayment due on tax losses = 30% × $24,000 = $7,200.

The double entry will be:

DEBIT	Tax receivable (statement of financial position)	$7,200	
CREDIT	Tax repayment (statement of comprehensive income)		$7,200

The tax receivable will be shown as an asset until the repayment is received from the tax authorities.

1.5 Measurement

Measurement of current tax liabilities (assets) for the current and prior periods is very simple. They are measured at the **amount expected to be paid to (recovered from) the tax authorities**. The tax rates (and tax laws) used should be those enacted (or substantively enacted) by the year end.

1.6 Recognition of current tax

Normally, current tax is recognised as income or expense and included in the net profit or loss for the period, except in two cases.

(a) Tax arising from a **business combination** which is an acquisition is treated differently (see Section 6 of this chapter).

(b) Tax arising from a transaction or event which is recognised **directly in equity** (in the same or a different period).

The rule in (b) is logical. If a transaction or event is charged or credited directly to equity, rather than to profit or loss, then the related tax should be also. An example of such a situation is where, under IAS 8, an adjustment is made to the **opening balance of retained earnings** due to either a change in accounting policy that is applied retrospectively, or to the correction of a fundamental error.

1.7 Presentation

In the statement of financial position, **tax assets and liabilities** should be shown separately from other assets and liabilities.

Current tax assets and liabilities can be **offset**, but this should happen only when certain conditions apply.

(a) The entity has a **legally enforceable right** to set off the recognised amounts.

(b) The entity intends to settle the amounts on a **net basis**, or to realise the asset and settle the liability at thc same time.

The **tax expense (income)** related to the profit or loss from ordinary activities should be shown in the income statement.

2 Deferred tax

FAST FORWARD

Deferred tax is an accounting measure, used to match the tax effects of transactions with their accounting impact. It is quite complex.

Exam focus point

Students invariably find deferred tax very confusing. It is an inherently difficult topic and as such is likely to appear frequently. You *must* understand the contents of the rest of this chapter.

2.1 What is deferred tax?

When a company recognises an asset or liability, it expects to **recover or settle the carrying amount** of that asset or liability. In other words, it expects to sell or use up assets, and to pay off liabilities. What happens if that recovery or settlement is likely to make future tax payments larger (or smaller) than they would otherwise have been if the recovery or settlement had no tax consequences? In these circumstances, IAS 12 requires companies to recognise a **deferred tax liability** (or **deferred tax asset**).

2.2 Definitions

Here are the definitions relating to deferred tax given in IAS 12.

Key terms

Deferred tax liabilities are the amounts of income taxes payable in future periods in respect of taxable temporary differences.

Deferred tax assets are the amounts of income taxes recoverable in future periods in respect of:

- Deductible temporary differences
- The carryforward of unused tax losses
- The carryforward of unused tax credits

Temporary differences are differences between the carrying amount of an asset or liability in the statement of financial position and its tax base. Temporary differences may be either:

- **Taxable temporary differences**, which are temporary differences that will result in taxable amounts in determining taxable profit (tax loss) of future periods when the carrying amount of the asset or liability is recovered or settled
- **Deductible temporary differences**, which are temporary differences that will result in amounts that are deductible in determining taxable profit (tax loss) of future periods when the carrying amount of the asset or liability is recovered or settled.

The **tax base** of an asset or liability is the amount attributed to that asset or liability for tax purposes.

(IAS 12)

2.3 Tax base

We can expand on the definition given above by stating that the **tax base of an asset** is the amount that will be deductible for tax purposes against any taxable economic benefits that will flow to the entity when it recovers the carrying value of the asset. Where those economic benefits are not taxable, the tax base of the asset is the same as its carrying amount.

Question — Tax base 1

State the tax base of each of the following assets.

(a) A machine cost $10,000. For tax purposes, depreciation of $3,000 has already been deducted in the current and prior periods and the remaining cost will be deductible in future periods, either as depreciation or through a deduction on disposal. Revenue generated by using the machine is taxable, any gain on disposal of the machine will be taxable and any loss on disposal will be deductible for tax purposes.

(b) Interest receivable has a carrying amount of $1,000. The related interest revenue will be taxed on a cash basis.

(c) Trade receivables have a carrying amount of $10,000. The related revenue has already been included in taxable profit (tax loss).

(d) A loan receivable has a carrying amount of $1m. The repayment of the loan will have no tax consequences.

(e) Dividends receivable from a subsidiary have a carrying amount of $5,000. The dividends are not taxable.

Answer

(a) The tax base of the machine is $7,000.
(b) The tax base of the interest receivable is nil.
(c) The tax base of the trade receivables is $10,000.
(d) The tax base of the loan is $1m.
(e) The tax base of the dividend is $5,000.

In the case of (e), in substance the entire carrying amount of the asset is deductible against the economic benefits. There is no taxable temporary difference. An alternative analysis is that the accrued dividends receivable have a tax base of nil and a tax rate of nil is applied to the resulting taxable temporary difference ($5,000). Under both analyses, there is no deferred tax liability.

In the case of a **liability**, the tax base will be its carrying amount, less any amount that will be deducted for tax purposes in relation to the liability in future periods. For revenue received in advance, the tax base of the resulting liability is its carrying amount, less any amount of the revenue that will *not* be taxable in future periods.

Question — Tax base 2

State the tax base of each of the following liabilities.

(a) Current liabilities include accrued expenses with a carrying amount of $1,000. The related expense will be deducted for tax purposes on a cash basis.

(b) Current liabilities include interest revenue received in advance, with a carrying amount of $10,000. The related interest revenue was taxed on a cash basis.

(c) Current assets include prepaid expenses with a carrying amount of $2,000. The related expense has already been deducted for tax purposes.

(d) Current liabilities include accrued fines and penalties with a carrying amount of $100. Fines and penalties are not deductible for tax purposes.

(e) A loan payable has a carrying amount of $1m. The repayment of the loan will have no tax consequences.

Answer

(a) The tax base of the accrued expenses is nil.
(b) The tax base of the interest received in advance is nil.
(c) The tax base of the accrued expenses is $2,000.
(d) The tax base of the accrued fines and penalties is $100.
(e) The tax base of the loan is $1m.

IAS 12 gives the following examples of circumstances in which the carrying amount of an asset or liability will be **equal to its tax base**.

- **Pre-paid expenses** have already been deducted in determining an entity's current tax liability for the current or earlier periods.
- A **loan payable** is measured at the amount originally received and this amount is the same as the amount repayable on final maturity of the loan.
- **Accrued expenses** will never be deductible for tax purposes.
- **Accrued income** will never be taxable.

2.4 Temporary differences

You may have found the definition of temporary differences somewhat confusing. Remember that accounting profits form the basis for computing **taxable profits**, on which the tax liability for the year is calculated. However, accounting profits and taxable profits are different. There are two reasons for the differences.

(a) **Permanent differences**. These occur when certain items of revenue or expense are excluded from the computation of taxable profits (for example, entertainment expenses may not be allowable for tax purposes).

(b) **Temporary differences**. These occur when items of revenue or expense are included in both accounting profits and taxable profits, but not for the same accounting period. For example, an expense which is allowable as a deduction in arriving at taxable profits for 20X7 might not be included in the financial accounts until 20X8 or later. In the long run, the total taxable profits and total accounting profits will be the same (except for permanent differences) so that timing differences originate in one period and are capable of reversal in one or more subsequent periods. Deferred tax is the tax attributable to **temporary differences.**

The distinction made in the definition between **taxable temporary differences** and **deductible temporary differences** can be made clearer by looking at the explanations and examples given in the standard and its appendices.

2.5 Section summary

- Deferred tax is an **accounting device**. It does *not* represent tax payable to the tax authorities.
- The **tax base** of an asset or liability is the value of that asset or liability for tax purposes.
- You should understand the difference between **permanent and temporary differences**.
- Deferred tax is the tax attributable to **temporary differences**.

3 Taxable temporary differences

FAST FORWARD

Deferred tax assets and liabilities arise from taxable and deductible temporary differences.

Exam focus point

The rule to remember here is that:

'All taxable temporary differences give rise to a deferred tax liability.'

The following are examples of circumstances that give rise to taxable temporary differences.

3.1 Transactions that affect the statement of comprehensive income

- **Interest revenue** received in arrears and included in accounting profit on the basis of time apportionment. It is included in taxable profit, however, on a cash basis.
- **Sale of goods revenue** is included in accounting profit when the goods are delivered, but only included in taxable profit when cash is received.
- **Depreciation** of an asset is accelerated for tax purposes. When new assets are purchased, allowances may be available against taxable profits which exceed the amount of depreciation chargeable on the assets in the financial accounts for the year of purchase.
- **Development costs** which have been capitalised will be amortised in profit or loss, but they were deducted in full from taxable profit in the period in which they were incurred.
- **Prepaid expenses** have already been deducted on a cash basis in determining the taxable profit of the current or previous periods.

3.2 Transactions that affect the statement of financial position

- **Depreciation of an asset** is not deductible for tax purposes. No deduction will be available for tax purposes when the asset is sold/scrapped.
- A borrower records a **loan** at proceeds received (amount due at maturity) less transaction costs. The carrying amount of the loan is subsequently increased by amortisation of the transaction costs against accounting profit. The transaction costs were, however, deducted for tax purposes in the period when the loan was first recognised.
- A **loan** payable is measured on initial recognition at net proceeds (net of transaction costs). The transaction costs are amortised to accounting profit over the life of the loan. Those transaction costs are not deductible in determining the taxable profit of future, current or prior periods.
- The liability component of a **compound financial instrument** (eg a convertible bond) is measured at a discount to the amount repayable on maturity, after assigning a portion of the cash proceeds to the equity component (see IAS 32). The discount is not deductible in determining taxable profit.

3.3 Fair value adjustments and revaluations

- **Current investments** or financial instruments are carried at fair value. This exceeds cost, but no equivalent adjustment is made for tax purposes.
- Property, plant and equipment is **revalued** by an entity (under IAS 16), but no equivalent adjustment is made for tax purposes. This also applies to long-term investments.

The standard also looks at the deferred tax implications of business combinations and consolidations. We will look at these in Section 7.

Remember the rule we gave you above, that all taxable temporary differences give rise to a deferred tax liability? There are **two circumstances** given in the standards where this does *not* apply.

(a) The deferred tax liability arises from the initial recognition of **goodwill**.

(b) The deferred tax liability arises from the **initial** recognition of an asset or liability in a transaction which:

(i) is *not* a business combination (see Section 6), *and*
(ii) at the time of the transaction affects neither accounting profit nor taxable profit.

Try to **understand the reasoning** behind the recognition of deferred tax liabilities on taxable temporary differences.

(a) When an **asset is recognised**, it is expected that its carrying amount will be recovered in the form of economic benefits that flow to the entity in future periods.
(b) If the carrying amount of the asset is **greater than** its tax base, then taxable economic benefits will also be greater than the amount that will be allowed as a deduction for tax purposes.
(c) The difference is therefore a **taxable temporary difference** and the obligation to pay the resulting income taxes in future periods is a **deferred tax liability**.
(d) As the entity recovers the carrying amount of the asset, the taxable temporary difference will **reverse** and the entity will have taxable profit.
(e) It is then probable that economic benefits will flow from the entity in the form of **tax payments**, and so the recognition of all deferred tax liabilities (except those excluded above) is required by IAS 12.

3.3.1 Example: Taxable temporary differences

A company purchased an asset costing $1,500. At the end of 20X8 the carrying amount is $1,000. The cumulative depreciation for tax purposes is $900 and the current tax rate is 25%.

Required

Calculate the deferred tax liability for the asset.

Solution

Firstly, what is the tax base of the asset? It is $1,500 – $900 = $600.

In order to recover the carrying value of $1,000, the entity must earn taxable income of $1,000, but it will only be able to deduct $600 as a taxable expense. The entity must therefore pay income tax of $400 × 25% = $100 when the carrying value of the asset is recovered.

The entity must therefore recognise a deferred tax liability of $400 × 25% = $100, recognising the difference between the carrying amount of $1,000 and the tax base of $600 as a taxable temporary difference.

3.4 Revalued assets

Under IAS 16 assets may be revalued. If this affects the taxable profit for the current period, the tax base of the asset changes and **no temporary difference** arises.

If, however (as in some countries), the revaluation does *not* affect current taxable profits, the tax base of the asset is not adjusted. Consequently, the taxable flow of economic benefits to the entity as the carrying value of the asset is recovered will differ from the amount that will be deductible for tax purposes. The difference between the carrying amount of a revalued asset and its tax base is a temporary difference and gives rise to a **deferred tax liability or asset**.

3.5 Initial recognition of an asset or liability

A temporary difference can arise on initial recognition of an asset or liability, eg if part or all of the cost of an asset will not be deductible for tax purposes. The **nature of the transaction** which led to the initial recognition of the asset is important in determining the method of accounting for such temporary differences.

If the transaction affects *either* accounting profit or taxable profit, an entity will **recognise any deferred tax liability** or asset. The resulting deferred tax expense or income will be recognised in profit or loss.

Where a transaction affects **neither accounting profit nor taxable profit** it would be normal for an entity to recognise a deferred tax liability or asset and adjust the carrying amount of the asset or liability by the same amount (unless exempted by IAS 12 as under Paragraph 3.6 above). However, IAS 12 does *not* permit this recognition of a deferred tax asset or liability as it would make the financial statements less transparent. This will be the case both on initial recognition and subsequently, nor should any subsequent changes in the unrecognised deferred tax liability or asset as the asset is depreciated be made.

3.6 Example: Initial recognition

As an example of the last paragraph, suppose Petros Co intends to use an asset which cost $10,000 in 20X7 through its useful life of five years. Its residual value will then be nil. The tax rate is 40%. Any capital gain on disposal would not be taxable (and any capital loss not deductible). Depreciation of the asset is not deductible for tax purposes.

Required

State the deferred tax consequences in each of years 20X7 and 20X8.

Solution

As at 20X7, as it recovers the carrying amount of the asset, Petros Co will earn taxable income of $10,000 and pay tax of $4,000. The resulting deferred tax liability of $4,000 would not be recognised because it results from the initial recognition of the asset.

As at 20X8, the carrying value of the asset is now $8,000. In earning taxable income of $8,000, the entity will pay tax of $3,200. Again, the resulting deferred tax liability of $3,200 is not recognised, because it results from the initial recognition of the asset.

The following question on accelerated depreciation should clarify some of the issues and introduce you to the calculations which may be necessary in the exam.

Question

Jonquil Co buys equipment for $50,000 and depreciates it on a straight line basis over its expected useful life of five years. For tax purposes, the equipment is depreciated at 25% per annum on a straight line basis. Tax losses may be carried back against taxable profit of the previous five years. In year 20X0, the entity's taxable profit was $25,000. The tax rate is 40%.

Required

Assuming nil profits/losses after depreciation in years 20X1 to 20X5 show the current and deferred tax impact in years 20X1 to 20X5 of the acquisition of the equipment.

Answer

Jonquil Co will recover the carrying amount of the equipment by using it to manufacture goods for resale. Therefore, the entity's current tax computation is as follows.

			Year		
	20X1	*20X2*	*20X3*	*20X4*	*20X5*
	$	$	$	$	$
Taxable income*	10,000	10,000	10,000	10,000	10,000
Depreciation for tax purposes	12,500	12,500	12,500	12,500	0
Taxable profit (tax loss)	(2,500)	(2,500)	(2,500)	(2,500)	10,000
Current tax expense (income) at 40%	(1,000)	(1,000)	(1,000)	(1,000)	4,000

* ie nil profit plus ($50,000 ÷ 5) depreciation add-back.

The entity recognises a current tax asset at the end of years 20X1 to 20X4 because it recovers the benefit of the tax loss against the taxable profit of year 20X0.

The temporary differences associated with the equipment and the resulting deferred tax asset and liability and deferred tax expense and income are as follows.

			Year		
	20X1	*20X2*	*20X3*	*20X4*	*20X5*
	$	$	$	$	$
Carrying amount	40,000	30,000	20,000	10,000	0
Tax base	37,500	25,000	12,500	0	0
Taxable temporary difference	2,500	5,000	7,500	10,000	0
Opening deferred tax liability	0	1,000	2,000	3,000	4,000
Deferred tax expense (income): bal fig	1,000	1,000	1,000	1,000	(4,000)
Closing deferred tax liability @ 40%	1,000	2,000	3,000	4,000	0

The entity recognises the deferred tax liability in years 20X1 to 20X4 because the reversal of the taxable temporary difference will create taxable income in subsequent years. The entity's income statement is as follows.

			Year		
	20X1	*20X2*	*20X3*	*20X4*	*20X5*
	$	$	$	$	$
Income	10,000	10,000	10,000	10,000	10,000
Depreciation	10,000	10,000	10,000	10,000	10,000
Profit before tax	0	0	0	0	0
Current tax expense (income)	(1,000)	(1,000)	(1,000)	(1,000)	4,000
Deferred tax expense (Income)	1,000	1,000	1,000	1,000	(4,000)
Total tax expense (income)	0	0	0	0	0
Net profit for the year	0	0	0	0	0

4 Deductible temporary differences

Refer again to the definition given in Section 2 above.

Exam focus point

> The rule to remember here is that:
>
> 'All deductible temporary differences give rise to a deferred tax asset.'

There is a proviso, however. The deferred tax asset must also satisfy the **recognition criteria** given in IAS 12. This is that a deferred tax asset should be recognised for all deductible temporary differences to the extent that it is **probable that taxable profit will be available** against which it can be utilised. This is an application of prudence. Before we look at this issue in more detail, let us consider the examples of deductible temporary differences given in the standard.

4.1 Transactions that affect the statement of comprehensive income

- **Retirement benefit costs** (pension costs) are deducted from accounting profit as service is provided by the employee. They are not deducted in determining taxable profit until the entity pays either retirement benefits or contributions to a fund. (This may also apply to similar expenses.)
- **Accumulated depreciation** of an asset in the financial statements is greater than the accumulated depreciation allowed for tax purposes up to the year end.
- The **cost of inventories** sold before the year end is deducted from accounting profit when goods/services are delivered, but is deducted from taxable profit when the cash is received. (*Note.* There is also a taxable temporary difference associated with the related trade receivable, as noted in Section 3 above.)
- The **NRV** of inventory, or the **recoverable amount** of an item of property, plant and equipment falls and the carrying value is therefore **reduced**, but that reduction is ignored for tax purposes until the asset is sold.
- **Research costs** (or organisation/other start-up costs) are recognised as an expense for accounting purposes but are not deductible against taxable profits until a later period.
- Income is **deferred** in the statement of financial position, but has already been included in taxable profit in current/prior periods.
- A **government grant** is included in the statement of financial position as deferred income, but it will not be taxable in future periods. (*Note.* A deferred tax asset may *not* be recognised here according to the standard.)

4.2 Fair value adjustments and revaluations

Current investments or **financial instruments** may be carried at fair value which is less than cost, but no equivalent adjustment is made for tax purposes.

Other situations discussed by the standard relate to **business combinations** and consolidation (see Section 6).

4.3 Recognition of deductible temporary differences

We looked earlier at the important recognition criteria above. As with temporary taxable differences, there are also circumstances where the overall rule for recognition of deferred tax asset is *not* allowed. This applies where the deferred tax asset arises from **initial recognition** of an asset or liability in a transaction which is not a business combination, *and* at the time of the transaction, affects neither accounting nor taxable profit/ tax loss.

Let us lay out the reasoning behind the recognition of deferred tax assets arising from deductible temporary differences.

(a) When a **liability is recognised**, it is assumed that its carrying amount will be settled in the form of outflows of economic benefits from the entity in future periods.

(b) When these resources flow from the entity, part or all may be deductible in determining taxable profits of a **period later** than that in which the liability is recognised.

(c) A **temporary tax difference** then exists between the carrying amount of the liability and its tax base.

(d) A **deferred tax asset** therefore arises, representing the income taxes that will be recoverable in future periods when that part of the liability is allowed as a deduction from taxable profit.

(e) Similarly, when the carrying amount of an asset is **less than its tax base**, the difference gives rise to a deferred tax asset in respect of the income taxes that will be recoverable in future periods.

4.3.1 Example: Deductible temporary differences

Pargatha Co recognises a liability of $10,000 for accrued product warranty costs on 31 December 20X7. These product warranty costs will not be deductible for tax purposes until the entity pays claims. The tax rate is 25%.

Required

State the deferred tax implications of this situation.

Solution

What is the tax base of the liability? It is nil (carrying amount of $10,000 less the amount that will be deductible for tax purposes in respect of the liability in future periods).

When the liability is settled for its carrying amount, the entity's future taxable profit will be reduced by $10,000 and so its future tax payments by $10,000 × 25% = $2,500.

The difference of $10,000 between the carrying amount ($10,000) and the tax base (nil) is a deductible temporary difference. The entity should therefore recognise a deferred tax asset of $10,000 × 25% = $2,500 **provided that** it is probable that the entity will earn sufficient taxable profits in future periods to benefit from a reduction in tax payments.

4.4 Taxable profits in future periods

When can we be sure that sufficient taxable profit will be available against which a deductible temporary difference can be utilised? IAS 12 states that this will be assumed when sufficient **taxable temporary differences** exist which relate to the same taxation authority and the same taxable entity. These should be expected to reverse as follows.

(a) In the same period as the expected reversal of the deductible temporary difference.

(b) In periods into which a tax loss arising from the deferred tax asset can be carried back or forward.

Only in these circumstances is the deferred tax asset **recognised**, in the period in which the deductible temporary differences arise.

What happens when there are **insufficient taxable temporary differences** (relating to the same taxation authority and the same taxable entity)? It may still be possible to recognise the deferred tax asset, but only to the following extent.

(a) **Taxable profits** are sufficient in the same period as the reversal of the deductible temporary difference (or in the periods into which a tax loss arising from the deferred tax asset can be carried forward or backward), ignoring taxable amounts arising from deductible temporary differences arising in future periods.

(b) **Tax planning opportunities** exist that will allow the entity to create taxable profit in the appropriate periods.

With reference to (b), **tax planning opportunities** are actions that an entity would take in order to create or increase taxable income in a particular period before the expiry of a tax loss or tax credit carryforward. For example, in some countries it may be possible to increase or create taxable profit by electing to have interest income taxed on either a received or receivable basis, or deferring the claim for certain deductions from taxable profit.

In any case, where tax planning opportunities **advance taxable profit** from a later period to an earlier period, the utilisation of a tax loss or a tax credit carryforward will still depend on the existence of future taxable profit from sources other than future originating temporary differences.

If an entity has a **history of recent losses**, then this is evidence that future taxable profit may not be available (see below).

4.5 Initial recognition of an asset or liability

Consider Paragraph 3.6 on **initial recognition of an asset or liability**. The example given by the standard is of a non-taxable government grant related to an asset, deducted in arriving at the carrying amount of the asset. For tax purposes, however, it is *not* deducted from the asset's depreciable amount (ie its tax base). The carrying amount of the asset is less than its tax base and this gives rise to a deductible temporary difference. Paragraph 3.6 applies to this type of transaction.

4.6 Unused tax losses and unused tax credits

An entity may have unused tax losses or credits (ie which it can offset against taxable profits) at the end of a period. Should a deferred tax asset be recognised in relation to such amounts? IAS 12 states that a deferred tax asset may be recognised in such circumstances **to the extent that it is probable future taxable profit will be available against which the unused tax losses/credits can be utilised**.

The **criteria for recognition** of deferred tax assets here is the same as for recognising deferred tax assets arising from deductible differences. The existence of **unused tax losses** is strong evidence, however, that future taxable profit may not be available. So where an entity has a history of recent tax losses, a deferred tax asset arising from unused tax losses or credits should be recognised only to the extent that the entity has sufficient taxable temporary differences or there is other convincing evidence that sufficient taxable profit will be available against which the unused losses/credits can be utilised by the entity.

In these circumstances, the following criteria should be considered when assessing the probability that taxable profit will be available against which unused tax losses/credits can be utilised.

- Existence of **sufficient taxable temporary differences** (same tax authority/taxable entity) against which unused tax losses/credits can be utilised before they expire
- Probability that the entity will have **taxable profits** before the unused tax losses/credits expire
- Whether the unused tax losses result from **identifiable causes**, unlikely to recur
- Availability of **tax planning opportunities** (see above)

To the extent that it is **not probable** that taxable profit will be available, the deferred tax asset is *not* recognised.

4.7 Reassessment of unrecognised deferred tax assets

For *all* unrecognised deferred tax assets, at each year end an entity should **reassess the availability of future taxable profits** and whether part or all of any unrecognised deferred tax assets should now be recognised. This may be due to an improvement in trading conditions which is expected to continue.

4.8 Section summary

- Deductible temporary differences give rise to a **deferred tax asset**.
- **Prudence** dictates that deferred tax assets can only be recognised when **sufficient future taxable profits** exist against which they can be utilised.

5 Measurement and recognition of deferred tax

FAST FORWARD

IAS 12 *Income taxes* covers both current and deferred tax. It has substantial presentation and disclosure requirements.

5.1 Basis of provision of deferred tax

IAS 12 adopts the full provision method of providing for deferred tax.

The **full provision method** has the **advantage** that it recognises that each timing difference at the year end has an effect on future tax payments. If a company claims an accelerated tax allowance on an item of plant, future tax assessments will be bigger than they would have been otherwise. Future transactions may well affect those assessments still further, but that is not relevant in assessing the position at the year end. The **disadvantage** of full provision is that, under certain types of tax system, it gives rise to large liabilities that may fall due only far in the future.

IAS 12 requires deferred tax assets and liabilities to be measured at the tax rates expected to apply in the period **when the asset is realised or liability settled**, based on tax rates and laws enacted (or substantively enacted) at the year end. In other words, IAS 12 requires the **liability method** to be used.

5.2 Example: Full provision

Suppose that Girdo Co begins trading on 1 January 20X7. In its first year it makes profits of \$5m, the depreciation charge is \$1m and the tax allowances on those assets is \$1.5m. The rate of corporation tax is 30%.

Solution: Full provision

The tax liability is \$1.35m again, but the debit to profit or loss is increased by the deferred tax liability of 30% × \$0.5m = \$150,000. The total charge to profit or loss is therefore \$1.5m which is an effective tax rate of 30% on accounting profits (ie 30% × \$5.0m). Again, no judgement is involved in using this method.

5.3 Different rates of tax

In addition, in some countries different tax rates apply to different levels of taxable income. In such cases, deferred tax assets and liabilities should be measured using the **average rates** that are expected to apply to the taxable profit (loss) of the periods in which the temporary differences are expected to reverse.

5.4 Manner of recovery or settlement

In some countries, the way in which an entity **recovers or settles** the carrying amount of an asset or liability may affect the following.

(a) The tax rate applying when the entity recovers/settles the carrying amount of the asset/liability
(b) The tax base of the asset/liability

In such cases, the entity must consider the expected manner of recovery or settlement. Deferred tax liabilities and assets must be measured accordingly, using an **appropriate tax rate and tax base**.

5.5 Example: Manner of recovery/settlement

Richcard Co has an asset with a carrying amount of \$10,000 and a tax base of \$6,000. If the asset were sold, a tax rate of 20% would apply. A tax rate of 30% would apply to other income.

Required

State the deferred tax consequences if the entity:

(a) sells the asset without further use.
(b) expects to return the asset and recover its carrying amount through use.

Solution

(a) A deferred tax liability is recognised of $(10,000 – 6,000) × 20% = $800.

(b) A deferred tax liability is recognised of $(10,000 – 6,000) × 30% = $1,200.

Question — Recovery 1

Emida Co has an asset which cost $100,000. In 20X9 the carrying value was $80,000 and the asset was revalued to $150,000. No equivalent adjustment was made for tax purposes. Cumulative depreciation for tax purposes is $30,000 and the tax rate is 30%. If the asset is sold for more than cost, the cumulative tax depreciation of $30,000 will be included in taxable income but sale proceeds in excess of cost will not be taxable.

Required

State the deferred tax consequences of the above. (*Hint.* Assume first that the entity expects to recover the carrying value through use, and secondly that it will not and therefore will sell the asset instead.)

Answer

The tax base of the asset is $70,000 ($150,000 – $80,000).

If the entity expects to recover the carrying amount by using the asset it must generate taxable income of $150,000, but will only be able to deduct depreciation of $70,000. On this basis there is a deferred tax liability of $24,000 ($80,000 × 30%).

If the entity expects to recover the carrying amount by selling the asset immediately for proceeds of $150,000, the deferred tax liability will be computed as follows.

	Taxable temporary difference	*Tax rate*	*Deferred tax liability*
	$		$
Cumulative tax depreciation	30,000	30%	9,000
Proceeds in excess of cost	50,000	Nil	–
Total	80,000		9,000

Note. The additional deferred tax that arises on the revaluation is charged directly to equity: see below.

Question — Recovery 2

The facts are as in Recovery 1 above, except that if the asset is sold for more than cost, the cumulative tax depreciation will be included in taxable income (taxed at 30%) and the sale proceeds will be taxed at 40% after deducting an inflation-adjusted cost of $110,000.

Required

State the deferred tax consequences of the above (use the same hint as in Recovery 1).

Answer

If the entity expects to recover the carrying amount by using the asset, the situation is as in Recovery 1 above in the same circumstances.

If the entity expects to recover the carrying amount by selling the asset immediately for proceeds of $150,000, the entity will be able to deduct the indexed costs of $110,000. The net profit of $40,000 will be taxed at 40%. In addition, the cumulative tax depreciation of $30,000 will be included in taxable income and taxed at 30%. On this basis, the tax base is $80,000 ($110,000 – $30,000), there is a taxable temporary difference of $70,000 and there is a deferred tax liability of $25,000 ($40,000 × 40% plus $30,000 × 30%).

Exam focus point

> If the tax base is not immediately apparent in Recovery 2 above, it may be helpful to consider the fundamental principle of IAS 12: that an entity should recognise a deferred tax liability (asset) whenever recovery or settlement of the carrying amount of an asset or liability would make future tax payments larger (smaller) than they would be if such recovery or settlement would have no consequences.

5.6 Discounting

IAS 12 states that deferred tax assets and liabilities **should not be discounted** because the complexities and difficulties involved will affect reliability. Discounting would require detailed scheduling of the timing of the reversal of each temporary difference, but this is often impracticable. If discounting were permitted, this would affect comparability, so it is barred completely. However, carrying amounts determine temporary differences even when such carrying amounts are discounted (eg retirement benefit obligations: see Chapter 9).

5.7 Carrying amount of deferred tax assets

The carrying amount of deferred tax assets should be **reviewed at each year end** and reduced where appropriate (insufficient future taxable profits). Such a reduction may be reversed in future years.

5.8 Recognition

As with current tax, deferred tax should normally be recognised as income or an expense and included in the net profit or loss for the period. The exceptions are where the tax arises from the events below.

(a) A transaction or event which is recognised (in the same or a different period) **directly in equity**
(b) A business combination that is an **acquisition**

The figures shown for deferred tax in profit or loss will consist of **two components**.

(a) Deferred tax relating to **timing differences**.

(b) Adjustments relating to **changes in the carrying amount of deferred tax assets/ liabilities** (where there is no change in timing differences), eg changes in tax rates/ laws, reassessment of the recoverability of deferred tax assets, or a change in the expected recovery of an asset.

Items in (b) will be recognised in the profit or loss, *unless* they relate to items previously charged/credited to equity.

Deferred tax (and current tax) should be **charged/credited directly to equity** if the tax relates to items also charged/credited directly to equity (in the same or a different period).

The following show examples of IASs which allow certain items to be credited/charged directly to equity.

(a) **Revaluations** of property, plant and equipment (IAS 16)

(b) The effect of a **change in accounting policy** (applied retrospectively) or correction of an **error** (IAS 8)

Where it is not possible to determinc the amount of current/deferred tax that relates to items credited/charged to equity, such tax amounts should be based on a reasonable **prorata allocation** of the entity's current/deferred tax.

5.9 Section summary

- You should understand and be able to explain the different **bases for provision** of deferred tax.
  - **Flow-through method** (no tax provided)
  - **Full provision method** (tax provided in full, as per IAS 12)
  - **Partial provision method** (tax provided to the extent it is expected to be paid)

- There are two methods of calculating deferred tax when **tax rates change**.
  - **Deferral method** (use tax rates current when differences **arise**)
  - **Liability method** (use tax rate expected when differences **reverse**: per IAS 12)
- Where different rates of tax apply to different rates of income, the **manner of recovery/settlement** of assets/liabilities is important.

6 Taxation in company accounts

FAST FORWARD

In the statement of financial position the liability for tax payable is the tax charge for the year. In the statement of comprehensive income the tax charge for the year is adjusted for transfers to or from deferred tax and for prior year under or over provisions.

We have now looked at the 'ingredients' of taxation in company accounts. There are two aspects to be learned:

(a) Taxation on profits in the statement of comprehensive income.
(b) Taxation payments due, shown as a liability in the statement of financial position.

6.1 Taxation in the statement of comprehensive income

The tax on profit on ordinary activities is calculated by **aggregating**:

(a) **Income tax** on taxable profits
(b) **Transfers to or from deferred taxation**
(c) Any **under provision or over provision** of income tax on profits of previous years

When income tax on profits is calculated, **the calculation is only an estimate of what the company thinks its tax liability will be. In subsequent dealings with the tax authorities, a different income tax charge might eventually be agreed.**

The difference between the estimated tax on profits for one year and the actual tax charge finally agreed for the year is made as an adjustment to taxation on profits in the following year, **resulting in the disclosure of either an under provision or an over provision of tax.**

Question — Tax payable

In the accounting year to 31 December 20X3, Neil Down Co made an operating profit before taxation of $110,000.

Income tax on the operating profit has been estimated as $45,000. In the previous year (20X2) income tax on 20X2 profits had been estimated as $38,000 but it was subsequently agreed at $40,500.

A transfer to the credit of the deferred taxation account of $16,000 will be made in 20X3.

Required

(a) Calculate the tax on profits for 20X3 for disclosure in the accounts.
(b) Calculate the amount of tax payable.

Answer

(a)

	$
Income tax on profits (liability in the statement of FP)	45,000
Deferred taxation	16,000
Under provision of tax in previous year $(40,500 – 38,000)	2,500
Tax on profits for 20X3 (income statement charge)	63,500

(b)

	$
Tax payable on 20X3 profits (liability)	45,000

6.2 Taxation in the statement of financial position

It should already be apparent from the previous examples that the income tax charge in the statement of comprehensive income will not be the same as income tax liabilities in the statement of financial position.

In the statement of financial position, there are several items which we might expect to find.

(a) **Income tax may be payable** in respect of (say) interest payments paid in the last accounting return period of the year, or accrued.

(b) If no tax is payable (or very little), then there might be an **income tax recoverable asset** disclosed in current assets (income tax is normally recovered by offset against the tax liability for the year).

(c) There will usually be a **liability for tax**, possibly including the amounts due in respect of previous years but not yet paid.

(d) We may also find a **liability on the deferred taxation account**. Deferred taxation is shown under 'non-current liabilities' in the statement of financial position.

Question

Tax charge

For the year ended 31 July 20X4 Norman Kronkest Co made taxable trading profits of $1,200,000 on which income tax is payable at 30%.

(a) A transfer of $20,000 will be made to the deferred taxation account. The balance on this account was $100,000 before making any adjustments for items listed in this paragraph.

(b) The estimated tax on profits for the year ended 31 July 20X3 was $80,000, but tax has now been agreed at $84,000 and fully paid.

(c) Tax on profits for the year to 31 July 20X4 is payable on 1 May 20X5.

(d) In the year to 31 July 20X4 the company made a capital gain of $60,000 on the sale of some property. This gain is taxable at a rate of 30%.

Required

(a) Calculate the tax charge for the year to 31 July 20X4.

(b) Calculate the tax liabilities in the statement of financial position of Norman Kronkest as at 31 July 20X4.

Answer

(a) *Tax charge for the year*

(i)

	$
Tax on trading profits (30% of $1,200,000)	360,000
Tax on capital gain	18,000
Deferred taxation	20,000
	398,000
Under provision of taxation in previous years $(84,000 – 80,000)	4,000
Tax charge on profit for the period	402,000

(ii) *Note.* The statement of comprehensive income will show the following.

	$
Profit before tax (1,200,000 + 60,000)	1,260,000
Income tax expense	(402,000)
Profit for the year	858,000

(b)

	$
Deferred taxation	
Balance brought forward	100,000
Transferred from profit or loss	20,000
Deferred taxation in the statement of financial position	120,000

The tax liability is as follows.

	$
Payable on 1 May 20X5	
Tax on profits (30% of $1,200,000)	360,000
Tax on capital gain (30% of $60,000)	18,000
Due on 1 May 20X5	378,000

Summary

	$
Current liabilities	
Tax, payable on 1 May 20X5	378,000
Non-current liabilities	
Deferred taxation	120,000

Note. It may be helpful to show the journal entries for these items.

		$	$
DEBIT	Tax charge (statement of comprehensive income)	402,000	
CREDIT	Tax payable		*382,000
	Deferred tax		20,000

* This account will show a debit balance of $4,000 until the under provision is recorded, since payment has already been made: (360,000 + 18,000 + 4,000). The closing balance will therefore be $378.000.

6.3 Presentation of tax assets and liabilities

These should be **presented separately** from other assets and liabilities in the statement of financial position. Deferred tax assets and liabilities should be distinguished from current tax assets and liabilities.

In addition, deferred tax assets/liabilities should *not* be classified as current assets/liabilities, where an entity makes such a distinction.

There are only limited circumstances where **current tax** assets and liabilities may be **offset**. This should only occur if two things apply

(a) The entity has a legally enforceable right to set off the recognised amounts.

(b) The entity intends either to settle on a net basis, or to realise the asset and settle the liability simultaneously.

Similar criteria apply to the **offset of deferred tax assets and liabilities**.

6.4 Presentation of tax expense

The tax expense or income related to the profit or loss for the period should be presented in the statement of comprehensive income.

7 Deferred taxation and business combinations

FAST FORWARD

You must appreciate the deferred tax aspects of **business combinations.**

7.1 Tax bases

Remember the definition of the tax base of an asset or liability given in Section 4 above? In relation to business combinations and consolidations, IAS 12 gives (in an appendix) examples of circumstances that give rise to taxable temporary differences and to deductible temporary differences.

7.1.1 Circumstances that give rise to taxable temporary differences

- The carrying amount of an asset is increased to **fair value** in a business combination that is an acquisition and no equivalent adjustment is made for tax purposes
- **Unrealised losses resulting from intragroup transactions** are eliminated by inclusion in the carrying amount of inventory or property, plant and equipment
- **Retained earnings** of subsidiaries, branches, associates and joint ventures are included in consolidated retained earnings, but income taxes will be payable if the profits are distributed to the reporting parent
- Investments in foreign subsidiaries, branches or associates or interests in foreign joint ventures are affected by **changes in foreign exchange rates**
- An entity accounts in its own currency for the cost of the non-monetary assets of a foreign operation that is **integral to the reporting entity's operations** but the taxable profit or tax loss of the foreign operation is determined in the foreign currency

Question — **Deferred tax and business combinations 1**

What are the consequences of the above situations?

Note. You may want to read through to the end of this section before you attempt this question.

Answer

(a) *Fair value adjustment*
On initial recognition, the resulting deferred tax liability increases goodwill or decreases negative goodwill.

(b) *Unrealised losses*
The tax bases of the assets are unaltered.

(c) *Consolidated earnings*
IAS 12 does not allow recognition of the resulting deferred tax liability if the parent, investor or venturer is able to control the timing of the reversal of the temporary difference and it is probable that the temporary difference will not reverse in the foreseeable future.

(d) *Changes in exchange rates: investments*
There may be either a taxable temporary difference or a deductible temporary difference in this situation. IAS 12 does not allow recognition of the resulting deferred tax liability if the parent, investor or venturer is able to control the timing of the reversal of the temporary difference and it is probable that the temporary difference will not reverse in the foreseeable future.

(e) *Changes in exchange rates: use of own currency*
Again, there may be either a taxable temporary difference or a deductible temporary difference. Where there is a taxable temporary difference, the resulting deferred tax liability is recognised, because it relates to the foreign operation's own assets and liabilities, rather than to the reporting **entity**'s investment in that foreign operation. The deferred tax is charged to profit or loss.

7.1.2 Circumstances that give rise to deductible temporary differences

- A **liability is recognised at its fair value** in a business combination that is an acquisition, but none of the related expense is deducted in determining taxable profit until a later period
- **Unrealised profits resulting from intragroup transactions** are eliminated from the carrying amount of assets, such as inventory or property, plant or equipment, but no equivalent adjustment is made for tax purposes
- Investments in foreign subsidiaries, branches or associates or interests in foreign joint ventures are affected by **changes in foreign exchange rates**
- A foreign operation accounts for its non-monetary assets in its own (functional) currency. If its taxable profit or loss is determined in a different currency (under the presentation currency method) changes in the exchange rate result in temporary differences. The resulting deferred tax is charged or credited to profit or loss.

Question — **Deferred tax and business combinations 2**

What are the consequences of the above situations?

Note. Again, you should read to the end of this section before you answer this question.

Answer

(a) *Fair value of liabilities*

The resulting deferred tax asset decreases goodwill or increases negative goodwill.

(b) *Unrealised profits*

As in above

(c) *Changes in exchange rates: investments*

As noted in Question 7, there may be a taxable temporary difference or a deductible temporary difference. IAS 12 requires recognition of the resulting deferred tax asset to the extent, and only to the extent, that it is probable that:

(i) the temporary difference will reverse in the foreseeable future; and
(ii) taxable profit will be available against which the temporary difference can be utilised.

(d) *Changes in exchange rates: use of own currency*

As noted in the question before this, there may be either a taxable temporary difference or a deductible temporary difference. Where there is a deductible temporary difference, the resulting deferred tax asset is recognised to the extent that it is probable that sufficient taxable profit will be available, because the deferred tax asset relates to the foreign operation's own assets and liabilities, rather than to the reporting **entity**'s investment in that foreign operation. The deferred tax is charged to profit or loss.

7.2 Taxable temporary differences

In a business combination, the cost of the acquisition must be allocated to the fair values of the identifiable assets and liabilities acquired as at the date of the transaction. Temporary differences will arise when the tax bases of the identifiable assets and liabilities acquired are not affected by the business combination or are affected differently. For example, the carrying amount of an asset is increased to fair value but the tax base of the asset remains at cost to the previous owner; a taxable temporary difference arises which results in a deferred tax liability and this will also affect goodwill.

7.3 Deductible temporary differences

In a business combination that is an acquisition, as in Paragraph 6.2 above, when a **liability** is recognised on acquisition but the related costs are not deducted in determining taxable profits until a later period, a deductible temporary difference arises resulting in a deferred tax asset. A deferred tax asset will also arise when the fair value of an identifiable asset acquired is less than its tax base. In both these cases goodwill is affected (see below).

7.4 Investments in subsidiaries, branches and associates and interests in joint ventures

When such investments are held, **temporary differences** arise because the carrying amount of the investment (ie the parent's share of the net assets including goodwill) becomes different from the tax base (often the cost) of the investment. Why do these differences arise? These are some examples.

- There are **undistributable profits** held by subsidiaries, branches, associates and joint ventures
- There are **changes in foreign exchange rates** when a parent and its subsidiary are based in different countries
- There is a **reduction in the carrying amount** of an investment in an associate to its recoverable amount

The **temporary difference in the consolidated financial statements** may be different from the temporary difference associated with that investment in the parent's separate financial statements when the parent carries the investment in its separate financial statements at cost or revalued amount.

IAS 12 requires entities to **recognise a deferred tax liability** for all taxable temporary differences associated with investments in subsidiaries, branches and associates, and interests in joint ventures, *except* to the extent that both of these conditions are satisfied:

(a) The parent/investor/venturer is able to **control the timing of the reversal** of the temporary difference

(b) It is probable that the temporary difference **will not reverse** in the foreseeable future.

As well as the fact of parent control over reversal of temporary differences, it would often be **impracticable** to determine the amount of income taxes payable when the temporary differences reverses. So when the parent has determined that those profits will not be distributed in the foreseeable future, the parent does not recognise a deferred tax liability. The same applies to investments in branches.

Where a foreign operation's taxable profit or tax loss (and therefore the tax base of its non-monetary assets and liabilities) is determined in a **foreign currency**, changes in the exchange rate give rise to temporary differences. These relate to the foreign entity's own assets and liabilities, rather than to the reporting entity's investment in that foreign operation, and so the reporting entity should recognise the resulting deferred tax liability or asset. The resulting deferred tax is charged or credited to profit or loss.

An investor in an **associate** does not control that entity and so cannot determine its dividend policy. Without an agreement requiring that the profits of the associate should not be distributed in the foreseeable future, therefore, an investor should recognise a deferred tax liability arising from taxable temporary differences associated with its investment in the associate. Where an investor cannot determine the exact amount of tax, but only a minimum amount, then the deferred tax liability should be that amount.

In a **joint venture**, the agreement between the parties usually deals with profit sharing. When a venturer can control the sharing of profits and it is probable that the profits will not be distributed in the foreseeable future, a deferred liability is not recognised.

IAS 12 then states that a **deferred tax asset** should be recognised for all deductible temporary differences arising from investments in subsidiaries, branches and associates, and interests in joint ventures, to the extent that (and *only* to the extent that) both these are probable:

(a) that the temporary difference will **reverse** in the foreseeable future, **and**

(b) that **taxable profit** will be available against which the temporary difference can be utilised.

The **prudence principles** discussed above for the recognition of deferred tax assets should be considered.

7.5 Recognition of deferred tax arising from business combinations

As noted above, temporary differences may arise in a business combination. IFRS 3 *Business combinations* requires an entity to recognise any resulting deferred tax assets (to the extent that they meet the relevant recognition criteria) or deferred tax liabilities as identifiable assets and liabilities at the date of acquisition. These deferred tax assets and liabilities, consequently, will **affect goodwill or negative goodwill**. An entity will not, however, recognise deferred tax liabilities arising from the initial recognition of goodwill.

An acquirer may consider that, as a result of a business combination, it is probable that it will **recover its own deferred tax asset** that was not recognised prior to the business combination, eg by utilising unused tax losses against the future taxable profit of the acquiree. The acquirer should recognise a deferred tax asset but does not take it into account in calculating goodwill.

If deferred tax assets of an acquiree were not originally recognised as identifiable assets at the acquisition date but are realised and **recognised subsequently**, deferred tax income is recognised in profit or loss. The acquirer should also:

(a) **Adjust (reduce) the carrying amount of goodwill** to the amount that would have been recognised if the deferred tax asset had been recognised at acquisition, and

(b) **Recognise the reduction in the carrying amount** of goodwill as an expense.

The acquirer cannot, however, recognise negative goodwill. In other words, the acquirer cannot recognise a gain in the statement of comprehensive income.

Question — Recognition

In 20X2 Jacko Co acquired a subsidiary, Jilly Co, which had deductible temporary differences of $3m. The tax rate at the date of acquisition was 30%. The resulting deferred tax asset of $0.9m was not recognised as an identifiable asset in determining the goodwill of $5m resulting from the business combination. Two years after the acquisition, Jacko Co decided that future taxable profit would probably be sufficient for the entity to recover the benefit of all the deductible temporary differences.

Required

(a) Consider the accounting treatment of the subsequent recognition of the deferred tax asset in 20X4.

(b) What would happen if the tax rate had risen to 40% by 20X4 or decreased to 20%?

Answer

(a) The entity recognises a deferred tax asset of $0.9m ($3m × 30%) and, in profit or loss statement, deferred tax income of $0.9m. It also reduces the cost of the goodwill by $0.9m and recognises an expense of $0.9m in profit or loss. The cost of goodwill is reduced to $4.1m, ie the amount that would have been recorded if a deferred tax asset of $0.9m had been recognised as an identifiable asset at the date of the business combination.

(b) If the tax rate rises to 40%, the entity should recognise a deferred tax asset of $1.2m ($3m × 40%) and, in profit or loss, deferred tax income of $0.12m.

If the tax rate falls to 20%, the entity should recognise a deferred tax asset of $0.6m ($3m × 20%) and deferred tax income of $0.6m.

In both cases, the entity will also reduce the cost of goodwill by $0.9m and recognise an expense for that amount in profit or loss.

7.6 Example: Deferred tax adjustments (1)

Red is a private limited company and has two 100% owned subsidiaries, Blue and Green, both themselves private limited companies. Red acquired Green on 1 January 20X2 for $5 million when the Fair value of the net assets was $4 million, and the tax base of the net assets was $3.5 million. The acquisition of Green and Blue was part of a business strategy whereby Red would build up the 'value' of the group over a three year period and then list its existing share capital on the stock exchange.

(a) The following details relate to the acquisition of Green, which manufactures electronic goods.

  (i) Part of the purchase price has been allocated to intangible assets because it relates to the acquisition of a database of key customers from Green. The recognition and measurement criteria for an intangible asset under IFRS 3 *Business combinations*/IAS 38 *Intangible assets* do not appear to have been met but the directors feel that the intangible asset of $0.5 million will be allowed for tax purposes and have computed the tax provision accordingly. However, the tax authorities could possibly challenge this opinion.

  (ii) Green has sold goods worth $3 million to Red since acquisition and made a profit of $1 million on the transaction. The inventory of these goods recorded in Red's statement of financial position at the year end of 31 May 20X2 was $1.8 million.

  (iii) The balance on the retained earnings of Green at acquisition was $2 million. The directors of Red have decided that, during the three years to the date that they intend to list the shares of the company, they will realise earnings through future dividend payments from the subsidiary amounting to $500,000 per year. Tax is payable on any remittance or dividends and no dividends have been declared for the current year.

(b) Blue was acquired on 1 June 20X1 and is a company which undertakes various projects ranging from debt factoring to investing in property and commodities. The following details relate to Blue for the year ending 31 May 20X2.

  (i) Blue has a portfolio of readily marketable government securities which are held as current assets. These investments are stated at market value in the statement of financial position with any gain or loss taken to the income statement. These gains and losses are taxed when the investments are sold. Currently the accumulated unrealised gains are $4 million.

  (ii) Blue has calculated that it requires a specific allowance of $2 million against loans in its portfolio. Tax relief is available when the specific loan is written off.

  (iii) When Red acquired Blue it had unused tax losses brought forward. At 1 June 20X1, it appeared that Blue would have sufficient taxable profit to realise the deferred tax asset created by these losses but subsequent events have proven that the future taxable profit will not be sufficient to realise all of the unused tax loss.

The current tax rate for Red is 30% and for public companies is 35%.

Required

Write a note suitable for presentation to the partner of an accounting firm setting out the deferred tax implications of the above information for the Red Group of companies.

Solution: Deferred tax adjustments (1)

Acquisition of the subsidiaries – general

Fair value adjustments have been made for consolidation purposes in both cases and these will **affect** the **deferred tax charge for the year**. This is because the deferred tax position is viewed **from the perspective of the group as a whole**. For example, it may be possible to recognise deferred tax assets which previously could not be recognised by individual companies, because there are now sufficient tax profits available within the group to utilise unused tax losses. Therefore a **provision** should be made for **temporary differences between fair values of the identifiable net assets acquired and their carrying values** ($4 million less $3.5 million in respect of Green). **No provision should be made for the temporary difference** of $1 million arising on goodwill recognised as a result of the combination with Green.

Future listing

Red plans to seek a listing in three years time. Therefore it will become a **public company** and will be subject to a **higher rate of tax**. IAS 12 states that deferred tax should be measured at the **average tax rates expected to apply in the periods in which the timing differences are expected to reverse**, based on current enacted tax rates and laws. This means that Red may be paying tax at the higher rate when some of its timing differences reverse and this should be taken into account in the calculation.

Acquisition of Green

(a) The directors have calculated the tax provision on the assumption that the intangible asset of $0.5 million will be allowed for tax purposes. However, this is not certain and the directors **may eventually have to pay the additional tax**. If the directors cannot be persuaded to adjust their calculations a **liability for the additional tax should be recognised**.

(b) The intra-group transaction has resulted in an **unrealised profit** of $0.6 million in the group accounts and this will be **eliminated on consolidation**. The tax charge in the group statement of comprehensive income includes the tax on this profit, for which **the group will not become liable to tax until the following period. From the perspective of the group, there is a temporary difference**. Because the temporary difference arises in the financial statements of Red, **deferred tax should be provided** on this difference (an asset) using the rate of tax payable by Red.

(c) **Deferred tax should be recognised on the unremitted earnings of subsidiaries** unless the parent is able to **control the timing of dividend payments** or it is **unlikely that dividends will be paid for the foreseeable future**. Red controls the dividend policy of Green and this means that there would normally be no need to make a provision in respect of unremitted profits. However, the profits of Green **will be distributed** to Red over the next few years and **tax will be payable** on the dividends received. Therefore a **deferred tax liability should be shown**.

Acquisition of Blue

(a) A **temporary difference arises** where non-monetary assets are **revalued upwards** and the **tax treatment of the surplus is different from the accounting treatment**. In this case, the revaluation surplus has been **recognised in profit or loss** for the current period, rather than in equity but no corresponding adjustment has been made to the tax base of the investments because the gains will be taxed in future periods. Therefore the company **should recognise a deferred tax liability on the temporary difference of $4 million**.

(b) A temporary difference arises when the provision for the loss on the loan portfolio is first recognised. The general allowance is expected to increase and therefore it is unlikely that the temporary difference will reverse in the near future. However, a **deferred tax liability should still be recognised**. The temporary difference gives rise to a **deferred tax asset**. IAS 12 states that **deferred tax assets should not be recognised unless it is probable that taxable profits will be available** against which the taxable profits can be utilised. **This is affected by the situation in point (c) below**.

(c) In theory, unused tax losses give rise to a deferred tax asset. However, IAS 12 states that **deferred tax assets should only be recognised to the extent that they are regarded as recoverable**. They should be regarded as recoverable to the extent that on the basis of all the evidence available it is **probable that there will be suitable taxable profits against which the losses can be recovered**. The future taxable profit of Blue **will not be sufficient to realise all the unused tax loss. Therefore the deferred tax asset is reduced to the amount that is expected to be recovered**.

This reduction in the deferred tax asset implies that it was **overstated at 1 June 20X1**, when it was acquired by the group. As these are the first post-acquisition financial statements, **goodwill should also be adjusted**.

7.7 Example: Deferred tax adjustments 2

You are the accountant of Pay it. Your assistant is preparing the consolidated financial statements of the year ended 31 March 20X2. However, he is unsure how to account for the deferred tax effects of certain transactions as he has not studied IAS 12. These transactions are given below.

Transaction 1

During the year, Pay it sold goods to a subsidiary for $10 million, making a profit of 20% on selling price. 25% of these goods were still in the inventories of the subsidiary at 31 March 20X2. The subsidiary and Pay it are in the same tax jurisdiction and pay tax on profits at 30%.

Transaction 2

An overseas subsidiary made a loss adjusted for tax purposes of $8 million ($ equivalent). The only relief available for this tax loss is to carry it forward for offset against future taxable profits of the overseas subsidiary. Taxable profits of the oversees subsidiary suffer tax at a rate of 25%.

Required

Compute the effect of both the above transactions on the deferred tax amounts in the consolidated statement of financial position of Pay it at 31 March 20X2. You should provide a full explanation for your calculations and indicate any assumptions you make in formulating your answer.

Solution: Deferred tax adjustments 2

Transaction 1

This intra-group sale will give rise to a **provision for unrealised profit** on the unsold inventory of $10,000,000 × 20% × 25% = $500,000. This provision must be made in the consolidated accounts. However, this profit has already been taxed in the financial statements of Payit. In other words there is a **timing difference.** In the following year when the stock is sold outside the group, the provision will be released, but the profit will not be taxed. The timing difference therefore gives rise to a **deferred tax asset.** The asset is 30% × $500,000 = $150,000.

Deferred tax assets are recognised to the extent that they are **recoverable.** This will be the case if **it is more likely than not** that **suitable tax profits** will exist from which the reversal of the timing difference giving rise to the asset can be deducted. The asset is carried forward on this assumption.

Transaction 2

An unrelieved tax loss gives rise to a **timing difference** because the loss is recognised in the financial statements but not yet allowed for tax purposes. When the overseas subsidiary generates sufficient taxable profits, the loss will be offset against these in arriving at taxable profits.

The amount of the deferred tax asset to be carried forward is 25% × $8m = $2m.
As with Transaction 1, deferred tax assets are recognised to the extent that they are **recoverable.** This will be the case if **it is more likely than not** that **suitable tax profits** will exist from which the reversal of the timing difference giving rise to the asset can be deducted.

7.8 Section summary

In relation to deferred tax and business combinations you should be familiar with:

- Circumstances that give rise to **taxable temporary differences**
- Circumstances that give rise to **deductible temporary differences**
- Their **treatment** once an acquisition takes place
- Reasons **why deferred tax arises** when investments are held
- **Recognition** of deferred tax on business combinations

Chapter Roundup

- Taxation consists of **two components.**
  - Current tax
  - Deferred tax
- **Current tax** is the amount payable to the tax authorities in relation to the trading activities during the period. It is generally straightforward.
- **Deferred tax** is an accounting measure, used to match the tax effects of transactions with their accounting impact. It is quite complex.
- **Deferred tax assets and liabilities** arise from taxable and deductible temporary differences.
- **IAS 12 *Income taxes*** covers both current and deferred tax. It has substantial presentation and disclosure requirements.
- In the statement of financial position the liability for tax payable is the tax charge for the year. In the statement of comprehensive income the tax charge is adjusted for transfers to or from deferred tax and for prior year under- or over- provisions.
- You must appreciate the deferred tax aspects of **business combinations.**

Quick Quiz

1 What is the difference between 'current tax' and 'deferred tax'?

2 How should current tax be measured?

A The total liability, including deferred tax
B The amount expected to be paid to (or recovered from) the tax authorities
C The amount calculated on profit at current tax rates
D The amount calculated on profit at future tax rates

3 A taxable temporary difference does *not* give rise to a deferred tax liability. *True or false*?

4 What is the basis of provision for deferred tax required by IAS 12?

5 What two methods can be used for calculating deferred tax when the tax rate changes?

6 Current tax assets and liabilities cannot be offset. *True or false*?

7 How do temporary differences arise when investments are held in subsidiaries, associates etc?

8 The tax expense related to the profit from ordinary activities should be shown on the face of the income statement.

True ☐ False ☐

9 Deferred tax liabilities are the amounts of income taxes payable in future periods in respect of ....

10 Give three examples of taxable temporary differences.

11 An entity has a tax over provision relating to the prior year of $3,000. Taxable temporary differences have increased by $6,000 and profit for the year is $150,000. Tax is at 30%.

What is the charge to profit or loss?

Answers to Quick Quiz

1 (a) Current tax is the amount actually payable to the tax authorities.
  (b) Deferred tax is used to match the tax effects of transactions with their accounting impact.

2 B The amount expected to be paid to (or recovered from) the tax authorities.

3 True.

4 Full provision

5
- Deferral method
- Liability method

6 False. They can be offset only if the entity has a legally enforceable right to offset *and* it intends to actually carry out the offset.

7 When the carrying amounts of the investment become different to the tax base of the investment.

8 True

9 Taxable temporary differences

10 Any three of:

- Interest revenue received in arrears
- Depreciation accelerated for tax purposes
- Development costs capitalised in the statement of financial position
- Prepayments
- Sale of goods revenue recognised before the cash is received

11 $43,800

	$
Tax on profit (150,000 × 30%)	45,000
Over provision	(3,000)
Deferred tax increase (6,000 × 30%)	1,800
	43,800

Now try the question below from the Exam Question Bank

Number	Level	Marks	Time
Q16	Introductory	15	27 mins

Foreign currency translation

12

Topic list	Syllabus reference
1 Foreign currency translation	3(e)
2 IAS 21: Individual company stage	3(e)
3 Functional and presentation currency	3(e)

Introduction

In a global economy most companies trade overseas, buying and selling assets in foreign currencies. You need to be able to record transactions in foreign currency and translate monetary and non-monetary items at the reporting date.

Study Guide

Section 12 – The effects of changes in foreign currency exchange rates

- Discuss the recording of transactions and translation of monetary/non-monetary items at the reporting date for individual entities
- Distinguish between reporting and functional currencies
- Determine an entity's functional currency

1 Foreign currency translation

FAST FORWARD

You may have to deal with the translation of foreign currency assets and liabilities for inclusion in the financial statements.

Exam focus point

A financial statements preparation question in the pilot paper and the June 2005 exam included a part dealing with foreign currency translation.

Foreign currency translation was also examined recently in December 2006, June 2008, June 2010 and in the Pilot Paper for exams from 2011 onwards.

If a company trades overseas, it will buy or sell assets in **foreign currencies**. For example, an Indian company might buy materials from Canada, and pay for them in US dollars, and then sell its finished goods in Germany, receiving payment in Euros, or perhaps in some other currency. If the company owes money in a foreign currency at the end of the accounting year, or holds assets which were bought in a foreign currency, those liabilities or assets must be translated into the local currency (in this text $), in order to be shown in the books of account.

A company might have a subsidiary abroad (ie a foreign enterprise that it owns), and the subsidiary will trade in its own local currency. The subsidiary will keep books of account and prepare its annual accounts in its own currency. However, at the year end, the holding company must 'consolidate' the results of the overseas subsidiary into its group accounts, so that somehow, the assets and liabilities and the **annual profits of the subsidiary must be translated from the foreign currency into $.**

If foreign currency exchange rates remained constant, there would be no accounting problem. As you will be aware, however, foreign exchange rates are continually changing, and it is not inconceivable for example, that the rate of exchange between the Polish zlotych and US Dollars might be Z3.3 to $1 at the start of the accounting year, and Z3.0 to $1 at the end of the year (in this example, a 10% increase in the relative strength of the zlotych).

There are two distinct types of foreign currency transaction, **conversion and translation**.

1.1 Conversion gains and losses

Conversion is the process of exchanging amounts of one foreign currency for another. For example, suppose a local company buys a large consignment of goods from a supplier in Germany. The order is placed on 1 May and the agreed price is €124,250. At the time of delivery the rate of foreign exchange was €3.50 to $1. The local company would record the amount owed in its books as follows.

DEBIT	Inventory account (124,250 ÷ 3.5)	$35,500	
CREDIT	Payables account		$35,500

When the local company comes to pay the supplier, it needs to obtain some foreign currency. By this time, however, if the rate of exchange has altered to €3.55 to $1, the cost of raising €124,250 would be (÷ 3.55) $35,000. The company would need to spend only $35,000 to settle a debt for inventories 'costing' $35,500. Since it would be administratively difficult to alter the value of the inventories in the company's books of account, it is more appropriate to record a profit on conversion of $500.

DEBIT	Payables account	$35,500	
CREDIT	Cash		$35,000
CREDIT	Profit on conversion		$500

Profits (or losses) on conversion would be included in the income statement for the year in which conversion (whether payment or receipt) takes place.

Suppose that another home company sells goods to a Chinese company, and it is agreed that payment should be made in Chinese Yuan at a price of Y116,000. We will further assume that the exchange rate at the time of sale is Y10.74 to $1, but when the debt is eventually paid, the rate has altered to Y10.79 to $1. The company would record the sale as follows.

DEBIT	Receivables account (116,000 ÷ 10.74)	$10,790	
CREDIT	Sales account		$10,790

When the Y116,000 are paid, the local company will convert them into $, to obtain (÷ 10.79) $10,740. In this example, there has been a loss on conversion of $50 which will be written off to the income statement:

DEBIT	Cash	$10,740	
DEBIT	Loss on conversion	$50	
CREDIT	Payables account		$10,790

There are **no accounting difficulties** concerned with foreign currency conversion gains or losses, and the procedures described above are uncontroversial.

1.2 Translation

Foreign currency translation, as distinct from conversion, does not involve the act of exchanging one currency for another. **Translation is required at the end of an accounting period when a company still holds assets or liabilities in its statement of financial position which were obtained or incurred in a foreign currency.**

These assets or liabilities might consist of any of the following.

(a) An individual home company holding individual **assets** or **liabilities** originating in a foreign currency 'deal'.

(b) An individual home company with a separate **branch** of the business operating abroad which keeps its own books of account in the local currency.

(c) A home company which wishes to consolidate the **results of a foreign subsidiary**.

There has been great **uncertainty** about the method which should be used to translate the following.

- Value of assets and liabilities from a foreign currency into $ for the year end statement of financial position
- Profits of an independent foreign branch or subsidiary into $ for the annual statement of comprehensive income

Suppose, for example, that a Belgian subsidiary purchases a piece of property for €2,100,000 on 31 December 20X7. The rate of exchange at this time was €70 to $1. During 20X8, the subsidiary charged depreciation on the building of $16,800, so that at 31 December 20X8, the subsidiary recorded the asset as follows.

	€
Property at cost	2,100,000
Less accumulated depreciation	(16,800)
Net book value	2,083,200

At this date, the rate of exchange has changed to €60 to $1.

The local holding company must translate the asset's value into $, but there is a **choice of exchange rates**.

(a) Should the rate of exchange for translation be the rate which existed at the date of purchase, which would give a net book value of 2,083,200 ÷ 70 = $29,760?

(b) Should the rate of exchange for translation be the rate existing at the end of 20X8 (the closing rate of €60 to $1)? This would give a net book value of $34,720.

Similarly, should depreciation be charged in the group income statement at the rate of €70 to $1 (the historical rate), €60 to $1 (the closing rate), or at an average rate for the year (say, €64 to $1)?

1.3 Consolidated accounts

If a parent has a subsidiary whose accounts are presented in a foreign currency, those accounts must be translated into the local currency before they can be included in the consolidated financial statements.

- Should the subsidiary's accounts be translated as if the subsidiary is an extension of the parent?
- Or should they be translated as if the subsidiary is a separate business?

Where the affairs of a foreign operation are very closely interlinked with those of the investing company, it should be included in the consolidated financial statements as if the transactions had been entered into by the investing company in its own currency. Non-monetary assets and depreciation are translated at **historical rate** and sales, purchase and expenses at **average rate**. **Exchange differences** arising on retranslation are reported as part of **profit or loss** on ordinary activities.

Where a foreign operation is effectively a separate business, the **closing rate** is used for most items in the financial statements. **Exchange differences** are taken **directly** to **equity**.

Note that foreign subsidiaries are specifically excluded from the syllabus and will not be examined.

2 IAS 21: Individual company stage

FAST FORWARD

The functional currency is the currency of the primary economic environment in which the entity operates.

The questions discussed above are addressed by IAS 21 *The effects of changes in foreign exchange rates.* We will examine those matters which affect single company accounts here.

2.1 Definitions

These are some of the definitions given by IAS 21.

Key terms

- **Foreign currency**. A currency other than the functional currency of the entity.
- **Functional currency**. The currency of the primary economic environment in which the entity operates.
- **Presentation currency**. The currency in which the financial statements are presented.
- **Exchange rate**. The ratio of exchange for two currencies.
- **Exchange difference**. The difference resulting from translating a given number of units of one currency into another currency at different exchange rates.
- **Closing rate**. The spot exchange rate at the reporting date.
- **Spot exchange rate**. The exchange rate for immediate delivery.
- **Monetary items**. Units of currency held and assets and liabilities to be received or paid in a fixed or determinable number of units of currency. *(IAS 21)*

Each entity – whether an individual company, a parent of a group, or an operation within a group (such as a subsidiary, associate or branch) – should determine its **functional currency** and **measure its results and financial position in that currency**.

For most individual companies the functional currency will be the currency of the country in which they are located and in which they carry out most of their transactions. Determining the functional currency is much more likely to be an issue where an entity operates as part of a group. IAS 21 contains detailed guidance on how to determine an entity's functional currency and we will look at this in more detail in Section 3.

An entity can present its financial statements in any currency (or currencies) it chooses. IAS 21 deals with the situation in which financial statements are presented in a currency other than the functional currency.

Again, this is unlikely to be an issue for most individual companies. Their presentation currency will normally be the same as their functional currency (the currency of the country in which they operate). A company's presentation currency may be different from its functional currency if it operates within a group and we will look at this in Section 3.

2.2 Foreign currency transactions: initial recognition

IAS 21 states that a foreign currency transaction should be recorded, on initial recognition in the functional currency, by applying the exchange rate between the reporting currency and the foreign currency **at the date of the transaction** to the foreign currency amount.

An **average rate** for a period may be used if exchange rates do not fluctuate significantly.

2.3 Reporting at subsequent reporting dates

The following rules apply at each subsequent reporting date.

(a) Report foreign currency **monetary items** using the **closing rate**.

(b) Report **non-monetary items** (eg non-current assets, inventories) which are carried at **historical cost** in a foreign currency using the **exchange rate at the date of the transaction** (historical rate).

(c) Report **non-monetary items** which are carried at **fair value** in a foreign currency using the exchange rates that existed **when the values were determined.**

2.4 Recognition of exchange differences

FAST FORWARD

Exchange differences occur when there is a **change in the exchange rate** between the transaction date and the date of settlement of monetary items arising from a foreign currency transaction.

Exchange differences occur when there is a **change in the exchange rate** between the transaction date and the date of settlement of monetary items arising from a foreign currency transaction.

Exchange differences arising on the settlement of monetary items (receivables, payables, loans, cash in a foreign currency) or on translating an entity's monetary items at rates different from those at which they were translated initially, or reported in previous financial statements, should be **recognised in profit or loss** in the period in which they arise.

There are two situations to consider.

(a) The transaction is **settled in the same period** as that in which it occurred: all the exchange difference is recognised in that period.

(b) The transaction is **settled in a subsequent accounting period**: the exchange difference recognised in each intervening period up to the period of settlement is determined by the change in exchange rates during that period.

In other words, where a monetary item has not been settled at the end of a period, it should be **restated using the closing exchange rate** and any gain or loss taken to the income statement.

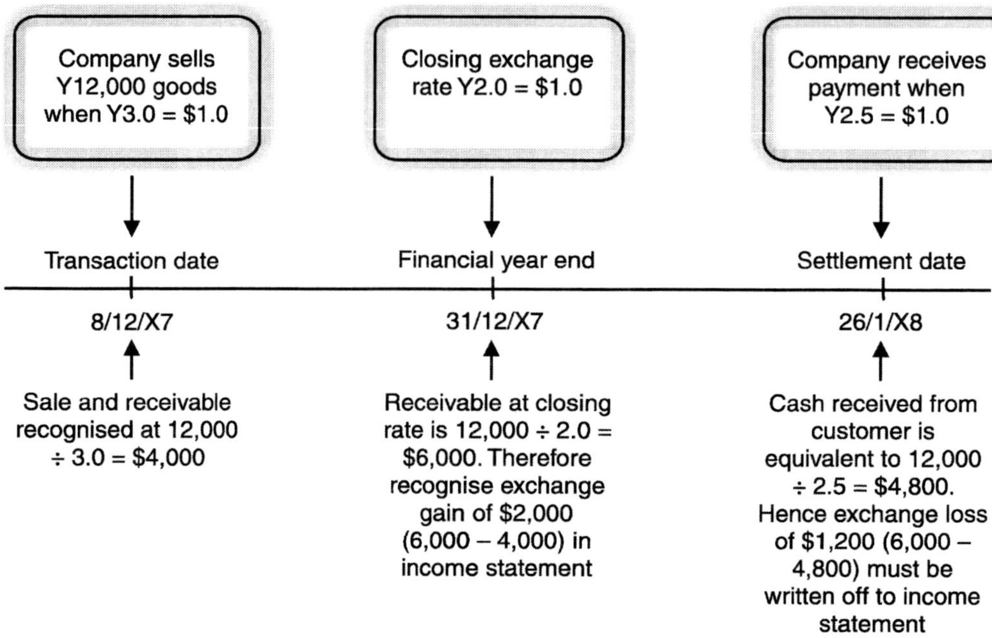

Question — Entries

Red Cabbage Co, whose year end is 31 December, buys some goods from Distan SA of France on 30 September. The invoice value is €40,000 and is due for settlement in equal instalments on 30 November and 31 January. The exchange rate moved as follows.

	€ = $1
30 September	1.60
30 November	1.80
31 December	1.90
31 January	1.85

Required

State the accounting entries in the books of Red Cabbage Co.

Answer

The purchase will be recorded in the books of Red Cabbage Co using the rate of exchange ruling on 30 September.

DEBIT	Purchases	$25,000	
CREDIT	Trade payables		$25,000

Being the $ cost of goods purchased for €40,000 (€40,000 ÷ €1.60/$1)

On 30 November, Red Cabbage must pay €20,000. This will cost €20,000 ÷ €1.80/$1 = $11,111 and the company has therefore made an exchange gain of $12,500 – $11,111 = $1,389.

DEBIT	Trade payables	$12,500	
CREDIT	Exchange gains: Profit or loss		$1,389
CREDIT	Cash		$11,111

On 31 December, the reporting date, the outstanding liability will be recalculated using the rate applicable to that date: €20,000 ÷ €1.90/$1 = $10,526. A further exchange gain of $1,974 has been made and will be recorded as follows.

DEBIT	Trade payables	$1,974	
CREDIT	Exchange gains: Profit or loss		$1,974

The total exchange gain of $3,363 will be included in the operating profit for the year ending 31 December.

On 31 January, Red Cabbage must pay the second instalment of €20,000. This will cost them $10,811 (€20,000 ÷ €1.85/$1).

DEBIT	Trade payables	$10,526	
	Exchange losses: Profit or loss	$285	
CREDIT	Cash		$10,811

When a gain or loss on a non-monetary item is recognised **directly in equity** (for example, where property is revalued), any **related exchange differences** should also be **recognised directly in equity.**

2.5 Disclosure

IAS 21 requires disclosure of the following.

(a) Amount of exchange differences recognised in profit or loss

(b) Net exchange differences (classified as equity) as a separate component of equity, and a reconciliation of the amount of such exchange differences at the beginning and end of the period

In addition, when the **presentation currency is different** from the functional currency, that fact should be stated and the functional currency should be disclosed. The reason for using a different presentation currency should also be disclosed.

Where there is a **change in the functional currency** of either the reporting entity or a significant foreign operation, that fact and the reason for the change in functional currency should be disclosed.

An entity may present its financial statements or other financial information in a currency that is different from either its functional currency or its presentation currency. For example, it may convert selected items only, or it may use a translation method that does not comply with IFRSs in order to deal with hyperinflation. In this situation the entity must:

(a) Clearly identify the information as supplementary information to distinguish it from information that complies with IFRSs

(b) Disclose the currency in which the supplementary information is displayed; and

(c) Disclose the entity's functional currency and the method of translation used to determine the supplementary information.

3 Functional and presentation currency

The following definitions are relevant here.

Key terms

- **Functional currency**. The currency of the primary economic environment in which the entity operates.
- **Presentation currency**. The currency in which the financial statements are presented. *(IAS 21)*

3.1 Determining functional currency

The primary economic environment an entity operates within is usually the environment where it generates and spends cash.

IAS 21 states that an entity should consider the following factors in determining its functional currency:

(a) The currency that mainly **influences sales prices** for goods and services (often the currency in which prices are denominated and settled)

(b) The currency of the **country whose competitive forces and regulations** mainly determine the sales prices of its goods and services; and

(c) The currency that mainly **influences labour, material and other costs** of providing goods or services (often the currency in which prices are denominated and settled).

Sometimes the functional currency of an entity is not immediately obvious. Management must then exercise judgement and may also need to consider:

(a) The currency in which **funds from financing activities** (raising loans and issuing equity) are generated

(b) The currency in which **receipts from operating activities** are usually retained.

Where a parent has a foreign operation a number of factors are considered:

(a) Whether the activities of the foreign operation are carried out as an **extension of the parent**, rather than being carried out with a **significant degree of autonomy**.

(b) Whether **transactions with the parent** are a high or a low proportion of the foreign operation's activities.

(c) Whether **cash flows** from the activities of the foreign operation **directly affect the cash flows of the parent** and are readily available for remittance to it.

(d) Whether the activities of the foreign operation are **financed from its own cash flows** or by **borrowing from the parent**.

To sum up: in order to determine the functional currency of a foreign operation it is necessary to consider the **relationship** between the foreign operation and its parent:

- If the foreign operation carries out its business as though it were an **extension of the parent's operations**, it almost certainly has the **same functional currency** as the parent.
- If the foreign operation is **semi-autonomous** it almost certainly has **a different functional currency** from the parent.

The translation method used has to reflect the economic reality of the relationship between the reporting entity (the parent) and the foreign operation.

Where the above indicators are mixed, management must judge the functional currency on the one that most fairly represents the transactions, events and conditions of the entity. Once functional currency has been determined it is not changed unless there are changes to the underlying conditions or transactions of the entity.

3.2 Presentation currency

The presentation currency is the currency the entity uses to present its financial statements. IAS 21 allows an entity to use any currency as its presentation currency.

A reporting entity may consist of a parent and subsidiaries. If the subsidiaries are located overseas from the parent, their functional currency may be different to that of the parent. Their financial statements must be translated into the presentation currency.

3.3 Accounting treatment: same functional currency as the reporting entity

In this situation, the foreign operation normally comes with the business as though it were an extension of the reporting entity's operations. The same standards and procedures identified in Section 2 above for individual company accounts should be applied to the financial statements of a foreign operation, **as if the transactions of the foreign operation had been those of the parent**.

We can summarise the treatment here.

(a) **Income statement**: translate using actual rates. An average for a period may be used, but not where there is significant fluctuation and the average is therefore unreliable.

(b) **Non-monetary items**: translate using an historical rate at the date of purchase (or revaluation to fair value, or reduction to realisable/recoverable amount). This includes inventories and long-term assets (and their depreciation).

(c) **Monetary items**: translate at the closing rate.

(d) **Exchange differences**: report as part of profit for the year.

3.4 Accounting treatment: different functional currency from the reporting entity

In this situation, the foreign operation operates in a semi-autonomous manner, its transactions occurring in its own local currency. The financial statements of the foreign operation must be translated to the functional currency of the parent. Different procedures must be followed here, because the functional currency of the parent is the **presentation currency** of the foreign operation.

(a) The **assets and liabilities** shown in the foreign operation's statement of financial position are translated at the **closing rate** at the reporting date, regardless of the date on which those items originated. The balancing figure on the translated statement of financial position represents the reporting entity's net investment in the foreign operation.

(b) Amounts in the **statement of comprehensive income** should be translated at the rate ruling at the date of the transaction (an **average rate** will usually be used for practical purposes).

(c) **Exchange differences** arising from the re-translation at the end of each year of the parent's net investment should be **taken to equity**, not through the profit or loss for the year, until the disposal of the net investment.

Chapter Roundup

- You may have to deal with the translation of foreign currency assets and liabilities for inclusion in the financial statements.
- The functional currency is the currency of the primary economic environment in which the entity operates.
- Exchange differences occur when there is a **change in the exchange rate** between the transaction date and the date of settlement of monetary items arising from a foreign currency transaction.

Quick Quiz

1 What is the difference between conversion and translation?

2 How should foreign currency transactions be recognised initially in an individual company's accounts?

3 How should foreign currency amounts be reported at each reporting date for an individual company?

4 How will the resulting exchange differences be treated?

Answers to Quick Quiz

1 Conversion exchanges one amount of foreign currency for another. Translation is required at the end of an accounting period, when an entity still holds assets or liabilities that were obtained or incurred in a foreign currency.

2 Use the exchange rate at the date of the transaction. An average rate for a period can be used if the exchange rates did not fluctuate significantly.

3 See 2.3

4 See 2.4

Now try the questions below from the Exam Question Bank

Number	Level	Marks	Time
Q17	Practice	10	18 mins

Accounting for agriculture and mineral resources

13

Topic list	Syllabus reference
1 IAS 41 Agriculture	2(k)
2 IFRS 6 Exploration for and evaluation of mineral resources: main proposals	2(m)

Introduction

In this chapter we deal with agriculture and biological assets (IAS 41) and mineral resources (IFRS 6).

Study Guide

Section 13 – Agriculture

- Recognise the scope of international accounting standards for agriculture
- Discuss the recognition and measurement criteria including treatment of gains and losses, and the inability to measure fair value reliably
- Identify and explain the treatment of government grants, and the presentation and disclosure of information relating to agriculture
- Report on the transformation of biological assets and agricultural produce at the point of harvest and account for agriculture related government grants

Section 15 – Exploration and evaluation expenditures

- Outline the need for an accounting standard in this area and clarify its scope
- Give examples of elements of cost that might be included in the initial measurement of exploration and evaluation assets
- Describe how exploration and evaluation assets should be classified and reclassified
- Explain when and how the exploration and evaluation assets should be tested for impairment

Section 6 – Intangible assets and goodwill

- Describe the method of accounting specified by the IASB for the exploration for and evaluation of mineral resources

1 IAS 41 Agriculture

FAST FORWARD

IAS 41 *Agriculture* is very topical internationally.

Exam focus point

The topic was examined in June and December 2008, in December 2004 and in a 25 mark question in the pilot paper. Please give it proper attention and bear in mind that it fits well with IAS 20.

As a rule, agriculture is a more important sector to the economies of the developing world than to those of the developed world. IAS 41 *Agriculture* is therefore likely to be of more significance to developing countries.

IAS 41 was issued by the old IASC in 2001, and is an instance of the IASC/IASB developing standards that are specific to individual industries where the accounting issues involved are of sufficient substance and significance.

IAS 41 has contributed to the international harmonisation of accounting standards, because agriculture in particular was characterised by a **great diversity in accounting treatments**. Cows, for instance, were accounted for as 'stocks' in Ireland but as 'fixed assets' in the UK. IAS 41 has helped to foster increased comparability between accounts produced in these different regions.

Question

Agriculture

If you work in agriculture, or if agriculture is important in your country, you may like to investigate the accounting treatment of items such as forestry activity or livestock activity in your country. Are there differences within your own country? How do these practices compare with other countries?

Perhaps more interestingly, it is quite difficult to apply **traditional accounting methods** to agricultural activities, which explains why agriculture is excluded from many IASs.

(a) When and how do you account for the **critical events** associated with biological transformation (growth, procreation, production and degeneration), which alter the substance of biological assets?

(b) **Statement of financial position classification** is made difficult by the variety and characteristics of the living assets of agriculture.

(c) The nature of the management of agricultural activities also causes problems, particularly determination of the **unit of measurement**, ie whether biological assets are a perpetual group of assets or a number of limited life assets.

The standard has improved and harmonised practice in accounting for agriculture, which demonstrates fundamental **differences in its nature and characteristics** to other business activities.

1.1 Definitions

The following definitions are used in IAS 41 (you should be familiar with the definitions of fair value and carrying amount by now).

Key terms

- **Agricultural activity** is the management by an enterprise of the biological transformation of biological assets for sale, into agricultural produce or into additional biological assets.
- **Agricultural produce** is the harvested product of an enterprise's biological assets.
- A **biological asset** is a living animal or plant.
- **Biological transformation** comprises the processes of growth, degeneration, production and procreation that cause qualitative and quantitative changes in a biological asset.
- A **group of biological assets** is an aggregation of similar living animals or plants.
- **Harvest** is the detachment of produce from a biological asset or the cessation of a biological asset's life processes
- **Fair value** is the amount for which an asset could be exchanged, or a liability settled, between knowledgeable, willing parties in an arm's length transaction.
- **Carrying amount** is the amount at which an asset is recognised in the statement of financial position.

(IAS 41)

Note the key parts of the definition of **agriculture**.

(a) **Biological**: agriculture relates to 'life phenomena', living animals and plants with an innate capacity of biological transformation which are dependent upon a combination of natural resources (sunlight, water, etc).

(b) **Transformation**: agriculture involves physical transformation, whereby animals and plants undergo a change in biological quantity (fat cover, density, etc) and/or quantity (progeny, live weight etc) over time, which is measured and monitored (increasingly objectively) as part of management control.

(c) **Management**: biological transformation is managed.

    (i) Conditions are stabilised or enhanced

    (ii) The transparency of the relationship between inputs and outputs is determined by the degree of control (intensive versus extensive)

    (iii) It is different from exploitation through extraction, where no attempt is made to facilitate the transformation

    (iv) Biological assets are managed in groups of plant or animal classes, using individual assets to ensure the sustainability of the group

    (v) Sustainability of an agricultural activity is a function of quality and quantity

(d) **Produce**: agricultural produce is diverse and may require further processing before ultimate consumption.

Question — Accounting issues

Before we look at the way the standard tackles accounting for agriculture, can you think of some of the main accounting issues, given some of the things we have looked at so far?

Answer

The standard lists the following.

(a) Biological assets meet the definition and recognition criteria of tangible assets (see IAS 16).

(b) Biological transformation is the source of sector uniqueness and significant events within agricultural activities.

(c) Biological transformations are critical events separable from the transactions entered into to facilitate them.

(d) In agricultural activities there is a general lack of clarity in the relationship between inputs and outputs which increases the complexity of the allocation process, ie between joint costs and joint products.

(e) A consistent basis of management must be applied to all outcomes to produce meaningful representations of current period performance, because of the range of outcomes and lack of traceability. This means that both biological assets and agricultural produce should be measured using the same basis.

(f) Active and efficient markets for both biological assets and agricultural produce increases the reliability of measures of net market value and existing use value respectively.

(g) Using the class or collective of biological assets as a unit of measurement has implications for: measurement (the class is more reliable than the individual, future benefits not confined to immediately available uses, values are normally expressed in the collective); for classification (a collective is a regenerative perpetual asset, even though individual members have a limited life); and for going concern (sustainability is an important indicator of going concern).

(h) Different agricultural activities have different risk and reward characteristics and will therefore be reported under different segments (see IFRS 8, Chapter 18).

1.2 Scope

FAST FORWARD

In relation to agriculture you should be able to discuss:

- Accounting for biological assets
- Transformation and changes in substance
- Unit of measurement and changes in the carrying amount

The standard applies to the three elements that form part of, or result from, agricultural activity.

- Biological assets
- Agricultural produce at the point of harvest
- Government grants

The standard does not apply to agricultural land (IASs 16 and 40) or intangible assets related to agricultural activity (IAS 38). After harvest, IAS 2 is applied.

1.3 Biological assets

We have seen the definition given above. Biological assets are the core income-producing assets of agricultural activities, held for their transformative capabilities. **Biological transformation** leads to various **different outcomes**.

- **Asset changes:**
  - Growth: increase in quantity and or quality
  - Degeneration: decrease in quantity and/or quality
- **Creation of new assets:**
  - Production: producing separable non-living products
  - Procreation: producing separable living animals

The above can be depicted as follows.

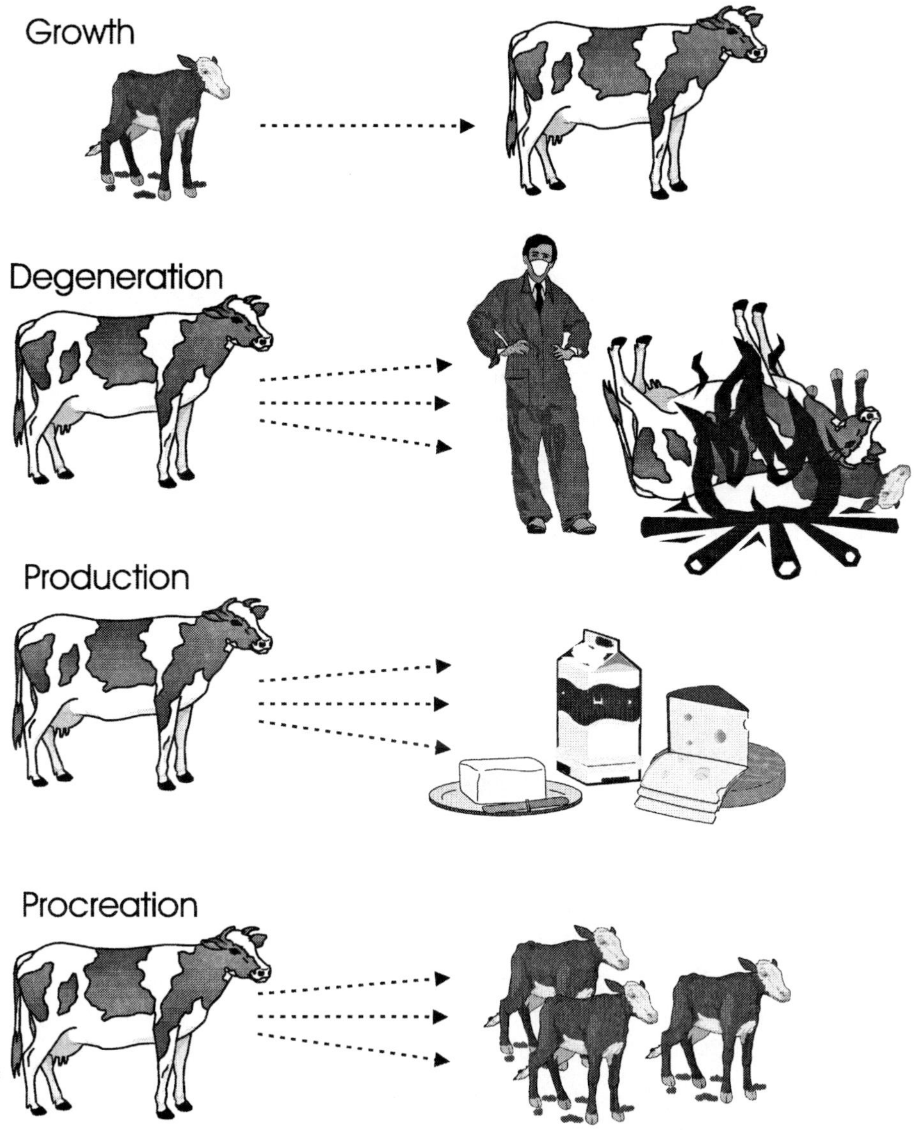

We can distinguish between the importance of these by saying that asset changes are **critical to the flow of future economic benefits** both in and beyond the current period, but the relative importance of new asset creation will depend on the purpose of the agricultural activity.

The IAS distinguishes therefore between two broad categories of agricultural production system.

(a) **Consumable**: animals/plants themselves are harvested
(b) **Bearer**: animals/plants bear produce for harvest

A few further points are made.

(a) Biological assets are usually managed in groups of animal or plant classes, with characteristics (eg male/female ratio) which allow **sustainability in perpetuity**.

(b) **Land often forms an integral part** of the activity itself in pastoral and other land-based agricultural activities.

The Standard then goes on to look at the principal issues in accounting for biological assets.

1.3.1 Recognition of biological assets

The recognition criteria are very **similar to those for other assets**, in that animals or plants should be recognised as assets in the following circumstances.

(a) The enterprise **controls** the asset as a result of past events
(b) It is probable that the **future economic benefits** associated with the asset will flow to the enterprise
(c) The fair value or cost of the asset to the enterprise can be **measured reliably**

The significant physical attributes of biological assets can be measured using various methods (which are used by markets to measure value) and generally indicate the source of future economic benefits. The **certainty** of the flow of rewards can be determined by formal ownership records, eg land title, branding. The availability of both cost and value for biological assets indicates the reliability aspect of the measurement criteria is fulfilled.

1.3.2 Measurement of biological assets

The IAS provides for a benchmark treatment and an allowed alternative treatment.

Benchmark treatment	Allowed alternative treatment
Fair value less estimated point of sale costs	Cost less accumulated depreciation and impairment losses

The alternative method is allowed, if a fair value cannot be determined because market-determined prices or values are not available.

This alternative basis is only allowed on **initial recognition.**

The **measurement basis** used to depict the fair value of a biological asset will differ depending on the existence of an active market, market efficiency and the use made of the asset.

In summary, it is felt that **fair value**, when compared to historical cost, has greater relevance, reliability, comparability and understandability as a measure of future economic benefits.

1.3.3 Determining fair value

The standard states that the primary indicator of fair value should be **net market value**. This is reasonable as efficient markets exist for most biological assets in most locations, and net market value is usually considered as providing the best evidence of fair value where an active market exists. Markets will generally differentiate between differing **qualities and quantities**. Market value is not generally predicted on management's intended use, however, but recognises alternative uses.

An active and efficient market may not be available for a class of biological assets in a specific location, or there may be imperfections in the market. The standard goes into some detail about **how fair value should be estimated** in such circumstances, but in summary, the valuation techniques should be consistent with the objectives of measuring fair value and should attain an appropriate balance between relevance and reliability.

1.3.4 Recognition

This is an important principle, whereby the change in the carrying amount for a group of biological assets should be allocated between:

(a) The change attributable to **differences in fair value,** and
(b) The **physical change** in biological assets held.

The total change in carrying value between the beginning and end of the period thus consists of two components. Although the separation of these two components might appear impractical, the Standard states that separate disclosure of each is **fundamental to appraising current period performance and future prospects**. This is because they will not be reported in the same way in the financial statements.

(a) The change in carrying amount attributable to the **physical change in biological assets** must be recognised as income or expense and described as the change in biological assets. This allows management's performance to be evaluated in relation to the production from, and maintenance and renewal of, biological assets. This is the 'operating' part of the change in carrying amount.

(b) The change in carrying amount attributable to **differences in fair value** should be recognised in the statement of non-owner movements in equity and presented in equity under the heading of surplus/(deficit) on fair valuation of biological assets. This is the 'holding' part of the change in carrying amount.

In the **statement of financial position** the biological assets must be shown at fair value, incorporating the consequences of all biological transformations. These assets, with their differing risk and return characteristics, should be identified clearly.

The recommended **method of separating the above components** is to calculate the change attributable to the differences in fair value by restating biological assets on hand at the opening reporting date using end of period fair values and comparing this with the closing carrying amount. The biological assets on hand at the beginning and end of the period will then be expressed in a common measurement unit, ie period-end fair value. This allows the relative significance of sales, disposals, purchases, additions and biological transformations to be evaluated in relation to the overall change in substance of the biological assets held during the period.

There are **exceptions to this approach** in certain situations. For example, in some agricultural systems the predominant activity has a production cycle of less than a year (eg broiler chickens, mushroom growing, cereal crops). In such cases the total change in carrying amount is reported in the income statement as a single item of income or expense.

On other occasions, the consequences of an **extraordinary item** may form part of the total change in biological assets. This should be disclosed separately as required by IAS 8 on the face of the income statement after the profit or loss on ordinary activities, rather than being included in the change in biological assets recognised as income or expense. It should also appear as a separate item in the reconciliation to determine the change attributable to biological transformation.

Any other events giving rise to a change in biological assets of such a **size, nature or incidence** that their disclosure is relevant to explain the entity's performance (as defined in IAS 8) should be included in the change in biological assets recognised as income or expense. They should, however, be shown as a separate item in the reconciliation required to determine the change attributable to biological transformation.

1.3.5 Presentation and disclosure

In the **statement of financial position** biological assets should be classified as a separate class of assets falling under neither current nor non-current classifications. This reflects the view of such assets as having an unlimited life on a collective basis; it is the total exposure of the entity to this type of asset that is important.

Biological assets should also be **sub-classified** (either on the face of the statement of financial position or as a note to the accounts).

(a) Class of animal or plant
(b) Nature of activities (consumable or bearer)
(c) Maturity or immaturity for intended purpose

Where activities are **consumable**, the maturity criterion will be attainment of harvestable specifications, whereas in **bearer** activities, it will be attainment of sufficient maturity to sustain economic harvests.

In the **statement of comprehensive income**, enterprises with significant agricultural activity are encouraged to provide, on the face of the statement of comprehensive income, an analysis of the income and expenses used in determining profit from operating activities based on the nature of income and expenses (ie rather than the cost of sales method).

The IAS also lists some detailed disclosure requirements including the measurement base used for fair value, the details of the reconciliation of the change in carrying value for the year and so on.

1.4 Agricultural produce

This was defined in the key terms above. It is **recognised at the point of harvest** (eg detachment from the biological asset). Agricultural produce is either incapable of biological process or such processes remain dormant (eg stored grain). **Recognition ends** once the produce enters trading activities or production processes within integrated agribusinesses, although processing activities that are incidental to agricultural activities and that do not materially alter the form of the produce (eg drying or cleaning) are not counted as processing. Following harvest, the provisions of IAS 2 apply.

1.4.1 Measurement and presentation

Following the treatment of biological assets above, the IAS states that agricultural produce should be **measured at each reporting date at fair value** less estimated point-of-sale costs, to the extent that it is sourced from an enterprise's biological assets, which are also valued at fair value. This is logical when you consider that, until harvest, the agricultural produce was valued at fair value anyway as part of the biological asset.

The **change in the carrying amount** of the agricultural produce held at two reporting dates should be recognised as **income or expense** in the income statement. This will be rare as such produce is usually sold or processed within a short time, so that produce held over two reporting dates is being held for a specific management purpose and the consequences of that should be reflected in the current period.

Agricultural produce that is harvested for **trading or processing activities** within integrated agricultural/ agribusiness operations should be measured at **fair value** at the date of harvest and this amount is deemed cost for application of IAS 2 to consequential inventories.

1.4.2 Presentation in the statement of financial position

Agricultural produce should be classified as inventory in the statement of financial position and disclosed separately either in the statement of financial position or in the notes.

1.5 Government grants

FAST FORWARD

In relation to government grants you should be able to explain treatment, presentation and disclosure.

An unconditional government grant related to a biological asset measured at its fair value less estimated point-of-sale costs should be recognised as income when, and only when, the grant becomes receivable.

If a government grant requires an enterprise not to engage in specified agricultural activity (eg the EU's set aside grant), an enterprise should only recognise the grant as income when, and only when, the conditions are met.

IAS 20 does not apply to a government grant on biological assets measured at fair value less estimated point-of-sale costs. However if a biological asset is measured at cost less accumulated depreciation and accumulated impairment losses then IAS 20 does apply.

The following should be disclosed.

- The nature and extent of government grants recognised in the financial statements.
- Unfulfilled conditions and other contingencies attaching to government grants.
- Significant decreases expected in the level of government grants.

1.6 Section summary

In relation to agriculture you should be able to discuss:

- Accounting for **biological assets**
- **Transformation** and changes in substance
- **Unit of measurement** and changes in the carrying amount

Exam focus point

In March 2000, the IASC Board decided to run a field test of fair value measurements to be completed by June 2000. This field test was designed to show that reliable measures of fair value for biological assets are available. The final Standard depended on the results of these field tests. Note that this is the first standard to have been field tested in this way.

2 IFRS 6 Exploration for and evaluation of mineral resources: main proposals

FAST FORWARD

IFRS 6 requires that mineral resources on initial recognition are measured at cost

- Subsequent measurement may be based on either the **cost model** or the **revaluation model**
- Assets must be assessed for impairment in accordance with IAS 36

2.1 Reasons for issuing IFRS 6

IFRS 6 is an interim standard. It is only a short-term solution to the problems of accounting in this area, and was issued so that entities had at least *some* guidance until a complete standard is issued in the future. Before IFRS, accounting practices varied greatly between national standard-setters, so it was important that, with more and more entities switching to IFRS, there was at least some IFRS guidance in the area. Since it had had to be specifically excluded from IAS 16 and IAS 38, the IASB developed and issued IFRS 6.

IFRS 6 is related to IAS 38's distinction between research and development phases, where research costs are expensed and development costs are capitalised. The problem is that the exploration for and evaluation of mineral resources is not quite research and not quite development – hence the need for IFRS 6.

2.2 Scope

The scope of IFRS 6 is intentionally very narrow. Entities must apply IFRS 6 to all exploration and evaluation expenditure incurred, but it does not address other aspects of their accounting.

Moreover, IFRS 6 only applies *after* the entity has obtained legal rights to explore in a specific area, but *before* extraction has been demonstrated to be both technically feasible and commercially viable.

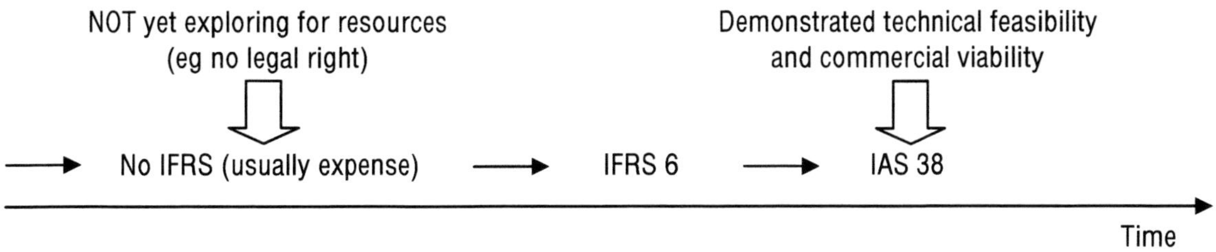

Key terms

Exploration and evaluation expenditures are expenditures incurred by an entity in connection with the exploration for and evaluation of mineral resources before the technical feasibility and commercial viability of extracting a mineral resource are demonstrable.

Exploration and evaluation assets are exploration and evaluation expenditures recognised as assets in accordance with the entity's accounting policy.

Exploration for and evaluation of mineral resources is the search for mineral resources, including minerals, oil, natural gas and similar non-regenerative resources after the entity has obtained legal rights to explore in a specific area, as well as the determination of the technical feasibility and commercial viability of extracting the mineral resource. *(IFRS 6)*

2.3 Recognition

Expenditure is recognised as an asset for IFRS 6 until the technical feasibility and commercial viability of extracting resources can be demonstrated. Note that this also means that the entity must have the necessary technical and financial means to extract the resources.

An entity can then choose its own accounting policy as long as it is line with IAS 8. Specifically, it must conform to IAS 8 paragraph 10, which states that **management should use its judgement** in developing an **accounting policy** that results in information that is **relevant** and **reliable**. After choosing their policy, entities must then **apply their policy consistently**.

Note that expenditure related to the **development** of mineral resources must not be recognised as exploration and evaluation assets under IFRS 6, as they come under IAS 38.

2.4 Measurement at recognition

At recognition, exploration and evaluation **assets must be measured at cost**.

The following are examples of expenditures an entity might incur in the initial measurement of exploration and evaluation assets:

(a) Acquisition of rights to explore
(b) Topographical geological, geochemical and geophysical studies
(c) Exploratory drilling
(d) Trenching
(e) Sampling
(f) Activities in relation to evaluating the technical feasibility and commercial viability of extracting a mineral resource

An entity should also recognise the cost of any obligations for removal and restoration, in line with IAS 37.

Exam focus point

Your syllabus explicitly states that you should be able to give examples of elements of cost that might be included in the initial recognition in the financial statements. It would be advisable to learn the above, non-exhaustive, list!

2.5 Example: Cost

Gold Diggers Co is a mining company currently exploring and evaluating the possibilities for extracting gold from the deserts of South Australia. It has incurred the following costs in the year ended 20X1.

	$'000
Legal expenses relating to acquisition of land in which exploration is to take place	15,000
Legal expenses relating to acquisition of right to explore land	12,000
Exploratory drilling costs	123,000
General administrative overheads allocated to exploration of land in S Australia	25,000
Costs of extracting gold	152,000

Which of the above costs may be capitalised as exploration and evaluation assets in accordance with IFRS 6?

Solution

The following costs **can** be capitalised in accordance with IFRS 6:

	$'000
Legal expenses relating to acquisition of right to explore land	12,000
Exploratory drilling costs	123,000

The following costs **cannot** be capitalised in accordance with IFRS 6:

	$'000
Legal expenses relating to acquisition of land in which exploration is to take place (*Note 1*)	15,000
General administrative overheads allocated to exploration of land in S Australia (*Note 2*)	25,000
Costs of extracting gold (*Note 3*)	152,000

Notes

1. The land is acquired before the process of exploration and evaluation beings (because by definition the entity cannot be exploring and evaluating resources on land it does not own). The legal expenses relating to the acquisition are therefore not accounted for in line with IFRS 6, and are expensed.
2. General administrative overheads do not relate to the exploration and evaluation of resources, and must be expensed.
3. The costs of extracting gold are incurred after the process of exploration and evaluation has ended, and are not therefore accounted for in accordance with IFRS 6. They are costs incurred in the ordinary course of the business, and will likely be expensed as they are unlikely to qualify as intangible assets under IAS 38.

2.6 Measurement after recognition

Entities must apply either the **cost model** or the **revaluation model** (taking the revaluation model either from IAS 16 or IAS 38).

2.7 Changes in accounting policies

These may be made if the change makes the financial statements more relevant to users. **IAS 8** criteria need to be applied.

2.8 Classification and reclassification

Exploration and evaluation assets are classified as **tangible or intangible according to the nature** of the assets acquired. For example, drilling rights would be intangible; vehicles or drilling rigs would be tangible. The classification must be applied consistently.

They should no longer be classified as exploration and evaluation assets when the technical feasibility and commercial viability of extracting a mineral resource are demonstrable. Any impairment loss on the assets must be recognised before classification.

2.9 Impairment

Exploration and evaluation assets must be **assessed for impairment when facts and circumstances suggest that the carrying amount of an asset may exceed its recoverable amount. Any resulting impairment loss must be measured, presented and disclosed in accordance with IAS 36.**

The following **factors** suggest exploration and evaluation assets should be tested for impairment:

(a) The period for which the entity has **exploration rights has expired** or is due to expire in the near future and is not expected to be reviewed.

(b) **Substantive expenditure** on further exploration in the specific area is **not budgeted** or planned.

(c) Exploration in a specific area has **not** led to the discovery of **commercially viable quantities** of mineral resources, and the entity has decided to discontinue activities in this area.

(d) Sufficient data indicates that whilst a development in a specific area may proceed, the **carrying value of the exploration and evaluation asset is unlikely to be recovered** from successful development and sale.

For impairment purposes, each cash generating unit or group of units to which an exploration and evaluation asset is allocated must not be larger than a segment as determined by IFRS 8 *Operating segments.*

2.10 Disclosures

These must identify and explain the amounts recognised in the accounts. Specifically, entities must explain:

- Accounting policies
- The amounts of assets, liabilities, income and expenses, and operating and investing cash flows

Chapter Roundup

- IAS 41 *Agriculture* is very topical internationally.
- In relation to agriculture you should be able to discuss:
  - Accounting for biological assets
  - Transformation and changes in substance
  - Unit of measurement and changes in the carrying amount
- In relation to government grants you should be able to explain treatment, presentation and disclosure.
- IFRS 6 requires that mineral resources at initial recognition are measured at cost.
  - Subsequent measurement may be based on either the **cost model** or the **revaluation model**.
  - Assets must be **tested for impairment** in accordance with IAS 36.

Quick Quiz

1 What is a biological asset?

2 What is agricultural produce?

3 Fill in the missing words.

Transformation refers to the .... transformation, whereby .... and .... undergo a change in .... quality and/or quantity over .... which is .... and monitored as part of .... control.

4 IAS 41 has abolished the concept of cost for measurement purposes.

True ☐ False ☐
[Question:]

5 An entity has just begun exploring a previously unexplored area of ocean for oil. It has discovered oil there and there is an active market to sell to. The entity is unsure, however, if it can raise the necessary funds to complete the exploration process. What is the required treatment of the exploration costs incurred?

Answers to Quick Quiz

1 A biological asset is a living animal or plant.

2 Agricultural produce is product harvested from biological assets.

3 Physical, animal, plants, biological, time, measured, management

4 False. Cost is still allowed if fair value is not available at initial recognition.

5 The costs are recognised as expenses in profit and loss, as the entity does not have the financial resources to bring any asset to market and to receive future benefits from it.

Now try the questions below from the Exam Question Bank

Number	Level	Marks	Time
Q18	Introductory	n/a	n/a

Share-based payment

14

Topic list	Syllabus reference
1 IFRS 2 *Share based payment*	2(I)
2 Deferred tax implications	2(I)
3 Recent developments	2(I)

Introduction

The increasing use of share-based payments to employees or third parties has raised questions about the accounting treatment of such payments. This is dealt with in IRS 2 **Share based payment**, a controversial area, explained in this chapter.

Study Guide

Section 14 – Share-based payment

- Understand the term 'share-based payment' (IFRS 2)
- Discuss the key issue that measurement of the transaction should be based on fair value
- Explain the difference between cash-settled share-based payment transactions and equity-settled share-based payment transactions
- Identify the principles applied to measuring both cash and equity settled share-based payment transactions
- Compute the amounts that need to be recorded in the statement of comprehensive income and the statement of financial position when an entity carries out a transaction where the payment is share based

1 IFRS 2 Share based payment

FAST FORWARD

Share-based payment transactions should be recognised in the financial statements. You need to understand and be able to advise on:

- Recognition
- Measurement
- Disclosure

of both equity settled and cash settled transactions.

Exam focus point

Share-based payment is a popular exam topic, as it is a relatively recent and controversial standard. It was examined in December 2007 as part of a longer question, and the December 2009 exam included a 25 mark question entirely on a share-based payment.

1.1 Background

Transactions whereby entities purchase goods or services from other parties, such as suppliers and employees, by **issuing shares or share options** to those other parties are **increasingly common.** Share schemes are a common feature of director and executive remuneration and in some countries the authorities may offer tax incentives to encourage more companies to offer shares to employees. Companies whose shares or share options are regarded as a valuable 'currency' commonly use share-based payment to obtain employee and professional services.

The increasing use of share-based payment has raised questions about the accounting treatment of such transactions in company financial statements.

Share options are often granted to employees at an exercise price that is equal to or higher than the market price of the shares at the date the option is granted. Consequently the options have no intrinsic value and so **no transaction is recorded in the financial statements**.

This leads to an **anomaly:** if a company pays its employees in cash, an expense is recognised in profit or loss, but if the payment is in share options, no expense is recognised.

1.1.1 Arguments against recognition of share-based payment in the financial statements

There are a number of arguments against recognition. The IASB has considered and rejected the arguments below.

(a) **No cost therefore no charge**

There is no cost to the entity because the granting of shares or options does not require the entity to sacrifice cash or other assets. Therefore a charge should not be recognised.

This argument is unsound because it ignores the fact that a transaction has occurred. The employees have provided valuable services to the entity in return for valuable shares or options.

(b) **Earnings per share is hit twice**

It is argued that the charge to profit or loss for the employee services consumed reduces the entity's earnings, while at the same time there is an increase in the number of shares issued.

However, the dual impact on earnings per share simply reflects the two economic events that have occurred.

(i) The entity has issued shares or options, thus increasing the denominator of the earnings per share calculation.

(ii) It has also consumed the resources it received for those shares or options, thus reducing the numerator.

(c) **Adverse economic consequences**

It could be argued that entities might be discouraged from introducing or continuing employee share plans if they were required to recognise them on the financial statements. However, if this happened, it might be because the requirement for entities to account properly for employee share plans had revealed the economic consequences of such plans.

A situation where entities are able to obtain and consume resources by issuing valuable shares or options without having to account for such transactions could be perceived as a distortion.

1.2 Objective and scope

IFRS 2 requires an entity to **reflect the effects of share-based payment transactions** in its profit or loss and financial position.

IFRS 2 applies to all share-based payment transactions. There are three types.

(a) **Equity-settled share-based payment transactions**, in which the entity receives goods or services in exchange for equity instruments of the entity (including shares or share options)

(b) **Cash-settled share-based payment transactions**, in which the entity receives goods or services in exchange for amounts of cash that are based on the price (or value) of the entity's shares or other equity instruments of the entity

(c) Transactions in which the entity receives or acquires goods or services and either the entity or the supplier has a **choice** as to whether the entity settles the transaction in cash (or other assets) or by issuing equity instruments

IFRS 2 was amended in June 2009 to address situations in those parts of the world where, for public policy or other reasons, companies give their shares or rights to shares to individuals, organisations or groups that have not provided goods or services to the company. An example is the issue of shares to a charitable organisation for less than fair value, where the benefits are more intangible than usual goods or services.

Certain transactions are **outside the scope** of the IFRS:

(a) Transactions with employees and others in their capacity as a holder of equity instruments of the entity (for example, where an employee receives additional shares in a rights issue to all shareholders)

(b) The issue of equity instruments in exchange for control of another entity in a business combination

Key terms

Share-based payment transaction A transaction in which the entity receives goods or services as consideration for equity instruments of the entity (including shares or share options), or acquires goods or services by incurring liabilities to the supplier of those goods or services for amounts that are based on the price of the entity's shares or other equity instruments of the entity.

Key terms (cont')

Share-based payment arrangement An agreement between the entity and another party (including an employee) to enter into a share-based payment transaction, which thereby entitles the other party to receive cash or other assets of the entity for amounts that are based on the price of the entity's shares or other equity instruments of the entity, or to receive equity instruments of the entity, provided the specified vesting conditions, if any, are met.

Equity instrument A contract that evidences a residual interest in the assets of an entity after deducting all of its liabilities.

Equity instrument granted The right (conditional or unconditional) to an equity instrument of the entity conferred by the entity on another party, under a share-based payment arrangement.

Share option A contract that gives the holder the right, but not the obligation, to subscribe to the entity's shares at a fixed or determinable price for a specified period of time.

Fair value The amount for which an asset could be exchanged, a liability settled, or an equity instrument granted could be exchanged, between knowledgeable, willing parties in an arm's length transaction.

Grant date The date at which the entity and another party (including an employee) agree to a share-based payment arrangement, being when the entity and the other party have a shared understanding of the terms and conditions of the arrangement. At grant date the entity confers on the other party (the counterparty) the right to cash, other assets, or equity instruments of the entity, provided the specified vesting conditions, if any, are met. If that agreement is subject to an approval process (for example, by shareholders), grant date is the date when that approval is obtained.

Intrinsic value The difference between the fair value of the shares to which the counterparty has the (conditional or unconditional) right to subscribe or which it has the right to receive, and the price (if any) the other party is (or will be) required to pay for those shares. For example, a share option with an exercise price of $15 on a share with a fair value of $20, has an intrinsic value of $5.

Measurement date The date at which the fair value of the equity instruments granted is measured. For transactions with employees and others providing similar services, the measurement date is grant date. For transactions with parties other than employees (and those providing similar services), the measurement date is the date the entity obtains the goods or the counterparty renders service.

Vest To become an entitlement. Under a share-based payment arrangement, a counterparty's right to receive cash, other assets, or equity instruments of the entity vests upon satisfaction of any specified vesting conditions.

Vesting conditions The conditions that must be satisfied for the counterparty to become entitled to receive cash, other assets or equity instruments of the entity, under a share-based payment arrangement. Vesting conditions include service conditions, which require the other party to complete a specified period of service, and performance conditions, which require specified performance targets to be met (such as a specified increase in the entity's profit over a specified period of time).

Vesting period The period during which all the specified vesting conditions of a share-based payment arrangement are to be satisfied. *(IFRS 2)*

1.3 Recognition: the basic principle

An entity should **recognise goods or services received or acquired in a share-based payment transaction when it obtains the goods or as the services are received.** Goods or services received or acquired in a share-based payment transaction **should be recognised as expenses unless they qualify for recognition as assets**. For example, services are normally recognised as expenses (because they are normally rendered immediately), while goods are recognised as assets.

If the goods or services were received or acquired in an **equity-settled** share-based payment transaction the entity should recognise **a corresponding increase in equity** (reserves).

If the goods or services were received or acquired in a **cash-settled** share-based payment transaction the entity should recognise a **liability.**

1.4 Equity-settled share-based payment transactions

1.4.1 Measurement

The issue here is how to measure the 'cost' of the goods and services received and the equity instruments (eg, the share options) granted in return.

The general principle in IFRS 2 is that when an entity recognises the goods or services received and the corresponding increase in equity, it should measure these at the **fair value of the goods or services received**. Where the transaction is with **parties other than employees**, there is a rebuttable presumption that the fair value of the goods or services received can be estimated reliably.

If the fair value of the goods or services received cannot be measured reliably, the entity should measure their value by reference to the **fair value of the equity instruments granted.**

Where the transaction is with a party other than an employee fair value should be measured at the date the entity obtains the goods or the counterparty renders service.

Where shares, share options or other equity instruments are granted to **employees** as part of their remuneration package, it is not normally possible to measure directly the services received. For this reason, the entity should measure the fair value of the employee services received by reference to the **fair value of the equity instruments granted**. The fair value of those equity instruments should be measured at **grant date**.

1.4.2 Determining the fair value of equity instruments granted

Where a transaction is measured by reference to the fair value of the equity instruments granted, fair value is based on **market prices** if available, taking into account the terms and conditions upon which those equity instruments were granted.

If market prices are not available, the entity should estimate the fair value of the equity instruments granted using a **valuation technique**, such as the option pricing model.

1.4.3 Transactions in which services are received

The issue here is **when** to recognise the transaction. When equity instruments are granted they may vest immediately, but often the counterparty has to meet specified conditions first. For example, an employee may have to complete a specified period of service. This means that the effect of the transaction normally has to be allocated over more than one accounting period.

If the equity instruments granted **vest immediately**, (ie, the counterparty is not required to complete a specified period of service before becoming unconditionally entitled to the equity instruments) it is presumed that the services have already been received (in the absence of evidence to the contrary). The entity should **recognise the services received in full**, with a corresponding increase in equity, **on the grant date**.

If the equity instruments granted do not vest until the counterparty completes a specified period of service, the entity should account for those services **as they are rendered** by the counterparty during the vesting period. For example if an employee is granted share options on condition that he or she completes three years' service, then the services to be rendered by the employee as consideration for the share options will be received in the future, over that three-year vesting period.

The entity should recognise an amount for the goods or services received during the vesting period based on the **best available estimate** of the **number of equity instruments expected to vest**. It should **revise** that estimate if subsequent information indicates that the number of equity instruments expected to vest differs from previous estimates. On **vesting date**, the entity should revise the estimate to **equal the number of equity instruments that actually vest**.

Once the goods and services received and the corresponding increase in equity have been recognised, the entity should make no subsequent adjustment to total equity after the vesting date.

1.5 Example: Equity-settled share-based payment transaction

On 1 January 20X1 an entity grants 100 share options to each of its 400 employees. Each grant is conditional upon the employee working for the entity until 31 December 20X3. The fair value of each share option is $20.

During 20X1 20 employees leave and the entity estimates that 20% of the employees will leave during the three year period.

During 20X2 a further 25 employees leave and the entity now estimates that 25% of its employees will leave during the three year period.

During 20X3 a further 10 employees leave.

Required

Calculate the remuneration expense that will be recognised in respect of the share-based payment transaction for each of the three years ended 31 December 20X3.

Solution

IFRS 2 requires the entity to recognise the remuneration expense, based on the fair value of the share options granted, as the services are received during the three year vesting period.

In 20X1 and 20X2 the entity estimates the number of options expected to vest (by estimating the number of employees likely to leave) and bases the amount that it recognises for the year on this estimate.

In 20X3 it recognises an amount based on the number of options that actually vest. A total of 55 employees left during the three year period and therefore 34,500 options (400 – 55 × 100) vested.

The amount recognised as an expense for each of the three years is calculated as follows:

		Cumulative expense at year-end	*Expense for year*
		$	$
20X1	40,000 × 80% × 20 × 1/3	213,333	213,333
20X2	40,000 × 75% × 20 × 2/3	400,000	186,667
20X3	34,500 × 20	690,000	290,000

Question — Share options

During its financial year ended 31 January 20X6, TSQ issued share options to several of its senior employees. The options vest immediately upon issue.

Which *one* of the following describes the accounting entry that is required to recognise the options?

A	DEBIT the statement of changes in equity	CREDIT liabilities
B	DEBIT the statement of changes in equity	CREDIT equity
C	DEBIT profit or loss	CREDIT liabilities
D	DEBIT profit or loss	CREDIT equity

Answer

D Under IFRS 2 a charge must be made to profit or loss

Question — Share based payment

On 1 January 20X9 an entity grants 250 share options to each of its 200 employees. The only condition attached to the grant is that the employees should continue to work for the entity until 31 December 20Y2. Five employees leave during the year.

The market price of each option was $12 at 1 January 20X9 and $15 at 31 December 20X9.

Required

Show how this transaction will be reflected in the financial statements for the year ended 31 December 20X9.

Answer

The remuneration expense for the year is based on the fair value of the options granted at the grant date (1 January 20X9). As five of the 200 employees left during the year it is reasonable to assume that 20 employees will leave during the four year vesting period and that therefore 45,000 options (250 × 180) will actually vest.

Therefore the entity recognises a remuneration expense of $135,000 (45,000 × 12 × ¼) in the profit or loss and a corresponding increase in equity of the same amount.

1.6 Cash-settled share-based payment transactions

Examples of this type of transaction include:

(a) **Share appreciation rights** granted to employees: the employees become entitled to a future cash payment (rather than an equity instrument), based on the increase in the entity's share price from a specified level over a specified period of time, or

(b) An entity might grant to its employees a right to receive a future cash payment by granting to them a **right to shares that are redeemable**

The basic principle is that the entity measures the goods or services acquired and the liability incurred at the **fair value of the liability**.

The entity should **remeasure** the fair value of the liability **at each reporting date** until the liability is settled **and at the date of settlement**. Any **changes** in fair value are recognised in **profit or loss** for the period.

The entity should recognise the services received, and a liability to pay for those services, **as the employees render service.** For example, if share appreciation rights do not vest until the employees have completed a specified period of service, the entity should recognise the services received and the related liability, over that period.

1.7 Example: cash-settled share-based payment transaction

On 1 January 20X1 an entity grants 100 cash share appreciation rights (SARS) to each of its 500 employees, on condition that the employees continue to work for the entity until 31 December 20X3.

During 20X1 35 employees leave. The entity estimates that a further 60 will leave during 20X2 and 20X3.

During 20X2 40 employees leave and the entity estimates that a further 25 will leave during 20X3.

During 20X3 22 employees leave.

At 31 December 20X3 150 employees exercise their SARs. Another 140 employees exercise their SARs at 31 December 20X4 and the remaining 113 employees exercise their SARs at the end of 20X5.

The fair values of the SARs for each year in which a liability exists are shown below, together with the intrinsic values at the dates of exercise.

	Fair value	*Intrinsic value*
	$	$
20X1	14.40	
20X2	15.50	
20X3	18.20	15.00
20X4	21.40	20.00
20X5		25.00

Required

Calculate the amount to be recognised in profit or loss for each of the five years ended 31 December 20X5 and the liability to be recognised in the statement of financial position at 31 December for each of the five years.

Solution

For the three years to the vesting date of 31 December 20X3 the expense is based on the entity's estimate of the number of SARs that will actually vest (as for an equity-settled transaction). However, the fair value of the liability is **re-measured** at each year-end.

The intrinsic value of the SARs at the date of exercise is the amount of cash actually paid.

		Liability at year-end		*Expense for year*
		$	$	$
20X1	Expected to vest (500 – 95):			
	405 × 100 × 14.40 × 1/3	194,400		194,400
20X2	Expected to vest (500 – 100):			
	400 × 100 × 15.50 × 2/3	413,333		218,933
20X3	Exercised:			
	150 ×100 × 15.00		225,000	
	Not yet exercised (500 – 97 – 150):			
	253 × 100 × 18.20	460,460	47,127	
				272,127
20X4	Exercised:			
	140 × 100 × 20.00		280,000	
	Not yet exercised (253 – 140):			
	113 × 100 × 21.40	241,820	(218,640)	
				61,360
20X5	Exercised:			
	113 × 100 × 25.00		282,500	
		Nil	(241,820)	
				40,680
				787,500

Transactions which either the entity or the other party has a choice of settling in cash or by issuing equity instruments.

If the entity has incurred a liability to settle in cash or other assets it should account for the transaction as a cash-settled share-based payment transaction.

If no such liability has been incurred the entity should account for the transaction as an equity-settled share-based payment transaction.

2 Deferred tax implications

FAST FORWARD

Deferred tax may arise where the tax deductibility of share-based payments occurs in a later period to that in which the expense is recognised.

2.1 Issue

An entity may receive a tax deduction that differs from related cumulative remuneration expense, and may arise in a later accounting period.

Eg: an entity recognises an expense for share options granted under IFRS 2, but does not receive a tax deduction until the options are exercised and receives the tax deduction at the share price on the exercise date.

2.2 Measurement

The deferred tax asset temporary difference is measured as:

Carrying amount of share-based payment expense	0
Less: tax base of share-based payment expense (estimated amount tax authorities will permit as a deduction in future periods, based on year end information)	(X)
Temporary difference	(X)
Deferred tax asset at X%	X

If the amount of the tax deduction (or estimated future tax deduction) exceeds the amount of the related cumulative remuneration expense, this indicates that the tax deduction relates also to an equity item.

The excess is therefore recognised directly in equity, and **not** reported in other comprehensive income.

2.3 Example: Deferred tax implications of share-based payment

On 1 January 20X2, Bruce granted 5,000 share options to an employee vesting two years later on 31 December 20X3. The fair value of each option measured at the grant date was $3.

Tax law in the jurisdiction in which the entity operates allows a tax deduction of the intrinsic value of the options on exercise. The intrinsic value of the share options was $1.20 at 31 December 20X2 and $3.40 at 31 December 20X3 on which date the options were exercised.

Assume a tax rate of 30%.

Required

Show the deferred tax accounting treatment of the above transaction at 31 December 20X2, 31 December 20X3 (before exercise), and on exercise.

Solution

	31/12/20X2	*31/12/20X3 before exercise*
Carrying amount of share-based payment expense	0	0
Less: Tax base of share-based payment expense (5,000 × $1.2 × ½)/(5,000 × $3.40)	(3,000)	(17,000)
Temporary difference	(3,000)	(17,000)
Deferred tax asset @ 30%	900	5,100
Deferred tax (Cr I/S) (5,100 – 900 – (Working) 600)	900	3,600
Deferred tax (Cr Equity) (Working)	0	600

On exercise, the deferred tax asset is replaced by a current tax one. The double entry is:

Debit deferred tax (I/S)	4,500	reversal
Debit deferred tax (equity)	600	
Credit deferred tax asset	5,100	

Debit current tax asset	5,100
Credit current tax (I/S)	4,500
Credit current tax (equity)	600

Working

Accounting expense recognised (5,000 × $3 × ½)/(5,000 × $3)	7,500	15,000
Tax deduction (5,000 × $1.20 × 1/2)/(5,000 × $3.40)	(3,000)	(17,000)
Excess temporary difference	0	(2,000)
Excess deferred tax asset to equity @ 30%	0	600

3 Recent developments

FAST FORWARD IFRS 2 was amended to define vesting conditions and clarify the accounting treatment of cancellations.

3.1 Amendment to IFRS 2

In 2008 IFRS 2 was amended to clarify:

- The definition of 'vesting conditions'
- The accounting treatment of cancellations by parties other than the entity.

3.1.1 Vesting conditions

The definition of vesting conditions is:

- Restricted to service conditions and performance conditions, and
- Excludes other features such as a requirement for employees to make regular contributions into a savings scheme.

3.1.2 Cancellations

Three types are identified:

- Cancellations by the entity
- Cancellations by the counterparty (eg the employee)
- Cancellations by a third party (eg a shareholder)

The amendment requires cancellations by the employee to be treated in the same way as cancellations by the employer, resulting in an **accelerated charge to profit or loss of the unamortised balance of the options granted**.

3.2 Further amendments to IFRS 2

3.2.1 The issue

Payment for goods or services received by an entity within a group may be made in the form of granting equity instruments of the parent company, or equity instruments of another group company. IFRS 2.3 states that this type of transaction qualifies as a share-based payment transaction within the scope of IFRS 2.

The standard was not, however clear as regards the following types of arrangements:

- Where the entity's suppliers (including employees) will receive cash payments that are linked to the price of the equity instruments of the entity
- Where the entity's suppliers (including employees) will receive cash payments that are linked to .the price of the equity instruments of the entity's parent

Under either arrangement, the entity's parent had an obligation to make the required cash payments to the entity's suppliers. The entity itself did not have any obligation to make such payments.

3.2.2 Amendments

The June 2009 amendment to IFRS 2 clarifies that IFRS 2 applies to arrangements such as those described above even if the entity that receives goods or services from its suppliers has no obligation to make the required share-based cash payments.

3.3 Section summary

IFRS 2 requires entities to **recognise** the goods or services received as a result of **share based payment transactions.**

- Equity settled transactions: DEBIT Asset/Expense, CREDIT Equity
- Cash settled transactions: DEBIT Asset/Expense, CREDIT Liability
- Transactions are **recognised when goods/services are obtained/received** (usually over the performance period)
- Transactions are measured at fair value

Chapter Roundup

- **Share-based payment** transactions should be recognised in the financial statements. You need to understand and be able to advise on:
  - Recognition
  - Measurement
  - Disclosure

  of both equity settled and cash settled transactions.
- Deferred tax may arise where the tax deductibility of share-based payments occurs in a later period to that in which the expense is recognised.
- IFRS 2 was amended to define vesting conditions and clarify the accounting treatment of cancellations

Quick Quiz

1 What is a cash-settled share based payment transaction?

2 What is a grant date?

3 If an entity has entered into an equity settled share-based payment transaction, what should it recognise in its financial statements?

4 Where an entity has granted share options to its employees in return for services, how is the transaction measured?

Answers to Quick Quiz

1 A transaction in which the entity receives goods or services in exchange for amounts of cash that are based on the price (or value) of the entity's shares or other equity instruments of the entity.

2 The date at which the entity and another party (including an employee) agree to a share based payment arrangement, being when the entity and the other party have a shared understanding of the terms and conditions of the arrangement.

3 The goods or services received and a corresponding increase in equity.

4 By reference to the fair value of the equity instruments granted, measured at grant date.

Now try the question below from the Exam Question Bank

Number	Level	Marks	Time
Q19	Introductory	6	11 mins

PART C

Presentation and additional disclosures

Presentation of published financial statements

15

Topic list	Syllabus reference
1 IAS 1 (revised): Presentation of financial statements	4
2 Structure and content of financial statements	4
3 Statement of financial position	4
4 The current/non-current distinction	4
5 Statement of comprehensive income	4
6 Income statement	4
7 Revision of basic accounts	4
8 Changes in equity	4
9 Notes to the financial statements	4
10 Problems with small entities	4
11 IAS 34: Interim financial reporting	3(d)

Introduction

We begin in this chapter by looking at the overall **content and format** of company financial statements. These are governed by IAS 1 (revised) *Presentation of financial statements.*

Study Guide

Section 16 – Presentation of the income statement and statement of comprehensive income

- State the objectives of international accounting standards governing presentation of financial statements
- Describe the structure and the content of income statements, including continuing operations
- Discuss 'fair presentation' and the accounting concepts/principles
- Recognise the content and format of interim financial statements

Exam Guide

The Dip IFR syllabus was changed for exams from 2011 onwards, with single entity financial statements no longer being examinable. However, in the groups question you could be asked for any of the primary financial statements. The question usually asks for an income statement and statement of financial position, but sometimes asks for a statement of changes in equity so you must be prepared for this.

These questions are a useful method of examining published financial statements as well as the content of accounting standards as there are always a number of adjustments to deal with.

1 IAS 1 (revised): Presentation of financial statements

1.1 Objective and scope

FAST FORWARD

IAS 1 *Presentation of financial statements* covers **accounting concepts**. You need to remember and be able to apply all the key terms such as going concern, accruals, consistency, materiality, aggregation and offsetting.

The main objective of IAS 1 is:

> 'to prescribe the basis for presentation of general purpose financial statements, in order to ensure comparability both with the entity's own financial statements of previous periods and with the financial statements of other entities.'

IAS 1 applies to all **general purpose financial statements** prepared in accordance with IASs, ie those intended to meet the needs of users who are not in a position to demand reports tailored to their specific needs.

1.2 Purpose of financial statements

The **objective of financial statements** is to provide information about the financial position, performance and cash flows of an entity that is useful to a wide range of users in making economic decisions. They also show the result of **management stewardship** of the resources of the entity.

This may be depicted by the following diagram.

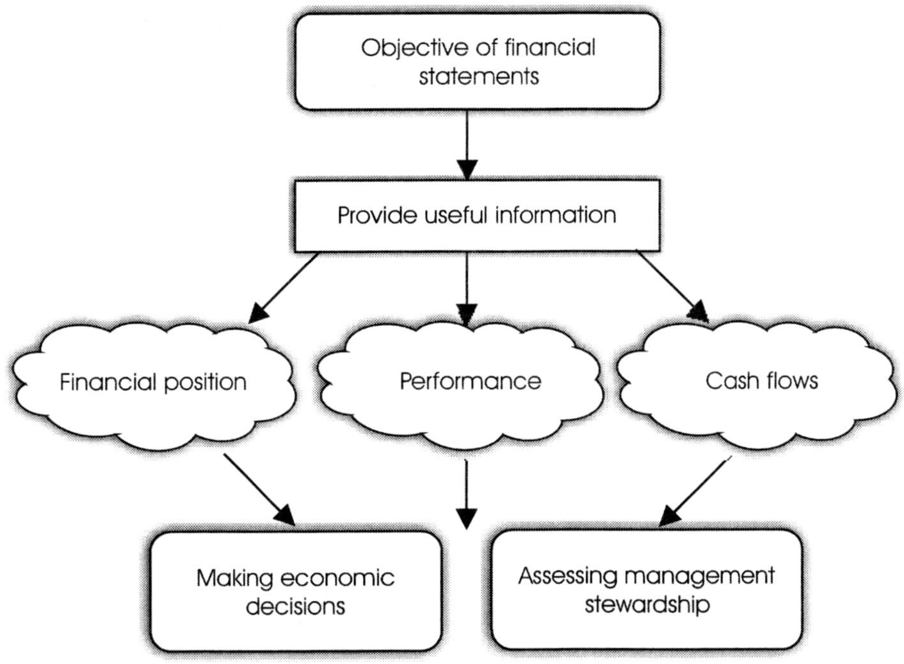

In order to fulfil this objective, financial statements must provide information about the following aspects of an entity's results.

- Assets
- Liabilities
- Equity
- Income and expenses (including gains and losses)
- Contributions by and distributions to owners in their capacity as owners
- Cash flows

This information, along with other information in the notes, assists users in predicting the entity's **future cash flows** and, in particular, their timing and certainty.

1.3 Responsibility for financial statements

Responsibility for the preparation and presentation of an entity's financial statements rests with the **board of directors** (or equivalent).

1.4 Components of financial statements

A complete set of financial statements includes the following components.

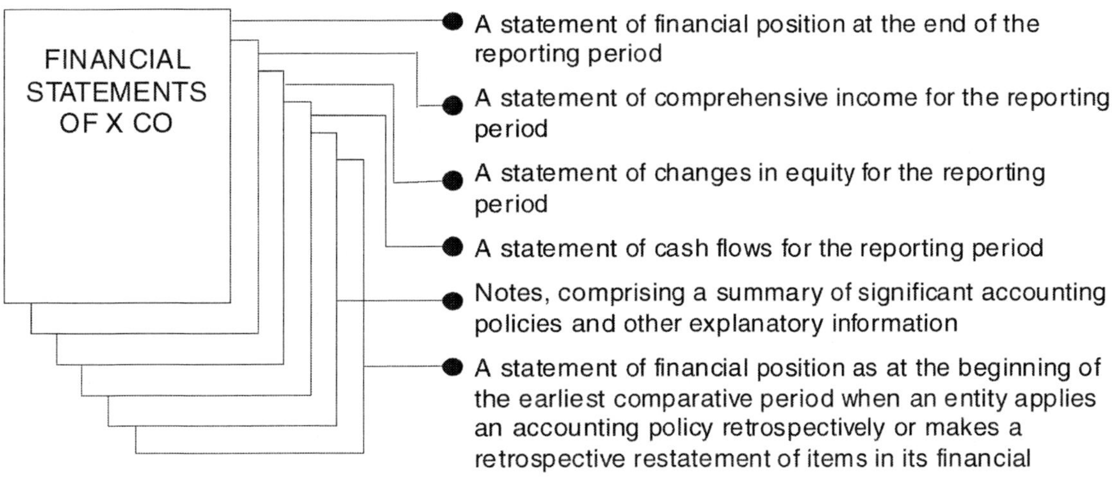

In addition, IAS 1 encourages, but does not require, a **financial review** by management (which is *not* part of the financial statements), explaining the main features of the entity's performance and position, and the principal uncertainties it faces. The report may include a review of the following.

(a) **Factors/influences determining performance**: changes in the environment in which the entity operates, the entity's response to those changes and their effect, and the entity's policy for investment to maintain and enhance performance, including its dividend policy

(b) Entity's **sources of funding**, the policy on **gearing** and its **risk management policies**

(c) **Strengths and resources** of the entity whose value is not reflected in the statement of financial position under IASs

Entities are encouraged to produce any other reports and statements which may aid users.

1.5 Fair presentation and compliance with IFRS

Most importantly, financial statements should **present fairly** the financial position, financial performance and cash flows of an entity. **Compliance with IFRS** is presumed to result in financial statements that achieve a fair presentation.

The following points made by IAS 1 expand on this principle.

(a) **Compliance with IFRS** should be disclosed

(b) **All relevant IFRS** must be followed if compliance with IFRS is disclosed

(c) Use of an **inappropriate accounting treatment** cannot be rectified either by disclosure of accounting policies or notes/explanatory material

There may be (very rare) circumstances when management decides that compliance with a requirement of an IFRS would be misleading. **Departure from the IFRS** is therefore required to achieve a fair presentation. The following should be disclosed in such an event.

(a) Management confirmation that the financial statements fairly present the entity's financial position, performance and cash flows

(b) Statement that all IFRS have been complied with *except* departure from one IFRS to achieve a fair presentation

(c) Details of the nature of the departure, why the IFRS treatment would be misleading, and the treatment adopted

(d) Financial impact of the departure

1.5.1 Extreme case disclosures

In very rare circumstances, management may conclude that compliance with a requirement in a Standard or interpretation may be so **misleading** that it would **conflict with the objective** of Financial Statements set out in the *Framework*, but the relevant regulatory framework prohibits departure from the requirements. In such cases the entity needs to reduce the perceived misleading aspects of compliance by **disclosing**:

(a) The title of the Standard, the nature of the requirement and the reason why management has reached its conclusion.

(b) For each period, the adjustment to each item in the Financial Statements that would be necessary to achieve fair presentation.

IAS 1 states what is required for a fair presentation.

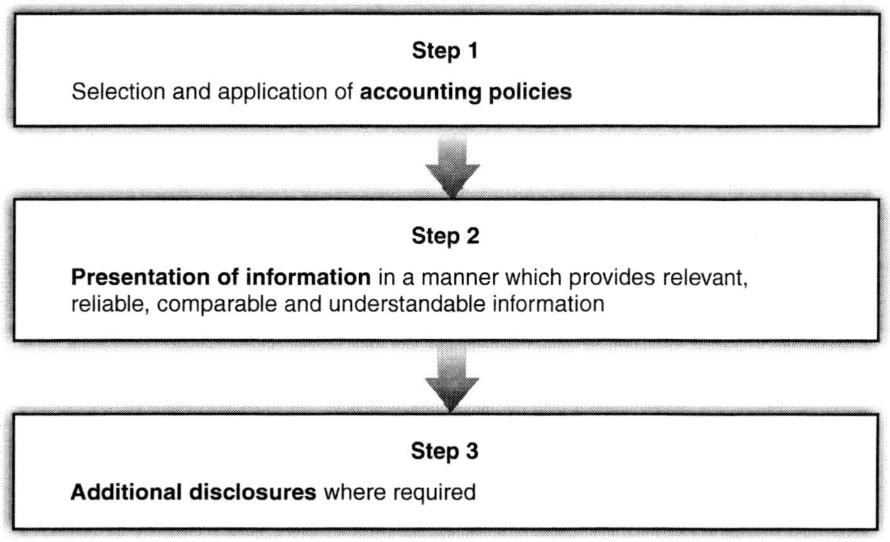

The IAS then goes on to consider certain important assumptions which underpin the preparation and presentation of financial statements, which we might call **fundamental assumptions.**

1.6 Going concern

Key term

> The entity is normally viewed as a **going concern**, that is, as continuing in operation for the foreseeable future. Financial statements are prepared on a going concern basis unless management intends to liquidate the entity or to cease trading.

This assumption is based on the notion that, when preparing a normal set of accounts, it is always expected that the business will **continue to operate** in approximately the same manner for the foreseeable future (at least the next 12 months should be considered). In particular, the entity will not go into liquidation or scale down its operations in a material way.

Various factors may be considered in assessing the going concern assumption.

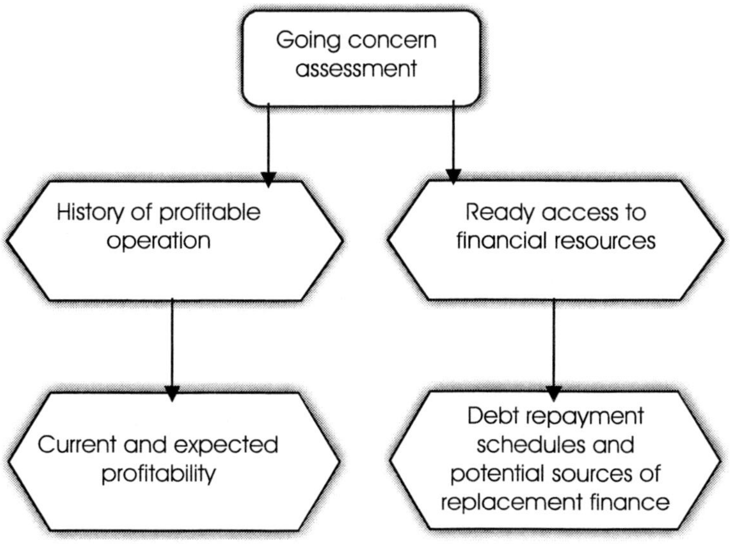

The main significance of the going concern assumption is that the assets of the business **should not be valued at their 'break-up' value**, which is the amount that they would sell for if they were sold off piecemeal and the business were thus broken up.

If the going concern assumption is not followed, that fact must be disclosed, together with:

- The **basis** on which the financial statements have been prepared
- The **reasons** why the entity is not considered to be a going concern

1.7 Accrual basis of accounting

Key term

> **Accrual basis of accounting.** Items are recognised as assets liabilities, equity, income and expenses when they satisfy the definition and recognition criteria for those elements in the *Framework*. *(IAS 1)*

Entities should prepare their financial statements on the basis that transactions are recorded in them, not as the cash is paid or received, but as the revenues or expenses are **earned or incurred** in the accounting period to which they relate.

According to the accrual assumption, then, in computing profit revenue earned must be **matched against** the expenditure incurred in earning it.

1.8 Consistency of presentation

To maintain consistency, the presentation and classification of items in the financial statements should **stay the same from one period to the next. There are two exceptions.**

(a) There is a significant change in the **nature of the operations** or a review of the financial statements presentation indicates a **more appropriate presentation**.

(b) A change in presentation is **required by an IFRS**.

1.9 Materiality and aggregation

All material items should be **disclosed** in the financial statements.

Amounts which are **immaterial** can be aggregated with amounts of a similar nature or function and need not be presented separately.

Key term

> **Materiality.** Omissions or misstatement of items are material if they could, individually or collectively, influence the economic decisions of users taken on the basis of the financial statements. Materiality depends on the size and nature of the omission or misstatement judged in the surrounding circumstances. The size or nature of the item, or a combination of both, could be the determining factor. *(IAS 1)*

An error which is too trivial to affect anyone's understanding of the accounts is referred to as **immaterial**. In preparing accounts it is important to assess what is material and what is not, so that time and money are not wasted in the pursuit of excessive detail.

Determining whether or not an item is material is a very **subjective exercise**. There is no absolute measure of materiality. It is common to apply a convenient rule of thumb (for example to define material items as those with a value greater than 5% of the net profit disclosed by the accounts). But some items disclosed in accounts are regarded as particularly sensitive and even a very small misstatement of such an item would be regarded as a material error. An example in the accounts of a limited liability company might be the amount of remuneration paid to directors of the company.

The assessment of an item as material or immaterial may **affect its treatment in the accounts**. For example, the income statement of a business will show the expenses incurred by the business grouped under suitable captions (heating and lighting expenses, rent and local taxes etc); but in the case of very small expenses it may be appropriate to lump them together under a caption such as 'sundry expenses', because a more detailed breakdown would be inappropriate for such immaterial amounts.

In assessing whether or not an item is material, it is not only the amount of the item which needs to be considered. The **context** is also important.

(a) If a statement of financial position shows non-current assets of $2 million and inventories of $30,000 an error of $20,000 in the depreciation calculations might not be regarded as material, whereas an error of $20,000 in the inventory valuation probably would be. In other words, the total of which the erroneous item forms part must be considered.

(b) If a business has a bank loan of $50,000 and a $55,000 balance on bank deposit account, it might well be regarded as a material misstatement if these two amounts were displayed on the statement of financial position as 'cash at bank $5,000'. In other words, incorrect presentation may amount to material misstatement even if there is no monetary error.

Users are assumed to have a personal knowledge of business and economic activities and accounting and a willingness to study the information with reasonable diligence.

1.10 Offsetting

IAS 1 does not allow **assets and liabilities to be offset** against each other unless such a treatment is required or permitted by another IFRS.

Income and expenses can be offset only when:

(a) an IAS requires/permits it; *or*

(b) gains, losses and related expenses arising from the same/similar transactions are not material (aggregate).

1.11 Comparative information

IAS 1 requires comparative information to be disclosed for the previous period for all **numerical information**, unless another IAS permits/requires otherwise. Comparatives should also be given in narrative information where helpful.

Comparatives should be **reclassified** when the presentation or classification of items in the financial statements is amended (see IAS 8: Chapter 16).

1.12 Disclosure of accounting policies

There should be a specific section for accounting policies in the notes to the financial statements and the following should be disclosed there.

(a) **Measurement bases** used in preparing the financial statements

(b) Each **specific accounting policy** necessary for a proper understanding of the financial statements

To be clear and understandable it is essential that financial statements should disclose the accounting policies used in their preparation. This is because **policies may vary**, not only from entity to entity, but also from country to country. As an aid to users, all the major accounting policies used should be disclosed in the same place.

There is a wide range of policies available in many accounting areas. Examples where such differing policies exist are as follows, although the list is not exhaustive and it contains some items which you will only meet later on in this text.

- **General**
  - Consolidation policy
  - Conversion/translation of foreign currencies, including the treatment of exchange gains/losses
  - Overall valuation policy (eg historical cost, general purchasing power, replacement value)
  - Events subsequent to the reporting date
  - Leases, hire purchase or instalment transactions and related interest
  - Taxes
  - Construction contracts
  - Franchises

- **Assets**
  - Receivables
  - Inventories and related cost of goods sold
  - Depreciable assets and depreciation
  - Growing crops
  - Land held for development and related development costs
  - Investments: subsidiary and associate companies and other investments
  - Research and development
  - Patents and trademarks
  - Goodwill
- **Liabilities and provisions**
  - Warranties
  - Commitments and contingencies
  - Pension costs and retirement plans
  - Severance and redundancy payments
- **Profits and losses**
  - Methods of revenue recognition
  - Maintenance, repairs and improvements
  - Gains and losses on disposals of property
  - Reserve accounting, statutory or otherwise, including direct charges and credits to surplus accounts

Have a go at the following questions as revision of IAS 1.

Question — Accounting concept

Compare the following two income statements prepared for a sole trader who wishes to show them to the bank manager to justify continuation of an overdraft facility.

YEAR ENDED 31 DECEMBER 20X7

	$	$
Sales revenue		25,150
Less: production costs	10,000	
selling and administration	7,000	
		17,000
Gross profit		8,150
Less interest charges		1,000
Profit after interest		7,150

YEAR ENDED 31 DECEMBER 20X8

	$
Sales revenue less selling costs	22,165
Less production costs	10,990
Gross profit	11,175
Less administration and interest	3,175
Net profit	8,000

Which accounting concept is being ignored here? Justify your choice.

How do you think the changes in the format of these financial statements affect the quality of the accounting information presented?

Answer

The accounting assumption breached here is that of **consistency**. This concept holds that accounting information should be presented in a way that facilitates comparisons from period to period.

In the income statement for 20X7 sales revenue is shown separately from selling costs. Also interest and administration charges are treated separately.

The new format is poor in itself, as we cannot know whether any future change in 'sales revenue less selling costs' is due to an increase in sales revenue or a decline in selling costs. A similar criticism can be levelled at the lumping together of administration costs and interest charges. It is impossible to divide the two.

It is not possible to 'rewrite' 20X7's accounts in terms of 20X8, because we do not know the breakdown in 20X7 between selling and administration costs.

The business's bank manager will not, therefore, be able to assess the business's performance, and might wonder if the sole trader has 'something to hide'. Thus the value of this accounting information is severely affected.

Question

Accounting assumptions

You are in business in a small town, whose main source of economic prosperity is the tourist trade. On 25 March 20X8 the town celebrated the 1,000th anniversary of its existence. The town held a number of festivals to mark this occasion and to bring in more tourists.

Your business has had the good fortune to be involved in the event. You have made 1,000 commemorative mugs. These were all made by 31 December 20X7 to be ready at the beginning of the year. They cost 40 cents each to make and during the anniversary year they were for sale at 75 cents each. At the end of the anniversary year, there are 200 still unsold. You estimate that you are unlikely to sell any more at 75 cents, but you might be able to sell them at 30 cents each.

Required

Which fundamental accounting assumptions and other matters will you consider when assessing a value for the mugs in your statement of financial position:

(a) At the end of 20X7?
(b) At the end of 20X8?

On the basis of your considerations, note down the value of the mugs you would include in the statement of financial position at 31 December 20X7 and 31 December 20X8.

Answer

The accounting assumption mainly involved is **accruals. Prudence** is also important when determining the accounting policy.

The accruals assumption states that income and expenditure should be matched in the same period if reasonably possible, whereas prudence dictates that revenue should not be anticipated. However, you are reasonably certain of selling the mugs, so you would value them in the statement of financial position at the beginning of the year at *cost*, as an *asset* (rather than treating them as an expense in the statement of comprehensive income for that earlier year).

At 31 December 20X8 you have 200 spare, whose selling price is less than the cost of making them. Prudence dictates therefore that they are valued in the statement of financial position at the lower of these two amounts (ie sales value if it is lower than cost).

You could argue that valuing them at a lower amount means a conflict with the accruals assumption, because the loss is accounted for before the sale. This is true. Normally, when accruals and prudence conflict, prudence should prevail.

As a consequence, at 31 December 20X7, the mugs would be valued at 40 cents each. At 31 December 20X8, the remaining mugs would be valued at 30 cents each.

Question

Materiality

You work for a multinational company and you are preparing two accounting documents.

(a) A statement for a customer, listing invoices and receipts, and detailing the amounts owed

(b) A report sent to the senior management of a division, who want a brief comparative summary of how well the firm is doing in Thailand and in Malaysia

How would considerations of **materiality** influence your preparation of each document?

Answer

Materiality as a 'fundamental concept' does have strict limitations. It refers primarily to financial *reporting*, but has no bearing at all on detailed procedural matters such as bank reconciliations or statements of account sent to customers.

Consequently, the statement sent to the customer, described in option (a), must be accurate to the last cent, however large it is. After all, if you receive a bill from a company for $147.50, you do not 'round it up' to $150 when you pay. Nor will the company billing you be prepared to 'round it down' to $145. A customer pays an agreed price for an agreed product or service. Paying more is effectively giving money away, and if you are going to do that, there might be worthier beneficiaries of your generosity. Paying less exposes your creditor to an unfair loss.

On the other hand, if you are preparing a performance report comparing how well the company is doing in Thailand and Malaysia, entirely different considerations apply.

There is little point in being accurate to the last cent (and inconsistencies might occur from the choice of currency rate used). This is because senior management are interested in the broad picture, and they are looking to identify comparisons between the overall performance of each division.

Assume that Thailand profits were $1,233,750.57 and profits in Malaysia were $1,373,370.75.

Malaysia	*Thailand*
$	$
1,373,370.75	1,233,750.57
or	or
$'000	$'000
1,373	1,234

The rounded figures are much easier to understand, and so the relative performance is easier to compare. Considerations of materiality would allow you to ignore the rounding differences, because they are so small and the information is used for comparative purposes only.

1.13 Section summary

Accounting policies are extremely important.

- Accounting policies must be **appropriate** and **applied consistently**
- Financial statements complying with IASs will normally **present fairly** the results of the entity
- Important **concepts** are: going concern, accruals, consistency, materiality, prudence and substance over form
- All accounting policies should be **fully disclosed**

2 Structure and content of financial statements

FAST FORWARD

IAS 1 covers the **form and content of** financial statements. The main components are:

- Statement of financial position
- Statement of comprehensive income
- Statement of changes in equity
- Statement of cash flows
- Notes to the financial statements

Each component must be **identified clearly**.

IAS 1 *Presentation of financial statements* gives substantial guidance on the form and content of published financial statements. It was revised in September 2007. The standard looks at the statement of financial position and statement of comprehensive income (the statement of cash flows is covered by IAS 7). First of all, some general points are made about financial statements.

2.1 Profit or loss for the period

The statement of comprehensive income is the most significant indicator of a company's financial performance. So it is important to ensure that it is not misleading.

IAS 1 stipulates that all items of income and expense recognised in a period shall be included in profit or loss unless a **Standard** or an **Interpretation** requires otherwise.

Circumstances where items may be excluded from profit or loss for the current year include the correction of errors and the effect of changes in accounting policies. These are covered in IAS 8.

2.2 How items are disclosed

IAS 1 specifies disclosures of certain items in certain ways.

- Some items must appear on the face of the statement of financial position or statement of comprehensive income
- Other items can appear in a **note to the financial statements** instead
- **Recommended formats** are given which entities may or may not follow, depending on their circumstances

Obviously, disclosures specified by **other standards** must also be made, and we will mention the necessary disclosures when we cover each statement in turn. Disclosures in both IAS 1 and other standards must be made either on the face of the statement or in the notes unless otherwise stated, ie disclosures cannot be made in an accompanying commentary or report.

2.3 Identification of financial statements

As a result of the above point, it is most important that entities **distinguish the financial statements** very clearly from any other information published with them. This is because all IASs/IFRSs apply *only* to the financial statements (ie the main statements and related notes), so readers of the annual report must be able to differentiate between the parts of the report which are prepared under IFRSs, and other parts which are not.

The entity should **identify each** financial statement and the notes very clearly. IAS 1 also requires disclosure of the following information in a prominent position. If necessary it should be repeated wherever it is felt to be of use to the reader in his understanding of the information presented.

- **Name** of the reporting entity (or other means of identification)
- Whether the accounts cover the **single entity** only or a group of entities
- The **date of the end of the reporting period** or the period covered by the financial statements (as appropriate)
- The **presentation currency**

- The **level of rounding** used in presenting amounts in the financial statements

Judgement must be used to determine the best method of presenting this information. In particular, the standard suggests that the approach to this will be very different when the financial statements are communicated electronically.

The **level of rounding** is important, as presenting figures in thousands or millions of units makes the figures more understandable. The level of rounding must be disclosed, however, and it should not obscure necessary details or make the information less relevant.

2.4 Reporting period

It is normal for entities to present financial statements **annually** and IAS 1 states that they should be prepared at least as often as this. If (unusually) the end of an entity's reporting period is changed, for whatever reason, the period for which the statements are presented will be less or more than one year. In such cases the entity should also disclose:

(a) the **reason(s) why** a period other than one year is used; and
(b) the fact that the comparative figures given **are not in fact comparable**.

For practical purposes, some entities prefer to use a period which **approximates to a year**, eg 52 weeks, and the IAS allows this approach as it will produce statements not materially different from those produced on an annual basis.

2.5 Timeliness

If the publication of financial statements is delayed too long after the reporting period, their usefulness will be severely diminished. The standard states that entities should be able to produce their financial statements **within six months of the end of the reporting period.** An entity with consistently complex operations cannot use this as a reason for its failure to report on a timely basis. Local legislation and market regulation imposes specific deadlines on certain entities.

IAS 1 looks at the statement of financial position and statement of comprehensive income. We will not give all the detailed disclosures as some are outside the scope of your syllabus. Instead we will look at a **'proforma' set of accounts** based on the Standard.

3 Statement of financial position

FAST FORWARD

IAS 1 suggests **formats** for the statement of financial position. Certain items are specified for **disclosure on the face of the financial statements**.

IAS 1 discusses the distinction between current and non-current items in some detail, as we shall see in the next section. First of all we can look at the **suggested format** of the statement of financial position (given in an appendix to the standard) and then look at further disclosures required.

3.1 Statement of financial position example

The example given by IAS 1 revised is as follows.

XYZ GROUP – STATEMENT OF FINANCIAL POSITION AT 31 DECEMBER

	20X9	*20X8*
Assets	$'000	$'000
Non-current assets		
Property, plant and equipment	350,700	360,020
Goodwill	80,800	91,200
Other intangible assets	227,470	227,470
Investments in associates	100,150	110,770
Available-for-sale financial assets	142,500	156,000
	901,620	945,460
Current assets		
Inventories	135,230	132,500
Trade receivables	91,600	110,800
Other current assets	25,650	12,540
Cash and cash equivalents	312,400	322,900
	564,880	578,740
Total assets	1,466,500	1,524,200
Equity and liabilities		
Equity attributable to owners of the parent		
Share capital	650,000	600,000
Retained earnings	243,500	161,700
Other components of equity	10,200	21,200
	903,700	782,900
Non-controlling interest	70,050	48,600
Total equity	973,750	831,500
Non-current liabilities		
Long-term borrowings	120,000	160,000
Deferred tax	28,800	26,040
Long-term provisions	28,850	52,240
Total non-current liabilities	117,650	238,280
Current liabilities		
Trade and other payables	115,100	187,620
Short-term borrowings	150,000	200,000
Current portion of long-term borrowings	10,000	20,000
Current tax payable	35,000	42,000
Short-term provisions	5,000	4,800
Total current liabilities	315,100	454,420
Total liabilities	492,750	692,700
Total equity and liabilities	1,466,500	1,524,200

IAS 1 (revised) specifies various items which must appear on the **face of the statement of financial position** as a minimum disclosure.

(a) Property, plant and equipment (Chapter 4)
(b) Investment property (Chapter 4)
(c) Intangible assets (Chapter 6)
(d) Financial assets (excluding amounts shown under (e), (h) and (i)) (Chapter 10)
(e) Investments accounted for using the equity method (Chapter 23)
(f) Biological assets (outside the scope of the syllabus)
(g) Inventories (Chapter 7)
(h) Trade and other receivables
(i) Cash and cash equivalents (Chapter 19)
(j) Assets classified as held for sale under IFRS 5

(k) Trade and other payables
(l) Provisions (Chapter 8)
(m) Financial liabilities (other than (j) and (k))
(n) Current tax liabilities and assets as in IAS 12 (Chapter 11)
(o) Deferred tax liabilities and assets (Chapter 11)
(p) Liabilities included in disposal groups under IFRS 5
(q) Non-controlling interests (Chapters 23 and 24)
(r) Issued capital and reserves

We will look at these items in the chapters marked.

Any **other line items**, headings or sub-totals should be shown on the face of the statement of financial position when it is necessary for an understanding of the entity's financial position.

The example shown above is for illustration only (although we will follow the format in this Study Text). The IAS, however, does not prescribe the order or format in which the items listed should be presented. It simply states that they **must be presented separately** because they are so different in nature or function from each other.

Whether additional items are presented separately depends on judgements based on the assessment of the following factors.

(a) **Nature and liquidity of assets and their materiality**. Thus goodwill and assets arising from development expenditure will be presented separately, as will monetary/non-monetary assets and current/non-current assets.
(b) **Function within the entity.** Operating and financial assets, inventories, receivables and cash and cash equivalents are therefore shown separately.
(c) **Amounts, nature and timing of liabilities**. Interest-bearing and non-interest-bearing liabilities and provisions will be shown separately, classified as current or non-current as appropriate.

The standard also requires separate presentation where **different measurement bases** are used for assets and liabilities which differ in nature or function. According to IAS 16, for example, it is permitted to carry certain items of property, plant and equipment at cost or at a revalued amount.

3.2 Information presented either on the face of the statement of financial position or by note

Further **sub-classification** of the line items listed above should be disclosed either on the face of the statement of financial position or in the notes. The classification will depend upon the nature of the entity's operations. As well as each item being sub-classified by its nature, any amounts payable to or receivable from any **group company or other related party** should also be disclosed separately.

The sub-classification details will in part depend on the requirements of IFRSs. The size, nature and function of the amounts involved will also be important and the factors listed above should be considered. **Disclosures** will vary from item to item and IAS 1 gives the following examples.

(a) **Property, plant and equipment** are classified by class as described in IAS 16, *Property, plant and equipment*
(b) **Receivables** are analysed between amounts receivable from trade customers, other members of the group, receivables from related parties, prepayments and other amounts
(c) **Inventories** are sub-classified, in accordance with IAS 2 *Inventories,* into classifications such as merchandise, production supplies, materials, work in progress and finished goods
(d) **Provisions** are analysed showing separately provisions for employee benefit costs and any other items classified in a manner appropriate to the entity's operations
(e) **Equity capital and reserves** are analysed showing separately the various classes of paid in capital, share premium and reserves

The standard then lists some **specific disclosures** which must be made, either on the face of the statement of financial position or in the related notes.

(a) **Share capital disclosures (**for each class of share capital)

(i) Number of shares authorised

(ii) Number of shares issued and fully paid, and issued but not fully paid

(iii) Par value per share, or that the shares have no par value

(iv) Reconciliation of the number of shares outstanding at the beginning and at the end of the year

(v) Rights, preferences and restrictions attaching to that class including restrictions on the distribution of dividends and the repayment of capital

(vi) Shares in the entity held by the entity itself or by related group companies

(vii) Shares reserved for issuance under options and sales contracts, including the terms and amounts

(b) Description of the nature and purpose of **each reserve** within owners' equity

Some types of entity have no share capital, eg partnerships. Such entities should disclose information which is **equivalent** to that listed above. This means disclosing the movement during the period in each category of equity interest and any rights, preferences or restrictions attached to each category of equity interest.

4 The current/non-current distinction

FAST FORWARD

You should appreciate the distinction between current and non-current assets and liabilities and the difference in treatment for operating cycle and other non-operating items which are due after twelve months.

4.1 The current/non-current distinction

An entity must present **current** and **non-current** assets as separate classifications on the face of the statement of financial position. A presentation based on liquidity should only be used where it provides more relevant and reliable information, in which case all assets and liabilities must be presented broadly **in order of liquidity**.

In either case, the entity should disclose any portion of an asset or liability which is expected to be recovered or settled **after more than twelve months**. For example, for an amount receivable which is due in instalments over 18 months, the portion due after more than twelve months must be disclosed.

The IAS emphasises how helpful information on the **operating cycle** is to users of financial statements. Where there is a clearly defined operating cycle within which the entity supplies goods or services, then information disclosing those net assets that are continuously circulating as **working capital** is useful.

This distinguishes them from those net assets used in the long-term operations of the entity. Assets that are expected to be realised and liabilities that are due for settlement within the operating cycle are therefore highlighted.

The liquidity and solvency of an entity is also indicated by information about the **maturity dates** of assets and liabilities. As we will see later, IFRS 7 *Financial instruments: disclosures* requires disclosure of maturity dates of both financial assets and financial liabilities. (Financial assets include trade and other receivables; financial liabilities include trade and other payables.) In the case of non-monetary assets, eg inventories, such information is also useful.

4.2 Current assets

Key term

> An asset should be classified as a **current asset** when it:
>
> - Is expected to be realised in, or is held for sale or consumption in, the normal course of the entity's operating cycle; or
> - Is held primarily for trading purposes or for the short-term and expected to be realised within twelve months of the end of the reporting period; or
> - Is cash or a cash equivalent asset which is not restricted in its use.
>
> All other assets should be classified as non-current assets. *(IAS 1)*

Non-current assets includes tangible, intangible, operating and financial assets of a long-term nature. Other terms with the same meaning can be used (eg 'fixed', 'long-term').

The term 'operating cycle' has been used several times above and the standard defines it as follows.

Key term

> The **operating cycle** of an entity is the time between the acquisition of assets for processing and their realisation in cash or cash equivalents. *(IAS 1)*

Current assets therefore include inventories and trade receivables that are sold, consumed and realised as part of the normal operating cycle. **This is the case even where they are not expected to be realised within twelve months.**

Current assets will also include **marketable securities** if they are expected to be realised within twelve months after the reporting period. If expected to be realised later, they should be included in non-current assets.

4.3 Current liabilities

Key term

> A liability should be classified as a **current liability** when it:
>
> - Is expected to be settled in the normal course of the entity's operating cycle; or
> - Is held primarily for the purpose of trading; or
> - Is due to be settled within twelve months after the reporting period; or
> - The entity does not have an unconditional right to defer settlement of the liability for at least twelve months after the reporting period.
>
> All other liabilities should be classified as non-current liabilities. *(IAS 1)*

The categorisation of current liabilities is very similar to that of current assets. Thus, some current liabilities are part of the **working capital** used in the normal operating cycle of the business (ie trade payables and accruals for employee and other operating costs). Such items will be classed as current liabilities **even where they are due to be settled more than twelve months after the end of the reporting period.**

There are also current liabilities which are not settled as part of the normal operating cycle, but which are due to be settled within twelve months of the end of the reporting period. These include bank overdrafts, income taxes, other non-trade payables and the current portion of interest-bearing liabilities. Any interest-bearing liabilities that are used to finance working capital on a long-term basis, and that are not due for settlement within twelve months, should be classed as **non-current liabilities**.

A **non-current financial liability** due to be **settled within twelve months** of the end of the reporting period should be classified as a **current liability**, even if an agreement to refinance, or to reschedule payments, on a long-term basis is completed after the end of the reporting period and before the financial statements are authorised for issue.

End of the reporting period	Agreement to refinance on long-term basis	Date financial statements authorised for issue	Settlement date <12 months after end of the reporting period therefore current liability

A **non-current financial liability** that is payable on **demand** because the entity **breached** a **condition** of its loan agreement should be classified as **current** at the end of the reporting period even if the **lender** has agreed **after the end of the reporting period**, and **before** the financial statements are **authorised for issue**, **not** to **demand payment** as a consequence of the breach.

Condition of loan agreement breached. Non-current liability becomes payable on demand	End of the reporting period	Lender agrees not to enforce payment resulting from breach	Date financial statements are authorised for issue. Loan shown as **current** liability

However, if the **lender** has **agreed** by the **end of the reporting period** to provide a **period of grace** ending **at least twelve months after the end of the reporting period** within which the entity can rectify the breach and during that time the lender cannot demand immediate repayment, the liability is classified as **non-current.**

5 Statement of comprehensive income

FAST FORWARD

IAS 1 (revised) requires all items of income and expense in a period to be shown in a **statement of comprehensive income**.

The revision of IAS 1 in 2007 introduced a new statement, the **statement of comprehensive income**. This shows both income statement items and items which would previously have gone to the statement of recognised income and expense.

5.1 Statement of comprehensive income – format

IAS 1 (revised) allows income and expense items to be presented either:

(a) in a single statement of comprehensive income; or
(b) in two statements: a separate income statement and statement of other comprehensive income.

The format for a single statement of comprehensive income is shown as follows in the standard. The section down to 'profit for the year' can be shown as a separate 'income statement' with an additional 'statement of other comprehensive income'. Note that not all of the items which would appear under 'other comprehensive income' are included in your syllabus.

Exam focus point

In the examinations, if a 'Statement of Comprehensive Income' is referred to, this will always relate to the single statement format. If 'Income Statements' are referred to, this relates to the statement from 'Revenue' to 'Profit for the year'. Exams may refer to 'Other Comprehensive Income' which relates to the 'other comprehensive income' section of the statement. In practice, the item of 'other comprehensive income' you are most likely to meet is a revaluation gain. Where we have used 'income statement' in this text, this can be taken to refer to the income statement section of the statement of comprehensive income or separate income statement.

XYZ GROUP – STATEMENT OF COMPREHENSIVE INCOME FOR THE YEAR ENDED 31 DECEMBER

	20X9	*20X8*
	$'000	$'000
Revenue	390,000	355,000
Cost of sales	(245,000)	(230,000)
Gross profit	145,000	125,000
Other income	20,667	11,300
Distribution costs	(9,000)	(8,700)
Administrative expenses	(20,000)	(21,000)
Other expenses	(2,100)	(1,200)
Finance costs	(8,000)	(7,500)
Share of profit of associates	35,100	30,100
Profit before tax	161,667	128,000
Income tax expense	(40,417)	(32,000)
Profit for the year from continuing operations	121,250	96,000
Loss for the year from discontinued operations	–	(30,500)
Profit for the year	121,250	65,500
Other comprehensive income:		
Exchange differences on translating foreign operations	5,334	10,667
Available-for-sale financial assets	(24,000)	26,667
Cash flow hedges	(667)	(4,000)
Gains on property revaluation	993	3,367
Actuarial gains (losses) on defined benefit pension plans	(667)	1,333
Share of other comprehensive income of associates	400	(700)
Income tax relating to components of other comprehensive income	4,667	(9,334)
Other comprehensive income for the year, net of tax	(14,000)	28,000
Total comprehensive income for the year	107,250	93,500
Profit attributable to:		
Owners of the parent	97,000	52,400
Non-controlling interest	24,250	13,100
	121,250	65,500
Total comprehensive income attributable to		
Owners of the parent	85,800	74,800
Non-controlling interest	21,450	18,700
	107,250	93,500
Earnings per share	0.46	0.30

Companies are given the option of presenting this information in two statements as follows:

XYZ GROUP – INCOME STATEMENT FOR THE YEAR ENDED 31 DECEMBER

	20X9	*20X8*
	$'000	$'000
Revenue	390,000	355,000
Cost of sales	(245,000)	(230,000)
Gross profit	145,000	125,000
Other income	20,667	11,300
Distribution costs	(9,000)	(8,700)
Administrative expenses	(20,000)	(21,000)
Other expenses	(2,100)	(1,200)
Finance costs	(8,000)	(7,500)
Share of profit of associates	35,100	30,100
Profit before tax	161,667	128,000
Income tax expense	(40,417)	(32,000)
Profit for the year from continuing operations	121,250	96,000
Loss for the year from discontinued operations	–	(30,500)
Profit for the year	121,250	65,500
Profit attributable to:		
Owners of the parent	97,000	52,400
Non-controlling interest	24,250	13,100
	121,250	65,500

XYZ GROUP – STATEMENT OF COMPREHENSIVE INCOME FOR THE YEAR ENDED 31 DECEMBER

	20X9	20X8
	$'000	$'000
Profit for the year	121,250	65,500
Other comprehensive income:		
Exchange differences on translating foreign operations	5,334	10,667
Available-for-sale financial assets	(24,000)	26,667
Cash flow hedges	(667)	(4,000)
Gains on property revaluation	933	3,367
Actuarial gains (losses) on defined benefit pension plans	(667)	1,333
Share of other comprehensive income of associates	400	(700)
Income tax relating to components of other comprehensive income	4,667	(9,334)
Other comprehensive income for the year, net of tax	(14,000)	28,000
Total comprehensive income for the year	107,250	93,500
Total comprehensive income attributable to		
Owners of the parent	85,800	74,800
Non-controlling interest	21,450	18,700
	107,250	93,500

6 Income statement

FAST FORWARD

IAS 1 offers two possible formats for the income statement section or separate income statement – by function or by nature. Classification by function is more common.

6.1 Examples of separate income statements

XYZ GROUP
INCOME STATEMENT FOR THE YEAR ENDED 31 DECEMBER 20X8

Illustrating the classification of expenses by function

	20X8	*20X7*
	$'000	$'000
Revenue	X	X
Cost of sales	(X)	(X)
Gross profit	X	X
Other income	X	X
Distribution costs	(X)	(X)
Administrative expenses	(X)	(X)
Other expenses	(X)	(X)
Finance costs	(X)	(X)
Share of profit of associates	X	X
Profit before tax	X	X
Income tax expense	(X)	(X)
Profit for the year	X	X
Attributable to:		
Owners of the parent	X	X
Non-controlling interest	X	X
	X	X

Illustrating the classification of expenses by nature

	20X8	*20X7*
	$'000	$'000
Revenue	X	X
Other operating income	X	X
Changes in inventories of finished goods and work in progress	(X)	X
Work performed by the entity and capitalised	X	X
Raw material and consumables used	(X)	(X)
Employee benefits expense	(X)	(X)
Depreciation and amortisation expense	(X)	(X)
Impairment of property, plant and equipment	(X)	(X)
Other expenses	(X)	(X)
Finance costs	(X)	(X)
Share of profit of associates	X	X
Profit before tax	X	X
Income tax expense	(X)	(X)
Profit for the year	X	X
Profit attributable to:		
Owners of the parent	X	X
Non-controlling interest	X	X
	X	X

Note: The usual method of presentation is expenses by function and this is the format likely to appear in your exam.

6.2 Information presented in the statement of comprehensive income or separate income statement

The standard lists the following as the **minimum** to be disclosed on the face of the income statement.

(a) Revenue
(b) Finance costs
(c) Share of profits and losses of associates and joint ventures accounted for using the equity method
(d) Tax expense
(e) A single amount comprising the post-tax profit or loss of discontinued operations, and the post-tax gain or loss recognised on measurement to fair value less costs to sell or on disposal of the assets of the discontinued operation.
(f) Profit or loss

The following items must be disclosed in the income statement as allocations of profit or loss for the period.

(a) Profit or loss attributable to non-controlling interest
(b) Profit or loss attributable to owners of the parent

The allocated amounts must not be presented as items of income or expense. (These relate to group accounts, covered later in this text.)

Income and expense items can only be **offset** when, and only when:

(a) It is permitted or required by an IFRS, or
(b) Gains, losses and related expenses arising from the same or similar transactions and events are immaterial, in which case they can be aggregated.

6.3 Information presented either in the statement or in the notes

An analysis of expenses must be shown either in the income statement section (as above, which is encouraged by the standard) or by note, using a classification based on *either* the nature of the expenses or their function. This **sub-classification of expenses** indicates a range of components of financial performance; these may differ in terms of stability, potential for gain or loss and predictability.

6.3.1 Nature of expense method

Expenses are not reallocated amongst various functions within the entity, but are aggregated in the income statement **according to their nature** (eg purchase of materials, depreciation, wages and salaries, transport costs). This is by far the easiest method, especially for smaller entities.

6.3.2 Function of expense/cost of sales method

You are likely to be more familiar with this method. Expenses are classified according to their function as part of cost of sales, distribution or administrative activities. This method often gives **more relevant information** for users, but the allocation of expenses by function requires the use of judgement and can be arbitrary. Consequently, perhaps, when this method is used, entities should disclose **additional information** on the nature of expenses, including staff costs, and depreciation and amortisation expense.

Which of the above methods is chosen by an entity will depend on **historical and industry factors**, and also the **nature of the organisation**. Under each method, there should be given an indication of costs which are likely to vary (directly or indirectly) with the level of sales or production. The choice of method should fairly reflect the main elements of the entity's performance. **This is the method you should expect to see in your exam.**

6.4 Dividends

IAS 1 also requires disclosure of the amount of **dividends per share** for the period covered by the financial statements. This is shown on the face of the income statement.

Further points

(a) All requirements previously set out in other Standards for the presentation of particular line items in the statement of financial position and income statement are now dealt with in IAS 1. These line items are: biological assets; liabilities and assets for current tax and deferred tax; and pre-tax gain or loss recognised on the disposal of assets or settlement of liabilities attributable to discontinued operations.

(b) The section that set out the **presentation requirements** for the **net profit or loss** for the period in **IAS 8** has now been **transferred** to **IAS 1** instead.

(c) The following disclosures are no longer required:

   (i) The results of operating activities, as a line item in the income statement. **'Operating activities'** are **not defined in IAS 1**

   (ii) **Extraordinary items**, as a line item in the income statement (note that the disclosure of 'extraordinary items' is now **prohibited**)

   (iii) The **number** of an **entity's employees**

(d) An entity must disclose, in the summary of significant accounting policies and/or other notes, the **judgements** made by management in **applying** the **accounting policies** that have the **most significant effect** on the amounts of items recognised in the financial statements.

(e) An entity must disclose in the notes information regarding **key assumptions** about the **future**, and other sources of **measurement uncertainty**, that have a significant **risk of** causing a **material adjustment** to the carrying amounts of assets and liabilities within the **next financial year**.

7 Revision of basic accounts

FAST FORWARD

The Study Guide requires you to be able to prepare a basic set of company accounts from a trial balance.

In the next part of this text we move on to the mechanics of preparing financial statements. It would be useful at this point to refresh your memory of the basic accounting you have already studied and these questions will help you. Make sure that you understand everything before you go on.

Question — Basics

A friend has bought some shares in a company quoted on a local stock exchange and has received the latest accounts. There is one page he is having difficulty in understanding.

Briefly, but clearly, answer his questions.

(a) What is a statement of financial position?
(b) What is an asset?
(c) What is a liability?
(d) What is share capital?
(e) What are reserves?
(f) Why does the statement of financial position balance?
(g) To what extent does the statement of financial position value my investment?

Answer

(a) A **statement of financial position** is a statement of the assets, liabilities and capital of a business as at a stated date. It is laid out to show either total assets as equivalent to total liabilities and capital or net assets as equivalent to capital. Other formats are also possible but the top half (or left hand) total will always equal the bottom half (or right hand) total.

(b) An **asset** is a resource controlled by a business and is expected to be of some future benefit. Its value is determined as the historical cost of producing or obtaining it (unless an attempt is being made to reflect rising prices in the accounts, in which case a replacement cost might be used). Examples of assets are:

(i) Plant, machinery, land and other **non-current assets**

(ii) **Current** assets such as inventories, cash and debts owed to the business with reasonable assurance of recovery: these are assets which are not intended to be held on a continuing basis in the business

(c) A **liability** is an amount owed by a business, other than the amount owed to its proprietors (capital). Examples of liabilities are:

(i) Amounts owed to the government (sales or other taxes)
(ii) Amounts owed to suppliers
(iii) Bank overdraft
(iv) Long-term loans from banks or investors

It is usual to differentiate between 'current' and 'long-term' liabilities. The former fall due within a year of the end of the reporting period.

(d) **Share capital** is the permanent investment in a business by its owners. In the case of a limited company, this takes the form of *shares* for which investors subscribe on formation of the company. Each share has a **nominal** or **par** (ie face) **value** (say $1). In the statement of financial position, total issued share capital is shown at its par value.

(e) If a company issues shares for more than their par value (at a **premium**) then (usually) by law this premium must be recorded separately from the par value in a 'share premium account'. This is an example of a reserve. It belongs to the shareholders but cannot be distributed to them, because it is a **capital reserve**. Other capital reserves include the revaluation surplus, which shows the surpluses arising on revaluation of assets which are still owned by the company.

Share capital and capital reserves are not distributable except on the winding up of the company, as a guarantee to the company's creditors that the company has enough assets to meet its debts. This is necessary because shareholders in limited liability companies have 'limited liability'; once they have paid the company for their shares they have no further liability to it if it becomes insolvent. The proprietors of other businesses are, by contrast, personally liable for business debts.

Retained earnings constitute accumulated profits (less losses) made by the company and can be distributed to shareholders as **dividends**. They too belong to the shareholders, and so are a claim on the resources of the company.

(f) Statements of financial position do not always balance on the first attempt, as all accountants know! However, once errors are corrected, all statement of financial position balance. This is because in **double entry bookkeeping** every transaction recorded has a dual effect. Assets are always equal to liabilities plus capital and so capital is always equal to assets less liabilities. This makes sense as the owners of the business are entitled to the net assets of the business as representing their capital plus accumulated surpluses (or less accumulated deficit).

(g) The statement of financial position is not intended as a statement of a business's worth at a given point in time. This is because, except where some attempt is made to adjust for the effects of rising prices, assets and liabilities are recorded at **historical cost** and on a prudent basis. For example, if there is any doubt about the recoverability of a debt, then the value in the accounts must be reduced to the likely recoverable amount. In addition, where non-current assets have a finite useful life, their cost is gradually written off to reflect the use being made of them.

Sometimes non-current assets are **revalued** to their market value but this revaluation then goes out of date as few assets are revalued every year.

The figure in the statement of financial position for capital and reserves therefore bears **no relationship** to the market value of shares. Market values are the product of a large number of factors, including general economic conditions, alternative investment returns (eg interest rates), likely future profits and dividends and, not least, market sentiment.

Question — Company financial statements

The accountant of Fiddles Co, a limited liability company, has begun preparing final accounts but the work is not yet complete. At this stage the items included in the list of account balances are as follows.

	$'000
Land	100
Buildings	120
Plant and machinery	170
Depreciation provision	120
Ordinary shares of $1	100
Retained earnings brought forward	200
Trade accounts receivable	200
Trade accounts payable	110
Inventory	190
Operating profit	80
Loan stock (16%)	180
Allowance for receivables	3
Bank balance (asset)	12
Suspense	1

Notes (i) to (vi) below are to be taken into account.

(i) The accounts receivable control account figure, which is used in the list of account balances, does not agree with the total of the sales ledger. A contra of $5,000 has been entered correctly in the individual ledger accounts but has been entered on the wrong side of both control accounts.

A batch total of sales of $12,345 had been entered in the double entry system as $13,345, although the individual ledger accounts entries for these sales were correct. The balance of $4,000 on the sales returns account has inadvertently been omitted from the trial balance though correctly entered in the ledger records.

(ii) A standing order of receipt from a regular customer for $2,000, and bank charges of $1,000, have been completely omitted from the records.

(iii) A receivable for $1,000 is to be written off. The allowance for receivables balance is to be adjusted to 1% of receivables.

(iv) The opening inventory figure had been overstated by $1,000 and the closing inventory figure had been understated by $2,000.

(v) Any remaining balance on the suspense account should be treated as purchases if a debit balance and as sales if a credit balance.

(vi) The loan stock was issued three months before the year end. No entries have been made as regards interest.

Required

(a) Prepare journal entries to cover items in notes (i) to (v) above. You are not to open any new accounts and may use only those accounts included in the list of account balances as given.

(b) Prepare final accounts for internal use within the limits of the available information. For presentation purposes all the items arising from notes (i) to (vii) above should be regarded as material.

Answer

(a) JOURNAL ENTRIES FOR ADJUSTMENTS

		Debit	Credit
		$	$
(i)	Trade accounts payable	10,000	
	Trade accounts receivable		10,000
	Operating profit	1,000	
	Trade accounts receivable		1,000
	Operating profit	4,000	
	Suspense		4,000
(ii)	Bank	2,000	
	Trade accounts receivable		2,000
	Operating profit	1,000	
	Bank		1,000
(iii)	Operating profit	1,000	
	Trade accounts receivable		1,000
	Allowance for receivables (W1)	1,140	
	Operating profit		1,140
(iv)	Inventories	2,000	
	Operating profit		2,000
	Retained earnings brought forward	1,000	
	Operating profit		1,000
(v)	Suspense	3,000	
	Operating profit		3,000

(b) FIDDLES CO
STATEMENT OF FINANCIAL POSITION

	$	$	$
Assets			
Non-current assets			
Land and buildings		220,000	
Plant and machinery		170,000	
Depreciation		(120,000)	
			270,000
Current assets			
Inventories (190 + 2)		192,000	
Accounts receivable (W1)	186,000		
Less allowance	(1,860)		
		184,140	
Bank (12 + 2 – 1)		13,000	
			389,140
Total assets			659,140
Equity and liabilities			
Equity			
Share capital		100,000	
Retained earnings		271,940	
			371,940
Non-current liabilities			
Loan stock			180,000
Current liabilities			
Accounts payable (110 – 10)		100,000	
Loan stock interest payable		7,200	
			107,200
Total equity and liabilities			659,140

FIDDLES CO

INCOME STATEMENT (note that this is not as per IAS 1, it is purely for internal purposes)

	$
Operating profit (W2)	80,140
Debenture interest ($180,000 × 16% × 3/12)	(7,200)
	72,940
Retained earnings brought forward ($200,000 – 1,000)	199,000
Retained earnings carried forward	271,940

Workings

1 *Accounts receivable*

	$
Per opening trial balance	200,000
Contra	(10,000)
Miscasting	(1,000)
Standing order	(2,000)
Written off	(1,000)
	186,000
Allowance b/f	3,000
Allowance required	1,860
Journal	1,140

2 *Operating profit*

	$
Per question	80,000
Wrong batch total	(1,000)
Returns	(4,000)
Bank charges	(1,000)
Irrecoverable debt	(1,000)
Allowance for receivables	1,140
Inventory (2,000 + 1,000)	3,000
Suspense (sales)	3,000
	80,140

Note: This question dealt with accounts for **internal** purposes. In accounts produced for publication the income statement would comply with the IAS 1 format. In the following chapter we will be dealing with all the issues involved in producing financial statements for publication.

8 Changes in equity 6/06, 12/07

FAST FORWARD

IAS 1 requires a statement of changes in equity. This shows the movement in the equity section of the statement of financial position. A full set of financial statements includes a statement of changes in equity.

Exam focus point

Your examiner has commented that students are often unable to prepare the statement of changes in equity. He is therefore quite likely to want to test it, so you should make sure that you are comfortable with the material here.

8.1 Format

This is the format of the statement of changes in equity.

XYZ GROUP – STATEMENT OF CHANGES IN EQUITY FOR THE YEAR ENDED 31 DECEMBER 20X9

	Share capital	*Retained earnings*	*Available for-sale financial assets*	*Revaluation surplus*	*Total*	*Non-controlling interest*	*Total equity*
	$'000	$'000	$'000	$'000	$'000	$'000	$'000
Balance at 1 January 20X8	600,000	118,100	1,600	–	719,700	29,800	749,500
Changes in accounting policy	–	400	–	–	400	100	500
Restated balance	600,000	118,500	1,600	–	720,100	29,900	750,000
Changes in equity							
Dividends	–	(10,000)	–	–	(10,000)	–	(10,000)
Total comprehensive income for the year	–	53,200	16,000	1,600	70,800	18,700	89,500
Balance at 31 December 20X8	600,000	161,700	17,600	1,600	780,900	48,600	829,500
Changes in equity for 20X9							
Issue of share capital	50,000	–	–	–	50,000	–	50,000
Dividends	–	(15,000)	–	–	(15,000)	–	(15,000)
Total comprehensive income for the year	–	96,600	(14,400)	800	83,000	21,450	104,450
Transfer to retained earnings	–	200	–	(200)	–	–	–
Balance at 31 December 20X9	650,000	243,500	3,200	2,200	898,900	70,050	968,950

Note that where there has been a change of accounting policy necessitating a retrospective restatement, the adjustment is disclosed for each period. So, rather than just showing an adjustment to the balance b/f on 1.1.X9, the balances for 20X8 are restated. Gains and losses on cash flow hedges or on the translation of foreign operations would be shown in additional columns.

Question

Statement of changes in equity

Delta Group is preparing its financial statements for the year ended 31 March 20X1. Using the following information, prepare the group statement of changes in equity along with relevant extracts from the statement of financial position.

STATEMENT OF FINANCIAL POSITION (EXTRACT) OF DELTA GROUP AS AT 31 MARCH 20X0

Equity and liabilities	
Equity	
Share capital	90,000
Retained earnings	40,000
Total equity	130,000
Non-controlling interest	25,000
	155,000

(a) On 1 April 20X0 a bond was issued carrying a zero interest rate but redeemable at an amount of $16,105,100 on 31 March 20X5. The total proceeds for the issue were $12m. As an alternative to redemption, the bond-holders have the option to convert the bond into equity shares. Had the option not been available, the bond-holders would have only been prepared to invest $10 million given their requirement for a 10% return on their investment.

(b) The total divided paid in the year to ordinary shareholders was $20m.

(c) The group's total comprehensive income for the year was $10m, of which $0.5m is attributable to the non-controlling interest.

Answer

STATEMENT OF CHANGES IN EQUITY OF DELTA GROUP FOR THE YEAR ENDED 31 MARCH 20X1

	Share capital	*Other reserves*	*Retained earnings*	*Total*	*Non-controlling interest*	*Total equity*
	$'000	$'000	$'000	$'000	$'000	$'000
Balance at 31 March 20X0	90,000	-	40,000	130,000	25,000	155,000
Total comprehensive income for the year			9,500	9,500	500	10,000
Dividend paid			(20,000)	(20,000)	-	(20,000)
Equity element of convertible bond (*Working*)		2,000		2,000		2,000
Balance at 31 March 20X1	90,000	2,000	29,500	121,500	25,500	147,000

STATEMENT OF FINANCIAL POSITION (EXTRACT) OF DELTA GROUP FOR THE YEAR ENDED 31 MARCH 20X1

Equity and liabilities	
Equity	
Share capital	90,000
Retained earnings	29,500
Other reserves	2,000
Total equity	121,500
Non-controlling interest	25,500
	147,000

Working: equity and debt elements of convertible bond

	$'000
Total proceeds from redeemable debt	12,000
Less: loan element of convertible	10,000
Equity element	2,000

9 Notes to the financial statements

FAST FORWARD

Some items need to be disclosed by way of note.

9.1 Contents of notes

The notes to the financial statements will **amplify** the information given in the statement of financial position, statement of comprehensive income, statement of cash flows and statement of changes in equity. We have already noted above the information which the IAS allows to be shown by note rather than in the statements. To some extent, then, the contents of the notes will be determined by the level of detail shown on the **face of the statements**.

9.2 Structure

The notes to the financial statements should perform the following functions.

(a) Provide information about the **basis on which the financial statements were prepared** and which **specific accounting policies** were chosen and applied to significant transactions/events

(b) Disclose any information, not shown elsewhere in the financial statements, which is **required by IFRSs**

(c) Show any additional information that is relevant to understanding which is not shown elsewhere in the financial statements

The way the notes are presented is important. They should be given in a **systematic manner** and **cross referenced** back to the related figure(s) in the statement of financial position, statement of comprehensive income, statement of cash flows, or statement of changes in equity.

Notes to the financial statements will amplify the information shown therein by giving the following.

(a) More **detailed analysis** or breakdowns of figures in the statements
(b) **Narrative information** explaining figures in the statements
(c) **Additional information**, eg contingent liabilities and commitments

IAS 1 suggests a **certain order** for notes to the financial statements. This will assist users when comparing the statements of different entities.

(a) Statement of **compliance** with IFRSs

(b) Statement of the **measurement basis** (bases) and accounting policies applied

(c) **Supporting information** for items presented in each financial statement in the same order as each line item and each financial statement is presented

(d) Other disclosures, eg:

 (i) Contingent liabilities, commitments and other financial disclosures
 (ii) Non-financial disclosures

The order of specific items may have to be varied occasionally, but a systematic structure is still required.

9.3 Presentation of accounting policies

The accounting policies section should describe the following.

(a) The **measurement basis** (or bases) used in preparing the financial statements

(b) The **other accounting policies** used, as required for a proper understanding of the financial statements

This information may be shown in the notes or sometimes as a **separate component** of the financial statements.

The information on measurement bases used is obviously fundamental to an understanding of the financial statements. Where **more than one basis is used**, it should be stated to which assets or liabilities each basis has been applied.

9.4 Other disclosures

An entity must disclose in the notes:

(a) The amount of dividends proposed or declared before the financial statements were authorised for issue but not recognised as a distribution to owners during the period, and the amount per share

(b) The amount of any cumulative preference dividends not recognised

IAS 1 ends by listing some **specific disclosures** which will always be required if they are not shown elsewhere in the financial statements.

(a) The domicile and legal form of the entity, its country of incorporation and the address of the registered office (or, if different, principal place of business)

(b) A description of the nature of the entity's operations and its principal activities

(c) The name of the parent entity and the ultimate parent entity of the group

Exam focus point

You will have to produce financial statements suitable for publication in your exam, so this chapter is important and you should refer back to it.

Question — Financial statements

The accountant of Wislon Co has prepared the following list of account balances as at 31 December 20X7.

	$'000
50c ordinary shares (fully paid)	450
10% debentures (secured)	200
Retained earnings 1.1.X7	242
General reserve 1.1.X7	171
Land and buildings 1.1.X7 (cost)	430
Plant and machinery 1.1.X7 (cost)	830
Accumulated depreciation	
Buildings 1.1.X7	20
Plant and machinery 1.1.X7	222
Inventory 1.1.X7	190
Sales	2,695
Purchases	2,152
Ordinary dividend	15
Debenture interest	10
Wages and salaries	254
Light and heat	31
Sundry expenses	113
Suspense account	135
Trade accounts receivable	179
Trade accounts payable	195
Cash	126

Notes

(a) Sundry expenses include $9,000 paid in respect of insurance for the year ending 1 September 20X8. Light and heat does not include an invoice of $3,000 for electricity for the three months ending 2 January 20X8, which was paid in February 20X8. Light and heat also includes $20,000 relating to salesmen's commission.

(b) The suspense account is in respect of the following items.

	$'000
Proceeds from the issue of 100,000 ordinary shares	120
Proceeds from the sale of plant	300
	420
Less consideration for the acquisition of Mary & Co	285
	135

(c) The net assets of Mary & Co were purchased on 3 March 20X7. Assets were valued as follows

	$'000
Available-for-sale financial assets	231
Inventory	34
	265

All the inventory acquired was sold during 20X7. The available-for-sale financial assets were still held by Wislon at 31.12.X7. Goodwill has not been impaired in value.

(d) The property was acquired some years ago. The buildings element of the cost was estimated at $100,000 and the estimated useful life of the assets was fifty years at the time of purchase. As at 31 December 20X7 the property is to be revalued at $800,000.

(e) The plant which was sold had cost $350,000 and had a net book value of $274,000 as on 1.1.X7. $36,000 depreciation is to be charged on plant and machinery for 20X7.

(f) The management wish to provide for:

(i) Debenture interest due
(ii) A transfer to general reserve of $16,000
(iii) Audit fees of $4,000

(g) Inventory as at 31 December 20X7 was valued at $220,000 (cost).

(h) Taxation is to be ignored.

Required

Prepare the financial statements of Wislon Co as at 31 December 20X7. You do not need to produce notes to the statements.

Answer

(a) Normal adjustments are needed for accruals and prepayments (insurance, light and heat, debenture interest and audit fees). The debenture interest accrued is calculated as follows.

	$'000
Charge needed in income statement (10% × $200,000)	20
Amount paid so far, as shown in list of account balances	10
Accrual: presumably six months' interest now payable	10

The accrued expenses shown in the statement of financial position comprise:

	$'000
Debenture interest	10
Light and heat	3
Audit fee	4
	17

(b) The misposting of $20,000 to light and heat is also adjusted, by reducing the light and heat expense, but charging $20,000 to salesmen's commission.

(c) Depreciation on the building is calculated as $\frac{\$100,000}{50} = \$2,000$.

The NBV of the property is then $430,000 – $20,000 – $2,000 = $408,000 at the end of the year. When the property is revalued a reserve of $800,000 – $408,000 = $392,000 is then created.

(d) The profit on disposal of plant is calculated as proceeds $300,000 (per suspense account) less NBV $274,000, ie $26,000. The cost of the remaining plant is calculated at $830,000 – $350,000 = $480,000. The depreciation provision at the year end is:

	$'000
Balance 1.1.X7	222
Charge for 20X7	36
Less depreciation on disposals (350 – 274)	(76)
	182

(e) Goodwill arising on the purchase of Mary & Co is:

	$'000
Consideration (per suspense account)	285
Assets at valuation	265
Goodwill	20

This is shown as an asset in the statement of financial position. The financial assets, being owned by Wislon at the year end, are also shown on the statement of financial position, whereas Mary's inventory, acquired and then sold, is added to the purchases figure for the year.

(f) The other item in the suspense account is dealt with as follows.

	$'000
Proceeds of issue of 100,000 ordinary shares	120
Less nominal value 100,000 × 50c	50
Excess of consideration over par value (= share premium)	70

(g) The transfer to general reserve increases it to $171,000 + $16,000 = $187,000.

We can now prepare the financial statements.

WISLON CO
STATEMENT OF COMPREHENSIVE INCOME FOR THE YEAR ENDED 31 DECEMBER 20X7

	$'000
Revenue	2,695
Cost of sales (W1)	(2,156)
Gross profit	539
Other income (profit on disposal of plant)	26
Administrative expenses (W2)	(437)
Finance costs	(20)
Profit for the year	108
Gain on property revaluation	392
Total comprehensive income for the year	500

Note

The only item of 'other comprehensive income' for the year was the revaluation gain. If there had been no revaluation gain, only an income statement would have been required.

Workings

1 *Cost of sales*

	$'000
Opening inventory	190
Purchases (2,152 + 34)	2,186
Closing inventory	(220)
	2,156

2 *Administrative expenses*

	$'000
Wages, salaries and commission (254 + 20)	274
Sundry expenses (113 – 6)	107
Light and heat (31 – 20 + 3)	14
Depreciation: buildings	2
plant	36
Audit fees	4
	437

WISLON CO
STATEMENT OF FINANCIAL POSITION AS AT 31 DECEMBER 20X7

	$'000	$'000
Assets		
Non-current assets		
Property, plant and equipment		
Property at valuation		800
Plant: cost	480	
Accumulated depreciation	(182)	
		298
Goodwill		20
Available-for-sale financial assets		231
Current assets		
Inventory	220	
Trade accounts receivable	179	
Prepayments	6	
Cash	126	
		531
Total assets		1,880
Equity and liabilities		
Equity		
50c ordinary shares	500	
Share premium	70	
Revaluation surplus	392	
General reserve	187	
Retained earnings	319	
		1,468
Non-current liabilities		
10% loan stock (secured)		200
Current liabilities		
Trade accounts payable	195	
Accrued expenses	17	
		212
Total equity and liabilities		1,880

WISLON CO
STATEMENT OF CHANGES IN EQUITY
FOR THE YEAR ENDED 31 DECEMBER 20X7

	Share capital	*Share premium*	*Retained earnings*	*General reserve*	*Revaluation Surplus*	*Total*
	$'000	$'000	$'000	$'000	$'000	$'000
Balance at 1.1.X7	450	–	242	171	–	863
Issue of share capital	50	70				120
Dividends			(15)			(15)
Total comprehensive income for the year			108		392	500
Transfer to reserve			(16)	16		
Balance at 31.12.X7	500	70	319	187	392	1,468

Note that the total comprehensive income is analysed into its components.

10 Problems with small entities

FAST FORWARD

In July 2009, the IASB issued the IFRS for Small and Medium-sized Entities.

In most countries the majority of companies or other types of entity are **very small**. They are generally owned and managed by one person or a family. The owners have invested their own money in the business and there are no outside shareholders to protect.

Large entities, by contrast, particularly companies listed on a stock exchange, may have shareholders who have invested their money, possibly through a pension fund, with no knowledge whatever of the company. These shareholders need protection and the regulations for such companies need to be more stringent.

It could therefore be argued that company accounts should be of two types:

(a) 'Simple' ones for small companies with fewer regulations and disclosure requirements
(b) 'Complicated' ones for larger companies with extensive and detailed requirements

This is sometimes called the **big GAAP/little GAAP divide**.

It is certainly the case that there are several IASs which very rarely have any bearing on small company accounts, whereas others almost always have an impact. In particular, almost all small companies will be affected by the IASs on:

- Property, plant and equipment
- Depreciation
- Inventories
- Presentation of financial statements
- Contingencies and events occurring after the reporting date
- Taxes on income
- Revenue

Does this mean that companies below a certain size should be exempt from other IASs? An alternative approach would be to reduce the exposure of small companies to IASs on a **standard by standard basis**. For those 'core' standards listed above, small companies would be required to follow all or most of their provisions. For more complicated standards, small companies would face nothing but very brief general obligations.

Question — Special rules

Are there special rules in your country which allow certain exemptions from accounting standards or legislation for small companies? Try to find out.

This was an area of discussion in IFRS accounting for many years. Many jurisdictions have their own standard for small and medium sized entities which reduce the reporting requirements for these entities. There has been no guidance on this area from the IASB until very recently.

In July 2009, the IASB issued the IFRS for Small and Medium-sized Entities. The IFRS is a stand-alone document providing guidance for smaller entities, and simplifying the accounting treatment of certain areas, including financial instruments.

The IFRS is intended to be used by small and medium entities that are not publicly accountable, ie are listed on a stock exchange or in the process of seeking a listing.

Exam focus point

The IFRS for SMEs is not on your Dip IFR syllabus, but you need to be aware of these general issues around it.

11 IAS 34: Interim financial reporting

FAST FORWARD

IAS 34 recommends that **entities should produce interim financial reports**, and for entities that do publish such reports, it lays down principles and guidelines for their production.

Exam focus point

The December 2004 exam included a six mark written question on IAS 34 *Interim financial reporting*.

The following definitions are used in IAS 34.

Key terms

- **Interim period** is a financial reporting period shorter than a full financial year.
- **Interim financial report** means a financial report containing either a complete set of financial statements (as described in IAS 1) or a set of condensed financial statements (as described in this standard) for an interim period. *(IAS 34)*

11.1 Scope

The standard does not make the preparation of interim financial reports **mandatory**, taking the view that this is a matter for governments, securities regulators, stock exchanges or professional accountancy bodies to decide within each country. The IASB does, however, strongly recommend to governments, etc, that interim financial reporting should be a requirement for companies whose equity or debt securities are **publicly traded**. The specific recommendations are that:

(a) An interim financial report should be produced by such companies for **at least the first six months of their financial year** (ie a half year financial report).

(b) The report should be **available no later than 60 days** after the end of the interim period.

Thus, a company with a year ending 31 December would be required as a minimum to prepare an interim report for the half year to 30 June and this report should be available before the end of August.

11.2 Minimum components

The proposed standard specifies the **minimum component elements** of an interim financial report.

- Condensed statement of financial position
- Condensed statement of comprehensive income
- Condensed statement of changes in equity
- Condensed statement of cash flows
- Selected note disclosures

The rationale for requiring only condensed statements and selected note disclosures is that entities need not duplicate information in their interim report that is contained in their report for the previous financial year. Interim statements should **focus more on new events, activities and circumstances**.

11.3 Form and content

Where **full financial statements** are given as interim financial statements, IAS 1 should be used as a guide, otherwise IAS 34 specifies minimum contents.

The **condensed statement of financial position** should include, as a minimum, each of the major components of assets, liabilities and equity as were in the statement of financial position at the end of the previous financial year, thus providing a summary of the economic resources of the entity and its financial structure.

The **condensed statement of comprehensive income** should include, as a minimum, each of the component items of income and expense as are shown in profit or loss for the previous financial year, together with the earnings per share and diluted earnings per share.

The **condensed statement of cash flows** should show, as a minimum, the three major sub-totals of cash flow as required in statements of cash flows by IAS 7, namely: cash flows from operating activities, cash flows from investing activities and cash flows from financing activities.

The **condensed statement of changes in equity** should include, as a minimum, each of the major components of equity as were contained in the statement of changes in equity for the previous financial year of the entity.

11.3.1 Selected explanatory notes

IAS 34 states that **relatively minor changes** from the most recent annual financial statements need not be included in an interim report. However, the notes to interim report should include the following (unless the information is contained elsewhere in the report).

- A statement that the **same accounting policies and methods of computation** have been used for the interim statements as were used for the most recent annual financial statements. If not, the nature of the differences and their effect should be described. (The accounting policies for preparing the interim report should only differ from those used for the previous annual accounts in a situation where there has been a change in accounting policy since the end of the previous financial year, and the new policy will be applied for the annual accounts of the current financial period.)
- Explanatory comments on the **seasonality or 'cyclicality'** of operations in the interim period. For example, if a company earns most of its annual profits in the first half of the year, because sales are much higher in the first six months, the interim report for the first half of the year should explain this fact
- The **nature and amount** of items during the interim period affecting assets, liabilities, capital, net income or cash flows, that are unusual, due to their nature, incidence or size
- The **issue or repurchase** of equity or debt securities
- Nature and amount of any **changes in estimates** of amounts reported in an earlier interim report during the financial year, or in prior financial years if these affect the current interim period
- **Dividends paid** on ordinary shares and the dividends paid on other shares
- **Segmental results** for the business segments or geographical segments of the entity (see IFRS 8)
- Any **significant events since the end of the interim period**
- Effect of the acquisition or disposal of subsidiaries during the interim period
- Any significant change in a **contingent liability or a contingent asset** since the date of the last annual statement of financial position

The entity should also disclose the fact that the interim report has been produced **in compliance with** IAS 34 on interim financial reporting.

Question — **Disclosures**

Give some examples of the type of disclosures required according to the above list of explanatory notes.

Answer

The following are examples.

(a) Write-down of inventories to net realisable value and the reversal of such a write-down

(b) Recognition of a loss from the impairment of property, plant and equipment, intangible assets, or other assets, and the reversal of such an impairment loss

(c) Reversal of any provisions for the costs of restructuring

(d) Acquisitions and disposals of items of property, plant and equipment

(e) Commitments for the purchase of property, plant and equipment

(f) Litigation settlements

(g) Corrections of fundamental errors in previously reported financial data

(h) Any debt default or any breach of a debt covenant that has not been corrected subsequently

(i) Related party transactions

11.4 Periods covered

The standard requires that interim financial reports should provide financial information for the following periods or as at the following dates.

- **Statement of financial position data** as at the end of the current interim period, and comparative data as at the end of the most recent financial year
- **Statement of comprehensive income data** for the current interim period and cumulative data for the current year to date, together with comparative data for the corresponding interim period and cumulative figures for the previous financial year
- **Statement of cash flows data** should be *cumulative* for the current year to date, with comparative cumulative data for the corresponding interim period in the previous financial year
- **Data for the statement of changes in equity** should be for both the current interim period and for the year to date, together with comparative data for the corresponding interim period, and cumulative figures, for the previous financial year

11.5 Materiality

Materiality should be assessed in relation to the interim period financial data. It should be recognised that interim measurements **rely to a greater extent on estimates** than annual financial data.

11.6 Recognition and measurement principles

A large part of IAS 34 deals with recognition and measurement principles, and guidelines as to their practical application. The **guiding principle** is that an entity should use the **same recognition and measurement principles in its interim statements as it does in its annual financial statements**.

This means, for example, that a cost that would not be regarded as an asset in the year-end statement of financial position should not be regarded as an asset in the statement of financial position for an interim period. Similarly, an accrual for an item of income or expense for a transaction that has not yet occurred (or a deferral of an item of income or expense for a transaction that has already occurred) is inappropriate for interim reporting, just as it is for year-end reporting.

Applying this principle of recognition and measurement may result, in a subsequent interim period or at the year-end, in a **remeasurement** of amounts that were reported in a financial statement for a previous interim period. **The nature and amount of any significant remeasurements should be disclosed**.

11.6.1 Revenues received occasionally, seasonally or cyclically

Revenue that is received as an occasional item, or within a seasonal or cyclical pattern, should not be anticipated or deferred in interim financial statements, if it would be inappropriate to anticipate or defer the revenue for the annual financial statements. In other words, the principles of revenue recognition should be applied consistently to the interim reports and year-end reports.

11.6.2 Costs incurred unevenly during the financial year

These should only be anticipated or deferred (ie treated as accruals or prepayments) if it would be appropriate to anticipate or defer the expense in the annual financial statements. For example, it would be appropriate to anticipate a cost for property rental where the rental is paid in arrears, but it would be inappropriate to anticipate part of the cost of a major advertising campaign later in the year, for which no expenses have yet been incurred.

The standard goes on, in an appendix, to deal with **specific applications** of the recognition and measurement principle. Some of these examples are explained below, by way of explanation and illustration.

11.6.3 Payroll taxes or insurance contributions paid by employers

In some countries these are assessed on an annual basis, but paid at an uneven rate during the course of the year, with a large proportion of the taxes being paid in the early part of the year, and a much smaller proportion paid later on in the year. In this situation, it would be appropriate to use an estimated average annual tax rate for the year in an interim statement, not the actual tax paid. This treatment is appropriate because it reflects the fact that the taxes are assessed on an annual basis, even though the payment pattern is uneven.

11.6.4 Cost of a planned major periodic maintenance or overhaul

The cost of such an event later in the year must not be anticipated in an interim financial statement *unless* there is a legal or constructive obligation to carry out this work. The fact that a maintenance or overhaul is planned and is carried out annually is not of itself sufficient to justify anticipating the cost in an interim financial report.

11.6.5 Other planned but irregularly-occurring costs

Similarly, these costs such as charitable donations or employee training costs, should not be accrued in an interim report. These costs, even if they occur regularly and are planned, are nevertheless discretionary.

11.6.6 Year-end bonus

A year-end bonus should not be provided for in an interim financial statement *unless* there is a constructive obligation to pay a year-end bonus (eg a contractual obligation, or a regular past practice) and the size of the bonus can be reliably measured.

11.6.7 Holiday pay

The same principle applies here. If holiday pay is an enforceable obligation on the employer, then any unpaid accumulated holiday pay may be accrued in the interim financial report.

11.6.8 Non-mandatory intangible assets

The entity might incur expenses during an interim period on items that might or will generate non-monetary intangible assets. IAS 38 *Intangible assets* requires that costs to generate non-monetary intangible assets (eg development expenses) should be recognised as an expense when incurred *unless* the costs form part of an identifiable intangible asset. Costs that were initially recognised as an expense cannot subsequently be treated instead as part of the cost of an intangible asset. IAS 34 states that interim financial statements should adopt the same approach. This means that it would be inappropriate in an interim financial statement to 'defer' a cost in the expectation that it will eventually be part of a non-monetary intangible asset that has not yet been recognised: such costs should be treated as an expense in the interim statement.

11.6.9 Depreciation

Depreciation should only be charged in an interim statement on non-current assets that have been acquired, not on non-current assets that will be acquired later in the financial year.

11.7 Foreign currency translation gains and losses

These should be calculated by the same principles as at the financial year end, in accordance with IAS 21.

11.7.1 Tax on income

An entity will include an expense for income tax (tax on profits) in its interim statements. The **tax rate** to use should be the estimated average annual tax rate for the year. For example, suppose that in a particular jurisdiction, the rate of tax on company profits is 30% on the first $200,000 of profit and 40% on profits above $200,000. Now suppose that a company makes a profit of $200,000 in its first half year, and expects to make $200,000 in the second half year. The rate of tax to be applied in the interim financial report should be 35%, not 30%, ie the expected average rate of tax for the year as a whole. This approach is appropriate because income tax on company profits is charged on an annual basis, and an effective annual rate should therefore be applied to each interim period.

As another illustration, suppose a company earns pre-tax income in the first quarter of the year of $30,000, but expects to make a loss of $10,000 in each of the next three quarters, so that net income before tax for the year is zero. Suppose also that the rate of tax is 30%. In this case, it would be inappropriate to anticipate the losses, and the tax charge should be $9,000 for the first quarter of the year (30% of $30,000) and a negative tax charge of $3,000 for each of the next three quarters, if actual losses are the same as anticipated.

Where the tax year for a company does not coincide with its financial year, a separate estimated weighted average tax rate should be applied for each tax year, to the interim periods that fall within that tax year.

Some countries give entities tax credits against the tax payable, based on amounts of capital expenditure or research and development, etc. Under most tax regimes, these credits are calculated and granted on an annual basis; therefore it is appropriate to include anticipated tax credits within the calculation of the estimated average tax rate for the year, and apply this rate to calculate the tax on income for interim periods. However, if a tax benefit relates to a specific one-time event, it should be recognised within the tax expense for the interim period in which the event occurs.

11.7.2 Inventory valuations

Within interim reports, inventories should be valued in the same way as for year-end accounts. It is recognised, however, that it will be necessary to rely more heavily on estimates for interim reporting than for year-end reporting.

In addition, it will normally be the case that the net realisable value of inventories should be estimated from selling prices and related costs to complete and dispose at interim dates.

11.8 Use of estimates

Although accounting information must be reliable and free from material error, it may be necessary to sacrifice some accuracy and reliability for the sake of timeliness and cost-benefits. This is particularly the case with interim financial reporting, where there will be much less time to produce reports than at the financial year end. The proposed standard therefore recognises that estimates will have to be used to a greater extent in interim reporting, to assess values or even some costs, than in year-end reporting.

An appendix to IAS 34 gives some examples of the use of estimates.

(a) **Inventories**. An entity might not need to carry out a full inventory count at the end of each interim period. Instead, it may be sufficient to estimate inventory values using sales margins.

(b) **Provisions**. An entity might employ outside experts or consultants to advise on the appropriate amount of a provision, as at the year end. It will probably be inappropriate to employ an expert to make a similar assessment at each interim date. Similarly, an entity might employ a professional valuer to revalue fixed assets at the year end, whereas at the interim date(s) the entity will not rely on such experts.

(c) **Income taxes**. The rate of income tax (tax on profits) will be calculated at the year end by applying the tax rate in each country/jurisdiction to the profits earned there. At the interim stage, it may be sufficient to estimate the rate of income tax by applying the same 'blended' estimated weighted average tax rate to the income earned in all countries/jurisdictions.

The principle of **materiality** applies to interim financial reporting, as it does to year-end reporting. In assessing materiality, it needs to be recognised that interim financial reports will rely more heavily on estimates than year-end reports. Materiality should be assessed in relation to the interim financial statements themselves, and should be independent of 'annual materiality' considerations.

11.9 Section summary

- IAS 34 in concept makes **straightforward proposals** for the production of interim financial reports by entities.
- It is essential to apply **principles of recognition and measurement** that will prevent entities from 'massaging' the interim figures.
- The **detail** in the guidelines is therefore very important, and the application of the recognition and measurement principles to particular valuations and measurements needs to be understood.

Chapter Roundup

- IAS 1 *Presentation of financial statements* covers **accounting concepts.** You need to remember and be able to apply all the key terms such as going concern, accruals, consistency, materiality, aggregation and offsetting.
- IAS 1 also covers the **form and content of** financial statements. The main components are:
  - Statement of financial position
  - Statement of comprehensive income
  - Statement of changes in equity
  - Statement of cash flows
  - Notes to the financial statements

  Each component must be **identified clearly**.
- IAS 1 suggests **formats** for the statement of financial position. Certain items are specified for **disclosure on the face of the financial statements.**
- You should appreciate the distinction between **current and non-current** assets and liabilities and the difference in treatment for operating cycle items and other non-operating items which are due after twelve months.
- IAS 1 (revised) requires all items of income and expense in a period to be shown in a statement of comprehensive income.
- IAS 1 offers two possible formats for the income statement section or separate income statement – by means function of by nature. Classification by function is more common.
- The Study Guide requires you to be able to prepare a basic set of company accounts from a trial balance.
- IAS 1 requires a statement of changes in equity. This shows the movement in the equity section of the statement of financial position. A full set of financial statements includes the statement of changes in equity.
- Some items need to be disclosed by way of note.
- In July 2009, the IASB issued the IFRS for Small and Medium-sized Entities.
- IAS 34 recommends that **entities should produce interim financial reports**, and for entities that do publish such reports, it lays down principles and guidelines for their production.

Quick Quiz

1 Financial statements provide information on financial position, performance and cash flow to help users do what?

(a) (b)

2 Which of the following are examples of current assets?

(a) Property, plant and equipment
(b) Prepayments
(c) Cash equivalents
(d) Manufacturing licences
(e) Accumulated profits

3 Provisions must be disclosed on the face of the statement of financial position.

True ☐ False ☐

4 Which of the following must be disclosed on the face of the income statement?

(a) Tax expense
(b) Analysis of expenses
(c) Net profit or loss for the period.

5 Fill in the blanks.

The accounting policies section of the notes describes:

The .... used in preparing the financial statements and the .... used that are relevant to an understanding of the financial statements.

6 Where are revaluation gains shown in the financial statements?

Answers to Quick Quiz

1 (a) Make economic decisions
(b) Assess management stewardship

2 (b) and (c) only

3 True

4 (a) and (c) only. (b) may be shown in the notes.

5 Measurement basis
Specific accounting policies

6 In the statement of comprehensive income and the statement of changes in equity

Now try the questions below from the Exam Question Bank

Number	Level	Marks	Time
Q20	Introductory	n/a	n/a
Q21	Examination	25	45 mins

16 Reporting financial performance

Topic list	Syllabus reference
1 IAS 10 (Revised) Events after the reporting period	3(a)
2 IAS 8 Accounting policies, changes in accounting estimates and errors	2, 3
3 Accounting policies	2, 3
4 Changes in accounting policies	2, 3
5 Changes in accounting estimates	2, 3
6 Errors	2, 3
7 IFRS 5 Non-current assets held for sale and discontinued operations	2, 3

Introduction

This long chapter is mainly concerned with the **income statement**. **IAS 8** deals with accounting policies. It also looks at certain circumstances and transactions which require different treatment to normal profit or loss items.

Study Guide

Section 18 – Accounting policies, changes in accounting estimates and errors

- Distinguish between and account for adjusting and non-adjusting events after the reporting period (IAS 10)
- Identify items requiring separate disclosure, including their accounting treatment and required disclosures
- Recognise the circumstances where a change in accounting policy is justified
- Define prior period adjustments and 'errors' and account for the correction of errors and changes in accounting policies (IAS 8)

1 IAS 10 (Revised) Events after the reporting period

FAST FORWARD

IAS 10 defines events occurring after the reporting period.

The financial statements are significant indicators of a company's success or failure. It is important, therefore, that they include all the information necessary for an understanding of the company's position.

IAS 10 *(Revised) Events after the reporting period* requires the provision of additional information in order to facilitate such an understanding. IAS 10 deals with events **after** the reporting date which may affect the position **at** the reporting date.

Note that the parts of IAS 10 that cover contingencies have been superseded by IAS 37, already covered in Chapter 8.

Exam focus point

The financial statements preparation question in the pilot paper included a part dealing with events after the reporting period.

The December 2003 exam asked candidates to:

- Explain why events after the reporting date might be of importance.
- Describe the circumstances where financial statements should, and should not, be adjusted.

Candidates were also required to recommend the accounting treatment for a series of events after the reporting period.

Events after the reporting period were also examined in June 2005 in the context of accounts preparation.

1.1 Definitions

The standard gives the following definition.

Key term

Events after the reporting period are those events, both favourable and unfavourable, that occur between the end of the reporting period and the date on which the financial statements are authorised for issue. Two types of events can be identified:

- Those that provide further evidence of conditions that existed at the end of the reporting period; and
- Those that are indicative of conditions that arose subsequent to the reporting period (IAS 10).

1.2 Events after the reporting period

Between the end of the reporting period and the date on which the financial statements are authorised (ie for issue outside the organisation), events may occur which show that assets and liabilities at the reporting date should be adjusted, or that disclosure of such events should be given.

1.3 Events requiring adjustment

FAST FORWARD

> Events after the reporting period which provide additional evidence of conditions existing at the reporting date, will cause adjustments to be made to the assets and liabilities in the financial statements.

The standard requires adjustment of assets and liabilities in certain circumstances.

FAST FORWARD

> An entity shall adjust the amounts recognised in its financial statements to reflect adjusting events after the reporting period. (IAS 10)

An **example** of additional evidence which becomes available after the reporting period is where a **customer goes bankrupt, thus confirming that the trade account receivable balance at the year end is uncollectable.**

In relation to going concern, the standard states that, where operating results and the financial position have deteriorated after the reporting period, it may be necessary to reconsider whether the going concern assumption is appropriate in the preparation of the financial statements.

1.4 Events not requiring adjustment

FAST FORWARD

> Events which do not affect the situation at the reporting date should not be adjusted for, but should be disclosed in the financial statements.

The standard then looks at events which do **not** require adjustment.

FAST FORWARD

> An entity shall not adjust the amounts recognised in its financial statements to reflect non-adjusting events after the reporting period. (IAS 10)

The **example** given by the standard of such an event is where the **value of an investment falls between the reporting date and the date the financial statements are authorised** for issue. The fall in value represents circumstances during the current period, not conditions existing at the previous reporting date, so it is not appropriate to adjust the value of the investment in the financial statements. Disclosure is an aid to users, however, indicating 'unusual changes' in the state of assets and liabilities after the reporting date.

The rule for **disclosure** of events occurring after the reporting period which relate to conditions that arose after that date, is that disclosure should be made if non-disclosure would hinder the user's ability to made **proper evaluations** and decision based on the financial statements. An example might be the acquisition of another business.

The distinction between an **adjusting event** and a **non-adjusting event** can be shown by the following diagram.

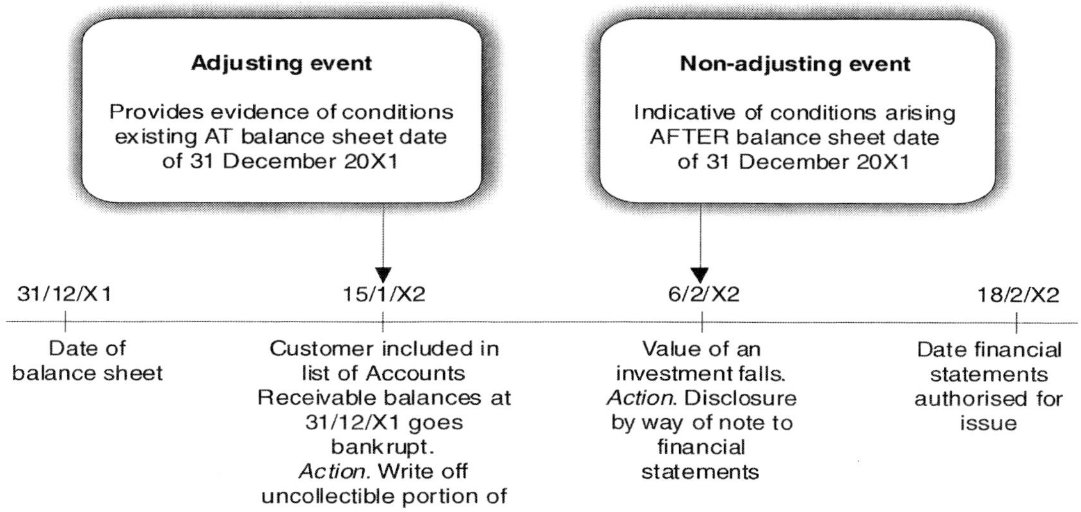

1.5 Dividends

Dividends declared by the entity after the end of the reporting period are a special case. Even if they are stated to be in respect of the period covered by the financial statements, they should **not** be **provided for**. They should simply be disclosed in the notes instead. This is because dividends proposed do not meet **IAS 37**'s criteria for recognising a provision.

1.6 Disclosures

The following **disclosure requirements** are given **for events** which occur after the reporting period which do *not* require adjustment. If disclosure of events occurring after the reporting period is required by this standard, the following information should be provided:

(a) The nature of the event
(b) An estimate of the financial effect, or a statement that such an estimate cannot be made

Question — Adjusting on non-adjusting

State whether the following events occurring after the reporting date require an adjustment to the assets and liabilities of the financial statements.

(a) Purchase of an investment
(b) A change in the rate of tax, applicable to the previous year
(c) An increase in pension benefits
(d) Losses due to fire
(e) A bad debt suddenly being paid
(f) The receipt of proceeds of sales or other evidence concerning the net realisable value of inventory
(g) A sudden decline in the value of property held as a long-term asset

Answer

(b), (e) and (f) require adjustment.

Of the other items, (a) would not need to be disclosed at all. Item (c) could need a disclosure if the cost to the company is likely to be material. Item (d) again would be disclosed if material, as would (g) if material.

Assuming that item (d) is material, it would be disclosed by way of the following note to the accounts. (The company year end is 31 December 20X8.)

Events after the reporting date

On 22 January 20X9, there was a fire at the company's warehouse. As a result, inventories costing a total of $250,000 were destroyed. These inventories are included in assets at the reporting date.

2 IAS 8 Accounting policies, changes in accounting estimates and errors

FAST FORWARD

IAS 8 is a very important standard and you should be familiar with it. You should be able to define and deal with:

- Accounting policy
- Changes in accounting policies
- Changes in accounting estimates
- Errors

Exam focus point

> The December 2003 paper asked for a description of the circumstances in which accounting policies may be changed and what constitutes a change of accounting policy. IAS 8 was examined in the June 2006 paper, with a question requiring the candidate to distinguish between the treatment of errors and revision in estimates.

IAS 8 deals with the treatment of changes in accounting estimates, changes in accounting policies and errors, as defined below.

The standard was extensively revised in December 2003. The new title reflects the fact that the material on determining net profit and loss for the period has been transferred to IAS1.

2.1 Definitions

The following definitions are given in the standard. Apart from the definition of accounting policies, most of the definitions are either new or heavily amended.

Key terms

- **Accounting policies** are the specific principles, bases, conventions, rules and practices adopted by an entity in preparing and presenting financial statements.
- A **change in accounting estimate** is an adjustment of the carrying amount of an asset or a liability or the amount of the periodic consumption of an asset, that results from the assessment of the present status of, and expected future benefits and obligations associated with, assets and liabilities. Changes in accounting estimates result from new information or new developments and, accordingly, are not corrections of errors.
- **Material**: as defined in IAS 1 (see Chapter 4)
- **Prior period errors** are omissions from, and misstatements in, the entity's financial statements for one or more prior periods arising from a failure to use, or misuse of, reliable information that:
  - (a) Was available when financial statements for those periods were authorised for issue, and
  - (b) Could reasonably be expected to have been obtained and taken into account in the preparation and presentation of those financial statements.

  Such errors include the effects of mathematical mistakes, mistakes in applying accounting policies, oversights or misinterpretations of facts, and fraud.
- **Retrospective application** is applying a new accounting policy to transactions, other events and conditions as if that policy had always been applied.
- **Retrospective restatement** is correcting the recognition, measurement and disclosure of amounts of elements of financial statements as if a prior period error had never occurred.
- **Prospective application** of a change in accounting policy and of recognising the effect of a change in an accounting estimate, respectively, are:
  - (a) Applying the new accounting policy to transactions, other events and conditions occurring after the date as at which the policy is changes; and
  - (b) Recognising the effect of the change in the accounting estimate in the current and future periods affected by the change.
- **Impracticable** Applying a requirement is impracticable when the entity cannot apply it after making every reasonable effort to do so. It is impracticable to apply a change in an accounting policy retrospectively or to make a retrospective restatement to correct an error if one of the following apply.
  - (a) The effects or the retrospective application or retrospective restatement are not determinable.
  - (b) The retrospective application or retrospective restatement requires assumptions about what management's intent would have been in that period.
  - (c) The retrospective application or retrospective restatement requires significant estimates of amounts and it is impossible to distinguish objectively information about those estimates

that: provides evidence of circumstances that existed on the date(s) at which those amounts are to be recognised, measured or disclosed; and would have been available when the financial statements for that prior period were authorised for issue from other information. (IAS 8)

3 Accounting policies

FAST FORWARD

An entity must select and apply its accounting policies for a period consistently.

The material on accounting policies has been **transferred** into IAS 8 from IAS 1.

Accounting policies are determined by **applying the relevant IFRS or IFRS Interpretation (IFRIC, SIC)** and considering any relevant Implementation Guidance issued by the IASB for that IFRS/IFRIC.

Where there is no applicable IFRS or IFRIC management should use its **judgement** in developing and applying an accounting policy that results in information that is **relevant** and **reliable**. Management should refer to:

(a) The requirements and guidance in IFRSs and IFRICs dealing with **similar** and **related issues**

(b) The definitions, recognition criteria and measurement concepts for assets, liabilities and expenses in the ***Framework***

Management may also consider the most recent pronouncements of **other standard setting bodies** that use a similar conceptual framework to develop standards, other accounting literature and accepted industry practices if these do not conflict with the sources above.

An entity must select and apply its accounting policies for a period **consistently** for similar transactions, other events and conditions, unless an IFRS or an IFRIC specifically requires or permits categorisation of items for which different policies may be appropriate. If an IFRS or an IFRIC requires or permits categorisation of items, an appropriate accounting policy must be selected and applied consistently to each category.

4 Changes in accounting policies

FAST FORWARD

Changes in accounting policies should be rare and should be made under specific circumstances.

The same accounting policies are usually adopted from period to period, to allow users to analyse trends over time in profit, cash flows and financial position. **Changes in accounting policy will therefore be rare** and should be made only if required by one of three things.

(a) By **statute**

(b) By an **accounting standard setting body**

(c) If the change will result in a **more appropriate presentation** of events or transactions in the financial statements of the entity

The standard highlights two types of event **which do not constitute changes in accounting policy**.

(a) Adopting an accounting policy for a **new type of transaction** or event not dealt with previously by the entity.

(b) Adopting a **new accounting policy** for a transaction or event which has not occurred in the past or which was not material.

In the case of tangible non-current assets, if a policy of revaluation is adopted for the first time then this is treated, not as a change of accounting policy under IAS 8, but as a revaluation under IAS 16 *Property, plant and equipment* (see Chapter 4). The following paragraphs do not therefore apply to a changes in policy to adopt revaluations.

A change in accounting policy **must be applied retrospectively**. **Retrospective application** means that the new accounting policy is applied to transactions and events as if it had always been in use. In other words, at the earliest date such transactions or events occurred, the policy is applied from that date.

Prospective application is **no longer allowed** under the revised IAS 8 unless it is **impracticable** (see Key Terms) to determine the cumulative amount of charge.

What would constitute a change in accounting policy? Examples are:

- A change from inventory valuation using FIFO to weighted average, or vice versa.
- A change in presentation, such as depreciation transferred from cost of sales to administrative expenses.

4.1 Adoption of an IAS/IFRS

Where a new IAS or IFRS is adopted, IAS 8 requires any transitional provisions in the new IAS itself to be followed. If none are given in the IAS which is being adopted, then IAS 8 offers a benchmark and an allowed alternative treatment.

4.2 Other changes in accounting policy

IAS 8 requires **retrospective application**, *unless* it is **impracticable** to determine the cumulative amount of charge. Any resulting adjustment should be reported as an adjustment to the opening balance of retained earnings. Comparative information should be restated unless it is impracticable to do so.

This means that all comparative information must be restated **as if the new policy had always been in force**, with amounts relating to earlier periods reflected in an adjustment to opening reserves of the earliest period presented.

Prospective application is allowed only when it is impracticable to determine the cumulative effect of the change

Certain **disclosures** are required when a change in accounting policy has a material effect on the current period or any prior period presented, or when it may have a material effect in subsequent periods.

(a) Reasons for the change

(b) Amount of the adjustment for the current period and for each period presented

(c) Amount of the adjustment relating to periods prior to those included in the comparative information

(d) The fact that comparative information has been restated or that it is impracticable to do so

An entity should also disclose information relevant to assessing the **impact of new IFRS** on the financial statements where these have **not yet come into force.**

Question — **Change in accounting policy**

Dudek Co was established on 1 January 20X0. In the first three years' accounts development expenditure was carried forward as an asset in the statement of financial position. During 20X3 the managers decided that for the current and future years, all development expenditure should be written off as it is incurred. This decision has not resulted from any change in the expected outcome of development projects on hand, but rather from a desire to favour the prudence concept. The following information is available.

(a) Movements on the development account.

Year	*Development expenditure incurred and capitalised during year*	*Transfer from capitalised development expenditure account to income statement*
	$'000	$'000
20X0	525	–
20X1	780	215
20X2	995	360

(b) The 20X2 accounts showed the following.

	$'000
Retained earnings b/f	2,955
Retained earnings for the year	1,825
Retained earnings c/f	4,780

(c) The retained profit for 20X3 after charging the actual development expenditure for the year was $2,030,000.

Required

Show how the change in accounting policy should be reflected in the reserves in the company's 20X3 accounts in accordance with IAS 8.

Ignore taxation.

Answer

If the new accounting policy had been adopted since the company was incorporated, the additional income statement charges for development expenditure would have been:

	$'000
20X0	525
20X1 (780 – 215)	565
	1,090
20X2 (995 – 360)	635
	1,725

This means that the reserves brought forward at 1 January 20X3 would have been $1,725,000 less than the reported figure of $4,780,000; while the reserves brought forward at 1 January 20X2 would have been $1,090,000 less than the reported figure of $2,955,000.

The statement of reserves in Dudek Co's 20X3 accounts should, therefore, appear as follows.

RETAINED EARNINGS

		Comparative (previous year) figures	
	20X3	*20X2*	
	$'000	$'000	
Retained earnings at the beginning of year			
Previously reported	4,780	2,955	
Retrospective change in accounting policy (note 1)	1,725	1,090	
Restated	3,055	1,865	
Retained earnings for the year	2,030	1,190	(note 2)
Retained earnings at the end of the year	5,085	3,055	

Notes

1 The accounts should include a note explaining the reasons for and consequences of the changes in accounting policy. (See above workings for 20X3 and 20X2.)

2 The retained profit shown for 20X2 is after charging the additional development expenditure of $635,000.

5 Changes in accounting estimates

FAST FORWARD

The changes in accounting estimates should be included in profit or loss of current and/or future periods.

Estimates arise in relation to business activities because of the **uncertainties inherent within them**. Judgements are made based on the most up to date information and the use of such estimates is a necessary part of the preparation of financial statements. It does *not* undermine their reliability. Here are some examples of accounting estimates.

- A necessary **bad debt provision**
- **Useful lives** of depreciable assets
- Provision for **obsolescence of inventory**

The rule here is that the **effect of a change in an accounting estimate** should be included in the determination of net profit or loss in one of:

(a) The period of the change, if the change affects that period only
(b) The period of the change *and* future periods, if the change affects both

Changes may occur in the circumstances which were in force at the time the estimate was calculated, or perhaps additional information or subsequent developments have come to light.

An example of a change in accounting estimate which affects only the **current period** is the bad debt estimate. However, a revision in the life over which an asset is depreciated would affect both the **current and future periods**, in the amount of the depreciation expense.

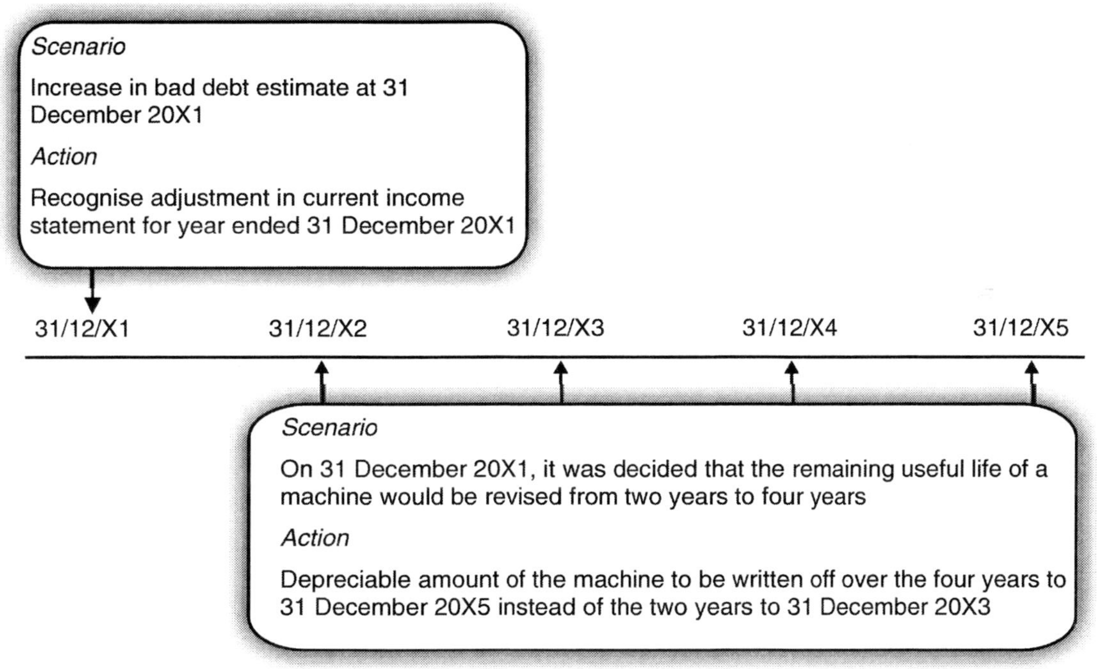

Reasonably enough, the effect of a change in an accounting estimate should be included in the **same income statement classification** as was used previously for the estimate. This rule helps to ensure **consistency** between the financial statements of different periods. Similarly, where an accounting estimate was previously reported as an extraordinary item, so the change of estimate should be too.

The **materiality** of the change is also relevant. The nature and amount of a change in an accounting estimate that has a material effect in the current period (or which is expected to have a material effect in subsequent periods) should be disclosed. If it is not possible to quantify the amount, this impracticability should be disclosed.

6 Errors

Errors discovered during a current period which **relate to a prior period** may have arisen through:

(a) Mathematical mistakes
(b) Mistakes in the application of accounting policies
(c) Misinterpretation of facts
(d) Oversights
(e) Fraud

A more formal definition was given in the Key Terms in Paragraph 2.1.

Most of the time these errors can be **corrected through net profit or loss for the current period**. Where they fulfil the definition of prior period errors (given earlier), however, this is not appropriate. The standard gives two alternative treatments.

6.1 Accounting treatment

Prior period errors: correct retrospectively.

This involves:

(a) Either restating the comparative amounts for the prior period(s) in which the error occurred,

(b) Or, when the error occurred before the earliest prior period presented, restating the opening balances of assets, liabilities and equity for that period

so that the financial statements are presented **as if the error had never occurred**.

Only where it is **impracticable** to determine the cumulative effect of an error on prior periods can an entity correct an error **prospectively**.

Various **disclosures** are required.

(a) **Nature** of the prior period error

(b) For each prior period, to the extent practicable, the **amount** of the correction.

  (i) For each financial statement line item affected
  (ii) If IAS 33 applies, for basic and diluted earnings per share

(c) The amount of the correction at the **beginning of the earliest prior** period presented

(d) If **retrospective restatement is impracticable** for a particular prior period, the **circumstances** that led to the existence of that condition and a description of how and from when the error has been corrected. Subsequent periods need not repeat these disclosures

Question — Prior period error

During 20X7 Prioska Co discovered that certain items had been included in inventory at 31 December 20X6, valued at $4.2m, which had in fact been sold before the year end. The following figures for 20X6 (as reported) and 20X7 (draft) are available.

	20X6	*20X7 (draft)*
	$'000	$'000
Sales	47,400	67,200
Cost of goods sold	(34,570)	(55,800)
Profit before taxation	12,830	11,400
Income taxes	(3,880)	(3,400)
Net profit	8,950	8,000

Reserves at 1 January 20X6 were $13m. The cost of goods sold for 20X7 includes the $4.2m error in opening inventory. The income tax rate was 30% for 20X6 and 20X7.

Required

Show the income statement of Prioska Co for 20X7, with the 20X6 comparative, and retained earnings.

Answer

PRIOSKA CO
INCOME STATEMENT

	20X6	20X7
	$'000	$'000
Sales	47,400	67,200
Cost of goods sold (W1)	(38,770)	(51,600)
Profit before tax	8,630	15,600
Income tax (W2)	(2,620)	(4,660)
Net profit	6,010	10,940

RETAINED EARNINGS

	20X6	20X7
Opening retained earnings		
As previously reported	13,000	21,950
Correction of prior period error (4,200 – 1,260)		(2,940)
As restated	13,000	19,010
Net profit for year	6,010	10,940
Closing retained earnings	19,010	29,950

Workings

1 *Cost of goods sold*

	20X6	20X7
	$'000	$'000
As stated in question	34,570	55,800
Inventory adjustment	4,200	(4,200)
	38,770	51,600

2 *Income tax*

	20X6	20X7
	$'000	$'000
As stated in question	3,880	3,400
Inventory adjustment (4,200 × 30%)	(1,260)	1,260
	2,620	4,660

7 IFRS 5 Non-current assets held for sale and discontinued operations

FAST FORWARD

IFRS 5 requires assets 'held for sale' to be presented separately on the face of the statement of financial position. The results of discontinued operations should be presented separately in the income statement.

Exam focus point

IFRS 5 is examined quite frequently. It often crops up as a discursive part of a question. Recently, it has been examined in June & December 2007, and December 2008.

7.1 Background

IFRS 5 is the result of a short-term convergence project with the US Financial Accounting Standards Board (FASB). It replaced IAS 35 *Discontinuing operations.*

IFRS 5 requires assets and groups of assets that are 'held for sale' to be **presented separately** on the face of the statement of financial position and the results of discontinued operations to be presented separately in the income statement. This is required so that users of financial statements will be better able to make **projections** about the financial position, profits and cash flows of the entity.

Key term

> **Disposal group:** a group of assets to be disposed of, by sale or otherwise, together as a group in a single transaction, and liabilities directly associated with those assets that will be transferred in the transaction. (In practice a disposal group could be a subsidiary, a cash-generating unit or a single operation within an entity.) *(IFRS 5)*

IFRS 5 does not apply to certain assets covered by other accounting standards:

(a) Deferred tax assets (IAS 12)
(b) Assets arising from employee benefits (IAS 19)
(c) Financial assets (IAS 39)
(d) Investment properties accounted for in accordance with the fair value model (IAS 40)
(e) Agricultural and biological assets that are measured at fair value less estimated point of sale costs (IAS 41)
(f) Insurance contracts (IFRS 4)

7.2 Classification of assets held for sale

A non-current asset (or disposal group) should be classified as **held for sale** if its carrying amount will be recovered **principally through a sale transaction** rather than **through continuing use**. A number of detailed criteria must be met:

(a) The asset must be **available for immediate sale** in its present condition.
(b) Its sale must be **highly probable** (ie, significantly more likely than not).

For the sale to be highly probable, the following must apply.

(a) Management must be **committed** to a plan to sell the asset.
(b) There must be an active programme to **locate a buyer.**
(c) The asset must be marketed for sale at a **price that is reasonable** in relation to its current fair value.
(d) The sale should be expected to take place **within one year** from the date of classification.
(e) It is unlikely that significant changes to the plan will be made or that the plan will be withdrawn.

An asset (or disposal group) can still be classified as held for sale, even if the sale has not actually taken place within one year. However, the delay must have been **caused by events or circumstances beyond the entity's control** and there must be sufficient evidence that the entity is still committed to sell the asset or disposal group. Otherwise the entity must cease to classify the asset as held for sale.

If an entity acquires a disposal group (eg, a subsidiary) exclusively with a view to its subsequent disposal it can classify the asset as held for sale only if the sale is expected to take place within one year and it is highly probable that all the other criteria will be met within a short time (normally three months).

An asset that is to be **abandoned** should not be classified as held for sale. This is because its carrying amount will be recovered principally through continuing use. However, a disposal group to be abandoned may meet the definition of a discontinued operation and therefore separate disclosure may be required (see below).

Question — Held for sale

On 1 December 20X8, a Biscan Co became committed to a plan to sell a manufacturing facility and has already found a potential buyer. The company does not intend to discontinue the operations currently carried out in the facility. At 31 December 20X8 there is a backlog of uncompleted customer orders. The subsidiary will not be able to transfer the facility to the buyer until after it ceases to operate the facility and has eliminated the backlog of uncompleted customer orders. This is not expected to occur until spring 20X9.

Required

Can the manufacturing facility be classified as 'held for sale' at 31 December 20X8?

Answer

The facility will not be transferred until the backlog of orders is completed; this demonstrates that the facility is not available for immediate sale in its present condition. The facility cannot be classified as 'held for sale' at 31 December 20X8. It must be treated in the same way as other items of property, plant and equipment: it should continue to be depreciated and should not be separately disclosed.

7.3 Measurement of assets held for sale

Key terms

Fair value: the amount for which an asset could be exchanged, or a liability settled, between knowledgeable, willing parties in an arm's length transaction.

Costs to sell: the incremental costs directly attributable to the disposal of an asset (or disposal group), excluding finance costs and income tax expense.

Recoverable amount: the higher of an asset's fair value less costs to sell and its value in use.

Value in use: the present value of estimated future cash flows expected to arise from the continuing use of an asset and from its disposal at the end of its useful life. *(IFRS 5)*

A non-current asset (or disposal group) that is held for sale should be measured at the **lower of** its **carrying amount** and **fair value less costs to sell**. Fair value less costs to sell is equivalent to net realisable value.

An impairment loss should be recognised where fair value less costs to sell is lower than carrying amount. Note that this is an exception to the normal rule. IAS 36 *Impairment of assets* requires an entity to recognise an impairment loss only where an asset's recoverable amount is lower than its carrying value. Recoverable amount is defined as the higher of net realisable value and value in use. IAS 36 does not apply to assets held for sale.

Non-current assets held for sale **should not be depreciated**, even if they are still being used by the entity.

A non-current asset (or disposal group) that is **no longer classified as held for sale** (for example, because the sale has not taken place within one year) is measured at the **lower of**:

(a) Its **carrying amount** before it was classified as held for sale, adjusted for any depreciation that would have been charged had the asset not been held for sale

(b) Its **recoverable amount** at the date of the decision not to sell

7.4 Presenting discontinued operations

Key terms

Discontinued operation: a component of an entity that has either been disposed of, or is classified as held for sale, and:

- Represents a separate major line of business or geographical area of operations
- Is part of a single co-ordinated plan to dispose of a separate major line of business or geographical area of operations, or
- Is a subsidiary acquired exclusively with a view to resale.

Component of an entity: operations and cash flows that can be clearly distinguished, operationally and for financial reporting purposes, from the rest of the entity. *(IFRS 5)*

An entity should **present and disclose information** that enables users of the financial statements to evaluate the financial effects of **discontinued operations** and disposals of non-current assets or disposal groups.

An entity should disclose a **single amount** on the **face of the income statement** comprising the total of:

(a) The **post-tax profit or loss** of discontinued operations and

(b) The post-tax gain or loss recognised on the **measurement to fair value less costs to sell** or on the disposal of the assets or disposal group(s) constituting the discontinued operation.

An entity should also disclose an **analysis** of the single amount into:

(a) The revenue, expenses and pre-tax profit or loss of discontinued operations

(b) The related income tax expense

(c) The gain or loss recognised on the measurement to fair value less costs to sell or on the disposal of the assets or the discontinued operation

(d) The related income tax expense

This may be presented either on the face of the income statement or in the notes. If it is presented on the face of the income statement it should be presented in a section identified as relating to discontinued operations, ie separately from continuing operations. This analysis is not required where the discontinued operation is a newly acquired subsidiary that has been classified as held for sale.

An entity should disclose the **net cash flows** attributable to the operating, investing and financing activities of discontinued operations. These disclosures may be presented either on the face of the statement of cash flows or in the notes.

Gains and losses on the remeasurement of a disposal group that is not a discontinued operation but is held for sale should be included in profit or loss from continuing operations.

7.5 Illustration

The following illustration is taken from the implementation guidance to IFRS 5. Profit for the period from discontinued operations would be analysed in the notes.

XYZ GROUP
INCOME STATEMENT
FOR THE YEAR ENDED 31 DECEMBER 20X9

	20X9	*20X8*
Continuing operations	$'000	$'000
Revenue	X	X
Cost of sales	(X)	(X)
Gross profit	X	X
Other income	X	X
Distribution costs	(X)	(X)
Administrative expenses	(X)	(X)
Other expenses	(X)	(X)
Finance costs	(X)	(X)
Share of profit of associates	X	X
Profit before tax	X	X
Income tax expense	(X)	(X)
Profit for the period from continuing operations	X	X
Discontinued operations		
Profit for the period from discontinued operations	X	X
Profit for the period	X	X

Profit attributable to:

	$'000	$'000
Owners of the parent		
Profit for the year from continuing operations	X	X
Profit for the year from discontinued operations	X	X
Profit for the year attributable to owners of the parent	X	X
Non-controlling interests		
Profit for the year from continuing operations	X	X
Profit for the year from discontinued operations	X	X
Profit for the year attributable to non-controlling interests	X	X

An alternative to this presentation would be to analyse the profit from discontinued operations in a separate column on the face of the income statement.

Question — **Closure**

On 20 October 20X9 the directors of a parent company made a public announcement of plans to close a steel works. The closure means that the group will no longer carry out this type of operation, which until recently has represented about 10% of its total turnover. The works will be gradually shut down over a period of several months, with complete closure expected in July 20Y0. At 31 December output had been significantly reduced and some redundancies had already taken place. The cash flows, revenues and expenses relating to the steel works can be clearly distinguished from those of the subsidiary's other operations.

Required

How should the closure be treated in the financial statements for the year ended 31 December 20X9?

Answer

Because the steel works is being closed, rather than sold, it cannot be classified as 'held for sale'. In addition, the steel works is not a discontinued operation. Although at 31 December 20X9 the group was firmly committed to the closure, this has not yet taken place and therefore the steel works must be included in continuing operations. Information about the planned closure could be disclosed in the notes to the financial statements.

7.6 Presentation of a non-current asset or disposal group classified as held for sale

Non-current assets and disposal groups classified as held for sale should be **presented separately** from other assets in the statement of financial position. The liabilities of a disposal group should be presented separately from other liabilities in the statement of financial position.

(a) Assets and liabilities held for sale **should not be offset**.

(b) The **major classes** of assets and liabilities held for sale should be **separately disclosed** either on the face of the statement of financial position or in the notes.

7.7 Additional disclosures

In the period in which a non-current asset (or disposal group) has been either classified as held for sale or sold the following should be disclosed.

(a) A **description** of the non-current asset (or disposal group)

(b) A description of the **facts and circumstances** of the disposal

(c) Any **gain or loss** recognised when the item was classified as held for sale

(d) If applicable, the **segment** in which the non-current asset (or disposal group) is presented in accordance with IFRS 8 *Operating Segments*

Where an asset previously classified as held for sale is **no longer held for sale**, the entity should disclose a description of the facts and circumstances leading to the decision and its effect on results.

Chapter Roundup

- IAS 10 defines events occurring after the reporting period.
- Events after the reporting date which provide additional evidence of conditions existing at the reporting date, will cause adjustments to be made to the assets and liabilities in the financial statements.
- An entity should adjust the amounts recognised in its financial statements to reflect adjusting events after the reporting period.
- Events which do not affect the situation at the reporting date should not be adjusted for, but should be disclosed in the financial statements.
- An entity should not adjust the amounts recognised in its financial statements to reflect non-adjusting events after the reporting period.
- IAS 8 is a very important standard and you should be familiar with it. You should be able to define and deal with:
  - Accounting policies
  - Changes in accounting policies
  - Changes in accounting estimates
  - Errors
- An entity must select and apply its accounting policies for a period consistently.
- Changes in accounting policies should be rare and should be made under specific circumstances.
- The changes in accounting estimates should be included in profit or loss of current and future periods.
- IFRS 5 requires assets 'held for sale' to be presented separately on the face of the statement of financial position. The results of discontinued operations should be presented separately in the income statement.

Quick Quiz

1 Define events occurring after the reporting date.

2 When does an event occurring after the reporting date require changes to the financial statements?

3 What treatment is required for dividends declared after the reporting date?

4 What disclosure is required when it is not possible to estimate the financial effect of an event not requiring adjustment?

5 A customer goes bankrupt after the reporting date and his debt must be written off.

Adjusting event ☐ Non-adjusting event ☐

6 Inventory is lost in a fire after the reporting date.

Adjusting event ☐ Non-adjusting event ☐

7 How should a prior period error be corrected under IAS 8?

8 Give three circumstances when a change in accounting policy might be required.

9 When can a non-current asset be classified as held for sale?

10 How should an asset held for sale be measured?

11 How does IFRS 5 define a discontinued operation?

Answers to Quick Quiz

1 Those events unfavourable and favourable, which occur between the reporting date and the date on which the financial statements are authorised for issue.

2 Assets and liabilities should be adjusted for events occurring after the reporting date when these provide additional evidence for estimates existing at the reporting date.

3 Dividends relating to the period covered by the financial statements, but declared after the reporting date, should be disclosed by way of note.

4 A statement of the nature of the event and the fact that a financial estimate of the event can not be made.

5 Adjusting

6 Non-adjusting

7 By adjusting the opening balance of retained earnings.

8 (a) By statute
(b) By the IASB
(c) For a more appropriate presentation

9 See Para 7.2

10 See Para 7.3

11 See Para 7.4 Key terms

Now try the questions below from the Exam Question Bank

Number	Level	Marks	Time
Q22	Examination	25	45 mins

17

Earnings per share

Topic list	Syllabus reference
1 IAS 33 Earnings per share	3(b)
2 Basic EPS	3(b)
3 Effect on EPS of changes in capital structure	3(b)
4 Diluted EPS	3(b)
5 Presentation, disclosure and other matters	3(b)

Introduction

Earnings per share (EPS) is widely used by investors as a measure of a company's performance and is of particular importance in:

(a) **Comparing the results** of a company over a **period of time**

(b) **Comparing the performance** of one company's equity against the performance of **another company's equity**, and also against the returns obtainable from loan stock and other forms of investment.

The purpose of any earnings yardstick is to achieve as far as possible clarity of meaning, comparability between one company and another, one year and another, and attributability of profits to the equity shares. IAS 33 *Earnings per share* goes some way to ensuring that all these aims are achieved.

Study Guide

Section 17 – Earnings per share

- Recognise the importance of comparability in relation to the calculation of earnings per share (EPS) and its importance as a stock market indicator
- Explain why the trend of EPS may be a more accurate indicator of performance than a company's profit trend
- Define earnings
- Calculate the EPS in the following circumstances
  - basic EPS
  - where there has been a bonus issue of shares/stock split during the year, and
  - where there has been a rights issue of shares during the year
- Explain the relevance to existing shareholders of the diluted EPS, and describe the circumstances that will give rise to a future dilution of the EPS
- Compute the diluted EPS in the following circumstances:
  - Where convertible debt or preference shares are in issue
  - Where share options and warrants exist
- Identify anti-dilutive circumstances

1 IAS 33 Earnings per share

FAST FORWARD

Earnings per share is a measurement of the amount of profits earned by a company for each ordinary share. Earnings are profits after tax and preferred dividends.

Exam focus point

IAS 33 is a fairly straightforward standard. You would be advised to make sure that you follow all the calculations and discussion points through so that you can tackle any questions that do come up.

Earnings per share (EPS) is widely used as a measure of a company's performance and is of particular importance in comparing results over a period of several years. A company must be able to sustain its earnings in order to pay dividends and re-invest in the business so as to achieve future growth. Investors also look for **growth** in the EPS from one year to the next.

Note that:

(a) EPS is a figure based on past data, and

(b) It is easily manipulated by changes in accounting policies and by mergers or acquisitions

The use of the measure in calculating management bonuses makes it particularly liable to manipulation.

1.1 Objective

The objective of IAS 33 is to improve the **comparability** of the performance of different entities in the same period and of the same entity in different accounting periods by prescribing methods for determining the number of shares to be included in the calculation of earnings per share and other amounts per share and by specifying their presentation.

1.2 Definitions

The following definitions are given in IAS 33, some of which are given in other IASs.

Key terms

Ordinary share: an equity instrument that is subordinate to all other classes of equity instruments.

Potential ordinary share: a financial instrument or other contract that may entitle its holder to ordinary shares.

Warrants or options: financial instruments that give the holder the right to purchase ordinary shares.

Financial instrument: any contract that gives rise to both a financial asset of one entity and a financial liability or equity instrument of another entity.

Equity instrument: any contract that evidences a residual interest in the assets of an entity after deducting all of its liabilities. *(IAS 33)*

1.2.1 Ordinary shares

There may be more than one class of ordinary shares, but ordinary shares of the same class will have the same rights to receive dividends. Ordinary shares participate in the net profit for the period **only after other types of shares**, eg preference shares.

1.2.2 Potential ordinary shares

IAS 33 identifies the following examples of financial instruments and other contracts generating potential ordinary shares.

(a) **Debt or equity instruments**, including preference shares, that are convertible into ordinary shares

(b) **Share warrants and options**

(c) **Employee plans** that allow employees to receive ordinary shares as part of their remuneration and other share purchase plans

(d) Shares that would be issued upon the satisfaction of **certain conditions** resulting from contractual arrangements, such as the purchase of a business or other assets

1.3 Scope

IAS 33 has the following scope restrictions.

(a) Only companies with (potential) ordinary shares which are **publicly traded** need to present EPS (including companies in the process of being listed).

(b) EPS need only be presented on the basis of **consolidated results** where the parent's results are shown as well.

(c) Where companies **choose** to present EPS, even when they have no (potential) ordinary shares which are traded, they must do so in accordance with IAS 33.

2 Basic EPS

FAST FORWARD

Basic EPS is calculated by dividing the net profit or loss for the period attributable to ordinary shareholders by the weighted average number of ordinary shares outstanding during the period.

2.1 Measurement

Basic EPS should be calculated by dividing the **net profit** or loss for the period attributable to ordinary shareholders by the **weighted average number of ordinary shares** outstanding during the period.

$$\text{Basic EPS} = \frac{\text{Net profit/(loss) attributable to ordinary shareholders}}{\text{Weighted average number of ordinary shares outstanding during the period}}$$

2.2 Earnings

Earnings includes **all items of income and expense** (including tax and non-controlling interests) *less* net profit attributable to **preference shareholders** (where preference shares are treated as equity), including preference dividends.

Preference dividends deducted from net profit consist of:

(a) Preference dividends on non-cumulative preference shares declared in respect of the period

(b) The full amount of the required preference dividends for cumulative preference shares for the period, *whether or not* they have been declared (*excluding* those paid/declared during the period in respect of previous periods)

2.3 Per share

The number of ordinary shares used should be the weighted average number of ordinary shares during the period. This figure (for all periods presented) should be **adjusted for events**, other than the conversion of potential ordinary shares, that have changed the number of shares outstanding without a corresponding change in resources.

The **time-weighting factor** is the number of days the shares were outstanding compared with the total number of days in the period; a reasonable approximation is usually adequate.

2.4 Example: weighted average number of shares

Justina Co, a listed company, has the following share transactions during 20X7.

Date	*Details*	*Shares issued*	*Treasury shares**	*Shares outstanding*
1 January 20X7	Balance at beginning of year	200,000	30,000	170,000
31 May 20X7	Issue of new shares for cash	80,000	–	250,000
1 December 20X7	Purchase of treasury shares	–	25,000	225,000
31 December 20X7	Balance at year end	280,000	55,000	225,000

* Treasury shares are an entity's own shares acquired. In some countries own shares cannot be held, but must be cancelled on acquisition.

Required

Calculate the weighted average number of shares outstanding for 20X7.

Solution

The weighted average number of shares can be calculated in two ways.

(a) (170,000 × 5/12) + (250,000 × 6/12) + (225,000 × 1/12) = 214,583 shares
(b) (170,000 × 12/12) + (80,000 × 7/12) – (25,000 × 1/12) = 214,583 shares

2.5 Consideration

Shares are usually included in the weighted average number of shares from the **date consideration is receivable** which is usually the date of issue; in other cases consider the specific terms attached to their issue (consider the substance of any contract). The treatment for the issue of ordinary shares in different circumstances is as follows.

Consideration	Start date for inclusion
In exchange for cash	When cash is receivable
On the voluntary reinvestment of dividends on ordinary or preferred shares	The dividend payment date
As a result of the conversion of a debt instrument to ordinary shares	Date interest ceases accruing

Consideration	Start date for inclusion
In place of interest or principal on other financial instruments	Date interest ceases accruing
In exchange for the settlement of a liability of the entity	The settlement date
As consideration for the acquisition of an asset other than cash	The date on which the acquisition is recognised
For the rendering of services to the entity	As services are rendered

Ordinary shares issued as **purchase consideration** in an acquisition should be included as of the date of acquisition because the acquired entity's results will also be included from that date.

If ordinary shares are **partly paid**, they are treated as a fraction of an ordinary share to the extent they are entitled to dividends relative to fully paid ordinary shares.

Contingently issuable shares (including those subject to recall) are included in the computation when all necessary conditions for issue have been satisfied.

Question

Basic EPS

Flame Co is a company with a called up and paid up capital of 100,000 ordinary shares of $1 each and 20,000 10% preferred shares of $1 each. The company manufactures gas appliances. During its financial year to 31 December the company had to pay $50,000 compensation and costs arising from an uninsured claim for personal injuries suffered by a customer while on the company premises.

The gross profit was $200,000. Flame Co paid the required preferred share dividend and declared an ordinary dividend of 42c per share. Assuming an income tax rate of 30% on the given figures show the trading results and EPS of the company.

Answer

FLAME CO
TRADING RESULTS FOR YEAR TO 31 DECEMBER

	$	$
Gross profit		200,000
Expense		(50,000)
Profit before tax		150,000
Tax at 30%		(45,000)
Profit for the financial year		105,000
Less dividends		
Preferred *	2,000	
Ordinary	42,000	
		44,000
		61,000

EARNINGS PER SHARE

$$\frac{103{,}000^*}{100{,}000} = 103c$$

*($105,000 – $2,000 preferred div = $103,000)

3 Effect on EPS of changes in capital structure

FAST FORWARD

You should know how to calculate **basic EPS** and how to deal with related complications (issue of shares for cash, bonus issue, share splits/reverse share splits, rights issues).

3.1 Introduction

We looked at the effect of issues of new shares or buy-backs of shares on basic EPS above. In these situations, the corresponding figures for EPS for the previous year will be comparable with the current year because, as the weighted average number of shares has risen or fallen, there has been a **corresponding increase or decrease in resources**. Money has been received when shares were issued, and money has been paid out to repurchase shares. It is assumed that the sales or purchases have been made at full market price.

3.2 Example: earnings per share with a new issue

On 30 September 20X2, Boffin Co made an issue at full market price of 1,000,000 ordinary shares. The company's accounting year runs from 1 January to 31 December. Relevant information for 20X1 and 20X2 is as follows.

	20X2	*20X1*
Shares in issue as at 31 December	9,000,000	8,000,000
Profits after tax and preferred dividend	$3,300,000	$3,280,000

Required

Calculate the EPS for 20X2 and the corresponding figure for 20X1.

Solution

	20X2	*20X1*
Weighted average number of shares		
9 months × 8 million	6,000,000	
3 months × 9 million	2,250,000	
	8,250,000	8,000,000
Earnings	$3,300,000	$3,280,000
EPS	40 cents	41 cents

In spite of the increase in total earnings by $20,000 in 20X2, the EPS is not as good as in 20X1, because there was extra capital employed for the final 3 months of 20X2.

There are other events, however, which change the number of shares outstanding, **without a corresponding change in resources**. In these circumstances it is necessary to make adjustments so that the current and prior period EPS figures are comparable.

Four such events are considered by IAS 33.

(a) **Capitalisation or bonus issue** (sometimes called a stock dividend)
(b) Bonus element in any other issue, eg a **rights issue** to existing shareholders
(c) **Share split**
(d) **Reverse share split** (consolidation of shares)

3.3 Capitalisation/bonus issue and share split/reverse share split

These two types of event can be considered together as they have a similar effect. In both cases, ordinary shares are issued to existing shareholders for **no additional consideration**. The number of ordinary shares has increased without an increase in resources.

This problem is solved by **adjusting the number of ordinary shares outstanding before the event** for the proportionate change in the number of shares outstanding as if the event had occurred at the beginning of the earliest period reported.

3.4 Example: earnings per share with a bonus issue

Greymatter Co had 400,000 shares in issue, until on 30 September 20X2 it made a bonus issue of 100,000 shares. Calculate the EPS for 20X2 and the corresponding figure for 20X1 if total earnings were $80,000 in 20X2 and $75,000 in 20X1. The company's accounting year runs from 1 January to 31 December.

Solution

	20X2		20X1	
Earnings	$80,000		$75,000	
Shares at 1 January	400,000		400,000	
Bonus issue	100,000		100,000	
	500,000	shares	500,000	shares
EPS	16c		15c	

The number of shares for 20X1 must also be adjusted if the figures for EPS are to remain comparable.

3.5 Rights issue

A rights issue of shares is an issue of new shares to existing shareholders **at a price below the current market value**. The offer of new shares is made on the basis of x new shares for every y shares currently held; eg a 1 for 3 rights issue is an offer of 1 new share at the offer price for every 3 shares currently held. This means that there is a bonus element included.

To arrive at figures for EPS when a rights issue is made, we need to calculate first of all the **theoretical ex-rights price**. This is a weighted average value per share, and is perhaps explained most easily with a numerical example.

3.6 Example: theoretical ex-rights price

Suppose that Egghead Co has 10,000,000 shares in issue. It now proposes to make a 1 for 4 rights issue at a price of $3 per share. The market value of existing shares on the final day before the issue is made is $3.50 (this is the 'with rights' value). What is the theoretical ex-rights price per share?

Solution

	$
Before issue 4 shares, value $3.50 each	14.00
Rights issue 1 share, value $3	3.00
Theoretical value of 5 shares	17.00

$$\text{Theoretical ex-rights price} = \frac{\$17.00}{5} = \$3.40 \text{ per share}$$

Note that this calculation can alternatively be performed using the total value and number of outstanding shares.

3.7 Procedures

The procedures for calculating the EPS for the current year and a corresponding figure for the previous year are now as follows.

(a) The **EPS for the corresponding previous period** should be multiplied by the following fraction. (*Note.* The market price on the last day of quotation is taken as the fair value immediately prior to exercise of the rights, as required by the standard.)

Formula to learn

$$\frac{\text{Theoretical ex-rights price}}{\text{Market price on last day of quotation (with rights)}}$$

(b) To obtain the **EPS for the current year**:

(i) Multiply the number of shares before the rights issue by the fraction of the year before the date of issue and by the following fraction

Formula to learn

$$\frac{\text{Market price on last day of quotation with rights}}{\text{Theoretical ex-rights price}}$$

(ii) Multiply the number of shares after the rights issue by the fraction of the year after the date of issue and add to the figure arrived at in (i)

The total earnings should then be divided by the total number of shares so calculated.

3.8 Example: earnings per share with a rights issue

Brains Co had 100,000 shares in issue, but then makes a 1 for 5 rights issue on 1 October 20X2 at a price of $1. The market value on the last day of quotation with rights was $1.60.

Calculate the EPS for 20X2 and the corresponding figure for 20X1 given total earnings of $50,000 in 20X2 and $40,000 in 20X1.

Solution

Calculation of theoretical ex-rights price:

	$
Before issue 5 shares, value × $1.60	8.00
Rights issue 1 share, value × $1.00	1.00
Theoretical value of 6 shares	9.00

Theoretical ex-rights price = $\frac{\$9}{6}$ = $1.50

EPS for 20X1

EPS as calculated before taking into account the rights issue = 40c ($40,000 divided by 100,000 shares).

EPS = $\frac{1.50}{1.60} \times 40c = 37\frac{1}{2}c$

(Remember: this is the corresponding value for 20X1 which will be shown in the financial statements for Brains Co at the end of 20X2.)

EPS for 20X2

Number of shares before the rights issue was 100,000. 20,000 shares were issued.

Stage 1:	$100{,}000 \times 9/12 \times \frac{1.60}{1.50}$ =	80,000
Stage 2:	$120{,}000 \times 3/12$ =	30,000
		110,000

EPS = $\frac{\$50{,}000}{110{,}000} = 45\frac{1}{2}c$

The figure for total earnings is the actual earnings for the year.

Question **Rights issue**

Marcoli Co has produced the following net profit figures for the years ending 31 December.

	$m
20X6	1.1
20X7	1.5
20X8	1.8

On 1 January 20X7 the number of shares outstanding was 500,000. During 20X7 the company announced a rights issue with the following details.

Rights:	1 new share for each 5 outstanding (100,000 new shares in total)
Exercise price:	$5.00
Last date to exercise rights:	1 March 20X7

The market (fair) value of one share in Marcoli immediately prior to exercise on 1 March 20X7 = $11.00.

Required

Calculate the EPS for 20X6, 20X7 and 20X8.

Answer

Computation of theoretical ex-rights price

This computation uses the total fair value and number of shares.

$$\frac{\text{Fair value of all outstanding shares + total received from exercise of rights}}{\text{No shares outstanding prior to exercise + no shares issued in exercise}}$$

$$= \frac{(\$11.00 \times 500{,}000) + (\$5.00 \times 100{,}000)}{500{,}000 + 100{,}000} = \$10.00$$

Computation of EPS

		20X6 $	*20X7* $	*20X8* $
20X6	EPS as originally reported $\frac{\$1{,}100{,}000}{500{,}000}$	2.20		
20X6	EPS restated for rights issue = $\frac{\$1{,}100{,}000}{500{,}000} \times \frac{10}{11}$	2.00		
20X7	EPS including effects of rights issue $\frac{\$1{,}500{,}000}{(500{,}000 \times 2/12 \times 11/10) + (600{,}000 \times 10/12)}$		2.54	
20X8	EPS = $\frac{\$1{,}800{,}000}{600{,}000}$			3.00

4 Diluted EPS

FAST FORWARD

Diluted EPS is calculated by adjusting the net profit attributable to ordinary shareholders and the weighted average number of shares outstanding for the effects of all dilutive potential ordinary shares.

4.1 Introduction

At the end of an accounting period, a company may have in issue some **securities** which do not (at present) have any 'claim' to a share of equity earnings, but **may give rise to such a claim in the future**. These securities include:

(a) A **separate class of equity shares** which at present is not entitled to any dividend, but will be entitled after some future date

(b) **Convertible loan stock** or **convertible preferred shares** which give their holders the right at some future date to exchange their securities for ordinary shares of the company, at a pre-determined conversion rate

(c) **Options** or **warrants**

In such circumstances, the future number of ordinary shares in issue might increase, which in turn results in a fall in the EPS. In other words, a **future increase** in the **number of ordinary shares will cause a dilution or 'watering down' of equity**, and it is possible to calculate a **diluted earnings per share** (ie the EPS that would have been obtained during the financial period if the dilution had already taken place). This will indicate to investors the possible effects of a future dilution.

4.2 Earnings

The earnings calculated for basic EPS should be adjusted by the **post-tax** (including deferred tax) effect of:

(a) Any **dividends** on dilutive potential ordinary shares that were deducted to arrive at earnings for basic EPS

(b) **Interest recognised** in the period for the dilutive potential ordinary shares

(c) Any **other changes in income or expenses** (fees and discount, premium accounted for as yield adjustments) that would result from the conversion of the dilutive potential ordinary shares

The conversion of some potential ordinary shares may lead to changes in **other income or expenses**. For example, the reduction of interest expense related to potential ordinary shares and the resulting increase in net profit for the period may lead to an increase in the expense relating to a non-discretionary employee profit-sharing plan. When calculating diluted EPS, the net profit or loss for the period is adjusted for any such consequential changes in income or expense.

4.3 Per share

The number of ordinary shares is the weighted average number of ordinary shares calculated for basic EPS plus the weighted average number of ordinary shares that would be issued on the conversion of all the **dilutive potential ordinary shares** into ordinary shares.

It should be assumed that dilutive ordinary shares were converted into ordinary shares at the **beginning of the period** or, if later, at the actual date of issue. There are two other points.

(a) The computation assumes the most **advantageous conversion rate** or exercise rate from the standpoint of the holder of the potential ordinary shares.

(b) **Contingently issuable** (potential) ordinary shares are treated as for basic EPS; if the conditions have not been met, the number of contingently issuable shares included in the computation is based on the number of shares that would be issuable if the end of the reporting period was the end of the contingency period. Restatement is not allowed if the conditions are not met when the contingency period expires.

4.4 Example: diluted EPS

In 20X7 Farrah Co had a basic EPS of 105c based on earnings of $105,000 and 100,000 ordinary $1 shares. It also had in issue $40,000 15% Convertible Loan Stock which is convertible in two years' time at the rate of 4 ordinary shares for every $5 of stock. The rate of tax is 30%. In 20X7 gross profit of $200,000 and expenses of $50,000 were recorded, including interest payable of $6,000.

Required

Calculate the diluted EPS.

Solution

Diluted EPS is calculated as follows.

Step 1 **Number of shares**: the additional equity on conversion of the loan stock will be 40,000 × 4/5 = 32,000 shares

Step 2 **Earnings**: Farrah Co will save interest payments of $6,000 but this increase in profits will be taxed. Hence the earnings figure may be recalculated:

	$
Gross profit	200,000
Expenses (50,000 – 6,000)	(44,000)
Profit before tax	156,000
Tax expense (30%)	(46,800)
Earnings	109,200

Step 3 **Calculation**: Diluted EPS = $\frac{\$109{,}200}{132{,}000}$ = 82.7c

Step 4 **Dilution**: the dilution in earnings would be 105c – 82.7c = 22.3c per share.

Question — Diluted EPS

Ardent Co has 5,000,000 ordinary shares of 25 cents each in issue, and also had in issue in 20X4:

(a) $1,000,000 of 14% convertible loan stock, convertible in three years' time at the rate of 2 shares per $10 of stock;

(b) $2,000,000 of 10% convertible loan stock, convertible in one year's time at the rate of 3 shares per $5 of stock.

The total earnings in 20X4 were $1,750,000.

The rate of income tax is 35%.

Required

Calculate the basic EPS and diluted EPS.

Answer

(a) Basic EPS = $\frac{\$1{,}750{,}000}{5 \text{ million}}$ = 35 cents

(b) We must decide which of the potential ordinary shares (ie the loan stocks) are dilutive (ie would decrease the EPS if converted).

For the 14% loan stock, incremental EPS = $\frac{0.65 \times \$140{,}000}{200{,}000 \text{ shares}}$

= 45.5c

For the 10% loan stock, incremental EPS = $\frac{0.65 \times \$200{,}000}{1.2\text{m shares}}$

= 10.8c

The effect of converting the 14% loan stock is therefore to **increase** the EPS figure, since the incremental EPS of 45.5c is greater than the basic EPS of 35c. The 14% loan stock is not dilutive and is therefore excluded from the diluted EPS calculation.

The 10% loan stock is dilutive.

Diluted EPS = $\frac{\$1.75\text{m} + \$0.13\text{m}}{5\text{m} + 1.2\text{m}}$ = 30.3c

It should be assumed that options were exercised and that the assumed proceeds would have been received from the issue of shares at **fair value**. Fair value for this purpose is calculated on the basis of the average price of the ordinary shares during the period. Calculations of this nature are beyond the scope of the Paper 2.5 syllabus.

4.5 Dilutive potential ordinary shares

According to IAS 33, potential ordinary shares should be treated as dilutive when, and only when, their conversion to ordinary shares would **decrease net profit per share** from continuing operations. This point was illustrated in the question above.

4.6 Restatement

If the number of ordinary or potential ordinary shares outstanding **increases** as a result of a capitalisation, bonus issue or share split, or decreases as a result of a reverse share split, the calculation of basic and diluted EPS for all periods presented should be **adjusted retrospectively**.

If these changes occur **after the reporting date** but before the financial statements are authorised for issue, the calculations per share for the financial statements and those of any prior period should be based on the **new number of shares** (and this should be disclosed).

In addition, basic and diluted EPS of all periods presented should be adjusted for the effects of **material errors**, and adjustments resulting from **changes** in **accounting policies**, dealt with in accordance with IAS 8.

An entity **does not restate diluted EPS** of any prior period for changes in the assumptions used or for the conversion of potential ordinary shares into ordinary shares outstanding.

Entities are encouraged to disclose a description of ordinary share transactions or potential ordinary share transactions, other than capitalisation issues and share splits, which occur **after the reporting date** when they are of such importance that non-disclosure would affect the ability of the users of the financial statements to make proper evaluations and decisions (see IAS 10). Examples of such transactions include the following.

(a) Issue of shares for cash

(b) Issue of shares when the proceeds are used to repay debt or preferred shares outstanding at the reporting date

(c) Redemption of ordinary shares outstanding

(d) Conversion or exercise of potential ordinary shares, outstanding at the reporting date, into ordinary shares

(e) Issue of warrants, options or convertible securities

(f) Achievement of conditions that would result in the issue of contingently issuable shares

EPS amounts are not adjusted for such transactions occurring after the reporting date because such transactions **do not affect the amount of capital used** to produce the net profit or loss for the period.

5 Presentation, disclosure and other matters

5.1 Presentation

Basic and diluted EPS should be presented by an entity on the **face of the statement of comprehensive income** for each class of ordinary share that has a different right to share in the net profit for the period. The basic and diluted EPS should be presented with **equal prominence** for all periods presented.

Disclosure must still be made where the EPS figures (basic and/or diluted) are **negative** (ie a loss per share).

5.2 Disclosure

An entity should disclose the following.

(a) The amounts used as the **numerators** in calculating basic and diluted EPS, and a **reconciliation** of those amounts to the net profit or loss for the period

(b) The weighted average number of ordinary shares used as the **denominator** in calculating basic and diluted EPS, and a **reconciliation** of these denominators to each other.

5.3 Alternative EPS figures

An entity may present **alternative EPS figures if it wishes**. However, IAS 33 lays out certain rules where this takes place.

(a) The weighted average number of shares as calculated under IAS 33 **must** be used.

(b) A **reconciliation** must be given between the component of profit used in the alternative EPS (if it is not a line item in the income statement) and the line item for profit reported in the income statement.

(c) Basic and diluted EPS must be shown with **equal prominence**.

5.4 Significance of earnings per share

Earnings per share (EPS) is one of the most frequently quoted statistics in financial analysis. Because of the widespread use of the price earnings **(P/E) ratio** as a yardstick for investment decisions, it became increasingly important.

It seems that reported and forecast EPS can, through the P/E ratio, have a **significant effect on a company's share price**. Thus, a share price might fall if it looks as if EPS is going to be low. This is not very rational, as EPS can depend on many, often subjective, assumptions used in preparing a historical statement, such as the income statement. It does not necessarily bear any relation to the value of a company, and of its shares. Nevertheless, the market is sensitive to EPS.

EPS has also served as a means of assessing the **stewardship and management** role performed by company directors and managers. Remuneration packages might be linked to EPS growth, thereby increasing the pressure on management to improve EPS. The danger of this, however, is that management effort may go into distorting results to produce a favourable EPS.

Chapter Roundup

- **Earnings per share** is a measure of the amount of profits earned by a company for each ordinary share. Earnings are profits after tax and preferred dividends.
- **Basic EPS** is calculated by dividing the net profit or loss for the period attributable to ordinary shareholders by the weighted average number of ordinary shares outstanding during the period.
- You should know how to calculate **basic EPS** and how to deal with related complications (issue of shares for cash, bonus issue, share splits/reverse share splits, rights issues).
- **Diluted EPS** is calculated by adjusting the net profit attributable to ordinary shareholders and the weighted average number of shares outstanding for the effects of all dilutive potential ordinary shares.

Quick Quiz

1 How is basic EPS calculated?

2 Give the formula for the 'bonus element' of a rights issue.

3 Define 'dilutive potential ordinary share'.

4 Which numerator is used to decide whether potential ordinary shares are dilutive?

5 Why is the numerator adjusted for convertible bonds when calculating diluted EPS?

Answers to Quick Quiz

1 $$\frac{\text{Net profit/(loss) attributable to ordinary shareholders}}{\text{Weighted average number of ordinary shares outstanding during the period}}$$

2 $$\frac{\text{Actual cum – rights price}}{\text{Theoretical ex – rights price}}$$

3 See Para 4.1

4 Net profit from continuing operations only.

5 Because the issue of shares will affect earnings (the interest will no longer have to be paid).

Now try the question below from the Exam Question Bank

Number	Level	Marks	Time
Q23	Examination	25	45 mins

Miscellaneous standards: related party disclosures and segment reporting

18

Topic list	Syllabus reference
1 IAS 24 Related party disclosures	3(c)
2 IFRS 8 Operating segments	3(f)

Introduction

In this chapter we look at a number of standards.

IAS 24 requires disclosure on related party transactions during the period in order to give a better indication of performance.

IFRS 8 on segment reporting requires quoted entities to provide additional information on their results in order for more detailed analysis to be possible.

Study Guide

Section 19 – Related party disclosures

- Define and apply the definition of related parties in accordance with international accounting standards
- Describe the potential to mislead users when related party transactions accounted for
- Explain the disclosure requirements for related party transactions

Section 20 – Operating segments

- Discuss the usefulness and problems associated with the provision of segment information
- Define an operating segment
- Identify a reportable segment (including applying the aggregation criteria and quantitative thresholds)

1 IAS 24 Related party disclosures

FAST FORWARD

IAS 24 is primarily a **disclosure statement**. It is concerned to improve the quality of information provided by financial statements and also to strengthen their stewardship role.

In the absence of information to the contrary, it is assumed that a reporting entity has **independent discretionary power** over its resources and transactions and pursues its activities independently of the interests of its individual owners, managers and others. Transactions are presumed to have been undertaken on an **arm's length basis**, ie on terms such as could have obtained in a transaction with an external party, in which each side bargained knowledgeably and freely, unaffected by any relationship between them.

These assumptions may not be justified when **related party relationships** exist, because the requisite conditions for competitive, free market dealings may not be present. Whilst the parties may endeavour to achieve arm's length bargaining the very nature of the relationship may preclude this occurring.

Exam focus point

You may be asked to explain the relevance of related party transactions and the importance of disclosure.

1.1 Objective

This is the related parties issue and IAS 24 tackles it by ensuring that financial statements contain the disclosures necessary to draw attention to the possibility that the reported financial position and results may have been affected by the existence of related parties and by material transactions with them. In other words, this is a standard which is primarily concerned with **disclosure**.

1.2 Scope

The standard requires disclosure of related party transactions and outstanding balances in the **separate financial statements** of a parent, venturer or investor presented in accordance with IAS 27 as well as in consolidated financial statements.

This is a **change** from the previous version of IAS 24, which did not require disclosure in the separate financial statements of a parent or wholly-owned subsidiary that are made available or published with consolidated financial statements for the group.

An entity's financial statements disclose related party transactions and outstanding balances with other entities in a group. **Intragroup** transactions and balances are **eliminated** in the preparation of consolidated financial statements.

1.3 Definitions

The following important definitions are given by the standard which was subjected to minor amendments in November 2009. Note that the definitions of **control** and **significant influence** are now the same as those given in IASs 27, 28 and 31.

Key terms

Related party. A party is related to an entity if:

(a) directly, or indirectly through one or more intermediaries, it:

- (i) Controls, is controlled by, or is under common control with, the entity (this includes parents, subsidiaries and fellow subsidiaries)
- (ii) Has an interest in the entity that gives it significant influence over the entity; or
- (iii) Has joint control over the entity

(b) it is an associate

(c) it is a joint venture in which the entity is a venturer

(d) it is a member of the key management personnel of the entity or its parent

(e) it is a close member of the family of any individual referred to in (a) or (d)

(f) it is an entity that is controlled, jointly controlled or significantly influenced by; or for which significant voting power in such entity resides with, directly or indirectly, any individual referred to in (d) or (e)

(g) both entities are joint ventures of the same third party

(h) one entity is a joint venture and the other is an associate of the same third party; or

(i) it is a post-employment benefit plan for the benefit of employees of the entity, or of any entity that is a related party of the entity.

Related party transaction. A transfer of resources, services or obligations between related parties, regardless of whether a price is charged.

Control is the power to govern the financial and operating policies of an entity so as to obtain benefits from its activities.

Significant influence is the power to participate in the financial and operating policy decisions of an entity, but is not control over these policies. Significant ownership may be gained by share ownership, statute or agreement.

Joint control is the contractually agreed sharing of control over an economic activity.

Key management personnel are those persons having authority and responsibility for planning, directing and controlling the activities of the entity, directly or indirectly, including any director (whether executive or otherwise) of that entity.

Close members of the family of an individual are those family members who may be expected to influence, or be influenced by, that individual in their dealings with the entity. They may include:

(a) The individual's domestic partner and children
(b) Children of the domestic partner; and
(c) Dependants of the individual or the domestic partner.

(IAS 24)

The most important point to remember here is that, when considering each possible related party relationship, attention must be paid to the **substance of the relationship, not merely the legal form**.

IAS 24 lists the following which are **not necessarily related parties**.

(a) **Two entities simply because they have a director or other key management in common** (notwithstanding the definition of related party above, although it is necessary to consider how that director would affect both entities).

(b) **Two venturers, simply because they share joint control over a joint venture.**

(c) Certain other bodies, simply as a result of their **role in normal business dealings** with the entity

  (i) Providers of finance
  (ii) Trade unions
  (iii) Public utilities
  (iv) Government departments and agencies

(d) **Any single customer, supplier, franchisor, distributor, or general agent** with whom the entity transacts a significant amount of business, simply by virtue of the resulting economic dependence.

1.4 Exemption for government-related entities

Before the 2009 revision of IAS 24, if a government controlled or significantly influenced an entity, the entity was required to disclose information about all transactions with other entities controlled, or significantly influenced, by the same government. The revised standard still requires disclosures that are significant to users of the financial statements, but **eliminates the need to disclose information that is costly to gather, and of less value to users**. It achieves this by limiting disclosure required to transactions that are individually or collectively significant.

1.5 Disclosure

As noted above, IAS 24 is almost entirely concerned with disclosure and its provisions are meant to **supplement** those disclosure requirements required by national company legislation and other IASs (particularly IASs 1, 22, 27 and 28).

The standard lists some **examples** of transactions that are disclosed if they are with a related party:

- Purchases or sales of goods (finished or unfinished)
- Purchases or sales of property and other assets
- Rendering or receiving of services
- Leases
- Transfer of research and development
- Transfers under licence agreements
- Provision of finance (including loans and equity contributions in cash or in kind)
- Provision of guarantees and collateral security
- Settlement of liabilities on behalf of the entity or by the entity on behalf of another party

1.6 Parents and subsidiaries

Relationships between **parents and subsidiaries** must be **disclosed irrespective** of **whether** any **transactions** have **taken place between** the related parties. An entity must disclose the **name** of its **parent** and, if different, the **ultimate controlling party**. This will enable a reader of the financial statements to be able to form a view about the effects of a related party relationship on the reporting entity.

If neither the parent nor the ultimate controlling party produces financial statements available for public use, the name of the next most senior parent that does so shall also be disclosed.

An entity should disclose key management personnel compensation in total for various categories:

Items of a similar nature may be **disclosed in aggregate** *unless* separate disclosure is necessary for an understanding of the effect on the financial statements.

Disclosures that related party transactions were made on terms equivalent to those that prevail in arm's length transactions are made only if such disclosures can be substantiated.

1.7 Management personnel

An entity should disclose **key management personnel compensation** in **total** and for **each** of the following **categories**:

(a) **Short-term employee benefits** (eg wages, salaries, social security contributions, paid annual leave and paid sick-leave, profit sharing and bonuses and non-monetary benefits such as medical care, housing, cars and free or subsidised goods or services)

(b) **Post-employment benefits** (eg pensions, other retirement benefits, life insurance and medical care)

(c) **Other long-term benefits** (eg long-service leave, sabbatical leave, long-term disability benefits and, if they are not payable within twelve months after the end of the period, profit sharing, bonuses and deferred compensation)

(d) **Termination benefits**; and

(e) **Equity compensation benefits**

Compensation includes amounts paid on behalf of a parent of the entity in respect of the entity.

1.8 Disclosures

Where **transactions have taken place** between related parties, the entity should disclose the **nature** of the related party relationships, as well as information about the **transactions and outstanding balances** necessary for an understanding of the potential effect of the relationship on the financial statements. As a minimum, disclosures must include:

(a) The **amount of the transactions**

(b) The **amount of outstanding balances** and

  (i) their terms and conditions, including whether they are secured, and the nature of the consideration to be provided in settlement

  (ii) details of any guarantees given or received

(c) Provisions for **doubtful debts** related to the amount of outstanding balances

(d) The **expense** recognised during the period in respect of **bad or doubtful debts** due from related parties.

The above disclosures shall be made separately for **each** of the following categories:

(a) The parent
(b) Entities with joint control or significant influence over the entity
(c) Subsidiaries
(d) Associates
(e) Joint ventures in which the entity is a venturer
(f) Key management personnel of the entity or its parent; and
(g) Other related parties.

Items of a similar nature may be **disclosed in aggregate** *unless* separate disclosure is necessary for an understanding of the effect on the financial statements.

Disclosures that related party transactions were made on terms equivalent to those that prevail in arm's length transactions are made only if such disclosures can be substantiated.

1.9 Section summary

IAS 24 is primarily concerned with **disclosure**. You should learn the following.

- **Definitions**: these are very important
- Relationships covered
- Relationships that **may not** necessarily be between related parties
- **Disclosures**: again, very important, representing the whole purpose of the standard

Question

Accounting issues

Fancy Feet Co is a UK company which supplies handmade leather shoes to a chain of high street shoe shops. The company is also the sole importer of some famous high quality Greek stoneware which is supplied to an upmarket shop in London's West End.

Fancy Feet Co was set up 30 years ago by Georgios Kostades who left Greece when he fell out with the military government. The company is owned and run by Mr Kostades and his three children.

The shoes are purchased from a French company, the shares of which are owned by the Kostades Family Trust (Monaco).

Required

Identify the financial accounting issues arising out of the above scenario.

Answer

Issues

(a) The basis on which Fancy Feet trades with the Greek supplier and the French company owned by the Kostades family trust.

(b) Whether the overseas companies trade on commercial terms with the UK company or do the foreign enterprises control the UK company.

(c) Who owns the Greek company: is this a related party under the provisions of IAS 24?

(d) Should the nature of trade suggest a related party controls Fancy Feet Co? Detailed disclosures will be required in the accounts.

2 IFRS 8 Operating segments

FAST FORWARD

An important aspect of reporting financial performance is **segment reporting**. This is covered by IFRS 8 *Operating segments,* which replaced IAS 14 *Segment reporting* in November 2006.

Exam focus point

This area was last tested in June 2009 with the requirement to apply the standard to a scenario and to discuss criticisms of treatment in IRFS 8.

2.1 Introduction

Large entities produce a wide range of products and services, often in several different countries. Further information on how the overall results of entities are made up from each of these product or geographical areas will help the users of the financial statements. This is the reason for **segment reporting**.

- The entity's **past performance** will be better understood
- The entity's **risks and returns** may be better assessed
- More **informed judgements** may be made about the entity as a whole

Risks and returns of a **diversified, multi-national company** can only be assessed by looking at the individual risks and rewards attached to groups of products or services or in different groups of products or services or in different geographical areas. These are subject to differing rates of profitability, opportunities for growth, future prospects and risks.

Segment reporting is covered by IFRS 8 *Operating segments*, which replaced IAS 14 *Segment reporting* in November 2006.

2.2 Objective

An entity must disclose information to enable users of its financial statements to evaluate the nature and financial effects of the business activities in which it engages and the economic environments in which it operates.

2.3 Scope

Only entities whose **equity or debt securities are publicly traded** (ie on a stock exchange) need disclose segment information. In group accounts, only **consolidated** segmental information needs to be shown. (The statement also applies to entities filing or in the process of filing financial statements for the purpose of issuing instruments.)

2.4 Definition of operating segment

FAST FORWARD

Reportable segments are **operating segments** or aggregation of operating segments that meet specified criteria.

You need to learn this definition, as it is crucial to the standard.

Key term

Operating segment: This is a component of an entity:

(a) That engages in business activities from which it may earn revenues and incur expenses (including revenues and expenses relating to transactions with other components of the same entity)

(b) Whose operating results are regularly reviewed by the entity's chief operating decision maker to make decisions about resources to be allocated to the segment and assess its performance, and

(c) For which discrete financial information is available.

IFRS 8

The term 'chief operating decision maker' identifies a function, not necessarily a manager with a specific title. That function is to allocate resources and to assess the performance of the entity's operating segments

2.5 Aggregation

Two or more operating segments may be **aggregated** if the segments have **similar economic characteristics**, and the segments are similar in *each* of the following respects:

- The **nature of the products or services**
- The **nature of the production process**
- The **type or class of customer for their products or services**
- The **methods used to distribute their products or provide their services**, and
- If applicable, the **nature of the regulatory environment**

2.6 Determining reportable segments

FAST FORWARD

IFRS 8 adopts a **management approach** to determining operating segments.

An entity must report separate information about **each operating segment** that:

(a) Has been identified as meeting the **definition of an operating segment**; and

(b) Segment total is **10% or more of total**:

    (i) **Revenue** (internal and external), or
    (ii) **Profit** of **all segments not reporting a loss** (or all segments in loss if greater), or
    (iii) **Assets**

At least **75% of the entity's total external revenue** must be reported by the operating segments identified. Where this is not the case, additional segments must be identified (even if they do not meet the 10% thresholds).

Two or more operating segments **below** the thresholds may be aggregated to produce a reportable segment if the segments have similar economic characteristics, and the segments are similar in a **majority** of the aggregation criteria above.

Operating segments that do not meet **any of the quantitative thresholds** may be reported separately if management believes that information about the segment would be useful to users of the financial statements.

2.6.1 Decision tree to assist in identifying reportable segments

FAST FORWARD

An operating segment is a component of an entity:

– That engages in business activities where it earns revenues and incurs expenses
– Whose results are regularly reviewed by the chief operating decision maker
– For which discrete, financial information is available

The following decision tree will assist in identifying reportable segments.

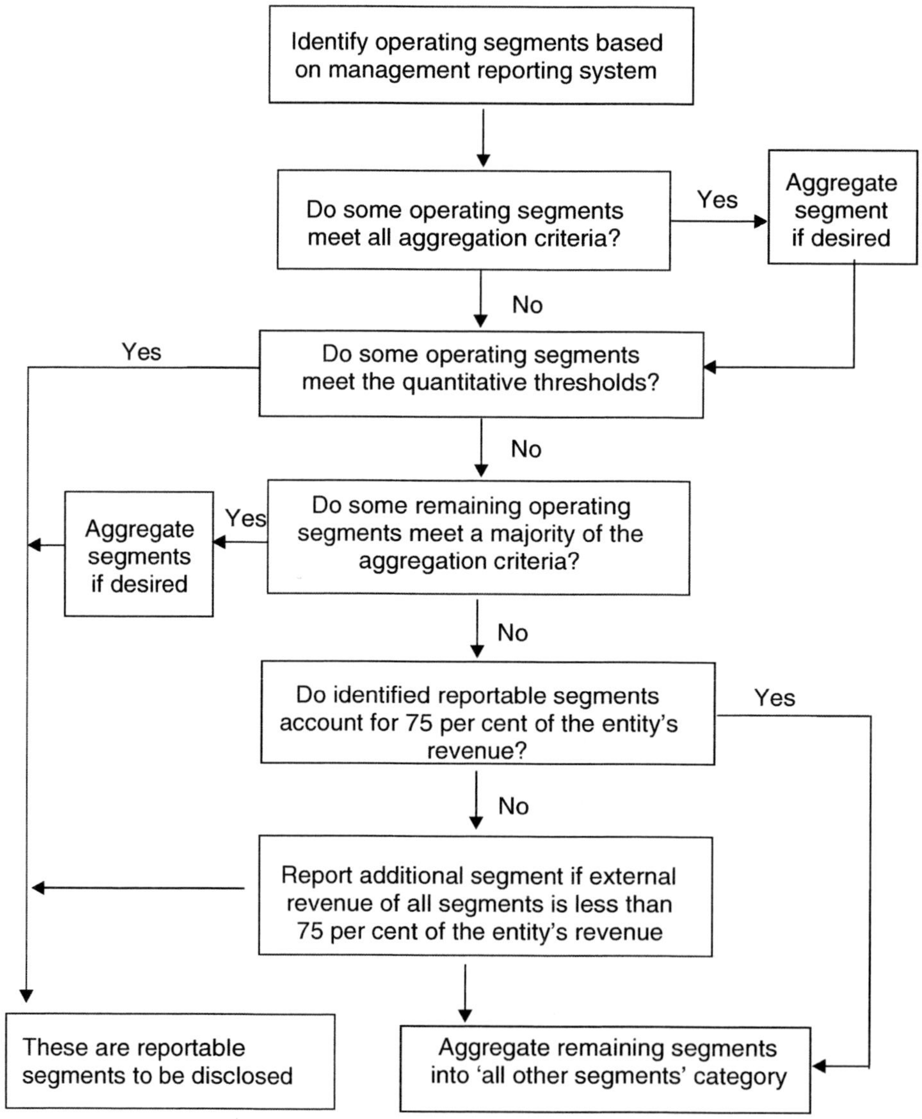

2.7 Disclosures

IFRS 8 disclosures are of:

- Operating segment profit or loss
- Segment assets
- Segment liabilities
- Certain income and expense items

Disclosures are also required about the revenues derived from products and services and about the countries in which revenues are earned or assets held, even if that information is not used by management in making decisions.

In April 2009 under the annual IFRS Improvements, IFRS 8 was amended to state that segment assets no longer have to be disclosed if they are not reported internally. This was effective from January 2010.

2.8 Key changes from IAS 14 *Segment reporting*

(a) IFRS 8 **converges with US GAAP** by adopting SFAS 131 Disclosures about segments of an enterprise and related information.

(b) The FASB managerial approach to identifying segments based on an internal organisation structure is used rather than the IAS 14 risk and returns approach.

(c) There is **no primary and secondary** (either business or geographical) **segment disclosure** hierarchy.

(d) There is no longer a requirement for more than 50% of revenue to be external for a segment to be reported separately.

(e) **Revenue, profit and assets** for reportable segment testing are **no longer defined**. The basis used depends on the information reported to the chief operating decision maker.

(f) The **level of compulsory segment disclosure** is **lower**, as only profit or loss and total assets are required figures. Other items are only disclosed if included in the figures reviewed by or regularly provided to the chief operating decision maker.

(g) The **scope of disclosure is widened** to include finance income, finance cost and income tax expense (if the specified amounts are included in the measure of segment profit or loss reviewed by the chief operating decision maker).

(h) New disclosures are required on **factors used to determine reportable segments** and types of products and services.

(i) **Geographical disclosures** are required on a **country by country** basis if material.

(j) There is no requirement to disclose capital expenditure on a geographical basis.

2.9 Advantages and disadvantages of the old and new segment definition approaches

	Advantages	**Disadvantages**
'Risks and Returns' approach (IAS 14)	• The information can be reconciled to the financial statements • It is a consistent method • The method helps to highlight the profitability, risks and returns of an identifiable segment	• Segment determination is the responsibility of directors and is subjective • Management may report segments which are not consistent for internal reporting and control purposes making its usefulness questionable
'Managerial' approach (IFRS 8)	• It is cost effective because the marginal cost of reporting segmental data will be low. • Users can be sure that the segment data reflects the operational strategy of the business	• The information may be commercially sensitive. • The segments may include operations with different risks and returns

2.10 Section summary

IFRS 8 is a **disclosure standard** which replaced IAS 14.

- **Segment reporting** is necessary for a better understanding and assessment of:
  - Past performance
  - Risks and returns
  - Informed judgements
- IFRS 8 adopts the **managerial approach** to identifying segments
- The standard gives guidance on how segments should be **identified** and **what information should be disclosed** for each

It also sets out **requirements for related disclosures** about products and services, geographical areas and major customers.

Chapter Roundup

- IAS 24 is primarily a **disclosure statement**. It is concerned to improve the quality of information provided by financial statements and also to strengthen their stewardship role.
- An important aspect of reporting financial performance is **segment reporting**. This is covered by IFRS 8 *Operating segments*, which replaced IAS 14 Segment reporting in November 2006.
- Reportable segments are **operating segments** or aggregation of operating segments that meet specified criteria.
- IFRS 8 adopts a **management approach** to determining operating segments.
- An operating segment is a component of an entity:
  - That engages in business activities where it earns revenues and incurs expenses
  - Whose results are regularly reviewed by the chief operating decision maker
  - For which discrete, financial information is available

Quick Quiz

1 What is a related party transaction?

2 Is a managing director of a company a related party?

3 Give two examples of situations in which a related party relationship does not necessarily exist.

4 What are the criteria to determine if an operating segment is reportable?

Answers to Quick Quiz

1 A transaction of resources, services or obligations between related parties, regardless of whether a price is charged.

2 True. A member of the key management personnel of an entity is a related party of that entity.

3 See Paragraph 1.3

4 See Paragraph 2.6

Now try the questions below from the Exam Question Bank

Number	Level	Marks	Time
Q24	Examination	25	45 mins

P A R T

D

Preparation of external financial reports for combined entities and joint ventures

Statement of cash flows

19

Topic list	Syllabus reference
1 IAS 7 Statements of cash flows	4(b)
2 Interpretation of statements of cash flows	4(b)

Introduction

The importance of the distinction between cash and profit and the scant attention paid to this by the income statement has resulted in the development of the statement of cash flows.

This chapter adopts a systematic approach to the preparation of cash flow statements in examinations; you should learn this method and you will then be equipped for any problems in the exam itself.

The third section of the chapter looks at the usefulness of the information which is provided by statements of cash flows and how this should be analysed.

Exam Guide

Statements of cash flows are specifically **excluded** from the Dip IFR syllabus from exams in 2011 onwards, and there are no syllabus references to them. However, IAS 7 *Statement of cash flows* is still an examinable document for the Dip IFR in 2011, so you could in principle be tested on it.

1 IAS 7 Statements of cash flows

FAST FORWARD

Statements of cash flows are a useful addition to the financial statements of companies because it is recognised that accounting profit is not the only indicator of a company's performance.

Exam focus point

Your examiner has stated that you are very unlikely to be asked to *prepare* a statement of cash flows in your exam. You should treat this chapter as background reading only. The focus of this part of your exam is highly likely to be on the other primary financial statements.

1.1 Introduction

It has been argued that 'profit' does not always give a useful or meaningful picture of a company's operations. Readers of a company's financial statements might even be **misled by a reported profit figure**.

(a) Shareholders might believe that if a company makes a profit after tax, of say, $100,000 then this is the amount which it could afford to **pay as a dividend**. Unless the company has **sufficient cash** available to stay in business and also to pay a dividend, the shareholders' expectations would be wrong.

(b) Employees might believe that if a company makes profits, it can afford to **pay higher wages** next year. This opinion may not be correct: the ability to pay wages depends on the **availability of cash**.

(c) Survival of a business entity depends not so much on profits as on its **ability to pay its debts when they fall due**. Such payments might include 'revenue' items such as material purchases, wages, interest and taxation etc, but also capital payments for new non-current assets and the repayment of loan capital when this falls due (for example on the redemption of debentures).

From these examples, it may be apparent that a company's performance and prospects depend not so much on the 'profits' earned in a period, but more realistically on liquidity or **cash flows**.

1.2 Funds flow and cash flow

FAST FORWARD

Statements of cash flows concentrate on the sources and uses of cash and are a useful indicator of a company's **liquidity and solvency**.

Some countries, either currently or in the past, have required the disclosure of additional statements based on **funds flow** rather than cash flow. However, the definition of 'funds' can be very vague and such statements often simply require a rearrangement of figures already provided in the statement of financial position and income statement. By contrast, a statement of cash flows is unambiguous and provides information which is additional to that provided in the rest of the accounts. It also lends itself to organisation by activity and not by classification in the statement of financial position.

Statements of cash flows are frequently given as an **additional statement**, supplementing the statement of financial position, statement of comprehensive income and related notes. The group aspects of statements of cash flows (and certain complex matters) have been excluded as they are beyond the scope of your syllabus.

1.3 Objective of IAS 7

The aim of IAS 7 is to provide information to users of financial statements about the entity's **ability to generate cash and cash equivalents**, as well as indicating the cash needs of the entity. The statement of cash flows provides *historical* information about cash and cash equivalents, classifying cash flows between operating, investing and financing activities.

1.4 Scope

A statement of cash flows should be presented as an **integral part** of an entity's financial statements. All types of entity can provide useful information about cash flows as the need for cash is universal, whatever the nature of their revenue-producing activities. Therefore **all entities are required by the standard to produce a statement of cash flows**.

1.5 Benefits of cash flow information

The use of statements of cash flows is very much **in conjunction** with the rest of the financial statements. Users can gain further appreciation of the change in net assets, of the entity's financial position (liquidity and solvency) and the entity's ability to adapt to changing circumstances by affecting the amount and timing of cash flows. Statements of cash flows **enhance comparability** as they are not affected by differing accounting policies used for the same type of transactions or events.

Cash flow information of a historical nature can be used as an indicator of the amount, timing and certainty of future cash flows. Past forecast cash flow information can be **checked for accuracy** as actual figures emerge. The relationship between profit and cash flows can be analysed as can changes in prices over time.

1.6 Definitions

The standard gives the following definitions, the most important of which are **cash** and **cash equivalents**.

Key terms

- **Cash** comprises cash on hand and demand deposits.
- **Cash equivalents** are short-term, highly liquid investments that are readily convertible to known amounts of cash and which are subject to an insignificant risk of changes in value.
- **Cash flows** are inflows and outflows of cash and cash equivalents.
- **Operating activities** are the principal revenue-producing activities of the entity and other activities that are not investing or financing activities.
- **Investing activities** are the acquisition and disposal of non-current assets and other investments not included in cash equivalents.
- **Financing activities** are activities that result in changes in the size and composition of the equity capital and borrowings of the entity. *(IAS 7)*

1.7 Cash and cash equivalents

The standard expands on the definition of cash equivalents: they are not held for investment or other long-term purposes, but rather to meet short-term cash commitments. To fulfil the above definition, an investment's **maturity date should normally be within three months from its acquisition date**. It would usually be the case then that equity investments (ie shares in other companies) are *not* cash equivalents. An exception would be where preferred shares were acquired with a very close maturity date.

Loans and other borrowings from banks are classified as investing activities. In some countries, however, **bank overdrafts** are repayable on demand and are treated as part of an entity's total cash management system. In these circumstances an overdrawn balance will be included in cash and cash equivalents. Such banking arrangements are characterised by a balance which fluctuates between overdrawn and credit.

Movements between different types of cash and cash equivalent are not included in cash flows. The investment of surplus cash in cash equivalents is part of cash management, not part of operating, investing or financing activities.

1.8 Presentation of a statement of cash flows

FAST FORWARD

You need to be aware of the **format** of the statement as laid out in **IAS 7**.

IAS 7 requires statements of cash flows to report cash flows during the period classified by **operating, investing and financing activities.**

1.9 Activities

The manner of presentation of cash flows between operating, investing and financing activities **depends on the nature of the entity**. By classifying cash flows between different activities in this way users can see the impact on cash and cash equivalents of each one, and their relationships with each other. We can look at each in more detail.

1.9.1 Operating activities

This is perhaps the key part of the statement of cash flows because it shows whether, and to what extent, companies can **generate cash from their operations**. It is these operating cash flows which must, in the end pay for all cash outflows relating to other activities, ie paying loan interest, dividends and so on.

Most of the components of cash flows from operating activities will be those items which **determine the net profit or loss of the entity**, ie they relate to the main revenue-producing activities of the entity. The standard gives the following as examples of cash flows from operating activities.

(a) Cash receipts from the sale of goods and the rendering of services
(b) Cash receipts from royalties, fees, commissions and other revenue
(c) Cash payments to suppliers for goods and services
(d) Cash payments to and on behalf of employees

Certain items may be included in the net profit or loss for the period which do *not* relate to operational cash flows, for example the profit or loss on the sale of a piece of plant will be included in net profit or loss, but the cash flows will be classed as **investing**.

1.9.2 Investing activities

The cash flows classified under this heading show the extent of new investment in **assets which will generate future profit and cash flows**. The standard gives the following examples of cash flows arising from investing activities.

(a) Cash payments to acquire property, plant and equipment, intangibles and other non-current assets, including those relating to capitalised development costs and self-constructed property, plant and equipment
(b) Cash receipts from sales of property, plant and equipment, intangibles and other non-current assets
(c) Cash payments to acquire shares or debentures of other entities
(d) Cash receipts from sales of shares or debentures of other entities
(e) Cash advances and loans made to other parties
(f) Cash receipts from the repayment of advances and loans made to other parties

1.9.3 Financing activities

This section of the statement of cash flows shows the share of cash which the entity's capital providers have claimed during the period. This is an indicator of **likely future interest and dividend payments**. The standard gives the following examples of cash flows which might arise under this heading.

(a) Cash proceeds from issuing shares
(b) Cash payments to owners to acquire or redeem the entity's shares
(c) Cash proceeds from issuing debentures, loans, notes, bonds, mortgages and other short or long-term borrowings
(d) Principal repayments of amounts borrowed under finance leases

Item (d) needs more explanation. Where the reporting entity uses an asset held under a finance lease, the amounts to go in the statement of cash flows as financing activities are repayments of the **principal (capital)** rather than the **interest**. The interest paid will be shown under operating activities.

1.10 Reporting cash flows from operating activities

The standard offers a choice of method for this part of the statement of cash flows.

(a) **Direct method:** disclose major classes of gross cash receipts and gross cash payments
(b) **Indirect method**: net profit or loss is adjusted for the effects of transactions of a non-cash nature, any deferrals or accruals of past or future operating cash receipts or payments, and items of income or expense associated with investing or financing cash flows

The **direct method is the preferred method** because it discloses information, not available elsewhere in the financial statements, which could be of use in estimating future cash flows. The example below shows both methods.

1.10.1 Using the direct method

There are different ways in which the **information about gross cash receipts and payments** can be obtained. The most obvious way is simply to extract the information from the accounting records. This may be a laborious task, however, and the indirect method below may be easier. The example and question above used the direct method.

1.10.2 Using the indirect method

This method is undoubtedly **easier** from the point of view of the preparer of the statement of cash flows. The net profit or loss for the period is adjusted for the following.

(a) Changes during the period in inventories, operating receivables and payables
(b) Non-cash items, eg depreciation, provisions, profits/losses on the sales of assets
(c) Other items, the cash flows from which should be classified under investing or financing activities.

A **proforma** of such a calculation, taken from the IAS, is as follows and this method may be more common in the exam. (The proforma has been amended to reflect changes to IFRS.)

	$
Cash flows from operating activities	
Profit before taxation	X
Adjustments for:	
Depreciation	X
Foreign exchange loss	X
Investment income	(X)
Interest expense	X
	X
Increase in trade and other receivables	(X)
Decrease in inventories	X
Decrease in trade payables	(X)
Cash generated from operations	X
Interest paid	(X)
Income taxes paid	(X)
Net cash from operating activities	X

It is important to understand why **certain items are added and others subtracted**. Note the following points.

(a) Depreciation is not a cash expense, but is deducted in arriving at profit. It makes sense, therefore, to eliminate it by adding it back.

(b) By the same logic, a loss on a disposal of a non-current asset (arising through underprovision of depreciation) needs to be added back and a profit deducted.

(c) An increase in inventories means less cash – you have spent cash on buying inventory.

(d) An increase in receivables means the company's debtors have not paid as much, and therefore there is less cash.

(e) If we pay off payables, causing the figure to decrease, again we have less cash.

1.10.3 Indirect versus direct

The direct method is encouraged where the necessary information is not too costly to obtain, but IAS 7 does not require it. In practice the indirect method is more commonly used, since it is quicker and easier.

1.11 Interest and dividends

Cash flows from interest and dividends received and paid should each be **disclosed separately**. Each should be classified in a consistent manner from period to period as either operating, investing or financing activities.

Dividends paid by the entity can be classified in **one of two ways**.

(a) As a **financing cash flow**, showing the cost of obtaining financial resources.

(b) As a component of **cash flows from operating activities** so that users can assess the entity's ability to pay dividends out of operating cash flows.

1.12 Taxes on income

Cash flows arising from taxes on income should be **separately disclosed** and should be classified as cash flows from operating activities *unless* they can be specifically identified with financing and investing activities.

Taxation cash flows are often **difficult to match** to the originating underlying transaction, so most of the time all tax cash flows are classified as arising from operating activities.

1.13 Components of cash and cash equivalents

The components of cash and cash equivalents should be disclosed and a **reconciliation** should be presented, showing the amounts in the statement of cash flows reconciled with the equivalent items reported in the statement of financial position.

It is also necessary to disclose the **accounting policy** used in deciding the items included in cash and cash equivalents, in accordance with IAS 1 *Presentation of Financial Statements*, but also because of the wide range of cash management practices worldwide.

1.14 Other disclosures

All entities should disclose, together with a **commentary by management**, any other information likely to be of importance, for example:

(a) Restrictions on the use of or access to any part of cash equivalents

(b) The amount of undrawn borrowing facilities which are available

(c) Cash flows which increased operating capacity compared to cash flows which merely maintained operating capacity

(d) Cash flows arising from each reported industry and geographical segment

1.15 Example of a statement of cash flows

1.15.1 Direct method

STATEMENT OF CASH FLOWS
YEAR ENDED 31 DECEMBER 20X7

	$m	$m
Cash flows from operating activities		
Cash receipts from customers	30,330	
Cash paid to suppliers and employees	(27,600)	
Cash generated from operations	2,730	
Interest paid	(270)	
Income taxes paid	(900)	
Net cash from operating activities		1,560
Cash flows from investing activities		
Purchase of property, plant and equipment	(900)	
Proceeds from sale of equipment	20	
Interest received	200	
Dividends received	200	
Net cash used in investing activities		(480)
Cash flows from financing activities		
Proceeds from issue of share capital	250	
Proceeds from long-term borrowings	250	
Dividends paid*	(1,290)	
Net cash used in financing activities		(790)
Net increase in cash and cash equivalents		290
Cash and cash equivalents at beginning of period (Note)		120
Cash and cash equivalents at end of period (Note)		410

* This could also be shown as an operating cash flow

1.15.2 Indirect method

Net cash from operating activities can also be calculated using the indirect method.

STATEMENT OF CASH FLOWS (INDIRECT METHOD)
YEAR ENDED 31 DECEMBER 20X7

	$m	$m
Cash flows from operating activities		
Profit before taxation	3,570	
Adjustments for:		
Depreciation	450	
Investment income	(500)	
Interest expense	400	
	3,920	
Increase in trade and other receivables	(500)	
Decrease in inventories	1,050	
Decrease in trade payables	(1,740)	
Cash generated from operations	2,730	
Interest paid	(270)	
Income taxes paid	(900)	
Net cash from operating activities		1,560
Cash flows from investing activities		
Purchase of property, plant and equipment	(900)	

Proceeds from sale of equipment	20	
Interest received	200	
Dividends received	200	
Net cash used in investing activities		(480)
Cash flows from financing activities		
Proceeds from issue of share capital	250	
Proceeds from long-term borrowings	250	
Dividends paid*	(1,290)	
Net cash used in financing activities		(790)
Net increase in cash and cash equivalents		290
Cash and cash equivalents at beginning of period		120
Cash and cash equivalents at end of period		410

* This could also be shown as an operating cash flow

2 Interpretation of statements of cash flows

FAST FORWARD

IAS 7 *Statement of cash flows* was introduced on the basis that it would provide better, more comprehensive and more useful information than what was already shown in the financial statements.

2.1 Introduction

So what kind of information does the statement of cash flows, along with its notes, provide?

Some of the main areas where IAS 7 should provide information not found elsewhere in the financial statements are as follows.

(a) The **relationships between profit and cash** can be seen clearly and analysed accordingly.
(b) **Cash equivalents** are highlighted, giving a better picture of the liquidity of the company.
(c) **Financing inflows and outflows must be shown, rather than simply passed through reserves**.

One of the most important things to realise at this point is that it is wrong to try to assess the health or predict the death of a reporting entity solely on the basis of a single indicator. When analysing cash flow data, the **comparison should not just be between cash flows and profit, but also between cash flows over a period of time** (say three to five years).

Cash is not synonymous with profit on an annual basis, but you should also remember that the 'behaviour' of profit and cash flows will be very different. **Profit is smoothed out** through accruals, prepayments, provisions and other accounting conventions. This does not apply to cash, so the **cash flow figures** are likely to be **'lumpy'** in comparison. You must distinguish between this 'lumpiness' and the trends which will appear over time.

The **relationship between profit and cash flows will vary constantly**. Healthy companies do not always have reported profits exceeding operating cash flows. Similarly, unhealthy companies can have operating cash flows well in excess of reported profit. The value of comparing them is in determining the extent to which earned profits are being converted into the necessary cash flows.

Profit is not as important as the extent to which a company can **convert its profits into cash on a continuing basis.** This process should be judged over a period longer than one year. The cash flows should be compared with profits over the same periods to decide how successfully the reporting entity has converted earnings into cash.

Cash flow figures should also be considered in terms of their specific relationships with each other over time. A form of **'cash flow gearing'** can be determined by comparing operating cash flows and financing flows, particularly borrowing, to establish the extent of dependence of the reporting entity on external funding.

Other relationships can be examined.

(a) Operating cash flows and investment flows can be related to match cash recovery from investment to investment.

(b) Investment can be compared to distribution to indicate the proportion of total cash outflow designated specifically to investor return and reinvestment.

(c) A comparison of tax outflow to operating cash flow minus investment flow will establish a 'cash basis tax rate'.

The 'ratios' mentioned above can be monitored **inter– and intra-firm** and the analyses can be undertaken in monetary, general price-level adjusted, or percentage terms.

2.2 The advantages of cash flow accounting

The advantages of cash flow accounting are as follows.

(a) Survival in business depends on the **ability to generate** cash. Cash flow accounting directs attention towards this critical issue.

(b) Cash flow is **more comprehensive** than 'profit' which is dependent on accounting conventions and concepts.

(c) **Creditors** (long and short-term) are more interested in an entity's ability to repay them than in its profitability. Whereas 'profits' might indicate that cash is likely to be available, cash flow accounting is more direct with its message.

(d) Cash flow reporting provides a better means of **comparing the results** of different companies than traditional profit reporting.

(e) Cash flow reporting **satisfies the needs of all users** better.

    (i) For **management**, it provides the sort of information on which decisions should be taken (in management accounting, 'relevant costs' to a decision are future cash flows); traditional profit accounting does not help with decision-making.

    (ii) For **shareholders and auditors**, cash flow accounting can provide a satisfactory basis for stewardship accounting.

    (iii) As described previously, the information needs of **creditors and employees** will be better served by cash flow accounting.

(f) Cash flow forecasts are **easier to prepare**, as well as more useful, than profit forecasts.

(g) They can in some respects be **audited more easily** than accounts based on the accruals concept.

(h) The accruals concept is confusing, and cash flows are **more easily understood**.

(i) Cash flow accounting should be both retrospective, and also include a forecast for the future. This is of **great information value** to all users of accounting information.

(j) **Forecasts** can subsequently be **monitored** by the publication of variance statements which compare actual cash flows against the forecast.

Question — Disadvantages

Can you think of some possible disadvantages of cash flow accounting?

Answer

The main disadvantages of cash accounting are essentially the advantages of accruals accounting (proper matching of related items). There is also the practical problem that few businesses keep historical cash flow information in the form needed to prepare a historical statement of cash flows and so extra record keeping is likely to be necessary.

2.3 Criticisms of IAS 7

The inclusion of **cash equivalents** has been criticised because it does not reflect the way in which businesses are managed: in particular, the requirement that to be a cash equivalent an investment has to be within three months of maturity is considered **unrealistic**.

The management of assets similar to cash (ie 'cash equivalents') is not distinguished from other investment decisions.

Chapter roundup

- **Statements of cash flows** are a useful addition to the financial statements of companies because it is recognised that accounting profit is not the only indicator of a company's performance.
- Statements of cash flows concentrate on the sources and uses of cash and are a useful indicator of a company's **liquidity and solvency**.
- You need to be aware of the **format** of the statement as laid out in **IAS 7**.
- IAS 7 *Statement of cash flows* was introduced on the basis that it would provide better, more comprehensive and more useful information than what was already shown in the financial statements.

Quick quiz

1 What is the aim of a statement of cash flows?

2 The standard headings in IAS 7 *Statement of cash flows* are:
- O................. a................
- I.................. a...................
- F.................. a.....................
- Net.................. in C..................... and ....

3 Cash equivalents are current asset investments which will mature or can be redeemed within three months of the year end.

True ☐ False ☐

4 Why are you more likely to encounter the indirect method as opposed to the direct method?

5 List five advantages of cash flow accounting.

Answers to quick quiz

1 To indicate an entity's ability to generate cash and cash equivalents.

2
- Operating activities
- Investing activities
- Financing activities
- Net increase (decrease) in cash and cash equivalents

3 False. See the definition in paragraph 1.6 if you are not sure about this.

4 The indirect method utilises figures which appear in the financial statements. The figures required for the direct method may not be readily available.

5 See paragraph 2.2

20

Constitution of a group

Topic list	Syllabus reference
1 Group accounts	4(a)-(b)
2 IAS 27 Consolidated and separate financial statements	4(a)-(b)
3 Content of group accounts and group structure	4(a)-(b)
4 Group accounts: the related party issue	4(a)-(b)

Introduction

Consolidation is an extremely important area of your Diploma in International Financial Reporting syllabus as you are almost certain to face a large consolidation question in the first question of the paper.

The key to consolidation questions in the examination is to adopt a logical approach and to practise as many questions as possible.

In this chapter we will look at the major definitions in consolidation and the relevant accounting standards. These matters are fundamental to your comprehension of group accounts, so make sure you can understand them and then **learn them**.

Study Guide

Section 21 – Preparation of group consolidated external reports

- Explain the concept of a group and the purpose of preparing consolidated financial statements
- Explain and apply the definition of subsidiary companies
- Identify the circumstances and reasoning when subsidiaries should be excluded from consolidated financial statements
- Explain the need for using coterminous year-ends and uniform accounting policies and preparing consolidated financial statements and describe how it is achieved in practice

Exam Guide

The preparation of group consolidated accounts is in question 1, and will contain a number of financial reporting issues in addition to the consolidation itself. This may be accompanied by a discursive part on related issues.

1 Group accounts

FAST FORWARD

Many large businesses consist of several companies controlled by one central or administrative company. Together these companies are called a **group**. The controlling company, called the **parent** or **holding company**, will own some or all of the shares in the other companies, called **subsidiaries**.

1.1 Introduction

There are many reasons for businesses to operate as groups; for the goodwill associated with the names of the subsidiaries, for tax or legal purposes and so forth. In many countries, company law requires that the results of a group should be presented as a whole. Unfortunately, it is not possible simply to add all the results together and this chapter and those following will teach you how to **consolidate** all the results of companies within a group.

In traditional accounting terminology, a **group of companies** consists of a **parent company** and one or more **subsidiary companies** which are controlled by the parent company.

1.2 Accounting standards

We will be looking at three accounting standards in this and the next three chapters.

- IAS 27 *Consolidated and separate financial statements*
- IFRS 3 *Business combinations*
- IAS 28 *Investments in associates*

These standards are all concerned with different aspects of group accounts, but there is some overlap between them, particularly between IFRS 3 and IAS 27.

In this and the next chapter we will concentrate on IAS 27, which covers the basic group definitions and consolidation procedures of a parent-subsidiary relationship. First of all, however, we will look at all the important definitions involved in group accounts, which **determine how to treat each particular type of investment** in group accounts.

1.3 Definitions

We will look at some of these definitions in more detail later, but they are useful here in that they give you an overview of all aspects of group accounts.

Exam focus point

All the definitions relating to group accounts are extremely important. You must **learn them** and **understand** their meaning and application.

Key terms

- **Control**. The power to govern the financial and operating policies of an entity so as to obtain benefits from its activities. *(IFRS 3, IASs 27, 28)*
- **Subsidiary**. An entity that is controlled by another entity (known as the parent). *(IFRS 3, IASs 27, 28)*
- **Parent**. An entity that has one or more subsidiaries. *(IFRS 3, IAS 27)*
- **Group**. A parent and all its subsidiaries. *(IAS 27)*
- **Associate**. An entity, including an unincorporated entity such as a partnership, in which an investor has significant influence and which is neither a subsidiary nor a joint venture of the investor. *(IAS 28)*
- **Significant influence** is the power to participate in the financial and operating policy decisions of an investee or an economic activity but is not control or joint control over those policies. *(IAS 28)*

We can summarise the different types of investment *and* the required accounting for them as follows.

Investment	Criteria	Required treatment in group accounts
Subsidiary	Control	Full consolidation
Associate	Significant influence	Equity accounting
Investment which is none of the above	Asset held for accretion of wealth	As for single company accounts per IAS 39

1.4 Investments in subsidiaries

The important point here is **control**. In most cases, this will involve the holding company or parent owning a majority of the ordinary shares in the subsidiary (to which normal voting rights are attached). There are circumstances, however, when the parent may own only a minority of the voting power in the subsidiary, *but* the parent still has control.

IAS 27 states that control can usually be assumed to exist when the parent **owns more than half (ie over 50%) of the voting power** of an entity *unless* it can be clearly shown that **such ownership does not constitute control** (these situations will be very rare).

What about situations where this ownership criterion does not exist? IAS 27 lists the following situations where control exists, even when the parent owns only 50% or less of the voting power of an entity.

(a) The parent has power over more than 50% of the voting rights by virtue of **agreement with other investors**

(b) The parent has power to **govern the financial and operating policies** of the entity by statute or under an agreement

(c) The parent has the power to **appoint or remove a majority of members of the board of directors** (or equivalent governing body)

(d) The parent has power to cast a **majority of votes at meetings of the board of directors**

IAS 27 also states that a parent loses control when it loses the power to govern the financial and operating policies of an investee. Loss of control can occur without a change in ownership levels. This may happen if a subsidiary becomes subject to the control of a government, court administrator or regulator (for example, in bankruptcy).

Exam focus point

You should learn the contents of the above paragraph as you may be asked to apply them in the exam.

1.4.1 Accounting treatment in group accounts

IAS 27 requires a parent to present consolidated financial statements, in which the accounts of the parent and subsidiary (or subsidiaries) are combined and presented **as a single entity**.

1.5 Investments in associates

This type of investment is something less than a subsidiary, but more than a simple investment. The key criterion here is **significant influence**. This is defined as the 'power to participate', but *not* to 'control' (which would make the investment a subsidiary).

Significant influence can be determined by the holding of voting rights (usually attached to shares) in the entity. IAS 28 states that if an investor holds **20% or more** of the voting power of the investee, it can be presumed that the investor has significant influence over the investee, *unless* it can be clearly shown that this is not the case.

Significant influence can be presumed *not* to exist if the investor holds **less than 20%** of the voting power of the investee, unless it can be demonstrated otherwise.

The **existence of significant influence** is evidenced in one or more of the following ways.

(a) Representation on the **board of directors** (or equivalent) of the investee
(b) Participation in the **policy making process**
(c) **Material transactions** between investor and investee
(d) Interchange of management personnel
(e) Provision of essential technical information

1.5.1 Accounting treatment in group accounts

IAS 28 requires the use of the **equity method** of accounting for investments in associates. This method will be explained in detail in Chapter 23.

Question — **Treatments**

The section summary after this question will give an augmented version of the table given in Paragraph 1.3 above. Before you look at it, see if you can write out the table yourself.

1.6 Section summary

Investment	Criteria	Required treatment in group accounts
Subsidiary	Control (> 50% rule)	Full consolidation (IAS 27)
Associate	Significant influence (20%+ rule)	Equity accounting (IAS 28)
Investment which is none of the above	Asset held for accretion of wealth	As for single company accounts (IAS 39)

2 IAS 27 Consolidated and separate financial statements

FAST FORWARD

IAS 27 requires a parent to present **consolidated** financial statements.

2.1 Introduction

Key term

> **Consolidated financial statements**. The financial statements of a group presented as those of a single economic entity. *(IAS 27)*

When a parent issues consolidated financial statements, it should consolidate **all subsidiaries**, both foreign and domestic.

2.2 Exemption from preparing group accounts

A parent **need not present** consolidated financial statements if and only if **all** of the following hold:

(a) The parent is itself a **wholly-owned subsidiary** or it is a **partially owned subsidiary** of another entity and its other owners, including those not otherwise entitled to vote, have been informed about, and do not object to, the parent not presenting consolidated financial statements

(b) Its securities are **not publicly traded**

(c) It is **not in the process of issuing securities** in public securities markets; and

(d) The **ultimate or intermediate parent** publishes consolidated financial statements that comply with International Financial Reporting Standards

A parent that does not present consolidated financial statements must comply with the IAS 27 rules on separate financial statements (discussed later in this section).

2.3 Potential voting rights

An entity may own share warrants, share call options, or other similar instruments that are **convertible into ordinary shares** in another entity. If these are exercised or converted they may give the entity voting power or reduce another party's voting power over the financial and operating policies of the other entity (potential voting rights). The **existence and effect** of potential voting rights, including potential voting rights held by another entity, should be considered when assessing whether an entity has control over another entity (and therefore has a subsidiary).

In assessing whether potential voting rights give rise to control, the entity examines all facts and circumstances that affect the rights (for example, terms and conditions), except the intention of management and the financial ability to exercise the rights or convert them into equity shares.

2.4 Exclusion of a subsidiary from consolidation

It has been argued in the past that subsidiaries should be excluded from consolidation on the grounds of **dissimilar activities**, ie the activities of the subsidiary are so different to the activities of the other companies within the group that to include its results in the consolidation would be misleading. IAS 27 rejects this argument: exclusion on these grounds is not justified because better (relevant) information can be provided about such subsidiaries by consolidating their results and then giving additional information about the different business activities of the subsidiary.

The previous version of IAS 27 permitted exclusion where the subsidiary operates under **severe long-term restrictions** and these significantly impair its ability to transfer funds to the parent. This exclusion has been **removed**. Control must actually be lost for exclusion to occur.

2.5 Different reporting dates

In most cases, all group companies will prepare accounts to the same reporting date. One or more subsidiaries may, however, prepare accounts to a different reporting date from the parent and the bulk of other subsidiaries in the group.

In such cases the subsidiary may prepare additional statements to the reporting date of the rest of the group, for consolidation purposes. If this is not possible, the subsidiary's accounts may still be used for the consolidation, *provided that* the gap between the reporting dates is **three months or less**.

Where a subsidiary's accounts are drawn up to a different accounting date, **adjustments should be made** for the effects of significant transactions or other events that occur between that date and the parent's reporting date.

2.6 Uniform accounting policies

Consolidated financial statements should be prepared using **the same accounting policies** for like transactions and other events in similar circumstances.

Adjustments must be made where members of a group use different accounting policies, so that their financial statements are suitable for consolidation.

2.7 Date of inclusion/exclusion

The results of subsidiary undertakings are included in the consolidated financial statements from:

(a) the date of 'acquisition', ie the **date control passes to the parent**, to
(b) the date of 'disposal', ie the **date control passes from the parent**.

Once an investment is no longer a subsidiary, it should be treated as an associate under IAS 28 (if applicable) or as an investment under IAS 39 (see Chapter 10).

2.8 Accounting for subsidiaries and associates in the parent's separate financial statements

A parent company will usually produce its own single company financial statements. In these statements, investments in subsidiaries and associates included in the consolidated financial statements should be *either*:

(a) Accounted for at **cost**, *or*
(b) In accordance with **IAS 39** (see Chapter 10).

Where subsidiaries are **classified as held for sale** in accordance with IFRS 5 they should be accounted for in accordance with IFRS 5 (see Chapter 16).

2.9 Disclosure

The disclosure requirements for **consolidated financial statements** are as follows.

(a) **Summarised financial information** of **subsidiaries** that are **not consolidated**, either individually or in groups, including the amounts of total assets, total liabilities, revenues and profit or loss
(b) The nature of the **relationship** between the parent and a **subsidiary** of which the **parent** does **not own**, directly or indirectly through subsidiaries, **more than half of the voting power**
(c) For an investee of which more than half of the voting or potential voting power is owned, directly or indirectly through subsidiaries, but which, because of the absence of control, is not a subsidiary, the reasons **why** the **ownership** does **not constitute control**
(d) The reporting date of the financial statements of a subsidiary when such financial statements are used to prepare consolidated financial statements and are as of a reporting date or for a period that is different from that of the parent, and the **reason** for using a **different reporting date or different period**
(e) The nature and extent of any **restrictions** on the ability of subsidiaries to **transfer funds** to the parent in the form of cash dividends, repayment of loans or advances (ie borrowing arrangements, regulatory restraints etc)

Where a parent chooses to take advantage of the exemptions from preparing consolidated financial statements (see above) the **separate financial statements** must disclose:

(a) The fact that the financial statements are separate financial statements; that the exemption from consolidation has been used; the name and country of incorporation of the entity whose consolidated financial statements that comply with IFRSs have been published; and the address where those consolidated financial statements are obtainable

(b) A list of significant investments in subsidiaries, jointly controlled entities and associates, including the name, country of incorporation, proportion of ownership interest and, if different, proportion of voting power held

(c) A description of the method used to account for the investments listed under (b)

When a parent prepares separate financial statements in addition to consolidated financial statements, the separate financial statements must disclose:

(a) The fact that the statements are separate financial statements and the reasons why they have been prepared if not required by law

(b) Information about investments and the method used to account for them, as above.

2.10 Section summary

IAS 27 covers the basic rules and definitions of the parent-subsidiary relationship. You should learn:

- **Definitions**
- Rules for **exemption** from preparing consolidated financial statements
- **Disclosure**

3 Content of group accounts and group structure

FAST FORWARD

It is important to distinguish between the parent company **individual accounts** and the **group accounts**.

3.1 Introduction

The information contained in the individual statements of a parent company and each of its subsidiaries does not give a picture of the group's total activities. A **separate set of group statements** can be prepared from the individual ones. Remember that a group has no separate (legal) existence, except for accounting purposes.

Consolidated accounts are one form of group accounts which combines the information contained in the separate accounts of a holding company and its subsidiaries as if they were the accounts of a single entity. 'Group accounts' and 'consolidated accounts' are terms often used synonymously.

In simple terms a set of consolidated accounts is prepared by **adding together** the assets and liabilities of the parent company and each subsidiary. The **whole** of the assets and liabilities of each company are included, even though some subsidiaries may be only partly owned. The 'equity and liabilities' section of the statement of financial position will indicate how much of the net assets are attributable to the group and how much to outside investors in partly owned subsidiaries. These **outside investors** are known as the **non-controlling interest**.

Key term

Non-controlling interest. The equity in a subsidiary not attributable, directly or indirectly, to a parent. *(IFRS 3, IAS 27)*

Non-controlling interest should be presented in the consolidated statement of financial position **within equity, separately from the parent shareholders' equity**.

Most parent companies present their own individual accounts and their group accounts in a single **package**. The package typically comprises the following.

- **Parent company financial statements**, which will include 'investments in subsidiary undertakings' as an asset in the statement of financial position, and income from subsidiaries (dividends) in the statement of comprehensive income
- **Consolidated statement of financial position**

- **Consolidated statement of comprehensive income** (or separate income statement)
- **Consolidated statement of cash flows**

It may not be necessary to publish all of the parent company's financial statements, depending on local or national regulations.

3.2 Group structure

With the difficulties of definition and disclosure dealt with, let us now look at group structures. The simplest are those in which a parent company has only a **direct interest** in the shares of its subsidiary companies. For example:

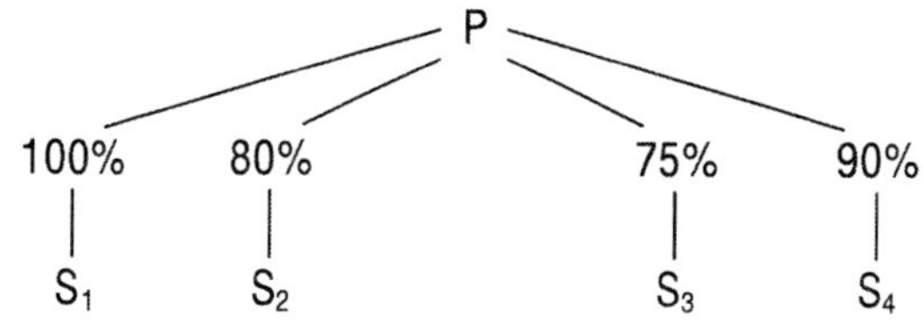

S_1 Co is a wholly owned subsidiary of P Co. S_2 Co, S_3 Co and S_4 Co are partly owned subsidiaries; a proportion of the shares in these companies is held by outside investors.

Often a parent will have **indirect holdings** in its subsidiary companies. This can lead to more complex group structures.

(a)

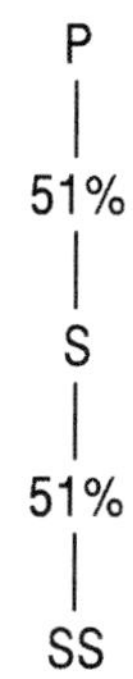

P Co owns 51% of the equity shares in S Co, which is therefore its subsidiary. S Co in its turn owns 51% of the equity shares in SS Co. SS Co is therefore a subsidiary of S Co and consequently a subsidiary of P Co. SS Co would describe S Co as its parent (or holding) company and P Co as its ultimate parent company.

Note that although P Co can control the assets and business of SS Co by virtue of the chain of control, its interest in the assets of SS Co is only 26%. This can be seen by considering a dividend of $100 paid by SS Co: as a 51% shareholder, S Co would receive $51; P Co would have an interest in 51% of this $51 = $26.01.

(b)

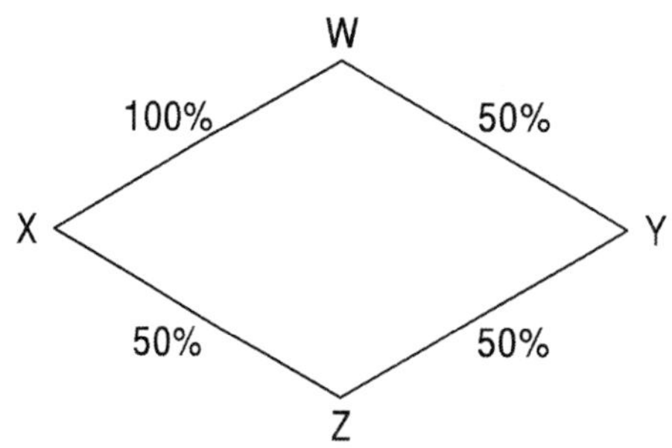

W Co owns 100% of the equity of X Co and 50% of the equity of Y Co. X Co and Y Co each own 50% of the equity of Z Co. Assume that:

(i) W Co does not control the composition of Y Co's board, nor can it cast a majority of votes on the board

(ii) W Co does not hold or control more than 50% of the **voting rights** in Y Co, either directly or by agreement with other investors

(iii) W Co does not have the power to govern the financial or operating policies of Y Co by virtue of statute or an agreement

(iv) None of the above apply to either X Co's or Y Co's holdings in Z Co

In other words, because W Co is not in co-operation with the holder(s) of the other 50% of the shares in Y Co, neither Y nor Z can be considered subsidiaries.

In that case:

(i) X Co is a subsidiary of W Co
(ii) Y Co is not a subsidiary of W Co
(iii) Z Co is not a subsidiary of either X Co or Y Co. Consequently, it is not a subsidiary of W Co

If Z Co pays a dividend of $100, X Co and Y Co will each receive $50. The interest of W Co in this dividend is as follows.

	$
Through X Co (100% × $50)	50
Through Y Co (50% × $50)	25
	75

Although W Co has an interest in 75% of Z Co's assets, Z Co is not a subsidiary of W Co.

(c)

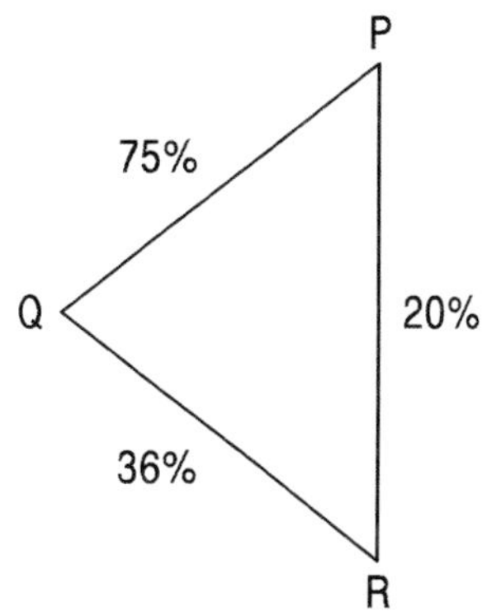

Q Co is a subsidiary of P Co. P Co therefore has indirect control over 36% of R Co's equity. P Co also has direct control over 20% of R Co's equity. R Co is therefore a subsidiary of P Co, although P Co's interest in R Co's assets is only 20% + (75% × 36%) = 47%.

Examples (b) and (c) illustrate an important point: in deciding whether a company A holds more than 50% of the equity (or equivalent) of an entity B it is necessary to aggregate:

- Shares (or equivalent) in B held directly by A
- Shares (or equivalent) in B held by entities which are subsidiaries of A

Question — Consolidated accounts

During the time until your examination you should obtain as many sets of the published accounts of large companies in your country as possible. Examine the accounting policies in relation to subsidiary and associated companies and consider how these policies are shown in the accounting and consolidation treatment. Consider the effect of any disposals during the year. Also, look at all the disclosures made relating to fair values, goodwill etc and match them to the disclosure requirements outlined in this chapter and in subsequent chapters on IFRS 3 and IAS 28.

Alternatively (or additionally) you should attempt to obtain such information from the financial press.

4 Group accounts: the related parties issue

FAST FORWARD

Parent companies and subsidiaries are **related parties** as per IAS 24. Bear in mind that this relationship can be exploited.

IAS 24 draws attention to the significance of related party relationships and transactions – that transactions between the parties may not be 'at arm's length' and that users of the accounts must be made aware of this, as it may affect their view of the financial statements.

4.1 Individual company accounts

The relationship between a parent and a subsidiary is the most obvious example of a related party relationship and it offers a number of opportunities for manipulating results. Some of these may be aimed at improving the parent's individual financial statements.

Any of the following could take place:

- The subsidiary sells goods to the parent company at an artificially low price. This increases parent company profit while reducing profit in the subsidiary, thus increasing profit available for distribution to parent company shareholders at the expense of the non-controlling interest.
- The parent sells goods to the subsidiary at an artificially high price. This has the same result as above.
- The subsidiary makes a loan to the parent at an artificially low rate of interest or the parent makes a loan to the subsidiary at an artificially high rate of interest. The loans will be cancelled on consolidation but the interest payments will transfer profits from the subsidiary to the parent.
- The parent can sell an asset to the subsidiary at an amount in excess of its carrying amount. This again serves to transfer profit (and cash) to the parent.

4.2 Consolidated accounts

The transactions above seek to improve the **individual** parent company accounts at the expense of the individual subsidiary accounts. Dividends are paid to shareholders on the basis of these individual company financial statements, not the consolidated financial statements.

The tightening up of the opportunities for excluding a subsidiary from consolidation under IAS 27 have reduced the opportunities for improving the appearance of the **consolidated** financial statements. Prior to this, a number of possibilities could be exploited:

- A group could obtain loans via a subsidiary, which was not then consolidated. The loan would not appear in the consolidated statement of financial position and group gearing (% of capital provided by loans) would appear lower than it actually was.
- Sale and leaseback transactions could be carried out in which assets were sold to a non-consolidated subsidiary and leased back under an operating lease. This enabled the asset and its associated borrowings to be removed from the statement of financial position.

4.3 Disposal of subsidiaries

While the situations above are all concerned with improving the appearance of the parent company or group financial statements at the expense of those of the subsidiary, there may be occasions where the **opposite** is the intention.

For instance, when a parent company has decided to dispose of its shares in a poorly-performing subsidiary, it may seek to enhance the results of that subsidiary for the purpose of selling at a profit. In this case, transactions such as those at 4.1 above may be undertaken in the other direction – to transfer profit from the **parent** to the **subsidiary**.

4.4 Effect on trading

Even where no related party transactions have taken place, the parent/subsidiary relationship can still affect how the parties do business. For instance if, prior to acquisition by the parent, the subsidiary had a major customer or supplier who was a competitor of the parent, that trading arrangement can be expected to cease. The subsidiary may itself have been a competitor of the parent, in which case it may now have had to withdraw from certain markets in favour of the parent.

Look out for any of these issues in a consolidated accounts question.

Chapter Roundup

- Many large businesses consist of several companies controlled by one central or administrative company. Together these companies are called a **group**. The controlling company, called the **parent** or **holding company** will own some or all of the shares in the other companies, called **subsidiaries**.
- IAS 27 requires a parent to present **consolidated** financial statements.
- It is important to distinguish between the parent company **individual accounts** and the **group accounts.**
- Parent companies and subsidiaries are **related parties** as per IAS 24. Bear in mind that this relationship can be exploited.

Quick Quiz

1 Define a 'subsidiary'.

2 When can control be assumed?

3 What accounting treatment does IAS 27 require of a parent company?

4 When is a parent exempted from preparing consolidated financial statements?

5 Under what circumstances should subsidiary undertakings be excluded from consolidation?

6 How should an investment in a subsidiary be accounted for in the separate financial statements of the parent?

7 What is a non-controlling interest?

Answers to Quick Quiz

1 An entity that is controlled by another entity.

2 When the parent owns more than half (ie over 50%) of the voting power of an entity, unless it can be clearly shown that such ownership does not constitute control.

3 The accounts of parent and subsidiary are combined and presented as a single entity.

4 When the parent is itself a wholly owned subsidiary, or a partially owned subsidiary and the non-controlling interests do not object.

5 There are no circumstances under which a subsidiary can be excluded from consolidation. See section 2.4.

6 (a) At cost, or
(b) In accordance with IAS 39.

7 The equity in a subsidiary not attributable, directly or indirectly, to a parent.

Now try the question below from the Exam Question Bank

Number	Level	Marks	Time
Q25	Introductory	n/a	n/a

21 The consolidated statement of financial position

Topic list		Syllabus reference
1	IAS 27 Summary of consolidation procedures	4(a), (b)
2	Non-controlling interests	4(a), (b)
3	Dividends paid by a subsidiary	4(a), (b)
4	Goodwill arising on consolidation	4(a), (b)
5	A technique of consolidation	4(a), (b)
6	Intra-group trading	4(a), (b)
7	Intra-group sales of non-current assets	4(a), (b)
8	Summary: consolidated statement of financial position	4(a), (b)
9	Acquisition of a subsidiary during its accounting period	4(a)-(d)
10	Fair values in acquisition accounting	4(a)-(d)

Introduction

This chapter introduces the **basic procedures** required in consolidation and gives a formal step plan for carrying out a statement of financial position consolidation. This step procedure should be useful to you as a starting guide for answering any question, but remember that you cannot rely on it to answer the question for you.

Each question must be approached and **answered on its own merits**. Examiners often put small extra or different problems in because, as they are always reminding students, it is not possible to 'rote-learn' consolidation.

The **method of consolidation** shown here uses schedules for workings (retained earnings, non-controlling interest etc) rather than the ledger accounts used in some other texts. This is because we believe that ledger accounts lead students to 'learn' the consolidation journals without thinking about what they are doing - always a dangerous practice in consolidation questions.

There are plenty of questions in this chapter - work through *all* of them carefully.

Study Guide

Section 21 – Preparation of group consolidated external reports

- Prepare a consolidated statement of financial position for a simple group dealing with pre and post acquisition profits, non-controlling interests and goodwill

Section 22 – Business combinations – intra-group adjustments

- Explain why intra-group transactions should be eliminated on consolidation
- Report the effects of intra-group trading and other transactions including:
  - Unrealised profits in inventory and non-current assets
  - Intra-group loans and interest and other intra-group charges
  - Intra-group dividends

Section 23 – Business combinations – fair value adjustments

- Explain why it is necessary for both the consideration paid for a subsidiary and the subsidiary's identifiable assets and liabilities to be accounted for at their fair values when preparing consolidated financial statements
- Prepare consolidated financial statements dealing with fair value adjustments (including their effect on consolidated goodwill) in respect of:
  - Depreciating and non-depreciating non-current assets
  - Inventory
  - Monetary liabilities
  - Assets and liabilities (including contingencies) not included in the subsidiary's own statement of financial position

1 IAS 27 Summary of consolidation procedures

FAST FORWARD

IAS 27 lays out the basic procedures for the preparation of consolidated financial statements.

1.1 Basic procedure

The financial statements of a parent and its subsidiaries are **combined on a line-by-line basis** by adding together like items of assets, liabilities, equity, income and expenses.

The following steps are then taken, in order that the consolidated financial statements should **show financial information about the group as if it was a single entity**.

(a) The carrying amount of the parent's **investment in each subsidiary** and the parent's **portion of equity** of each subsidiary are **eliminated or cancelled**

(b) **Non-controlling interests in the net income of consolidated subsidiaries** are adjusted against group income, to arrive at the net income attributable to the owners of the parent

(c) **Non-controlling interests in the net assets of consolidated subsidiaries** should be presented separately in the consolidated statement of financial position

Other matters to be dealt with include the following.

(a) **Goodwill on consolidation** should be dealt with according to IFRS 3

(b) **Dividends paid** by a subsidiary must be accounted for

IAS 27 states that all intragroup balances and transactions, and the resulting **unrealised profits**, should be **eliminated in full**. **Unrealised losses** resulting from intragroup transactions should also be eliminated *unless* cost can be recovered. This will be explained later in this chapter.

1.2 Cancellation and part cancellation

FAST FORWARD

The mechanics of preparing simple **consolidated statements of financial position** can be summarised into the following main procedures:

- Cancellation
- Calculation of non-controlling interests
- Calculation of goodwill arising on consolidation

The preparation of a consolidated statement of financial position, in a very simple form, consists of two procedures.

(a) Take the individual accounts of the parent company and each subsidiary and **cancel out items** which appear as an asset in one company and a liability in another.

(b) Add together all the uncancelled assets and liabilities throughout the group.

Items requiring cancellation may include the following.

(a) The asset **'shares in subsidiary companies'** which appears in the parent company's accounts will be matched with the liability 'share capital' in the subsidiaries' accounts.

(b) There may be **intra-group trading** within the group. For example, S Co may sell goods on credit to P Co. P Co would then be a receivable in the accounts of S Co, while S Co would be a payable in the accounts of P Co.

1.3 Example: cancellation

P Co regularly sells goods to its one subsidiary company, S Co, which it has owned since S Co's incorporation. The statement of financial position of the two companies on 31 December 20X6 are given below.

STATEMENT OF FINANCIAL POSITION AS AT 31 DECEMBER 20X6

		P Co	*S Co*
		$	$
Assets			
Non-current assets			
Property, plant and equipment		35,000	45,000
Investment in 40,000 $1 shares in S Co at cost		40,000	
		75,000	
Current assets			
Inventories		16,000	12,000
Receivables:	S Co	2,000	
	Other	6,000	9,000
Cash at bank		1,000	
Total assets		100,000	66,000
Equity and liabilities			
Equity			
40,000 $1 ordinary shares			40,000
70,000 $1 ordinary shares		70,000	
Retained earnings		16,000	19,000
		86,000	59,000
Current liabilities			
Bank overdraft			3,000
Payables:	P Co		2,000
Payables:	Other	14,000	2,000
Total equity and liabilities		100,000	66,000

Required

Prepare the consolidated statement of financial position of P Co at 31 December 20X6.

Solution

The cancelling items are:

(a) P Co's asset 'investment in shares of S Co' ($40,000) cancels with S Co's liability 'share capital' ($40,000);

(b) P Co's asset 'receivables: S Co' ($2,000) cancels with S Co's liability 'payables: P Co' ($2,000).

The remaining assets and liabilities are added together to produce the following consolidated statement of financial position.

P CO
CONSOLIDATED STATEMENT OF FINANCIAL POSITION AS AT 31 DECEMBER 20X6

Assets	$	$
Non-current assets		
Property, plant and equipment		80,000
Current assets		
Inventories	28,000	
Receivables	15,000	
Cash at bank	1,000	
		44,000
Total assets		124,000
Equity and liabilities		
Equity		
70,000 $1 ordinary shares	70,000	
Retained earnings	35,000	
	105,000	
Current liabilities		
Bank overdraft	3,000	
Payables	16,000	
		19,000
Total equity and liabilities		124,000

Note the following.

(a) P Co's bank balance is **not netted off** with S Co's bank overdraft. To offset one against the other would be less informative and would conflict with the principle that assets and liabilities should not be netted off.

(b) The share capital in the consolidated statement of financial position is the **share capital of the parent company alone**. This must *always* be the case, no matter how complex the consolidation, because the share capital of subsidiary companies must *always* be a wholly cancelling item.

1.4 Part cancellation

An item may appear in the statements of financial position of a parent company and its subsidiary, but not at the same amounts.

(a) The parent company may have acquired **shares in the subsidiary** at a price **greater or less than their par value**. The asset will appear in the parent company's accounts at cost, while the liability will appear in the subsidiary's accounts at par value. This raises the issue of **goodwill**, which is dealt with later in this chapter.

(b) Even if the parent company acquired shares at par value, it **may not** have **acquired all the shares of the subsidiary** (so the subsidiary may be only partly owned). This raises the issue of **non-controlling interests**, which are also dealt with later in this chapter.

(c) The inter-company trading balances may be out of step because of **goods or cash in transit**.

(d) One company may have **issued loan stock** of which a **proportion only** is taken up by the other company.

The following question illustrates the techniques needed to deal with items (c) and (d) above. The procedure is to **cancel as far as possible**. The remaining uncancelled amounts will appear in the consolidated statement of financial position.

unsecured stock delivered to an entity that has furnished a loan for a company.

(a) **Uncancelled loan stock** will appear as a **liability of the group**.

(b) **Uncancelled balances on intra-group accounts** represent **goods or cash in transit**, which will appear in the consolidated statement of financial position.

Question — Cancellation

The statements of financial position of P Co and of its subsidiary S Co have been made up to 30 June. P Co has owned all the ordinary shares and 40% of the loan stock of S Co since its incorporation.

P CO
STATEMENT OF FINANCIAL POSITION AS AT 30 JUNE

	$	$
Assets		
Non-current assets		
Property, plant and equipment	120,000	
Investment in S Co, at cost		
80,000 ordinary shares of $1 each	80,000	
$20,000 of 12% loan stock in S Co	20,000	
		220,000
Current assets		
Inventories	50,000	
Receivables	40,000	
Current account with S Co	18,000	
Cash	4,000	
		112,000
Total assets		332,000
Equity and liabilities		
Equity		
Ordinary shares of $1 each, fully paid	100,000	
Retained earnings	95,000	
		195,000
Non-current liabilities		
10% loan stock		75,000
Current liabilities		
Payables	47,000	
Taxation	15,000	
		62,000
Total equity and liabilities		332,000

S CO
STATEMENT OF FINANCIAL POSITION AS AT 30 JUNE

	$	$
Assets		
Property, plant and equipment		100,000
Current assets		
Inventories	60,000	
Receivables	30,000	
Cash	6,000	
		96,000
Total assets		196,000

	$	$
Equity and liabilities		
Equity		
80,000 ordinary shares of $1 each, fully paid	80,000	
Retained earnings	28,000	
		108,000
Non-current liabilities		
12% loan stock		50,000
Current liabilities		
Payables	16,000	
Taxation	10,000	
Current account with P Co	12,000	
		38,000
Total equity and liabilities		196,000

The difference on current account arises because of goods in transit.

Required

Prepare the consolidated statement of financial position of P Co.

Answer

P CO
CONSOLIDATED STATEMENT OF FINANCIAL POSITION AS AT 30 JUNE

	$	$
Assets		
Non-current assets		
Property, plant and equipment (120,000 + 100,000)		220,000 ✓
Current assets		
Inventories (50,000 + 60,000)	110,000✓	
Goods in transit (18,000 – 12,000)	6,000	
Receivables (40,000 + 30,000)	70,000✓	
Cash (4,000 + 6,000)	10,000✓	
		196,000
Total assets		416,000
Equity and liabilities		
Equity		
Ordinary shares of $1 each, fully paid (parent)	100,000✓	
Retained earnings (95,000 + 28,000)	123,000✓	
		223,000
Non-current liabilities		
10% loan stock	75,000	
→ 12% loan stock (50,000 × 60%)	30,000	
		105,000
Current liabilities		
Payables (47,000 + 16,000)	63,000✓	
Taxation (15,000 + 10,000)	25,000✓	
		88,000
Total equity and liabilities		416,000

Note especially how:

(a) The uncancelled loan stock in S Co becomes a liability of the group
(b) The goods in transit is the difference between the current accounts ($18,000 – $12,000)
(c) The investment in S Co's shares is cancelled against S Co's share capital

2 Non-controlling interests

FAST FORWARD

In the consolidated statement of financial position it is necessary to distinguish non-controlling interests from those net assets attributable to the group and financed by shareholders' equity.

2.1 Introduction

It was mentioned earlier that the total assets and liabilities of subsidiary companies are included in the consolidated statement of financial position, even in the case of subsidiaries which are only partly owned. A proportion of the net assets of such subsidiaries in fact belongs to investors from outside the group (**non-controlling interests**).

IFRS allows two alternative ways of calculating non-controlling interest in the group statement of financial position. Non-controlling interest can be valued at:

(a) Its proportionate share of the fair value of the subsidiary's net assets; or

(b) Full (or fair) value (usually based on the market value of the shares held by the non-controlling interest).

You are required to be able to apply both of these methods in your examination. The exam question will tell you which method to use. If you are required to use the 'full (or fair) value' method, then you will be given the share price or told what the fair value of the non-controlling interest is.

The following example shows non-controlling interest calculated at its proportionate share of the subsidiary's net assets.

2.2 Example: non-controlling interest

P Co has owned 75% of the share capital of S Co since the date of S Co's incorporation. Their latest statements of financial position are given below.

P CO
STATEMENT OF FINANCIAL POSITION

	$	$
Assets		
Non-current assets		
Property, plant and equipment	50,000	
30,000 $1 ordinary shares in S Co at cost	30,000	
		80,000
Current assets		45,000
Total assets		125,000
Equity and liabilities		
Equity		
80,000 $1 ordinary shares	80,000	
Retained earnings	25,000	
		105,000
Current liabilities		20,000
Total equity and liabilities		125,000

S CO
STATEMENT OF FINANCIAL POSITION

	$	$
Assets		
Property, plant and equipment		35,000
Current assets		35,000
Total assets		70,000

	$	$
Equity and liabilities		
Equity		
40,000 $1 ordinary shares	40,000	
Retained earnings	10,000	
		50,000
Current liabilities		20,000
Total equity and liabilities		70,000

Required

Prepare the consolidated statement of financial position.

Solution

All of S Co's net assets are consolidated despite the fact that the company is only 75% owned. The amount of net assets attributable to non-controlling interests is calculated as follows.

	$
Non-controlling share of share capital (25% × $40,000)	10,000
Non-controlling share of retained earnings (25% × $10,000)	2,500
	12,500

Of S Co's share capital of $40,000, $10,000 is included in the figure for non-controlling interest, while $30,000 is cancelled with P Co's asset 'investment in S Co'.

The consolidated statement of financial position can now be prepared.

P GROUP
CONSOLIDATED STATEMENT OF FINANCIAL POSITION

	$	$
Assets		
Property, plant and equipment		85,000
Current assets		80,000
Total assets		165,000
Equity and liabilities		
Equity attributable to owners of the parent		
Share capital	80,000	
Retained earnings $(25,000 + (75% × $10,000))	32,500	
		112,500
Non-controlling interest		12,500
		125,000
Current liabilities		40,000
Total equity and liabilities		165,000

2.3 Procedure

(a) Aggregate the assets and liabilities in the statement of financial position ie 100% P + 100% S irrespective of how much P actually owns.

This shows the amount of net assets **controlled** by the group.

(b) Share capital is that of the parent only.

(c) Calculate the non-controlling interest share of the subsidiary's net assets (share capital plus reserves).

(d) Balance of subsidiary's reserves are consolidated (after cancelling any intra-group items).

Question

Set out below are the draft statement of financial position of P Co and its subsidiary S Co. You are required to prepare the consolidated statement of financial position. The non-controlling interest is valued at its proportional share of the fair value of the subsidiary's net assets.

P CO

	$	$
Assets		
Non-current assets		
Property, plant and equipment		31,000
Investment in S Co		
12,000 $1 ordinary shares at cost	12,000	
$8,000 10% loan stock at cost	8,000	
		20,000
		51,000
Current assets		21,000
Total assets		72,000
Equity and liabilities		
Equity		
Ordinary shares of $1 each	40,000	
Retained earnings	22,000	
		62,000
Current liabilities		10,000
Total equity and liabilities		72,000

S CO

	$	$
Assets		
Property, plant and equipment		34,000
Current assets		32,000
Total assets		66,000
Equity and liabilities		
Equity		
Ordinary shares of $1 each	20,000	
Revaluation surplus	6,000	
Retained earnings	4,000	
		30,000
Non-current liabilities		
10% loan stock		26,000
Current liabilities		10,000
Total equity and liabilities		66,000

Answer

The group structure is:

P Co
↓ 60%
S Co

Partly cancelling items are the components of P Co's investment in S Co, ie ordinary shares, loan stock. Non-controlling shareholders have an interest in 40% (8,000/20,000) of S Co's ordinary shares, including reserves.

You should now aggregate the assets and liabilities and produce workings for non-controlling interest, revaluation surplus and retained earnings as follows.

Workings

1 *Non-controlling interest*

	$
S Co's net assets (66,000 – 36,000)	30,000
× 40%	12,000

2 *Revaluation surplus*

	$
P Co	–
Share of S Co's revaluation surplus (60% × 6,000)	3,600
	3,600

3 *Retained earnings*

	$
P Co	22,000
Share of S Co's retained earnings (60% × 4,000)	2,400
	24,400

The results of the workings are now used to construct the consolidated statement of financial position.

P GROUP
CONSOLIDATED STATEMENT OF FINANCIAL POSITION

	$	$
Assets		
Property, plant and equipment		65,000
Current assets		53,000
Total assets		118,000
Equity and liabilities		
Equity attributable to owners of the parent		
Ordinary shares of $1 each	40,000	
Revaluation surplus (W2)	3,600	
Retained earnings (W3)	24,400	
		68,000
Non-controlling interest (W1)		12,000
		80,000
Non-current liabilities		
10% loan stock (26,000 – 8,000)		18,000
Current liabilities		20,000
Total equity and liabilities		118,000

Notes

(a) S Co is a subsidiary of P Co because P Co owns 60% of its ordinary capital.

(b) As always, the share capital in the consolidated statement of financial position is that of the parent company alone. The share capital in S Co's statement of financial position was partly cancelled against the investment shown in P Co's statement of financial position, while the uncancelled portion was credited to non-controlling interest.

(c) The figure for non-controlling interest comprises the interest of outside investors in the share capital and reserves of the subsidiary. The uncancelled portion of S Co's loan stock is not shown as part of non-controlling interest but is disclosed separately as a liability of the group.

3 Dividends paid by a subsidiary

FAST FORWARD

Complexities arise when dividends are paid shortly after the acquisition with some dividend relating to pre-acquisition profits.

When a subsidiary company pays a **dividend** during the year the accounting treatment is not difficult. Suppose S Co, a 60% subsidiary of P Co, pays a dividend of $1,000 on the last day of its accounting period. Its total reserves before paying the dividend stood at $5,000.

(a) $400 of the dividend is paid to non-controlling shareholders. The cash leaves the group and will not appear anywhere in the consolidated statement of financial position.

(b) The parent company receives $600 of the dividend, debiting cash and crediting profit or loss. This will be cancelled on consolidation.

(c) The remaining balance of retained earnings in S Co's statement of financial position ($4,000) will be consolidated in the normal way. The group's share (60% × $4,000 = $2,400) will be included in group retained earnings in the statement of financial position; the non-controlling interest share (40% × $4,000 = $1,600) is credited to the non-controlling interest account in the statement of financial position.

However, the situation is more complicated when a subsidiary pays a dividend shortly after acquisition and some of that dividend is deemed to been paid from pre-acquisition profits. This situation is considered in Section 10.

4 Goodwill arising on consolidation

FAST FORWARD

In practice the cost of shares acquired by the parent company is seldom equal to the par value of those shares.

We consider such examples below.

4.1 Accounting

To begin with, **we will examine the entries made by the parent company in its own statement of financial position when it acquires shares.**

When a company P Co wishes to **purchase shares** in a company S Co it must pay the previous owners of those shares. The most obvious form of payment would be in **cash**. Suppose P Co purchases all 40,000 $1 shares in S Co and pays $60,000 cash to the previous shareholders in consideration. The entries in P Co's books would be:

DEBIT	Investment in S Co at cost	$60,000	
CREDIT	Bank		$60,000

However, the previous shareholders might be prepared to accept some other form of consideration. For example, they might accept an agreed number of **shares** in P Co. P Co would then issue new shares in the agreed number and allot them to the former shareholders of S Co. This kind of deal might be attractive to P Co since it avoids the need for a heavy cash outlay. The former shareholders of S Co would retain an indirect interest in that company's profitability via their new holding in its parent company.

Continuing the example, suppose the shareholders of S Co agreed to accept one $1 ordinary share in P Co for every two $1 ordinary shares in S Co. P Co would then need to issue and allot 20,000 new $1 shares. How would this transaction be recorded in the books of P Co?

The simplest method would be as follows.

DEBIT	Investment in S Co	$20,000	
CREDIT	Share capital		$20,000

However, if the 40,000 $1 shares acquired in S Co are thought to have a value of $60,000 this would be misleading. The former shareholders of S Co have presumably agreed to accept 20,000 shares in P Co because they consider each of those shares to have a value of $3. This view of the matter suggests the following method of recording the transaction in P Co's books.

DEBIT	Investment in S Co	$60,000	
CREDIT	Share capital		$20,000
	Share premium account		$40,000

The second method is the one which should normally be used in preparing consolidated accounts.

The amount which P Co records in its books as the cost of its investment in S Co may be more or less than the book value of the assets it acquires. Suppose that S Co in the previous example has nil reserves and nil liabilities, so that its share capital of $40,000 is balanced by tangible assets with a book value of $40,000. For simplicity, assume that the book value of S Co's assets is the same as their market or fair value.

Now when the directors of P Co agree to pay $60,000 for a 100% investment in S Co they must believe that, in addition to its tangible assets of $40,000, S Co must also have intangible assets worth $20,000. This amount of $20,000 paid over and above the value of the tangible assets acquired is called **goodwill arising on consolidation** (sometimes **premium on acquisition**).

Following the normal cancellation procedure the $40,000 share capital in S Co's statement of financial position could be cancelled against $40,000 of the 'investment in S Co' in the statement of financial position of P Co. This would leave a $20,000 debit uncancelled in the parent company's accounts and this $20,000 would appear in the consolidated statement of financial position under the caption 'Intangible non-current assets: goodwill arising on consolidation'.

4.2 Goodwill and pre-acquisition profits

Up to now we have assumed that S Co had nil retained earnings when its shares were purchased by P Co. Assuming instead that S Co had earned profits of $8,000 in the period before acquisition, its statement of financial position just before the purchase would look as follows.

	$
Total assets	48,000
Share capital	40,000
Retained earnings	8,000
	48,000

If P Co now purchases all the shares in S Co it will acquire total assets worth $48,000 at a cost of $60,000. Clearly in this case S Co's intangible assets (goodwill) are being valued at $12,000. It should be apparent that any earnings retained by the subsidiary **prior to its acquisition** by the parent company must be **incorporated in the cancellation** process so as to arrive at a figure for goodwill arising on consolidation. In other words, not only S Co's share capital, but also its **pre-acquisition** retained earnings, must be cancelled against the asset 'investment in S Co' in the accounts of the parent company. The uncancelled balance of $12,000 appears in the consolidated statement of financial position.

The consequence of this is that **any pre-acquisition retained earnings of a subsidiary company are not aggregated with the parent company's retained earnings** in the consolidated statement of financial position. The figure of consolidated retained earnings comprises the retained earnings of the parent company plus the **post-acquisition retained earnings only of subsidiary companies**. The post-acquisition retained earnings are simply retained earnings now *less* retained earnings at acquisition.

4.3 Example: goodwill and pre-acquisition profits

Sing Co acquired the ordinary shares of Wing Co on 31 March when the draft statements of financial position of each company were as follows.

SING CO
STATEMENT OF FINANCIAL POSITION AS AT 31 MARCH

	$
Assets	
Non-current assets	
Investment in 50,000 shares of Wing Co at cost	80,000
Current assets	40,000
Total assets	120,000
Equity and liabilities	
Equity	
Ordinary shares	75,000
Retained earnings	45,000
Total equity and liabilities	120,000

WING CO
STATEMENT OF FINANCIAL POSITION AS AT 31 MARCH

	$
Current assets	60,000
Equity	
50,000 ordinary shares of $1 each	50,000
Retained earnings	10,000
	60,000

Prepare the consolidated statement of financial position as at 31 March.

Solution

The technique to adopt here is to produce a new working: 'Goodwill'. A proforma working is set out below.

Goodwill

	$	$
Consideration transferred		X
Non-controlling interest at acquisition		X
		X
Net assets acquired as represented by:		
Ordinary share capital	X	
Share premium	X	
Retained earnings on acquisition	X	
		(X)
Goodwill		X

Applying this to our example the working will look like this.

	$	$
Consideration transferred		80,000
Non-controlling interest		-
		80,000
Net assets acquired as represented by:		
Ordinary share capital	50,000	
Retained earnings on acquisition	10,000	
		(60,000)
Goodwill		20,000

SING CO
CONSOLIDATED STATEMENT OF FINANCIAL POSITION AS AT 31 MARCH

	$
Assets	
Non-current assets	
Goodwill arising on consolidation	20,000
Current assets	100,000
	120,000

	$
Equity	
Ordinary shares	75,000
Retained earnings	45,000
	120,000

4.4 Goodwill and non-controlling interest

Not let us look at what would happen if Sing Co had obtained less than 100% of the shares of Wing Co.

If Sing Co had paid $80,000 for 40,000 shares in Wing Co, the goodwill working would be as follows:

	$
Consideration transferred	80,000
Non-controlling interest (60,000 × 20%)	12,000
Net assets acquired	(60,000)
Goodwill	32,000

The goodwill has been increased by the non-controlling interest – Sing Co has paid the same amount but acquired a smaller shareholding.

Note: Work out the net assets and **then** the non-controlling interest.

4.5 Non-controlling interest at fair value

IFRS 3 (revised) gives entities the option of valuing non-controlling interest at fair value. The thinking behind this is that the non-controlling interest, in purchasing their shares, also purchased goodwill in the subsidiary, and that the traditional method of consolidation does not show this goodwill.

IFRS 3 revised suggests that the closest approximation to fair value will be the market price of the shares held by non-controlling shareholders just before acquisition by the parent.

Continuing our example above, we will assume that the market price of the shares was $1.25. The goodwill calculation will then be as follows:

	$
Consideration transferred	80,000
Non-controlling interest (10,000 × $1.25)	12,500
Net assets at acquisition	(60,000)
Goodwill	32,500

Goodwill is $500 higher than goodwill calculated measuring non-controlling interest at its share of the net assets of the subsidiary. This $500 represents the **goodwill attributable to the non-controlling interest**.

4.6 Non-controlling interest at year end

Where the option is used to value non-controlling interest at fair value, this applies only to **non-controlling interest at acquisition**. At the year end, the non-controlling interest is measured at its share of the subsidiary's year end net assets, subject to adjustments for intra-group trading which we will cover later in this chapter.

However, **where the fair value option has been used**, goodwill at the year end will include the additional goodwill attributable to the non-controlling interest, in the example above $500. The other side of the entry is to **add the goodwill onto the non-controlling interest at the year end**.

This is illustrated in the following worked example.

4.7 Worked example

P acquired 75% of the shares in S on 1 January 2007 when S had retained earnings of $15,000. The market price of S's shares just before the date of acquisition was $1.60. P values non-controlling interest at fair value. Goodwill is not impaired.

The statements of financial position of P and S at 31 December 20X7 were as follows:

	P	S
	$	$
Property, plant and equipment	60,000	50,000
Shares in S	68,000	–
Current assets	128,000	50,000
	52,000	35,000
	180,000	85,000
Share capital – $1 shares	100,000	50,000
Retained earnings	70,000	25,000
	170,000	75,000
Current liabilities	10,000	10,000
	180,000	85,000

Prepare the consolidated statement of financial position of the P Group.

4.8 Solution

CONSOLIDATED STATEMENT OF FINANCIAL POSITION

	$
Assets	
Property plant and equipment (60,000 + 50,000)	110,000
Goodwill (W1)	23,000
Current assets (52,000 + 35,000)	87,000
Total assets	220,000
Equity and liabilities	
Equity attributable to the owners of P	
Share capital	100,000
Retained earnings (W2)	77,500
	177,500
Non-controlling interest (W3)	22,500
Total equity	200,000
Current liabilities (10,000 + 10,000)	20,000
	220,000

Workings

1. *Goodwill*

	$
Consideration transferred	68,000
Non-controlling interest at acquisition (12,500 shares @ $1.60)	20,000
Net assets of S at acquisition (50,000 + 15,000)	(65,000)
Goodwill (parent and non-controlling interest)	23,000
Non-controlling interest at fair value (as above)	20,000
Non-controlling share of net assets at acquisition (65,000 × 25%)	(16,250)
Goodwill attributable to non-controlling interest	3,750

2. *Retained earnings*

	P	S
	$	$
Per statement of financial position	70,000	25,000
Less pre- acquisition		(15,000)
		10,000
Group share of S (10,000 × 75%)	7,500	
Group retained earnings	77,500	

3. *Non-controlling interest at year end*

	$
Share of net assets of S (75,000 × 25%)	18,750
Goodwill (W1)	3,750
	22,500

4.9 Effect of non-controlling interest at fair value

You can see from the above example that the use of the fair value option increases goodwill and non-controlling interest by the same amount. That amount represents goodwill attributable to the shares held by non-controlling shareholders. It is not necessarily proportionate to the goodwill attributed to the parent. The parent may have paid more to acquire a controlling interest. If non-controlling interest was valued under the usual method (share of net assets) goodwill and non-controlling interest in the example above would be as follows:

W1 Goodwill

	$
Considered transferred	68,000
Non-controlling interest ((50,000 + 15,000) × 25%)	16,250
Net assets of S at acquisition (50,000 + 15,000)	(65,000)
	19,250

W3 Non-controlling interest at year end

	$
Share of net assets of S (75,000 × 25%)	18,750

Compare these with goodwill and non-controlling interest in the solution above and you will see that both have been reduced by $3,750 – the goodwill attributable to the non-controlling interest. So whether non-controlling interest is valued at share of net assets or at fair value, the statement of financial position will still balance.

Exam focus point

The option to value non-controlling interest at fair value is introduced by the revised IFRS 3, but it is just an **option**. Companies can choose to adopt it or to continue to value non-controlling interest at share of net assets. In the exam, unless you are directed to apply the fair value option, you should value non-controlling interest at share of net assets. It is likely that the examiner will specifically tell you this. If you are required to use the fair value option, the examiner has stated that there are three possible options:

1. You may be given the share price of the subsidiary just before acquisition.
2. You may be told that the non-controlling interest is valued at a certain amount.
3. You may be given the amount of goodwill attributable to the non-controlling interest. In this case you would calculate goodwill and non-controlling interest under the traditional method and then add the goodwill to both of them.

In the exam, the consolidation question will tell you which method to use. It will state either:

'It is the group policy to value the non-controlling interest at full (or fair) value;' or

'It is the group policy to value the non-controlling interest at its proportionate share of the (fair value of the) subsidiary's identifiable net assets'.

4.10 Impairment of goodwill

Goodwill arising on consolidation is subjected to an annual impairment review and impairment may be expressed as an amount or as a percentage. The double entry to write off the impairment is:

DEBIT Group retained earnings CREDIT Goodwill

However, when non-controlling interest is valued at **fair value** the goodwill in the statement of financial position includes goodwill attributable to the non-controlling interest. In this case the double entry will reflect the non-controlling interest proportion based on their shareholding as follows:

DEBIT Group retained earnings CREDIT Goodwill
DEBIT Non-controlling interest

In our solution above in 4.8 the non-controlling interest holds 25%. If the goodwill of $23,000 was impaired by 20% the double entry for this would be:

	$		$
DEBIT Retained earnings	3,450	CREDIT Goodwill	4,600
DEBIT Non-controlling interest	1,150		

Non-controlling interest at the year end would then be $21,350.

4.11 Gain on a bargain purchase

Goodwill arising on consolidation is one form of **purchased goodwill**, and is governed by IFRS 3. As explained in an earlier chapter IFRS 3 requires that goodwill arising on consolidation should **be capitalised in the consolidated statement of financial position** and **reviewed for impairment every year**.

Goodwill arising on consolidation is the difference between the cost of an acquisition and the value of the subsidiary's net assets acquired. This difference can be **negative**: the aggregate of the fair values of the separable net assets acquired may **exceed** what the parent company paid for them. IFRS 3 refers to this as a 'bargain purchase'. In this situation:

(a) An entity should first **re-assess** the amounts at which it has measured both the cost of the combination and the acquiree's identifiable net assets. This exercise should **identify any errors.**

(b) Any **excess remaining** should be **recognised immediately in profit or loss.**

4.12 Forms of consideration

The consideration paid by the parent for the shares in the subsidiary can take different forms and this will affect the calculation of goodwill. Here are some examples:

4.12.1 Contingent consideration

The parent acquired 60% of the subsidiary's $100m share capital on 1 Jan 20X6 for a cash payment of $150m and a further payment of $50m on 31 March 20X7 if the subsidiary's post acquisition profits have exceeded an agreed figure by that date.

In the financial statements for the year to 31 December 20X6 $50m will be added to the cost of the combination, discounted as appropriate.

IFRS 3 requires the acquisition-date **fair value** of contingent consideration to be recognised as part of the consideration for the acquiree. In an examination question students will be told the acquisition-date fair value or told how to calculate it.

The acquirer may be required to pay contingent consideration in the form of equity or of a debt instrument or cash. A debt instrument should be presented as under IAS 32. Contingent consideration can also be an asset, if the consideration has already been transferred and the acquirer has the right to return of some of it, if certain considerations are met.

Note: The previous version of IFRS 3 only required contingent consideration to be recognised if it was **probable** that it would become payable. IFRS 3 revised dispenses with this requirement – **all contingent consideration is now recognised**. It is possible that the fair value of the contingent consideration may change after the acquisition date. If this is due to additional information obtained that affects the position at acquisition date goodwill should be remeasured. If the change is due to events after the acquisition date (such as a higher earnings target has been met, so more is payable) it should be accounted for under IAS 39 if the consideration is in the form of a financial instrument (such as loan notes) or under IAS 37 as an increase in a provision if it is cash. Any equity instrument is not remeasured.

4.12.2 Deferred consideration

The parent acquired 75% of the subsidiary's 80m $1 shares on 1 Jan 20X6. It paid $3.50 per share and agreed to pay a further $108m on 1 Jan 20X8.

The parent company's cost of capital is 8%.

In the financial statements for the year to 31 December 20X6 the cost of the combination will be as follows:

	$m
80m shares × 75% × $3.50	210
Deferred consideration:	
$108m × 1/1.08	100
Total consideration	310

At 31 December 20X7, the cost of the combination will be unchanged but $8 will be charged to finance costs, being the unwinding of the discount on the deferred consideration.

4.12.3 Share exchange

The parent has acquired 12,000 $1 shares in the subsidiary by issuing 5 of its own $1 shares for every 4 shares in the subsidiary. The market value of the parent company's shares is $6.

Cost of the combination:

	$
12,000 × 5/4 × $6	90,000

Note that this is credited to the share capital and share premium of the parent company as follows:

	DR	*CR*
Investment in subsidiary	90,000	
Share capital ($12,000 × 5/4)		15,000
Share premium ($12,000 × 5/4 × 5)		75,000

4.12.4 Expenses and issue costs

Expenses of the combination, such as lawyers and accountants fees are written off as incurred. However, IFRS 3 requires that the costs of issuing equity are treated as a deduction from the proceeds of the equity issue. Share issue costs will therefore be debited to the share premium account. Issue costs of financial instruments are deducted from the proceeds of the financial instrument.

4.13 Adjustments to goodwill

At the date of acquisition the parent recognises the assets, liabilities and contingent liabilities of the subsidiary at their fair value at the date when control is acquired. It may be that some of these assets or liabilities had not previously been recognised by the acquiree.

For instance, the subsidiary may have tax losses brought forward, but had not recognised these as an asset because it could not foresee future profits against which they could be offset. If it now appears that taxable profits will be forthcoming, the deferred tax asset can be recognised.

An entity has acquired a 60% interest in another entity which has brought forward tax losses unutilised of $200,000. The tax losses can now be utilised.

The adjustment will be:

	DR	*CR*
Deferred tax (subsidiary)	200,000	
Goodwill		200,000

5 A technique of consolidation

FAST FORWARD

A **seven-stage drill** is made up of the following stages:

- Update the draft statements of financial position to take account of any dividend paid but not accounted for
- Agree intra-group current accounts by adjusting for items in transit
- Cancel items common to both statements in financial position
- Non-controlling interests
- Goodwill
- Retained earnings
- Consolidated statement of financial position

1 Aggregate the assets and liabilities on the statement of financial position. Cancel common items.
2 Calculate goodwill.
3 Calculate non-controlling interest.
4 Calculate retained earnings.

Question — Consolidated statement of financial position

The draft statements of financial position of Ping Co and Pong Co on 30 June 20X4 were as follows.

PING CO
STATEMENT OF FINANCIAL POSITION AS AT 30 JUNE 20X4

	$	$
Assets		
Non-current assets		
Property, plant and equipment	50,000	
20,000 ordinary shares in Pong Co at cost	30,000	
		80,000
Current assets		
Inventory	3,000	
Receivables	16,000	
Cash	2,000	
		21,000
Total assets		101,000
Equity and liabilities		
Equity		
Ordinary shares of $1 each	45,000	
Revaluation surplus	12,000	
Retained earnings	26,000	
		83,000
Current liabilities		
Owed to Pong Co	8,000	
Trade payables	10,000	
		18,000
Total equity and liabilities		101,000

PONG CO
STATEMENT OF FINANCIAL POSITION AS AT 30 JUNE 20X4

	$	$
Assets		
Property, plant and equipment		40,000
Current assets		
Inventory	8,000	

Owed by Ping Co	10,000	
Receivables	7,000	
		25,000
Total assets		65,000
Equity and liabilities		
Equity		
Ordinary shares of $1 each	25,000	
Revaluation surplus	5,000	
Retained earnings	28,000	
		58,000
Current liabilities		
Trade payables		7,000
Total equity and liabilities		65,000

Ping Co acquired its investment in Pong Co on 1 July 20X1 when the retained earnings of Pong Co stood at $6,000. There have been no changes in the share capital or revaluation surplus of Pong Co since that date. At 30 June 20X4 Pong Co had invoiced Ping Co for goods to the value of $2,000 which had not been received by Ping Co.

There is no impairment of goodwill. It is group policy to value non-controlling interest at its proportionate share of the subsidiary's identifiable net assets.

Prepare the consolidated statement of financial position of Ping Co as at 30 June 20X4.

Answer

1 **Agree current accounts.**

Ping Co has goods in transit of $2,000 making its total inventory $3,000 + $2,000 = $5,000 and its liability to Pong Co $8,000 + $2,000 = $10,000.

Cancel common items: these are the current accounts between the two companies of $10,000 each.

2 **Calculate goodwill.**

Goodwill

	$	$
Consideration transferred		30,000
Non-controlling interest (W3)		7,200
Net assets acquired as represented by:		37,200
Ordinary share capital	25,000	
Revaluation surplus on acquisition	5,000	
Retained earnings on acquisition	6,000	
		(36,000)
Goodwill		1,200

This goodwill must be capitalised in the consolidated statement of financial position.

3 **Calculate non-controlling interest.**

(a) *at acquisition*

	$
Pong Co's net assets (W2)	36,000
× 20%	7,200

(b) *at year end*

	$
Pong Co's net assets (65,000 – 7,000)	58,000
× 20%	11,600

4 **Calculate consolidated reserves.**

Consolidated revaluation surplus

	$
Ping Co	12,000
Share of Pong Co's post acquisition revaluation surplus	–
	12,000

Consolidated retained earnings

	Ping	*Pong*
	$	$
Retained earnings per question	26,000	28,000
Less pre-acquisition		(6,000)
		22,000
Share of Pong: 80% × $22,000	17,600	
	43,600	

5 Prepare the consolidated statement of financial position.

PING CO
CONSOLIDATED STATEMENT OF FINANCIAL POSITION AS AT 30 JUNE 20X4

	$	$
Assets		
Non-current assets		
Property, plant and equipment ($50,000 + $40,000)		90,000
Intangible asset: goodwill		1,200
Current assets		
Inventories ($5,000 + $8,000)	13,000	
Receivables ($16,000 + $7,000)	23,000	
Cash	2,000	
		38,000
Total assets		129,200
Equity and liabilities		
Equity		
Ordinary shares of $1 each	45,000	
Revaluation surplus	12,000	
Retained earnings	43,600	
		100,600
Non-controlling interest		11,600
		112,200
Current liabilities		
Trade payables ($10,000 + $7,000)		17,000
Total equity and liabilities		129,200

5.1 Non-controlling interest at fair value

Now we will look at how the answer to the question above would appear if the non-controlling interest was at fair value. We will take a share price of $1.50. The non-controlling interest would become:

	$
5,000 shares at $1.50	7,500

Now let us look at how this affects the goodwill calculation:

	$
Consideration transferred	30,000
Non-controlling interest	7,500
Net assets of Pong Co	(36,000)
Goodwill	1,500

The non-controlling interest at acquisition has increased by $300 (7,500 – 7,200) and the goodwill has increased by the same amount (1,500 – 1,200). If the share price were $1.25, the non-controlling interest would be $6,250, a reduction of $950 from the original value of $7,200 and the goodwill would be (30,000 + 6,250 – 36,000 = 250) – a reduction of $950 from the original value of $1,200.

Note: In this text, unless stated otherwise, non-controlling interest is valued at share of fair value of net assets.

Exam focus point

A consolidated statement of financial position will come up as regularly as clockwork. There will nearly always be an adjustment for intra-group trading, which we look at next.

6 Intra-group trading

FAST FORWARD

There are consolidation adjustments necessary when group companies **trade with or sell non-current assets to each other**.

- The guiding principle is thtat the consolidated statement of financial position must show assets at their cost to the group
- Any profit arising on intra-group transaction must be eliminated from the group retained earnings unless and until it is realised by a sale outside the group.

6.1 Unrealised profit

Any receivable/payable balances outstanding between the companies are cancelled on consolidation. No further problem arises if all such intra-group transactions are **undertaken at cost**, without any mark-up for profit.

However, each company in a group is a separate trading entity and may wish to treat other group companies in the same way as any other customer. In this case, a company (say A Co) may buy goods at one price and sell them at a higher price to another group company (B Co). The accounts of A Co will quite properly include the profit earned on sales to B Co; and similarly B Co's statement of financial position will include inventories at their cost to B Co, ie at the amount at which they were purchased from A Co.

This gives rise to two problems.

(a) Although A Co makes a profit as soon as it sells goods to B Co, the group does not make a sale or achieve a profit until an outside customer buys the goods from B Co.

(b) Any purchases from A Co which remain unsold by B Co at the year end will be included in B Co's inventory. Their value in the statement of financial position will be their cost to B Co, which is not the same as their cost to the group.

The objective of consolidated accounts is to present the financial position of several connected companies as that of a single entity, the group. This means that **in a consolidated statement of financial position the only profits recognised should be those earned by the group** in providing goods or services to outsiders; and similarly, inventory in the consolidated statement of financial position should be valued at cost to the group.

Suppose that a holding company P Co buys goods for $1,600 and sells them to a wholly owned subsidiary S Co for $2,000. The goods are in S Co's inventory at the year end and appear in S Co's statement of financial position at $2,000. In this case, P Co will record a profit of $400 in its individual accounts, but from the group's point of view the figures are:

Cost	$1,600
External sales	nil
Closing inventory at cost	$1,600
Profit/loss	nil

If we add together the figures for retained earnings and inventory in the individual statements of financial position of P Co and S Co the resulting figures for consolidated retained earnings and consolidated inventory will each be overstated by $400. A **consolidation adjustment** is therefore necessary as follows.

DEBIT	Group retained earnings
CREDIT	Group inventory (statement of financial position)

with the amount of **profit unrealised** by the group.

Question — Unrealised profit

P Co acquired all the shares in S Co one year ago when the reserves of S Co stood at $10,000. Draft statements of financial position for each company are as follows.

	P Co		*S Co*	
	$	$	$	$
Assets				
Non-current assets				
Property, plant and equipment	80,000			40,000
Investment in S Co at cost	46,000			
		126,000		
Current assets		40,000		30,000
Total assets		166,000		70,000
Equity and liabilities				
Equity				
Ordinary shares of $1 each	100,000		30,000	
Retained earnings	45,000		22,000	
		145,000		52,000
Current liabilities		21,000		18,000
Total equity and liabilities		166,000		70,000

During the year S Co sold goods to P Co for $50,000, the profit to S Co being 20% of selling price. At the end of the reporting period, $15,000 of these goods remained unsold in the inventories of P Co. At the same date, P Co owed S Co $12,000 for goods bought and this debt is included in the trade payables of P Co and the receivables of S Co. The goodwill arising on consolidation has been impaired. The amount of the impairment is $1,500.

Required

Prepare a draft consolidated statement of financial position for P Co.

Answer

1 *Goodwill*

	$	$
Consideration transferred		46,000
Non-controlling interest		-
Net assets acquired as represented by		
Share capital	30,000	
Retained earnings	10,000	
		(40,000)
Goodwill		6,000

2 *Retained earnings*

	P Co	*S Co*
	$	$
Retained earnings per question	45,000	22,000
Unrealised profit: 20% × $15,000	(3,000)	
	42,000	
Pre-acquisition		(10,000)
		12,000
Share of S Co	12,000	
Goodwill impairment loss	(1,500)	
	52,500	

P CO
CONSOLIDATED STATEMENT OF FINANCIAL POSITION

	$	$
Assets		
Non-current assets		
Property, plant and equipment	120,000	
Goodwill (6,000 – 1,500)	4,500	
		124,500
Current assets (W1)		55,000
Total assets		179,500
Equity and liabilities		
Equity		
Ordinary shares of $1 each	100,000	
Retained earnings	52,500	
		152,500
Current liabilities (W2)		27,000
Total equity and liabilities		179,500

Workings

1 *Current assets*

	$	$
In P Co's statement of financial position		40,000
In S Co's statement of financial position	30,000	
Less S Co's current account with P Co cancelled	(12,000)	
		18,000
		58,000
Less unrealised profit excluded from inventory valuation		(3,000)
		55,000

2 *Current liabilities*

	$
In P Co's statement of financial position	21,000
Less P Co's current account with S Co cancelled	(12,000)
	9,000
In S Co's statement of financial position	18,000
	27,000

6.2 Non-controlling interests in unrealised intra-group profits

A further problem occurs where a subsidiary company which is **not wholly owned is involved in intra-group trading** within the group. If a subsidiary S Co is 75% owned and sells goods to the parent company for $16,000 cost plus $4,000 profit, ie for $20,000 and if these items are unsold by P Co at the end of the reporting period, the 'unrealised' profit of $4,000 earned by S Co and charged to P Co will be partly owned by the non-controlling interest of S Co. As far as the non-controlling interest of S Co is concerned, their share (25% of $4,000) amounting to $1,000 of profit on the sale of goods would appear to have been fully realised. It is only the group that has not yet made a profit on the sale.

There are three different possibilities for the treatment of these intra-group profits.

(a) Remove only the group's share of the profit loading
(b) **Remove the whole profit loading, charging the non-controlling interest with their proportion**
(c) Remove the whole of the profit without charging the non-controlling interest (to reduce group retained earnings by the whole profit loading)

The method given under (b) is usually considered best practice and the double entry is therefore as follows.

Entries to learn

DEBIT	Group retained earnings
DEBIT	Non-controlling interest
CREDIT	Group inventory (statement of financial position)

6.3 Example: non-controlling interests and intra-group profits

P Co has owned 75% of the shares of S Co since the incorporation of that company. During the year to 31 December 20X2, S Co sold goods costing $16,000 to P Co at a price of $20,000 and these goods were still unsold by P Co at the end of the year. Draft statements of financial position of each company at 31 December 20X2 were as follows.

	P Co		*S Co*	
Assets	$	$	$	$
Non-current assets				
Property, plant and equipment	125,000		120,000	
Investment: 75,000 shares in S Co at cost	75,000		–	
		200,000		120,000
Current assets				
Inventories	50,000		48,000	
Trade receivables	20,000		16,000	
		70,000		64,000
Total assets		270,000		184,000
Equity and liabilities				
Equity				
Ordinary shares of $1 each fully paid	80,000		100,000	
Retained earnings	150,000		60,000	
		230,000		160,000
Current liabilities		40,000		24,000
Total equity and liabilities		270,000		184,000

Required

Prepare the consolidated statement of financial position of P Co at 31 December 20X2. It is the group policy to value the non-controlling interest at its proportionate share of the subsidiary's net assets.

Solution

The profit earned by S Co but unrealised by the group is $4,000 of which $3,000 (75%) is attributable to the group and $1,000 (25%) to the non-controlling interest. Remove the whole of the profit loading, charging the non-controlling interest with their proportion.

	P Co	*S Co*
	$	$
Retained earnings		
Per question	150,000	60,000
Less unrealised profit		(4,000)
		56,000
Share of S Co: $56,000 × 75%	42,000	
	192,000	
Non-controlling interest		
S Co's net assets (184,000 – 24,000)		160,000
Unrealised profit		(4,000)
		156,000
× 25%		39,000

P CO
CONSOLIDATED STATEMENT OF FINANCIAL POSITION AS AT 31 DECEMBER 20X2

	$	$
Assets		
Property, plant and equipment		245,000
Current assets		
Inventories $(50,000 + 48,000 – 4,000)	94,000	
Trade receivables	36,000	
		130,000
Total assets		375,000
Equity and liabilities		
Equity		
Ordinary shares of $1 each	80,000	
Retained earnings	192,000	
		272,000
Non-controlling interest		39,000
		311,000
Current liabilities		64,000
Total equity and liabilities		375,000

7 Intra-group sales of non-current assets

7.1 Accounting treatment

In their individual accounts the companies concerned will treat the transfer just like a sale between unconnected parties: the selling company will record a profit or loss on sale, while the purchasing company will record the asset at the amount paid to acquire it, and will use that amount as the basis for calculating depreciation.

On consolidation, the usual **'group entity' principle applies**. The consolidated statement of financial position must show assets at their cost to the group, and any depreciation charged must be based on that cost. Two consolidation adjustments will usually be needed to achieve this.

(a) An adjustment to alter retained earnings and non-current assets cost so as to remove any element of unrealised profit or loss. This is similar to the adjustment required in respect of unrealised profit in inventory.

(b) An adjustment to alter retained earnings and accumulated depreciation is made so that consolidated depreciation is based on the asset's cost to the group.

In practice, these steps are combined so that the retained earnings of the entity making the unrealised profit are debited with the unrealised profit less the additional depreciation.

The double entry is as follows.

(a) Sale by parent

DEBIT Group retained earnings
CREDIT Non-current assets

with the profit on disposal, less the additional depreciation.

(b) Sale by subsidiary

DEBIT Group retained earnings (P's share of S)
DEBIT Non-controlling interest (NCI's share of S)
CREDIT Non-current assets

with the profit on disposal, less additional depreciation

7.2 Example: intra-group sale of non-current assets

P Co owns 60% of S Co and on 1 January 20X1 S Co sells plant costing $10,000 to P Co for $12,500. The companies make up accounts to 31 December 20X1 and the balances on their retained earnings at that date are:

P Co	after charging depreciation of 10% on plant	$27,000
S Co	including profit on sale of plant	$18,000

Required

Show the working for consolidated retained earnings.

Solution

Retained earnings

	P Co	*S Co*
	$	$
Per question	27,000	18,000
Disposal of plant		
Profit		(2,500)
Depreciation: 10% × $2,500		250
		15,750
Share of S Ltd: $15,750 × 60%	9,450	
	36,450	

Notes

1. The non-controlling interest in the retained earnings of S Co is 40% × $15,750 = $6,300.
2. The asset is written down to cost and depreciation on the 'profit' element is removed. The group profit for the year is thus reduced by a net (($2,500 – $250) × 60%) = $1,350.

8 Summary: consolidated statement of financial position

Purpose	To show the net assets which P controls and the ownership of those assets.
Net assets	Always 100% P plus 100% S providing P holds a majority of voting rights.
Share capital	P only.
Reason	Simply reporting to the parent company's shareholders in another form.
Retained earnings	100% P plus group share of post-acquisition retained earnings of S less consolidation adjustments.
Reason	To show the extent to which the group actually owns total assets less liabilities.
Non-controlling interest	NCI share of S's consolidated net assets, or valuation at fair value.
Reason	To show the equity in a subsidiary not attributable to the parent.

9 Acquisition of a subsidiary during its accounting period

FAST FORWARD

When a subsidiary is acquired **during its accounting period**, its **pre-acquisition profits** will include a **proportion of its total profits** for the accounting period.

9.1 Accounting problem

FAST FORWARD

In the absence of information to the contrary, the profits earned during the period may be assumed to have **accrued evenly** and should be allocated accordingly.

As we have already seen, at the end of the accounting year it will be necessary to prepare consolidated accounts.

The subsidiary company's accounts to be consolidated will show the subsidiary's profit or loss for the whole year. For consolidation purposes, however, it will be necessary to distinguish between:

(a) Profits earned before acquisition
(b) Profits earned after acquisition

In practice, a subsidiary company's profit may not accrue evenly over the year; for example, the subsidiary might be engaged in a trade, such as toy sales, with marked seasonal fluctuations. Nevertheless, the assumption can be made that **profits accrue evenly** whenever it is impracticable to arrive at an accurate split of pre- and post-acquisition profits.

Once the amount of pre-acquisition profit has been established the appropriate consolidation workings (goodwill, retained earnings) can be produced.

Bear in mind that in calculating **non-controlling interests** at the year end, the distinction between pre- and post-acquisition profits is irrelevant. The non-controlling shareholders are simply credited with their share of the subsidiary's total net assets at the end of the reporting period.

It is worthwhile to summarise what happens on consolidation to the retained earnings figures extracted from a subsidiary's statement of financial position. Suppose the accounts of S Co, a 60% subsidiary of P Co, show retained earnings of $20,000 at the end of the reporting period, of which $14,000 were earned prior to acquisition. The figure of $20,000 will appear in the consolidated statement of financial position as follows.

	$
Non-controlling interests working: their share of total retained earnings at the end of the reporting period (40% × $20,000)	8,000
Goodwill working: group share of pre-acquisition retained earnings (60% × $14,000)	8,400
Consolidated retained earnings working: group share of post-acquisition retained earnings (60% × $6,000)	3,600
	20,000

Question

Acquisition

Hinge Co acquired 80% of the ordinary shares of Singe Co on 1 April 20X5. On 31 December 20X4 Singe Co's accounts showed a share premium account of $4,000 and retained earnings of $15,000. The statements of financial position of the two companies at 31 December 20X5 are set out below. Neither company has paid any dividends during the year. Non-controlling interest should be valued at its proportionate share of net assets.

You are required to prepare the consolidated statement of financial position of Hinge Co at 31 December 20X5. There has been no impairment of goodwill.

HINGE CO
STATEMENT OF FINANCIAL POSITION AS AT 31 DECEMBER 20X5

	$	$
Assets		
Non-current assets		
Property, plant and equipment	32,000	
16,000 ordinary shares of 50c each in Singe Co	50,000	
		82,000
Current assets		85,000
Total assets		167,000

	$	$
Equity and liabilities		
Equity		
Ordinary shares of $1 each	100,000	
Share premium account	7,000	
Retained earnings	40,000	
		147,000
Current liabilities		20,000
Total equity and liabilities		167,000

SINGE CO
STATEMENT OF FINANCIAL POSITION AS AT 31 DECEMBER 20X5

	$	$
Assets		
Property, plant and equipment		30,000
Current assets		43,000
Total assets		73,000
Equity and liabilities		
Equity		
20,000 ordinary shares of 50c each	10,000	
Share premium account	4,000	
Retained earnings	39,000	
		53,000
Current liabilities		20,000
Total equity and liabilities		73,000

Answer

Singe Co has made a profit of $24,000 ($39,000 – $15,000) for the year. In the absence of any direction to the contrary, this should be assumed to have arisen evenly over the year; $6,000 in the three months to 31 March and $18,000 in the nine months after acquisition. The company's pre-acquisition retained earnings are therefore as follows.

	$
Balance at 31 December 20X4	15,000
Profit for three months to 31 March 20X5	6,000
Pre-acquisition retained earnings	21,000

The balance of $4,000 on share premium account is all pre-acquisition.

The consolidation workings can now be drawn up.

1 *Goodwill*

	$	$
Consideration transferred		50,000
Non-controlling interest (W2)		7,000
Net assets acquired		57,000
represented by		
Ordinary share capital	10,000	
Retained earnings (pre-acquisition)	21,000	
Share premium	4,000	
		(35,000)
Goodwill		22,000

2 *Non-controlling interest at acquisition*

	$	$
Share capital	10,000	
Share premium	4,000	
Retained earnings 31.12.X4	15,000	
Earnings 3 months to 31.03.X5	6,000	
		35,000
NCI 20%		7,000

3 *Non-controlling interest at reporting date*

	$
Singe Co net assets (73,000 – 20,000)	53,000
× 20%	10,600

4 *Retained earnings*

	Hinge Co	*Singe Co*
	$	$
Per question	40,000	39,000
Pre-acquisition (see above)		(21,000)
		18,000
Share of Singe: $18,000 × 80%	14,400	
	54,400	

5 *Share premium account*

	$
Hinge Co	7,000
Share of Singe Co's post-acquisition share premium	–
	7,000

HINGE CO
CONSOLIDATED STATEMENT OF FINANCIAL POSITION AS AT 31 DECEMBER 20X5

	$	$
Assets		
Property, plant and equipment		62,000
Goodwill (W1)		22,000
Current assets		128,000
Total assets		212,000
Equity and liabilities		
Equity		
Ordinary shares of $1 each	100,000	
Reserves		
Share premium account (W5)	7,000	
Retained earnings (W4)	54,400	
		161,400
Non-controlling interest (W3)		10,600
		172,000
Current liabilities		40,000
Total equity and liabilities		212,000

9.2 Example: pre-acquisition losses of a subsidiary

As an illustration of the entries arising when a subsidiary has pre-acquisition *losses*, suppose P Co acquired all 50,000 $1 ordinary shares in S Co for $20,000 on 1 January 20X1 when there was a debit balance of $35,000 on S Co's retained earnings. In the years 20X1 to 20X4 S Co makes profits of $40,000 in total, leaving a credit balance of $5,000 on retained earnings at 31 December 20X4. P Co's retained earnings at the same date are $70,000.

Solution

The consolidation workings would appear as follows.

1 *Goodwill*

	$	$
Consideration transferred		20,000
Net assets acquired		
as represented by		
Ordinary share capital	50,000	
Retained earnings	(35,000)	
		(15,000)
Goodwill		5,000

2 *Retained earnings*

	P Co	*S Co*
	$	$
At the end of the reporting period	70,000	5,000
Pre-acquisition loss		35,000
		40,000
S Co – share of post-acquisition retained earnings		
(40,000 × 100%)	40,000	
	110,000	

10 Fair values in acquisition accounting

FAST FORWARD

The accounting requirements and disclosures of the **fair value exercise** are covered by **IFRS 3**.

10.1 Goodwill

To understand the importance of fair values in the acquisition of a subsidiary consider again what we mean by goodwill.

Key term

Goodwill. Any excess of the consideration transferred over the acquirer's interest in the fair value of the identifiable assets and liabilities acquired as at the date of the exchange transaction. *(IFRS 3)*

The **statement of financial position of a subsidiary company** at the date it is acquired may not be a guide to the fair value of its net assets. For example, the market value of a freehold building may have risen greatly since it was acquired, but it may appear in the statement of financial position at historical cost less accumulated depreciation.

10.2 What is fair value?

Fair value is defined as follows by IFRS 3 and various other standards – it is an important definition.

Key term

Fair value. The amount for which an asset could be exchanged, or a liability settled, between knowledgeable, willing parties in an arm's length transaction. *(IFRS 3)*

We will look at the requirements of IFRS 3 regarding fair value in more detail below. First let us look at some practical matters.

10.3 Fair value adjustment calculations

Until now we have calculated goodwill as the difference between the consideration transferred and the **carrying amount** of net assets acquired by the group. If this calculation is to comply with the definition above we must ensure that the carrying amount of the subsidiary's net assets is the same as their **fair value**.

There are two possible ways of achieving this.

(a) The **subsidiary company** might **incorporate any necessary revaluations** in its own books of account. In this case, we can proceed directly to the consolidation, taking asset values and reserves figures straight from the subsidiary company's statement of financial position.

(b) The **revaluations** may be made as a **consolidation adjustment without being incorporated** in the subsidiary company's books. In this case, we must make the necessary adjustments to the subsidiary's statement of financial position as a working. Only then can we proceed to the consolidation.

Note. Remember that when depreciating assets are revalued there may be a corresponding alteration in the amount of depreciation charged and accumulated.

10.4 Example: fair value adjustments

P Co acquired 75% of the ordinary shares of S Co on 1 September 20X5. At that date the fair value of S Co's non-current assets was $23,000 greater than their net book value, and the balance of retained earnings was $21,000. The statements of financial position of both companies at 31 August 20X6 are given below. S Co has not incorporated any revaluation in its books of account.

P CO
STATEMENT OF FINANCIAL POSITION AS AT 31 AUGUST 20X6

	$	$
Assets		
Non-current assets		
Property, plant and equipment	63,000	
Investment in S Co at cost	51,000	
		114,000
Current assets		82,000
Total assets		196,000
Equity and liabilities		
Equity		
Ordinary shares of $1 each	80,000	
Retained earnings	96,000	
		176,000
Current liabilities		20,000
Total equity and liabilities		196,000

S CO
STATEMENT OF FINANCIAL POSITION AS AT 31 AUGUST 20X6

	$	$
Assets		
Property, plant and equipment		28,000
Current assets		43,000
Total assets		71,000
Equity and liabilities		
Equity		
Ordinary shares of $1 each	20,000	
Retained earnings	41,000	
		61,000
Current liabilities		10,000
Total equity and liabilities		71,000

If S Co had revalued its non-current assets at 1 September 20X5, an addition of $3,000 would have been made to the depreciation charged for 20X5/X6.

Required

Prepare P Co's consolidated statement of financial position as at 31 August 20X6. Non-controlling interest is to be valued at its proportionate share of the fair value of the subsidiary's identifiable net assets.

Solution

P CO CONSOLIDATED STATEMENT OF FINANCIAL POSITION AS AT 31 AUGUST 20X6

	$	$
Non-current assets		
Property, plant and equipment $(63,000 + 48,000)*	111,000	
Goodwill (W1)	3,000	
		114,000
Current assets		125,000
		239,000
Equity and liabilities		
Equity		
Ordinary shares of $1 each	80,000	
Retained earnings (W3)	108,750	
		188,750
Non-controlling interest (W2)		20,250
		209,000
Current liabilities		30,000
		239,000

* (28,000 + 23,000 – 3,000)

1 *Goodwill*

	$	$
Consideration transferred		51,000
Non-controlling interest (64,000 × 25%)		16,000
		67,000
Net assets acquired as represented by		
Ordinary share capital	20,000	
Retained earnings	21,000	
Fair value adjustment	23,000	
		(64,000)
Goodwill		3,000

2 *Non-controlling interest at reporting date*

	$
S Co's net assets (71,000 – 10,000)	61,000
Fair value adjustment (23,000 – 3,000)	20,000
	81,000
× 25%	20,250

3 *Retained earnings*

	P Co $	*S Co* $
Per question	96,000	41,000
Pre acquisition profits		(21,000)
Depreciation adjustment		(3,000)
Post acquisition S Co		17,000
Group share in S Co ($17,000 × 75%)	12,750	
Group retained earnings	108,750	

Question

An asset is recorded in S Co's books at its historical cost of $4,000. On 1 January 20X5 P Co bought 80% of S Co's equity. Its directors attributed a fair value of $3,000 to the asset as at that date. It had been depreciated for two years out of an expected life of four years on the straight line basis. There was no expected residual value. On 30 June 20X5 the asset was sold for $2,600. What is the profit or loss on disposal of this asset to be recorded in S Co's accounts and in P Co's consolidated accounts for the year ended 31 December 20X5?

Answer

S Co: NBV at disposal (at historical cost) = $4,000 × 1½/4 = $1,500
∴ Profit on disposal = $1,100 (depreciation charge for the year = $500)

P Co: NBV at disposal (at fair value) = $3,000 × 1½/2 = $2,250
∴ Profit on disposal for consolidation = $350 (depreciation for the year = $750).

The non-controlling interest would be credited with 20% of both the profit on disposal and the depreciation charge as part of the one line entry in the consolidated income statement .

10.5 IFRS 3 Fair values

FAST FORWARD

Goodwill arising on consolidation is the difference between the consideration transferred plus the non-controlling interest and the fair value of the identifiable assets and liabilities acquired. **Goodwill** should be calculated **after revaluing** the subsidiary company's assets to fair value. If the subsidiary does not incorporate the revaluation in its own accounts, it should be done as a **consolidation adjustment.**

IFRS 3 sets out **general principles** for arriving at the fair values of a subsidiary's assets and liabilities. The acquirer should recognise the acquiree's identifiable assets, liabilities and contingent liabilities at the acquisition date only if they satisfy the following criteria.

(a) In the case of an **asset** other than an intangible asset, it is **probable** that any associated **future economic benefits** will flow to the acquirer, and its fair value can be **measured reliably.**

(b) In the case of a **liability** other than a contingent liability, it is probable that an **outflow** of resources embodying economic benefits will be required to settle the obligation, and its fair value can be **measured reliably**.

(c) In the case of an **intangible asset** or a **contingent liability**, its fair value can be **measured reliably**.

The acquiree's identifiable assets and liabilities might include assets and liabilities **not previously recognised** in the acquiree's financial statements. For example, a tax benefit arising from the acquiree's tax losses that was not recognised by the acquiree may be recognised by the group if the acquirer has future taxable profits against which the unrecognised tax benefit can be applied.

10.5.1 Restructuring and future losses

An acquirer **should not recognise liabilities for future losses** or other costs expected to be incurred as a result of the business combination.

IFRS 3 explains that a plan to restructure a subsidiary following an acquisition is not a present obligation of the acquiree at the acquisition date. Neither does it meet the definition of a contingent liability. Therefore an acquirer **should not recognise a liability for** such **a restructuring plan** as part of allocating the cost of the combination unless the subsidiary was already committed to the plan before the acquisition.

This **prevents creative accounting**. An acquirer cannot set up a provision for restructuring or future losses of a subsidiary and then release this to profit or loss in subsequent periods in order to reduce losses or smooth profits.

10.5.2 Intangible assets

The acquiree may have **intangible assets**, such as development expenditure. These can be recognised separately from goodwill only if they are **identifiable**. An intangible asset is identifiable only if it:

(a) Is **separable**, ie capable of being separated or divided from the entity and sold, transferred, or exchanged, either individually or together with a related contract, asset or liability, or

(b) Arises from contractual or other legal rights

10.5.3 Contingent liabilities

Contingent liabilities of the acquirer are **recognised** if their **fair value can be measured reliably**. This is a departure from the normal rules in IAS 37; contingent liabilities are not normally recognised, but only disclosed.

After their initial recognition, the acquirer should measure contingent liabilities that are recognised separately at the higher of:

(a) The amount that would be recognised in accordance with IAS 37
(b) The amount initially recognised

10.5.4 Cost of a business combination

The general principle is that the acquirer should measure the cost of a business combination as the total of the **fair values**, at the date of exchange, **of assets given**, liabilities incurred or assumed, and equity instruments issued by the acquirer, in exchange for control of the acquiree.

Sometimes all or part of the cost of an acquisition is deferred (ie, does not become payable immediately). The fair value of any deferred consideration is determined by **discounting** the amounts payable to their **present value** at the date of exchange.

Where equity instruments (eg, ordinary shares) of a quoted entity form part of the cost of a combination, the **published price** at the date of exchange normally provides the best evidence of the instrument's fair value and except in rare circumstances this should be used.

Future losses or other costs expected to be incurred as a result of a combination should not be included in the cost of the combination.

Costs **attributable** to the combination, for example professional fees and administrative costs, should not be included: they are recognised as an expense when incurred. **Costs of issuing debt instruments and equity shares** are covered by IAS 32 *Financial instruments: presentation*, which states that such costs should **reduce the proceeds from the debt issue or the equity issue**.

Question — **Goodwill on consolidation**

On 1 September 20X7 Tyzo Co acquired 6 million $1 shares in Kono Co at $2.00 per share. At that date Kono Co produced the following interim financial statements.

	$m		$m
Property, plant and equipment		Trade payables	3.2
(note 1)	16.0	Taxation	0.6
Inventories (note 2)	4.0	Bank overdraft	3.9
Receivables	2.9	Long-term loans	4.0
Cash in hand	1.2	Share capital ($1 shares)	8.0
		Retained earnings	4.4
	24.1		24.1

Notes

1 The following information relates to the property, plant and equipment of Kono Co at 1 September 20X7.

	$m
Gross replacement cost	28.4
Net replacement cost (gross replacement cost less depreciation)	16.6
Economic value	18.0
Net realisable value	8.0

2 The inventories of Kono Co which were shown in the interim financial statements are raw materials at cost to Kono Co of $4 million. They would have cost $4.2 million to replace at 1 September 20X7.

3 On 1 September 20X7 Tyzo Co took a decision to rationalise the group so as to integrate Kono Co. The costs of the rationalisation were estimated to total $3.0 million and the process was due to start on 1 March 20X8. No provision for these costs has been made in the financial statements given above.

Required

Compute the goodwill on consolidation of Kono Co that will be included in the consolidated financial statements of the Tyzo Co group for the year ended 31 December 20X7, explaining your treatment of the items mentioned above. You should refer to the provisions of relevant accounting standards.

Answer

Goodwill on consolidation of Kono Co

	$m	$m
Consideration ($2.00 × 6m)		12.0
Non-controlling interest (13.2 × 25%)		3.3
		15.3
Fair value of net assets acquired		
Share capital	8.0	
Pre-acquisition reserves	4.4	
Fair value adjustments		
Property, plant and equipment (16.6 – 16.0)	0.6	
Inventories (4.2 – 4.0)	0.2	
		(13.2)
Goodwill		2.1

Notes on treatment

(a) Share capital and pre-acquisition profits represent the book value of the net assets of Kono Co at the date of acquisition. Adjustments are then required to this book value in order to give the fair value of the net assets at the date of acquisition. For short-term monetary items, fair value is their carrying value on acquisition.

(b) IFRS 3 states that the fair value of property, plant and equipment should be determined by market value or, if information on a market price is not available (as is the case here), then by reference to depreciated replacement cost, reflecting normal business practice. The net replacement cost (ie $16.6m) represents the gross replacement cost less depreciation based on that amount, and so further adjustment for extra depreciation is unnecessary.

(c) IFRS 3 also states that raw materials should be valued at replacement cost. In this case that amount is $4.2m.

(d) The rationalisation costs cannot be reported in pre-acquisition results under IFRS 3 as they are not a liability of Kono Co at the acquisition date.

10.5.5 Example: cost of a business combination

Rather than pay cash for Kono Co's shares, Tyzo has funded the acquisition by issuing 4.5m of its own shares to Kono Co's shareholders.

Tyzo's shares have a market value of $3. The costs of the share issue amounted to $500,000 and Tyzo paid a total of $750,000 to lawyers and accountants to carry out the combination.

Calculate the goodwill.

Solution

	$
Consideration:	
Share issue (4.5m × $3)	13.5
Non-controlling interest (as above)	3.3
	16.8
Net assets acquired (as above)	(13.2)
Goodwill	3.6

Note. The share issue costs are debited to share premium and the $750,000 expenses are written off.

10.6 Goodwill arising on acquisition

Goodwill should be carried in the statement of financial position at **cost less any accumulated impairment losses**. Refer back to paragraph 4.10 for more detail on this.

Chapter Roundup

- IAS 27 lays out the basic procedures for the preparation of consolidated financial statements.
- The mechanics of preparing simple **consolidated statements of financial position** can be summarised into the following main procedures:
  - Cancellation
  - Calculation of non-controlling interests
  - Calculation of goodwill arising on consolidation
- In the consolidated statement of financial position it is necessary to distinguish non-controlling interests from those net assets attributable to the group and financed by shareholders' equity.
- Complexities arise when dividends are paid shortly after the acquisition with some dividend relating to pre-acquisition profits.
- In practice the cost of shares acquired by the parent company is seldom equal to the par value of those shares.
- A **seven-stage drill** is made up of the following stages:
  - Update the draft statements of financial position to take account of any dividend paid but not accounted for
  - Agree intra-group current accounts by adjusting for items in transit
  - Cancel items common to both statements of financial position
  - Non-controlling interests
  - Goodwill
  - Retained earnings
  - Consolidated statement of financial position
- There are consolidation adjustments necessary when group companies **trade with or sell non-current assets to each other.**
  - The guiding principle is that the consolidated statement of financial position must show assets at their cost to the group.
  - Any profit arising on intra-group transactions must be eliminated from the group retained earnings unless and until it is realised by a sale outside the group.
- When a subsidiary is acquired **during its accounting period**, its **pre-acquisition profits** will include a **proportion of its total profits** for the accounting period.
- In the absence of information to the contrary, the profits earned during the period may be assumed to have **accrued evenly** and should be allocated accordingly.
- **Goodwill arising on consolidation** is the difference between the consideration transferred plus the non-controlling interest and the fair value of the identifiable assets and liabilities acquired. **Goodwill** should be calculated **after revaluing** the subsidiary company's assets to fair value. If the subsidiary does not incorporate the revaluation in its own accounts, it should be done as a **consolidation adjustment**.
- The accounting requirements and disclosures of the **fair value exercise** are covered by **IFRS 3**.

Quick Quiz

1 Chicken Co owns 80% of Egg Co. Egg Co sells goods to Chicken Co at cost plus 50%. The total invoiced sales to Chicken Co by Egg Co in the year ended 31 December 20X9 were $900,000 and, of these sales, goods which had been invoiced at $60,000 were held in inventory by Chicken Co at 31 December 20X9. What is the reduction in aggregate group gross profit?

2 Major Co, which makes up its accounts to 31 December, has an 80% owned subsidiary Minor Co. Minor Co sells goods to Major Co at a mark-up on cost of 33.33%. At 31 December 20X8, Major had $12,000 of such goods in its inventory and at 31 December 20X9 had $15,000 of such goods in its inventory.

What is the amount by which the consolidated profit attributable to Major Co's shareholders should be adjusted in respect of the above?

Ignore taxation

A $1,000 Debit
B $800 Credit
C $750 Credit
D $600 Debit

3 What are the components making up the figure of non-controlling interest in a consolidated statement of financial position?

4 Goodwill is always positive. True or false?

5 A parent company can assume that, for a subsidiary acquired during its accounting period, profits accrue evenly during the year. True or false?

6 What entries are made in the workings to record the pre-acquisition profits of a subsidiary?

7 What entries are made in the parent company's accounts to record a dividend received from a subsidiary's pre-acquisition profits?

8 Describe the requirement of IFRS 3 in relation to the revaluation of a subsidiary company's assets to fair value at the acquisition date.

9 What guidelines are given by IFRS 3 in relation to valuing land and buildings fairly?

Answers to Quick Quiz

1 $\$60,000 \times \frac{50}{150} = \$20,000$

2 D $(15,000 - 12,000) \times \frac{33.3}{133.3} \times 80\%$

3 The non-controlling interests' share of ordinary shares, reserves and retained earnings *or* the market value of their shares.

4 False. Goodwill can be negative if the purchaser has 'got a bargain'.

5 Not necessarily – the examiner will advise you on this.

6 See Para 4.2

7 DEBIT Cash
CREDIT Investment in subsidiary

8 See para 11.5

9 Market value is the best guideline.

Now try the question below from the Exam Question Bank

Number	Level	Marks	Time
Q26	Introductory	15	27 mins
Q27	Introductory	14	27 mins

22

The consolidated income statement

Topic list	Syllabus reference
1 The consolidated income statement	4(b)
2 The consolidated statement of comprehensive income	4(b)

Introduction

This chapter deals with the consolidated income statement and the consolidated statement of comprehensive income.

Most of the consolidation adjustments will involve the **income statement**, so that is the focus of this chapter.

Study Guide

Section 21 – Preparation of group consolidated external reports

- Prepare a consolidated income statement, statement of comprehensive income and statement of changes in equity for a simple group, including an example where an acquisition occurs during the year and there is a non-controlling interest

1 The consolidated income statement

FAST FORWARD

The source of the consolidated income statement is the individual accounts of the separate companies in the group.

1.1 Consolidation procedure

It is customary in practice to prepare a working paper (known as a **consolidation schedule**) on which the individual income statements are set out side by side and totalled to form the basis of the consolidated income statement.

Exam focus point

In an examination it is very much quicker not to do this. Use workings to show the calculation of complex figures such as the non-controlling interest and show the derivation of others on the face of the income statement, as shown in our examples.

FAST FORWARD

In the consolidated income statement non-controlling interest is brought in as a one-line adjustment at the end of the income statement.

1.2 Simple example: consolidated income statement

P Co acquired 75% of the ordinary shares of S Co on that company's incorporation in 20X3. The summarised income statements and movement on retained earnings of the two companies for the year ending 31 December 20X9 are set out below.

	P Co	*S Co*
	$	$
Sales revenue	75,000	38,000
Cost of sales	(30,000)	(20,000)
Gross profit	45,000	18,000
Administrative expenses	(14,000)	(8,000)
Profit before tax	31,000	10,000
Income tax expense	(10,000)	(2,000)
Profit for the year	21,000	8,000
Note: Movement on retained earnings		
Retained earnings brought forward	87,000	17,000
Profit for the year	21,000	8,000
Retained earnings carried forward	108,000	25,000

Required

Prepare the consolidated income statement and extract from the statement of changes in equity showing retained earnings and non-controlling interest.

Solution

P CO
CONSOLIDATED INCOME STATEMENT
FOR THE YEAR ENDED 31 DECEMBER 20X9

	$
Sales revenue (75 + 38)	113,000
Cost of sales (30 + 20)	(50,000)
Gross profit	63,000
Administrative expenses (14 + 8)	(22,000)
Profit before tax	41,000
Income tax expense	(12,000)
Profit for the year	29,000
Profit attributable to:	
Owners of the parent	27,000
Non-controlling interest ($8,000 × 25%)	2,000
	29,000

STATEMENT OF CHANGES IN EQUITY (EXTRACT)

	Retained Earnings	*Non-controlling Interest*	*Total Equity*
	$	$	$
Balance b/f	99,750	4,250	104,000
Profit for the year	27,000	2,000	29,000
	126,750	6,250	133,000

Notice how the non-controlling interest is dealt with.

(a) Down to the line **'profit for the year'** the **whole** of S Co's results is included without reference to group share or non-controlling share. A **one-line adjustment** is then inserted to deduct the non-controlling share of S Co's profit.

(b) The non-controlling share ($4,250) of S Co's retained earnings brought forward (17,000 × 25%) is **excluded** from group retained earnings. This means that the carried forward figure of $126,750 is the figure which would appear in the statement of financial position for group retained earnings.

This last point may be clearer if we construct the working for group retained earnings.

Group retained earnings

	P Co	*S Co*
	$	$
At reporting date	108,000	25,000
Less pre-acquisition retained earnings		–
		25,000
S Co – share of post acquisition retained earnings (25,000 × 75%)	18,750	
	126,750	

The non-controlling share of S Co's retained earnings comprises the non-controlling interest in the $17,000 profits brought forward plus the non-controlling interest ($2,000) in $8,000 retained profits for the year.

Notice that a consolidated income statement **links up** with a consolidated statement of financial position exactly as in the case of an individual company's accounts: the figure of retained earnings carried forward at the bottom of the income statement appears as the figure for retained earnings in the statement of financial position.

We will now look at the complications introduced by **inter-company trading**, **inter-company dividends** and **pre-acquisition profits** in the subsidiary.

1.3 Intra-group trading

FAST FORWARD

Intra-group sales and purchases are eliminated from the consolidated income statement.

Like the consolidated statement of financial position, the consolidated income statement should deal with the results of the group as those of a single entity. When one company in a group sells goods to another an identical amount is added to the sales revenue of the first company and to the cost of sales of the second. Yet as far as the entity's dealings with outsiders are concerned no sale has taken place.

The consolidated figures for sales revenue and cost of sales should represent **sales to**, and **purchases from, outsiders**. An adjustment is therefore necessary to reduce the sales revenue and cost of sales figures by the value of intra-group sales during the year.

We have also seen in an earlier chapter that any unrealised profits on intra-group trading should be excluded from the figure for group profits. This will occur whenever goods sold at a profit within the group remain in the inventory of the purchasing company at the year end. The best way to deal with this is to **calculate the unrealised profit on unsold inventories at the year end and reduce consolidated gross profit by this amount**. Cost of sales will be the balancing figure.

1.4 Example: intra-group trading

Suppose in our earlier example that S Co had recorded sales of $5,000 to P Co during 20X9. S Co had purchased these goods from outside suppliers at a cost of $3,000. One half of the goods remained in P Co's inventory at 31 December 20X9. Prepare the revised consolidated income statement.

Solution

The consolidated income statement for the year ended 31 December 20X9 would now be as follows.

	$
Sales revenue (75 + 38 – 5)	108,000
Cost of sales (30 + 20 – 5 + 1*)	(46,000)
Gross profit (45 + 18 – 1*)	62,000
Administrative expenses	(22,000)
Profit before taxation	40,000
Income tax expense	(12,000)
Profit for the year	28,000
Profit attributable to :	
Owners of the parent	26,250
Non-controlling interest	1,750
	28,000

Note:

Retained earnings brought forward	99,750
Profit for the year	26,250
Retained earnings carried forward	126,000

*Unrealised profit: ½ × ($5,000 – $3,000)

An adjustment will be made for the unrealised profit against the inventory figure in the consolidated statement of financial position.

1.5 Intra-group dividends

In our example so far we have assumed that S Co retains all of its after-tax profit. It may be, however, that S Co distributes some of its profits as dividends. As before, the **non-controlling interest** in the subsidiary's profit should be calculated immediately after the figure of after-tax profit. For this purpose, no account need be taken of how much of the non-controlling interest is to be distributed by S Co as dividend.

Note that group retained earnings are only adjusted for dividends paid to the parent company shareholders. Dividends paid by the subsidiary to the parent are cancelled on consolidation and dividends paid to the non-controlling interest are replaced by the allocation to the non-controlling interest of their share of the profit for the year of the subsidiary.

1.6 Pre-acquisition profits

FAST FORWARD

Only the **post acquisition** profits of the subsidiary are brought into the consolidated income statement.

As explained above, the figure for retained earnings carried forward must be the same as the figure for retained earnings in the consolidated statement of financial position. We have seen in previous chapters that retained earnings in the consolidated statement of financial position comprise:

(a) The **whole of the parent company's** retained earnings

(b) A **proportion of the subsidiary company's** retained earnings. The proportion is the **group's share of post-acquisition retained earnings** in the subsidiary. From the total retained earnings of the subsidiary we must therefore **exclude** both the **non-controlling share** of total retained earnings and the **group's share of pre-acquisition** retained earnings.

A **similar procedure is necessary in the consolidated income statement** if it is to link up with the consolidated statement of financial position. Previous examples have shown how the non-controlling share of profits is excluded in the income statement. Their share of profits for the year is deducted from profit after tax, while the figure for profits brought forward in the consolidation schedule includes only the group's proportion of the subsidiary's profits.

In the same way, when considering examples which include pre-acquisition profits in a subsidiary, the figure for profits brought forward should include only the group's share of the post-acquisition retained profits. If the subsidiary is **acquired during the accounting year**, it is therefore necessary to apportion its profit for the year between pre-acquisition and post-acquisition elements. The part year method is used.

With the part-year method, the entire income statement of the subsidiary is split between pre-acquisition and post-acquisition proportions. Only the post-acquisition figures are included in the consolidated income statement.

Question

Acquisition

P Co acquired 60% of the equity of S Co on 1 April 20X5. The income statements of the two companies for the year ended 31 December 20X5 are set out below.

	P Co	*S Co*	*S Co* ($^9/_{12}$)
	$	$	$
Sales revenue	170,000	80,000	60,000
Cost of sales	65,000	36,000	27,000
Gross profit	105,000	44,000	33,000
Other income – dividend received S Co	3,600		
Administrative expenses	43,000	12,000	9,000
Profit before tax	65,600	32,000	24,000
Income tax expense	23,000	8,000	6,000
Profit for the year	42,600	24,000	18,000
Note			
Dividends (paid 31 December)	12,000	6,000	
Profit retained	30,600	18,000	
Retained earnings brought forward	81,000	40,000	
Retained earnings carried forward	111,600	58,000	

Prepare the consolidated income statement and retained earnings extract from the statement of changes in equity.

Answer

The shares in S Co were acquired three months into the year. Only the post-acquisition proportion (9/12ths) of S Co's income statement is included in the consolidated income statement. This is shown above for convenience.

P CO CONSOLIDATED INCOME STATEMENT
FOR THE YEAR ENDED 31 DECEMBER 20X5

	$
Sales revenue (170 + 60)	230,000
Cost of sales (65 + 27)	(92,000)
Gross profit	138,000
Administrative expenses (43 + 9)	(52,000)
Profit before tax	86,000
Income tax expense (23 + 6)	(29,000)
Profit for the year	57,000
Profit attributable to:	
Owners of the parent	49,800
Non-controlling interest (18 × 40%)	7,200
	57,000

STATEMENT OF CHANGES IN EQUITY

	Retained earnings
	$
Balance brought forward*	81,000
Dividend paid (P)	(12,000)
Total comprehensive income for the year	49,800
Balance carried forward	118,800

* All of S Co's profits brought forward are pre-acquisition.

Question

Non-controlling interest

The following information relates to Brodick Co and its subsidiary Lamlash Co for the year to 30 April 20X7.

	Brodick Co	*Lamlash Co*
	$'000	$'000
Sales revenue	1,100	500
Cost of sales	(630)	(300)
Gross profit	470	200
Administrative expenses	(105)	(150)
Dividend from Lamlash Co	24	–
Profit before tax	389	50
Income tax expense	(65)	(10)
Profit for the year	324	40
Note		
Dividends paid	200	30
Profit retained	124	10
Retained earnings brought forward	460	106
Retained earnings carried forward	584	116

Additional information

(a) The issued share capital of the group was as follows.

Brodick Co : 5,000,000 ordinary shares of $1 each.
Lamlash Co : 1,000,000 ordinary shares of $1 each.

(b) Brodick Co purchased 80% of the issued share capital of Lamlash Co in 20X0. At that time, the revenue reserves of Lamlash amounted to $56,000.

Required

Insofar as the information permits, prepare the Brodick group consolidated income statement for the year to 30 April 20X7 in accordance with IASs, and the extract from the statement of changes in equity showing retained earnings.

Answer

BRODICK GROUP
CONSOLIDATED INCOME STATEMENT
FOR THE YEAR TO 30 APRIL 20X7

	$'000
Sales revenue (1,100 + 500)	1,600
Cost of sales (630 + 300)	(930)
Gross profit	670
Administrative expenses (105 + 150)	(255)
Profit before tax	415
Income tax expense (65 + 10)	(75)
Profit for the year	340

Profit attributable to:

	$
Owners of the parent	332
Non-controlling interest	8
	340

STATEMENT OF CHANGES IN EQUITY	*Retained earnings*
	$
Balance brought forward (W2)	500
Dividend paid (parent)	(200)
Total comprehensive income for the year	332
Balance carried forward	632

Workings

1 *Non-controlling interests*

	$'000
In Lamlash (20% × 40)	8

2 *Retained earnings brought forward*

	Brodick Co	*Lamlash Co*
	$'000	$'000
Per question	460	106
Less pre-aqn		(56)
		50
Share of Lamlash: 80% × 50	40	
	500	

1.7 Section summary

The table below summarises the main points about the consolidated income statement.

Purpose	To show the results of the group for an accounting period as if it were a single entity.
Sales revenue to profit for year	100% P + 100% S (excluding adjustments for inter-company transactions).
Reason	To show the results of the group which were controlled by the parent company.
Intra-group sales	Strip out inter-company activity from both sales revenue and cost of sales.
Unrealised profit on intra-group sales	(a) Goods sold by P. Increase cost of sales by unrealised profit. (b) Goods sold by S. Increase cost of sales by full amount of unrealised profit and decrease non-controlling interest by their share of unrealised profit.
Depreciation	If the value of S's non-current assets have been subjected to a fair value uplift then any additional depreciation must be charged in the consolidated income statement. The non-controlling interest will need to be adjusted for their share.
Transfer of non-current assets	Expenses must be increased by any profit on the transfer and reduced by any additional depreciation arising from the increased carrying value of the asset.
Non-controlling interests	S's profit after tax (PAT) — X Less: * unrealised profit — (X) * profit on disposal of non-current assets — (X) additional depreciation following FV uplift — (X) Add: ** additional depreciation following disposal of non-current assets — X X NCI% — X * Only applicable if sales of goods and non-current assets made by subsidiary. ** Only applicable if sale of non-current assets made by subsidiary.
Reason	To show the extent to which profits generated through P's control are in fact owned by other parties.
Reserves carried forward	As per the calculations for the statement of financial position.

2 The consolidated statement of comprehensive income

FAST FORWARD

The consolidated statement of comprehensive income is produced using the consolidated income statement as a basis.

The only items of other comprehensive income that are included in your syllabus are revaluation gains and losses, so a consolidated statement of comprehensive income will be easy to produce once you have done the income statement.

We will take the last question and add an item of comprehensive income to illustrate this.

2.1 Example: Consolidated statement of comprehensive income

The consolidated income statement of the Brodrick Group is as in the answer to the last question. In addition, Lamlash made a $200,000 revaluation gain on one of its properties during the year.

2.2 Solution

BRODRICK GROUP
CONSOLIDATED STATEMENT OF COMPREHENSIVE INCOME FOR THE YEAR TO 30 APRIL 20X7

	$'000
Sales revenue	1,600
Cost of sales	(930)
Gross profit	670
Administrative expenses	(255)
Profit before tax	415
Income tax expense	(75)
Profit for the year	340
Other comprehensive income:	
Gain on property revaluation	200
Total comprehensive income for the year	540
Profit attributable to:	
Owners of the parent	332
Non-controlling interest	8
	340
Total comprehensive income attributable to:	
Owners of the parent (332 + (200 × 80%))	492
Non-controlling interest (8 + (200 × 20%))	48
	540

2.3 Consolidated statement of comprehensive income (separate statement)

If we were using the two-statement format (as explained in Chapter 15) we would produce a separate income statement and statement of comprehensive income.

2.4 Example: Statement of comprehensive income

BRODRICK GROUP
CONSOLIDATED STATEMENT OF COMPREHENSIVE INCOME

Profit for the year	340
Other comprehensive income:	
Gain on property revaluation	200
Total comprehensive income for the year	540
Total comprehensive income attributable to:	
Owners of the parent (332 + (200 × 80%))	492
Non-controlling interest (8 + (200 × 20%)	48
	540

2.5 Consolidated statement of changes in equity

These amounts would appear in the consolidated statement of changes in equity as follows:

	Retained earnings	*Revaluation surplus*	*Total*	*Non-controlling interest*	*Total*
	$'000	$'000	$'000	$'000	$'000
Total comprehensive income for the year	332	160	492	48	540

Chapter Roundup

- The source of the consolidated income statement is the individual accounts of the separate companies in the group.
- In the consolidated income statement non-controlling interest is brought in as a one-line adjustment after 'profit for the year'.
- Intra-group sales and purchases are eliminated from the consolidated income statement.
- Only the **post acquisition** profits of the subsidiary are brought into the consolidated income statement.
- The consolidated statement of comprehensive income is produced using the consolidated income statement as a basis.

Quick Quiz

1 Where does unrealised profit on intra-group trading appear in the income statement?

2 At the beginning of the year a 75% subsidiary transfers a non-current asset to the parent for $500,000. It's carrying value was $400,000 and it has 4 years of useful life left. How is this accounted for at the end of the year in the consolidated income statement?

Answers to Quick Quiz

1 As a deduction from consolidated gross profit.

2

	$
Unrealised profit	100,000
Additional depreciation (100 ÷ 4)	(25,000)
Net charge to income statement	75,000

	DR	*CR*
	$	$
Non-current asset		100,000
Additional depreciation	25,000	
Group profit (75%)	56,250	
Non-controlling interest (25%)	18,750	
	100,000	100,000

Now try the questions below from the Exam Question Bank

Number	Level	Marks	Time
Q28	Examination	25	45 mins
Q29	Introductory	15	27 mins
Q30	Introductory	20	36 mins

23 Accounting for associates

Topic list	Syllabus reference
1 Accounting for associates	4(c)
2 The equity method	4(c)
3 Income statement and statement of financial position	4(c)

Introduction

In this chapter we deal with the treatment of associates in the consolidated financial statements. As the group's share of profit in the associate appears in the income statement section, we have concentrated on the separate income statement.

Study Guide

Section 24 – Business combinations – associates and joint ventures

- Define associates and joint ventures (ie jointly controlled operations, assets and entities)
- Distinguish between equity accounting and proportional consolidation
- Describe and prepare accounts under the two formats of proportional consolidation
- Prepare consolidated financial statements to include a single subsidiary and an associated company or a joint venture (both methods)

1 Accounting for associates

FAST FORWARD

IAS 28 requires that, in consolidated accounts, **associates** should be accounted for using **equity accounting principles**.

1.1 Definitions

We looked at some of the important definitions in Chapter 20; these are repeated here with some additional important terms.

Key terms

- **Associate**. An entity, including an unincorporated entity such as a partnership, over which an investor has significant influence and which is neither a subsidiary nor an interest in a joint venture.
- **Significant influence** is the power to participate in the financial and operating policy decisions of the investee but is not control or joint control over those policies.
- **Equity method**. A method of accounting whereby the investment is initially recorded at cost and adjusted thereafter for the post-acquisition change in the investor's share of net assets of the investee. The profit or loss of the investor includes the investor's share of the profit or loss of the investee. *(IAS 28)*

We have already looked at how the **status** of an investment in an associate should be determined. Go back to Section 1 of Chapter 20 to revise it. (Note that, as for an investment in a subsidiary, any **potential voting rights** should be taken into account in assessing whether the investor has **significant influence** over the investee.)

IAS 28 requires all investments in associates to be accounted for in the consolidated accounts using the equity method, *unless* the investment is classified as 'held for sale' in accordance with IFRS 5 in which case it should be accounted for under IFRS 5 (see Chapter 16), or the exemption in the paragraph below applies.

An investor is exempt from applying the equity method if:

(a) It is a parent exempt from preparing consolidated financial statements under IAS 27, or

(b) All of the following apply:

   (i) The investor is a **wholly-owned subsidiary** or it is a **partially owned subsidiary** of another entity and its other owners, including those not otherwise entitled to vote, have been informed about, and do not object to, the investor not applying the equity method;

   (ii) The investor's securities are **not publicly traded**

   (iii) It is **not in the process of issuing securities** in public securities markets; and

   (iv) The **ultimate or intermediate parent** publishes consolidated financial statements that comply with International Financial Reporting Standards.

The revised version of IAS 28 **no longer allows** an investment in an associate to be excluded from equity accounting when an investee operates under severe long-term restrictions that significantly impair its ability to transfer funds to the investor. Significant influence must be lost before the equity method ceases to be applicable.

The use of the equity method should be **discontinued** from the date that the investor **ceases to have significant influence.**

From that date, the investor shall account for the investment in accordance with IAS 39 *Financial instruments: recognition and measurement.* The carrying amount of the investment at the date that it ceases to be an associate shall be regarded as its cost on initial measurement as a financial asset under IAS 39.

1.2 Separate financial statements of the investor

If an investor **issues consolidated financial statements** (because it has subsidiaries), an investment in an associate should be *either*:

(a) Accounted for at **cost**, or
(b) In accordance with **IAS 39** (at fair value)

in its separate financial statements.

If an investor that does ***not*** **issue consolidated financial statements** (ie it has no subsidiaries) but has an investment in an associate this should similarly be included in the financial statements of the investor either at cost, or in accordance with IAS 39 (see Chapter 10).

2 The equity method

2.1 Application of the equity method: consolidated accounts

Some of the procedures required to apply the equity method are the same as are required for full consolidation. In particular, **intra-group unrealised profits** must be excluded.

Goodwill is calculated as the difference (positive or negative) between the cost of acquisition and the investor's share of the fair values of the net identifiable assets of the associate. This should be treated as required by IFRS 3 (see Chapter 6).

Point to note

It is vital that you don't confuse associates with subsidiaries. While there are some similarities between the accounting rules for each of them, there are also some very important differences.

2.1.1 Consolidated income statement

The basic principle is that the investing company (X Co) should take account of its **share of the earnings** of the associate, Y Co, whether or not Y Co distributes the earnings as dividends. X Co achieves this by adding to consolidated profit the group's share of Y Co's profit after tax.

Notice the difference between this treatment and the **consolidation** of a subsidiary company's results. If Y Co were a subsidiary then X Co would take credit for the whole of its sales revenue, cost of sales etc and would then make a one-line adjustment to remove any non-controlling share.

However, under equity accounting, the associate's sales revenue, cost of sales and so on are ***not*** **amalgamated** with those of the group. Instead the group share only of the associate's profit before tax and tax charge for the year is added to the corresponding lines of the parent company and its subsidiaries.

2.1.2 Consolidated statement of financial position

A figure for **investment in associates** is shown which at the time of the acquisition must be stated at cost. This amount will increase (decrease) each year by the amount of the group's share of the associated company's profit (loss) for the year.

2.2 Example: associate

P Co, a company with subsidiaries, acquires 25,000 of the 100,000 $1 ordinary shares in A Co for $60,000 on 1 January 20X8. In the year to 31 December 20X8, A Co earns profits after tax of $24,000, from which it pays a dividend of $6,000.

How will A Co's results be accounted for in the individual and consolidated accounts of P Co for the year ended 31 December 20X8?

Solution

In the **individual accounts** of P Co, the investment will be recorded on 1 January 20X8 at cost. Unless there is an impairment in the value of the investment (see below), this amount will remain in the individual statement of financial position of P Co permanently. The only entry in P Co's individual income statement will be to record dividends received. For the year ended 31 December 20X8, P Co will:

DEBIT	Cash	$1,500	
CREDIT	Income from shares in associates		$1,500

In the **consolidated accounts** of P Co equity accounting principles will be used to account for the investment in A Co. Consolidated profit after tax will include the group's share of A Co's profit after tax (25% × $24,000 = $6,000). To the extent that this has been distributed as dividend, it is already included in P Co's individual accounts and will automatically be brought into the consolidated results. That part of the group's share of profit in the associate which has not been distributed as dividend ($4,500) will be brought into consolidation by the following adjustment.

DEBIT	Investment in associates	$4,500	
CREDIT	Income from shares in associates		$4,500

The asset 'Investment in associates' is then stated at $64,500, being cost plus the group share of post-acquisition retained profits.

Exam focus point

A common mistake made by struggling students is to add the associate's accounts line-by-line into the rest of the group's, as if it were a subsidiary. You need to make sure you apply the equity accounting rules to associates.

3 Income statement and statement of financial position

3.1 Consolidated income statement

FAST FORWARD

In the **consolidated income statement** the investing group takes credit for its **share of the after-tax profits** of associates whether or not they are distributed as dividends.

A **consolidation schedule** may be used to prepare the consolidated income statement of a group with associates. The treatment of associates' profits in the following example should be studied carefully.

3.2 Illustration

The following **consolidation schedule** relates to the P Co group, consisting of the parent company, an 80% owned subsidiary (S Co) and an associate (A Co) in which the group has a 30% interest.

CONSOLIDATION SCHEDULE

	Group	*P Co*	*S Co*	*A Co*
	$'000	$'000	$'000	$'000
Sales revenue	1,400	600	800	300
Cost of sales	770	370	400	120
Gross profit	630	230	400	180
Administrative expenses	290	110	180	80
	340	120	220	100
Interest receivable	30	30	–	–
	370	150	220	100
Interest payable	(20)	–	(20)	–
Share of profit of associate ((100 – 43) × 30%)	17	–	–	
	367	150	200	100
Income tax expense				
Group	(145)	(55)	(90)	
Associate		–	–	(43)
Profit for the year	222	95	110	57
Non-controlling interest (110× 20%)	(22)	–	(22)	–
	200	95	88	57
Inter-company dividends	–	20	(18)	(2)
Group profit	200	115	70	55

Note the following

(a) Group sales revenue, group gross profit and costs such as depreciation etc exclude the sales revenue, gross profit and costs etc of associated companies.

(b) The group share of the associated company profits is credited to the group income statement. If the associated company has been acquired during the year, it would be necessary to deduct the pre-acquisition profits (remembering to allow for tax on current year profits).

(c) The non-controlling interest will only ever apply to subsidiary companies.

3.3 Pro-forma consolidated income statement

The following is a **suggested layout** (using the figures given in the illustration above) for the consolidated income statement for a company having subsidiaries as well as associated companies.

	$'000
Sales revenue	1,400
Cost of sales	770
Gross profit	630
Administrative expenses	290
	340
Other income: interest receivable	30
	370
Finance costs	(20)
	350
Share of profit of associate (30 – 13)	17
Profit before taxation	367
Income tax expense	(145)
Profit for the year	222
Profit attributable to:	
Owners of the parent	200
Non-controlling interest	22
	222

3.4 Consolidated statement of financial position

FAST FORWARD

In the **consolidated statement of financial position** the investment in associates should be shown as:

- **Cost of the investment in the associate**; plus
- Group share of post acquisition profits; less
- Any amounts paid out as dividends; less any amount written off the investment

As explained earlier, the consolidated statement of financial position will contain an **asset 'Investment in associates'**. The amount at which this asset is stated will be its original cost plus the group's share of any **profits earned since acquisition** which have not been distributed as dividends.

3.5 Example: consolidated statement of financial position

On 1 January 20X6 the net tangible assets of A Co amount to $220,000, financed by 100,000 $1 ordinary shares and revenue reserves of $120,000. P Co, a company with subsidiaries, acquires 30,000 of the shares in A Co for $75,000. During the year ended 31 December 20X6 A Co's profit after tax is $30,000, from which dividends of $12,000 are paid.

Show how P Co's investment in A Co would appear in the consolidated statement of financial position at 31 December 20X6.

Solution

CONSOLIDATED STATEMENT OF FINANCIAL POSITION
AS AT 31 DECEMBER 20X6 (extract)

	$
Non-current assets	
Investment in associated company	
Cost	75,000
Group share of post-acquisition retained profits	
(30% × $18,000)	5,400
	80,400

Question — Associate I

Set out below are the draft accounts of Parent Co and its subsidiaries and of Associate Co. Parent Co acquired 40% of the equity capital of Associate Co three years ago when the latter's reserves stood at $40,000.

SUMMARISED STATEMENTS OF FINANCIAL POSITION

	Parent Co & subsidiaries	*Associate Co*
	$'000	$'000
Tangible non-current assets	220	170
Investment in Associate at cost	60	–
Loan to Associate Co	20	–
Current assets	100	50
Loan from Parent Co	–	(20)
	400	200
Share capital ($1 shares)	250	100
Retained earnings	150	100
	400	200

SUMMARISED INCOME STATEMENTS

	Parent Co & subsidiaries	*Associate Co*
	$'000	$'000
Net profit	95	80
Taxation	35	30
	60	50

You are required to prepare the summarised consolidated accounts of Parent Co.

Notes

(1) Assume that the associate's assets/liabilities are stated at fair value.

(2) Assume that there are no non-controlling interests in the subsidiary companies.

Answer

PARENT CO
CONSOLIDATED INCOME STATEMENT

	$'000
Net profit	95
Share of profits of associated company (80 × 40%)	32
Profit before tax	127
Taxation (35 + (30 × 40%) note (a))	47
Profit attributable to the members of Parent Co	80

Notes

(a) The note to the tax charge would disclose that $12,000 is the share of Associate's tax.

(b) The accounts should disclose the amount of the profit attributable to the members of Parent Co which has been dealt with in that company's own accounts. In this example there is insufficient information to do this.

PARENT CO
CONSOLIDATED STATEMENT OF FINANCIAL POSITION

	$'000
Assets	
Tangible non-current assets	220
Interest in associated company (see note)	104
Current assets	100
Total assets	424
Equity and liabilities	
Share capital	250
Retained earnings (W1)	174
Total equity and liabilities	424

Note

	$'000
Interest in associate	
Cost of investment	60
Share of post-acquisition retained earnings (W1)	24
Loan to associate	20
	104

Workings

1

Retained earnings	*Parent & Subsidiaries*	*Associate*
	$'000	$'000
Per question	150	100
Pre-acquisition		40
Post-acquisition		60
Group share in associate ($60 × 40%)	24	
Group retained earnings	174	

Question — Associate II

Alfred Co bought a 25% shareholding on 31 December 20X8 in Grimbald Co at a cost of $38,000.

During the year to 31 December 20X9 Grimbald Co made a profit before tax of $82,000 and the taxation charge on the year's profits was $32,000. A dividend of $20,000 was paid on 31 December out of these profits.

Calculate the entries for the associate which would appear in the consolidated accounts of the Alfred group, in accordance with the requirements of IAS 28.

Answer

CONSOLIDATED INCOME STATEMENT

	$
Group share of profit of associate (82,000 × 25%)	20,500
Less taxation (32,000 × 25%)	(8,000)
Share of profit of associate	12,500

CONSOLIDATED STATEMENT OF FINANCIAL POSITION

	$
Interest in associate	45,500

Working

	$
Cost of investment	38,000
Share of post-acquisition retained earnings ((82,000 – 32,000 – 20,000) × 25%)	7,500
	45,500

The following points are also relevant and are similar to a parent-subsidiary consolidation situation.

(a) Use financial statements drawn up to the **same reporting date.**

(b) If this is impracticable, adjust the financial statements for **significant transactions/ events** in the intervening period. The difference between the reporting date of the associate and that of the investor must be no more than three months.

(c) Use **uniform accounting policies** for like transactions and events in similar circumstances, adjusting the associate's statements to reflect group policies if necessary.

3.6 'Upstream' and 'downstream' transactions

'Upstream' transactions are, for example, sales from an associate to the investor. 'Downstream' transactions are, for example, sales from the investor to an associate.

Unrealised profits resulting from 'upstream' and 'downstream' transactions between an investor (including its consolidated subsidiaries) and an associate are eliminated to the extent of the investor's interest in the associate. This is very similar to the procedure for eliminating intra-group transactions between a parent and a subsidiary. The important thing to remember is that **only the group's share is eliminated**.

3.7 Example: downstream transaction

A Co, a parent with subsidiaries, holds 25% of the equity shares in B Co. During the year, A Co makes sales of $1,000,000 to B Co at cost plus a 25% mark-up. At the year-end, B Co has all these goods still in inventories.

Solution

A Co has made an unrealised profit of $200,000 (1,000,000 × 25/125) on its sales to the associate. The group's share (25%) of this must be eliminated:

DEBIT	Cost of sales (consolidated income statement)	$50,000	
CREDIT	Investment in associate (consolidated statement of financial position)		$50,000

Because the sale was made to the associate, the group's share of the unsold inventory forms part of the investment in the associate at the year-end. If the associate had made the sale to the parent, the adjustment would have been:

DEBIT	Cost of sales (consolidated income statement)	$50,000	
CREDIT	Inventories (consolidated statement of financial position)		$50,000

The group's share of the revenue must also be eliminated from the consolidated income statement.

DEBIT	Revenue (25% × 1,000,000)	$250,000	
CREDIT	Cost of sales		$250,000

3.8 Associate's losses

When the equity method is being used and the investor's share of losses of the associate equals or exceeds its interest in the associate, the investor should **discontinue** including its share of further losses. The investment is reported at nil value. The interest in the associate is normally the carrying amount of the investment in the associate, but it also includes any other long-term interests, for example, long term receivables or loans.

After the investor's interest is reduced to nil, **additional losses** should only be recognised where the investor has incurred obligations or made payments on behalf of the associate (for example, if it has guaranteed amounts owed to third parties by the associate).

3.9 Impairment losses

IAS 39 sets out a list of indications that a financial asset (including an associate) may have become impaired. Any impairment loss is recognised in accordance with IAS 36 *Impairment of assets* for each associate individually.

In the case of an associate, any impairment loss will be deducted from the carrying amount in the statement of financial position.

The working would be as follows.

	$
Cost of investment	X
Share of post-acquisition retained earnings	X
	X
Impairment loss	(X)
Investment in associate	X

Exam focus point

It is not unusual in the exam to have both an associate and a subsidiary to account for in a consolidation.

The statements of financial position of J Co and its investee companies, P Co and S Co, at 31 December 20X5 are shown below.

STATEMENTS OF FINANCIAL POSITION AS AT 31 DECEMBER 20X5

	J Co	*P Co*	*S Co*
	$'000	$'000	$'000
Non-current assets			
Freehold property	1,950	1,250	500
Plant and machinery	795	375	285
Investments	1,500	–	–
	4,245	1,625	785
Current assets			
Inventory	575	300	265
Trade receivables	330	290	370
Cash	50	120	20
	955	710	655
Total assets	5,200	2,335	1,440
Equity and liabilities			
Equity			
Share capital – $1 shares	2,000	1,000	750
Retained earnings	1,460	885	390
	3,460	1,885	1,140
Non-current liabilities			
12% loan stock	500	100	
Current liabilities			
Trade payables	680	350	300
Bank overdraft	560	–	–
	1,240	350	300
Total equity and liabilities	5,200	2,335	1,440

Additional information

(a) J Co acquired 600,000 ordinary shares in P Co on 1 January 20X0 for $1,000,000 when the retained earnings of P Co were $200,000.

(b) At the date of acquisition of P Co, the fair value of its freehold property was considered to be $400,000 greater than its value in P Co's statement of financial position. P Co had acquired the property in January 20W0 and the buildings element (comprising 50% of the total value) is depreciated on cost over 50 years.

(c) J Co acquired 225,000 ordinary shares in S Co on 1 January 20X4 for $500,000 when the retained earnings of S Co were $150,000.

(d) P Co manufactures a component used by both J Co and S Co. Transfers are made by P Co at cost plus 25%. J Co held $100,000 inventory of these components at 31 December 20X5 and S Co held $80,000 at the same date.

(e) The goodwill in P Co is impaired and should be fully written off. An impairment loss of $92,000 is to be recognised on the investment in S Co.

Required

Prepare, in a format suitable for inclusion in the annual report of the J Group, the consolidated statement of financial position at 31 December 20X5.

Answer

J GROUP CONSOLIDATED STATEMENT OF FINANCIAL POSITION AS AT 31 DECEMBER 20X5

	$'000
Non-current assets	
Freehold property (W2)	3,570.00
Plant and machinery (795 + 375)	1,170.00
Investment in associate (W8)	475.20
	5,215.20
Current assets	
Inventory (W3)	855.00
Receivables (W4)	620.00
Cash (50 + 120)	170.00
	1,645.00
Total assets	6,860.20
Equity and liabilities	
Equity	
Share capital	2,000.00
Retained earnings (W9)	1,778.12
	3,778.12
Non-controlling interest (W6)	892.08
	4,670.20
Non-current liabilities	
12% loan stock (500 + 100)	600.00
Current liabilities (W5)	1,590.00
Total equity and liabilities	6,860.20

Workings

1 *Group structure*

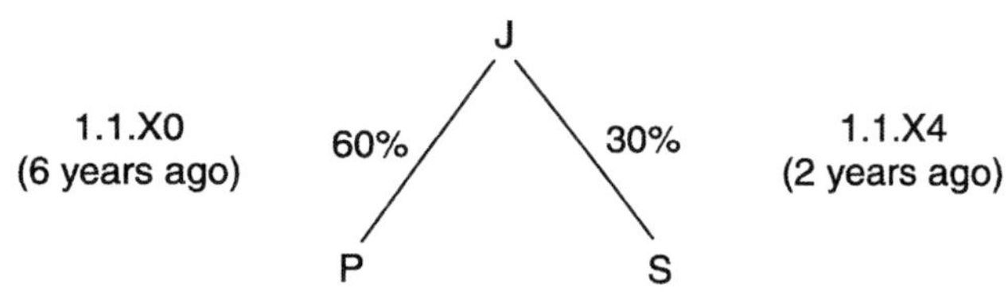

2 *Freehold property*

	$'000
J Co	1,950
P Co	1,250
Fair value adjustment	400
Additional depreciation (400 × 50% ÷ 40) × 6 years (20X0-20X5)	(30)
	3,570

3 *Inventory*

	$'000
J Co	575
P Co	300
PUP (100 × $^{25}/_{125}$)	(20)
	855

4 *Receivables*

	$'000
J Co	330
P Co	290
	620

5 *Current liabilities*

		$'000
J Co:	bank overdraft	560
	trade payables	680
P Co:	trade payables	350
		1,590

6 *Non-controlling interest at reporting date*

	$'000
Net assets of P Co	1,885.0
Fair value adjustment (W11)	370.0
Less PUP: sales to J Co	(20.0)
sales to S Co (80 × $^{25}/_{125}$ × 30%)	(4.8)
	2,230.2
Non-controlling interest (40%)	892.08

7 *Goodwill*

	$'000	$'000
P Co		
Consideration transferred		1,000
Non-controlling interest at acquisition (1,600 × 40%)		640
Net assets acquired		
Share capital	1,000	
Retained earnings	200	
Fair value adjustment	400	
		(1,600)
Goodwill at acquisition		40
Impairment loss		(40)
		0

8 *Investment in associate*

	$'000
Cost of investment	500.00
Share of post-acquisition profit (390 – 150) × 30%	72.00
Less PUP	(4.80)
Less impairment loss	(92.00)
	475.20

9 *Retained earnings*

	J	*P*	*S*
	$'000	$'000	$'000
Retained earnings per question	1,460.0	885.0	390.0
Adjustments			
Unrealised profit (W10)		(24.8)	
Fair value adjustments (W11)		(30.0)	
		830.2	390.0
Less pre-acquisition reserves		(200.0)	(150.0)
	1,460.0	630.2	240.0
P: 60% × 630.2	378.1		
S: 30% × 240	72.0		
Less impairment losses : P	(40.0)		
S	(92.0)		
	1,778.1		

10 *Unrealised profit (PUP)*

	$'000
On sales to J (parent co) 100 × 25/125	20.0
On sales to S (associate) 80 × 25/125 × 30%	4.8
	24.8

11 *Fair value adjustments*

	Difference at acquisition	*Difference now*
	$'000	$'000
Property	400	400
Additional depreciation: 200 × 6/40	–	(30)
	400	370

∴ Charge $30,000 to retained earnings

Chapter Roundup

- IAS 28 requires that, in consolidated accounts, **associates** should be accounted for using **equity accounting principles.**
- In the **consolidated income statement** the investing group takes credit for its **share of the after-tax profits** of associates, whether or not they are distributed as dividends.
- In the **consolidated statement of financial position,** the investment in associates should be shown as:
  - **Cost of the investment in the associate**; plus
  - Group share of post-acquisition profits; less
  - Any amounts paid out as dividends; less any amount written off this investment

Quick Quiz

1 Barley Co has owned 100% of the issued share capital of Oats Co for many years. Barley Co sells goods to Oats Co at cost plus 20%. The following information is available for the year:

Revenue	– Barley Co	$460,000
	– Oats Co	$120,000

During the year Barley Co sold goods to Oats Co for $60,000 of which $18,000 were still held in inventory by Oats at the year end.

At what amount should revenue appear in the consolidated income statement?

2 Horace Co acquired 75% of the ordinary share capital of Sylvia Co several years ago. The income statement of Sylvia Co for the year ended 28 February 20X0 showed the following:

	$
Profit on ordinary activities after tax	4,000
Ordinary dividend	(2,000)
	2,000

What is the non-controlling interest in the consolidated income statement of Horace Co for the year ended 28 February 20X0?

3 Saroti Co owns 70% of the ordinary shares of Macari Co. An extract from Macari Co's income statement is as follows:

	$
Profit after tax	10,000
Ordinary dividend paid	(5,000)
Retained profit	5,000

What amount for non-controlling interest should be shown in the consolidated income statement of Saroti Co?

4 Define an associate.

5 How should associates be accounted for in the separate financial statements of the investor?

6 What is the effect of the equity method on the consolidated income statement and statement of financial position?

Answers to Quick Quiz

1 Revenue: 460 + 120 – 60 = $520,000

2 25% × $4,000 = $1,000

3 30% × $10,000 = $3,000

4 An entity in which an investor has a significant influence, but which is not a subsidiary or a joint venture of the investor.

5 Either at cost or in accordance with IAS 39.

6 (a) *Income statement.* Investing company includes its share of the earnings of the associate, by adding its share of profit after tax.

(b) *Statement of financial position.* Investment in associates is initially included in assets at cost. This will increase or decrease each year according to whether the associated company makes a profit or loss.

Now try the questions below from the Exam Question Bank

Number	Level	Marks	Time
Q31	Examination	25	45 mins

Accounting for joint ventures

24

Topic list	Syllabus reference
1 IAS 31 Interests in joint ventures	4(d)

Introduction

IAS 31 covers all types of **joint venture**. It looks at how joint ventures are accounted for in individual accounts and in consolidated accounts. This is covered in full as an important standard.

Study Guide

Section 24 – Business combinations – associates and joint ventures

- Define associates and joint ventures (ie jointly controlled operations, assets and entities)
- Distinguish between equity accounting and proportional consolidation
- Describe and prepare accounts under the two formats of proportional consolidation
- Prepare consolidated financial statements to include a single subsidiary and an associated company or a joint venture (both methods)

1 IAS 31 Interests in joint ventures

FAST FORWARD

IAS 31 *Financial reporting of interests in joint ventures* is concerned with how venturers **report their interests** in joint ventures in their accounts.

Two or more persons may decide to enter into a business venture together without wishing to form a formal long-term partnership. Usually the venturers agree to place limitations on their activities, for example, a joint venture to manufacture and sell 'total eclipse of the sun' souvenirs could be limited by time, while a joint venture to buy and sell a bankrupt's inventory (a fairly common occurrence in practice) comes to an end when all the inventory has been sold.

Joint ventures are often found when each party can **contribute in different ways** to the venture. For example, one venturer may provide finance, another purchases or manufactures goods, while a third offers his marketing skills.

Joint ventures generally have the following characteristics.

- They are **limited by time and/or activity**
- The venturers usually **carry on their principal businesses** at the same time
- **Separate books** for the venture are **not** normally maintained
- The venturers usually agree to a **profit/loss sharing ratio** for the purpose of the venture

IAS 31 *Interests in joint ventures* covers all types of joint ventures. It is not concerned with the accounts of the joint venture itself (if separate accounts are maintained), but rather **how the interest in a joint venture is accounted for by each joint venturer** (ie each 'partner' in the joint venture).

The assets and liabilities, income and expenses of the joint venture must be reported in the financial statements of the venturers and investors, whatever the form of the joint venture.

IAS 31 looks at the various forms of joint venture which may be undertaken and then looks at how joint ventures are dealt with in the **individual financial statements** of the venturer *and* the **group financial statements**.

1.1 Definitions

The IAS begins by listing some important definitions.

Key terms

Joint venture. A contractual arrangement whereby two or more parties undertake an economic activity which is subject to joint control.

Control. The power to govern the financial and operating policies of an economic activity so as to obtain benefits from its activities.

Joint control. The contractually agreed sharing of control over an economic activity.

Significant influence. The power to participate in the financial and operating policy decisions of an economic activity but is not control or joint control over those policies.

Venturer. A party to a joint venture that has joint control over that joint venture.

Key terms (cont'd)

Proportionate consolidation. A method of accounting whereby a venturer's share of each of the assets, liabilities, income and expenses of a jointly controlled entity is combined line-by-line with similar items in the venturer's financial statements or reported as separate line items in the venturer's financial statements.

Equity method. A method of accounting whereby an interest in a jointly controlled entity is initially recorded at cost and adjusted thereafter for the post acquisition change in the venturer's share of net assets of the jointly controlled entity. The income statement reflects the venturer's share of the profit or loss of the jointly controlled entity. *(IAS 31)*

1.2 Forms of joint venture

The **form and structure** of joint ventures can vary enormously. There are, however, three main types identified by the standard.

- **Jointly controlled operations**
- **Jointly controlled assets**
- **Jointly controlled entities**

We will look at each of these below. They are all usually described as joint ventures and fulfil the definition of a joint venture given above.

Whatever the form and structure, every joint venture will have **two characteristics.**

- Two (or more) venturers are bound by a **contractual arrangement**.
- The contractual relationship establishes **joint control**.

1.2.1 Contractual arrangement

The existence of a contractual agreement distinguishes a joint venture from an investment in an associate. **If there is no contractual arrangement, then a joint venture does not exist**.

Evidence of a contractual arrangement could be in one of several forms.

- **Contract** between the venturers
- **Minutes** of discussion between the venturers
- Incorporation in the **articles or by-laws** of the joint venture

The contractual arrangement is usually **in writing**, whatever its form, and it will deal with the following issues surrounding the joint venture.

- **Its activity, duration and reporting obligations**
- The appointment of its **board of directors** (or equivalent) and the **voting rights** of the venturers
- **Capital contributions** to it by the venturers
- How its output, income, expenses or results are **shared** between the venturers

It is the contractual arrangement which establishes **joint control** over the joint venture, so that no single venturer can control the activity of the joint venture on its own.

One venturer, identified by the contractual agreement, may be the **operator of the joint venture**. This does *not* mean that the operator controls the joint venture, the operator must act within the policies (financial and operation) agreed by all the venturers as laid out in the contractual arrangement. If this is not the case, if the operator effectively controls the joint venture rather than only acting within the arrangements delegated to it, then the activity is *not* a joint venture.

1.3 Section summary

- There are three **common types of joint venture**: jointly controlled operations, assets or entities
- A **contractual arrangement** must exist which establishes joint control
- **Joint control** is important: an **operator** must not be able to govern the financial and operating policies of the joint venture

1.4 Forms of joint venture

FAST FORWARD

There are three usual forms of joint venture.

- Jointly controlled operations
- Jointly controlled assets
- Jointly controlled entities

1.4.1 Jointly controlled operations

In this type of joint venture, there is no separate entity set up to deal with the joint venture, whether in the form of a corporation, partnership or other entity. Instead, the venturers **use their own assets and resources** for the joint venture, ie their own property, plant and equipment is used and they carry their own inventories.

The venturers also incur their own expenses and liabilities, and raise their own finance which then represent their own obligations. In these situations, the activities of the joint venture will often be performed by the venturers' staff alongside the venturers' **other similar activities**. The way that income and expenses are shared between the venturers is usually laid out in the joint venture agreement.

Question **Joint venture**

Can you think of an example of a situation where such a joint venture might occur?

Answer

IAS 31 uses the example of building an aircraft. Say that Boeing is to build the body of the aircraft and the engines are to be built by Rolls Royce as specified by the airline customer for the aircraft. You can see that different parts of the manufacturing process are carried out by each of the venturers. In the Rolls Royce factory, workers will work on the engines for the Boeing plane alongside others working on engines for different aircraft.

Each venturer, Boeing and Rolls Royce, bears its own costs and takes a share of revenue from the aircraft sale. That share is decided in the contractual arrangement between the venturers.

Can you think of other examples?

1.4.2 Accounting treatment

FAST FORWARD

Joint ventures are characterised by **joint control** evidenced by a **contractual arrangement.**

When a joint venture in the nature of jointly controlled operations exists, IAS 31 requires a venturer to recognise the following in its financial statements.

(a) The **assets** it controls and the **liabilities** it incurs

(b) The **expenses** it incurs and the **income** it earns from the sale of goods or services by the joint venture

Separate accounts for the joint venture are not required, although the venturers may prepare management accounts for the joint venture, in order to assess its performance.

1.4.3 Jointly controlled assets

In this type of joint venture, the venturers have **joint control**, and often **joint ownership** of some or all of the assets in the joint venture. These assets may have been contributed to the joint venture or purchased for the purpose of the joint venture, but in any case they are **dedicated to the activities of the joint venture**. These assets are used to produce benefits for the venturers; each venturer takes a share of the output and bears a share of the incurred expenses.

As with jointly controlled operations, this type of joint venture does *not* involve setting up a corporation, partnership or any other kind of entity. The venturers **control their share of future economic benefits** through their share in the jointly controlled asset.

Question — **Jointly controlled asset**

Can you think of examples of situations where this type of joint venture might take place?

Answer

IAS 31 gives examples in the oil, gas and mineral extraction industries. In such industries companies may, say, jointly control and operate on oil or gas pipeline. Each company transports its own products down the pipeline and pays an agreed proportion of the expenses of operating the pipeline (perhaps based on volume).

A further example is a property which is jointly controlled, each venturer taking a share of the rental income and bearing a portion of the expense.

Accounting treatment

IAS 31 requires each venturer to recognise (ie include in their financial statements) the following in respect of its interest in jointly controlled assets.

(a) Its **share of the jointly controlled assets**, classified by their nature, eg a share of a jointly controlled oil pipeline should be classified as property, plant and equipment

(b) Any **liabilities** it has incurred, eg in financing its share of the assets

(c) Its share of any **liabilities incurred jointly** with the other venturers which relate to the joint venture

(d) Any **income** from the sale or use of its share of the joint venture's output, together with its share of any **expenses** incurred by the joint venture

(e) Any **expenses** which it has incurred in respect of its interest in the joint venture, eg those relating to financing the venturer's interest in the assets and selling its share of the output

This treatment of jointly controlled assets reflects the **substance and economic reality,** and (usually) the legal form of the joint venture. Separate accounting records need not be kept for the joint venture and financial statements for the joint venture need not be prepared. Management accounts may be produced, however, in order to monitor the performance of the joint venture.

1.4.4 Jointly controlled entities

FAST FORWARD

Jointly controlled entities may be accounted for in different ways:

- **Proportionate consolidation**: combine items on a line by line basis
- **Equity method**: see above

This type of joint venture involves the setting up of a corporation, partnership or other entity. This **operates in the same way as any other entity**, except that the venturers have a contractual arrangement establishing their joint control over the economic activity of the entity.

A jointly controlled entity effectively operates as a **separate entity**: it controls the joint venture's assets, incurs liabilities and expenses and earns income. It can, as a separate entity, enter into contracts in its own name and raise finance to fund the activities of the joint venture. The venturers share the results of the jointly controlled entity, and in some cases they may also share the output of the joint venture.

Question — Jointly controlled entities

Can you think of some examples of situations where jointly controlled entities might be set up?

Answer

A common situation is where two or more entities transfer the relevant assets and liabilities to a jointly controlled entity in order to combine their activities in a particular line of business.

In other situations, an entity wishing to start operations in a foreign country will set up a jointly controlled entity with the government of the foreign country (or an agency of it).

The **substance** of jointly controlled entities are often similar in substance to the joint ventures discussed above (jointly controlled assets/operations). In the case of the oil/gas pipeline mentioned in Question 4, the asset might be transferred to a jointly controlled entity for tax or similar reasons. In other circumstances, a jointly controlled entity may be set up to deal with only certain aspects of the jointly controlled operations, eg marketing or after-sales service, design or distribution.

As a separate entity, the jointly controlled entity must maintain its **own accounting records** and will **prepare financial statements** according to national requirements and IASs. The accounting treatment for jointly controlled entities is discussed in the next section.

1.4.5 Transactions between a venturer and a joint venture

A venturer may **sell or contribute assets** to a joint venture. The value attributed to such assets may create a gain or loss. However, any such gain or loss should only be recognised to the extent that it reflects the substance of the transaction.

What this means is that only the **gain** attributable to the interest of the other venturers should be recognised. However, the full amount of any **loss** should be recognised when the transaction shows evidence that the net realisable value of current assets is less than cost, or that there is an impairment loss (determined by applying IAS 36).

Question — Inventories

Kirstan Co contributes inventories to a 50:50 joint venture it has undertaken with Pirstan Co. The recorded historical cost of the inventories is $2m.

What gain or loss should Kirstan Co recognise in its financial statements when the fair value (net realisable value) of the inventories is estimated at the date of transfer and recorded by the joint venture as:

(a) $2.2m?
(b) $1.8m?

Answer

(a) Kirstan Co has made a profit of $0.2m, but only 50% of this can be considered as realised, ie that part attributable to the other venturer. Kirstan Co should therefore recognise a gain of $0.1m.

(b) A loss of $0.2m has been made on the inventories, the entire amount of which should be recognised by Kirstan Co. It is known that the loss will be made, even though the inventories have not yet been sold, and so prudence requires that the full loss should be recognised.

A venturer may **purchase assets** from a joint venture. When it does so, the venturer should not recognise its share of the profit made by the joint venture on the transaction in question until it resells the assets to an independent third party, ie until the profit is realised. Losses should be treated in the same way, *except* losses should be recognised immediately if they represent a reduction in the net realisable value of current assets, or a permanent decline in the carrying amount of non-current assets.

1.4.6 Investors in joint ventures

There may be investors in joint ventures who **do *not* have joint control**. Such interests should be reported in accordance with IAS 39 (see Chapter 7) or IAS 28 *Investments in associates* (see Section 1), depending on the circumstances.

1.4.7 Operators of joint ventures

Operators of joint ventures will often **receive fees** for their work in directly managing the joint venture. Such fees should be accounted for according to IAS 18 *Revenue*. Such management fees will be treated by the joint venture as an expense.

1.4.8 Special purpose entities

These are dealt with here because they do not fit in readily anywhere else! An entity may be created to accomplish a specific, defined objective. Examples include research and development, or securitisation of financial assets. Such special purpose entities (SPE) may be incorporated or unincorporated. Often there are strict and permanent limits on the decision-making powers of their governing board or other management. They operate on 'autopilot', ie the policy guiding their activities cannot be modified other than perhaps by their sponsor. The sponsor frequently transfers assets to the SPE or performs services for it.

SPEs are dealt with in SIC 12 *Consolidation – special purpose entities*. The SIC states that **an SPE should be consolidated** when the **substance of the relationship between an entity and the SPE indicates that the SPE is controlled by that entity**. There are several circumstances which might indicate **control**.

1.5 Accounting treatment of jointly controlled entities

1.5.1 Separate financial statements of a venturer

IAS 31 states that where a venturer prepares separate financial statements (as a single company), investments in jointly controlled entities should be *either*:

(a) accounted for at **cost**, *or*
(b) in accordance with **IAS 39**.

The same accounting treatment must be applied consistently to all jointly controlled entities.

Exam focus point

This type of joint venture is the one most likely to appear in your examination.

1.5.2 Consolidated financial statements of a venturer

IAS 31 requires all interests in jointly controlled entities to be accounted for using *either* proportionate consolidation *or* the equity method.

However, several exemptions are available and neither of these methods need be applied where:

(a) The interest is classified as held for sale in accordance with IFRS 5, or

(b) The venturer is a parent exempt from preparing consolidated financial statements under IAS 27, or

(c) All of the following apply:

 (i) The venturer is a **wholly-owned subsidiary** or it is a **partially owned subsidiary** of another entity and its other owners, including those not otherwise entitled to vote, have been informed about, and do not object to, the investor not applying proportionate consolidation or the equity method.

 (ii) Its securities are **not publicly traded.**

 (iii) It is **not in the process of issuing securities** in public securities markets; and

 (iv) The **ultimate or intermediate parent** publishes consolidated financial statements that comply with International Financial Reporting Standards.

Where an interest is classified as held for sale it should be accounted for in accordance with IFRS 5 (see Chapter 15).

1.5.3 Proportionate consolidation

A venturer should report its interest in a jointly controlled entity in its consolidated financial statements using one of the two reporting formats for **proportionate consolidation**.

IAS 31 maintains that this treatment reflects the **substance and economic reality** of the arrangement, ie the control the venturer has over its share of future economic benefits through its share of the assets and liabilities of the venture.

The proportionate consolidation method differs from normal consolidation in that only the group share of assets and liabilities, income and expenses are brought into account. There is therefore **no non-controlling interest**.

There are **two different formats** with which the proportionate consolidation method can be used.

(a) **Combine on a line-by-line basis** the venturer's share of each of the assets, liabilities, income and expenses of the jointly controlled entity with the similar items in the venturer's consolidated financial statements.

(b) Include in the venturer's consolidated financial statements **separate line items** for the venturer's share of the assets and liabilities, income and expenses of the jointly controlled entity.

1.5.4 Example: Proportionate consolidation

Both of the above methods produce exactly the same results and they are demonstrated in this example. We will use similar information as in the question above.

Set out below are the draft accounts of Parent Co and its subsidiaries and of Joint Venture Co. Parent Co acquired 50% of the equity capital of Joint Venture Co three years ago when the latter's retained earnings stood at $40,000.

SUMMARISED STATEMENTS OF FINANCIAL POSITION

	Parent Co & subsidiaries	*Joint Venture Co*
	$'000	$'000
Tangible non-current assets	220	170
Investment in joint venture	75	–
Current assets	100	50
Loan to Joint Venture	20	–
	415	220
Share capital ($1 shares)	250	100
Retained earnings	165	100
Loan from Parent Co	–	20
	415	220

SUMMARISED INCOME STATEMENTS

	Parent Co & subsidiaries	*Joint Venture Co*
	$'000	$'000
Profit before tax	95	80
Income tax expense	35	30
	60	50
Dividends paid	(50)	(10)
Profit for the year	10	40

Parent Co has taken credit for the dividend paid by Joint Venture Co.

You are required to prepare the summarised consolidated statement of financial position of Parent Co, under both the formats of proportionate consolidation recommended by IAS 31.

Solution: Line-by-line format

PARENT CO
CONSOLIDATED STATEMENT OF FINANCIAL POSITION

	$'000
Goodwill (W1)	5
Tangible non-current assets (220 + (50% × 170))	305
Current assets (100 + (50% × 50))	125
Loan to joint venturer (note)	10
	445
Share capital	250
Retained earnings (W2)	195
	445

Note. The loan is the proportion of the $20,000 lent to the other venturer.

Workings

1 *Goodwill*

	$'000
Consideration transferred	75
Share of net assets acquired (50% × 140)	(70)
Premium on acquisition	5

2 *Retained earnings*

	Parent Co & subsidiaries	*Joint Venture Co*
	$'000	$'000
Per individual	165	100
Pre-acquisition		(40)
Post-acquisition		60
Group share in joint venture ($60 × 50%)	30	
Group retained earnings	195	

Solution: Separate line method

PARENT CO
CONSOLIDATED STATEMENT OF FINANCIAL POSITION

	$'000	$'000
Goodwill (as above)		5
Tangible non-current assets		
Group	220	
Joint venture (170 × 50%)	85	
		305
Current assets		
Group	100	
Joint venture (50% × 50)	25	
		125
Loan to joint venturer		10
		445
Share capital		250
Retained earnings (as above)		195
		445

In both these cases the **consolidated income statements** would be shown in the same way.

The use of the proportionate consolidation method should be **discontinued** from the date the venturer ceases to have joint control over the entity.

1.5.5 Equity method

A venturer can report its interest in a joint venture in its consolidated financial statements under the **equity method**, as discussed in Section 1. The argument for this method is that it is misleading to combine controlled items with jointly controlled items. It is also felt by some that venturers have significant influence over the entity, not merely joint control.

IAS 31 does not agree with this approach, preferring the proportionate consolidation method for the reasons given above, but it allows the equity method, **as laid out in IAS 28**, to be used.

The use of the equity method should be **discontinued** from the date on which the venturer ceases to have joint control over, or have significant influence on, a jointly controlled entity.

1.5.6 Section summary

In **consolidated accounts**, two treatments are allowed for the consolidation of an investment in a jointly controlled entity.

- **Proportionate consolidation**, using either of two formats
  - **Line-by-line combined results**
  - **Separate line item method**
- **Equity method** as under IAS 28

Chapter Roundup

- IAS 31 *Financial reporting of interests in joint ventures* is concerned with how venturers **report their interests** in joint ventures in their accounts.
- There are three usual **forms of joint venture.**
  - Jointly controlled operations
  - Jointly controlled assets
  - Jointly controlled entities
- Joint ventures are characterised by **joint control** evidenced by a **contractual arrangement.**
- **Jointly controlled entities** may be accounted for in different ways:
  - **Proportionate consolidation**: combine items on a line by line basis
  - **Equity method**: see above

Quick Quiz

1. A joint venture is a ______________ whereby two or more parties undertake an economic activity which is subject to ______________ . *Complete the blanks.*
2. What forms of evidence of a contractual agreement might exist?
3. How should a venturer account for its share of jointly controlled operations?
4. Which standard should an operator of a joint venture follow when dealing with management fees received?
5. What is the procedure for proportionate consolidation?

Answers to Quick Quiz

1 A joint venture is a **contractual arrangement** whereby two or more parties undertake an economic activity which is subject to **joint control**.

2
- Contractual arrangement
- Joint control

3 (a) The assets it controls and the liabilities it incurs
(b) The expenses it incurs and the income it earns

4 IAS 18 *Revenue*

5 (a) Line-by-line basis with venturer's own assets, liabilities, income and expenses.
(b) Show as separate line items within the venturer's accounts.

Note. Remember only the venturer's share is included, so there is **no** non-controlling interest.

Now try the question 33 from the Exam Question Bank

Number	Level	Marks	Time
Q32	Introductory	15	27 mins

Exam question bank

1 Setting and regulating standards

(a) Explain the objectives of the IASB.

(b) Describe how the IASB goes about developing and issuing new international financial reporting standards.

(c) Briefly describe the potential barriers to harmonisation of financial reporting standards across the globe.

(d) Briefly outline the role of IFRS Interpretations Committee.

2 Regulators

State three different regulatory influences on the preparation of the published accounts of quoted companies and briefly explain the role of each one. Comment briefly on the effectiveness of this regulatory system.

3 Europa

> *Note.* Although the dates in this question relate to first time adoption which took place in 2005, the principles are still relevant for companies which adopt IFRS for the first time. An example may be a company that becomes listed for the first time.

Europa is a listed company incorporated in the European Union. It will adopt International Financial Reporting Standards (IFRSs) for the first time in its financial statements for the year ended 31 December 2005.

The directors of Europa are unclear as to the impact of IFRS 1 First-time Adoption of International Financial Reporting Standards.

Required:

Advise the directors of Europa on the following in this question.

(a) The procedure for preparing IFRS financial statements for the first time (as required by IFRS 1)

(b) The practical steps that the company should take in order to ensure an efficient transfer to accounting under IFRS

(c) In its previous financial statements for 31 December 2003 and 2004, which were prepared under local GAAP, the company:

  (i) Made a number of routine accounting estimates, including accrued expenses and provisions, and

  (ii) did not recognise a provision for a court case arising from events that occurred in September 2004. When the court case was concluded on 30 June 2005, Europa was required to pay $10 million and paid this on 10 July 2005.

In the opinion of the directors, the company's estimates of accrued expenses and provisions under local GAAP were made on a basis consistent with IFRSs.

Required

Discuss how the matters above should be dealt with in the financial statements of Europa for the year ended 31 December 2005.

4 Revision of accounting concepts

Explain the following accounting concepts.

(a) The business entity concept

(b) The historical cost convention

(c) The realisation concept

5 Conceptual framework

(a) Outline the role of the IASB *Framework* in the development of international financial reporting standards.

(b) State the objectives of financial statements.

(c) State the definition of assets and liabilities.

(d) Explain the IASB approach to the application of prudence, neutrality and reliability in the preparation of financial statements.

6 Jenson - solution p.510 **45 mins**

The timing of revenue (income) recognition has long been an area of debate and inconsistency in accounting. Industry practice in relation to revenue recognition varies widely, the following are examples of different points in the operating cycle of businesses that revenue and profit can be recognised.

(a) On the acquisition of goods
(b) During the manufacture or production of goods
(c) On delivery/acceptance of goods
(d) When certain conditions have been satisfied after the goods have been delivered
(e) Receipt of payment for credit sales
(f) On the expiry of a guarantee or warranty

In the past the 'critical event' approach has been used to determine the timing of revenue recognition. The International Accounting Standards Board (IASB) in its *Framework for the Preparation and Presentation of Financial Statements (Framework)'* has defined the 'elements' of financial statements, and it uses these to determine when a gain or loss occurs.

Required

(a) Explain what is meant by the critical event in relation to revenue recognition and discuss the criteria used in the framework for determining when a gain or loss arises. **(5 marks)**

(b) For each of the states of the operating cycle identified above, explain why it may be an appropriate point to recognise revenue and, where possible, give a practical example of an industry where it occurs. **(12 marks)**

(c) Jenson has entered into the following transactions/agreements in the year to 31 March 20X0.

   (i) Goods, which had cost of $20,000, were sold to Wholesaler for $35,000 on 1 June 20W9. Jenson has an option to repurchase the goods from Wholesaler at any time within the next two years. The repurchase price will be $35,000 plus interest charged at 12% per annum from the date of sale to the date of repurchase. It is expected that Jenson will repurchase the goods.

   (ii) Jenson owns the rights to a fast food franchise. On 1 April 20W9 it sold the right to open a new outlet to Mr Cody. The franchise is for five years. Jenson received an initial fee of $50,000 for the first year and will receive $5,000 per annum thereafter. Jenson has continuing service obligations on its franchise for advertising and product development that amount to approximately $8,000 per annum for franchised outlet. A reasonable profit margin on the provision of the continuing services is deemed to be 20% of revenues received

   (iii) On 1 September 20W9 Jenson received subscriptions in advance of $240,000. The subscriptions are for 24 monthly publications of a magazine produced by Jenson. At the year end Jenson had produced and despatched six of the 24 publications. The total cost of producing the magazine is estimated at $192,000 with each publication costing a broadly similar amount.

Required

Describe how Jenson should treat each of the above examples in its financial statements in the year to 31 March 20X0. **(8 marks)**

(Total = 25 marks)

7 D'Urberville **45 mins**

The financial controller of D'Urberville Inc is preparing forecast statements of financial position as at 31 December 20X4, 20X5, 20X6 and 20X7.

The 20X4 forecast has been prepared and shows the following figure in respect of motor vehicles.

	$'000
Cost	540
Accumulated depreciation	130
Net book value	410

Depreciation on motor vehicles is charged at 25% on the reducing balance. A full year's depreciation is charged in the year of purchase and none in the year of sale.

The assistant accountant has collated the following information in order to help the financial controller prepare his forecast.

FORECAST PURCHASES OF MOTOR VEHICLES
FOR THE YEARS ENDED 31 DECEMBER

	20X5	*20X6*	*20X7*
	$'000	$'000	$'000
List price			
Cash purchase	180	300	450
Leased vehicles	–	400	500
Trade discount (20%)			
Cash purchase	36	60	90
Leased vehicles	–	80	100
Cash discount (5% of net price)	7	12	18
Delivery costs (paid to supplier)	10	12	15
Costs of valeting old vehicles to prepare them for sale	2	3	4
Trade-in allowances on old vehicles to be set off against finance lease first year rental		25	20
Finance lease first year rental		65	90
		(80 – 25)	(110 – 20)
Total cash to be paid to the suppliers of the new vehicles in the year of outright purchase	147	77	105
	(180 – 36 – 7 + 10)	(65 + 12)	(90 + 15)

FORECAST DISPOSALS OF MOTOR VEHICLES (AT COST)
IN THE YEARS ENDED 31 DECEMBER

	20X5	*20X6*	*20X7*
	$'000	$'000	$'000
Vehicle			
Originally acquired in years ended 31 December			
20X0	30		
20X1	40		
20X2		45	
20X3		65	
20X4			75

The following methods of purchase will be used to acquire the vehicles.

Year ended 31 December 20X5: cash purchase.

Year ended 31 December 20X6: cash purchase and finance lease agreement. A rental of $80,000 will be payable in arrears for six years. The fair value of the vehicles was $320,000.

Year ended 31 December 20X7: cash purchase and finance lease agreement. A rental of $110,000 will be payable in arrears for six years. The fair value of the vehicles was $400,000.

Required

For the non-current asset (motor vehicles) in the forecast statements of financial position of D'Urberville Inc as at 31 December 20X5, 20X6, 20X7, produce a schedule showing cost, accumulated depreciation and net book value. You should show all your workings and make all calculations to the nearest $'000.

(25 marks)

8 Yorana — 45 mins

Yorana Aggregates Co wish to expand their transport fleet and purchased three heavy lorries with a list price of $18,000 each. Yorana has negotiated lease finance to fund this expansion, and the company has entered into a finance lease agreement with Gregory Garages Co on 1 January 20X1. The agreement states that Yorana Aggregates will pay a deposit of $9,000 on 1 January 20X1, and two annual instalments of $24,000 on 31 December 20X1, 20X2 and a final instalment of $20,391 on 31 December 20X3.

Interest is to be calculated at 25% on the balance outstanding on 1 January each year and paid on 31 December each year.

The depreciation policy of Yorana Aggregates Co is to write off the vehicles over a four year period using the straight line method and assuming a scrap value of $1,333 for each vehicle at the end of its useful life.

The cost of the vehicles to Gregory Garages is $14,400 each.

Required

(a) Account for the above transactions in the books of Yorana Aggregates Co showing the entries in the income statement and statement of financial position for the years 20X1, 20X2, 20X3. This is the only lease transaction undertaken by this company.

(b) Account for the above transactions in the books of Gregory Garages Co, showing the entries in the lease trading account for the years 20X1, 20X2 and 20X3. This is the only lease transaction undertaken by this company.

Calculations to the nearest $. **(25 marks)**

9 Bulwell — 45 mins

Bulwell Aggregates Co wish to expand their transport fleet and purchased three heavy lorries with a list price of $18,000 each. Robert Bulwell has negotiated lease finance to fund this expansion, and the company has entered into a finance lease agreement with Granby Garages Co on 1 January 20X1. The agreement states that Bulwell Aggregates will pay a deposit of $9,000 on 1 January 20X1, and two annual instalments of $24,000 on 31 December 20X1, 20X2 and a final instalment of $20,391 on 31 December 20X3.

Interest is to be calculated at 25% on the balance outstanding on 1 January each year and paid on 31 December each year.

The depreciation policy of Bulwell Aggregates Co is to write off the vehicles over a four year period using the straight line method and assuming a scrap value of $1,333 for each vehicle at the end of its useful life.

The cost of the vehicles to Granby Garages is $14,400 each.

Required

(a) Account for the above transactions in the books of Bulwell Aggregates Co showing the entries in the income statement and statement of financial position for the years 20X1, 20X2, 20X3. This is the only lease transaction undertaken by this company. **(15 marks)**

(b) Account for the above transactions in the books of Granby Garages Co, showing the entries in the lease trading account for the years 20X1, 20X2 and 20X3. This is the only lease transaction undertaken by this company. **(10 marks)**

Calculations to the nearest $. **(Total = 25 marks)**

10 Winger — 45 mins

The following list of account balances relates to Winger at 31 March 20X1.

	$'000	$'000
Sales revenue (note 1)		358,450
Cost of sales	185,050	
Distribution costs	28,700	
Administration expenses	15,000	
Lease rentals (note 2)	20,000	
Debenture interest paid	2,000	
Interim dividends (note 6)	12,000	
Property at cost (note 3)	200,000	
Plant and equipment cost	154,800	
Depreciation 1 April 20X0 – plant and equipment		34,800
Development expenditure (note 4)	30,000	
Profit on disposal of non-current assets		45,000
Trade accounts receivable	55,000	
Inventories: 31 March 20X1	28,240	
Cash and bank	10,660	
Trade accounts payable		29,400
Taxation: over provision in year to 31 March 20X0		2,200
Equity shares of 25c each		150,000
8% debenture (issued in 20W9)		50,000
Accumulated profits 1 April 20X0		71,600
	741,450	741,450

The following notes are relevant.

(a) Included in sales revenue is $27 million, which relates to sales made to customers under sale or return agreements. The expiry date for the return of these goods is 30 April 20X1. Winger has charged a mark-up of 20% on cost for these sales.

(b) A lease rental of $20 million was paid on 1 April 20X0. It is the first of five annual payments in advance for the rental of an item of equipment that has a cash purchase price of $80 million. The auditors have advised that this is a finance lease and have calculated the implicit interest rate in the lease as 12% per annum. Leased assets should be depreciated on a straight-line basis over the life of the lease.

(c) On 1 April 20X0 Winger acquired a new property at a cost of $200 million. For the purpose of calculating depreciation only, the asset has been separated into the following elements.

Separate asset	*Cost*	*Life*
	$'000	
Land	50,000	freehold
Heating system	20,000	10 years
Lifts	30,000	15 years
Building	100,000	50 years

The depreciation of the elements of the property should be calculated on a straight-line basis. The new property replaced an existing one that was sold on the same date for $95 million. It had cost $50 million and had a carrying value of $80 million at the date of sale. The profit on this property has been calculated on the original cost. It had not been depreciated on the basis that the depreciation charge would not be material.

Plant and machinery is depreciated at 20% on the reducing balance basis.

(d) The figure for development expenditure in the list of account balances represents the amounts deferred in previous years in respect of the development of a new product. Unfortunately, during the current year, the government has introduced legislation which effectively bans this type of product. As a consequence of this the project has been abandoned. The directors of Winger are of the opinion that writing off the development expenditure, as opposed to its previous deferment, represents a change of accounting policy and therefore wish to treat the write off as a prior period adjustment.

(e) A provision for income tax for the year to 31 March 20X1 of $15 million is required.

(f) The company has paid an interim equity dividend and half of the annual debenture interest. The average annual dividend yield (interim plus final) for companies in Winger's market sector is 4%. The current market price of Winger's equity shares is $1.25. The directors have declared, but not yet accounted for, a final dividend which will give Winger's equity shareholders a return equal to the average gross yield for the sector.

Required

(a) Prepare the income statement of Winger for the year to 31 March 20X1. **(9 marks)**

(b) Prepare a statement of financial position as at 31 March 20X1 in accordance with International Accounting Standards as far as the information permits. **(11 marks)**

(c) Discuss the acceptability of the company's previous policy in respect of non-depreciation of property. **(5 marks)**

(Total = 25 marks)

Note. As you have not yet covered IAS (revised) *Presentation of Financial Statements*, you do not need to comply with its detailed requirements.

11 Global Konstruckshen

Global Konstrukshen Co is a civil engineering company. It started work on two long-term projects during the year ended 31 December 20X0. The following figures relate to those projects at the reporting date.

	Alpine bypass	*World Ecology Centre*
	$'000	$'000
Contract price	9,000	8,000
Costs incurred to date	1,400	2,900
Estimated costs to completion	5,600	5,200
Value of work certified to date	2,800	3,000
Cash received from contractee	2,600	3,400

An old mineshaft has been discovered under the site for the World Ecology Centre and the costs of dealing with this have been taken into account in the calculation of estimated costs to completion. Global's lawyers are reasonably confident that the customer will have to bear the additional costs which will be incurred in stabilising the land. If negotiations are successful then the contract price will increase to $10m.

Global recognises turnover and profits on long-term (construction) contracts on the basis of work certified to date.

Required

(a) Calculate the figures which would appear in Global Konstrukshen's financial statements in respect of these two projects.

(b) It has been suggested that profit on construction contracts should not be recognised until the contract is completed. Briefly explain whether you believe that this suggestion would improve the quality of financial reporting for long-term contracts.

12 Provisions **45 mins**

IAS 37 *Provisions, contingent liabilities and contingent assets* was issued in July 1998. Prior to its publication, there was no International Accounting Standard that dealt with the general subject of accounting for provisions.

Extract prepares its financial statements to 31 December each year. During the years ended 31 December 20X0 and 31 December 20X1, the following event occurred.

Extract is involved in extracting minerals in a number of different countries. The process typically involves some contamination of the site from which the minerals are extracted. Extract makes good this contamination only where legally required to do so by legislation passed in the relevant country.

The company has been extracting minerals in Copperland since January 20W8 and expects its site to produce output until 31 December 20X5. On 23 December 20X0, it came to the attention of the directors of Extract that the government of Copperland was virtually certain to pass legislation requiring the making good of mineral extraction sites. The legislation was duly passed on 15 March 20X1. The directors of Extract estimate that the cost of making good the site in Copperland will be $2 million. This estimate is of the actual cash expenditure that will be incurred on 31 December 2005.

Required

(a) Explain why there was a need for an accounting standard dealing with provisions, and summarise the criteria that need to be satisfied before a provision is recognised. **(12 marks)**

(b) Compute the effect of the estimated cost of making good the site on the financial statements of Extract for BOTH of the years ended 31 December 20X0 and 20X1. Give full explanations of the figures you compute.

The annual discount rate to be used in any relevant calculations is 10%. **(13 marks)**

(Total = 25 marks)

13 Jerzy

During the year ended 30 November 20X3, the directors of Jerzy decided to form a defined benefit pension scheme for the employees of the company and contributed cash of $160 million to it. The following details relate to the scheme at 30 November 20X3:

	$m
Present value of obligation	208
Fair value of plan assets	200
Current service cost	176
Interest cost – scheme liabilities	32
Expected return on pension scheme assets	16

The only entry in the financial statements made to date is in respect of the cash contribution which has been included in trade receivables. The directors have been uncertain as to how to deal with the above pension scheme in the consolidated financial statements because of the significance of the potential increase in the charge to the income statement relating to the pension scheme. They wish to recognise any actuarial gain immediately.

Required:

Show how the defined benefit pension scheme should be dealt with in the financial statements for the year ended 30 November 20X3.

14 Tall

(a) Two standards have been published by the IASB to deal with the complex area of financial instruments.

(i) IAS 32 *Financial instruments: Presentation*
(ii) IAS 39 *Financial instruments: Recognition and measurement*

Required

What are the problems with the way that financial instruments have been accounted for in the past that these standards were issued to correct?

(b) You are the accountant of Tall. The entity is planning a number of acquisitions in 20Y0 and so you are aware that additional funding will be needed. Today's date is 30 November 20X9. The balance sheet of the company at 30 September 20X9 (the financial year-end of Tall) showed the following balances.

	$m
Equity share capital	100.0
Share premium account	35.8
Retained earnings	89.7
	225.5
Net assets	225.5

On 1 October 20X9 Tall raised additional funding as follows:

- Tall issued 15 million $1 bonds at par. The bonds pay no interest but are redeemable on 1 October 20Y4 at $1.61 – the total payable on redemption being $24.15m. As an alternative to redemption, bondholders can elect to convert their holdings into $1 equity shares on the basis of one equity share for every bond held. The current price of a $1 share is $1.40 and it is reckonable that this will grow by at least 5 percent per annum for the next five years.
- Tall issued 10 million $1 preferred shares at $1.20 per share, incurring costs of $100,000. The preferred shares carry no dividend and are redeemable on 1 October 20Y5 at $2.35 per share – the total payable on redemption being $23.5m.

Your assistant is unsure how to reflect the additional funding in the financial statements of Tall. He expresses the opinion that both the new financial instruments should logically be reflected in the equity (capital and reserves) section of the statement of financial position . He justifies this as follows.

- The preferred shares are legally shares and so equity is the appropriate place to present them.
- The bonds and the preferred shares seem to have similar terms of issue and is quite likely that the bonds will *become* shares in five years' time, given the projected growth in the equity share price.

He has no idea how to show the finance costs of the financial instruments in the income statement. He knows that IAS 39 *Financial Instruments: recognition and measurement* is the relevant accounting standard but is unaware of the details.

In addition, the entity is due to borrow a substantial sum ($100m) for three months on 15 November 20X9. The treasurer has been concerned that interest rates may rise, and on 15 August 20X9 covered the position by selling 200 three-month interest rate futures. Interest rates have indeed risen since 15 August and the interest futures look likely to yield a profit. Given that no cash has been laid out, other than the initial deposit on the futures contract, your assistant is uncertain as to what action, if any, to take.

Required

(i) Write a memorandum to your assistant which evaluates the comments he has made regarding the presentation of the financial instruments and explains the correct treatment where necessary. Your memorandum should refer to the provisions of relevant accounting standards.

(ii) Prepare a response to your assistant which explains the correct treatment of the interest futures.

(iii) Calculate the finance cost that will be required to be shown in the income statement of Tall for the year ended 30 September 20Y0 for the bonds and the preferred shares. You may assume that both will be treated as held-to-maturity investments in accordance with IAS 39.

15 Dennis **45 mins**

The following transactions and events have arisen during the preparation of the draft financial statements of Dennis for the year to 31 March 20X0.

(a) On 1 April 20W9 Dennis issued $80 million 8% convertible loan stock at par. The stock is convertible into equity shares, or redeemable at par, on 31 March 20X4, at the option of the stockholders. The terms of conversion are that each $100 of loan stock will be convertible into 50 equity shares of Dennis. A finance consultant has advised that if the option to convert to equity had not been included in the terms of the issue, then a coupon (interest) rate of 12% would have been required to attract subscribers for the stock.

The value of $1 receivable at the end of each year at a discount rate of 12% can be taken as:

Year	$
1	0.89
2	0.80
3	0.71
4	0.64
5	0.57

Required

Calculate the income statement finance charge for the year to 31 March 20X0 and the statement of financial position extracts at 31 March 20X0 in respect of the issue of the convertible loan stock. (5 marks)

(b) On 1 January 20X0 Dennis acquired Steamdays, a company that operates a scenic railway along the coast of a popular tourist area. The summarised statement of financial position at fair values of Steamdays on 1 January 20X0, reflecting the terms of the acquisition was:

	$'000
Goodwill	200
Operating licence	1,200
Property – train stations and land	300
Rail tack and coaches	300
Two steam engines	1,000
Purchase consideration	3,000

The operating licence is for ten years. It was renewed on 1 January 20X0 by the transport authority and is stated at the cost of its renewal. The carrying values of the property and rail track and coaches are based on their value in use. The engines, and other net assets are valued at their net selling prices.

On 1 February 20X0 the boiler of one of the steam engines exploded, completely destroying the whole engine. Fortunately no one was injured, but the engine was beyond repair. Due to its age a replacement could not be obtained. Because of the reduced passenger capacity the estimated value in use of the whole of the business after the accident was assessed at $2 million.

Passenger numbers after the accident were below expectations even allowing for the reduced capacity. A market research report concluded that tourists were not using the railway because of their fear of a similar accident occurring to the remaining engine. In the light of this the value in use of the business was re-assessed on 31 March 20X0 at $1.8 million. On this date Dennis received an offer of $900,000 in respect of the operating licence (it is transferable). The realisable value of the other net assets has not changed significantly.

Required

Calculate the carrying value of the assets of Steamdays (in Dennis's consolidated statement of financial position) at 1 February 20X0 and 31 March 20X0 after recognising the impairment losses.

(c) Dennis is in the intermediate stage of a construction contract for the building of a new privately owned road bridge over a river estuary. The original details of the contract are:

Approximate duration of contract:	3 years
Date of commencement:	1 October 20W8
Total contract price:	$40 million
Estimated total cost:	$28 million

An independent surveyor certified the value of the work in progress as follows:

– on 31 March 20W9	$12 million
– on 31 March 20X0	$30 million (including the $12 million in 20W9
Total costs incurred at:	
– 31 March 20W9	$9 million
– 31 March 20X0	$28.5 million (including the $9 million in 20W9
Progress billings at 31 March 20X0 were £25 million	

On 1 April 20W9 Dennis agreed to a contract variation that would involve an additional $5 million with associated additional estimated costs of $2 million.

The costs incurred during the year to 31 March 2000 include $2.5 million relating to the replacement of some bolts which had been made from material that had been incorrectly specified by the firm of civil engineers who were contracted by Dennis to design the bridge. These costs were not included in the original estimates, but Dennis is hopeful that they can be recovered from the firm of civil engineers.

Dennis calculates profit on construction contracts using the percentage of completion method. The percentage of completion of the contract is based on the value of the work certified to date compared to the total contract price.

Required

Prepare the extracts of the statement of comprehensive income and the statement of financial position in respect of the contract for the year to 31 March 20X0 only. **(25 marks)**

16 DT Group **27 mins**

DT, a public limited company, has decided to adopt the provisions of IFRSs for the first time in its financial statements for the year ending 30 November 20X1. The amounts of deferred tax provided as set out in the notes of the group financial statements for the year ending 30 November 20X0 were as follows:

	$m
Tax depreciation in excess of accounting depreciation	38
Other temporary differences	11
Liabilities for health care benefits	(12)
Losses available for offset against future taxable profits	(34)
	3

The following notes are relevant to the calculation of the deferred tax liability as at 30 November 20X1:

(a) DT acquired a 100% holding in a foreign company on 30 November 20X1. The subsidiary does not plan to pay any dividends for the financial year to 30 November 20X1 or in the foreseeable future. The carrying amount in DT's consolidated financial statements of its investment in the subsidiary at 30 November 20X1 is made up as follows:

	$m
Carrying value of net assets acquired excluding deferred tax	76
Goodwill (before deferred tax and impairment losses)	14
Carrying amount/cost of investment	90

The tax base of the net assets of the subsidiary at acquisition was $60m. No deduction is available in the subsidiary's tax jurisdiction for the cost of the goodwill.

Immediately after acquisition on 30 November 20X1, DT had supplied the subsidiary with inventories amounting to $30m at a profit of 20% on selling price. The inventories had not been sold by the year end and the tax rate applied to the subsidiary's profit is 25%. There was no significant difference between the fair values and carrying values on the acquisition of the subsidiary.

(b) The carrying amount of the property, plant and equipment (excluding that of the subsidiary) is \$2,600m and their tax base is \$1,920m. Tax arising on the revaluation of properties of \$140m, if disposed of at their revalued amounts, is the same at 30 November 20X1 as at the beginning of the year. The revaluation of the properties is included in the carrying amount above.

Other taxable temporary differences (excluding the subsidiary) amount to \$90m as at 30 November 20X1.

(c) The liability for health care benefits in the statement of financial position had risen to \$100m as at 30 November 20X1 and the tax base is zero. Health care benefits are deductible for tax purposes when payments are made to retirees. No payments were made during the year to 30 November 20X1.

(d) Under the tax law of the country, tax losses can be carried forward for three years only. The taxable profits for the years ending 30 November were anticipated to be as follows:

20X1	*20X2*	*20X3*
\$m	\$m	\$m
110	100	130

The auditors are unsure about the availability of taxable profits in 20X3 as the amount is based upon the projected acquisition of a profitable company. It is anticipated that there will be no future reversals of existing taxable temporary differences until after 30 November 20X3.

(e) Income tax of \$165m on a property disposed of in 20X0 becomes payable on 30 November 20X4 under the deferral relief provisions of the tax laws of the country. There had been no sales or revaluations of property during the year to 30 November 20X1.

(f) Income tax is assumed to be 30% for the foreseeable future in DT's jurisdiction and the company wishes to discount any deferred tax liabilities at a rate of 4% if allowed by IAS 12.

(g) There are no other temporary differences other than those set out above. The directors of DT have calculated the opening balance of deferred tax using IAS 12 to be \$280m.

Required

Calculate the liability for deferred tax required by the DT Group at 30 November 20X1 and the deferred tax expense in profit or loss for the year ending 30 November 20X1 using IAS 12, commenting on the effect that the application of IAS 12 will have on the financial statements of the DT Group.

17 Courtney — 18 Mins

The following transactions relate to Courtney for the year ended 31 December 20X7.

(a) Courtney purchased 6,000 kg of materials on December 20X7 to use in their production process. The supplier is located in Erehwon where the currency is the Won.

The goods cost 300,000 Wons and have not been paid for at the year end.

The relevant exchange rates are:

1 December	US\$1 = 20 Wons
31 December	US\$1 = 16 Wons

Show how this transaction will be included in the financial statements at 31 December 20X7.

(b) Courtney's finance manager does not understand the difference between functional and presentation currencies. Courtney's local currency is the US\$. They are a wholly owned autonomous subsidiary of a large corporation based in Europe who reports group results in Euros.

Define functional and presentation currencies in relation to Courtney and in its parent.

(10 marks)

18 Farmer Gyles

Gyles has just bought a farm in Europe and would like to know various things about IAS 41 *Agriculture.*

(a) Distinguish a biological asset from agricultural produce.

(b) State four ways in which biological assets can be transformed.

(c) State the general rule for **measuring** biological assets.

(d) Briefly explain the issues relating to **recognition** of agricultural produce.

19 Share-based payment **11 mins**

J&B granted 200 options on its $1 ordinary shares to each of its 800 employees on 1 January 20X1. Each grant is conditional upon the employee being employed by J&B until 31 December 20X3.

J&B estimated at 1 January 20X1 that:

(i) The fair value of each option was $4 (before adjustment for the possibility of forfeiture).

(ii) Approximately 50 employees would leave during 20X1, 40 during 20X2 and 30 during 20X3 thereby forfeiting their rights to receive the options. The departures were expected to be evenly spread within each year.

The exercise price of the options was $1.50 and the market value of a J&B share on 1 January 20X1 was $3.

In the event, only 40 employees left during 20X1 (and the estimate of total departures was revised down to 95 at 31 December 20X1), 20 during 20X2 (and the estimate of total departures was revised to 70 at 31 December 20X2) and none during 20X3, spread evenly during each year.

Required

The directors of J&B have asked you to illustrate how the scheme is accounted for under IFRS 2 *Share-based Payment.*

(a) Show the double entries for the charge to profit or loss for employee services over the three years and for the share issue, assuming all employees entitled to benefit from the scheme exercised their rights and the shares were issued on 31 December 20X3.

(b) Explain how your solution would differ had J&B offered its employees cash based on the share value rather than share options. **(6 marks)**

20 IAS 1

IAS 1 (revised) states that there are overall considerations that ensure the fair presentation of financial statements and compliance with International Accounting Standards.

Required

(a) List and explain briefly three of the overall considerations.

  (i) Materiality and aggregation
  (ii) Offsetting
  (iii) Consistency of presentation

  as the terms are used in IAS 1 (Revised).

(b) Explain and give an example of the effect on a set of published financial statements of a company, if the going concern convention is held *not* to apply.

(c) The IASB produced a document called 'The Framework for the Preparation and Presentation of Financial Statements'.

Required

Explain in general terms what the framework is trying to achieve. Do you think that IAS 1 (Revised) is achieving this aim? Give reasons for your answer.

21 Hewlett

Hewlett is a quoted company reporting under IFRS. During the year end 31 December 20X2, the company changed its accounting policy with respect to property valuation. There are also a number of other issues that need to be finalised before the financial statements can be published.

Hewlett's trial balance from the general ledger at 31 December 20X2 showed the following balances:

		$'m	$'m
Revenue			2,648
Loan note interest paid		3	
Purchases		1,669	
Distribution costs		514	
Administrative expenses		345	
Interim dividend paid		6	
Inventories at 1 January 20X2		444	
Trade receivables		545	
Trade payables			434
Cash and cash equivalents		28	
50c ordinary shares			100
Share premium			244
General reserve			570
Retained earnings at 1 January 20X2			349
4% loan note repayable 20X8 (issued 20X0)			150
Land and buildings:	cost (including $60m land)	380	
	accumulated depreciation at 1 January 20X2		64
Plant and equipment:	cost	258	
	accumulated depreciation at 1 January 20X2		126
Investment property at 1 January 20X2		548	
Rental income			48
Proceeds from sale of equipment			7
		4,740	4,740

Further information to be taken into account:

(i) Closing inventories were counted and amounted to $388m at cost. However, shortly after the year end out-of-date inventories with a cost of $15m were sold for $8m.

(ii) The company decided to change its accounting policy with respect to its 10 year old land and buildings from the cost model to the revaluation model. The revalued amounts at 1 January 20X2 were $800m (including $100m for the land). No further revaluation was necessary at 31 December 20X2. The company wishes to treat the revaluation surplus as being realised over the life of the asset.

(iii) Due to a change in the company's product portfolio plans, an item of plant with a carrying value $22m at 31 December 20X1 (after adjusting for depreciation for the year) may be impaired due to a change in use. An impairment test conducted at 31 December, revealed its fair value less costs to sell to be $16m. The asset is now expected to generate an annual net income stream of $3.8m for the next 5 years at which point the asset would be disposed for $4.2m. An appropriate discount rate is 8%. 5 year discount factors at 8% are:

Simple	*Cumulative*
0.677	3.993

(iv) The income tax liability for the year is estimated at $27m. Ignore deferred tax.

(v) An interim dividend of 3c per share was paid on 30 June 20X2. A final dividend of 1.5c per share was declared by the directors on 28 January 20X3. No dividends were paid or declared in 20X1.

(vi) During the year, Hewlett Co disposed of some malfunctioning equipment for $7m. The equipment had cost $15m and had accumulated depreciation brought forward at 1 January 20X2 of $3m.

There were no other additions or disposal to property, plant and equipment in the year.

(vii) The company treats depreciation on plant and equipment as a cost of sale and on land and buildings as an administration cost. Depreciation rates as per the company's accounting policy note are as follows:

Buildings	Straight line over 50 years
Plant and equipment	20% reducing balance

Hewlett's accounting policy is to charge a full year's depreciation in the year of an asset's purchase and none in the year of disposal.

(viii) During the year on 1 July 20X2, Hewlett made a 1 for 4 bonus issue, capitalising its general reserve. This transaction had not yet been accounted for. The fair value of the company's shares on the date of the bonus issue was $7.50 each.

(ix) Hewlett uses the fair value model of IAS 40. The fair value of the investment property at 31 December 20X2 was $586m.

Required

Prepare the statement of comprehensive income and statement of changes in equity for Hewlett Co for the year to 31 December 20X2 and a statement of financial position at that date in accordance with IFRS insofar as the information permits.

Notes to the financial statements are not required, but all workings should be clearly shown.

Work to the nearest $1m. Comparative information is not required. **(25 marks)**

22 Halliday Inns **45 mins**

Halliday Inns is a quoted company which owns a large number of hotels throughout the UK. The company's latest trial balance at 31 December 20X0 is as follows.

	$'000	$'000
Administrative expenses	3,000	
Bank	300	
Payables		1,700
Distribution costs	4,000	
Food purchases	2,100	
Heating and lighting	3,000	
Hotel buildings: cost	490,000	
depreciation to date		46,200
Hotel fixtures and fittings: cost	18,000	
depreciation to date		9,400
Interest	4,950	
Interim dividend paid	1,000	
Loans, repayable 20X8		110,000
Reserves		86,000
Sales of accommodation and food		68,500
Share capital: $1 shares, fully paid		220,000
Inventory as at 31 December 20X9	400	
Taxation	50	
Wages: administrative staff	6,000	
housekeeping and restaurant staff	9,000	
	541,800	541,800

Additional information

(a) During the year the company spent a total of $12m on a new hotel and purchased new fixtures for $7m. These acquisitions have been included in the relevant trial balance totals.

(b) Hotels are to be depreciated by 2 per cent of cost, and fixtures and fittings by 25 per cent of the reducing balance, with a full year's depreciation to be charged in the year of acquisition or revaluation.

(c) Closing inventories of foodstuffs and other consumables were valued at $470,000 on 31 December 20X0.

(d) The balance on the taxation account is the amount remaining after the settlement of the corporation tax liability for the year ended 31 December 20W9. The directors have estimated the corporation tax liability for the year ended 31 December 20X0 at $10.2m.

(e) The directors have proposed a final dividend of $6m. This was proposed before the year end.

Required

Prepare Halliday Inns income statement for the year ended 31 December 20X0 and its statement of financial position at that date.

Notes to the accounts are not required. **(25 marks)**

23 Cher **45 mins**

Note. To answers parts (b) to (d) of this question, you will need to refer to the income statements in the appendix at the end of the question.

(a) 'Reported earnings per share is a very important indicator of performance for a quoted company.'

Why do you think that this is, and do you agree?

(b) Cher Inc was formed fifteen years ago. As at 1 July 20X3, the issued share capital of the group was as follows, all shares being issued at par.

Ordinary $1 shares fully paid	800,000
Ordinary $1 shares 60c paid	200,000
	1,000,000

On 1 October 20X3, Cher Inc received the monies due on the partly paid shares.

Required

Calculate the earnings per share figure for the year ended 30 June 20X4, as it would appear in the financial statements of the group.

(c) On 28 February 20X5 Cher (Holdings) Co made a 1 for 4 rights issue at $1.30 per share. The actual *cum rights* price was $1.90 per share on the last day of quotation *cum rights*.

Required

(i) Calculate earnings per share for the year ended 30 June 20X5. Show the comparative figure for 20X4.

(ii) Explain the reasoning behind your calculation in part (c)(i).

(d) On 1 January 20X6, a new group Sonny Inc was formed. Its purpose was to take over the business of Cher Inc, and the need to do so arose from the fact that Cher Inc was becoming linked in the mind of the public with an unconnected, somewhat disreputable group, Sheer Inc. Sonny Inc was to issue 2 shares for every 1 share in Cher Inc. In preparing the financial statements of Sonny Inc, which is essentially a continuation of Cher Inc, the uniting of interests method allowed by IAS 22 was adopted.

Required

Calculate earnings per share for the year ended 30 June 20X6. Show the comparative figure for 20X5.

APPENDIX: INCOME STATEMENTS

	Cher Inc		Sonny Inc
Year ended 30 June	*20X4*	*20X5*	*20X6*
	$'000	$'000	$'000
Turnover	2,000	3,400	4,500
Cost of sales	900	800	1,500
Gross profit	1,100	2,600	3,000
Distribution costs	150	240	310
Administrative expenses	260	410	420
Profit on ordinary activities before tax	690	1,950	2,270
Taxation	230	640	750
Profit on ordinary activities after tax	460	1,310	1,520
Dividends	100	200	250
Retained earnings for the financial year	360	1,110	1,270

(25 marks)

24 Engina **45 mins**

Engina, a foreign company, has approached a partner in your firm to assist in obtaining a local Stock Exchange listing for the company. Engina is registered in a country where transactions between related parties are considered to be normal but where such transactions are not disclosed. The directors of Engina are reluctant to disclose the nature of their related party transactions as they feel that although they are a normal feature of business in their part of the world, it could cause significant problems politically and culturally to disclose such transactions.

The partner in your firm has requested a list of all transactions with parties connected with the company and the directors of Engina have produced the following summary.

(a) Every month, Engina sells $50,000 of goods per month to Mr Satay, the financial director. The financial director has set up a small retailing business for his son and the goods are purchased at cost price for him. The annual turnover of Engina is $300 million. Additionally Mr Satay has purchased his company car from the company for $45,000 (market value $80,000). The director, Mr Satay, earns a salary of $500,000 a year, and has a personal fortune of many millions of pounds.

(b) A hotel property had been sold to a brother of Mr Soy, the Managing Director of Engina, for $4 million (net of selling cost of $0.2 million). The market value of the property was $4.3 million but in the overseas country, property prices were falling rapidly. The carrying value of the hotel was $5 million and its value in use was $3.6 million. There was an over supply of hotel accommodation due to government subsidies in an attempt to encourage hotel development and the tourist industry.

(c) Mr Satay owns several companies and the structure of the group is as follows.

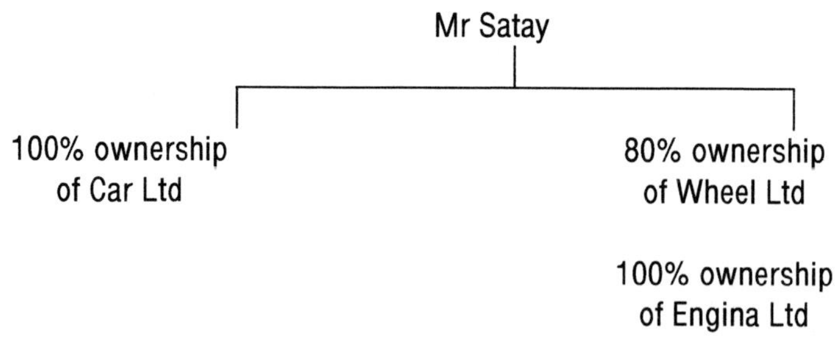

Engina earns 60% of its profit from transactions with Car and 40% of its profit from transactions with Wheel.

Required

Write a report to the directors of Engina setting out the reasons why it is important to disclose related party transactions and the nature of any disclosure required for the above transactions under IAS 24 Related party disclosures.

The mark allocation will be as follows:

		Marks
Style/layout of report		4
Reasons		8
Transaction	(a)	4
	(b)	5
	(c)	4
		25

(25 marks)

25 Group accounts

In many countries, companies with subsidiaries have been required to publish group accounts, usually in the form of consolidated accounts. You are required to state why you feel the preparation of group accounts is necessary and to outline their limitations, if any.

26 Barcelona and Madrid — 18 mins

Barcelona acquired 60% of Madrid's ordinary share capital on 30 June 20X2 at a price $1.06 per share. The balance on Madrid's retained earnings at that date was $104m and the general reserve stood at $11m.

Their respective statements of financial position as at 30 September 20X6 are as follows:

	Barcelona	*Madrid*
	$m	$m
Non-current assets:		
Property, plant & equipment	2,848	354
Patents	45	–
Investment in Madrid	159	–
	3,052	354
Current assets		
Inventories	895	225
Trade and other receivables	1,348	251
Cash and cash equivalents	212	34
	2,455	510
	5,507	864
Equity		
Share capital (20c ordinary shares)	920	50
General reserve	775	46
Retained earnings	2,086	394
	3,781	490
Non-current liabilities		
Long-term borrowings	558	168
Current liabilities		
Trade and other payables	1,168	183
Current portion of long-term borrowings	–	23
	1,168	206
	5,507	864

Annual impairment tests have revealed cumulative impairment losses relating to recognised goodwill of $17m to date.

Required

Produce the consolidated statement of financial position for the Barcelona Group as at 30 September 20X6. It is the group policy to value the non-controlling interest at its proportionate share of the fair value of the subsidiary's identifiable net assets. **(10 marks)**

27 Reprise **36 mins**

Reprise purchased 75% of Encore for $2,000,000 10 years ago when the balance on its retained earnings was $1,044,000. The statements of financial position of the two companies as at 31 March 20X4 are as follows:

	Reprise	*Encore*
	$'000	$'000
NON-CURRENT ASSETS		
Investment in Encore	2,000	–
Land and buildings	3,350	–
Plant and equipment	1,010	2,210
Motor vehicles	510	345
	6,870	2,555
CURRENT ASSETS		
Inventories	890	352
Trade receivables	1,372	514
Cash and cash equivalents	89	51
	2,351	917
	9,221	3,472
EQUITY		
Share capital – $1 ordinary shares	1,000	500
Revaluation surplus	2,500	–
Retained earnings	4,225	2,610
	7,725	3,110
NON-CURRENT LIABILITIES		
10% debentures	500	–
CURRENT LIABILITIES		
Trade payables	996	362
	9,221	3,472

The following additional information is available:

(1) Included in trade receivables of Reprise are amounts owed by Encore of $75,000. The current accounts do not at present balance due to a payment for $39,000 being in transit at the year end from Encore.

(2) Included in the inventories of Encore are items purchased from Reprise during the year for $31,200. Reprise marks up its goods by 30% to achieve its selling price.

(3) $180,000 of the recognised goodwill arising is to be written off due to impairment losses.

(4) Encore shares were trading at $4.40 just prior to acquisition by Reprise.

Required

Prepare the consolidated statement of financial position for the Reprise group of companies as at 31 March 20X4. It is the group policy to value the non-controlling interest at full (or fair) value. **(20 marks)**

28 War **45 mins**

(a) When an acquisition takes place, the purchase consideration may be in the form of share capital. Where no suitable market price exists (for example, shares in an unquoted company) how may the fair value of the purchase consideration be estimated? **(4 marks)**

(b) On 1 May 20X7, War Co acquired 70% of the ordinary share capital of Peace Co by issuing to Peace Co's shareholders 500,000 ordinary $1 shares at a market value of $1.60c per share. The costs associated with the share issue were $50,000.

As at 30 June 20X7, the following financial statements for War Co and Peace Co were available.

INCOME STATEMENTS
FOR THE YEAR ENDED 30 JUNE 20X7

	War Co	*Peace Co*
	$'000	$'000
Revenue	3,150	1,770
Cost of sales	(1,610)	(1,065)
Gross profit	1,540	705
Distribution costs	(620)	(105)
Administrative expenses	(325)*	(210)
Interest payable	(70)	(30)
Dividends from Peace Co	42	–
Profit before taxation	567	360
Income tax expense	(283)	(135)
Profit for the year	284	225

*Note. The issue costs of $50,000 on the issue of ordinary share capital are included in this figure.

Dividends paid during the year were:	War Co:	$38,000
	Peace Co:	$60,000

STATEMENTS OF FINANCIAL POSITION AT 30 JUNE 20X7

	War Co	*Peace Co*
	$'000	$'000
Assets		
Non-current assets		
Property, plant and equipment	1,750	350
Investment in Peace Co	800	–
	2,550	350
Current assets		
Inventory	150	450
Receivables	238	213
Cash	187	112
	575	775
Total assets	3,125	1,125
Equity and liabilities		
Shares of $1 each	750	100
Share premium	300	150
Retained earnings	625	450
	1,675	700
Non-current liabilities	1,050	175
Current liabilities	400	250
Total equity and liabilities	3,125	1,125

You have been asked to prepare the consolidated financial statements, taking account of the following further information.

(i) There was no impairment in the value of goodwill.

(ii) War Co accounts for pre-acquisition dividends by treating them as a deduction from the cost of the investment. Peace Co paid an ordinary dividend of 60c per share on 1 June 20X7. No dividends were proposed as at 30 June 20X7.

(iii) The profit of Peace Co may be assumed to accrue evenly over the year.

(iv) The property, plant and equipment of Peace Co had a net realisable value of $400,000 at the date of acquisition. Their fair value was $500,000. It has been decided that, as Peace Co was acquired so close to the year end, no depreciation adjustment will be made in the group accounts; the year end value will be taken as the carrying value of the property, plant and equipment in the accounts of Peace Co. The remaining assets and liabilities of Peace Co were all stated at their fair value as at 1 May 20X7.

(v) Peace Co did not issue any shares between the date of acquisition and the year end.

(vi) There were no intercompany transactions during the year.

Required

Prepare the consolidated statement of financial position and the consolidated income statement of the War Group Co for the year ended 30 June 20X7. It is the group policy to value the non-controlling interest at its proportionate share of the fair value of the subsidiary's identifiable net assets. **(21 marks)**

(Total = 25 marks)

29 Fallowfield and Rusholme **27 mins**

Fallowfield acquired a 60% holding in Rusholme three years ago when Rusholme's retained earnings balance stood at $16,000. Both businesses have been very successful since the acquisition and their respective income statements for the year ended 30 June 20X8 are as follows:

	Fallowfield	*Rusholme*
	$	$
Revenue	403,400	193,000
Cost of sales	(201,400)	(92,600)
Gross profit	202,000	100,400
Distribution costs	(16,000)	(14,600)
Administrative expenses	(24,250)	(17,800)
Dividends from Rusholme	15,000	
Profit before tax	176,750	68,000
Income tax expense	(61,750)	(22,000)
Profit for the year	115,000	46,000

STATEMENT OF CHANGES IN EQUITY (EXTRACT)

	Fallowfield Retained earnings	*Rusholme Retained earnings*
	$	$
Balance at 1 July 20X7	163,000	61,000
Dividends	(40,000)	(25,000)
Profit for the year	115,000	46,000
Balance at 30 June 20X8	238,000	82,000

Additional information

During the year Rusholme sold some goods to Fallowfield for $40,000, including 25% mark up. Half of these items were still in inventories at the year-end.

Required

Produce the consolidated income statement of Fallowfield Co and its subsidiary for the year ended 30 June 20X8, and an extract from the statement of changes in equity, showing retained earnings. Goodwill is to be ignored. **(15 marks)**

30 Panther Group 27 mins

Panther operated as a single company, but in 20X4 decided to expand its operations. Panther acquired a 60% interest in Sabre on 1 July 20X4 for $2,000,000. The statements of comprehensive income of Panther and Sabre for the year ended 31 December 20X4 are as follows:

	Panther	*Sabre*
	$'000	$'000
Revenue	22,800	4,300
Cost of sales	(13,600)	(2,600)
Gross profit	9,200	1,700
Distribution costs	(2,900)	(500)
Administrative expenses	(1,800)	(300)
Finance costs	(200)	(70)
Finance income	50	–
Profit before tax	4,350	830
Income tax expense	(1,300)	(220)
PROFIT FOR THE YEAR	3,050	610
Other comprehensive income for the year, net of tax	1,600	180
TOTAL COMPREHENSIVE INCOME FOR THE YEAR	4,650	790

Since acquisition, Panther purchased $320,000 of goods from Sabre. Of these, $60,000 remained in inventories at the year end. Sabre makes a mark-up on cost of 20% under the transfer pricing agreement between the two companies. The fair value of the identifiable net assets of Sabre on purchase were $200,000 greater than their book value. The difference relates to properties with a remaining useful life of 20 years.

On the acquisition date Panther advanced a loan to Sabre amounting to $800,000 at a preferential interest rate of 5%. The loan is due for repayment in 20X9.

Statement of changes in equity (extracts) for the two companies:

	Panther Reserves	*Sabre Reserves*
	$'000	$'000
Balance at 1 January 20X4	12,750	2,480
Dividend paid	(900)	–
Total comprehensive income for the year	4,650	790
Balance at 31 December 20X4	16,500	3,270

Panther and Sabre had $400,000 and $150,000 of share capital in issue throughout the period respectively.

Required

Prepare the consolidated statement of comprehensive income and statement of changes in equity (extract for reserves) for the Panther Group for the year ended 31 December 20X4.

No adjustments for impairment losses were necessary in the group financial statements.

Assume income and expenses (other than intragroup items) accrue evenly. **(15 marks)**

31 Hever **45 mins**

Hever has held shares in two companies, Spiro and Aldridge, for a number of years. As at 31 December 20X4 they have the following statements of financial position:

	Hever	*Spiro*	*Aldridge*
	$'000	$'000	$'000
Non-current assets			
Property, plant & equipment	370	190	260
Investments	218	–	–
	588	190	260
Current assets:			
Inventories	160	100	180
Trade receivables	170	90	100
Cash	50	40	10
	380	230	290
	968	420	550
Equity			
Share capital ($1 ords)	200	80	50
Share premium	100	80	30
Retained earnings	568	200	400
	868	360	480
Current liabilities			
Trade payables	100	60	70
	968	420	550

You ascertain the following additional information:

(1) The 'investments' in the statement of financial position comprise solely Hever's investment in Spiro ($128,000) and in Aldridge ($90,000).

(2) The 48,000 shares in Spiro were acquired when Spiro's retained earnings balance stood at $20,000.

The 15,000 shares in Aldridge were acquired when that company had a retained earnings balance of $150,000.

(3) When Hever acquired its shares in Spiro the fair value of Spiro's net assets equalled their book values with the following exceptions:

	$'000
Property, plant and equipment	50 higher
Inventories	20 lower (sold during 20X4)

Depreciation arising on the fair value adjustment to non-current assets since this date is $5,000.

(4) During the year, Hever sold inventories to Spiro for $16,000, which originally cost Hever $10,000. Three-quarters of these inventories have subsequently been sold by Spiro.

(5) No impairment losses on goodwill had been necessary by 31 December 20X4.

Required

Produce the consolidated statement of financial position for the Hever group (incorporating the associate). It is the group policy to value the non-controlling interest at its proportionate share of the fair value of the subsidiary's identifiable net assets. **(25 marks)**

32 Joint ventures **18 mins**

What are the advantages and disadvantages of accounting for joint ventures using the proportionate consolidation method? **(10 marks)**

Exam answer bank

1 Setting and regulating standards

(a) The objectives of the IASB are to:

(i) Develop high quality financial reporting standards to provide users with **transparent** and **comparative information** in financial statements.

(ii) Promote rigorous application of its standards.

(iii) Collaborate with local standard-setters to achieve convergence/harmonisation.

(b) The overall agenda of the IASB will initially be set by discussion with the Standards Advisory Council. The process for developing an individual standard would involve the following steps:

Step 1 During the early stages of a project, IASB may establish an **Advisory Committee** to give advice on issues arising in the project. Consultation with the Advisory Committee and the

Standards Advisory Council occurs throughout the project.

Step 2 IASB may develop and publish **Discussion Documents** for public comment.

Step 3 Following the receipt and review of comments, IASB would develop and publish an

Exposure Draft for public comment.

Step 4 Following the receipt and review of comments, the IASB would issue a final **International Financial Reporting Standard**.

The period of exposure for public comment is normally 90 days. However, in exceptional circumstances, proposals may be issued with a comment period of 60 days.

(c) **Barriers to harmonisation**

(i) **Different purposes of financial reporting**. In some countries the purpose is solely for tax assessment, while in others it is for investor decision-making.

(ii) **Different legal systems**. These prevent the development of certain accounting practices and restrict the options available.

(iii) **Different user groups**. Countries have different ideas about who the relevant user groups are and their respective importance. In the USA investor and creditor groups are given prominence, while in Europe employees enjoy a higher profile.

(iv) **Needs of developing countries**. Developing countries are obviously behind in the standard setting process and they need to develop the basic standards and principles already in place in most developed countries.

(v) **Nationalism** is demonstrated in an unwillingness to accept another country's standard.

(vi) **Cultural differences** result in objectives for accounting systems differing from country to country.

(vii) **Unique circumstances**. Some countries may be experiencing unusual circumstances which affect all aspects of everyday life and impinge on the ability of companies to produce proper reports, for example hyperinflation, civil war, currency restriction and so on.

(viii) **The lack of strong accountancy bodies**. Many countries do not have strong independent accountancy or business bodies which would press for better standards and greater harmonisation.

(d) The role of the IFRS Interpretations Committee is to:

(i) Review on a timely basis, newly identified financial **reporting issues not specifically addressed in IFRSs**.

(ii) **Clarify issues** where **unsatisfactory** or **conflicting** interpretations have developed, or seem likely to develop in the absence of authoritative guidance with a view to reaching a consensus on the appropriate treatment.

2 Regulators

> **Tutor's hint:**. It is best to use headings to divide up your answer, as we do here.

Stock Exchange

A listed company is a company whose shares are bought and sold on a stock exchange. This involves the signing of an agreement which requires compliance with the rules of that stock exchange. This would normally contain amongst other things the stock exchange's detailed rules on the information to be disclosed in listed companies' accounts. This, then, is one regulatory influence on a listed company's accounts. The stock exchange may enforce compliance by **monitoring accounts** and reserving the right to withdraw a company's shares from the stock exchange: ie the company's shares would no longer be traded through the stock exchange. In many countries there is, however, no statutory requirement to obey these rules.

Local legislation

In most countries, companies have to comply with the local companies legislation, which lays down **detailed requirements** on the **preparation of accounts**. Company law is often quite detailed, partly because of external influences such as EU Directives. Another reason to increase statutory regulation is that listed companies are under great pressure to **show profit growth** and an obvious way to achieve this is to **manipulate accounting policies**. If this involves breaking the law, as opposed to ignoring professional guidance, company directors may think twice before bending the rules – or, at least, this is often a government's hope.

Standard-setters

Professional guidance is given by the national and international standard-setters. Prescriptive guidance is given in accounting standards which must be applied in all accounts required to show a **'true and fair view' or 'present fairly** in all material aspects'. IASs and national standards are issued after extensive consultation and are revised as required to reflect economic or legal changes. In some countries, legislation requires details of non-compliance to be disclosed in the accounts. 'Defective' accounts can be revised under court order if necessary and directors signing such accounts can be prosecuted and fined (or even imprisoned).

The potential for the **IASB's influence** in this area is substantial. It must pursue **excellence in standards** with absolute rigour to fulfil that potential.

3 Europa

(a) Europa's first IFRS financial statements will be for the year ended 31 December 2005. IFRS 1 requires that at least one year's comparative figures are presented and therefore the date of transition to IFRSs is the beginning of business on 1 January 2004 (or close of business on 31 December 2003).

Therefore the procedure for adopting IFRSs is:

(i) identify accounting policies that comply with IFRSs effective at 31 December 2005 (the reporting date for the first IFRS financial statements);

(ii) restate the opening statement of financial position at 1 January 2004 (the date of transition) using these IFRSs retrospectively, by:

- recognising all assets and liabilities whose recognition is required by IFRSs;
- not recognising items as assets or liabilities if IFRSs do not permit such recognition;
- reclassifying items that were recognised under previous GAAP as one type of asset, liability or component of equity, but are a different type of asset liability or component of equity under IFRSs; and
- measuring all recognised assets and liabilities in accordance with IFRSs.

The company will almost certainly need to change some of its accounting policies and to adjust some of the amounts that it reported previously at the same dates using local GAAP. It should recognise these adjustments directly in retained earnings (ie, in equity).

(iii) Explain the effect of the transition from local GAAP to IFRSs, by presenting:

- a reconciliation of equity reported under local GAAP to equity under IFRSs at the date of transition and at the reporting date; and
- a reconciliation of the profit or loss reported under local GAAP to profit or loss reported under IFRSs for the period.

If Europa presented a statement of cash flows under local GAAP, it should also explain any material adjustments to the statement of cash flows.

Although the general rule is that all IFRSs should be applied retrospectively, a number of exemptions are available. These are intended to cover cases in which the cost of complying fully with a particular requirement would outweigh the benefits to users of the financial statements. Europa may choose to take advantage of any or all of the exemptions, which relate to fair values and revaluation; business combinations; employee benefits; cumulative foreign currency translation differences; compound financial instruments; and assets and liabilities of subsidiaries, associates and joint ventures.

(b) Changing from local GAAP to IFRSs is likely to be a complex process and should be carefully planned. Although local GAAP and IAS/IFRS may follow broadly the same principles there are still likely to be many important differences in the detailed requirements of individual standards.

If Europa has overseas subsidiaries outside the EU it will also need to ensure that they comply with any local reporting requirements. This may mean that subsidiaries have to prepare two sets of financial statements: one using their local GAAP; and one using IFRSs (for the consolidation).

The process will be affected by the following:

(i) The differences between local GAAP and IFRSs as they affect the group financial statements in practice. The company will need to carry out a detailed review of current accounting policies, paying particular attention to areas where there are significant differences between local GAAP and IFRSs. These will probably include deferred tax, business combinations, employee benefits and foreign currency translation. It should be possible to estimate the effect of the change by preparing pro-forma financial statements using IFRSs.

(ii) The level of knowledge of IFRSs of current finance staff (including internal auditors). It will probably be necessary to organise training and the company may need to recruit additional personnel.

(iii) The group's accounting systems. Management will need to assess whether computerised accounting systems can produce the information required to report under IFRSs. They will also need to produce new consolidation packages and accounting manuals.

Lastly, the company should consider the impact of the change to IFRSs on investors and their advisers. For this reason management should try to quantify the effect of IFRSs on results and other key performance indicators as early as possible.

(c) (i) *Accounting estimates*

Estimates under IFRSs at the date of transition must be consistent with those made at the same date under previous GAAP, (after adjustments to reflect any difference in accounting policies). The only exception to this is if the company has subsequently discovered that these estimates were in error. This is not the case here and therefore the estimates are not adjusted in the first IFRS financial statements.

(ii) *Court case*

The treatment of this depends on the reason why Europa did not recognise a provision under local GAAP at 31 December 2004.

If the requirements of local GAAP were consistent with IAS 37 *Provisions, Contingent Liabilities and Contingent Assets*, presumably the directors concluded that an outflow of economic benefit was not probable and that the recognition criteria were not met. In this case, Europa's assumptions under IFRSs are consistent with its previous assumptions under local GAAP. Europa does not recognise a provision at 31 December 2004 and accounts for the payment in the year ended 31 December 2005.

If the requirements of local GAAP were not consistent with IAS 37, Europa must determine whether it had an obligation at 31 December 2004. The directors should take account of all available evidence, including any additional evidence provided by events after the reporting date. Similarly, under IAS 10 *Events after the reporting period*, the resolution of a court case after the reporting date is an adjusting event if it confirms that the company had a present obligation at that date.

The outcome of the court case confirms that Europa had a liability in September 2004 (when the events that resulted in the case occurred). Therefore the company should recognise a provision at 31 December 2004.

4 Revision of accounting concepts

(a) **The business entity concept**

The concept is that accountants regard a business as a separate entity, **distinct from its owners** or managers. The concept applies whether the business is a limited liability company (and so recognised in law as a separate entity) or a sole proprietorship or partnership (in which case the business is not separately recognised by the law.

(b) **The historical cost convention**

A basic principle of accounting (some writers include it in the list of fundamental accounting assumptions) is that resources are normally stated in accounts at historical cost, ie at the amount which the **business paid to acquire them**. An important advantage of this procedure is that the **objectivity** of accounts is **maximised**: there is usually objective, documentary evidence to prove the amount paid to purchase an asset or pay an expense.

In general, accountants prefer to deal with costs, rather than with 'values'. This is because **valuations** tend to be **subjective** and to vary according to what the valuation is for. For example, suppose that a company acquires a machine to manufacture its products. The machine has an expected useful life of four years. At the end of two years the company is preparing a statement of financial position and has to decide what monetary amount to attribute to the asset.

Numerous possibilities might be considered.

(i) The original cost (historical cost) of the machine
(ii) Half of the historical cost, on the ground that half of its useful life has expired
(iii) The amount the machine might fetch on the **secondhand** market
(iv) The amount it would cost to replace the machine with an identical machine
(v) The amount it would cost to **replace** the machine with a more modern machine incorporating the technological advances of the previous two years
(vi) The machine's economic value, ie the amount of the **profits** it is expected to **generate** for the company during its remaining life

> **Tutor's hint**. Here we clarify what historical cost means by reference to other alternative bases of measurement.

All of these valuations have something to commend them, but the great advantage of the first two is that they are based on a figure (the machine's historical cost) which is objectively verifiable. (Some authors regard objectivity as an accounting concept in its own right.) The subjective judgement involved in the other valuations, particularly (f), is so great as to lessen the **reliability** of any accounts in which they are used.

(c) **The realisation concept**

The realisation concept states that revenue and profits are not anticipated but are recognised by inclusion in the income statement only when *realised* in the form either of **cash or of other assets** the **ultimate cash realisation** of which can be **assessed with reasonable certainty**. Provision is made for all known liabilities (expenses and losses) whether the amount of these is known with certainty or is a best estimate in the light of the information available.

There are some **exceptions** to the rule, notably for **land and buildings**. With dramatic rises in property prices in some countries, it has been a **common practice to revalue land and buildings periodically** to a current value, to avoid having a misleading statement of financial position. Even if the sale of the property is not contemplated, such **revaluations create an unrealised profit**:

DEBIT	Land and buildings account
CREDIT	Reserve account

This profit is sometimes known as a *holding gain*, because it is a profit which arises in the course of **holding** the asset as a result of its increase in value above cost.

In spite of such exceptions, however, the realisation principle has long been accepted by all practising accountants and it is standard practice that only profits realised at the reporting date should be included in profit or loss.

Unfortunately there is **no standard definition of realised profits** and losses it could be said that they are such profits or losses of a company as fall to be treated as realised in accordance with **principles generally accepted at the time** when the accounts are prepared, with respect to the determination for accounting purposes of realised profits. One aspect of the problem is the question: *At what point in the business cycle should revenue be recognised as earned?*

5 Conceptual framework

(a) The role of the IASB *Framework* in the development of IFRSs may be summarised as follows.

(i) Assist the Board of the IASB in the **development of future IFRSs** and in its review of existing IASs/IFRSs.

(ii) Assist the Board of the IASB in **promoting harmonisation** of regulations, accounting standards and procedures relating to the presentation of financial statements by providing a basis for reducing the number of alternative accounting treatments permitted by IASs/IFRSs.

(iii) Assist **national standard-setting bodies** in developing national standards.

(iv) Assist **preparers of financial statements** in applying IASs/IFRSs and in dealing with topics that have yet to form the subject of an IFRS.

(v) Assist **auditors** in forming an opinion as to whether financial statements conform with IASs/IFRSs.

(vi) Assist **users of financial statements** in interpreting the information contained in financial statements prepared in conformity with IASs/IFRSs.

(vii) Provide those who are interested in the work of IASB with **information** about its approach to the formulation of IASs/IFRSs.

(b) The *Framework* states that:

'The objective of financial statements is to provide information about the financial position, performance and changes in financial position of an enterprise that is useful to a wide range of users in making economic decisions.'

Such financial statements will meet the needs of most users. The information is, however, **restricted**.

(i) It is based on **past events** not expected future events.

(ii) It does not necessarily contain **non-financial information**.

The statements also show the **results** of **management's stewardship**.

(c) An asset is a **resource controlled** by an enterprise as a result of **past events** and from which **future economic benefits** are expected to flow to the enterprise.

A liability is a **present obligation** of an enterprise arising from **past events**, the settlement of which is expected to result in an **outflow** from the enterprise of **resources embodying economic benefits**.

(d) Information must be neutral ie **free from bias** to be **reliable**. Neutrality is lost if the financial statements are prepared so as to influence the user to make a judgement or decision in order to achieve a predetermined outcome.

Uncertainties exist in the preparation of financial information, eg the collectability of doubtful receivables. These uncertainties are recognised through disclosure and through the application of **prudence**. Prudence does not, however, allow the creation of hidden reserves or excessive provisions, understatement of assets or income or overstatement of liabilities or expenses.

Hence, where there is **uncertainty**, **prudence** must be exercised. However, prudence also implies **neutrality** or **freedom from bias** – **otherwise** the figures involved will not be **reliable**.

Prudence must be adopted where there is uncertainty but also the existence of uncertainty is a pre-condition before you can resort to prudence.

This approach is designed to **obviate** the use of prudence as a management tool for **smoothing results**.

6 Jenson

Tutor's hint. This is an important conceptual subject and it is closely linked with the IASB's *Framework,* which you should have discussed, rather than IAS 18, the accounting standard on revenue recognition. You need to use your imagination to come up with examples in (b).

(a) In revenue recognition, the 'critical event' is the point in the earnings process or operating cycle at which the transaction is deemed to have been **sufficiently completed** to allow the **profit** arising from the transaction, or a distinct component part of it, to be **recognised** in income in a particular period. This has to be addressed in order to allocate transactions and their effects to different accounting periods and is a direct result of the episodic nature of financial reporting. For most companies the **normal earnings cycle** is the purchase of raw materials which are transformed through a manufacturing process into saleable goods, for which orders are subsequently received, delivery is made and then payment received.

In the past the approach has been to **match costs with revenues** and record both once the critical event has passed; in most systems this critical event has been full or **near full performance of the transaction**, so that no material uncertainties surround either the transaction being completed or the amounts arising from the transaction. This is encompassed in the notion of prudence, so that revenue is recognised only in cash or near cash form. However, any point in the cycle could be deemed to be the critical event. This approach leaves the statement of financial position as a statement of uncompleted transaction balances, comprising unexpired costs and undischarged liabilities.

In contrast, the IASB's **Framework** defines gains and losses (or income and expenses) in terms of **changes** in assets and liabilities other than those arising from transactions with owners as owners, not in terms of an earnings or matching process. The statement of financial position thus assumes primary importance in the recognition of earnings and profits. A gain **can only be recognised** if there is an **increase** in the equity (ie net assets) of an entity not resulting from contributions from owners. Similarly, a loss is recognised if there is a **decrease** in the ownership interest of an entity not resulting from distributions to owners. Thus gains arise from recognition of assets and derecognition of liabilities, and losses arise from derecognition of assets and recognition of liabilities. The Statement explains that it is not possible to reverse this definitional process, ie by defining assets and liabilities in terms of gains and losses, because it has not been possible to formulate robust enough base definitions of gains and losses (partly because the choice of critical event can be subjective). Nevertheless commentators often attempt to link the two approaches by asserting that **sufficient evidence** for recognition or derecognition will be met at the critical event in the operating cycle.

(b)

Tutor's hint. You can argue these examples either way – what matters is that you marshal your arguments properly. Remember that this matter is still being clarified, for example by standard setters in the UK.

On the acquisition of goods
This would be **unlikely** to be a critical event for most businesses. However, for some the acquisition of the raw materials is the most important part of the process, eg extraction of gold from a mine, or the harvesting of coffee beans. Only where the goods in question could **be sold immediately in a liquid market** would it be appropriate to recognise revenue, ie they would have to have a **commodity value.**

During the manufacture or production of goods
This is also **unlikely** to be the critical event for most businesses because **too many uncertainties** remain, eg of damaged goods or overproduction leading to obsolete stock. An **exception** would **be long-term contracts** for the construction of specific assets, which tend to earn the constructing company revenues over the length of the contract, usually in stages, ie there is a **series of critical events** in the operating cycle (according to the *Framework*). It would **not** be appropriate to recognise all the revenue at the end of the contract, because this would reflect profit earned in past periods as well as the present period. Profit is therefore recognised during manufacture or production, usually through certification of a qualified valuer. Some would argue that this is not really a critical event approach, but rather an 'accretion approach'.

On delivery/acceptance of goods
Goods are frequently sold on **credit**, whereby the vendor hands over the inventory asset and receives in its place **a financial asset of a debt** due for the price of the goods. At that point legal title passes and **full performance** has taken place. In general, the bulk of the risks of the transaction have gone and the only ones remaining relate to the creditworthiness of the purchaser and any outstanding warranty over the goods. Many trade sales take place in this way, with periods of credit allowed for goods delivered, eg 30 days. This therefore tends to be the critical event for many types of business operating cycles.

Where certain conditions have been satisfied after the goods have been delivered
In these situations the customer had a right of return of the goods without reason or penalty, but usually within a time and non-use condition. A good example is clothes retailers who **allow non-faulty goods to be returned.** Another example is that the goods need only be paid for once they are sold on to a third party. Traditionally, recognition of revenue is delayed until, eg **the deadline to allowed return passes.** However, in circumstances where goods are never returned, it might be argued that the substance of the transaction is a sale on delivery.

Receipt or payment for credit sales
Once payment is received, only warranty risk remains. A company may wait until this point to recognise income if receipt is considered uncertain, eg when goods have been sold to a company resident in a country that has exchange controls. It would otherwise be **rare** to delay recognition until payment.

On the expiry of a guarantee or warranty
Many businesses may feel unable to recognise revenue in full because of **outstanding warranties,** eg a construction company which is subject to fee retention until some time after completion of the contract. Other businesses, such as car manufacturers, may make a **general provision** for goods

returned under warranty as it will not be possible to judge likely warranty costs under individual contracts.

(c) (i) This agreement is worded as a **sale**, but it is fairly obvious from the terms and assessed substance that it is in fact a **secured loan.** Jensen should therefore continue to recognise the stock on balance sheet and should treat the receipt from Wholesaler as a loan, not revenue. Finance costs will be charged to the income statement, of $35,000 × 12% × 9/12 = £3,150.

(ii) Years 2 to 5 of the franchise contract would be **loss making** for Jensen and hence, under IAS 18, part of the initial fee of $50,000 should be **deferred over the life of the contract.** Since Jensen should be making a profit margin of 20% on this type of arrangement, revenues of $10,000 will be required to match against the costs of $8,000. The company will receive $5,000 pa and so a further $5,000 × 4 = $20,000 of the initial fee should be deferred, leaving $50,000 – $20,000 = $30,000 to be recognised in the first year. However, this may not represent a liability under IAS 37 *Provisions, Contingent Liabilities and Contingent Assets*, where a liability is defined as an obligation to transfer economic benefits as a result of past transactions or events. It will be necessary to consider the terms of the initial fee and whether it is returnable.

(iii) The cost of the first 6 months' publications is $192,000 ÷ 24 × 6 = $48,000. On an accruals basis, income of $240,000 ÷ 24 × 6 = 60,000 should be recognised. This would leave deferred income of $240,000 – $60,000 = £180,000 in Jensen's statement of financial position (ie as a liability). As in (ii), however, this may not represent a liability. In fact, the liability of the company may only extend to the cost of the future publications, ie $192,000 – $48,000 = $144,000. This would allow Jensen to **recognise all the profit** on the publications **immediately**. In want of an accounting standard on revenue recognition, it will be necessary to consider the extent of Jensen's commitments under this arrangement.

7 D'Urberville

Tutor's hint. The figures for 20X5 are fairly easy. For 20X6 and 20X7 you have a finance lease to deal with, which requires a bit more thought.

Non-current assets

SCHEDULE OF MOTOR VEHICLES
FOR THE YEARS ENDED 31 DECEMBER 20X5, 20X6, 20X7

			$'000
20X5			
Cost:	At 1 January 20X5		540
	Additions		147
	Disposals		70
	At 31 December 20X5		617
Accumulated depreciation:		At 1 January 20X5	130
		Disposals (W1)	50
		Charge for year 25% × (617 – (130 – 50))	134
		At 31 December 20X5	214
Net book value at 31 December 20X5			403
20X6			
Cost:	At 1 January 20X6		617
	Additions*		252
	Held under finance leases		320
	Disposals		110
	At 31 December 20X6		1,079

		$'000
Accumulated depreciation:	At 1 January 20X6	214
	Disposals (W2)	68
	Charge for year 25% (759 – (214 – 68)) + (25% × 320)	233
	At 31 December 20X6	379
Net book value at 31 December 20X6		700

***Tutor's hint**. The acquisitions in 20X6 are capitalised at cash price less trade discount (for cash purchases), plus delivery costs $(300 – 60 + 12) = $252,000. Disclosure of the value of the assets held subject to finance leases is required by IAS 17.

20X7		$'000
Cost:	At 1 January 20X7	1,079
	Additions**	375
	Held under finance leases	400
	Disposals	75
	At 31 December 20X7	1,779

Accumulated depreciation:	At 1 January 20X7	379
	Disposals (W3)	(43)
	Charge for year 25% (1,379 – (379 – 43) + (400 × 25%))	361
	At 31 December 20X7	697
Net book value at 31 December 20X5		1,082

****Tutor's hint**. The acquisitions in 20X7 are capitalised at cash price less trade discount (for cash purchase) plus delivery cost: $(450 – 90 + 15) = $375.

Workings

1 Accumulated depreciation on 20X5 disposals

Vehicles acquired in 20X0:

		$
20X0	25% × $30,000	7,500
20X1	25% × $(30,000 – 7,500)	5,625
20X2	25% × $(30,000 – (7,500 + 5,625))	4,219
20X3	25% × $(30,000 – (7,500 + 5,625 + 4,219))	3,164
20X4	25% × $(30,000 – (7,500 + 5,625 + 4,219 + 3,164))	2,373
Total		22,881

Vehicles acquired in 20X1:

		$
20X1	25% × $40,000	10,000
20X2	25% × $(40,000 – 10,000)	7,500
20X3	25% × $(40,000 – (10,000 + 7,500))	5,625
20X4	25% × $(40,000 – (10,000 + 8,500 + 5,625))	4,219
Total		27,344

Total accumulated depreciation on disposals: $(22,881 + 27,344) = $50,225.

2 *Accumulated depreciation on 20X6 disposals*

Vehicles acquired in 20X2:

		$
20X2	25% × $45,000	11,250
20X3	25% × $(45,000 – 11,250)	8,438
20X4	25% × $(45,000 – (11,250 + 8,438))	6,328
20X5	25% × $(45,000 – (11,250 + 8,438 + 6,328))	4,746
Total		30,762

Vehicles acquired in 20X3:

		$
20X3	25% × $65,000	16,250
20X4	25% × $(65,000 – 16,250)	12,188
20X5	25% × $(65,000 – (16,250 + 12,188))	9,141
Total		37,579

Total accumulated depreciation on 20X6 disposals $(30,762 + 37,579) = $68,341

3 *Accumulated depreciation on 20X7 disposals*

Vehicles acquired in 20X2:

		$
20X4	25% × $75,000	18,750
20X5	25% × $(75,000 – 18,750)	14,063
20X6	25% × $(75,000 – (18,750 + 14,063)	10,547
Total		43,360

Tutor's hint. Note that the question does not ask for the details of the obligations under the finance leases which would be disclosed under long and short term payables in accordance with the requirements of IAS 17.

8 Yorana

Tutor's hint. The most important part of this question is the working apportioning the lease instalments between interest and the capital. The rest of the accounting follows on for this.

(a) BOOKS OF YORANA AGGREGATES CO

LORRIES ACCOUNT

		$			$
20X1					
1 Jan	Gregory Garages	54,000			

PROVISION FOR DEPRECIATION ON LORRIES

		$			$
20X1			*20X1*		
			31 Dec	Income statement: ¼ ×	
31 Dec	Balance c/d	12,500		$(54,000 – (3 × 1,333))	12,500
20X2			*20X2*		
31 Dec	Balance c/d	25,000	1 Jan	Balance b/d	12,500
			31 Dec	Income statement	12,500
		25,000			25,000
20X3			*20X3*		
31 Dec	Balance c/d	37,500	1 Jan	Balance b/d	25,000
			31 Dec	Income statement	12,500
		37,500			37,500
20X4			*20X4*		
31 Dec	Balance c/d	50,000	1 Jan	Balance b/d	37,500
			31 Dec	Income statement	12,500
		50,000			50,000
			20X5		
			1 Jan	Balance b/d	50,000

Tutor's hint. The above workings are very straightforward and can be done without worrying about the leasing aspects.

LEASE INTEREST PAYABLE

20X1		$	*20X1*		$
31 Dec	Bank (W)	11,250	31 Dec	Income statement	11,250
20X2			*20X2*		
31 Dec	Bank (W)	8,063	31 Dec	Income statement	8,063
20X3			*20X3*		
31 Dec	Bank (W)	4,078	31 Dec	Income statement	4,078

GREGORY GARAGES CO

20X1		$	*20X1*		$
1 Jan	Bank – deposit	9,000	1 Jan	Lorries a/c	54,000
31 Dec	Bank (W)	12,750			
	Balance c/d	32,250			
		54,000			54,000
20X2			*20X2*		
31 Dec	Bank (W)	15,937	1 Jan	Balance b/d	32,250
	Balance c/d	16,313			
		32,250			32,250
20X3			*20X3*		
31 Dec	Bank (W)	16,313	1 Jan	Balance b/d	16,313

INCOME STATEMENTS (EXTRACTS)

	20X1	*20X2*	*20X3*	*20X4*
	$	$	$	$
Lease interest	11,250	8,063	4,078	
Depreciation on lorries	12,500	12,500	12,500	12,500

STATEMENTS OF FINANCIAL POSITION AT 31 DECEMBER (EXTRACTS)

	20X1	*20X2*	*20X3*	*20X4*
	$	$	$	$
Non-current assets				
Lorries: at cost	54,000	54,000	54,000	54,000
Depreciation	12,500	25,000	37,500	50,000
	41,500	29,000	16,500	4,000
Current liabilities				
Finance lease obligations	15,937	16,313	–	–
Non-current liabilities				
Finance lease obligations	16,313	–	–	–

(b)

Tutor's hint. As you will see, the lessor's books are a mirror image of the lessee's.

BOOKS OF GREGORY GARAGES CO

YORANA AGGREGATES CO

20X1		$	*20X1*		$
1 Jan	Sales	54,000	1 Jan	Bank	9,000
			31 Dec	Bank	12,750
				Balance c/d	32,250
		54,000			54,000

20X2			*20X2*			
1 Jan	Balance b/d	32,250	31 Dec	Bank		15,937
				Balance c/d		16,313
		32,250				32,250
20X3			*20X3*			
1 Jan	Balance b/d	16,313	31 Dec	Bank		16,313

LEASE INTEREST RECEIVABLE

20X1		$	*20X1*		$
31 Dec	Income statement	11,250	31 Dec	Bank	11,250
20X2			*20X2*		
31 Dec	Income statement	8,063	31 Dec	Bank	8,063
20X3			*20X3*		
31 Dec	Income statement	4,078	31 Dec	Bank	4,078

INCOME STATEMENTS (EXTRACTS)

		20X1	*20X2*	*20X3*
	$	$	$	$
Sales	54,000		–	–
Cost of sales on lease	43,200		–	–
Gross profit on lease sales		10,800	–	–
Lease interest receivable		11,250	8,063	4,078

Working

Apportionment of lease instalments between interest and capital repayment.

	20X1	*20X2*	*20X3*
	$	$	$
Opening liability (after deposit)	45,000	32,250	16,313
Add interest at 25%	11,250	8,063	4,078
	56,250	40,313	20,391
Less instalment	24,000	24,000	20,391
Closing liability	32,250	16,313	Nil
Interest element as above	11,250	8,063	4,078
∴ Capital repayment	12,750	15,937	16,313
Total instalment	24,000	24,000	20,391

9 Bulwell

Tutor's hint. The most important part of this question is the working apportioning the lease instalments between interest and the capital. The rest of the accounting follows on from this.

(a) BOOKS OF BULWELL AGGREGATES CO

LORRIES ACCOUNT

20X1		$	$
1 Jan	Granby Garages	54,000	

ACCUMULATED DEPRECIATION ON LORRIES

20X1		$	*20X1*		$
			31 Dec	Income statement: ¼ ×	
31 Dec	Balance c/d	12,500		$(54,000 – (3 × 1,333))	12,500
20X2			*20X2*		
31 Dec	Balance c/d	25,000	1 Jan	Balance b/d	12,500
			31 Dec	Income statement	12,500
		25,000			25,000
20X3			*20X3*		
31 Dec	Balance c/d	37,500	1 Jan	Balance b/d	25,000
			31 Dec	Income statement	12,500
		37,500			37,500
20X4			*20X4*		
31 Dec	Balance c/d	50,000	1 Jan	Balance b/d	37,500
			31 Dec	Income statement	12,500
		50,000			50,000
			20X5		
			1 Jan	Balance b/d	50,000

Tutor's hint. The above workings are very straightforward and can be done without worrying about the leasing aspects.

LEASE INTEREST PAYABLE

20X1		$	*20X1*		$
31 Dec	Bank (W)	11,250	31 Dec	Income statement	11,250
20X2			*20X2*		
31 Dec	Bank (W)	8,063	31 Dec	Income statement	8,063
20X3			*20X3*		
31 Dec	Bank (W)	4,078	31 Dec	Income statement	4,078

GRANBY GARAGES CO

20X1		$	*20X1*		$
1 Jan	Bank – deposit	9,000	1 Jan	Lorries a/c	54,000
31 Dec	Bank (W)	12,750			
	Balance c/d	32,250			
		54,000			54,000
20X2			*20X2*		
31 Dec	Bank (W)	15,937	1 Jan	Balance b/d	32,250
	Balance c/d	16,313			
		32,250			32,250
20X3			*20X3*		
31 Dec	Bank (W)	16,313	1 Jan	Balance b/d	16,313

INCOME STATEMENTS (EXTRACTS)

	20X1	*20X2*	*20X3*	*20X4*
	$	$	$	$
Lease interest	11,250	8,063	4,078	
Depreciation on lorries	12,500	12,500	12,500	12,500

STATEMENTS OF FINANCIAL POSITION AT 31 DECEMBER (EXTRACTS)

	20X1	20X2	20X3	20X4
	$	$	$	$
Non-current assets				
Lorries: at cost	54,000	54,000	54,000	54,000
Depreciation	12,500	25,000	37,500	50,000
	41,500	29,000	16,500	4,000
Current liabilities				
Finance lease obligations	15,937	16,313	–	–
Non-current liabilities				
Finance lease obligations	16,313	–	–	–

(b)

> **Tutor's hint**. As you will see, the lessor's books are a mirror image of the lessee's.

BOOKS OF GRANBY GARAGES CO

BULWELL AGGREGATES CO

		$			$
20X1			*20X1*		
1 Jan	Sales	54,000	1 Jan	Bank	9,000
			31 Dec	Bank	12,750
				Balance c/d	32,250
		54,000			54,000
20X2			*20X2*		
1 Jan	Balance b/d	32,250	31 Dec	Bank	15,937
				Balance c/d	16,313
		32,250			32,250
20X3			*20X3*		
1 Jan	Balance b/d	16,313	31 Dec	Bank	16,313

LEASE INTEREST RECEIVABLE

		$			$
20X1			*20X1*		
31 Dec	Income statement	11,250	31 Dec	Bank	11,250
20X2			*20X2*		
31 Dec	Income statement	8,063	31 Dec	Bank	8,063
20X3			*20X3*		
31 Dec	Income statement	4,078	31 Dec	Bank	4,078

INCOME STATEMENTS (EXTRACTS)

		20X1	20X2	20X3
	$	$	$	$
Sales	54,000		–	–
Cost of sales on lease	43,200		–	–
Gross profit on lease sales		10,800	–	–
Lease interest receivable		11,250	8,063	4,078

Working

Apportionment of lease instalments between interest and capital repayment.

	20X1	*20X2*	*20X3*
	$	$	$
Opening liability (after deposit)	45,000	32,250	16,313
Add interest at 25%	11,250	8,063	4,078
	56,250	40,313	20,391
Less instalment	24,000	24,000	20,391
Closing liability	32,250	16,313	Nil
Interest element as above	11,250	8,063	4,078
∴ Capital repayment	12,750	15,937	16,313
Total instalment	24,000	24,000	20,391

10 Winger

Tutor's hint. As with consolidated accounts questions, a question on the preparation of a single company's accounts needs a methodical approach. Lay out proformas and fill the numbers in gradually by systematically working through the question. Points are as follows to which

(a) Exclude 'sale or return' goods from both sales and cost of sales.

(b) Abandonment of research project hits retained profit as well as current year profits.

(c) Exclude from the finance lease interest charge the $20 m down payment – interest does not accrue on this.

(d) When calculating the base creditor, you need to accrue one year's interest but no more. You know that $20m is due within one year, so the long term liability is the balance of the total creditor.

(a) WINGER PLC
INCOME STATEMENT FOR THE
YEAR ENDED 31 MARCH 20X1

	$'000	$'000
Sales revenues (358,450 – 27,000)		331,450
Cost of sales (W1)		(208,550)
Gross profit		122,900
Distribution expenses		(28,700)
Administration expenses		(15,000)
Operating profit		79,200
Profit on disposal of land and buildings (95,000 – 80,000)		15,000
Loss on abandonment of research project		(30,000)
Profit before interest		64,200
Finance cost (W3)		(11,200)
Profit before tax		53,000
Income tax (15,000 – 2,200)		(12,800)
Profit for the year		40,200
Dividends: interim	12,000	
final (W4)	18,000	
		(30,000)
Retained profit for the period		10,200
Accumulated profits b/f (71,600 + 30,000)		101,600
Accumulated profits c/f		111,800

(b) STATEMENT OF FINANCIAL POSITION
AS AT 31 MARCH 20X1

	$'000	$'000
Assets		
Tangible non current assets		
Property (200,000 – 6,000 (W2))		194,000
Plant and equipment (W5)		160,000
		354,000
Current assets		
Inventories (28,240 + 22,500 (W1))	50,740	
Accounts receivable (55,000 – 27,000 (W1))	28,000	
Cash	10,660	
		89,400
Total assets		443,400
Equity and liabilities		
Capital and reserves		
Equity shares 25c each		150,000
Accumulated profits (see (a))		111,800
		261,800
Non-current liabilities		
Leasing obligations (W6)	47,200	
8% loan notes	50,000	
		97,200
Current liabilities		
Trade and other accounts payable (W7)	51,400	
Income tax	15,000	
Proposed dividends	18,000	
		84,400
Total equity and liabilities		443,400

Workings

1 *Cost of sales*

	$'000
Per question	185,050
Less sale/return goods (27,000 × 100/120)	(22,500)
Add depreciation (W2)	46,000
	208,550

2 *Depreciation*

	$'000
Building (100,000 ÷ 50)	2,000
Heating system (20,000 ÷ 10)	2,000
Lifts (30,000 ÷ 15)	2,000
	6,000
Leased plant (80,000 × 20%)	16,000
Owned plant (154,800 – 34,800) × 20%	24,000
	46,000

3 *Finance cost*

	$'000
Debenture interest (50,000 × 8%)	4,000
Finance lease (80,000 – 20,000) × 12%	7,200
	11,200

4 *Final dividend*

	$'000
Total dividend required $1.25 × 4% × (150,000 × 4)	30,000
Interim dividend paid	(12,000)
Final dividend required	18,000

5 *Plant and equipment*

		$'000
Cost:	owned plant	154,800
	leased plant	80,000
		234,800
Depreciation:	owned plant (34,800 + 24,000 (W2))	(58,800)
	Leased plant (80,000 × 20%)	(16,000)
		160,000

6 *Leasing obligations*

	$'000
Total payments due	80,000
Less amount paid	(20,000)
	60,000
Add accrued interest (60,000 × 12%)	7,200
Total creditor	67,200
Due within one year	20,000
Due after one year	47,200

7 *Trade and other payables*

	$'000
Trial balance	29,400
Lease creditor (W7)	20,000
Accrued debenture interest	2,000
	51,400

(c) Companies often used to justify the non-depreciation of buildings on several grounds, including:

(i) That the current value of the buildings was **higher than cost**.
(ii) That the level of **maintenance** meant that no deterioration or consumption had taken place.
(iii) That the depreciation charge would **not be material.**

However, IAS 16 requires the **depreciable amount** of an asset to be charged against profit over its useful life. That depreciable amount is obtained by comparing the cost of the asset with its **estimated residual value** at the end of its useful economic life. By requiring the residual value to be estimated at **current prices** (under the benchmark treatment), the standard removes any **potential inflationary effects** which would otherwise increase the residual value and hence reduce, even to zero, the depreciable amount. This overcomes the argument that high residual values remove the need for depreciation, unless the value of a second-hand asset has greater value than the same asset new – an unlikely proposition.

The argument regarding **immateriality** of the depreciation charge because of a long economic life may have some validity. Although it is not addressed directly by IAS 16, accounting standards generally only apply to **material items,** according to the *Framework*. However, under this principle, it will be necessary to consider not only each year's potential depreciation charge, but also the **accumulated depreciation** that would need to be provided against the asset. Over time, this latter amount would inevitably become material and the 'long life' argument would cease to hold.

Thus, Winger's **previous policy** was not appropriate and the change to depreciate assets was necessary to comply with IAS 16.

The directors' treatment of the deferred development expenditure is also incorrect. It needs to be written off because its **value** has become **impaired due to adverse legislation, not a change of accounting policy**. It now has no effective value. There has therefore not been a change of accounting policy, so it cannot be treated as a prior period adjustment. It must be written off to the income statement.

11 Global Konstrukshen

Tutor's hint. Calculate profit or loss on the contract and cost of sales comes out as a balancing figure. You can then work out the accrued cost of sales and accrued future losses.

(a)

	Alpine bypass	*World Ecology centre*
	$'000	$'000
Turnover	2,800	3,000
Profit/(loss) (W)	622	(100)
Cost of sales	2,178	3,100
Current assets		
Amount recoverable on contract (2,800 – 2,600)	200	–
Current liabilities		
Payment on account (3,400 – 3,000)	–	(400)
Accrued cost of sales (2,178 – 1,400)	(778)	–
Accrued future losses (3,100 – 2,900)	–	(200)

(W) Alpine: $(9{,}000 - (1{,}400 + 5{,}600)) \times \frac{2{,}800}{9{,}000} = 622$

World Ecology: 8,000 – (2,900 + 5,200) = 100

(b) Construction contracts are recognised as such when they cover at **least two accounting periods**. If they were not to be treated as they are under IAS 11 then the costs incurred during the early years of the contract would be recognised but with no corresponding turnover. This would lead to several years of losses then one year of high profits regardless of how profitable the contract really was. The advantage of this approach however would be that there would be no need to use estimates and forecasts.

The current treatment **matches an element of the turnover to the costs incurred**. There is an attempt to maintain **prudence** by ensuring that any **foreseeable** losses are **accounted for immediately**. This gives a fairer representation of the underlying financial substance of the transaction and makes it easier for the user of the accounts to assess the financial position of the company.

12 Provisions

Tutor's hint. A good knowledge of IAS 37 is needed in this question. Do not disregard the discounting aspects, these calculations are quite straightforward as you are given the formulae in the exam.

(a) Why there was a need for an accounting standard dealing with provisions

IAS 37 *Provisions, contingent liabilities and contingent assets* was issued to prevent entities from using provisions for creative accounting. It was common for entities to recognise material provisions for items such as future losses, restructuring costs or even expected future expenditure on repairs and maintenance of assets. These could be combined in one large provision (sometimes known as the 'big bath'). Although these provisions reduced profits in the period in which they were recognised (and were often separately disclosed on grounds of materiality), they were then released to enhance profits in subsequent periods. To make matters worse, provisions were often recognised where there was no firm commitment to incur expenditure. For example, an entity might set up a provision for restructuring costs and then withdraw from the plan, leaving the provision available for profit smoothing.

The criteria that need to be satisfied before a provision is recognised

IAS 37 states that a provision should not be recognised unless:

(i) An entity has a present obligation to transfer economic benefits as a result of a past transaction or event, and

(ii) It is probable that a transfer of economic benefits will be required to settle the obligation; and

(iii) A reliable estimate can be made of the amount of the obligation.

An obligation can be legal or constructive. An entity has a constructive obligation if:

(i) It has indicated to other parties that it will accept certain responsibilities (by an established pattern of past practice or published policies), and

(ii) As a result, it has created a valid expectation on the part of those other parties that it will discharge those responsibilities.

(b) Extract should recognise a provision for the estimated costs of making good the site because:

(i) It has a present obligation to incur the expenditure as a result of a past event. In this case the obligating event occurred when it became virtually certain that the legislation would be passed. Therefore the obligation existed at 31 December 20X0; and

(ii) A transfer of economic benefits is probable, and

(iii) It is possible to make a reliable estimate of the amount.

Effect on the financial statements

For the year ended 31 December 20X0:

- A provision of \$1,242,000 (2,000,000 × 0.621) is reported as a liability under provisions.
- A non-current asset of \$1,242,000 is also recognised. The provision results in a corresponding asset because the expenditure gives the company access to future economic benefits; there is no effect on the income statement for the year.

For the year ended 31 December 20X1:

- Depreciation of \$248,400 (1,242,000 × 20%) is charged to profit or loss. The non-current asset is depreciated over its remaining useful economic life of 5 years from 31 December 20X0 (the site will cease to produce output on 31 December 20X5).
- Therefore at 31 December 20X1 the net book value of the non-current asset will be \$993,600 (1,242,000 – 248,400).
- At 31 December 20X1 the provision will be \$1,366,000 (2,000,000 × 0.683).
- The increase in the provision of \$124,000 (1,366,000 – 1,242,000) is recognised in the profit or loss as a finance cost. This arises due to the unwinding of the discount.

Note. This answer takes the view that the obligation to make good the site gives rise to future economic benefits because the company could not continue to generate income from the site without incurring the expenditure. For this reason an asset is recognised at the same time as the provision. Unlike the equivalent UK standard, IAS 37 does not deal with this issue. An alternative answer would be possible:

For the year ended 31 December 20X0:

- A provision of \$1,242,000 (2,000,000 × 0.621) is reported as a liability under provisions.
- There is a corresponding charge of \$1,242,000 to profit or loss. If this is material it is disclosed separately as required by IAS 8.

For the year ended 31 December 20X1:

- At 31 December 2001 the provision will be \$1,366,000 (2,000,000 × 0.683).
- The increase in the provision of \$124,000 (1,366,000 – 1,242,000) is recognised in profit or loss as a finance cost. This arises due to the unwinding of the discount.

13 Jerzy

The defined benefit pension scheme is treated in accordance with IAS 19 *Employee benefits.*

The pension scheme has a deficit of liabilities over assets:

	$m
Fair value of plan assets	200
Present value of obligation	(208)
	(8)

The deficit is reported as a liability in the statement of financial position

The statement of comprehensive income for the year includes:

	$m
Current service cost	176
Interest cost	32
Expected return on plan assets	(16)
	192

The company proposes to recognise the $24,000,000 actuarial gain, although under IAS 19 it is not required to do so. IAS 19 requires actuarial gains and losses at the end of the previous accounting period to be recognised using the '10% corridor approach'. Alternatively, they may be recognised more quickly, or immediately. There were no actuarial gains or losses at the start of the current period.

However, recognising the gain provides useful information to users of the financial statements, given that the pension scheme is new and results in a significant additional charge to the income statement. Under IAS 19 an actuarial gain cannot be recognised in the income statement, but must be taken to equity (reserves). The statement of changes in equity for the year includes:

	$m
Actuarial gain on defined benefit pension scheme assets	24

Adjustment to the financial statements:

Dr Accumulated profits	$168 million	
Cr Receivables		$160 million
Cr Defined benefit pension scheme liability		$8 million

Working

	$m
Scheme assets:	
Contributions paid	160
Expected return on plan assets	16
Actuarial gain (balancing figure)	24
Fair value of plan assets	200
Scheme liabilities:	
Current service cost	176
Interest cost	32
Present value of obligation	208
Net pension liability	5

14 Tall

This answer is based on IAS 39.

(a) The international financial community is **concerned over the way that financial instruments in general, and derivatives in particular, are reported in financial statements.** In summary, the concerns are that financial instruments can rapidly transform the risk profile of an entity in a way that is not made apparent under present reporting practices. For example, a derivative, acquired for nil cost (and hence not recognised on the statement of financial position), can be used to convert a dollar floating rate liability into a sterling fixed rate one. Or a derivative may be used to 'hedge' the risk that sales expected to occur next year in dollars may be worth less when converted into sterling because sterling may strengthen in the meantime. In both cases, the value of the derivative can change very significantly so that it represents a substantial asset or liability by the year-end. This may not be apparent to the reader under present accounting standards.

Furthermore, in some cases derivatives and other financial instruments have been used unwisely, **exposing entities to potentially large losses**. Under the present, historical cost based, system of reporting, such gains and losses are often not reported as they arise but are deferred until realised. Among other things, this gives rise to the abuse of cherry picking (eg in a bad year selling instruments with an unrealised gain so as to boost reported profits).

(b) **MEMORANDUM**

To: Assistant accountant
From: Accountant
Date: 30 November 20X9
Subject: **Funding**

(i) *Presentation of financial instruments*

1.1 Your suggestion that both the preference shares and bonds should be included in the shareholders' funds section is incorrect.

1.2 IAS 32 governs the presentation and disclosure of financial instruments.

1.3 Under IAS 32 there is a distinction made between debt and equity. This depends on whether the issuer is required contractually to issue cash or another financial asset to the holder of the financial instrument.

1.4 The bonds would be regarded as debt instruments as they have to be redeemed on the maturity date. They will go in the long-term liability section of the statement of financial position.

1.5 The preference share are legally shares but, under IAS 32, they are treated as long-term liabilities. The reason is because there is an obligation to pay dividends **and to redeem the shares on the maturity date.**

(ii) *Treatment of interest futures*

2.1 IAS 39 deals with the recognition and measurement of financial instruments.

2.2 The only action that has been taken at the reporting date is to make the initial deposit on the futures contract.

2.3 An interest-rate future is the right to receive a fixed amount of cash at a specific future date. It is, therefore, a financial instrument.

2.4 It is also a derivative because the value is derived from the interest rate levels.

2.5 Therefore cost-based valuations do not apply because the cost bears no relation to its value.

2.6 Under IAS 39, the changes in the market values of derivative financial instruments should be recognised in the income statement for the period.

2.7 Therefore the profit arising between 15 and 31 August 20X9 should be included in the accounts for 20X9.

(iii) *Finance cost of bonds*

$$\frac{\text{Carrying value}}{\text{Value on redemption}} = \frac{15}{24.15} = 0.621$$

From present value tables, implicit interest rate (5 years) is 10%.

∴ Interest for the year is 10% × \$15m = \$1.5m.

Finance cost of preferred shares

$$\frac{\text{Carrying value}}{\text{Value on redemption}} = \frac{11.9}{23.5} = 0.506$$

From present value tables, implicit interest rate (6 years) is 12%.

∴ Interest for the year is $11.9m × 12% = $1,428,000.

15 Dennis

Tutor's hint. Compound or hybrid instruments such as convertible loan stock (part (a)) are required by IASs 32 and 39 to be treated according to the substance of the contractual agreement. Here, the equity element and liability (debt) element must be separately identified on the statement of financial position. Although in theory this split can be calculated in many ways, with the information available in the question, the only available methodology is the 'residual value of equity' approach. This involves calculating the present value of the cash flows attributable to the 'pure' debt element and treating the difference with the proceeds received as the equity component.

This answer is based on IAS 39.

(a) STATEMENT OF COMPREHENSIVE INCOME (EXTRACTS)

	$'000	$'000
Loan stock interest paid (£80m × 8%)	6,400	
Required accrual of finance cost	1,844	
Total finance cost (£68.704m (W) × 12%)		8,244

STATEMENT OF FINANCIAL POSITION (EXTRACTS)

	$'000	$'000
Equity		
Share options (W)		11,296
Non-current liabilities		
8% loan stock 20X4 (W)	68,704	
Accrual of finance costs	1,844	
		70,548

Working

Year		*Cash flow*	*Factor*	*PV cash flow*
		$'000		$'000
1	Interest	6,400	0.89	5,696
2	Interest	6,400	0.80	5,120
3	Interest	6,400	0.71	4,544
4	Interest	6,400	0.64	4,096
5	Interest + capital	86,400	0.57	49,248
PV of debt cash flows				68,704
Residual equity element (= share options)				11,296
				80,000

(b)

Tutor's hint. Impairment is a difficult subject, so make sure you understand where you went wrong – if at all!

The impairment losses are allocated as required by IAS 36 *Impairment of assets.*

	Asset @ 1.1.20X0	*1st provision (W1)*	*Assets @ 1.2.20X0*	*2nd provision (W2)*	*Revised asset*
	$'000	$'000	$'000	$'000	$'000
Goodwill	200	(200)	–	–	–
Operating licence	1,200	(200)	1,000	(100)	900
Property: stations/land	300	(50)	250	(50)	200
Rail track/coaches	300	(50)	250	(50)	200
Steam engines	1,000	(500)	500	–	500
	3,000	(1,000)	2,000	(200)	1,800

Workings

1 *First provision*

$500,000 relates directly to an engine and its recoverable amount can be assessed directly (ie zero) and it is no longer part of the cash generating unit

IAS 36 then requires goodwill to be written off. Any further impairment must be written off the remaining assets pro rata, except the engine which must not be reduced below its net selling price of $500,000

2 *Second provision*

The first $100,000 of the impairment loss is applied to the operating licence to write it down to net selling price.

The remainder is applied pro rata to assets carried at other than their net selling prices, ie $50,000 to both the property and the rail track and coaches.

(c) *Statement of comprehensive income*

	$m
Contract revenue (W2)	18.0
Cost of sales (balancing figure)	(14.1)
Profit (W3)	3.9

Statement of financial position	$m
Current assets	
Receivables: amounts recoverable on long-term contracts (W6)	11.0

Workings

1 *Percentage completion*

$$\text{Percentage completion} = \frac{\text{Work certified}}{\text{Contract price}}$$

20W9 $\frac{\$12\text{m}}{\$40\text{m}} = 30\%$

20X0 (including variation) $\frac{\$30\text{m}}{\$45\text{m}} = 66.7\%$ (ie $\frac{2}{3}$)

2 *Contract revenue*

Accumulated turnover to 31 March 20X0 = $45m × $\frac{2}{3}$ = £30m

In 20X0 turnover = $30m – $12m (20W9) = $18m

3 *Profit*

Revised estimated total profit = $45m – $30m = $15m
Accumulated to 31 March 20X0 = $15m × $\frac{2}{3}$ =$10m

Total profit for year ended 31 March 20X0:

	$m
Accumulated to date	10.0
Less 20W9 profit taken (W4)	(3.6)
Less rectification costs	(2.5)
	3.9

4 *Profit for 20W9*

	$m
Turnover	12.0
Cost of sales (bal fig)	(8.4)
Profit = ($40m – $28m) × 30%	3.6

5 *Receivables due from customers*

	$m
Costs incurred to date	28.5
Add recognised profits (3.6 + 3.9)	7.5
Less progress billings	(25.0)
	11.0

16 DT Group

Calculation of deferred tax liability

	Carrying	*Tax*	*Temporary*
Goodwill (note 1)	14	–	–
Subsidiary (note 1)	76	60	16
Inventories (note 2)	24	30	(6)
Property, plant and equipment (note 3)	2,600	1,920	680
Other temporary differences			90
Liability for health care benefits	100		(100)
Unrelieved tax losses (note 4)			(100)
Property sold – tax due 30.11.20X4 (165/0.3)		–	550
Temporary differences			1,130

Deferred tax liability	1,320	at 30%	396
Deferred tax liability	16	at 25%	4
Deferred tax asset	(200)	at 30%	(60)
	(6)	at 25%	(1.5)
	1,130		338.5
Less: opening deferred tax liability			(280)
deferred tax attributable to subsidiary to goodwill (76 – 60) × 25%			(4)
Deferred tax expense for the year			54.5

Notes

1 As no deduction is available for the cost of goodwill in the subsidiary's tax jurisdiction, then the tax base of goodwill is zero. Paragraph 15(a) of IAS 12, states that DT should not recognise a deferred tax liability of the temporary difference associated in B's jurisdiction with the goodwill. Goodwill will be increased by the amount of the deferred tax liability of the subsidiary i.e. $4 million.

2 Unrealised group profit eliminated on consolidation are provided for at the receiving company's rate of tax (i.e. at 25%).

3 The tax that would arise if the properties were disposed of at their revalued amounts which was provided at the beginning of the year will be included in the temporary difference arising on the property, plant and equipment at 30 November 20X1.

4 DT has unrelieved tax losses of ($34m + $56m)/0.3 i.e. $300m. This will be available for offset against current year's profits ($110m) and against profits for the year ending 30 November 20X2 ($100m). Because of the uncertainty about the availability of taxable profits in 2003, no deferred tax asset can be recognised for any losses which may be offset against this amount. Therefore, a deferred tax asset may be recognised for the losses to be offset against taxable profits in 20X2. That is $100m × 30% i.e. $30m.

Comment

The deferred tax liability of DT will rise in total by $335.5 million ($338.5m – $3m), thus reducing net assets, distributable profits, and post-tax earnings. The profit for the year will be reduced by $54.5 million which would probably be substantially more under IAS 12 than the old method of accounting for deferred tax. A prior period adjustment will occur of $280m – $3m as IAS are being applied for the first time (IFRS 1) i.e. $277m. The borrowing position of the company may be affected and the directors may decide to cut dividend payments. However, the amount of any unprovided deferred tax, analysed into its major components, was required to be disclosed under the previous standard used. IAS 12 brings this liability onto the statement of financial position but because the bulk of the liability has already been disclosed the impact on the share price should be minimal.

17 Courtney

(a) Courtney must recognise the purchase of goods at the exchange rate in place at the date of the transaction.

Therefore:

300,000 Wons/20 = $15,000

DR	Purchases	$15,000	
	CR Trade payables		$15,000

At the year end, the supplier has not been paid, so the liability is still outstanding. It must be translated at the closing rate at the year end and any exchange gains or losses recognised in the income statement.

The liability at 31 December 20X7 is:

3000,000 Wons/16 = $18,750

It has increased and Courtney must recognise an exchange loss of $3,750 (18,750 – 15,000).

DR	Income statement	$3,750	
	CR Trade payables		$3,750

(b) Functional currency is the currency of the primary economic environment in which the entity operates.

Determining an entity's functional currency involves looking at the currency that influences sales prices and costs. Additionally, if an entity raises finance in its home currency, that is likely to be its functional currency.

In Courtney's case, it operates in US$, which is the functional currency.

The presentation currency is the currency in which the financial statements are presented. Courtney may well prepare financial statements in their functional currency (US$), but the parent company reports in Euros, so Courtney's results will have to be translated into Euros so that they can be consolidated. The group presentation currency is the Euro.

18 Farmer Gyles

(a) A **biological asset** is a **living animal** or **plant** whereas **agricultural produce** is the **harvested produce** of an enterprise's biological assets. Harvest, in turn, is the detachment of produce from a biological asset or the cessation of a biological asset's life processes.

(b) Asset changes

(i) **Growth**: increase in quality and/or quality
(ii) **Degeneration**: decrease in quantity and/or quality

Creation of new assets

(i) **Production**: producing saleable non-living products
(ii) **Procreation**: producing separate living animals

(c) IAS 41 requires that at each reporting date, all **biological assets** should be measured **at fair value less estimated point-of-sale costs**.

If at **initial recognition**, **fair value cannot be determined** because market determined prices or values are not available, they may be valued at **cost less accumulated depreciation and impairment losses**.

(d) **Agricultural produce**. It is **recognised at the point of harvest** (eg detachment from biological asset). Agricultural produce is either incapable of biological process or such processes remain dormant (eg stored grain). **Recognition ends** once the produce enters trading activities or production processes within integrated agribusinesses, although processing activities that are incidental to agricultural activities and that do not materially alter the form of the produce (eg drying or cleaning) are not counted as processing. Following harvest, the provisions of IAS 2 apply.

19 Share-based payment

(a) **Accounting entries**

		$	$
31.12.X1			
DEBIT	Profit or loss (Staff costs)	188,000	
CREDIT	Equity reserve ((800 – 95) × 200 × $4 × 1/3)		188,000
31.12.X2			
DEBIT	Profit or loss (Staff costs) (W1)	201,333	
CREDIT	Equity reserve		201,333
31.12.X3			
DEBIT	Profit or loss (Staff costs) (W2)	202,667	
CREDIT	Equity reserve		202,667
Issue of shares:			
DEBIT	Cash (740 × 200 × $1.50)	222,000	
DEBIT	Equity reserve	592,000	
CREDIT	Share capital (740 × 200 × $1)		148,000
CREDIT	Share premium (balancing figure)		666,000

Workings

1 *Equity reserve at 31.12.X2*

	$
Equity b/d	188,000
∴ P/L charge	201,333
Equity c/d ((800 – 70) × 200 × $4 × 2/3)	389,333

2 *Equity reserve at 31.12.X3*

Equity b/d	389,333
∴ P/L charge	202,667
Equity c/d ((800 – 40 – 20) × 200 × $4 × 3/3)	592,000

(b) **Cash-settled share-based payment**

If J&B had offered cash payments based on the value of the shares at vesting date rather than options, in each of the three years an accrual would be shown in the statement of financial position representing the expected amount payable based on the following:

No of employees estimated at the year end to be entitled to rights at the vesting date	×	Number of rights each	×	Fair value of each right at year end	×	Cumulative proportion of vesting period elapsed

The movement in the accrual would be charged to profit or loss representing further entitlements received during the year and adjustments to expectations accrued in previous years.

The accrual would continue to be adjusted (resulting in a profit or loss charge) for changes in the fair value of the right over the period between when the rights become fully vested and are subsequently exercised. It would then be reduced for cash payments as the rights are exercised.

20 IAS 1

Tutor's hint. Easy marks are to be gained in Part (a). Parts (b) and (c) require more thought.

(a) (i) **Materiality and aggregation**. Items which are material need to be shown separately in the financial accounts. Amounts which are not material, can be added together and the sub total can be shown.

(ii) **Offsetting**. Assets and liabilities should not be set off, unless it is permitted in a standard. This is because it hinders the users of financial statements understanding what the transactions are.

(iii) **Consistency**. Transactions should be treated on a similar basis from year to year. Also, transactions of the same kind should be treated in the same way in each accounting period.

(b)

Tutor's hint. Start with a simple explanation of what the concept means.

The **going concern assumption** is that an entity will continue in operational existence for the foreseeable future. This means that the financial statements of an entity are prepared on the assumption that the entity will **continue** trading. If this were not the case, various adjustments would have to be made to the accounts: provisions for losses; revaluation of assets to their possible market value; all non-current assets and liabilities would be reclassified as current; and so forth.

Unless it can be assumed that the business is a going concern, other accounting assumptions cannot apply.

Tutor's hint. Having made this assertion, you need to clarify it with examples.

For example, it is meaningless to speak of consistency from one accounting period to the next when this is the final accounting period.

The **accruals basis** of accounting states that items are recognised as assets, liabilities, equity, income and expenses when they satisfy the definitions and recognition criteria I the *Framework.* The effect of this is that revenue and expenses which are related to each other are matched, so as to be dealt with in the same accounting period, without regard to when the cash is actually paid or received. This is particularly relevant to the purchase of non-current assets. The cost of a non-current asset is spread over the accounting periods expected to benefit from it, thus matching costs and revenues. In the absence of the going concern convention, this cannot happen, as an example will illustrate.

Suppose a company has a machine which cost $10,000 two years ago and now has a net book value of $6,000. The machine can be used for another three years, but as it is obsolete, there is no possibility of selling it, and so it has no market value.

If the going concern assumption applies, the machine will be shown at **cost less depreciation** in the accounts (ie $6,000), as it still has a part to play in the continued life of the entity. However, if the assumption cannot be applied, the machine will be given a nil value and other assets and liabilities will be similarly revalued on the basis of winding down the company's operations.

(c) IAS 1 (revised) is the standard whose overall objectives are to further the user's understanding of financial statements by promoting an improvement in the quality of information disclosed. To achieve this it follows the principles and guidance in the **Framework** document by the IASB.

Tutor's hint. You now need to state what problems the *Framework* was brought in to address.

One of the ideas behind such a framework is to **avoid the fire-fighting approach**, which has characterised the development of accounting standards to date, and instead develop an underlying philosophy as a basis for consistent accounting principles so that each standard fits into the whole framework. Research began from an analysis of the fundamental objectives of accounting and their relationship to the information needs of accounts users. The framework has gone behind the requirements of existing accounting standards, which define accounting treatments for particular assets, liabilities, income and expenditure, to define the nature of assets, liabilities, income and expenditure.

IAS 1 (revised) is a positive step towards the adoption of such a framework as it includes the **basis for presenting the items in the financial statements** in order to give the users of financial statements the maximum disclosure in a clear and **understandable, neutral fashion**.

21 Hewlett

HEWLETT CO

STATEMENT OF COMPREHENSIVE INCOME FOR THE YEAR ENDED 31 DECEMBER 20X2

	$'m
Revenue	2,648
Cost of sales (W1)	(1,765)
Gross profit	883
Distribution costs (W1)	(514)
Administrative expenses (W1)	(363)
Finance costs (4% × 150)	(6)
Fair value gain on investment properties (586 – 548)	38
Rental income	48
Profit before tax	86
Income tax expense (note iv)	(27)
PROFIT FOR THE YEAR	59
Other comprehensive income:	
Gain on property revaluation	484
TOTAL COMPREHENSIVE INCOME FOR THE YEAR	543

STATEMENT OF FINANCIAL POSITION AS AT 31 DECEMBER 20X2

	$'m
ASSETS	
Non-current assets	
Property, plant and equipment (W2)	874
Investment properties (note x)	586
	1,460
Current assets	
Inventories (388 – (15 – 8))	381
Trade receivables	545
Cash and cash equivalents	28
	954
	2,414
EQUITY AND LIABILITIES	
Equity	
Share capital	125
Share premium	244
Retained earnings	413
General reserve	545
Revaluation surplus	473
	1,800
Non-current liabilities	
4% loan notes 20X8	150
Current liabilities	
Trade payables	434
Income tax payable (note v)	27
Interest payable ((4% × 150) – 3)	3
	464
	2,414

STATEMENT OF CHANGES IN EQUITY FOR THE YEAR ENDED 31 DECEMBER 20X2

	Share capital	*Share premium*	*Retained earnings*	*General reserve*	*Revaluation surplus*	*Total*
	$'m	$'m	$'m	$'m	$'m	$'m
Balance at 1 January 20X2	100	244	349	570	-	1,263
Changes in equity for 20X2						
Issue of share capital (W4)	25			(25)		-
Dividends (W5)			(6)			(6)
Total comprehensive income for the year			59		484	543
Transfer to retained earnings (W2)			11		(11)	-
Balance at 31 December 20X2	125	244	413	545	473	1,800

* The initial application of a policy to revalue assets under IAS 16 is a change in accounting policy dealt with as a revaluation in accordance with IAS 16, rather than IAS 8 (which would require restatement of the opening figures).

Workings

1 *Expenses*

	Cost of sales	*Distribution*	*Admin*
	$'m	$'m	$'m
Per TB	1,669	514	345
Opening inventories	444		
Depreciation of buildings (W2)			18
Depreciation of plant and equipment (W2)	24		
Impairment loss on plant (W3)	4		
Loss on sale of equipment (12 – 7)	5		
Closing inventories (388 – (15 – 8))	(381)		
	1,765	514	363

2 *Property, plant and equipment*

	Land	*Buildings*	*Plant & equipment*	*Total*
	$'m	$'m	$'m	$'m
Cost	60	320	258	
Accumulated depreciation	–	(64)	(126)	
NBV b/d at 1 January 20X2	60	256	132	
Change in accounting policy (bal)	40	444		484
	100	700	132	
Disposal of equipment (15 – 3)			(12)	
	100	700	120	
Depreciation during year				
Buildings ($700m/(50 – 10))	–	(18)		
Plant & equipment ($120m × 20%)			(24)	
Impairment loss on plant (W3)			(4)	
NBV c/d at 31 December 20X2	100	682	92	874

	$'m
Realisation of revaluation surplus on buildings:	
Surplus	444
Realised over remaining 40 years (444/40):	11

3 *Impairment loss on plant*

	$'m
Carrying value	22
Recoverable amount (Value in use: (3.8m × 3.993) + (4.2m × 0.677))	(18)
	(4)

Recoverable amount is the higher of value in use ($18m) and fair value less costs to sell ($16m).

4 *Bonus issue*

DR General reserve ($100m /$0.50 × 1/4 = 50m shares × $0.50)	$25m
CR Share capital	$25m

5 *Dividends (proof)*

	$'m
Interim ($100m /$0.50 = 200m shares × $0.03)	6 per trial balance

The final dividend has not been paid and is not a liability of the company at the year end.

22 Halliday Inns

INCOME STATEMENT
FOR THE YEAR ENDED 31 DECEMBER 20X0

	$'000
Turnover	68,500
Cost of sales (W2)	(25,980)
Gross profit	42,520
Distribution costs	(4,000)
Administrative expenses (W3)	(9,000)
Operating profit	29,520
Interest	(4,950)
Profit before tax	24,570
Taxation (10,200 + 50) (W5)	(10,250)
	14,320

STATEMENT OF FINANCIAL POSITION AS AT 31 DECEMBER 20X0

	$'000	$'000
Assets		
Tangible non-current assets (W4)		440,450
Current assets		
Inventory	470	
Cash at bank	300	
	770	
Creditors: amount due within one year		
Trade payables	1,700	
Taxation	10,200	
	11,900	
Net current liabilities		(11,130)
		429,320
Creditors: amount due after one year		
Loans		(110,000)
		319,320
Capital and reserves		
Share capital		220,000
Reserves	93,320	
Proposed dividend	6,000	
		99,320
		319,320

Workings

1 *Depreciation*

	$'000
Hotels 490,000 @ 2%	9,800
Fixtures and fittings (18,000 – 9,400) @ 25%	2,150
	11,950

2 *Cost of sales*

	$'000
Food purchases	2,100
Heating and lighting	3,000
Housekeeping and restaurant staff	9,000
Opening inventory	400
Closing inventory	(470)
Depreciation	11,950
	25,980

3 *Administrative expenses*

	$'000
Administration	3,000
Staff wages	6,000
	9,000

4 *Tangible non-current assets*

	Hotels	*Fixtures and fittings*	*Total*
	$'000	$'000	$'000
Cost or valuation			
As at 1 January 20X0	478,000	11,000	489,000
Additions	12,000	7,000	19,000
As at 31 December 20X0	490,000	18,000	508,000
Depreciation			
As at 1 January 20X0	46,200	9,400	55,600
Charge for the year	9,800	2,150	11,950
As at 31 December 20X0	56,000	11,550	67,550
Net book value as at 31 December 20X0	434,000	6,450	440,450
Net book value as at 1 January 20X0	431,800	1,600	433,400

5 *Taxation*

	$'000
Taxation charge for the year	10,200
Underprovision from the previous year	50
	10,250

23 Cher

Tutor's hint. The calculations involved in this question are not particularly complicated. However, a large number of marks are available for explanations and understanding. Part (d), particularly requires you to think very carefully about the implications of the uniting of interests method for EPS.

(a) Earnings per share (EPS) is one of the most frequently quoted statistics in financial analysis. Because of the widespread use of the price earnings (P/E) ratio as a yardstick for investment decisions, it became increasingly important.

It seems that reported and forecast EPS can, through the P/E ratio, have a significant effect on a company's share price. Thus, a share price might fall if it looks as if EPS is going to be low. This is not very rational, as EPS can depend on many, often subjective, assumptions used in preparing a historical statement, namely the income statement. It does not necessarily bear any relation to the value of a company, and of its shares. Nevertheless, the market is sensitive to EPS.

EPS has also served as a means of assessing the stewardship and management role performed by company directors and managers. Remuneration packages might be linked to EPS growth, thereby increasing the pressure on management to improve EPS. The danger of this, however, is that management effort goes into distorting results to produce a favourable EPS.

The IASB believed that the comparison of different entities' performance should be possible and issued IAS 33 in order to achieve this.

(b) CHER INC

EARNINGS PER SHARE FOR THE YEAR ENDED 30 JUNE 20X4

Earnings		$460,000
Number of shares		
In issue for full year		800,000
In issue 1.7.X3 – 30.9.X3		
200,000 × $^3/_{12}$ × 60%	30,000	
In issue 1.10.X3 – 30.6.X4		
200,000 × $^9/_{12}$ × 100%	150,000	
		180,000
		980,000

$$\text{Earnings per share} = \frac{460,000}{980,000} = 46.9c$$

(c) (i) Theoretical ex rights price per share

	$
Value of 4 shares before rights issue (4 × 1.90)	7.60
Value of 1 rights issue share	1.30
Value of 5 shares after rights issue	8.90

$$\text{Theoretical ex rights price } \frac{8.90}{5} = \$1.78$$

Earnings		$1,310,000
Number of shares in issue		
1.7.X4 – 28.2.X5		
$1,000,000 \times \frac{8}{12} \times \frac{1.90}{1.78}$	711,610	
1.3.X5 – 30.6.X5		
1,250,000 × $^4/_{12}$	416,667	
		1,128,277

$$\text{EPS } \frac{1,310,000}{1,128,277} = 116.1c$$

Revised EPS calculation for 20X4

$$46.9c \times \frac{1.78}{1.90} = 43.9c$$

	20X5	*20X4*
	116.1c	43.9c

(ii)

Tutor's hint. The main point to get across is that a rights issue is like a bonus issue combined with an issue at full market price

A rights issue is a popular method through which public companies are able to access the stock market for further capital. Under the terms of such an issue, existing shareholders are given the opportunity to acquire further shares in the company on a pro-rata basis to their existing shareholdings.

The 'rights' shares will usually be offered at a discount to the market price. In such cases, the issue is equivalent to a bonus issue combined with an issue at full market price. Bonus issues are treated as though they have been in issue for the whole year and are also taken into account in the previous year's EPS calculation to give a comparable result.

The bonus element of the rights issue is given by the following fraction, sometimes referred to as the *bonus fraction*.

$$\frac{\text{Actual cum rights price on last day of quotation cum rights}}{\text{Theoretical ex rights price}}$$

The 'cum rights price' is the *actual* price at which the shares are quoted inclusive of the right to take up the future shares under the rights issue.

The 'ex rights price' is the *theoretical* price at which the shares would be quoted, other stock market factors apart, after the rights issue shares have been issued.

In order to calculate earnings per share with a rights issue, the shares are time apportioned before and after the date of the rights issue. The number of shares is calculated in two stages as follows.

Before rights issue

Number of shares × Bonus fraction × Fraction of year
before rights issue   before rights issue

After rights issue

Number of shares after rights issue × Fraction of year after rights issue

The two figures produced by the above calculations are added together to give the denominator for the fraction required in calculating earnings per share.

When calculating the revised earnings per share for the previous year, the latter has to be adjusted to take account of the bonus element by multiplying it by the following

$$\frac{\text{Theoretical ex rights price}}{\text{Actual cum rights}}$$

This makes the previous year's figure comparable with that of the current year.

(d) *Current year*

Earnings		$1,520,000
Number of shares		
As at 1 July 20X5 (the new share capital after the rights issue)	1,250,000	
2 Sonny for 1 Cher	× 2	2,500,000

$$\text{EPS} = \frac{1,520,000}{2,500,000} = 60.8\text{c}$$

Tutor's hint. We are told in the question that the principles of the uniting of interests method have been adopted. This means that the shares in issue at the end of the year are assumed to have been in issue for the whole of the year. There is therefore no need to time apportion as we had to with the rights issue. The previous year's EPS figure will have to be adjusted to reflect the number of shares deemed to have been in issue in that year, ie twice as many as were in fact in issue.

Previous year
EPS = 116.1p × ½ = 58.05c

SONNY INC
EARNINGS PER SHARE FOR THE YEAR ENDED 30 JUNE

20X6	*20X5*
60.8c	58.05c

24 Engina

REPORT

To: The Directors
Engina Co
Zenda
Ruritania

From: A N Accountant
Date: 12 May 20X1

Related Party Transactions

The purpose of this report is to explain why it is necessary to disclose related party transactions. We appreciate that you may regard such disclosure as politically and culturally sensitive. However, there are **sound reasons for the required disclosures.** It should be emphasised that related party transactions are a normal part of business life, and the disclosures are required to give a fuller picture to the users of accounts, rather than because they are problematic.

Prior to the issue of IAS 24, disclosures in respect of related parties were often required by local regulatory authorities but were largely concerned with directors and their relationship with the group. The IASB has extended this definition and also the required disclosures. This reflects the objective of the IASB to provide useful data for investors not merely for companies to report on stewardship activities.

Unless investors know that transactions with related parties have not been carried out at **'arm's length'** between independent parties, they may fail to ascertain the true financial position.

Related party transactions typically take place on **terms which are significantly different** from those undertaken on normal commercial terms.

It should be noted that related party transactions are not necessarily fraudulent or intended to deceive. Without proper disclosures, investors may be disadvantaged – IAS 24 seeks to remedy this.

Sale of goods to the directors

Disclosure of related party transactions is only necessary when the transactions are **material.** IAS 24 applies only to material related party transactions. For the purposes of IAS 24, however, transactions are material when their disclosure might be expected to influence decisions made by users of the financial statements, irrespective of their amount. Moreover, the materiality of a related party transaction with an individual, for example a director, must be judged by reference to that individual and not just the company. In addition, disclosure of contracts of significance with directors may be required by the local Stock Exchange.

Mr Satay has purchased $600,000 (12 × $50,000) worth of goods from the company and a car for $45,000, which is just over half its market value. The transactions are not material to the company, and because Mr Satay has considerable personal wealth, they are not material to him either. However, **while not material**, any transactions with directors could be viewed as **sensitive**, and therefore ought to be disclosed in accordance with **best practice and good corporate governance.**

Hotel property

The hotel property sold to the Managing Director's brother is a **related party transaction**, and it appears to have been undertaken at **below market price**. IAS 24 requires disclosure of 'any other elements of the transactions necessary for an understanding of the financial statements'.

However, not only must the transaction be disclosed, but the question of **impairment** needs to be considered. The value of the hotel has become impaired due to the fall in property prices, so the carrying value needs to be adjusted in accordance with IAS 36 *Impairment of assets.* The hotel should be shown at the lower of carrying value ($5m) and the recoverable amount. The recoverable amount is the higher of fair value less costs to sell ($4.3m – $0.2m = $4.1m) and value in use ($3.6m). Therefore the hotel should be shown at $4.1m.

The sale of the property was for $100,000 below this impaired value, and it is this amount which needs to be disclosed.

Group structure

Companies legislation and the Stock Exchange require **disclosure of director's interests** in a company's share capital. Thus Mr Satay would need to disclose his ownership of the share capital of Engina, through his ownership of Wheel. IAS 24 also requires disclosure of transactions with Wheel, despite the fact that Wheel is a 100% owned subsidiary.

Engina's transactions with Car will also need to be disclosed. IAS 24 states that companies under **common control** are related parties, and the two companies are under the common control of Mr Satay.

25 Group Accounts

Tutor's hint. This is a general question to get you thinking about the nature of a group. The question strongly hints that there *are* limitations to group discounts.

The object of annual accounts is to help shareholders exercise control over their company by providing information about how its affairs have been conducted. The shareholders of a holding company would not be given sufficient information from the accounts of the holding company on its own, because not enough would be known about the nature of the assets, income and profits of all the subsidiary companies in which the holding company has invested. The primary purpose of group accounts is to provide a true and fair view of the position and earnings of the holding company group as a whole, from the standpoint of the shareholders in the holding company.

A number of arguments have been put forward, however, which argue that group accounts have certain limitations.

(a) Group accounts may be misleading.

  (i) The solvency (liquidity) of one company may hide the insolvency of another.

  (ii) The profit of one company may conceal the losses of another.

  (iii) They imply that group companies will meet each others' debts (this is certainly not true: a parent company may watch creditors of an insolvent subsidiary go unpaid without having to step in).

(b) There may be some difficulties in defining the group or 'entity' of companies, although company law and accounting standards have removed many of the grey areas here.

(c) Where a group consists of widely diverse companies in different lines of business, a set of group accounts may obscure much important detail unless supplementary information about each part of the group's business is provided.

26 Barcelona and Madrid

CONSOLIDATED STATEMENT OF FINANCIAL POSITION AS AT 30 SEPTEMBER 20X6

	$m
Non-current assets	
Property, plant & equipment (2,848 + 354)	3,202
Patents	45
Goodwill (W2)	43
	3,290
Current assets	
Inventories (895 + 225)	1,120
Trade and other receivables (1,348 + 251)	1,599
Cash and cash equivalents (212 + 34)	246
	2,965
	6,255

	$m
Equity attributable to owners of the parent	
Share capital	920
General reserve (W4)	796
Retained earnings (W3)	2,243
	3,959
Non-controlling interest (490 × 40%)	196
	4,155
Non-current liabilities	
Long-term borrowings (558 + 168)	726
Current liabilities	
Trade and other payables (1,168 + 183)	1,351
Current portion of long-term borrowings	23
	1,374
	6,255

Workings

1 *Group structure*

Barcelona

| 60% (30.6.X2)

Madrid

2 *Goodwill*

	$m	$m
Consideration transferred (250m × 50% × $1.06)		159
Non-controlling interest at acquisition (165 × 40%)		66
Net assets at acquisition:		
Share capital	50	
General reserve	11	
Retained earnings	104	
		(165)
Goodwill at acquisition		60
Impairment losses to date		(17)
Goodwill at end of reporting period		43

Goodwill – alternative working

	$m	$m
Consideration transferred		159
Net assets at acquisition (as above)	165	
Group share 60%		(99)
Goodwill at acquisition		60
Impairment		17
Goodwill at end of reporting period		43

3 *Retained earnings*

	Barcelona	*Madrid*
	$m	$m
Per question	2,086	394
Pre-acquisition	–	(104)
	2,086	290
Madrid – share of post acquisition earnings (290 × 60%)	174	
Less: goodwill impairment losses to date	(17)	
	2,243	

4 *General reserve*

	Barcelona	*Madrid*
	$m	$m
Per question	775	46
Pre-acquisition	–	(11)
	775	35
Madrid – share of post acquisition general reserve		
(35 × 60%)	21	
	796	

27 Reprise

REPRISE GROUP CONSOLIDATED STATEMENT OF FINANCIAL POSITION AS AT 31 MARCH 20X4

	$'000
Non-current assets	
Land and buildings	3,350
Plant and equipment (1,010 + 2,210)	3,220
Motor vehicles (510 + 345)	855
Goodwill (W4)	826
	8,251
Current assets	
Inventories (890 + 352 – (W2) 7.2)	1,234.8
Trade receivables (1,372 + 514 – 39 – (W3) 36)	1,811
Cash and cash equivalents (89 + 39 + 51)	179
	3,224.8
	11,475.8
Equity attributable to owners of the parent	
Share capital	1,000
Revaluation surplus	2,500
Retained earnings (W7)	5,257.3
	8,757.3
Non-controlling interest (W6)	896.5
	9,653.8
Non-current liabilities	
10% debentures	500
Current liabilities	
Trade payables (996 + 362 – (W3) 36)	1,322
	11,475.8

Workings

1 *Group structure*

R
|
| 75% ∴ non-controlling interest = 25%
|
E

2 *Unrealised profit on inventories*

Unrealised profit included in inventories is:

$$\$31,200 \times \frac{30}{130} = \$7,200$$

3 *Trade receivables/trade payables*

Intragroup balance of $75,000 is reduced to $36,000 once cash-in-transit of $39,000 is followed through to its ultimate destination.

4 *Goodwill*

	$'000	$'000
Consideration transferred		2,000
Non-controlling interest (125,000 × $4.40)		550
		2,550
Net assets acquired as represented by:		
Share capital	500	
Retained earnings	1,044	
		(1,544)
Goodwill at acquisition		1,006
Impairment losses to date		(180)
Goodwill at end of reporting period		826

Goodwill – alternative working

	$'000	$'000
Consideration transferred		2,000
Net assets acquired	1,544	
Group share 75%		(1,158)
Goodwill attributable to parent		842
Impairment (180 × 75%)		(135)
		707
Goodwill attributable to NCI (W5)		164
Impairment (180 × 25%)		(45)
		119
Total goodwill (707 + 119)		826

5 *Goodwill attributable to non-controlling interest*

	$'000
Non-controlling interest at fair value (W4)	550
Share of net assets at acquisition (1,544 × 25%)	(386)
	164

6 *Non-controlling interest at year end*

	$'000
Share of Encore's net assets at 31 March 20X4 (3,110 × 25%)	777.5
Goodwill (W5)	164
	941.5
Goodwill impairment (180 × 25%)	(45)
	896.5

Note: Goodwill impairment charged to the NCI is in proportion to the NCI shareholding.

7 *Consolidated retained earnings*

	Reprise $'000	*Encore* $'000
Per question	4,225	2,610
PUP (W2)	(7.2)	
Pre-acquisition retained earnings		(1,044)
	4,217.8	1,566
Encore – share of post acquisition retained earnings (1,566 × 75%)	1,174.5	
Less goodwill impairment losses to date (180 × 75%)	(135)	
	5,257.3	

28 War

Tutor's hint. This question may look intimidating because it involves an acquisition part of the way through the year, some fair value issues and both the consolidated income statement and statement of financial position. It is, however, fairly straightforward.

(a) IFRS 3 *Business combinations* states that shares offered as consideration should be valued at fair value, which for listed shares will be market price on the date of acquisition. However, the standard acknowledges that the market price may be difficult to determine if it is unreliable because of an inactive market. In particular, where the shares are not listed, there may be no suitable market. In such cases the value must be estimated using the best methods available. This may involve the use of:

(i) The value of similar listed securities
(ii) The present value of the cash flows of the shares
(iii) Any cash alternative which was offered
(iv) The value of any underlying security into which there is an option to convert

It may be necessary to undertake a valuation of the company in question should none of the above methods prove feasible.

Direct expenses incurred such as professional fees of lawyers and accountants also form part of the cost of the combination. However, issue costs of equity are treated as a deduction from the proceeds of the equity issue, rather than part of the cost of the combination.

(b) WAR GROUP
CONSOLIDATED STATEMENT OF FINANCIAL POSITION AS AT 30 JUNE 20X7

	$'000
Assets	
Non-current assets	
Property, plant and equipment (1,750 + 350 + 150)	2,250
Goodwill (W3)	189
	2,439
Current assets	
Inventories	600
Receivables	451
Cash at bank and in hand	299
	1,350
Total assets	3,789
Equity and liabilities	
Ordinary shares of $1 each	750
Share premium (W6)	250
Retained earnings (W5)	659
Non-controlling interest (W4)	255
	1,914
Non-current liabilities	1,225
Current liabilities	650
Total equity and liabilities	3,789

WAR GROUP
CONSOLIDATED INCOME STATEMENT FOR THE YEAR ENDED 30 JUNE 20X7

	$'000
Revenue	3,445
Cost of sales	(1,788)
Gross profit	1,657
Distribution costs	(638)
Administrative expenses (W7)	(310)
Operating profit	709
Interest payable	(75)
Profit before tax	634
Income tax	(306)
Profit for the year	328
Attributable to:	
Owners of the parent	317
Non-controlling interest	11
	328

Workings

1 *Fair value adjustment*

	$'000
Peace Co: property, plant and equipment at fair value	500
Carrying value	350
Fair value adjustment	150

Tutor's hint. Before you can work out the goodwill, you need to work out the pre-acquisition element of the dividend, as this will give you the cost of the investment.

2 *Pre-acquisition dividend*

Dividend paid by Peace to War: $42,000

Pre-acquisition element $^{10}/_{12} \times \$42,000 = \$35,000$

3 *Goodwill*

	$'000	$'000
Consideration transferred		800
Less pre-acquisition dividend (W2)		(35)
		765
Non-controlling interest (823 × 30%)		247
Share capital	100	
Share premium	150	
Fair value adjustment (W1)	150	
Retained earnings		
Prior year: 450 – 165 (225 – 60)	285	
Current year: $^{10}/_{12} \times 165$	138	
Total net assets		(823)
Goodwill		189

Goodwill – alternative working

	$'000	$'000
Consideration transferred		765
Total net assets	823	
Group share 70%		(576)
Goodwill		189

4 *Non-controlling interest at year end (statement of financial position)*

	$'000
Peace Co net assets (1,125 – 175 – 250)	700
Fair value adjustment (W1)	150
	850
× 30%	255

5 *Retained earnings*

	War Co	*Peace Co*
	$'000	$'000
Per statement of financial position	625	450
Pre-acquisition dividend	(35)	
Issue costs	50	
Pre-acquisition profits:		
Prior year (450 – 165 (W3))		(285)
10 months to 1 May 20X7 ((450 – 285)× 10/12)		(138)
		27
Group share of Peace (70% × 27)	19	
Group retained earnings	659	

6 *Share premium account*

	$'000
War Co	300
Less issue costs	(50)
	250

7 *Administrative expenses*

	$'000
War Co	325
Peace Co ($^2/_{12}$ × 210)	35
	360
Less issue costs	(50)
	310

8 *Non-controlling interest (income statement)*

$225,000 × $^2/_{12}$ × 30% = $11,250

29 Fallowfield and Rusholme

CONSOLIDATED INCOME STATEMENT FOR THE YEAR ENDED 30 JUNE 20X8

	$
Revenue (403,400 + 193,000 – 40,000)	556,400
Cost of sales (201,400 + 92,600 – 40,000 + 4,000)	(258,000)
Gross profit	298,400
Distribution costs (16,000 + 14,600)	(30,600)
Administrative expenses (24,250 + 17,800)	(42,050)
Profit before tax	225,750
Income tax expense (61,750 + 22,000)	(83,750)
Profit for the year	142,000
Profit attributable to:	
Owners of the parent	125,200
Non-controlling interest (W2)	16,800
	142,000

STATEMENT OF CHANGES IN EQUITY (EXTRACT)

	Retained earnings
	$
Balance at 1 July 20X7 (W3)	190,000
Dividends	(40,000)
Profit for the year	125,200
Balance at 30 June 20X8 (W4)	275,200

Workings

1 *Group structure*

Fallowfield
| 60% 3 years ago
| Pre-acquisition ret'd earnings: $16,000
Rusholme

2 *Non-controlling interest*

	$
Rusholme – profit for the period	46,000
Less: PUP (40,000 × ½ × 25/125)	4,000
	42,000
Non-controlling share 40%	16,800

3 *Retained earnings brought forward*

	Fallowfield	*Rusholme*
	$	$
Per question	163,000	61,000
Pre-acquisition retained earnings	–	(16,000)
	163,000	45,000
Rusholme – share of post acquisition retained earnings (45,000 × 60%)	27,000	
	190,000	

4 *Retained earnings carried forward*

	Fallowfield	*Rusholme*
	$	$
Per question	238,000	82,000
PUP	–	(4,000)
Pre-acquisition retained earnings		(16,000)
	238,000	62,000
Rusholme – share of post acquisition retained earnings (62,000 × 60%)	37,200	
	275,200	

30 Panther Group

PANTHER GROUP

CONSOLIDATED STATEMENT OF COMPREHENSIVE INCOME FOR THE YEAR ENDED 31 DECEMBER 20X4

	$'000
Revenue [22,800 + (4,300 × 6/12) – 320]	24,630
Cost of sales [13,600 + (2,600 × 6/12) – 320 + (W2) 10 + (W4) 5]	(14,595)
Gross profit	10,035
Distribution costs (2,900 + (500 × 6/12))	(3,150)
Administrative expenses (1,800 + (300 × 6/12))	(1,950)
Finance costs [200 + ((70 – (W3) 20) × 6/12)]	(225)
Finance income (50 – (W3) 20)	30
Profit before tax	4,740
Income tax expense [1,300 + (220 × 6/12)]	(1,410)
PROFIT FOR THE YEAR	3,330
Other comprehensive income for the year, net of tax [1,600 + (180 × 6/12)]	1,690
TOTAL COMPREHENSIVE INCOME FOR THE YEAR	5,020
Profit attributable to:	
Owners of the parent (3,330 – 112)	3,218
Non-controlling interest (W5)	112
	3,330
Total comprehensive income attributable to:	
Owners of the parent (5,020 – 148)	4,872
Non-controlling interest (W5)	148
	5,020

CONSOLIDATED STATEMENT OF CHANGES IN EQUITY FOR THE YEAR ENDED 31 DECEMBER 20X4 (EXTRACT)

	$'000 *Reserves*
Balance at 1 January 20X4 (Panther only)	12,750
Dividend paid	(900)
Total comprehensive income for the year	4,872
Balance at 31 December 20X4 (W6)	16,722

Workings

1 *Timeline*

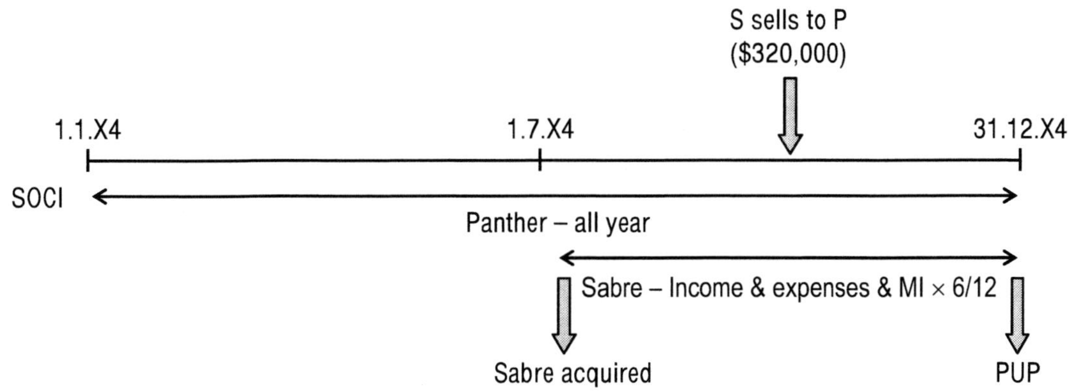

2 *Unrealised profit on intragroup trading*

Sabre to Panther = $\$60,000 \times \frac{20\%}{120\%} = \$10,000$

Adjust cost of sales and non-controlling interest in books of seller (Sabre).

3 *Interest on intragroup loan*

$\$800,000 \times 5\% \times 6/12 = \$20,000$

Cancel in books of Panther and Sabre.

4 *Fair value adjustments*

	At acq'n 1.7.X4	*Movement*		*At year end 31.12.X4*
	$'000		$'000	$'000
Property	200	(200/20 × 6/12)	(5)	195

5 *Non-controlling interest*

	$'000		$'000
Profit for the year ((610 + (W3) 20*) × 6/12)	315		
Less: Post acquisition interest* (W3)	(20)		
Less: PUP (W2)	(10)		
Additional depreciation on fair value adjustment (W4)	(5)		
	280	× 40%	112
Other comprehensive income (180 × 6/12)	90	× 40%	36
Total comprehensive income			148

* The interest on the loan is specific to the post-acquisition period. Therefore, it is added back before time apportioning the remainder of the profits, and then deducted in full as it is a post-acquisition expense.

6 *Group reserves carried forward (proof)*

	Panther	*Sabre*
	$'000	$'000
Reserves per question	16,500	3,270
PUP (W2)		(10)
Fair value change (W3)		(5)
Pre acquisition reserves (2,480 + (610 + 20 (W3) + 180) × 6/12)		(2,885)
		370
Sabre – share of post acquisition reserves (370 × 60%)	222	
	16,722	

31 Hever

CONSOLIDATED STATEMENT OF FINANCIAL POSITION AS AT 31 DECEMBER 20X4

	$'000
Non-current assets	
Property, plant & equipment (370 + 190 + (W3) 45)	605
Goodwill (W4)	2
Investment in associate (W5)	165
	772
Current assets	
Inventories (160 + 100 – (W2) 1.5)	258.5
Trade receivables (170 + 90)	260
Cash (50 + 40)	90
	608.5
	1,380.5
Equity attributable to owners of the parent	
Share capital	200
Share premium reserve	100
Retained earnings (W7)	758.5
	1,058.5
Non-controlling interest (W6)	162
	1,220.5
Current liabilities	
Trade payables (100 + 60)	160
	1,380.5

Workings

1 *Group structure*

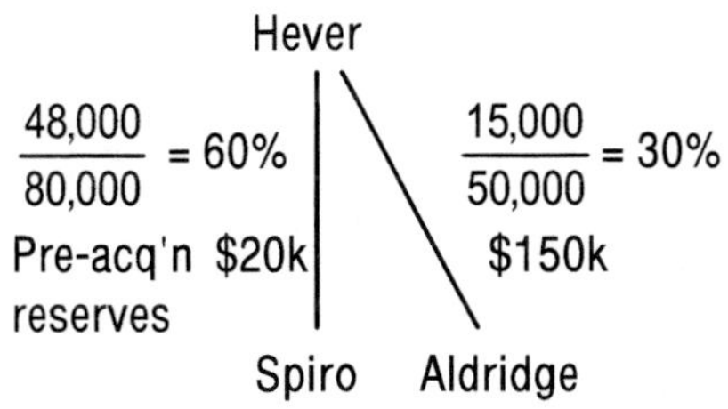

∴ In the absence of information to the contrary, Spiro is a subsidiary, and Aldridge an associate of Hever.

2 *Unrealised profit on inventories*

Mark-up = 6,000 ∴ ¼ × 6,000 = $1,500

3 *Fair values – adjustment to net assets*

	At Acquisition	*Movement*	*At balance sheet date*
Property, plant and equipment	50	(5)	45
Inventories	(20)	20	0
	30	15	45

4 *Goodwill on consolidation – Spiro*

	$'000	$'000
Consideration transferred		128
Non-controlling interest (210 × 40%)		84
Net assets at acquisition		
Share capital	80	
Retained earnings	20	
Share premium	80	
Fair value adjustments (W3)	30	
		(210)
Goodwill arising on consolidation		2

Goodwill – alternative working

	$'000	$'000
Consideration transferred		128
Net assets	210	
Group share 60%		(126)
Goodwill arising on consolidation		2

5 *Investment in associate*

	$'000
Cost of associate	90
Share of post-acquisition retained reserves ((400 – 150) × 30%)	75
	165

Note: it is not necessary to calculate the goodwill arising on the investment in Aldridge as there are no impairment losses.

6 *Non-controlling interest*

	$'000	$'000
Net assets	360	
Fair value adjustment (W3)	45	
	405	
Non-controlling share (40%)		162

7 *Retained earnings*

	Hever	*Spiro*	*Aldridge*
	$'000	$'000	$'000
Per question	568	200	400
PUP (W2)	(1.5)	–	–
Fair value adjustment (W3)		15	
Pre-acquisition retained earnings		(20)	(150)
		195	250
Spiro – share of post acquisition earnings (195 × 60%)	117		
Aldridge – share of post acquisition earnings (250 × 30%)	75		
Less: goodwill impairment losses to date	(0)		
Less: impairment losses on associate to date	(0)		
	758.5		

32 Joint ventures

Advantages

(a) This method clearly shows the size of an investor's interest in a joint venture and any related liabilities. The financing and structure of the venture is also shown, in relating to the rest of the group. All this information helps users to judge past performance and assess future prospects.

(b) This method treats the investment as if the investor had direct control of its share of the assets and results of the joint venture, which is very close to the reality of the situation, even though in fact it shares control of the entire venture.

(c) Proportional consolidation is used for joint ventures which consist of a sharing of facilities and so other joint ventures should use this method for consistency.

Disadvantages

(a) It may not be made clear (and it may not be possible to make clear) which assets and liabilities are controlled (directly or indirectly) by the group and those which are not. This will muddy the waters around the group results and confuse users of accounts. In particular, group figures which include consolidated *and* proportionately consolidated figures might be seen as meaningless.

(b) The assets and liabilities included in the group accounts from the joint venture do not meet the definitions of assets and liabilities in the IASB's *Framework*. 'Assets' include the ability to control rights or other access to benefits, but in a joint venture this control is not present; the investor only controls the net investment.

(c) What does 50% of a piece of machinery mean? Taking fractions of items and adding them into the group accounts may only confuse users.

List of Key Terms and Index

Note: are **Key Terms** and their page references given in **bold.**

REVIEW FORM & FREE PRIZE DRAW

All original review forms from the entire BPP range, completed with genuine comments, will be entered into a draw on 31 July 2011 and 31 January 2012. The names on the first four forms picked out will be sent a cheque for £50.

Name: ______________________ **Address:** ______________________

____

How have you used this Text?
(Tick one box only)

- ☐ Home study (book only)
- ☐ On a course: college ______________
- ☐ With 'correspondence' package
- ☐ Other ______________

Why did you decide to purchase this Text?
(Tick one box only)

- ☐ Have used BPP Texts in the past
- ☐ Recommendation by friend/colleague
- ☐ Recommendation by a lecturer at college
- ☐ Saw advertising
- ☐ Other ______________

During the past six months do you recall seeing/receiving any of the following?
(Tick as many boxes as are relevant)

- ☐ Our advertisement in *ACCA's publication*
- ☐ Our brochure with a letter through the post
- ☐ Website

Which (if any) aspects of our advertising do you find useful?
(Tick as many boxes as are relevant)

- ☐ Prices and publication dates of new editions
- ☐ Information on text content
- ☐ Facility to order books off-the-page
- ☐ None of the above

Your ratings, comments and suggestions would be appreciated on the following areas

	Very useful	*Useful*	*Not useful*
Introductory section	☐	☐	☐
Learning objectives	☐	☐	☐
Executive summaries	☐	☐	☐
Quality of explanations	☐	☐	☐
Examples	☐	☐	☐
Questions and answers in each chapter	☐	☐	☐
Illustrative diagrams	☐	☐	☐
Exam focus points	☐	☐	☐
Icons	☐	☐	☐
Chapter roundups	☐	☐	☐
Exam question bank	☐	☐	☐
Answer bank	☐	☐	☐
Index	☐	☐	☐

	Excellent	*Good*	*Adequate*	*Poor*
Overall opinion of this Text	☐	☐	☐	☐

Do you intend to continue using BPP Products? ☐ Yes ☐ No

Please note any further comments and suggestions/errors on the reverse of this page

Please return to: Benjamin Smith, BPP Learning Media Ltd, FREEPOST, London, W12 8AA or e-mail benjaminsmith@bpp.com

REVIEW FORM & FREE PRIZE DRAW (continued)

Please note any further comments and suggestions/errors below

FREE PRIZE DRAW RULES

1 Closing date for 31 July 2011 draw is 30 June 2011. Closing date for 31 January 2012 draw is 31 December 2011.

2 No purchase necessary. Entry forms are available upon request from BPP Learning Media Ltd. No more than one entry per title, per person. Draw restricted to persons aged 16 and over.

3 Winners will be notified by post and receive their cheques not later than 6 weeks after the draw date.

4 The decision of the promoter in all matters is final and binding. No correspondence will be entered into.